1997
The Supreme Court Review

199
The

"Judges as persons, or courts as institutions, are entitled to
no greater immunity from criticism than other persons
or institutions . . . [J]udges must be kept mindful of their limitations and
of their ultimate public responsibility by a vigorous
stream of criticism expressed with candor however blunt."
—*Felix Frankfurter*

". . . while it is proper that people should find fault when
their judges fail, it is only reasonable that they should recognize the
difficulties. . . . Let them be severely brought to book,
when they go wrong, but by those who will take the trouble
to understand them."
—*Learned Hand*

THE LAW SCHOOL

THE UNIVERSITY OF CHICAGO

Supreme Court Review

EDITED BY

DENNIS J. HUTCHINSON
DAVID A. STRAUSS
AND GEOFFREY R. STONE

THE UNIVERSITY OF CHICAGO PRESS

CHICAGO AND LONDON

INTERNATIONAL STANDARD BOOK NUMBER: 0-226-36314-7

LIBRARY OF CONGRESS CATALOG CARD NUMBER: 60-14353

THE UNIVERSITY OF CHICAGO PRESS, CHICAGO 60637

THE UNIVERSITY OF CHICAGO PRESS, LTD., LONDON

© 1998 BY THE UNIVERSITY OF CHICAGO, ALL RIGHTS RESERVED, PUBLISHED 1998

PRINTED IN THE UNITED STATES OF AMERICA

The paper used in this publication meets the minimum requirements of American National Standard for Information Sciences–Permanence of Paper for Printed Library Materials, ANSI Z39.48-1984. ♾

TO

D. M. Q.

AND

D. B. R.

With deep delight

CONTENTS

WHICH QUESTION? WHICH LIE? REFLECTIONS ON THE
PHYSICIAN-ASSISTED SUICIDE CASES   1
  Martha Minow

THE VALUE OF SEEING THINGS DIFFERENTLY: BOERNE V
FLORES AND CONGRESSIONAL ENFORCEMENT OF THE
BILL OF RIGHTS   31
  David Cole

CONGRESSIONAL POWER AND RELIGIOUS LIBERTY AFTER
CITY OF BOERNE V FLORES   79
  Christopher L. Eisgruber and Lawrence G. Sager

FREEDOM OF SPEECH, SHIELDING CHILDREN, AND
TRANSCENDING BALANCING   141
  Eugene Volokh

PRINTZ, STATE SOVEREIGNTY, AND THE LIMITS OF
FORMALISM   199
  Evan H. Caminker

O'HAGAN'S PROBLEMS   249
  Victor Brudney

TRAFFIC STOPS, MINORITY MOTORISTS, AND THE
FUTURE OF THE FOURTH AMENDMENT   271
  David A. Sklansky

ENTRENCHING THE DUOPOLY: WHY THE SUPREME
COURT SHOULD NOT ALLOW THE STATES TO
PROTECT THE DEMOCRATS AND REPUBLICANS FROM
POLITICAL COMPETITION   331
  Richard L. Hasen

"THE IDEAL NEW FRONTIER JUDGE"   373
  Dennis J. Hutchinson

THE COURT AND THE CORPORATION: JURISPRUDENCE,
LOCALISM, AND FEDERALISM   403
  Gregory A. Mark

DO NOT GO GENTLY INTO THAT GOOD RIGHT:
THE FIRST AMENDMENT IN THE HIGH COURT
OF AUSTRALIA   439
  Gerald N. Rosenberg and John M. Williams

MARTHA MINOW

WHICH QUESTION? WHICH LIE? REFLECTIONS ON THE PHYSICIAN-ASSISTED SUICIDE CASES

The imminence of death sharpens awareness. Tolstoy's Ivan Ilyich screams during his last days as he contemplates what suddenly comes to seem a squandered and squalid life as a lawyer.[1] For John Donne, thinking about even the deaths of others heightened a sense of human interdependence.[2] Approaching death led Gertrude Stein to consider the contingency of meanings and conclu-

Martha Minow is Professor, Harvard Law School.

AUTHOR'S NOTE: Comments from and conversations with Newton Minow, Frank Michelman, Joseph Singer, Elizabeth V. Spelman, Marc Spindelman, Carol Steiker, and Laurence Tribe gave help, and more questions, as I worked on this piece. Many students offered comments and assistance; I especially wish to thank Manuel Cachan, Julian Castro, Chris Campbell, David Melaugh, Deborah Perlstein, John Pierce, and Michael Siegel. And thanks to Laurie Corzett for help with citations.

[1] Leo Tolstoy, *The Death of Ivan Ilyich* (1960). Ronald Dworkin and Seth Kreimer both invoke this classic novella in their discussions of physician-assisted suicide. Ronald Dworkin, *Law's Dominion* at 203 (1995); Seth F. Kreimer, *Does Pro-Choice Mean Pro-Kevorkian? An Essay on Roe, Casey, and the Right to Die*, 44 Am U L Rev 803, 813 (1995). Dworkin invokes the story to show how people can reflect on their lives and find them wasted; Kreimer emphasizes Tolstoy's message of the possibility of redemption even in the very last moments of life.

[2] Hence, his observation, "No man is an island, entire of itself; every man is a piece of the continent, a part of the main. If a clod be washed away by the sea, Europe is the less, as well as if a promontory were, as well as if a manor of thy friend's or of thine own were; any man's death diminishes me, because I am involved in mankind; and therefore never send to know for whom the bell tolls; it tolls for thee." J. Donne, Meditation No. 17, in A. Aspa, ed, *Devotions Upon Emergent Occasions* at 86, 87 (1987) (quoted in *Vacco v Quill*, and *Washington v Glucksberg*, 117 S Ct 2258, 2293, 2304, 2305 & n 8 (1997) (Stevens, J, concurring in the judgments)).

sions on the questions humans ask.[3] Reportedly, her dying words were, "What *is* the answer? . . . In that case, what is the question?"[4]

The contemplation of death reminds us that what we ask frames what we answer. This insight animates and at times instructs the Supreme Court Justices who recently focused their attention on death, and more specifically, the challenges brought by dying patients and their doctors to state bans on physician-assisted death. In the two linked cases, *Washington v Glucksberg* and *Vacco v Quill*, five separate opinions all reach the same result: the Court rejects challenges to the state restrictions.[5] Yet the opinions diverge emphatically over the right question to be addressed.[6]

The opinions present five formulations of the liberty interest at stake.[7] They frame competing expressions of the methods of review authorized by the Due Process Clause of the Fourteenth Amendment. The Justices also debate how to articulate the equal protection objection and whether it adds anything to the analysis.[8] Some of the Justices characterize the challenges to the state statutes in the cases as facial attacks, while others construct the cases instead as challenges to the laws' applications. They further dispute whether the right question to ask involves the competencies and

---

[3] Quoted in *The Beacon Book of Quotations by Women* at 16 (compiled by Rosalie Maggio, 1992).

[4] Stein, supra.

[5] *Washington v Glucksberg*, 117 S Ct 2258 (1997); *Vacco v Quill*, 117 S Ct 2293 (1997) (hereafter cited as *Glucksberg* and *Quill*).

[6] In *Quill*, plaintiffs posed an equal protection challenge to a ban on physician-assisted suicide; in *Glucksberg*, plaintiffs framed a substantive due process challenge to a similar law in the state of Washington. Chief Justice Rehnquist wrote majority opinions for each case; Justice O'Connor wrote one concurring opinion for both cases (in which Justice Ginsburg substantially joined and Justice Breyer joined except insofar as Justice O'Connor's opinion joined the opinions of the Court). Justice Stevens wrote one opinion, concurring in the result, for both cases. Justice Souter wrote a short opinion concurring in the judgment in *Quill*, and a lengthy one concurring in the judgment in *Glucksberg*. Justice Breyer wrote one opinion concurring in the judgments in both cases. Perhaps this profusion of opinions occurred because Chief Justice Rehnquist chose to assign the authorship of the opinions to himself, despite the fact that a majority of the Court holds views more solicitous to the challenges than the ones he expressed in his opinions.

[7] For each of the following debates, see infra. Still other formulations are possible. See, e.g., Ronald D. Dworkin, *Life's Dominion* 195 (1993) (exploring justifications for euthanasia based on both religious and secular views of life's sacredness); Matthew P. Previn, *Note: Assisted Suicide and Religion: Conflicting Conceptions of the Sanctity of Human Life*, 84 Georgetown L J 589 (1996) (arguing for access to assisted suicide on religious freedom grounds).

[8] Compare *Vacco v Quill*, 117 S Ct 2293, 2297–98 (1997), with *Washington v Glucksberg* and *Vacco v Quill*, 117 S Ct 2302, 2309–10 (1997) (Stevens, J, concurring).

relationships between courts and legislatures or whether the relationships among the branches emerge in practice, over time, not by permanent announcements by one branch.

Perhaps because the Justices all agree about what to do for now, they use their opinions to lay the ground for future debates, in and out of the Court. Perhaps, because the Chief Justice exercised his prerogative in assigning the majority opinions to himself, he invited a contest over his formulation of the issues. Perhaps because of agreement on the result, the Justices felt at liberty to reveal the significance in their thinking of the choice of formulations, and to create an opportunity to instruct lawyers in the future about potentially winning frameworks for analysis. Yet I think amid all the competing formulations of questions at hand, the Justices leave unacknowledged a choice the cases unavoidably presented. That, as I explain later, is the choice about which lie to endorse.[9] But first, let us consider the choices the Justices did announce and contest.

I. WHAT'S THE QUESTION?

Formulating the question crucially shapes the answers courts give. No wonder the Justices explicitly wrangle over how the questions before them should be formulated, urging more narrow or more general, more blunt or more complex expressions of the issues at hand.[10] The justices implicitly instruct one another, advocates, and the general public about how framing issues influences results. The most explicit instruction appears in Justice Souter's opinion, while apparently discussing something else: the common law reasoning in the kind of Due Process analysis he ad-

---

[9] For the operative definition of "lie," see text at note 90 & note 90. Edward L. Rivet II, legislative director of Right to Life of Michigan, charges advocates of euthanasia as engaging in a lie; it differs from the ones I discuss in the context of physician-assisted suicide. He argues that with legislative or judicial rights to die, "[t]he big lie is that the patient has control" in euthanasia when, in fact, right-to-die legislation would give decisional authority to committees of doctors. See Nelvia Van't Hul, *Walker Conference Explores Right to Die*, LSA Magazine (University of Michigan) 36 (Fall 1997).

[10] See, e.g., *Glucksberg* and *Quill*, 117 S Ct 2302, 2303 (O'Connor, J, concurring) (question is narrower than the generalized right to suicide); id at 2311 (Breyer, J, concurring in the judgments) (question is whether there is something roughly described as a right to die with dignity); *Glucksberg*, 117 S Ct 2258, 2275 (Souter, J, concurring in the judgment) ("question is whether the statute sets up one of those 'arbitrary impositions' or 'purposeless restraints' at odds with the Due Process Clause").

vocates. In that context, almost like an actor turning to directly address the audience, Justice Souter exquisitely sketches the potential effect of contrasting versions of expression on judicial results:

> When identifying and assessing the competing interests of liberty and authority, for example, the breadth of expression that a litigant or a judge selects in stating the competing principles will have much to do with the outcome and may be dispositive.[11]

His lesson proceeds with a combination of avuncular advice and anthropological observation about the curious practices of legal argumentation:

> As in any process of rational argumentation, we recognize that when a generally accepted principle is challenged, the broader the attack the less likely it is to succeed. The principle's defenders will, indeed, often try to characterize any challenge as just such a broadside, perhaps by couching the defense as if a broadside attack had occurred.[12]

Justice Souter illustrates this comment with a reference to the *Dred Scott* decision, where the Court "treated prohibition of slavery in the Territories as nothing less than a general assault on the concept of property."[13] *Dred Scott*, the harbinger of that Civil War, was the nadir in judicial protection of individual freedom. Citing *Dred Scott* in this way, Justice Souter underscores the potentially disastrous consequences of an escalating game of generality in characterizing constitutional claims and rejoinders. Whether intended or not, this comment sets a suitably admonishing tone while the Justices vie for advantage while disputing which question to address.

A. WHAT LIBERTY?

In *Glucksberg*, Chief Justice Rehnquist's opinion for the Court's majority asserts that "the question before us is whether the 'liberty' specially protected by the Due Process Clause includes a right to commit suicide which itself includes a right to assistance in doing

---

[11] *Glucksberg*, 117 S Ct at 2284 (Souter, J, concurring in the judgment).

[12] Id.

[13] Id.

so."[14] Especially because it follows a lengthy description of the long-standing legal traditions condemning suicide and any efforts to promote it, the formulation effectively implies its negative answer.

Justice O'Connor announces that given the majority's formulation, she too would agree that "our Nation's history, legal traditions, and practices do not support the existence of such a right," but urges attention to a "narrower question" framed by the plaintiffs. The question is narrower in the sense that a smaller class of people are allegedly burdened, wrongly, by the state bans. Justice O'Connor's narrower question is "whether a mentally competent person who is experiencing great suffering has a constitutionally cognizable interest in controlling the circumstances of his or her imminent death."[15]

This phrasing allows Justice O'Connor a neat exit from the cases' dilemmas. She focuses on the part of the question dealing with the control of suffering, and observes that no parties in the cases dispute that a dying person near death has a right to control his or her great suffering. In both the states of Washington and New York, no legal barrier prevents physicians from administering medication to control the pain of dying patients, even where such prescription would hasten death.[16] Since that is not disputed, the portion of the question that Justice O'Connor treats as central does not require judicial attention.[17]

What remains in need of decision, then, is the permissible scope of state regulation to guard those persons who fall outside the nar-

---

[14] Id at 2269.

[15] *Glucksberg* and *Quill*, 117 S Ct at 2303 (O'Connor, J, concurring).

[16] Id. This is the vaunted doctrine of "double effect," taken from the concept in philosophy and bioethics that an action permissible when aimed to effect one intention does not become impermissible when it carries with it another, unintended effect. Accordingly, a physician's administration of medication to relieve the pain of a dying patient is justifiable, even if an unintended, though foreseeable, effect is to hasten death. The physician regretfully expects the death of the patient but does not intend that death. See Philip E. Devine, *Ethics of Homicide* 105–13 (1978); Helga Kuhse, *The Sanctity-of-Life Doctrine in Medicine: A Critique* 83–90 (1987); Thomas Nagel, *The View from Nowhere* 179 (1986).

[17] Justice O'Connor thus equates control over great suffering while nearing death with control over the circumstances of the death. While the two are close, they are not identical; palliative care in the form of sufficient medication to block severe pain may indeed control suffering while at the same time inducing loss of consciousness and a death more drawn out than one produced by direct administration of a fatal dosage. This distinction was much emphasized by some briefs before the Court, see, e.g., *Vacco v Quill*, No 95-1858, Brief for Respondents.

row question. Because the class of people who are both dying and competent can select pain medication even when it hastens death, in Justice O'Connor's view, the state bans only forbid physicians from assisting the deaths of others, who are not competent, not dying, or not voluntarily choosing death. Given her view, Justice O'Connor can join the majority's result, while having comforted any who are concerned about capable, choosing individuals trapped in painful, dying bodies. Indeed, it is precisely such a concern that most directly animates the push for physician-assisted suicide. Justice O'Connor in essence announces that as long as sufficient medication to lose consciousness and then die is available, the indignities of death can be managed. Her approach avoids even having to attribute a constitutional right or protected interest for these persons because she points to the absence of any current threat to such a potential right or interest.[18] Along the way, Justice O'Connor elides the difference between controlling pain in a way that may hasten death, and securing control over the moment of death.

Justice Breyer endorses Justice O'Connor's formulation, but also offers another of his own.[19] His opinion embraces the benefits of posing a question that emphasizes controlling pain, rather than achieving death.[20] Those seizing this framework can emphasize the availability of pain control even when it hastens death; they can cast doubt on a legal regime that would curtail such availability; they can imply support for a liberty or interest protected by such availability; and they can nonetheless endorse the bans on assisted suicide at issue in the case. Expending minimal judicial resources, this line of analysis still can reassure both those who fear painful deaths and those who fear a growth industry of Jack Kevorkians.[21]

---

[18] "[E]ven assuming that we would recognize such an interest, I agree that the State's interests in protecting those who are not truly competent or facing imminent death, or those whose decisions to hasten death would not be truly voluntary, are sufficiently weighty to justify a prohibition against physician-assisted suicide." *Glucksberg* and *Quill*, 117 S Ct at 2303 (O'Connor, J, concurring).

[19] *Glucksberg* and *Quill*, 117 S Ct at 2310 (Breyer, J, concurring in the judgments). Justice Ginsburg also endorsed Justice O'Connor's view but without elaboration.

[20] Justice Breyer implicitly acknowledges the apparent elision of controlling death in the formulation that uses controlling pain with use of parentheses: "in my view, the avoidance of severe physical pain (connected with death) would have to comprise an essential part of any successful claim." Id at 2311.

[21] Now stripped of his medical license in Michigan, Jack Kevorkian has become a household name in his effort to defy the ban on assisted suicide and offer the means for suicide

Yet even as he aligns with Justice O'Connor's approach, Justice Breyer actually offers yet another formulation. Explicitly rejecting the Court's "formulation of that claimed 'liberty' interest" as a "'right to commit suicide with another's assistance,'" Justice Breyer identifies an alternate "formulation that would use words roughly like a 'right to die with dignity.'"[22] Highlighting the artifice of word choice, Justice Breyer casts his formulation as "roughly like," and then resists any strong attachment to a particular formulation by gesturing to a right, "irrespective of the exact words used" to describe it.[23] Trying to speak without words does not work, of course, yet Justice Breyer both seeks to guard against any direct assault on his own choice of words while pointing toward an alternate expression of the interest at stake.[24] Thus, at the "core" of Justice Breyer's version of the liberty interest worth consideration "would lie personal control over the manner of death, professional medical assistance, and the avoidance of unnecessary and severe physical suffering—combined."[25]

Still another set of phrases receive Justice Stevens's approval. His opinion identifies "an interest in hastening death." Unlike his colleagues, Justice Stevens takes the next step and responds to the

---

to a wide variety of suffering patients. See Mark Hosenball, *The Real Jack Kevorkian*, Newsweek 28 (Dec 6, 1993). Although even defenders of physician-assisted suicide tend to criticize his practices, e.g., Timothy E. Quill, *Risk Taking by Physicians in Legally Gray Areas*, 57 Albany L Rev 693, 698 (1994), Kevorkian can be credited with overcoming the taboo of mentioning the subject and ushering in an era of popular discussion of assisted suicide.

[22] *Glucksberg* and *Quill*, 117 S Ct at 2311 (Breyer, J, concurring in the judgments). Later, he reminds readers that this is simply what he has called it, not the interest itself: "what I have called the core interest in dying with dignity." Id at 2312.

[23] Id at 2311.

[24] It is almost as if he is in the midst of a debate with Ludwig Wittgenstein about whether there really are any meanings apart from language. See, e.g., Ludwig Wittgenstein, *Philosophical Investigations* 48–49 (G. E. M. Anscombe trans, Basil Blackwell, 2d ed 1958) (paragraph 120) ("When I talk about language (words, sentences, etc.) I must speak the language of every day. Is this language somehow too coarse and material for what we want to say? *Then how is another one to be constructed?* And how strange that we should be able to do anything at all with the one we have! . . . Your questions refer to words; so I have to talk about words. You say: the point isn't the word, but is meaning, and you think of the meaning as a thing of the same kind as the word, though also different from the word. Here the word, there the meaning. The money, and the cow that you can buy with it. (But contrast: money, and its use)." See also id at 41 (paragraph 88) (discussing "inexact" which does not mean "unusable"); 107 (paragraph 329) ("When I think in language, there aren't 'meanings' going through my mind in addition to the verbal expressions: the language is itself the vehicle of thought").

[25] The "—combined," skipping an implied verb with an informal dash—etches still further the intent to avoid a formulation that can be examined fully.

overarching question: Does the interest, however defined, exist? Justice Stevens asserts that, at least at times, the liberty interest as he stated it is entitled to constitutional protection.[26] At stake, for Justice Stevens, is not only individual dignity, but also the ability to decide "how, rather than whether, a critical threshold shall be crossed."[27] His articulation brings a steady focus on death itself, not the pain surrounding it. His touchstone is the Court's treatment of withdrawal of life support in *Cruzan v Director, Missouri Department of Health*.[28] Justice Stevens's formulation also notably accentuates individuals' interests in influencing how they will be remembered after death. Consistent with his dissenting opinion in the Court's previous encounter with rights surrounding a dying patient,[29] Justice Stevens emphasizes an individual's interests in affecting the memories others will have of her.[30]

Here, and elsewhere, Justice Stevens is the most insistent Justice on the point that constitutional protection would restrict state regulation of an individual's decisions surrounding death.[31] Yet he is also the one who most emphatically stresses human interdependence and relationships. A dying person rightly worries how others will remember her. Remembering one who has died as dignified and vibrant, or dependent and pathetic, involves the others at least as much as the deceased. This guiding attention to relationships becomes apparent even when Justice Stevens grants his support for the Court's basic rejection of a right to commit suicide. For this Justice, there should be no such right, not only so the state may

---

[26] *Glucksberg* and *Quill*, 117 S Ct at 2305 (Stevens, J, concurring in the judgments).

[27] Id at 2307.

[28] See id at 2305–07 (discussing *Cruzan*, 497 US 261 (1990)).

[29] *Cruzan v Director, Missouri Department of Health*, 497 US 261, 344 (1990) (Stevens, J, dissenting) ("But Nancy Cruzan's interest in life, no less than that of any other person, includes an interest in how she will be thought of after her death by those whose opinions mattered to her. There can be no doubt that her life made her dear to her family and to others. How she dies will affect how that life is remembered.").

[30] Allowing an individual rather than the state to make decisions surrounding death "gives proper recognition to the individual's interest in choosing a final chapter that accords with her life story, rather than one that demeans her values and poisons memories of her." *Glucksberg* and *Quill*. See also id at 2306 & n 11 (discussing how Nancy Cruzan's death will influence the memories others have of her, and why this represents an interest deserving protection).

[31] *Glucksberg* and *Quill*, 117 S Ct 2302, 2308 (1997) (Stevens, J, concurring in the judgments); *Cruzan v Director, Missouri Department of Health*, 497 US 261 (1990) (Stevens, J, dissenting).

fully guard individuals against their own mistaken acts of self-inflicted death. There should be no right to suicide because of the value that every human being provides to others.[32] This emphasis on communal memories and the value people bring to one another joins what would otherwise seem a disconnection between his formulation of an individual's right to hasten death and his articulation of state powers to guard against any individual's death.[33]

Justice Souter slices the subject differently. His extensive discussion of the proper methods to be deployed in analysis of substantive due process claims warns against any statement of the liberty interest that is so general that it would require many, and therefore too many, exceptions.[34] He therefore rejects presentations of the claim as historically grounded "rights either to suicide or to assistance in committing it."[35] Instead, the claim he wants to address is "the option to obtain the services of a physician" to gain "the benefit of advice and medical help" of the sort physicians are generally free to provide; physicians ordinarily can "advise and aid those who exercise other rights to bodily autonomy."[36] Therefore, at stake is not simply a right to bodily autonomy, nor a general right to medical care, but instead an interest in both "bodily integrity and the concomitant tradition of medical assistance."[37]

---

[32] *Glucksberg* and *Quill* at 2305 (citing John Donne). The opinion continues: "The State has an interest in preserving and fostering the benefits that every human being may provide to the community—a community that thrives on the exchange of ideas, expressions of affection, shared memories and humorous incidents as well as on the material contributions that its members create and support. The value to others of a person's life is far too precious to allow the individual to claim a constitutional entitlement to complete autonomy in making a decision to end that life." Id.

[33] Justice Stevens has pursued the mutability, and importance, of conceptions of social and communal meaning in other contexts. See, e.g., *Board of Educ. of Kiryas Joel Village Sch. Dist. v Grumet*, 114 S Ct 2481, 2495 (Stevens, J, concurring) (explaining that the discrimination experienced by disabled Hasidic children who attended public school could be redressed by attending to the relationships they develop and attitudes of other children and adults).

[34] See *Glucksberg*, 117 S Ct at 2289–90 (Souter, J, concurring in the judgment). See also infra at pp 419–21 (discussing Justice Souter's approach to substantive due process analysis).

[35] Id at 2286.

[36] Id.

[37] Id at 2287. In this way, Justice Souter seeks a kind of precise, or indeed, compound right. His chosen guide is Justice Harlan's dissenting opinion in *Poe v Ullman*, where, crucially, the right to use contraceptives was asserted in combination with the right to enjoy the privacy of the marital bedroom. Id at 2284 (citing *Poe v Ullman*, 367 US 497 (1961) (Harlan, J, dissenting, at 543, 552–53)). Similar compound rights include parental and religious liberties at issue in the choices over children's schooling, see *Wisconsin v Yoder*. Yet recognizing the conjunction or convergence of two protected interests does not guarantee

By emphasizing the individual's right to receive consultation and assistance from a physician, Justice Souter moves the circumstance of physician-assisted suicide toward an analogy to physician-conducted abortions. In particular, he revives the emphasis on the relationship between physician and patient that pervaded *Roe v Wade*, although not many subsequent abortion decisions.[38] "Without physician assistance in abortion, the woman's right would have too often amounted to nothing more than a right to self-mutilation, and without a physician to assist in the suicide of the dying, the patient's right will often be confined to crude methods of causing death, most shocking and painful to the decedent's survivors."[39] Justice Souter presses the analogy further to evoke an image of physician respect for the whole person,[40] whether pregnant or dying.

Along the way, Justice Souter joins Justice Stevens in stressing that in death, not just an end to pain is at issue: "The patients here sought not only an end to pain (which they might have had, although perhaps at the price of stupor) but an end to their short remaining lives with a dignity that they believed would be denied them by powerful pain medication, as well as by their consciousness of dependency and helplessness as they approached death."[41] Justice Souter's construction of the interests as a conjunction of personal autonomy and medical consultation may seem narrower than Justice O'Connor's emphasis on the individual's control over pain. Yet Justice Souter's version reaches precisely the issue Justice

---

they will remain joined as constitutional interpretation proceeds. See *Eisenstadt v Baird* (extending *Griswold* to single persons); civil commitment (recognizing parental prerogatives as child is committed to mental hospital). Similarly, the conjunction between bodily autonomy and a right to consult a physician that infused the Court's initial ruling on abortion gradually left the physician consultation dimension aside. Compare *Roe v Wade*, 410 US 113 (1973), with *Planned Parenthood of Southeastern Pa. v Casey*, 505 US 833 (1992).

[38] See *Planned Parenthood of Southeastern Pa. v Casey*, 505 US 833 (1992) (little discussion of the physician's role).

[39] *Glucksberg*, 117 S Ct at 2288.

[40] "[I]n the course of holding that the decision to perform an abortion called for a physician's assistance, the Court recognized that the good physician is not just a mechanic of the human body whose services have no bearing on a person's moral choices, but one who does more than treat symptoms, one who ministers to the patient. . . . [F]or just as the decision about abortion is not directed to correcting some pathology, so the decision in which a dying patient seeks help is not so limited." Id. For a thoughtful treatment of the comparison of legal interests implicated in abortion and physician-assisted suicide, see Kreimer (cited in note 1).

[41] Id at 2289.

O'Connor elides: whether the interests at stake reach control over the moment and manner of death, not simply relief from physical suffering. At the same time, Justice Souter refrains from announcing a constitutional right of any sort, much less a fundamental right, at least for now, although "I accord the claims . . . a high degree of importance, requiring a commensurate justification."[42]

Many lines of agreement and disagreement appear in these competing formulations of the liberty interest. Chief Justice Rehnquist knows that the Court would never recognize a right to commit suicide or to gain assistance in so doing, as all the other Justices confirm. Yet at least five Justices make it clear that some kind of interest could indeed obtain constitutional solicitude in another, future case. With endorsements of Justices Ginsburg and Breyer, Justice O'Connor's emphasis on assuring sufficient pain control, even unto death, implies a warning to states that would restrict even that. Justice Breyer explicitly announces that any such restriction would invite reconsideration of the Court's conclusions.[43] Justice Stevens and Justice Souter directly identify patients' desires to secure death, not merely to control pain, even as they articulate quite different versions of the kind of liberty interest involved. Is there, or could there be, a liberty interest? For now, it depends on which version is framed, and by whom.

B. WHAT METHOD?

No small amount of explanation for the variety of liberty interests considered arises from the Justices' competing views about the proper method of judicial review of statutes under the Due Process Clause of the Fourteenth Amendment. While each claims to state the settled traditions of the Court on this subject, the Justices present starkly contrasting versions and steps.

Both the majority opinion and Justice Souter's concurrence claim fine and lengthy pedigrees for their methods. Where the majority characterizes its method as the one used "in all due process cases,"[44] Justice Souter presents essentially a scholarly treatise

---

[42] *Vacco*, 117 S Ct at 2302 (Souter, J, concurring in the judgment). In *Glucksberg*, he declares, "In my judgment, the importance of the individual interests here, as within the class of 'certain interests' demanding careful scrutiny of the State's contrary claim [citing Justice Harlan's dissent in *Poe v Ullman*], cannot be gainsaid." *Glucksberg*, 117 S Ct at 2290.

[43] *Glucksberg* and *Quill*, 117 S Ct at 2312 (Breyer, J, concurring in the judgments).

[44] *Glucksberg*, 117 S Ct at 2262.

on the origins and development of substantive review, both before and after the adoption of the Fourteenth Amendment.[45] The truly crucial moment, and text, for Justice Souter is the dissenting opinion of Justice Harlan in *Poe v Ullman*, the dissent that is often cited as the inspiration and basis for the Court's ultimate decision in *Griswold v Connecticut*.[46] Yet Justice Souter treats even Justice Harlan's dissent as an expression of the enduring tradition of American constitutional practice[47] and a manifestation of common law reasoning.[48]

Perhaps most strikingly, Justice Souter elevates the methodological question, and Justice Harlan's formulation of it, to his opening statement of the issue presented: "The question is whether the statute sets up one of those 'arbitrary impositions' or 'purposeless restraints' at odds with the Due Process Clause."[49] For Justice Souter, then, the central choice over formulation pertains less to the statement of the potential liberty at issue than to the statement of the framework for analyzing state restraints on individual liberties.

Unlike the method described and deployed by the majority, Justice Souter calls for scrutiny of the challenged legislative resolution of clashing principles. The task is to ask whether that legislative resolution falls outside the realm of the reasonable, in the sense of being arbitrary and purposeless, based crucially on explicit attention to detailed accounts of the two sides in the controversy.[50] This statement of the task requires careful delineation of the specific private interests at issue,[51] and attention to the competing state interests insofar as they address "specific features of the claim."[52]

---

[45] Id at 2277–83 (Souter, J, concurring in the judgment).

[46] 381 US 479 (1965), cited at 117 S Ct at 2280.

[47] 117 S Ct at 2280. In this way, he in part seeks to rescue the substantive due process inquiry from the bad reputation of one of its strands, used by the Court to strike down economic regulations. See id at 2279–80.

[48] Id at 2284.

[49] *Glucksberg* at 2275 (Souter, J, concurring in the judgment) (quoting *Poe v Ullman*, 367 US 497, 543 (1961) (Harlan, J, dissenting)).

[50] Id at 2281–90. He does acknowledge the framework that has become a catechism for law students. Id at 2285 n 12 (fundamental liberties trigger inquiry into whether the state's interests are compelling and the means selected is narrowly tailored).

[51] See supra (discussing Justice Souter's claim that the private interest conjoins consultation with medical professionals and advancement of personal autonomy).

[52] Id at 2290.

It is this framework that allows Justice Souter to dispense with consideration of the state's asserted interests in promoting life generally and in discouraging suicide. These are too general and imbued with moral judgment.[53] Yet the state's third rationale is suitably specific to warrant Justice Souter's attention and ultimate deference. The state's interest is in protecting "nonresponsible individuals and those who do not stand in relation either to death or to their physicians" as do the competent patients facing imminent death who desire physicians' aid in hastening that inevitable end.[54] Here Justice Souter essentially joins with Justice O'Connor's recognition of the dangers of abuse should assisted suicide be lawful. He also acknowledges the risk of the slippery slope, or slide into voluntary and involuntary euthanasia,[55] given psychological and economic pressures on physicians.[56] His chosen due process framework, however, permits Justice Souter to give his strong endorsement of the importance of individual interests at stake while conceding the state's justifiable caution.[57]

C. LINE-DRAWING OR ILLUSIONS?

Vacco v Quill directly posed an equal protection objection to bans on physician-assisted suicide, and yet only the Chief Justice's opinion for the Court spends much time addressing that claim. Even that opinion dispenses with the claim rather quickly. No fundamental rights or suspect classifications are involved, given the analysis in *Glucksberg*.[58] Chief Justice Rehnquist's opinion accepts the question as posed (and answered in the negative) by the Court of Appeals for the Second Circuit: Is there a rational basis for the

---

[53] Id.

[54] Id.

[55] Usually, euthanasia refers to death administered by someone other than the patient. Active euthanasia requires the administration of a drug or other device to produce death; passive euthanasia involves failure to give life-supporting or life-reviving treatment. When voluntary, the act of euthanasia is at the patient's request; when involuntary, it is not. See generally Lundberg, 'It's Over Debbie' and the Euthanasia Debate, 259 JAMA 2142, 2143 (1988) (identifying six categories of euthanasia, ranging from passive to active).

[56] 117 S Ct at 2291 (Souter, J, concurring in the judgment).

[57] Although line-drawing problems also occur, in Justice Souter's view, with permitted pain medication and disconnection of life support, the purposes there are not to cause death, and thus give smaller grounds for concern. Id at 2291 nn 16 & 17.

[58] *Quill*, 117 S Ct at 2297–98.

distinction between the withdrawal of life-sustaining treatment permitted by state law and the forbidden assistance of suicide?

Is there reason for this line of distinction, thus drawn? Yes, answers the Court's majority, given the long-standing legal tradition punishing suicide and aid to suicide, and given the legal conceptions of causation and intention.[59] The cause of death for someone removed from life support is the underlying disease, while "the cause of death from lethal medication is just that."[60] In addition, "a physician who withdraws, or honors a patient's refusal to begin, life-sustaining medical treatment purposefully intends, or may so intend, only to respect his patient's wishes," while one who prescribes lethal medication intends death.[61]

It is this focus on legal conceptions of intention that allows the Chief Justice to distinguish provision of aggressive pain treatment that may hasten a patient's death from suicide assistance.[62] Lawyers often use intention to distinguish two actions that may have the same result, and legislatures join in drawing the precise line between withdrawal of life-supporting treatment and self-infliction of deadly harm.[63] Analysis, and contemporary practices, framed by lawyers, support the distinction and thus defeat a claim of unequal treatment. A brief submitted by a distinguished group of philosophers took issue, however, with the distinction as ultimately framed by the majority.[64] The question, argued the philosophers' brief, is not whether there is a difference between killing a patient or letting a patient die from underlying medical causes, but whether there is a distinction between intending to kill a patient and intending to fulfill the patient's request for a lethal medication that would enable the patient to terminate his or her life.[65]

Yet the majority's formulation also captures the approval of Jus-

---

[59] This is the terrain covered by the concept of "double-effect" (see note 16).

[60] 117 S Ct at 2298.

[61] Id at 2298–99.

[62] Id at 2299 and 2301 n 11. The Court relied heavily on the report of the New York Task Force on Life and the Law, *When Death Is Sought: Assisted Suicide and Euthanasia in the Medical Context* (1994).

[63] Id at 2299.

[64] Ronald Dworkin et al, *Assisted Suicide: The Philosopher's Brief*, NY Rev of Books (March 27, 1997), at 41, 45. The philosophers signing the brief were Ronald Dworkin, Thomas Nagel, Robert Nozick, John Rawls, Thomas Scanlon, and Judith Jarvis Thompson.

[65] See id.

tice Souter. He similarly endorses the distinction between assistance to suicide, on the one side, and terminating artificial life support and death-hastening medication, on the other.[66] There is no further analysis; Justice Souter simply points to his conclusion that the ban on assisted suicide is not arbitrary under the due process standard to indicate reasons for the distinction at hand.

Only Justice Stevens directly disagrees, but by shifting the formulation from a question across the board to a question about some instances. He can concur in the judgment to reject the equal protection challenge because "the distinction between permitting death to ensue from an underlying fatal disease and causing it to occur by the administration of medication or other means provides a constitutionally sufficient basis for the State's classification."[67] Yet, "I am not persuaded that there will in fact be a significant difference between the intent of the physicians, the patients or the families in the two situations."[68]

His opinion proceeds to call any differences in intent or causation "illusory."[69] Justice Stevens supports the majority's result, which relies on the allegedly illusory distinction, only because he construes the case as a facial challenge to the statute, leaving open "the possibility that some applications of the New York statute may impose an intolerable intrusion on the patient's freedom."[70] The majority acknowledges in response that indeed a future plaintiff could bring a challenge to the application of the statute.[71] Still, the majority asserts, only different and "considerably stronger arguments" would prevail in such a future case.[72] After all, asserts the majority, the state can proceed with a reasonable distinction in the absence of omniscience about all the circumstances in which it might end up being untenable.[73]

Justice Stevens displaces ambivalence about the distinction be-

---

[66] *Quill*, 117 S Ct at 2302 (Souter, J, concurring in the judgment).

[67] *Glucksberg* and *Quill*, 117 S Ct at 2309–10 (Stevens, J, concurring in the judgments).

[68] Id at 2310.

[69] Id.

[70] Id. See id at 2304–05 (specific dying patients are no longer before the Court, so what remains is a facial challenge).

[71] Id at 2302 n 13.

[72] Id.

[73] *Quill* at 2302 n 12.

tween assisted suicide and pain medications, sufficient to kill, onto a distinction between facial and applied statutory challenges. His shift in gears speeds a concession from the majority, unleashing fuel for future challenges. Justice Souter offers still a further contrasting frame, recasting *Glucksberg* itself as a challenge to the application of the state statutes.[74] The terminally ill patients who filed as plaintiffs had already died; four physicians remained as plaintiffs and continued to request declaratory and injunctive relief "for their own benefit in discharging their obligations to other dying patients who request their help."[75] Because Justice Souter ends up accepting the state rationales for the statutes in general, it is not clear how characterizing the challenge as facial alters the result. Perhaps his goal is to accentuate the degree to which future challenges, whether to other particular applications of the statute or to the statute on its face, could gain judicial consideration. In any case, together with Justice Stevens, Justice Souter injects the issue of facial versus applied challenges not only as further wrinkles, but also future handles for prospective litigants. The issue even opens up avenues for creative exploration of remedies for the particular groups of individuals not at risk from physician-assisted death.[76]

D. WHO'S COMPETENT?

An intensely familiar device for framing adjudication shifts the question from the merits to one about who should decide the merits.[77] Sometimes the "who decides" question addresses the split between state and federal governments; sometimes it turns to the selection among branches of government; sometimes it mixes and matches the two.[78] Without noting the irony, or parallel in the word choice, most of the opinions in the physician-assisted suicide

---

[74] *Glucksberg*, 117 S Ct at 2275 n 2 (Souter, J, concurring in the judgment).

[75] Id at 2275.

[76] See Sylvia A. Law, *Physician-Assisted Death: An Essay on Constitutional Rights and Remedies*, 55 Md L Rev 292 (1996).

[77] See Martha Minow, *Who Speaks for the Child? Are Rights Right for Children?* 1987 ABF Res J 203 (1987); Joseph William Singer, *Property Law: Rules, Policies and Practices* 370–72 (1997) (outlining standard arguments on institutional competence and role).

[78] See John Ely, *The Irrepressible Myth of Erie*, 87 Harv L Rev 693 (1974) (identifying presence of both separation of powers and federalism choices in *Erie v Tomkins*); Lawrence Lessig, *Erie—Effects of Volume 110: An Essay on Context in Interpretive Theory*, 110 Harv L Rev 1755 (1997).

cases discuss this selection of institutional decision maker in terms of the very notion—competence—also used to distinguish the patients who could be self-determining from those who cannot be.

Justice O'Connor notes the present "extensive and serious evaluation of physician-assisted suicide" by state legislatures. Given the array of interests that include those of mentally competent dying patients, patients lacking competence or facing pressure, and family members, she finds no reason to distrust the democratic process and indeed endorses the opportunity for experimentation in the laboratories of the states.[79] Here, the allocation of power among the branches seems to be a matter of trust in balancing competing interests. Preserving the Court's role as ultimate arbiter, Justice O'Connor suggests no reason to distrust the state legislatures in this matter.

Dispelling distrust of the democratic process is less Justice Souter's concern than accentuating its greater competence precisely over issues such as physician-assisted suicide. He claims that legislative fact-finding is better suited than adjudication to address disputes over the meaning of data on the Netherlands, the only locale with empirical study of practical experience with physician-assisted suicide and euthanasia.[80] Legislatures have more flexible fact-finding mechanisms and can experiment, and evaluate experiments; courts, instead, must seek finality and durability in their judgments, especially when recognizing unenumerated rights that displace legislative action.[81]

Chief Justice Rehnquist implicitly treats the existence of widespread national debate as evidence that courts should recede and leave the law to elected representatives. Characterizing the nationwide debate about "the morality, legality and practicality" of physician-assisted suicide as "earnest and profound," the majority opinion in *Glucksberg* applauds the continuation of this debate and the Court's refusal to curtail it.[82]

---

[79] *Glucksberg* and *Quill*, 117 S Ct at 2303 (O'Connor, J, concurring).

[80] *Glucksberg*, 117 S Ct at 2292–93 (Souter, J, concurring in the judgment). This opinion, and others in the case, show an unusual degree of interest in comparative law, or at least, comparative practice.

[81] Id at 2292–93.

[82] Id at 2275. This seems an implicit reference to work by scholars such as Professor Mary Ann Glendon that argues that Supreme Court intrusion in widespread debate over abortion interfered with responsible legislative resolutions. See Mary Ann Glendon, *Abortion and Divorce in Western Law* (1987). The majority opinion may also be a basic endorsement

This closing comment by the majority is so salient for Justice Stevens that he chooses his opening paragraph to reply with an effort to reframe the debate over who should decide. Yes, debate should continue, but not only in the legislatures; he emphasizes the "room for further debate about the limits that the Constitution places on the power of the States to punish the practice."[83] For Justice Stevens, the proper precedents are the capital punishment cases.[84] Although the Court upheld the constitutionality of capital punishment in 1976, it continued to review, monitor, critique, and reject state practices in the area.[85] Accordingly, upholding the constitutionality of bans on physician-assisted suicide should not preclude further, and indeed, ongoing, judicial review in the area.

At stake in his exchange with the majority is precisely how to characterize the selection of institutional decision makers. Is this to be governed by the seriousness and breadth of public debate, or instead by readings of the Constitution's protection for individuals? Once again, Justice Souter injects yet another take on the subject. The choice of institutional decision maker should also reflect an obligation to act and not drag behind urgent public claims. For this proposition, he cites the Supreme Court's decision to reject racially segregated schools, the emblem of legitimate judicial activism even in this still racially divided society.[86] Yet, no foot-dragging can be attributed to legislatures in the assisted suicide context, only uncertainty about the effectiveness of guards against abuse. To resolve that kind of uncertainty, legislative competence is superior—but judicial action at some future date may be needed. Justice Souter's formulation thus invites more interaction among the branches, nuanced assessment of particular competencies in

---

of the Court's emerging trend toward enlarging the prerogatives of states and constricting the prerogatives of the federal government. See *Seminole Tribe of Florida v Florida*, 116 S Ct 1114 (1966) (Commerce Clause did not give Congress the power to intrude upon the states given Eleventh Amendment immunity); *United States v Lopez*, 514 US 548 (1995) (federal Gun-Free School Zones Act exceeds authority under the Commerce Clause absent demonstrable nexus between interstate commerce and gun possession in a school zone); *Gregory v Ashrcroft*, 501 US 452 (1991) (no federal authority could challenge state mandatory retirement age for state judges).

[83] *Glucksberg* and *Quill*, 117 S Ct at 2304 (Stevens, J, concurring in the judgments).

[84] Id at 2304.

[85] Id.

[86] *Glucksberg*, 117 S Ct at 2293 (citing *Bolling v Sharpe,* 347 US 497 (1954)) (Souter, J, concurring in the judgment).

particular circumstances, and obligations for judicial action even when legislatures might be better suited.

E. FRAMING DEVICES

Lawyers and judges learn to express the very same points in alternate forms.[87] Broadening and narrowing claims and defenses, rendering them abstract and then concrete, using lines and erasing them, shifting from merits questions to questions about methods or institutions, these are basic techniques in the legal tool kit. It is not unusual, therefore, to find Supreme Court opinions clashing with one another in their uses of such techniques. In the physician-assisted suicide cases, members of the Court explicitly dispute one another's formulations within familiar frames but also fight about the choice of relevant frameworks. Thus, not only do the opinions diverge over how properly to frame the liberty at stake, the method of due process analysis, the equality claim, or the assessment of institutional competencies; they also use the process of reframing the question at issue to move across these categories of analysis.

Standing back from all the details, we can see how the members of the Court painted two pictures of the problem. One presents a choice of two goods: respect for individual autonomy and self-determination versus respect for life and the protection of the vulnerable.[88] The second offers a choice between two bad options: forcing some people to end their days in undignified stupor or unremitting agony, or permitting the pressures of families and health care bureaucracies to accelerate some people's deaths.[89] Either picture presents conflicting commitments and values; neither the pros nor the cons line up simply on one side. What remains most intriguing to me, however, is another framework the justices do not discuss.

II. THE CHOICE OF LIES

Perhaps it is because judges do not usually talk this way. Nonetheless, I think the most honest statement of the issues pre-

---

[87] See generally Morton Horwitz, *Framing Devices*, *BRIDGE Project* (Compact Disk, 1997) (discussing rules vs. balancing, time frames, general vs. particular).

[88] For example, *Glucksberg*, 117 S Ct at 2281 (Souter, J, concurring in the judgment).

[89] For example, *Glucksberg* and *Quill*, 117 S Ct at 2307–08 (Stevens, J, concurring in the judgments).

sented in the physician-assisted suicide cases is this: the Court
faced a choice of two lies to countenance. By lie I mean knowing
misrepresentation; by countenance to extend approval or tolera-
tion.[90] The first lie is that physicians do *not* already, and regularly,
participate in assisting dying patients to end their lives. Every physician I have encountered acknowledges as much; many have written about it.[91] The Court certainly was presented with such accounts through briefs.[92] Indeed, the en banc opinion in *Glucksberg*
so indicated.[93] Because physicians assist the deaths of dying patients
already in the states banning assisted suicide, a Court approving

---

[90] By a lie, I mean statements intended to mislead. See Sisela Bok, *Lying: Moral Choice in Public and Private Life* 6–16 (1978). I do not mean to suggest that the Court generated or created either lie, nor that the members of the Court had the intention to mislead that produced the lies. Instead, a lie, such as the first one I will describe, may be an unacknowl-edged accompaniment to existing practice. A lie, such as the second one I will describe, may instead fail to disclose the effects of a proposed change in legal practice. The Court would countenance one or the other, and could do so explicitly, but instead left the matter implicit. Either way, the Court would be less than candid, in the sense defined by David Shapiro: candor is not only lacking when one has an intent to deceive, but also when one is indifferent to whether the listener is deceived. David L. Shapiro, *In Defense of Judicial Candor*, 100 Harv L Rev 731 (1987). I address the issue of candor in Section III.

Instead of the word, "lie," I could have used "fiction" or "illusion." "Fiction" has the advantage of a suitable definition: "an assumption of a possibility as a fact irrespective of the question of its truth." *Webster's Seventh New Collegiate Dictionary* 310 (G. & C. Merriam, 1971). It has the disadvantage of widespread use, often appreciative, in describing standard legal practices. See, e.g., Lon Fuller, *Legal Fictions* (1967). "Illusion" has a greater emphasis on deception and disordered perception than I mean to imply.

[91] For example, Marcia Angell, 319 New England J Med 1348 (1988).

[92] For example, *Vacco v Quill*, No 95-1858, Brief for Respondents, pp 38–42; Brief Amicus Curiae of the American Medical Student Association and a Coalition of Distinguished Med-ical Professionals in Support of Respondents, pp 18–19; Brief of Amicus Curiae of the Coalition of Hospice Professionals, pp 16–17; Brief Amicus Curiae of State Legislation in Support of Respondents, pp 3–4. At the oral argument, Justice Stevens asked William Wil-liams, who represented the state of Washington, about actual practice of physician-assisted suicide and any subsequent legal responses. Justice Stevens remarked: "it's hard to believe that it has never been committed." *Washington v Glucksberg*, No 96–110, US Supreme Court Official Transcript (Wed Jan 8, 1997), 1997 WL 13671, *57. Williams replied, "I don't disagree with that," and conceded that he knew of no successful prosecutions. Id. See also Timothy E. Quill, *Risk Taking by Physicians in Legally Gray Areas*, 57 Albany L Rev 693, 700–703 (1994) (recounting his own involvement in assisting the suicide of a terminally-ill patient) (hereinafter cited as *Risk Taking*). Timothy E. Quill, *Death and Dig-nity: A Case of Individualized Decision-Making*, 324 New England J Med 691 (1991). Dr. Quill, one of the named plaintiffs in the Ninth Circuit case, concluded: "We also know that there is a secret practice of physician-assisted death in this country. It is hard to get reliable data about the magnitude because it is legally dangerous to talk about it openly. Methodologically flawed research suggests that, in their careers, from three to thirty-seven percent of clinicians have actively assisted at least one patient to die." *Risk Taking* at 699 (citing studies).

[93] *Compassion in Dying v Washington*, 79 F3d 790, 827–28 (CA 9 1996).

such bans participates in the pretense that such prohibitions are in place and enforced.

The second lie is that permitting such assistance would *not* systematically and routinely be used to push dying people into death. The problem is not merely risks of abuse; the problem arises from the inauguration of a regime in which people would have to justify continuing to live.[94] Rooting the permission in a right or protected interest, based in autonomy or dignity, would not save individuals from pressures to die imposed directly or indirectly by family members, physicians, managed care providers, or the patients' own sense of guilt and burden.[95] Naming it a constitutionally protected claim might hide this systematic and foreseeable consequence from view, but even thus veiled, that is the consequence the Supreme Court would authorize if it accepted the challenges before it.[96]

Most of the Justices addressed aspects of what I am calling the second lie as risks of abuse that justify state prohibition of the practice.[97] Their discussions include candid and even eloquent acknowledgments of the variety of risks.[98] Some individuals may not

---

[94] Kreimer (cited in note 1) at 816, 854; Susan R. Martyn and Henry J. Bourguignon, *Physician-Assisted Suicide: The Lethal Flaws of the Ninth and Second Circuit Opinions*, 85 Cal L Rev 371, 408 (1997).

[95] Some may characterize my argument as an effort to justify paternalism, or governmental second-guessing of what would otherwise be the choices made by individuals. This is a special problem for political and legal theories that place respect for individual autonomy and choice at their heart. See Mark Strasser, *The New Paternalism*, 2 Bioethics 104 (1988). Paternalism can carry a range of meanings conveying restrictions on a person's choice-making justified in some sense for that person's own good, see George J. Annas and Joan E. Densberger, *Competence to Refuse Medical Treatment: Autonomy vs. Paternalism*, 15 Toledo L Rev 561, 562 n 2 (1984), and many powerful arguments within a liberal tradition can be proffered for at least some acts of governmental paternalism. See Gerald Dworkin, *Paternalism*, 56 Monist 64 (1972). Moreover, despite the importance of individual autonomy in our Constitution, ours is not a legal system that forbids every constraint on personal autonomy except where necessary to prevent harm to others. Instead, consistent with the mixture of public purposes embraced by the Constitution, a broad range of self-chosen conduct is properly subject to legislative regulation. See Marc Spindelman, *Are the Similarities Between a Woman's Right to Choose an Abortion and the Alleged Right to Assisted Suicide Really Compelling?* 29 U Mich J L Ref 775, 800–804 (1996).

[96] But note the possible interaction between the two lies: if everyone were to know they could get lethal medication—and thus see through lie number 1, would this drift into lie number 2 territory? Thanks to Frank Michelman for this complication; yet hence my emphasis on the difference between a sub rosa practice and a declaration of a right.

[97] See supra (discussing opinions).

[98] The majority opinion respects each of the defenses: preservation of life; responding to the public health problem of suicide, especially among vulnerable groups; protecting the integrity of the medical profession; and guarding against abuse and prejudice toward the elderly, the poor, and disabled persons. *Glucksberg*, 117 S Ct at 2272–74. Justice O'Connor finds sufficient the state interest in protecting those who are not truly competent or facing

be mentally competent, or may be depressed, or may have so much unmanaged pain that they cannot be seen as making a rational, unfettered choice to die. Others may not actually be dying, but may be led to think so. Or they may indeed have a fatal illness, but not be close yet to the hour of death.[99] Still others, both competent and dying, may recoil from the experience of burdening their loved ones financially and emotionally. Physicians who become familiar with assisting the competent, dying, and unpressured patient may wish, out of compassion, exhaustion, or efficiency to extend the same help to others who do not fit that mold.

One can begin to add up all these groups and find that they comprise a sizable majority. Apparently, it is actually a rather small class of people who would evade "abuse" of assisted suicide. It would be a lie, in short, to maintain that any regime permitting physician-assisted suicide would safeguard large numbers of people against abuse. No one on the Court, of course, implied such a lie; all were persuaded that the risks justified the state legislation. But that is not the lie that concerns me.

The lie I mean depends on the very idea that some line would remain between abuse and nonabuse in a regime permitting assisted suicide. The lie is the denial that such a regime reaches beyond vulnerable patients to all patients, dying and not; to all family members, self-serving or not; and to all physicians, those who endorse suicide assistance and those who do not. The option of medical assistance in dying would alter the menu for all involved. It would turn the continuation of living into a question, open for debate, doubt, and persuasion.

Exits change what it means to be here. A right to terminate treatment makes continuing treatment a daily choice.[100] A right to abort a pregnancy makes continuing the pregnancy a deliberate act. A right to divorce makes maintaining a marriage a matter of volition. Even with inertia and the pulls of continuity at work, of-

---

imminent death or whose decisions to die are not truly voluntary. Id at 2303 (O'Connor, J, concurring). Justice Souter acknowledges risks to terminally ill patients from involuntary suicide and euthanasia, but more tellingly identifies the difficulty distinguishing knowing and voluntary patient decisions from their supposed opposites. Id at 2290–91 (Souter, J, concurring in the judgment).

[99] See *Vacco v Quill*, Brief of the American Medical Association et al, No 95-1858, p 12.

[100] And rigorous restrictions on terminating treatment make it necessary to have advance written directives or written appointments of proxy decision makers, a situation which Susan Wolf has described as requiring "a document to die."

fering a way out makes staying a subject for decision, argument, and justification. A right to the aid of a doctor in ending your life means that dying patients will be invited to think about its exercise, family members will consider it, hospitals and nursing homes will institutionalize it, popular culture will elaborate it, and young, vibrant people will contemplate it. None of the Justices articulated these consequences of the interests asserted by the plaintiffs.

Nor did the Justices discuss the first lie, the one ultimately given new life by their opinions. Justice Stevens came close. He noted that "physicians are already involved in making decisions that hasten the death of terminally ill patients—through termination of life support, withholding of medical treatment, and terminal sedation—" so "there is in fact significant tension between the traditional view of the physician's role and the actual practice in a growing number of cases."[101] The attached footnote does not, however, pursue practice, but instead surveys of physicians' views that demonstrate significant support for the practice.[102] The briefs before the Court, as well as published accounts, made it clear that substantial numbers of physicians already assist the suicides of terminal patients,[103] so the Justice made the choice not to include such references.

Ultimately, choosing which lie to endorse is a horrible choice. Neither is appealing. Putting public power to the service of a lie should never be appealing, although it is often expedient. Yet the difficulty, for the Court, is even deeper. Should the choice be made explicit? What greater good could justify retreating from candor?

III. The Choice on Candor

Scholars debate the values of judicial candor, introspection, and attention to appearance.[104] Guido Calebresi has explained and

---

[101] *Glucksberg*, 117 S Ct at 2309 (Stevens, J, concurring in the judgment).

[102] Id at 2309 n 12.

[103] See note 92.

[104] See, e.g., Guido Calebresi and Philip Bobbit, *Tragic Choices* (1978); Scott Altman, *Beyond Candor*, 89 Mich L Rev 296 (1990); Guido Calebresi, *Bakke as Pseudo-Tragedy*, 28 Cath U L Rev 427 (1979); Deborah Hellmann, *The Importance of Appearing Principled*, 37 Ariz L Rev 1107 (1995); Shapiro (cited in note 90). See also Martha Minow, *Judging Inside Out*, 61 Colum L Rev 795 (1990) (considering differences between what judges and outside observers can describe about what they do).

at times justified the practice of social subterfuge, with euthanasia as a prime example.[105] We retain laws against it, and even at times prosecute, but do not convict; we use juries to produce acquittals without needing reasons as they exercise their subversive power of nullification. David Shapiro prefers candor, which includes overcoming indifference to whether the listener is deceived,[106] to promote respect for the judiciary and to the trust necessary in carrying on in human affairs.[107] Thus, he would render explicit for the jury their power to acquit if they find the accused physician not blameworthy; he would prefer even more the development of explicit processes of individual self-governance through "living wills," or advance directives.[108]

Decision without reasons is not available to the Supreme Court. The Court should appear principled, argues Deborah Hellmann, in order to maintain and build the esteem with which it is held.[109] The physician-assisted suicide cases, then, present the problem of how candid to be. Full candor might cut against the appearance of principled reasoning, if I am right in asserting that the Court faced a choice between which lie to countenance. For no lines of precedent, methods of constitutional analysis, or other tools for giving reasons offer guidance about choosing among lies. Simply picking offers no reasons; the most likely reasons depend on calculating social and personal harms, about which the Court as a whole and its members as individuals may have little knowledge or competence to predict.

Imagining how individual members of the Court might contemplate the choice of lies is, of course, almost as difficult as imagining how they each contemplated the issues of death and dying directly presented in the case. The two subjects, though, may be intimately connected. For considering death is not just an abstract question for adults, especially adults who are aging, and whose parents,

---

[105] See Calebresi (cited in note 104).

[106] Shapiro at 732 (cited in note 90).

[107] Id at 736–37.

[108] Id at 747–48. The validity of these documents could be questioned, however, if social, economic, and familial pressures turn these devices of voluntary consent into paper excuses for devaluing the lives of the dying. Since relatively few people currently undertake to write such documents, however, it is difficult to find them significant in demonstrating either consent or its opposite.

[109] Hellmann at 1120–30 (cited in note 104).

spouses, friends, and colleagues have died. That the subject touches even the Justices personally is apparent at least in Justice O'Connor's opinion. She writes in the first person plural: "Death will be different for each of us. . . . Every one of us at some point may be affected by our own or a family member's terminal illness."[110]

In this very candid disclosure, Justice O'Connor departs from the third-person distance in surrounding opinions. Acknowledging awareness of how personally and directly the topic reaches, her opinion nevertheless remains the one less candid in the choices presented. For hers is the opinion that elides the difference between access to pain medication that would have the additional effect of hastening death and control over the moment and circumstances of death.[111] Perhaps, then, we have a dialectic or tension between disclosure and dissembling around the topic of dying.

Certainly observers of American culture assert massive national inability to deal with dying and death.[112] Perhaps the Court's lack of candor in issues surrounding physician-assisted death should simply be predicted as a reflection of the surrounding cultural discomfort. Indeed, in this light, the Court's discussions and open debates are fresh, explicit, and potentially salutary in inspiring popular commentary and dinner-table conversations. Yet the discomfort with death and dying, observers say, also helps to explain the growing preoccupation with assisted suicide, and other techniques for sanitizing and controlling the dying process, as well as exaggerated hopes that medicine can extend life.[113] From this vantage point, the Court's biggest failure lies in its assumption that death should be feared and managed rather than experienced. The failure to discuss this assumption, though, simply means that the Justices, and most of those who argued before them, reflect the times and place in which they live.

In contrast, neglecting to discuss the two lies presented to the Court could reflect a deliberate decision to prefer the appearance

---

[110] *Glucksberg* at 2303 (O'Connor, J, concurring).

[111] See text at notes 15–33.

[112] See Daniel Calahan, *The Troubled Dream of Life* (1993); Sherwin B. Nuland, *How We Die: Reflections on Life's Final Chapter* (1993); Kathleen M. Boozang, *An Intimate Passing: Restoring the Role of Family and Religion in Dying*, 58 U Pitt L Rev 549, 556 (1997).

[113] See Boozang at 556–58 (cited in note 112).

of principle to the practice of disclosure. It could manifest the workings of subconscious processes of denial. Or it could result from a decision to leave such processes in place to the extent they exist in the minds of the public.

In any of these cases, to discuss the lies is to expose them to view, to disrupt the split-screen that allows us to say we forbid assisted suicide and yet know friends, physicians, and talk-show guests participating in it, and made-for-television movies depicting and sometimes advocating it. To discuss the choice of lies is to raise to visibility the social meanings that are taken for granted, that "rely for their source upon expectations or understandings not themselves (then) in question."[114] Neither lie could operate the way they otherwise would if made transparent in opinions of the Supreme Court. The Justices either hoped to leave the social practices at stake uncontested, or else fell prey to that very lack of contest in their own unawareness of the stakes before them.[115] In this light, I return with even greater wonder at the heightened self-consciousness in these opinions about how to talk, how to phrase what was at issue.[116]

IV. Don't Ask, Don't Tell[117]

The Court's formulations—balancing liberty and respect for life and human vulnerabilities; comparing the bad deaths with involuntary killings[118]—are not dishonest. Yet they are incomplete. Neglecting the lies that would be countenanced by either decision tragically runs the risk of simplifying the conflict presented.[119] For if the two lies are confronted, further complications ensue.

The first involves questions of equality. This is not the equal

---

[114] Lawrence Lessig, *The Regulation of Social Meaning*, 62 U Chi L Rev 943, 959 (1995).

[115] The high degree of legislative, public, and scholarly debate generated in advance, and after, the case suggests, however, that contests are already well under way.

[116] See Section I.

[117] For a powerful treatment of the "Don't Ask, Don't Tell, Don't Pursue" policy on homosexuality in the military—and comparisons with issues of racial identity—see Sharon Elizabeth Rush, *Equal Protection Analogies—Identity and 'Passing': Race and Sexual Orientation*, 13 Harv Blackletter L J 65 (1997).

[118] See supra (offering these formulations).

[119] Compare Martha Nussbaum, *The Fragility of Goodness: Luck and Ethics in Greek Tragedy and Philosophy* 49–82 (1986) (exploring tragedy in failures to acknowledge complexity of problems and competing demands).

protection challenge presented to the Court, which contested the availability of physician-assisted death for those on life support or those who could justify sedated death.[120] Instead, the questions involve inequality in access. If we acknowledge that assisted suicide is already going on, we should then address, for whom? Some, by dint of economic clout or trusting connections with doctors, can secure sufficient prescriptions for barbiturates or other death-giving medications. Many others cannot. This circumstance most likely presents policy and regulatory issues rather than matters amenable to constitutional adjudication, but it is reminiscent of abortion restrictions and the debates that they have engendered.[121]

Many inequality issues that would arise if physician-assisted suicide became permitted did surface in the Court's opinions. Hence, the discussions of greater risks of abuse for vulnerable persons, and even, in the majority opinion, consideration of "prejudice, negative and inaccurate stereotypes and societal indifference" toward disabled and terminally ill people.[122] Unmentioned by the Justices is the special set of risks for women, who, experts predict, might numerically predominate if assisted suicide is legitimated.[123]

Yet even beyond those very real concerns are once again problems of access. If, as Justice Souter explores, the crucial reasons to seek *physician*-assisted suicide rather than simply suicide is to obtain wise counsel, treating the whole person and not just the body,[124] who would have access to such kinds of physician assistance, and who would not? The specter of managed health care, and the 37 million Americans lacking health insurance for some of the year, are problematic here not only because it would be

---

[120] See text at notes 58–76 (discussing equal protection claim).

[121] See *Harris v McRae*, 448 US 297, reh'g denied, 448 US 917 (1980) (ban on use of public funds for abortions does not impinge upon a fundamental right because it does not place a direct obstacle in the path of exercising that right). For a discussion of this and other bans on the use of Medicaid for abortions, see Linda M. Vanzi, *Freedom at Home: State Constitutions and Medicaid Funding for Abortions*, 26 NM L Rev 433 (1996).

[122] *Glucksberg*, 117 S Ct at 2273.

[123] Women face disproportionate probabilities of depression, untreated depression, and bias in medical treatment. See Susan M. Wolf, *Gender, Feminism and Death: Physician-Assisted Suicide and Euthanasia*, in Susan M. Wolf, ed, *Feminism and Bioethics: Beyond Reproduction* 282 (Oxford University Press, 1996); Susan M. Wolf, *Physician-Assisted Suicide, Abortion, and Treatment Refusal: Using Gender to Analyze the Difference*, in Robert F. Weir, ed, *Physician-Assisted Suicide* 167, 179–80, 185 (Indiana University Press, 1997).

[124] *Glucksberg*, 117 S Ct at 2288–89 (Souter, J, concurring in the judgment).

cheaper to offer assisted suicide than treatment or palliative care.[125] Even those privileged to have managed care will be unlikely to have easy access, sustained relationships, or effective opportunities for communication with individual physicians.[126] The risk that the suicide option will be misused arises for all who do not have close and long-term ties to physicians. This risk arises, indeed, for all who do not have physicians who are themselves unfettered by economic incentives to kill or to foreshorten conversations.

Confronting the choice of lies would also expose to view basic issues of governing. Acknowledging that assisted suicide proceeds, usually secretly, especially in jurisdictions that ban it, would unmask for discussion the fundamental character of criminal prohibitions. Banning a practice means the government cannot regulate it. Banning a practice drives it underground and creates a market for it among the unscrupulous and dishonest. Banning a practice makes even those who have integrity reluctant to discuss it or consult about it.[127] When are these dangers worth the symbolic benefits, and marginal deterrent effects, of prohibition? The subject has been much discussed in the context of alcohol, marijuana, and prostitution.[128] The contours of a given situation, however, require particular attention. An honest discussion of the costs and benefits of prohibiting and regulating assisted suicide could now ensue in states, authorized as they are to experiment.[129] Yet explicit ac-

---

[125] See Martyn & Bourguignon at 419 (cited in note 94).

[126] Id at 423–25. The authors also note the sobering results of studies that show that physicians as a group would treat patients less aggressively than patients themselves would choose. Id at 424 & n 261.

[127] Id at 418 (noting that Dr. Quill was reluctant to consult with others about the individual who sought his assistance with suicide for fear of his and her legal jeopardy).

[128] A total ban on activities or products deemed harmful can communicate social disapproval while creating incentives for a black market; legalization and regulation can lessen the symbolic disapproval while enabling public monitoring and enforceable restrictions. See John F. Decker, *Prostitution: Regulation and Control* 67–74, 273–362 (1979). For a comparison of the ban on prostitution in the United States and the regulatory approach in the Netherlands, see Jessica N. Drexler, *Government's Role in Turning Tricks: The World's Oldest Profession in the Netherlands and the United States*, 15 Dickinson J Int'l L 201 (1996).

[129] Oregon may soon provide the first experiment with a law legalizing assisted suicide. The state's Death with Dignity Act permits a mentally competent person deemed likely to die within six months to obtain a lethal drug after consultation with two doctors and a fifteen-day waiting period. Although a federal district court overturned the act as an equal protection affront to the treatment of terminally-ill patients, the Court of Appeals for the Ninth Circuit reversed on the ground that the plaintiffs had not actually been harmed by the law and therefore lacked standing to sue. *Lee v State of Oregon*, 107 F3d 1382 (CA 9 1997), cert denied, *Lee v Harcleroad*, 1997 WL 274930 (U.S. Oct 14, 1997). Because the Supreme Court declined to accept certiorari, the law is left in place. In the meantime, the

knowledgment of these issues by the Court would have launched a more fruitful process of dialogue and learning, across the branches.

Another more basic governance question, likely to emerge if the choice of lies became transparent, involves how much communication or commerce ought there be between those who enforce the laws and those who are to obey them. The question has been well stated by Meir Dan-Cohen, in what he calls the "acoustic separation" of rules for decision makers and rules for the governed.[130] If, for whatever reasons, the decision makers implement a less rigorous standard than the one announced to the governed, it may be best not to disclose this, in order to promote more conduct approximating the announced rule. Disclosing the more lenient decision-making practice, in contrast, would likely expand the numbers of violations of the rule of conduct.[131] In other words, if it were known that most, or all, physicians who assist in suicides for dying patients evade either prosecution or conviction, fewer physicians would refrain from such conduct.

A Court that explicitly addressed the choice of lies would narrow the "acoustic separation" in the field of physician-assisted suicide, or at least render open for discussion the apparent distance between the prohibition and practices. Even with this Court's silence, it would be hard, if not impossible, now, to keep secret the leniency of prosecutors and juries when faced with physicians who help dying patients die. Once again, considering the choice of lies might help the legislatures now considering varied regimes to prohibit, permit, and regulate assisted suicide. In any case, considering the choice of lies would point to the issues of equality and governance that otherwise may lie too low to be picked up on the radar of watching publics.

Yet perhaps not talking of such things is the best avenue toward

---

Oregon legislature decided to put the issue to the voters again with a referendum by mail balloting.

Other experiments are under way in the Netherlands, the Northern Territories of Australia, and Switzerland. See Ronald Dworkin, *Assisted Suicide: The Philosopher's Brief* (cited in note 64), at 41 n 3.

[130] Meir Dan-Cohen, *Decision Rules and Conduct Rules: On Acoustic Separation in Criminal Law*, 97 Harv L Rev 625 (1984).

[131] Analogous issues arise for lawyers whose clients might choose to violate the law if the lawyers disclose a low likelihood of detection or prosecution by the relevant law enforcement agency. See David B. Wilkins, *Making Context Count: Regulating Lawyers After Kaye, Scholer*, 66 S Cal L Rev 1145, 1172 (1993).

some preferred ends. Antonio Cassesse, the Chief Judge for the Bosnia War Crimes Tribunal, startled me as I interviewed him about his work by referring to euthanasia, the practice neighboring assisted suicide, but involving the physician directly in killing the patient.[132] I had asked why his Court had not considered granting immunity or amnesty to certain indicted criminals in order to obtain their testimony to advance other prosecutions. He immediately responded that it reminded him of his views on euthanasia. He said he knows it goes on, and he wants those who engage in it to live every day suspended before the uncertainty over whether they may be prosecuted. Yet, like so many indicted and unindicted war criminals, most doctors who assist the deaths of the patients will not be caught or charged. The degree of uncertainty and angst encircling the physicians will depend, in no small measure, on the degree of distance between them and the actual practices of the legal system.

It is for reasons implied by Cassesse that I believe the Supreme Court picked, without acknowledging it, the better lie to countenance in the physician-assisted suicide cases. For now, at least, it is better to live with the lie that prohibition prevents the practice than the lie that its approval would not cost all of us, deeply. It is better to live with the lie that prohibition works so that, at the margin, those who engage in it do so with trembling. And even those jurisdictions that explore its authorization do so with humility and caution.

Veiling realities of law can heighten its power. Mysteries surrounding death increase its terror. Candor about veils and mysteries can distract us, temporarily, from power and terror. But how we talk about, and decide, how we and others die, tells us all how we mean to live.

---

[132] Interview, Nov 1996, The Hague.

DAVID COLE

THE VALUE OF SEEING THINGS DIFFERENTLY: BOERNE v FLORES AND CONGRESSIONAL ENFORCEMENT OF THE BILL OF RIGHTS

On June 19, 1997, the Supreme Court let stand a death sentence against Joseph Roger O'Dell III, who had been sentenced to death under procedures that the Court acknowledged violated the Constitution.[1] The jury that sentenced O'Dell to die did so because it found that he posed a threat of future danger. The jury never learned that O'Dell's only alternative sentence was life without parole, because the state court barred O'Dell's lawyer from informing the jury of that fact. In 1994, the Supreme Court ruled that denying the jury such information contravenes due process.[2] But O'Dell's conviction had become final six years earlier, and in 1997, the Court reasoned that because its 1994 ruling was not " 'dictated by precedent existing at the time the defendant's conviction became final,' " it could not be relied upon to vacate O'Dell's sentence.[3] Although the state's procedures had violated

David Cole is Professor, Georgetown University Law Center.

AUTHOR'S NOTE: I would like to thank for their comments and input my colleagues Alex Aleinikoff, Bill Eskridge, Nina Pillard, Michael Seidman, Mark Tushnet, and Carlos Vazquez, and my research assistants Andrew J. Camelio and Jeff Smagula.

[1] *O'Dell v Netherland*, 117 S Ct 1969 (1997).

[2] *Simmons v South Carolina*, 512 US 154 (1994).

[3] *O'Dell*, 117 S Ct at 1973 (quoting *Teague v Lane*, 489 US 288, 301 (1989)). Mr. O'Dell's sentence had become "final" in 1988, when the Supreme Court declined to review his state court conviction.

O'Dell's constitutional rights, its interpretation of the Constitution was not unreasonable at the time, and therefore the Court deferred to the state and let it execute O'Dell.

The *O'Dell* case received some public attention, but for reasons unrelated to the issue before the Supreme Court; the Pope, among others, had intervened on O'Dell's behalf. As a doctrinal matter, however, the Supreme Court's decision broke no new ground. The Court simply followed *Teague v Lane*,[4] a 1989 decision holding that "new" constitutional rules should not be applied on federal habeas corpus review to upset state court convictions that became final before the "new" rule was announced. A rule is "new," according to this doctrine, whenever a reasonable jurist could have reached a different conclusion about what the Constitution substantively requires, and the Court in *O'Dell* simply found that that deferential standard had been met.

Less than one week later, the Court held unconstitutional the Religious Freedom Restoration Act (RFRA).[5] RFRA's infirmity, according to the six-person majority, was that Congress enacted it pursuant to an understanding of the Free Exercise Clause different from the Court's own view. In 1990, in *Employment Division v Smith*,[6] the Court had ruled that religious groups have no constitutional right to object to generally applicable laws that have the effect of burdening their religion—such as laws banning home schooling, or generally denying unemployment compensation to people who cannot work on Saturdays. RFRA was a response to the decision that accommodation is not constitutionally required; it sought to extend to religious groups a statutory right to accommodation where neutral laws substantially burdened their religious practices. Citing Section 5 of the Fourteenth Amendment, RFRA's defenders maintained that Congress was "enforc[ing], through appropriate legislation" the due process guarantee of the Fourteenth Amendment, which the Supreme Court had read to include the right of free exercise of religion. In *Boerne v Flores*,[7] the Court rejected that argument, reasoning that Congress had overstepped its authority to "enforce" due process, and had impermissibly

---

[4] 489 US 288 (1989).

[5] *Boerne v Flores*, 117 S Ct 2157 (1997).

[6] 494 US 872 (1990).

[7] 117 S Ct 2157.

sought to redefine the constitutional content of due process by providing religious groups more legal protection than the Supreme Court had said the Constitution required.

At first blush, *O'Dell* and *Flores* seem to have little in common. One addresses the retroactivity of constitutional decisions when state criminal convictions are reviewed in federal court, and the other the power of Congress to provide broader protection to civil rights and civil liberties than the Court itself has provided. But a comparison of the two cases reveals a basic tension in the Supreme Court's conception of constitutional interpretation.

O'Dell and *Teague* are premised on an understanding that reasonable people can and do disagree about the meaning and content of many of the Constitution's most basic provisions. Where a constitutional rule is " 'susceptible to debate among reasonable minds,' " the Court explained in *O'Dell*, it would be unfair to impose that rule "retroactively" through federal habeas review to invalidate state court convictions—even if it means that a person will be executed pursuant to a procedure that we now acknowledge was fundamentally unfair. Where the meaning of a constitutional provision is open to reasonable disagreement, comity to the states counsels against imposing today's constitutional understanding on yesterday's criminal processes, even where the result is tomorrow's execution.

Flores is predicated on a very different view of the Constitution. Under *Flores*, the Constitution means precisely what a majority of the Supreme Court says it means, and there is no room for reasonable disagreement. RFRA fell because Congress sought to extend statutory protection to religious freedom that the Supreme Court had said was not required by the Free Exercise Clause of the First Amendment. The Court reasoned that Congress's Section 5 power to enforce liberty does not extend to enforcing a substantive understanding of free exercise that differs in any respect from the Court's substantive understanding. It did not matter that reasonable people can and do disagree about the substantive content of the Free Exercise Clause. It did not matter that the Supreme Court itself had disagreed, and for more than twenty-five years prior to the *Smith* decision had interpreted the Free Exercise Clause much as Congress did in RFRA. It did not matter that four (presumably reasonable) Justices dissented in *Smith* itself, reading the Constitution as Congress later did in RFRA. And it did not matter that

RFRA expanded legal protections for religious freedom without contravening any express constitutional prohibition.[8] Congress had disagreed with the Court on what the Constitution means, and that was unacceptable.

Thus, under *O'Dell* and *Teague*, the Court views the Constitution as open-ended and subject to change, justifying deference to state judges who make "reasonable" mistakes in interpreting it. But under *Flores*, the Constitution has a determinate meaning that only the Supreme Court can divine, and if Congress deviates from the Court's substantive understanding in any way, its actions are per se invalid.

This article explores the implications of the contrasting understandings of constitutional interpretation that underlie *O'Dell* and *Flores*. My focus will be on *Flores*; *O'Dell* is discussed principally as a foil for the theory of constitutional interpretation that informs the Court's rationale in *Flores*. I do not seek to replay the extensive debate on Congress's power to enforce liberty under Section 5 of the Fourteenth Amendment, but rather to reveal the unspoken theories of constitutional interpretation that underlie the Court's most recent position in that continuing debate. The debate is far from over, and despite *Flores*'s air of certainty, the decision raises more questions than it answers.[9] But my principal point is that the answer *Flores* does give is the wrong one. A proper recognition of the relationship between constitutional interpretation and institutional roles would afford Congress far more deference than the Court gave it in *Flores* when Congress extends statutory protection to liberty under Section 5 of the Fourteenth Amendment.

The root of the difficulty presented by the Fourteenth Amendment is that unlike most provisions in the Constitution, it empowers two branches with concurrent authority to enforce its guarantees: the Court and Congress. Most constitutional provisions are enforceable by only one branch, with the other branches performing a checking function. Thus, the federal courts have authority to enforce the Bill of Rights against the federal government,

---

[8] Only Justice Stevens thought that RFRA contravened an express constitutional prohibition, the Establishment Clause. *Flores*, 117 S Ct at 2172 (Stevens concurring). See note 18.

[9] For a more optimistic view of *Flores*'s implications for Congress's power to enforce liberty, see Christopher Eisgruber and Lawrence Sager, *Congressional Power and Religious Liberty After City of Boerne*, 1997 Supreme Court Review 311.

subject to the checks of appointment, impeachment, and control of jurisdiction. And Congress has authority to enforce most of the provisions in Article I, Section 8, such as the taxing and spending powers, subject to the presidential veto, and judicial review. But the Fourteenth Amendment simultaneously vests both Congress and the judiciary with authority to enforce its guarantees. Two questions are raised by the vesting of concurrent power: Who has the final say, and what standard of review should the branch with final say apply to the other's actions?

In *Flores*, the Supreme Court confused these questions. It treated a claim that the Court should deferentially review Congress's constitutional interpretations under Section 5 as equivalent to a claim that the Court should surrender its final say on constitutional matters. It therefore rejected a deferential approach, and interpreted Section 5 as giving Congress only remedial authority, that is, the power to specify remedies for violations of "equal protection" and "due process" as the Court has substantively defined those terms. The Court flatly rejected the notion that equal protection, due process, or any of the rights incorporated in the Due Process Clause might have different substantive meanings for purposes of judicial and legislative enforcement. Because Congress adopted a different substantive understanding of the Free Exercise Clause than the Court had, RFRA was invalid.

In my view, the *Flores* Court failed to consider the institutional implications of the Fourteenth Amendment's grant of concurrent enforcement power. Congress and the Court are very different bodies, with different competences and different limitations that cannot help but influence their respective constitutional interpretations. The Court is constrained in its interpretations by concerns about institutional manageability, by the case or controversy requirement, which precludes the Court from acting proactively, and by the knowledge that its constitutional dictates are relatively difficult to change. Congress, by contrast, has broader investigatory and agenda-setting powers, and the ability to create and fund extensive structural mechanisms to protect rights. In addition, congressional enforcement of the Constitution (by statute) is more susceptible to change than judicial enforcement (by decree). In light of these differences, it would be surprising if the two branches interpreted the Constitution identically for purposes of their respective enforcement authorities. The Court's decision in *Flores* failed to acknowledge these differences, and treated the Constitution as if it can have only one meaning, no matter which branch is enforcing or interpreting it.

The notion that concurrent enforcement authority may properly give rise to different substantive understandings of legal norms is illustrated by two other areas of concurrent power: the Commerce Clause and administrative law. Like the Fourteenth Amendment, and unlike most other provisions of the Constitution, the Commerce Clause has been interpreted to authorize concurrent judicial and legislative enforcement. But under the Commerce Clause, unlike the Fourteenth Amendment, the Court recognizes that judicial interpretation and congressional interpretation need not be identical. Congress has much more leeway in enforcing the Commerce Clause through legislation than does the Court in enforcing the Commerce Clause through adjudication. The Court would be unlikely, for example, to find that a minimum wage law was required by the Commerce Clause, but Congress nonetheless may choose to impose one. Congress's power to regulate pursuant to the Commerce Clause is not limited to the substantive meaning that the Court assigns to the so-called Dormant Commerce Clause. Nor should Congress's power to enforce the Fourteenth Amendment be limited to the precise substantive meaning the Court gives that Amendment when the Court enforces it itself.

Institutional differences also lead to different substantive results in administrative law. Many federal statutes are subject to enforcement by two institutions: administrative agencies and the judiciary. Yet the Court does not require that administrative agencies hew to the precise substantive meaning that the Court itself would assign to a statute. Under *Chevron USA, Inc. v NRDC*,[10] the judiciary defers to an administrative agency's interpretation of an ambiguous statute that the agency enforces, even where the agency interpretation differs from the judiciary's interpretation, as long as the administrative agency adopts a reasonable construction. This deference is justified in part by the fact that the courts and administrative agencies have different institutional competences. A similar understanding about Congress supports deferential judicial review of Congress's substantive interpretations of liberty under Section 5 of the Fourteenth Amendment.

---

[10] 467 US 837, 843–44 (1984).

Part I of this article introduces the issue presented in *Flores*. Part II addresses the first of the two infirmities that the Court identified in RFRA, namely, the claim that Congress violated the separation of powers by intruding upon the judiciary's constitutional province. I argue that this criticism is a red herring, because congressional legislation pursuant to a constitutional provision is quite different in its effects and consequences from a judicial interpretation of that same provision, and in no way infringes on judicial power. Part III addresses the more substantial objection to RFRA, namely, that it intrudes on state sovereignty by extending federal dictates beyond Congress's enumerated powers. I argue that this objection also fails, because any federalism-based objection would apply with even more force to judicial interpretation and enforcement of the Fourteenth Amendment.

Part IV identifies and criticizes the theory of constitutional interpretation that underlies *Flores*. The Court fails to acknowledge the significance of the institutional differences between congressional and judicial enforcement of the Constitution; once those differences are considered, a much more deferential approach to Congress's Section 5 powers is appropriate. This is not to say that judicial supremacy in interpreting the Constitution is unwarranted. The Court should and must continue to play a role in assessing whether Congress's Section 5 actions are consistent with the substantive values of the Fourteenth Amendment. But in doing so, the Court should defer to Congress's substantive interpretive choices, upholding them as long as they are reasonable, even if they do not track precisely the Court's determination of the Amendment's meaning for purposes of judicial enforcement. The differences between legislative and judicial enforcement of the Constitution— wholly ignored in *Flores*—justify a substantive gap between the Court's interpretation of the Fourteenth Amendment and Congress's.

Finally, Part V returns to the retroactivity doctrine applied in *O'Dell* and the structurally similar qualified immunity doctrine, to illustrate that in other settings the Court does defer to government actors' reasonable interpretations of the Constitution that depart from its own. The arguments for deference to Congress under Section 5 are at least as strong as those for deference to state courts and government officials that inform the Court's habeas and qualified immunity doctrines.

I. Smith, RFRA, and Their Critics

The Religious Freedom Restoration Act was so titled because it sought to restore the protection for religious freedom that
had governed the United States for more than two decades prior
to the Supreme Court's decision in *Employment Division v Smith*.
The Act said as much. It described its purpose as "to restore the
compelling interest test as set forth in *Sherbert v Verner*, 374 U.S.
398 (1963) and *Wisconsin v Yoder*, 406 U.S. 205 (1972) and to guarantee its application in all cases where free exercise of religion is
substantially burdened."[11] In *Sherbert* and *Yoder*, the Court had
held that where facially neutral laws of general applicability impose
a substantial burden on the exercise of religion, they must be justified by a compelling government interest. In *Smith*, a closely divided Court effectively reversed those cases, and held that facially
neutral laws of general applicability raise no free exercise issue
even if they impose extreme burdens on religious practices.[12] The
Court limited free exercise claims to laws that are specifically targeted at or intended to burden religious practices.

The line the Court drew in *Smith* is a familiar one in constitutional law; in essence, it replaced an "effects" test with an "intent"
test. Under prior free exercise doctrine, a law's burdensome effect
on religious practice would trigger strict scrutiny; after *Smith*, only
laws intended to burden or facially targeted at religion receive such
review. This is the same line the Court has drawn in equal protection doctrine, where it has ruled that strict scrutiny is triggered
only by laws and practices that intend to discriminate on the basis
of a suspect classification or that are facially predicated on such
classifications. It also resonates with the Court's speech jurisprudence, where laws targeted at the content of speech are subject to
strict scrutiny, but laws that only have incidental effects on speech
are subject to minimal rationality review.

Just as the rejection of an effects test in equal protection doctrine has come under intense criticism, so too did the *Smith* decision. Critics maintained that it was insensitive to the character of

---

[11] The Religious Freedom Restoration Act, 42 USC § 2000bb(b)(1) (1996).

[12] The Court did not technically reverse *Yoder* and *Sherbert*, choosing instead to distinguish them on various grounds. But the Court did expressly reject the test that those cases
had applied.

most legal impediments to free exercise. Only rarely do legislators or government officials openly target religious practices because of animus toward the practices themselves. Far more common are laws and practices of general applicability that simply fail to take into account their often severe impact on the religious practices of minority religions. The unemployment compensation laws struck down in *Sherbert v Verner*[13] and *Thomas v Review Board*,[14] which required that recipients be willing to work on Saturdays in order to be eligible for benefits, were not enacted for the purpose of burdening the religious practices of those who observe the Sabbath on Saturday, but they nonetheless had that effect. Similarly, there was no evidence that the compulsory schooling law in *Wisconsin v Yoder*[15] was intended to burden the Amish, yet it had that effect. Free exercise jurisprudence prior to *Smith* mandated that legislators consider the costs that generally applicable laws imposed on religious practices, and consider accommodation. *Smith* eliminated that mandate, and critics feared that legislatures would adopt laws that ignored the special needs of minority religions.

RFRA was Congress's response. Conservatives and liberals, Republicans and Democrats joined together to enact it in an unusual bipartisan effort—only three members of Congress voted against its passage, and President Clinton enthusiastically signed it into law.[16] RFRA embraced as a statutory matter the test that the Court had employed as a constitutional matter before *Smith*, by providing that government could not "substantially burden" the exercise of religion unless: (1) it had "a compelling government interest" for doing so, and (2) the law or practice in question was "the least restrictive means of furthering that compelling government interest."[17]

RFRA's critics launched two principal attacks, both of which the Supreme Court in *Flores* accepted. First, they contended that the statute violated the separation of powers, intruding on the judiciary's province by attempting to override a constitutional decision

---

[13] 374 US 398 (1963).

[14] 450 US 707 (1981).

[15] 406 US 205 (1972).

[16] Remarks on Signing the Religious Freedom Restoration Act of 1993, 29 Weekly Comp Pres Doc 2377 (Nov 16, 1993).

[17] 42 USC § 2000bb-1(a),(b) (1996).

through ordinary legislation. Second, they argued that it exceeded Congress's powers vis-à-vis the states, impermissibly intruding into areas of state sovereignty without authorization from the Constitution. The first criticism, I will argue, is a red herring—whatever else one might say about RFRA, it did not violate the separation of powers. The second criticism is far more substantial, but I believe it ultimately founders on a failure to consider adequately the institutional dimensions of constitutional interpretation.[18]

II. Separation of Powers

The first contention, stressed by lawyers for the City of Boerne, was that Congress had stepped on the Court's toes. By seeking to "reverse" *Smith*, the City argued, Congress had failed to respect the principle that it is the Court's province "to say what the law is."[19] The City argued that "Congress has taken over the judicial function of interpreting the Constitution," and has thereby "co-opted the Court's interpretive role."[20]

The Supreme Court agreed. Its substantive analysis begins and ends with references to *Marbury v Madison* and the separation of powers. The Court concluded that "RFRA contradicts vital principles necessary to maintain separation of powers."[21] By "interpret[ing] the Constitution, [Congress] ha[d] acted within the province of the Judicial Branch."[22] In particular, by adopting an

---

[18] In addition, some critics argued that by requiring accommodation to religious practices, RFRA violated the Establishment Clause. See Christopher L. Eisgruber and Lawrence G. Sager, *Why the Religious Freedom Restoration Act Is Unconstitutional*, 69 NYU L Rev 437 (1994). Justice Stevens was the only Justice to take this argument seriously. *Boerne v Flores*, 117 S Ct at 2172 (Stevens concurring). Sager and Eisgruber's claim is that by requiring states to favor religious adherents over anyone else who holds a deep moral conviction, RFRA effects an establishment of religion. This argument is beyond the scope of this article, but at first blush it is difficult to square with historical and contemporary doctrine. The Supreme Court itself at least purported to apply something akin to the RFRA standard for twenty-five years, and while it abandoned that standard in *Smith*, the Court never suggested that its own prior free exercise standard violated the Establishment Clause. It is also difficult to square with the long-accepted view that accommodation of religion by lifting burdens imposed upon it does not constitute an establishment violation. If Sager and Eisgruber are right, accommodation of religion would always be unconstitutional unless all other holders of deep moral convictions were similarly accommodated.

[19] *Marbury v Madison*, 5 US (1 Cranch) 137, 177 (1803).

[20] Brief for Petitioner, *Boerne v Flores*, No 95-2074.

[21] *Flores*, 117 S Ct at 2172.

[22] Id at 2172.

understanding of the Free Exercise Clause that the Court had rejected in *Smith*, Congress had impermissibly "alter[ed] the meaning of the Free Exercise Clause."[23] The danger posed by such action, according to the Court, was nothing less than a devaluation of the Constitution:

> If Congress could define its own powers by altering the Fourteenth Amendment's meaning, no longer would the Constitution be "superior paramount law, unchangeable by ordinary means." It would be "on a level with ordinary legislative acts, and, like other acts, . . . alterable when the legislature shall please to alter it." Under this approach it is difficult to conceive of a principle that would limit congressional power. Shifting legislative majorities could change the Constitution and effectively circumvent the difficult and detailed amendment process contained in Article V.[24]

The separation of powers argument, however, is easily rebutted. The argument's premise is that, in enacting RFRA, Congress sought to "alter[ ] the Fourteenth Amendment's meaning." But it did no such thing. RFRA provided a statutory right, not a constitutional right. It did not change the Constitution, but only the United States Code. It cannot possibly be inconsistent with the separation of powers for Congress to protect, by statute, rights not protected directly by the Constitution. Innumerable federal statutes—directed at private and government conduct alike—do precisely that.[25]

Perhaps the Court overlooked this point because Congress's action, in establishing a statutory right, was expressly predicated on Congress's disagreement with the Court's interpretation of the Constitution—as the reference to "Restoration" in the Act's title suggests. But the separation of powers does not bar Congress from disagreeing with the Court's interpretation of the Constitution. If Congress were to attempt to interfere with the Court's decision in a specific case, that might raise a separation of powers ques-

---

[23] Id at 2164.

[24] Id at 2168 (citations omitted), quoting *Marbury v Madison*, 5 US (1 Cranch) at 177.

[25] Civil Rights Act of 1964, Title VII, 42 USC § 2000a et seq (1994); Voting Rights Act of 1965, 42 USC §§ 1971, 1973 (1994); Age Discrimination in Employment Act of 1967, 26 USC § 621 et seq (1994); Americans With Disabilities Act, 42 USC § 1211 (1994).

tion.[26] But unlike deciding specific cases, making judgments about what the Constitution means is not the judiciary's exclusive province. Congress is sometimes—for example, when considering whether to enact legislation that might be unconstitutional—obligated to interpret the Constitution itself. The mere fact that Congress disagrees with the Court on a constitutional question is not a separation of powers problem.

Rather, whether there is a separation of powers issue depends on what Congress does after it makes its judgment. If it merely enacts a statute—subject to judicial review—creating statutory rights, it has not violated the separation of powers, even if the Court concludes later that the statute violates the Constitution. The mere fact that Congress disagreed with the Court is not a separation of powers issue. Presumably Congress may, for example, apply RFRA to federal actions, even if it does so because it believes, contrary to the Court, that those activities violate the Free Exercise Clause.[27] Yet such an application of RFRA presents the same separation of powers issue as does RFRA's application to the states. If Congress cannot rely on its disagreement about the meaning of the Constitution as a basis for regulating the states under RFRA, the reason is federalism, not the separation of powers.

This is not to say that a statute by definition can never violate the separation of powers, but only that the mere fact that the law originated from a different understanding of the Constitution's meaning is not in itself a separation of powers problem. Congress might violate the separation of powers, for example, by requiring the judiciary to engage in tasks beyond the Court's Article III powers, such as rendering advisory opinions.[28] Conversely, Congress

---

[26] See *Plaut v Spendthrift Farm, Inc.*, 514 US 211 (1995) (holding that Congress infringed on federal courts' Article III powers by requiring courts to reopen final judgments); *United States v Klein*, 80 US (13 Wall) 128 (1871).

[27] See, for example, *EEOC v Catholic Univ.*, 83 F3d 455 (DC Cir 1996) (applying RFRA to federal government).

[28] See, for example, *Lujan v Defenders of Wildlife*, 504 US 555 (1992) (separation of powers bars Congress from granting standing to sue where Article III "case or controversy" requirements are not met); see generally Antonin Scalia, *The Doctrine of Standing as an Element of the Separation of Powers*, 17 Suffolk U L Rev 891 (1983).

One could make such an argument about RFRA, but no one on the Court did. The *Smith* decision suggested that the task of identifying which practices were "central" to a person's religion for purposes of applying the *Sherbert* test was "'not within the judicial ken.'" *Smith*, 494 US at 872, quoting *Hernandez v Commissioner*, 490 US 680, 699 (1989). It might follow, then, that RFRA's resurrection of that test directed the Court to do some-

might violate the separation of powers by barring the Supreme Court from performing its essential functions. A statute that took away the Court's jurisdiction to adjudicate the constitutionality of federal statutes might violate the separation of powers. But RFRA did not deprive the Court of any of its essential functions. The Court remained the final expositor of the Constitution, and the Court retained its power to determine the constitutional validity of RFRA itself.

As an analytical matter, the separation of powers portion of *Flores* is a makeweight. But it also more than that. The Court's separation of powers analysis is driven ultimately by what appears to be an intuitive sense that it is improper or disrespectful for Congress to disagree with the Court's view of the Free Exercise Clause. That intuition underlies not only the separation of powers holding, but also the more important federalism holding. And that intuition is fundamentally mistaken, for reasons I will discuss below.

III. FEDERALISM

The more substantial critique of RFRA, advanced most powerfully by several state attorneys general in an amicus brief in *Flores*,[29] was that it intruded on the prerogative of the states. They argued that Congress had acted beyond its constitutionally enumerated powers in enacting RFRA. The Constitution limits Congress to specified enumerated powers, and reserves all other power to the states. Absent an affirmative source in the Constitution, the

---

thing it could not do. See Mark Tushnet, *Two Versions of Judicial Supremacy*, forthcoming Wm & Mary L Rev. But as the separate opinions in *Smith* suggested, determinations of centrality may not be necessary to apply the *Sherbert* standard, and in any event the courts had applied the *Sherbert* standard for twenty-five years. *Smith*, 494 US at 906–07 (O'Connor concurring in judgment); id at 919 (Blackmun dissenting). To hold RFRA unconstitutional on this ground would have required the Court to admit that it had been acting beyond its Article III authority for a quarter century.

For a more sophisticated version of the judicial supremacy argument, see Larry Alexander and Frederick Schauer, *On Extrajudicial Constitutional Interpretation*, 110 Harv L Rev 1359 (1997). While I agree with Alexander and Schauer that there are good arguments for judicial supremacy in matters of constitutional interpretation, the argument advanced here is not inconsistent with judicial supremacy. It merely contends that where concurrent enforcement authority has been extended to Congress and the Court, the Court should review congressional interpretations of the Constitution with deference to the institutional differences between judicial and legislative enforcement. The Court retains final say over the Constitution's meaning.

[29] Brief for Amici States of Ohio, et al, in Support of Petitioner, *Boerne v Flores*, No 95-2074.

states maintained, RFRA violated principles of federalism. Moreover, RFRA effected a particularly radical extension of federal power, because it imposed its stringent federal accommodation requirement on all state and local government acts, from zoning ordinances to antidiscrimination laws to state tax codes.

The Court adopted this argument, finding that Congress had improperly intruded on state authority by acting beyond its powers to enforce liberty under Section 5 of the Fourteenth Amendment. Section 5, the Court ruled, limits Congress to creating remedies for violations of the Constitution as substantively defined by the Court. This conclusion, however, is not supported by the text, history, or subsequent applications of Section 5. And the Court's unquestioned power to give substance to the Constitution is a greater threat to federalism than the power Congress asserted.

A. SECTION 5 AND ITS HISTORY

The Civil War Amendments "were specifically designed as an expansion of federal power and intrusion on state sovereignty,"[30] and therefore if RFRA was a proper exercise of authority under Section 5 of the Fourteenth Amendment, the federalism objections would fail. Section 5 authorizes Congress "to enforce, by appropriate legislation, the provisions of this article." RFRA's defenders characterized the statute as an "enforcement" of the liberty provisions of the Fourteenth Amendment, which in turn have long been interpreted to incorporate the Free Exercise Clause of the First Amendment. But the challengers responded that RFRA could not be said to "enforce" the Free Exercise Clause, since it required states to justify laws and practices that the Supreme Court had said pose no free exercise problem at all—namely, neutral laws of general applicability. Thus, the issue squarely posed by RFRA was whether Section 5 authorizes Congress to reach by legislation conduct that, according to the Supreme Court, does not violate Section 1 of the Fourteenth Amendment.

This question about congressional power is not a new one; it has split the Court for decades, and has generated mountains of legal scholarship. As noted above, the persistence of debate about Section 5 stems from the Fourteenth Amendment's peculiar dele-

---

[30] *City of Rome v United States*, 446 US 156, 179 (1980).

gation of concurrent authority to the judiciary and Congress to enforce its provisions against the states. The Section 5 issue took on particular prominence in the 1960s and 1970s, as Congress repeatedly enacted civil rights statutes that went beyond the protection the Court had afforded those rights through constitutional interpretation. In light of the heated history of this debate, the Supreme Court's response in *Flores* was perhaps most remarkable for its relative quiescence. While three Justices dissented, they did not part company with the majority on its interpretation of Section 5, but instead dissented on the independent ground that *Smith* itself should have been reconsidered.

The absence of a single voice in favor of RFRA on Section 5 grounds was all the more surprising in light of the fact that its proponents had two strong precedents in their favor: Title VII and the Voting Rights Act. In *Fitzpatrick v Bitzer*,[31] the Court had upheld Title VII's application to state government employers as a legitimate exercise of Section 5 power. Title VII gives employees a cause of action for facially neutral employment practices that have a disparate impact on racial minorities.[32] As the Court reads it, however, the Equal Protection Clause recognizes no such cause of action; it requires a showing of intentional discrimination.[33] Yet Congress has, pursuant to Section 5, imposed a disparate impact test on public employers as a way of "enforcing" the Equal Protection Clause.[34]

The Voting Rights Act story is similar. Section 2 of the Fifteenth Amendment parallels Section 5 of the Fourteenth Amendment. In 1980, the Court interpreted the Fifteenth Amendment to prohibit only state action intended to deprive persons of the right to vote.[35] Yet on the same day, the Court upheld a Voting Rights Act provision that prohibits state actions that have the effect of diluting votes, even where there is no intent to do so.[36] And while the Court has ruled that the Fifteenth Amendment of its

---

[31] 427 US 445 (1976).

[32] *Griggs v Duke Power Co*, 401 US 424 (1971).

[33] *Washington v Davis*, 426 US 229 (1976).

[34] Title VII, of course, also applies to private employers, but in that respect it is founded upon the Commerce Clause.

[35] *Mobile v Bolden*, 446 US 55 (1980).

[36] *City of Rome v United States*, 446 US 156 (1980).

own force does not prohibit literacy tests for voters,[37] it has upheld another statutory provision prohibiting such tests regardless of the intent underlying their imposition.[38] Thus, in reviewing both the Voting Rights Act and Title VII, the Court has permitted Congress to prohibit government conduct with a disparate impact on minority populations even where it has held that the substantive constitutional provisions these acts "enforce" are themselves violated only by intentional discrimination. RFRA was of the same character; it prohibited state action that had a burdensome effect on religious exercise where the Court had interpreted the Free Exercise Clause to require a showing of intentional discrimination. In light of these precedents, it is hardly surprising that most of the lower courts had upheld RFRA.[39]

B. THE FLORES COURT'S ANALYSIS AND THE REMEDIAL/
   SUBSTANTIVE DISTINCTION

The Supreme Court determined that RFRA was different. It acknowledged that Congress may reach "conduct which is not itself unconstitutional and intrudes into 'legislative spheres of autonomy previously reserved to the States,'" but only so long as the legislation "deters or remedies constitutional violations."[40] The Court distinguished between remedial or preventive legislation, which Section 5 permits, and substantive "legislation which alters the meaning of the Free Exercise Clause," which is beyond Congress's Section 5 power.[41] In what probably qualifies as the understatement of the term, the Court admitted that "the line between measures that remedy or prevent unconstitutional actions and measures that make a substantive change in the governing law is not easy to discern," but nonetheless insisted that "the distinction exists and must be observed."[42]

---

[37] *Lassiter v Northampton County Bd of Elections*, 360 US 45 (1959).

[38] *Katzenbach v Morgan*, 384 US 641 (1966).

[39] Judge Richard Posner of the Seventh Circuit and Judge Patrick Higginbotham of the Fifth Circuit, for example, both wrote opinions upholding RFRA, and did not appear to consider it even a close question. See *Sasnett v Sullivan*, 91 F3d 1018 (7th Cir 1996); *Flores v City of Boerne*, 73 F3d 1352 (5th Cir 1996).

[40] *Flores*, 117 S Ct at 2163.

[41] Id at 2164.

[42] Id.

The Court was careful to underscore that the line between remedial and substantive legislation does not limit Congress to forbidding only conduct that the Court would independently find unconstitutional. Congress may prohibit otherwise constitutional
state conduct as a means of remedying or deterring unconstitutional conduct, as that conduct is defined by the Court. And the
Court insisted that it would grant "much deference" to Congress's
determination on the question of what remedial or preventive
means are appropriate. But the Court's deference has limits. In
order to qualify as remedial or preventive, the Court explained, a
statutory prohibition must be "proportional" to the legitimate
ends of remedy and deterrence. RFRA, the Court concluded, "is
so out of proportion to a supposed remedial or preventive object
that it cannot be understood as responsive to, or designed to prevent, unconstitutional behavior."[43]

Beyond noting that the Court's "proportionality" standard provides little if any principled guidance as to where the line will be
drawn in any particular case, I do not want to quibble with the
Court's evaluation of RFRA as "substantive" rather than "remedial." While a decent argument can be made that RFRA was "remedial" or "preventive,"[44] it is certainly reasonable to conclude
that RFRA was not designed to remedy or prevent intentionally
discriminatory burdens on religious freedom. Congress's concern,
as stated in the Act's findings, was that "laws 'neutral' toward religion may burden religious exercise as surely as laws intended to
interfere with religious exercise."[45] In other words, Congress was
concerned with laws that have the effect of burdening religion,
regardless of their intent. The point was to require states to become
conscious of religion, and to take care not to impede it unnecessarily, because otherwise the states might unthinkingly impose substantial but needless burdens on minority religions. Congress's
judgment was that such laws should have to be justified precisely
because of their burdensome effects, and that requiring justification only where laws specifically and intentionally target religious

---

[43] Id at 2172.

[44] The United States argued, for example, that RFRA was designed to deter violations
of the Free Exercise Clause, to flush out illegal purpose, and to protect adherents of minority religions from discrimination. See *Flores v Boerne*, 73 F3d 1352, 1359–60 (5th Cir 1996)
(discussing these arguments).

[45] 42 USC § 2000bb(a)(2).

practices, as the *Smith* decision did, would leave many burdens on religious freedom unremedied. So one might well classify RFRA as a substantive statute.[46]

But the same characterization could fairly be made of the disparate effects aspects of the Voting Rights Act and Title VII. They also reflect judgments by Congress that disparate effects are problematic irrespective of their connection to invidious intentional discrimination. The Supreme Court has acknowledged, for example, that when Congress enacted Title VII, it targeted the "consequences of [discriminatory] employment practices, not simply the motivation."[47] Accordingly, the Court has interpreted Title VII to provide that, irrespective of intent, "[i]f an employment practice which operates to exclude Negroes cannot be shown to be related to job performance, the practice is prohibited."[48] When Congress endorsed the *Griggs* interpretation in 1972, it stated that "[e]xperts familiar with the subject generally describe the problem in terms of 'systems' and 'effects' rather than simply intentional wrongs."[49] Yet while facially neutral employment practices that have a disparate impact on minority groups do not violate the Equal Protection Clause,[50] the Court has upheld Title VII as a proper exercise of Section 5 power.[51]

Similarly, in 1982, Congress amended the Voting Rights Act to permit challenges to voting practices that have the "result" of ' discriminating against minorities, even where the result is wholly unintentional. Much as RFRA was a response to the Supreme Court's interpretation of the Constitution to require a showing of intentional religious discrimination in *Smith*, so the 1982 amendments to the Voting Rights Act were a response to the Supreme

---

[46] Indeed, one of RFRA's architects (and defenders before the Court in *Flores*), Professor Douglas Laycock, has admitted that "RFRA is based on the substantive theory in that Congress says that the definition of free exercise in *Employment Division v Smith* is wrong." Douglas Laycock, *RFRA, Congress, and the Ratchet*, 56 Mont L Rev 145, 153 (1995).

[47] *Griggs v Duke Power Co*, 401 US 424, 432 (1971) (interpreting Title VII to prohibit employment practices that are not intended to discriminate, but have disparate effects on minority groups).

[48] 401 US at 431.

[49] HR Rep No 92-238, 92d Cong, 1st Sess 8, reprinted in 1972 USCCAN 2137, 2144; see also HR Rep No 92-238 at 24, reprinted in 1972 USCCAN at 2164; S Rep No 92-415, 92d Cong, 1st Sess 1, 14–15 (1971); *Connecticut v Teal*, 457 US 440, 447 n 8 (1982).

[50] *Washington v Davis*, 426 US 229 (1976).

[51] *Fitzpatrick v Bitzer*, 427 US 445 (1976).

Court's decision in *City of Mobile v Bolden*, which held that the Fifteenth Amendment requires a showing of intentional vote dilution.[52] As the Court itself described the 1982 amendments, "Congress substantially revised §2 [of the Voting Rights Act] to make clear that a violation could be proved by showing discriminatory *effect* alone."[53] Thus, both the Voting Rights Act and Title VII were designed to prohibit conduct that the Supreme Court had held was not unconstitutional, and both statutes could, like RFRA, be characterized as reflecting Congress's disagreement with the Court over the substantive reach of the Constitution.

The principal question raised by *Flores*, therefore, is not whether RFRA was remedial or substantive, but why anything should turn on the distinction. The Court relied on the text of the Amendment, its legislative history, and case law to support the significance of the distinction, but none of these sources is persuasive. The text of Section 5 says that Congress "shall have power to enforce, by appropriate legislation, the provisions of this article." The *Flores* Court reasoned that the power to "enforce" is distinct from the power "to determine what constitutes a constitutional violation."[54] But the word "enforce" cannot bear the weight of that claim; after all, it is just as natural to speak of the Court as "enforcing" the Constitution when it "determine[s] what constitutes a constitutional violation." Section 5 does not say that "Congress shall have the power to provide remedies for constitutional violations identified by the courts." Instead, it gives Congress the power to "enforce" the provisions of Section 1, limited only by the requirement that its means be "appropriate" to that end. As the Supreme Court acknowledged in prior cases, this language of authorization is as broad as the "necessary and proper" clause.[55] Had the Framers sought to restrict Congress's power to remedial measures, they could have done so expressly. Thus, nothing in Sec-

---

[52] *City of Mobile v Bolden*, 446 US 55 (1980).

[53] *Thornburgh v Gingles*, 478 US 30, 35 (1986).

[54] *Flores*, 117 S Ct at 2164.

[55] *The Civil Rights Cases*, 109 US 3, 13–14 (1883); see also *Ex Parte Virginia*, 100 US 339, 345–46 (1879) (adopting deferential approach to Section 5); *South Carolina v Katzenbach*, 383 US 301, 326 (1966) (quoting deferential standard from *McCulloch v Maryland*, 17 US (4 Wheat) 316, 421 (1819) and applying it to Section 5); *James Everard's Breweries v Day*, 265 US 545, 560 (1924) (interpreting Congress's analogous enforcement power under Section 2 of the Eighteenth Amendment to extend to "any eligible and appropriate means to make [the Amendment's] prohibition effective").

tion 5 itself is inconsistent with granting Congress some deference to determine what constitutes a constitutional violation in the process of enforcing the Fourteenth Amendment. Indeed, the very fact that the Fourteenth Amendment includes Section 5 suggests an affirmative choice to empower Congress as well as the courts to act "appropriately" in enforcing liberty and equality norms against the states.[56] As Douglas Laycock has suggested, the Framers may well have been skeptical that enforcement of the Fourteenth Amendment could be left solely to the judiciary, particularly to a Supreme Court that had so recently decided *Dred Scott v Sandford.*[57]

The legislative history is similarly unpersuasive. The *Flores* Court relied heavily on the fact that the Framers rejected an earlier version of the Fourteenth Amendment, introduced by Representative John Bingham, which authorized Congress to:

> make all laws which shall be necessary and proper to secure to the citizens of the States all privileges and immunities of citizens in the several States, and to all persons in the several States equal protection in the rights of life, liberty, and property.[58]

The Court noted that one of the objections to Bingham's provision was that it would grant Congress too much power over state-law matters. But that was only one of two principal concerns expressed. The other was that the provision as drafted was not self-executing, that is, directly enforceable by individuals in court. Without judicial enforcement, the amendment would only have as much effect as the shifting majorities in Congress would give it at any given moment.[59]

The Fourteenth Amendment as drafted is different from the Bingham proposal, but the principal difference is that it authorizes direct judicial enforcement. On its face the Amendment as adopted responds to only one of the two objections to the earlier draft. In

---

[56] Douglas Laycock, 56 Mont L Rev at 158–62 (cited in note 46).

[57] 60 US (19 How) 393 (1857). Congress's skepticism toward the Court is further reflected in the extraordinary lengths to which it went to deprive the Court of the ability to rule on the validity of the Reconstruction government. *Ex parte McCardle*, 74 US (7 Wall) 506 (1869).

[58] Cong Globe, 39th Cong, 1st Sess 1034 (1866).

[59] *Flores*, 117 S Ct at 2165, quoting Cong Globe, 39th Cong, 1st Sess 1095 (1866) (Rep Hotchkiss).

fact, Representative Hale, an opponent of the Bingham proposal because it gave Congress too much power, objected to Section 5 on the very same grounds, characterizing it as giving Congress "absolute" and "broad" power to "legislat[e] in the first instance" and to "select in [its] own discretion all measures appropriate to the end in view."[60] It may be that responding to the criticism regarding the lack of judicial enforcement was all that was necessary to garner sufficient votes for the final version's passage. It does not follow, nor is there any evidence to suggest, that Section 5 as written and adopted was intended to preclude Congress from giving substantive meaning through its statutes to the open-ended provisions of Section 1, or as the Court put it in *Flores*, that "Congress's role was no longer plenary but remedial."[61] True, Congress's role was no longer plenary; making the provisions self-executing meant that the Court would also play an independent role in enforcing the Fourteenth Amendment's norms. But the opposite of plenary is not remedial. The legislative history of the Fourteenth Amendment's adoption could just as easily be read to authorize Congress to provide substantive meaning through statutory action to the constitutional values in Section 1, so long as its statutory means were "appropriate."[62]

The *Flores* Court's review of the legislative history of the Fourteenth Amendment confused two distinct issues: whether the Fourteenth Amendment regulates only state action or applies to private action as well, and whether it independently authorizes

---

[60] Cong Globe, 43d Cong, 2d Sess 979 (1875) (Rep Hale).

[61] *Boerne v Flores*, 117 S Ct at 2165.

[62] The Framers described Congress's Section 5 powers in broad terms. It was described as "cast[ing] upon Congress the responsibility of seeing to it, for the future, that all the sections of the amendment are carried out in good faith," Cong Globe, 39th Cong, 1st Sess 2768, and as reflecting "a direct affirmative delegation to Congress to carry out all the principles of all these guarantees." Id at 2766.

The fact that Section 5 extended to Congress the power to enact "appropriate" legislation, while the Bingham proposal gave Congress the power to enact "necessary and proper" legislation, is irrelevant, as the "appropriate" standard simply reflected the Court's interpretation of the "necessary and proper" language. As Senator Thurman explained:

What is meant by this term 'appropriate legislation'? We know where the term comes from. We know it comes from an old opinion of Chief Justice Marshall, and was applied by him simply to the old provision of the Constitution that Congress has power to make all laws necessary and proper for carrying into effect the foregoing powers.

Cong Globe, 41st Cong, 2d Sess 602 (1870).

Congress to interpret "due process" and "equal protection" in order to enforce those norms. The history the *Flores* Court relied upon is addressed to the first issue. Critics of the Bingham proposal expressed concern that the proposal would give Congress general police power to regulate private conduct, thereby supplanting the states.[63] And descriptions of Section 5 stressed that it authorized Congress to act only against state action.[64] Thus, Representative Stevens described Section 5 as "allow[ing] Congress to correct the unjust legislation of the States."[65] Similarly, Senator Howard described Section 5 as "enabl[ing] Congress, in case the States shall enact laws in conflict with the principles of the amendment, to correct that legislation by a formal congressional enactment."[66] This history supports the view that the Framers understood the Fourteenth Amendment not to apply to private conduct directly, but it suggests nothing about whether they considered Congress's Section 5 power to be remedial or substantive. A determination that Congress is limited to responding to state action simply does not speak to the distinct question of the extent to which Congress's powers are constrained by the Court's substantive interpretations of due process and equal protection. None of the evidence marshalled by the *Flores* Court addresses the latter question.

Finally, the case law does not support the remedial/substantive distinction. The *Flores* Court began its review of the case law by making the same mistake in reading *The Civil Rights Cases*[67] that it made in interpreting the legislative history of the Fourteenth Amendment. It quoted the earlier Court's determination that Section 5 did not authorize Congress to enact "general legislation upon the rights of the citizen, but corrective legislation; that is, such as may be necessary and proper for counteracting such laws as the States may adopt or enforce, and which, by the amendment, they are prohibited from making or enforcing."[68] It reasoned from

---

[63] *Flores*, 117 S Ct at 2164–65.

[64] Id.

[65] Cong Globe, 39th Cong, 1st Sess 2459 (1866).

[66] Id at 2768.

[67] 109 US 3 (1883).

[68] *Flores*, 117 S Ct at 2166, quoting *The Civil Rights Cases*, 109 US at 13–14.

this statement that the Court saw "Congress's § 5 power as corrective or preventive, not definitional." But nothing in *The Civil Rights Cases* justifies that leap. To say that the Fourteenth Amendment does not reach private action does not imply that Congress may not restrict by statute state conduct that the Court has not restricted by judicial decree. Moreover, the quotation the *Flores* Court highlighted supports a deferential view of Congress's power under Section 5, because it uses the terms "necessary and proper," the very terms found in Article I, Section 8.[69]

At best, the decisions since *The Civil Rights Cases* reflect confusion about how far Congress's power should extend; at worst, they are disingenuous. At times, the Court has adopted a substantive theory of Congress's Section 5 power. In *Katzenbach v Morgan*,[70] for example, the Court stated that Section 5 gives Congress independent authority to consider all the value judgments that the Court would take into account in interpreting and enforcing the Fourteenth Amendment, and that the Court must uphold Congress's interpretation so long as it can "perceive a basis upon which the Congress might resolve the conflict as it did."[71] At other times, the Court has suggested that Congress's Section 5 power is remedial, but has characterized as remedial statutes that are at least as substantive as RFRA.[72] In *Oregon v Mitchell*,[73] the Court came closest to rejecting the notion that Congress has substantive authority under Section 5, but only four Justices took that view.[74] In short,

---

[69] One might argue, although the *Flores* Court did not, that the very fact that the Court in *The Civil Rights Cases* invalidated a federal statute enacted pursuant to the Fourteenth Amendment implicitly supports the view that the Court, and not Congress, has the final word in defining the scope of the Fourteenth Amendment. And if saying Congress has substantive power to define Section 1 meant that Congress had the last word, then *The Civil Rights Cases* would support the Court's rejection of that position in *Flores*. But the claim that Congress has substantive power under Section 5 is not a claim that Congress can give the Fourteenth Amendment any meaning it wants, but only that the Court should defer to Congress's substantive understanding so long as it is reasonable and does not infringe on any constitutional rights. *The Civil Rights Cases* can be understood as holding that the Court did not consider it reasonable to interpret the Fourteenth Amendment to reach private conduct.

[70] 384 US 641 (1966).

[71] Id at 658.

[72] See text at notes 47–53 (discussion of Title VII and Voting Rights Act cases).

[73] 400 US 112 (1970).

[74] Chief Justice Burger and Justices Harlan, Stewart, and Blackmun rejected the notion that Congress has substantive authority under Section 5, 400 US at 153–54 (Harlan concurring in part and dissenting in part); id at 293 (Stewart concurring in part and dissenting

the Court has not always insisted on the remedial/substantive distinction, and even where it has said that the distinction matters, it has treated as remedial legislation no less substantive than RFRA. Thus, neither the text, history, nor judicial elaboration of Section 5 supports the remedial/substantive distinction applied in *Flores.*

There is a difference between RFRA and the civil rights statutes, but it is not the difference between remedy and substance, and it does not ultimately justify different treatment of the statutes. Justice Scalia explored this issue at oral argument in *Flores*,[75] but it received no attention in the opinions for the Court. The difference is that RFRA does not directly enforce Section 1 of the Fourteenth Amendment, but rather enforces the First Amendment as it has been incorporated and applied to the states through the Fourteenth Amendment's Due Process Clause. The paradoxical result is that an amendment expressly written to *restrict* Congress's own power to encroach on religious freedom has been transformed, via incorporation, into a positive *authorization* of congressional power to regulate the states. The First Amendment, after all, provides that "Congress shall make no law . . . ." Yet once incorporated through the Due Process Clause and viewed through the lens of Section 5, it effectively reads, "Congress shall have the power to enforce, by appropriate legislation, the principle that states shall make no law . . . ." RFRA dramatically illustrated that the consequence of incorporation is not merely federal judicial oversight over previously unregulated state domains, but congressional oversight as well.

In addition, because virtually all provisions of the Bill of Rights have been incorporated, Congress's Section 5 authority is potentially quite expansive. It would conceivably support broad federal legislation directed at the states in the criminal justice area, where Congress might impose additional warrant requirements to enforce the Fourth Amendment, require provision of legal counsel in all interrogations to enforce the Fifth Amendment, or bar the

in part), but Justice Black provided the fifth vote, on the ground that Congress's broad Section 5 authority should be limited to the area of race discrimination. Id at 129–30 (Black announcing judgment of Court).

[75] Transcript of oral argument in *Boerne v Flores*, 1997 WL 87109 at 5 (1997) (SCT–ORALARG database).

regulation of obscenity as an enforcement of the First Amendment. Indeed, Congress could conceivably go still further, enacting a "Free Speech Act" requiring that all laws that have an incidental effect on speech satisfy strict scrutiny, or an "Abortion Rights Restoration Act," requiring that all regulation of abortion be justified by strict scrutiny rather than the "undue burden" test.[76]

While the incorporation issue may differentiate RFRA from the civil rights statutes, the distinction should not affect the scope of Section 5 authority, as the Court in *Flores* acknowledged.[77] Incorporation effected a major shift in federal-state power, but once incorporation has been established, there is no independent ground beyond Section 5 for distinguishing between the federal courts' power to enforce the incorporated provisions of the Bill of Rights against the states and Congress's power to do so.

The potential sweep of Section 5, when combined with the effects of incorporation, is dramatic, but from the standpoint of individual liberty, that sweep is unproblematic. The Bill of Rights as incorporated through the Fourteenth Amendment creates a floor, not a ceiling. States are free to adopt rules more protective of individual rights than the Bill of Rights. And the federal courts may impose prophylactic rules on the states that are not literally required by the Bill of Rights provisions they are designed to further. The two most noteworthy examples are the exclusionary rule and *Miranda* warnings.[78] The *Miranda* warnings, for example, apply to all custodial interrogations, whether or not those interrogations would independently infringe the Fifth Amendment. Such rules have been characterized as "constitutional common law," because they are court-made rules that go beyond the literal requirements of the Constitution.[79] These cases are sometimes seen as excep-

---

[76] For a parade of horribles along these lines, see William W. Van Alstyne, *The Failure of the Religious Freedom Restoration Act Under Section 5 of the Fourteenth Amendment*, 46 Duke L J 291 (1996). The extreme unlikeliness of most of these hypotheticals suggests that the perceived dangers to federalism and separation of powers contemplated by the Court in *Flores* are greatly exaggerated.

[77] *Flores*, 117 S Ct at 2163 ("We agree with respondent, of course, that Congress can enact legislation under § 5 enforcing the constitutional right to the free exercise of religion" because it has been incorporated through the Due Process Clause).

[78] *Mapp v Ohio*, 367 US 643 (1961) (exclusionary rule); *Miranda v Arizona*, 384 US 436 (1966).

[79] Henry P. Monaghan, *Foreword: Constitutional Common Law*, 89 Harv L Rev 1 (1974).

tions, but as others have noted, in fact, constitutional common law is not the exception but the rule.[80] There is very little that the Constitution requires of its own force; virtually all of constitutional doctrine consists of judicial elaboration of the document's open-ended principles. For example, the language of the Fourth Amendment does not literally provide that all searches presumptively require a warrant and probable cause, yet the Court has imposed that rule on the states (subject, of course, to innumerable exceptions, none of which are set forth in the Fourth Amendment either). And virtually all of First Amendment doctrine is judge-made law.[81]

From the standpoint of individual liberty, as long as states and federal courts create prophylactic rules that do not fall below the floor set by the Constitution, there is no constitutional problem. And from the standpoint of individual liberty, there should be no problem with Congress creating similar prophylactic rules. (In fact, the Supreme Court invited as much in *Miranda*, where it provided that an equally effective congressional substitute might supplant the judicially required warnings.[82]) To the extent that any particular prophylactic rule infringes on a constitutionally protected liberty, it would be invalid, whether adopted by a federal court, state legislature, state court, or the U.S. Congress. Thus, a statute designed to further the Establishment Clause might violate the free speech provisions of the First Amendment, and if it did, it would be invalidated.[83] But short of such affirmative prohibitions, efforts to promulgate rules above the constitutional floor pose no liberty

---

[80] See David Strauss, *The Ubiquity of Prophylactic Rules*, 55 U Chi L Rev 190 (1988) (arguing that prophylactic rules, like the *Miranda* rules, are the norm in constitutional adjudication); see also Martha Field, *Sources of Law: The Scope of Federal Common Law*, 99 Harv L Rev 881 (1986) (arguing that any court-made rule of federal law that is "not clearly suggested by federal enactments—constitutional or congressional" is federal common law); Richard H. Fallon, Jr., Daniel J. Meltzer, and David L. Shapiro, *Hart & Wechsler's The Federal Courts and the Federal System* 755–77 (4th ed, 1996) (noting that federal common law "cannot be sharply distinguished from statutory or constitutional interpretation").

[81] See Strauss, 55 U Chi L Rev at 195–204 (cited in note 80).

[82] *Miranda*, 384 US 436, 467 (1966).

[83] See, for example, *Rosenberger v Rectors of the Board of Univ of Virginia*, 515 US 819 (1995) (declaring unconstitutional under Free Speech Clause a state university policy designed to avoid an Establishment Clause violation); *Lamb's Chapel v Center Moriches Union Free Sch. Dist.*, 508 US 384 (1993) (same).

issue, irrespective of whether they originate in the states, the Court, or the Congress.[84]

What drives the Court in *Flores*, of course, is not individual liberty, but federalism. From the standpoint of federalism, there is a critical difference between a state enacting a rule that "overprotects" a constitutional liberty, and Congress doing the same thing. States have plenary power to act, so long as they do not violate a constitutional prohibition. In contrast, absent some affirmative constitutional source of authority, the federal government has no power to act, and authority rests with the states. It is this concern that led the *Flores* Court to treat its interpretations of constitutional liberties as setting not merely a floor but also a ceiling vis-à-vis Congress. As a result, the Court's pronouncement of a constitutional liberty now has two implications. In order to protect the constitutional liberty, neither Congress nor the states is free to take actions that fall below the announced constitutional standard. But correlatively, in order to protect the states, Congress is not free to take actions that impose requirements beyond the substantive constitutional standard as the Supreme Court has enforced it itself. If Congress does so, it is acting beyond its enumerated powers, and infringing on states' rights.

This is at best a curious result, particularly given the federal courts' authority to create rules that extend beyond the Constitution's literal terms and intrude upon state authority. A constitutional interpretation that too expansively interprets a constitutional right can certainly infringe on state autonomy and undermine federalism. But judicial interpretations pose this danger to federal-

---

[84] One civil-liberties-based objection to authorizing Congress to go further than the Supreme Court in "enforcing" the Constitution would be that it might let the Court off the hook too easily. In difficult cases, the Court might be inclined to be more cautious in extending rights protections if it knows that Congress has independent ability to do so. In the same way that the existence of an appeal may reduce the gravity with which people treat an initial trial, *Evitts v Lucey*, 469 US 387 (1985), the fact that Congress can theoretically respond to a claim of constitutional right may lead the Court to hesitate. And where civil rights and civil liberties are at stake, they are usually at stake precisely because the majority has been insensitive to them. Thus, it will be the rare situation where Congress will respond. However, the Court already has this excuse, because states may go further than the Court says the Constitution demands. See, for example, *McCleskey v Kemp*, 481 US 279, 292 (1986) (declining to declare Georgia death penalty statute unconstitutional based on showing of statistically significant racial disparities in its implementation, and stating that such arguments are better presented to state legislatures). And in the end, the legislative alternative is not an equal one, since Congress's power is limited to enacting statutory rights, far more vulnerable than constitutional rights.

ism as much as, if not more than, congressional interpretations do.

The Court, unlike Congress, is not structurally suited to consider state interests. While today's Court happens to feature a majority of Justices committed to protecting state prerogatives, there is no institutional reason why that would generally be so. The Supreme Court is not a representative body, and its authority stems entirely from federal sources. Congress, by contrast, consists exclusively of representatives from the fifty states. Those representatives must be re-elected in their home districts, and therefore must be responsive to local concerns. As Professor Herbert Wechsler famously argued, that structure makes it likely that Congress will consider the interests of the states as a matter of course.[85] Congress will not intrude on state prerogatives unless a consensus emerges among the states' representatives that federal action displacing state authority is indeed warranted. While critics have challenged Wechsler's view of political dynamics as too simple,[86] it is certainly fair to say that Congress is, as an institutional matter, more likely to be sensitive to states' interests than is the Court. So if federalism concerns do not preclude the Court from creating prophylactic rules as a means of enforcing the Constitution, why should such concerns preclude Congress from doing so?

It might be thought that federal judicial power is less threatening to states' rights than federal legislative power because of the limitations of Article III. Federal courts can act only where cases and controversies are presented to them; Congress is not comparably limited. But as history has illustrated, Article III is not much of a constraint from a states' rights perspective. While Congress has displaced state regulatory authority in many areas, Wechsler's theory has been borne out dramatically in the area of enforcement of constitutional rights. The Court has repeatedly limited state authority where Congress has not. The incorporation doctrine, a judge-made rule, applied the Bill of Rights to the states, and made

[85] Herbert Wechsler, *The Political Safeguards of Federalism—The Role of the States in the Composition and Selection of the National Government*, 54 Colum L Rev 543 (1954); see also Jesse Choper, *Judicial Review and the National Political Process: A Functional Reconsideration of the Role of the Supreme Court* (1980); *Garcia v San Antonio Metropolitan Transit Authority*, 469 US 528 (1985).

[86] Lewis B. Kaden, *Politics, Money, and State Sovereignty: The Judicial Role*, 79 Colum L Rev 847 (1979).

such judicial intrusion possible in the first place. And ever since, the Court has consistently gone further than Congress in enforcing constitutional rights against the states. Consider the Court's decisions under the First Amendment, the Takings Clause, the Fourth, Fifth, and Sixth Amendment rights of the criminally accused, and procedural and substantive due process. Even in the area of race discrimination, the Court often took the first steps, only to be followed by more aggressive congressional interventions. One reason for the relatively few precedents on the issue decided in *Flores* is that Congress has been far less willing than the Court to restrict what the states may do on the basis of a judgment that the state conduct is unconstitutional. Even with respect to RFRA, Congress did not act until the Court had blazed the trail and then retreated. Thus, to the extent that federalism is the source of the Court's decision in *Flores*, the Court got it backwards. The Court presents a greater danger to states' rights than Congress does.

IV. Section 5 and the Institutional Determinants of Constitutional Interpretation

As shown in the preceding sections, neither separation of powers, federalism, nor liberty concerns necessitate restricting Congress's power to enforce constitutional liberties to a "remedial" function. At bottom, the Court's insistence on a remedial/substantive distinction appears to rest on a misguided notion of constitutional interpretation, namely, that when the Court defines the scope of a constitutional liberty for purposes of judicial enforcement, it also determines the scope of that liberty for purposes of congressional enforcement. But there are important institutional differences between judicial and congressional enforcement (and interpretation) of the Constitution. In light of those differences, the Fourteenth Amendment's substantive meaning for purposes of judicial enforcement need not be identical to its substantive meaning for legislative enforcement purposes. As long as Congress's interpretation is reasonable and does not transgress a constitutional prohibition, its authority to legislate pursuant to Section 5 should be at least as extensive as its authority to legislate under its other enumerated powers.

The Court and Congress have concurrent responsibility and authority to enforce the Fourteenth Amendment, and that duty cannot be performed without engaging in an act of interpretation. There are sound reasons why Congress and the Court might adopt different interpretations of the same constitutional provision, and there are equally sound reasons why the Court should tolerate such differences. Some of these reasons are captured in Professor Lawrence Sager's argument that institutional constraints may inhibit courts from enforcing a constitutional norm "to its conceptual limit."[87] In adopting the intent standard in equal protection jurisprudence, for example, the Court pointed to the institutional difficulties that would be posed by applying an effects test, and suggested that the issue is more appropriately addressed by the legislature.[88] The Court used virtually identical reasoning in *Employment Division v Smith*, noting that a free exercise "effects" test would potentially require courts to review an unmanageable range of generally applicable laws, and suggesting that these issues are better left to the political process.[89] Sager argues that where the federal courts fail to enforce a constitutional norm fully for institutional reasons, Congress should be free to enforce it to that limit. Sager, however, would distinguish between analytical and institutional constraints on judicial interpretations of the Constitution, and would not permit Congress's Section 5 power to extend beyond a judicial interpretation where the limits on that interpretation were analytical rather than institutional.

Sager's argument provides an important insight, but ironically, he fails to take it to its conceptual limit. All of the Court's interpretations of the Constitution are necessarily constrained by its institutional role (as are all of Congress's interpretations). Interpretation is a situated activity, and the circumstances and perspective of the reader cannot help but affect the outcome of the interpretive process. The Court is never free of its institutional constraints, and its every act of interpretation inevitably will reflect those lim-

---

[87] Lawrence Gene Sager, *Fair Measure: The Legal Status of Underenforced Constitutional Norms*, 91 Harv L Rev 1212 (1978).

[88] *Washington v Davis*, 426 US 229, 248 (1976) (because strict scrutiny for disparate impact "would raise serious questions about, and perhaps invalidate, a whole range of . . . statutes," Court holds that "extension of [strict scrutiny] beyond those areas where it is already applicable by reason of statute . . . should await legislative prescription"); *McCleskey v Kemp*, 481 US 279, 315–19 (same).

[89] 494 US at 889–90.

its. The same is true of Congress, but it operates under different institutional constraints. These differences may lead both institutions to adopt interpretations short of the Constitution's "conceptual limit."

More fundamentally still, the institutional character of interpretation raises questions about the meaning of Sager's "conceptual limit." From what institutional stance is the "conceptual limit" defined, if the Court, Congress, and the Executive (and for that matter, law professors) each bring their own particular institutional concerns to the act of interpretation? It may make more sense to say that the "conceptual limit" of a particular constitutional provision turns at least in part on which entity is enforcing it. The best explanation for the constitutionality of the Voting Rights Act is that the Fifteenth Amendment means one thing for purposes of direct judicial enforcement and something else for purposes of legislative enforcement. A court could not have enforced the Fifteenth Amendment through judicial decree in the way that Congress has through the Voting Rights Act. This institutional argument does not mean that anything goes, or that there is no ground to stand on in assessing the validity of particular interpretations, but simply that the very project of interpreting the Constitution must acknowledge that institutional differences may justify different interpretations of the same provision.

Three constraints in particular play a critical role in judicial interpretation of the Constitution. First, the Court's readings of the Constitution must (and cannot help but) take into account the limits of its own enforcement powers. In the equal protection area, for example, this constraint explains, at least in part, why the Court has adopted a formal conception of equality; it is far more "judicially manageable" than the competing conceptions.[90]

Second, and perhaps more importantly, the Court must (and cannot help but) consider the fact that its constitutional decisions are far less susceptible to change than Congress's. The Court is bound by stare decisis and rule-of-law norms that do not constrict Congress. While stare decisis has less weight in the constitutional area,[91] the Court nonetheless incurs costs to its legitimacy if it too

---

[90] *Washington v Davis*, 426 US at 248; see generally Stephen F. Ross, *Legislative Enforcement of Equal Protection*, 72 Minn L Rev 311, 321–26 (1987).

[91] *Payne v Tennessee*, 501 US 808 (1991).

regularly reverses its prior constitutional decisions.[92] In addition, the Court's constitutional decisions are virtually immune to correction by the political process, because amending the Constitution is so difficult. These constraints are likely to lead the Court to act cautiously, for it knows that in many cases there is no real check on its actions.

Third, the Court is limited to deciding cases and controversies. It is less free to set its own agenda and to address an issue comprehensively. Even if it feels that a broader factual record would assist it in deciding a particular issue, it has extremely limited ability to generate one if the parties do not take the initiative. Again, these constraints may lead the Court to adopt more cautious interpretations of rights, because it is aware that it is unable to consider the problem in all of its variations.

Congress, by contrast, can devise innovative enforcement mechanisms and allocate resources to implement them. It can conduct broad-based factfinding, and can hire its own investigators, call hearings, and subpoena witnesses on its own initiative. It can more effectively create structural reform, as exemplified by the Voting Rights Act. Of equal importance, when Congress enacts a statute to enforce a constitutional provision, it can change its mind whenever it concludes that it has made a mistake. It is not bound by principles like stare decisis. It need not be as concerned as the Court about the appearance of objectivity and neutrality. As a result, Congress may be able to address liberty and equality issues more comprehensively than the Court might.

At the same time, Congress acts subject to its own institutional constraints that limit its ability to protect constitutional rights. Its interpretations are necessarily developed with one eye on the electorate. If Congress's interpretations of the Constitution are unacceptable, its members can be voted out of office, or pressured to repeal the laws in question. Thus, in its interpretive process, Congress must (and cannot help but) consider the interests of the various local majorities its members represent. In addition, congres-

---

[92] *Planned Parenthood v Casey*, 505 US 833, 866 (1992) ("There is . . . a point beyond which frequent overruling would overtax the country's belief in the Court's good faith . . . . There is a limit to the amount of error that can plausibly be imputed to prior Courts. If that limit is exceeded, disturbance of prior rulings would be taken as evidence that justifiable reexamination of principle had given way to drives for particular results in the short term.").

sional interpretations of the Constitution are more subject to the passions of interest group politics, and accordingly may be more likely to reflect compromise over principle.

The differences between Congress and the Court outlined here are of course relative. The Court can and does change its mind on constitutional matters. Congress would also probably incur some costs if it too often changed its mind, and legislative inertia limits its flexibility in revisiting issues. Moreover, the Supreme Court's certiorari jurisdiction gives it some agenda-setting power. Nonetheless, the differences sketched here remain significant in the general run of cases.

In light of these institutional differences, one should expect to find that the Court and Congress will sometimes have different views of at least some of the substantive terms of the Constitution. The Court might well conclude that its institutional limits mean that it can only enforce an intent-based conception of free exercise or equal protection, while Congress may conclude that as a statutory matter it can enforce effects-based conceptions of these rights. One might nonetheless insist that where the Court and Congress disagree, the Court's substantive judgment must prevail. At this point in the *Flores* opinion, familiar separation of powers rhetoric reappears; the Court cites *Marbury* and declares it has the final say. But this misses the issue. There are, of course, very good reasons for assigning the Court, a countermajoritarian institution, the final say in enforcing the Constitution, a document of countermajoritarian principles. But who has the final say on a constitutional issue does not answer the more germane question of what standard the Court ought to apply in reviewing a congressional statute under Section 5. Some judges and scholars have suggested that to defer to Congress's substantive understanding of constitutional liberty under Section 5 where it differs from the Court's would constitute abdication of the judicial role.[93] But as so much of the Court's jurisprudence demonstrates, deference is not equivalent to abdication. Deferential judicial review is still review. The Court retains the final say.

---

[93] *Katzenbach v Morgan*, 384 US 641, 666 (1966) (Harlan dissenting); Alexander Bickel, *The Voting Rights Cases*, 1966 Supreme Court Review 79, 101–02; William Van Alstyne, *The Failure of the Religious Freedom Restoration Act Under Section 5 of the Fourteenth Amendment*, 46 Duke L J 291, 323 (1996).

The pertinent question raised by congressional disagreements such as those reflected in RFRA, Title VII, and the Voting Rights Act is what standard of review the Court should use when reviewing the action of an institution that has been assigned concurrent authority to enforce a legal norm. As two other areas of law illustrate, where the courts share concurrent enforcement authority with another institution, judicial supremacy is not undermined by exercising deferential review of the other institution's interpretations.

First, consider the Court's Commerce Clause/Dormant Commerce Clause jurisprudence. Here, as in the Fourteenth Amendment, the Court has found concurrent enforcement authority. Congress can prohibit state actions that it determines interfere with interstate commerce. And under the so-called Dormant Commerce Clause, the Court can do the same thing. The "Dormant" label does not hide the fact that in both instances, the sole authority for federal enforcement is the Commerce Clause. But here, the Court does not require Congress to adopt the same interpretation of the Commerce Clause that it adopts. Rather, this doctrine recognizes that there is a difference between what the Constitution "of its own force" precludes—that is, what the Constitution authorizes the Court to preclude, since the Constitution does not literally act "of its own force"—and what the Constitution authorizes Congress to forbid. Under the Commerce Clause, Congress has broad leeway to regulate the nation's economy, and its exercise of that power precludes contrary state regulation. So long as Congress acts reasonably in addressing an area that affects interstate commerce, the Court will uphold its acts. *United States v Lopez*[94] shows that the Court has not abdicated all review, but even under *Lopez*, the Court's review of Congress's legislative actions under the Commerce Clause remains extremely deferential.[95] At the same time, where Congress has not acted, the Commerce Clause "of its own force" (or more accurately, by judicial enforcement) prohibits certain state laws and practices. The scope of the Dormant Commerce Clause—that which the Constitution authorizes the judiciary to prohibit through judicial decree—is far less extensive than

[94] 514 US 549 (1995).

[95] Id at 557 ("the Court has . . . undertaken to decide whether a rational basis existed for concluding that a regulated activity sufficiently affects interstate commerce").

the scope of the affirmative Commerce Clause—that which Congress is authorized to prohibit by statute.

The Court's Dormant Commerce Clause jurisprudence, of course, is not uncontroversial. But the principal critiques of the doctrine—that it is judge-made law without a sufficient foundation in the Constitution, and that its standards are incoherent and judicially unmanageable[96]—do not affect the point I make here. I do not need to defend the Court's jurisprudence in this area; it is enough to say that it illustrates that where the Court has found concurrent enforcement authority over a legal norm, it does not follow that the Court's and Congress's substantive interpretations of that norm must be identical.[97]

A second area of the law that illustrates this point is the doctrine requiring courts to defer to administrative agencies' interpretations of statutes that the agencies administer. Courts and administrative agencies have concurrent authority to enforce certain statutes, much as Congress and the courts have concurrent authority to enforce the Fourteenth Amendment. On questions of statutory interpretation, the courts have final say vis-à-vis agencies, much as they do vis-à-vis Congress on questions of constitutional interpretation.

---

[96] See, for example, *West Lynn Creamery, Inc. v Healy*, 512 US 186, 207 (1994) (Scalia concurring in judgment); Lisa Heinzerling, *The Commercial Constitution*, 1996 Supreme Court Review 217.

[97] The Commerce Clause, one might object, cannot be compared to the Fourteenth Amendment because the former is an express grant of congressional authority, while the latter is simultaneously a grant of authority to the courts to protect individual liberty and equality norms, and a grant of congressional authority. But that difference goes to the Court's authority, not Congress's. The Court stands on much firmer ground in relying on the Fourteenth Amendment to invalidate state laws and practices than it does in reading the Commerce Clause to have that effect by negative implication. The fact that the Court has stronger authority to act independently under the Fourteenth Amendment does not speak to whether Congress's affirmative grants of authority under Article I, Section 8 and Section 5 of the Fourteenth Amendment should be interpreted differently.

In Dormant Commerce Clause jurisprudence, Congress has the final say (so long as by overturning a judicial Dormant Commerce Clause decision it does not violate some other provision of the Constitution). Under the Fourteenth Amendment, by contrast, the Court should retain the final say. But this fact does not diminish the point that the Court and Congress may and do interpret and enforce the Commerce Clause differently.

Finally, once Congress speaks on a particular Dormant Commerce Clause issue, the Court may not differ from Congress's interpretation, even reasonably. But that is because the Court's authority to enforce in this area turns on Congress's silence; once Congress speaks, the Court has no authority to act. Under the Fourteenth Amendment, however, the same is not true, because Section 5 does not authorize Congress to act only where the Court has been silent. As the Voting Rights Act decisions discussed above illustrate, Congress can and does speak even after the Court has, and need not agree with the Court's conclusions.

But in this area of concurrent enforcement competence, the courts do not require administrative agencies to adopt the same interpretations that the courts would. Under *Chevron USA, Inc. v NRDC,*[98] courts reviewing agency interpretations of statutes will defer to the agency's interpretation of an ambiguous statute it administers. "[A] court may not substitute its own construction of a statutory provision for a reasonable interpretation made by the administrator of an agency."[99] Such deference reflects at least in part an acknowledgment that the courts and administrative agencies are different institutions, with different competences.[100]

There is good reason to adopt a similar understanding of the relationship between what Section 1 of the Fourteenth Amendment authorizes the Court to prohibit by judicial decree and what Section 5 authorizes Congress to prohibit by legislation. As the Supreme Court before *Flores* had repeatedly recognized, Section 5's authorization of "appropriate" legislation is functionally identical to the Necessary and Proper Clause in Article I.[101] Both the Necessary and Proper Clause and Section 5 presuppose a substantial degree of room for congressional value judgments about how best to enforce their respective substantive constitutional provisions. Recognition of that room for congressional judgment does not mean abdication of the judicial role in policing the limits of the authority vested in Congress, any more than deference to agency interpretations of statutes constitutes judicial abdication. The Court enforces the Commerce Clause's outer limits by rejecting Congress's judgments only where they lack "a rational basis . . . for concluding that a regulated activity sufficiently affect[s] interstate commerce,"[102] and so, too, should it enforce Section 5's outer limits by rejecting Congress's judgments only where they are predicated on an unreasonable interpretation of the substantive constitutional liberty enforced.

It might be said that the institutional differences between the

[98] 467 US 837 (1984).

[99] Id at 843–44.

[100] See generally Colin S. Diver, *Statutory Interpretation in the Administrative State*, 133 U Pa L Rev 549, 571–92 (1985) (discussing institutional differences between agency and judicial interpretations of statutes).

[101] See note 55.

[102] *United States v Lopez*, 514 US at 557.

Court and Congress are already reflected in the *Flores* Court's distinction between remedy and substance. On this view, the Court should defer to Congress on remedial questions because Congress's institutional advantages make it relatively good at creating effective remedies. It can investigate the full scope of the problem, set up structural mechanisms to realize constitutional rights on a national scale, consider the costs and benefits of alternative plans from multiple perspectives, and design and modify implementation schemes with more flexibility than the Court. The Court is less able to establish and oversee a national remedial scheme, principally because of the case or controversy limitations on its perspective and power. By contrast, the Court's countermajoritarian character and commitment to principled legal analysis are likely to make it better than Congress at expounding upon the Constitution's substantive meaning. Congress's institutional makeup is more adept at reaching messy compromises than clear principles. These are strong arguments for drawing a remedial/substantive line.

But two problems remain with the distinction. The first is the inextricable relationship between right and remedy discussed above, and acknowledged by the *Flores* Court itself.[103] If right and remedy cannot easily be divided, then Congress's "remedial" measures are just as likely to affect the substantive scope of the right at issue as the Court's "substantive" interpretations are likely to determine the remedies available. Thus, it may be impossible to draw the line the Court asserts. If the remedial/substantive distinction cannot be maintained in practice, the fact that it might be defended as a theoretical matter is not of much significance.

The second and more fundamental point is that the Court's institutional concerns often affect not merely its willingness to provide remedies, but also its substantive definition of a right. Equal protection doctrine, for example, was driven to formal definitions of equality by the difficulty of implementing the remedy of substantive equality. It makes perfect sense that concerns about remedy would inevitably affect the Court's substantive definition of a right. The Court cannot count on Congress to provide remedies for every constitutional right it announces, and therefore it must

---

[103] See text at notes 47–53.

be prepared to recognize and enforce remedies for those rights itself. Few things undermine legitimacy like promises not kept. If the Court fears that it cannot make good on the remedy, it will be inclined to define the right in a manner more susceptible to judicial enforcement. As a result, concern about limits on remedies will generally have a strong impact on the Court's substantive definition of the right in the first place.

One of the principal objections to theories advocating judicial deference to "substantive" congressional interpretations of the Fourteenth Amendment is that deference is double-edged. Critics argue that if the Court must defer when Congress enacts RFRA, a statute "overprotecting" a constitutional right, it must also defer when Congress enacts statutes that undermine constitutional rights, by authorizing states to engage in action that the Supreme Court has determined to be unconstitutional.[104] Both an overprotective and an undermining statute might, after all, be characterized as adopting a different substantive interpretation of the constitutional liberty at stake, and if institutional concerns require the Court to defer to substantive interpretations in one (liberty-enhancing) direction, why should they not compel deference in the other (liberty-restricting) direction as well?

The first thing to say about this objection is that it applies equally to the Court's remedial/substantive distinction. As the Court itself has demonstrated over the last twenty years, one of the most effective ways to undermine a constitutional right is to restrict the remedies available for its violations. The Court has, for example, radically undermined rights protections by erecting numerous procedural hurdles to habeas corpus relief, by creating and applying the qualified immunity doctrine to protect government officials from damages actions for constitutional violations, by broadly construing the Eleventh Amendment to protect states from damages actions, and by creating the good faith exception to the exclusionary rule. If the Court were to defer symmetrically to Congress on questions of remedy under Section 5, Congress would have the same power to dilute and eviscerate substantive rights protections in the name of adjusting "remedies."[105] Thus, all judi-

---

[104] See, for example, *Katzenbach v Morgan*, 384 US at 666–68 (Harlan dissenting).

[105] See, for example, *Schweiker v Chilicky*, 487 US 412 (1988) (allowing congressional remedial scheme to preclude judicial damages action for constitutional violation, even where

cial deference to Congress, whether limited to remedial issues or extending also to substantive disagreements, poses the same problem: does judicial deference to congressional efforts to expand rights protections or remedies also require deference to legislative efforts to limit rights protections or remedies through Section 5?

I believe the best answer to this familiar problem requires, once again, attention to the institutional differences between Congress and the Court, in particular, their relative competences to address civil liberties and rights issues on the one hand, and federalism issues on the other. As Professor William Cohen has observed, when Congress passes a statute limiting a constitutional right, the interest potentially undermined is a civil right or civil liberty.[106] The protection of civil rights and civil liberties is the paradigmatic countermajoritarian act, and is therefore more appropriately a judicial duty.[107] Precisely because they are not answerable to the political process, the federal courts are better suited to protect civil rights and civil liberties, and should not defer to the Congress. Deference in that setting would undermine constitutional liberties, which are best protected by a countermajoritarian institution. But when a statute overprotects a constitutional right, the interest potentially undermined is federalism. And for the reasons stated above, Congress should be more effective than the courts in protecting the interests of the states.

Cohen would therefore read Section 5 to permit Congress to overprotect constitutional liberties to the same extent that the states may. That interpretation, I believe, goes too far. As noted above, the states have plenary power to regulate, and the only constraint on their ability to recognize and create rights is that they may not contravene an affirmative prohibition in the federal Constitution. Congress, as a body of limited and enumerated powers, lacks such plenary authority, precisely in order to protect the states' sovereign authority. Accordingly, the Court does play an appropriate role in protecting the interests of the states by enforcing the limits on Congress's authority that our system of enumer-

---

congressional remedy not an equally effective remedy); *Bush v Lucas*, 462 US 367 (1983) (same).

[106] William Cohen, *Congressional Power to Interpret Due Process and Equal Protection*, 27 Stan L Rev 603 (1975).

[107] *United States v Carolene Products Co.*, 304 US 144, 153 n 4 (1938).

ated powers necessarily implies. On this view, however, the Court's enforcement of the federalism limits on Congress's Section 5 power should be no different from its enforcement of federalism limits on Congress's Article I, Section 8 powers. Where Congress acts pursuant to one of its affirmative powers and does not contravene any affirmative constitutional prohibition, its actions should be upheld so long as they reflect a reasonable construction of the affirmative constitutional authority pursuant to which it has acted, whether it be Article I, Section 8, or Section 5 of the Fourteenth Amendment.

Unlike Professor Cohen's proposal, the "reasonableness" standard I advocate would provide some federal judicial protection for states' rights; it would enforce an outer limit beyond which the Congress may not go, even where a majority of the states' representatives think it should. In other words, I do not suggest that judicial restrictions on federalism grounds are inappropriate, but simply that they should take into account the possibility that the Constitution may have different meanings for purposes of judicial and legislative enforcement where both branches have been assigned the authority to enforce a provision. Judicial enforcement of federalism constraints remains appropriate because while states' interests have built-in structural protections in Congress, the Constitution does not limit federalism protections to the structure of the federal government. Rather, the Tenth Amendment inscribes federalism values as an explicit countermajoritarian norm in the Constitution itself, and these values deserve some protection from the countermajoritarian Court.[108] But a deferential "reasonableness" standard of review would reflect an understanding that Congress is institutionally likely to consider states' interests, and that the Constitution may legitimately have different meanings for purposes of legislative and judicial enforcement. Specifically, where a statute enacted pursuant to Section 5 does not undermine individual rights or liberties (as determined by the Court), Congress should be authorized to "enforce" the Fourteenth Amendment by statute to the full extent of a reasonable construction of the Amendment's substantive provisions, even if the Court might not

---

[108] See US Const, Amend X; William W. Van Alstyne, *The Second Death of Federalism*, 83 Mich L Rev 1709 (1985).

adopt the same substantive construction for purposes of direct judicial enforcement.

To analogize once more to the Commerce Clause, the remedial/substantive distinction that the Court has drawn in *Flores* is strikingly reminiscent of the direct/indirect and manufacturing/commerce distinctions that the Court once drew under the Commerce Clause.[109] Those distinctions proved not only difficult to draw but misguided in an integrated national economy, and eventually the Court abandoned them for a more deferential approach that left Congress substantial leeway in determining what conduct affects interstate commerce and requires regulation. The distinction between remedy and substance is similarly problematic given the inextricable interconnections between right and remedy. But more importantly, it misses the point, and treats the Constitution as a document that can have only a single determinate meaning, no matter which institution is enforcing it. An understanding of the institutional differences between judicial and congressional enforcement of a constitutional principle argues in favor of judicial deference to Congress's reasonable interpretations of the Constitution where Congress and the Court have concurrent enforcement authority.

V. DEFERENCE AND CONSTITUTIONAL INTERPRETATION

The *O'Dell* case with which this article opened serves as a reminder that in other contexts, the Court acknowledges that interpreting the Constitution is a fluid enterprise and defers to reasonable interpretations adopted by other government actors. When criminal defendants raise constitutional objections to their convictions on habeas corpus review, the Court declines to apply so-called "new" rules retroactively.[110] If any reasonable jurist could have reached a different conclusion on a constitutional issue at the time the conviction became final, the Court will deem the rule

---

[109] See, for example, *United States v EC Knight*, 156 US 1 (1895) (manufacturing/commerce distinction); *Carter v Carter Coal Co.*, 298 US 238, 304 (1936) (distinguishing between mining and commerce); *ALA Schechter Poultry Corp. v United States*, 295 US 495, 550 (1935) (distinguishing between indirect and direct effects on interstate commerce).

[110] *Teague v Lane*, 489 US 288 (1989).

sought by the habeas petitioner "new," and deny relief. This definition of a "new" rule extends substantial deference to state courts on matters of constitutional interpretation. Indeed, virtually every time since *Teague* that the Court has asked whether a habeas petitioner is invoking a "new" rule, it has answered in the affirmative, deferred to the state court process, and denied relief.[111]

The Court shows similarly broad deference to reasonable interpretations of the Constitution by other government actors under the judge-made doctrine of qualified immunity.[112] This doctrine holds that personal liability will not extend to government officials who violate individuals' constitutional rights where their actions did not violate "clearly established" constitutional law. The Court's definition of "clearly established" law, like its definition of a "new" rule, is highly deferential to government officials' interpretations of constitutional law. Under this standard, the Court has explained, "all but the plainly incompetent or those who knowingly violate the law" will be protected from liability.[113]

With respect to both issues—the retroactivity of constitutional rules on habeas corpus and the personal liability of government officials for unconstitutional conduct—the Court defers to government officials' interpretations of the Constitution even when the officials turn out to have been "wrong" about the Constitution's substantive requirements. Yet in *Flores*, the Court refused to defer to Congress, even where the Constitution assigned Congress express constitutional authority to "enforce" the provision at issue, and Congress had adopted a view of the Free Exercise Clause that the Court itself had followed for twenty-five years.[114]

Admittedly, the Court has given reasons for why it defers on matters of constitutional interpretation in the retroactivity and qualified immunity settings. Comity to the states and an interest in the finality of criminal judgments is said to support the deference paid to state court interpretations of the Constitution in habeas corpus proceedings.[115] In addition, the Court has reasoned,

---

[111] The only Supreme Court cases in which *Teague* has been addressed and the claim survived were *Penry v Lynaugh*, 492 US 302 (1989), and *Stringer v Black*, 503 US 222 (1992).

[112] *Harlow v Fitzgerald*, 457 US 800 (1982).

[113] *Malloy v Briggs*, 475 US 335, 341 (1986).

[114] RFRA states that it seeks to restore the pre-*Smith* doctrine "as set forth in prior Federal court rulings." 42 USC § 2000bb(a)(5).

[115] *Teague v Lane*, 489 US at 310.

deterrence is served by holding state courts to the constitutional requirements that exist when they decide a case, but is not served by faulting state courts for failing to forecast a change in constitutional law that was not predictable at the time.[116] Qualified immunity is justified by a sense that it is unfair to hold government officials personally liable for doing their jobs where the law is unclear, and a concern that officials might be "overdeterred" into taking little action at all for fear of liability if the standard is too strict.[117]

It is not the purpose of this essay to criticize these rationales; they have been soundly criticized elsewhere.[118] Whether or not these justifications are persuasive, my point is that they are premised on a very different understanding of constitutional interpretation and enforcement from that which operated in *Flores*. The retroactivity and qualified immunity doctrines make sense only to the extent that one accepts that enforcing the Constitution requires its interpretation, and that different actors within the legal system acting reasonably are likely to reach different understandings of the Constitution's substance in interpreting and enforcing it. When the same understanding is applied to Section 5, the arguments for deference to Congress are at least as persuasive as the arguments for deference to state courts and government officials accepted in *Teague* and *Harlow*.

It might be argued that the Court's deference in the habeas and qualified immunity settings is limited in important ways. These doctrines, after all, address the remedial impact of "mistakes," and not the substantive meaning of the Constitution itself. The doctrines do not extend deference to every effort by a state court or government official to interpret or enforce the Constitution. The Court shows no deference to state court interpretations of the Constitution, for example, when reviewing a state conviction on direct appeal as opposed to habeas corpus. And the Court similarly

---

[116] Id at 309.

[117] *Harlow v Fitzgerald*, 475 US 800.

[118] Linda Meyer, *"Nothing We Say Matters": Teague and New Rules*, 61 U Chi L Rev 423 (1994); Ann Woolhandler, *Demodeling Habeas*, 45 Stan L Rev 575 (1993); James S. Liebman, *More Than "Slightly Retro:" The Rehnquist Court's Rout of Habeas Corpus Jurisdiction in Teague v Lane*, 18 NYU Rev L & Soc Change 537 (1990–91); David Rudovsky, *The Qualified Immunity Doctrine in the Supreme Court: Judicial Activism and the Restriction of Constitutional Rights*, 138 U Pa L Rev 23 (1989).

shows no deference to government officials' constitutional interpretations when injunctive relief rather than damages is sought for a constitutional rights violation. This might be taken to support the view that the deference the Court does accord is predicated not so much on an understanding of the effects of institutional role on constitutional interpretation as on concerns about the fairness of second-guessing government actors who made reasonable mistakes. But these exceptions are in fact far less significant than they might at first appear. The Supreme Court rarely considers a state court conviction on direct review, preferring as an institutional matter to let the lower federal courts handle these matters in the first instance through habeas corpus petitions. And the Court has erected such formidable barriers to injunctive relief that in many cases it is damages or nothing where individuals' rights have been violated by official misconduct.[119] Thus, what in theory is only partial deference may be, in practice, virtually complete.

What may be more significant in comparing the retroactivity and qualified immunity doctrines to Section 5 jurisprudence is the way the Court's deference (or lack thereof) runs. All of these settings pose the same basic tension between individual rights and government authority. In the first two, the Court defers to reasonable, even if mistaken, interpretations of the Constitution that favor government authority and undermine individual rights. In construing Section 5, however, the Court brooks no disagreement with its own interpretation of the Constitution, even where Congress acts only to provide more statutory protection for a right than the Constitution demands.

What unites all three doctrines is that they favor governmental authority over individual rights. O'Dell was sentenced to die by an unconstitutional procedure, but the Court's deferential approach treated the violation as a "new" rule, thus favoring the state's in-

---

[119] See, for example, *Lyons v City of Los Angeles,* 461 US 95 (1983) (denying standing to victim of police chokehold to seek injunctive relief against police policy on chokeholds); *O'Shea v Littleton,* 414 US 488 (1974) (denying standing to individuals to challenge allegedly racially discriminatory prosecutorial policies); *Rizzo v Goode,* 423 US 362 (1976) (denying standing to challenge pattern of police brutality); *Armstrong v United States,* 116 S Ct 1480 (1996) (denying discovery in selective prosecution case despite evidentiary showing that all crack cocaine cases closed by Federal Public Defender's office that year had been against black defendants, and that non-black crack defendants were prosecuted in state court, where penalties were substantially lower).

terests in comity and finality over O'Dell's interest in due process. Similarly, the deferential qualified immunity standard sacrifices individual rights to government authority, denying any remedy to individuals whose rights have been violated as long as the violation was not obvious under settled law. Under Section 5, by contrast, the Court eschews deference in the one setting where a deferential approach would have the effect of favoring individual rights over state authority. But as Professor Cohen has shown, there is a much better argument for deference when Congress overprotects a constitutional right than when it (or indeed any government official) violates an individual constitutional right. The Court is the best guardian of individual rights, but not necessarily of federalism. Yet today's Court's deference is consistent only in that it always favors states' rights.

VI. CONCLUSION

Flores is another in an increasingly long line of cases reaffirming the importance to today's Court of states' interests.[120] Whether *Flores* will in the end impose a significant constraint on Congress's Section 5 powers remains to be seen, much as the consequences of *United States v Lopez*[121] for Commerce Clause jurisprudence remain to be seen. The Court in both *Flores* and *Lopez* went to great pains to insist that it was simply applying established doctrines, but in both cases seems to have retooled the old rules to protect the states. The Court's effort to make *Flores* look like its Section 5 precedents led the Court to insist that it would extend deference to Congress on the issue of what constitutes an appropriate remedial or preventive measure, if not on the question of a constitutional provision's substantive meaning. If it remains true

---

[120] In retrospect, this line of cases probably began with the revolution in habeas corpus, in which, out of deference to state criminal processes, the Court reinterpreted the writ of habeas corpus to cut off many convicted individuals' ability to present their federal claims in a federal court. See, for example, *Teague v Lane*, 489 US 288 (1989); *Wainwright v Sykes*, 433 US 72 (1977) (defendant waives right to pursue constitutional claim in habeas corpus if lawyer fails to preserve it in state court proceedings); *Stone v Powell*, 428 US 465 (1976) (Fourth Amendment violations may not be raised on habeas corpus). It continues with such cases as *New York v United States*, 505 US 144 (1992), *United States v Lopez*, 514 US 549 (1995), *Seminole Tribe v Florida*, 116 S Ct 1114 (1996), and *Printz v United States*, 117 S Ct 2365 (1997).

[121] 115 S Ct 1624 (1995).

to its word, *Flores* may prove a relatively insignificant case. Remedy and substance are inextricably linked, and a Congress that knows it must speak the language of remedy and prevention when acting under Section 5 should generally be able to do so.

RFRA was an unusual statute—it marked virtually unanimous congressional disagreement with the Court on a constitutional matter. The Court in *Flores* appeared to take umbrage at Congress's critical assessment, and treated the statute as a challenge to the Court's power to interpret and enforce the Constitution, virtually akin to Arkansas Governor Orville Faubus's blocking the schoolhouse door in Little Rock in defiance of a federal court desegregation decree. But despite the overheated rhetoric of RFRA's critics (the spirit of which made its way into the majority opinion), nothing in RFRA challenged the Court's ability to interpret and enforce the Constitution. RFRA's enactment did reflect Congress's disagreement with the Court over the meaning of the Free Exercise Clause, but it did not alter or amend the Constitution; it merely created a statutory cause of action. The fact that RFRA was only a statute, and not a constitutional amendment, had significant institutional consequences that should have played a greater role in the Court's assessment of its constitutionality.

Flores speaks in terms of federalism and separation of powers, but at bottom the case stands or falls on the validity of the Court's conception of constitutional interpretation as an enterprise that is unaffected by the interpreter's institutional character or by the consequences of the interpretation. The Court treated judicial enforcement of the Constitution as indistinguishable from congressional enforcement, and therefore saw no room for disagreements over the substance of the Free Exercise Clause. But in fact there are substantial institutional differences between Congress's interpretation of the Free Exercise Clause and the Court's. When the Court interprets a constitutional provision, it creates rights that cannot be altered except by a judicial departure from stare decisis or a constitutional amendment. And when the Court interprets the Fourteenth Amendment to impose duties on the states, it does so without the benefit of state representation. When Congress interprets the Fourteenth Amendment for purposes of statutory enforcement, by contrast, its interpretations are subject to amendment at any time by majority vote, and its deliberations structurally reflect the interests of the states. As a result, Congress ought to be more free to develop innovative approaches to further the values of the Fourteenth Amendment; its experiments come at less institutional cost.[122] As long as a statute enacted pursuant to Section 5 does not infringe an individual liberty or right protected by the Constitution, and represents a reasonable interpretation of the substance of the Fourteenth Amendment, it should be upheld, even if the Court would not reach the same interpretation for purposes of judicial enforcement of the Constitution.

To insist that the Constitution may have different substantive meanings for purposes of judicial and congressional enforcement is not to suggest that the Constitution has no determinate meaning. Rather, it is simply to note that all members of our federal government are sworn to uphold the Constitution, and that because of significant differences in their institutional competences, powers, and constraints, different institutions might reasonably differ about what the Constitution means for purposes of their respective enforcement obligations. Under Section 5, Congress should be permitted to go further than the Court in its interpretation of what equal protection or due process requires. The Court, of course, remains the final arbiter of constitutional meaning. But where the Constitution has created concurrent enforcement authority, as in the Fourteenth Amendment, the Court ought not confuse deference for abdication.

---

[122] Indeed, to the extent that one of the functional arguments in favor of federalism is that it provides "laboratories for experimentation," one would think that a functional federalist would also support this federal mechanism for experimentation.

CHRISTOPHER L. EISGRUBER
AND LAWRENCE G. SAGER

CONGRESSIONAL POWER AND RELIGIOUS LIBERTY AFTER CITY OF BOERNE v FLORES

I. Introduction

For the last seven years, Congress and the Supreme Court have wrestled over the meaning of the Free Exercise Clause. Their confrontation reflects the confused legacy of the 1963 decision in *Sherbert v Verner*.[1] In *Sherbert*, the Court seemed to endorse the proposition that religiously motivated persons are constitutionally exempt from otherwise valid laws unless the imposition of those laws is necessary to secure "a compelling state interest."[2] But *Sherbert*'s fierce invocation of the compelling state interest test was never reflected in practice: in only four cases after *Sherbert* did the Supreme Court find that religious believers were entitled to exemptions, and three of those were minor variations on *Sherbert*

Christopher L. Eisgruber is Professor of Law, New York University School of Law. Lawrence G. Sager is Robert B. McKay Professor of Law, New York University School of Law.

Authors' note: For helpful comments on earlier drafts, the authors thank Vicki Been, Abner Greene, Ira C. Lupu, Derek Parfit, and participants in the NYU Constitutional Theory Colloquium and in a Constitutional Theory Workshop organized by John Jeffries at the University of Virginia Law School. Stephanie Pare, Megan Lewis, and Alex Reinert provided excellent research assistance, and the Filomen D'Agostino and Max E. Greenberg Faculty Research Fund provided generous financial support.

[1] 374 US 398 (1963).

[2] Id at 403 (internal quotation marks omitted).

itself—they were cases in which states denied unemployment insurance benefits after ruling that claimants who left jobs for religious reasons lacked "good cause" for their resignation.[3] Most attempts to exempt religiously motivated persons from the obligation to comply with otherwise valid laws failed, just as they had always failed before *Sherbert*.[4]

The failure of *Sherbert*'s bold rhetoric posed an interesting jurisprudential puzzle, but the underlying question of religious exemptions remained a quiet and somewhat obscure corner of constitutional law for more than a quarter century—a decidedly unlikely venue for pitched conflict between the Court and Congress. Then, in 1990, the Supreme Court decided *Employment Division, Department of Human Resources of Oregon v Smith*.[5] Smith involved a Native American religious ritual which required participants to ingest peyote; practitioners of the religion claimed that the Free Exercise Clause exempted them from Oregon's prohibition of the consumption of peyote. The Court not only refused this claim as it had more or less routinely refused the exemption claims of other religiously motivated persons: it went on to formally renounce the *Sherbert* test as the general rule in religious exemption cases. In the eyes of the *Smith* Court, "the right of free exercise does not relieve an individual of the obligation to comply with a 'valid and neutral law of general applicability on the ground that the law proscribes (or prescribes) conduct that his religion prescribes (or proscribes).' "[6]

Smith touched a sensitive nerve. A coalition of religious interests, civil liberties groups, and law professors decried the case as

---

[3] The four cases are *Wisconsin v Yoder*, 406 US 205 (1972); *Thomas v Review Bd of the Indiana Empl. Sec. Division*, 450 US 707 (1981); *Hobbie v Unemployment Appeals Commission of Florida*, 480 US 136 (1987); and *Frazee v Illinois Department of Empl. Sec.*, 489 US 829 (1989). All but *Yoder* involved claims for unemployment insurance benefits.

[4] We review *Sherbert*'s legacy in Section III. We have done so in more detail in Christopher L. Eisgruber and Lawrence G. Sager, *Why the Religious Freedom Restoration Act Is Unconstitutional*, 69 NYU L Rev 437, 445–48 (1994), and Christopher L. Eisgruber and Lawrence G. Sager, *The Vulnerability of Conscience: The Constitutional Basis for Protecting Religious Conduct*, 61 U Chi L Rev 1245, 1246–47, 1273–82 (1994). We extended our theoretical framework to other religious liberty issues in Christopher L. Eisgruber and Lawrence G. Sager, *Unthinking Religious Freedom*, 74 Tex L Rev 577 (1996).

[5] 494 US 872 (1990).

[6] Id at 879 (quoting *United States v Lee*, 455 US 252, 263 n 3 (1982) (Stevens concurring)).

an affront to religious freedom. Congress took up their cause, and in 1993 was nearly unanimous in enacting the Religious Freedom Restoration Act ("RFRA").[7] RFRA provided that "[g]overnment shall not substantially burden a person's exercise of religion" unless it first demonstrates that "application of the burden to the person" is the "least restrictive means" to further "a compelling government interest."[8] This, of course, was a direct and explicit rejection of the *Smith* Court's understanding of the Free Exercise Clause, and set Congress and the Court on a collision course. RFRA claimants would be advancing statutory rather than constitutional rights, but these statutory rights derived from Congress's distinct understanding of the Free Exercise Clause. Congress maintained that its authority under Section 5 of the Fourteenth Amendment to enforce the liberty-bearing provisions of the Bill of Rights permitted it to disagree—and as with RFRA, to disagree quite sharply—with the Court's view of constitutional liberty.[9]

In relatively short order, the Supreme Court found the occasion to consider whether Congress could, in the fashion of RFRA, legislate a dissenting view of constitutional liberty. Late in its most recent term, the Court decided *City of Boerne v Flores*.[10] *Flores* arose out of a zoning dispute in a small town not far from San Antonio. St. Peter's Catholic Church was located in the downtown historic district in Boerne, Texas. The church's membership was swelling, and the church wanted to expand. The church invoked RFRA to claim an exemption from the restrictions imposed upon buildings located in the historic district. The Court's response was blunt and forceful: RFRA exceeded the scope of Congress's authority under Section 5 of the Fourteenth Amendment and was constitutionally invalid. Period.

Flores may not or may not end the matter. Within weeks of the *Flores* decision, Florida Congressman Charles Canady convened

---

[7] 42 USC §§ 2000bb–2000bb-4 (1994).

[8] Id § 2000bb-1(a)–(b).

[9] The Senate and House Reports on RFRA both characterized the statute as an exercise of power granted Congress by Section 5 of the Fourteenth Amendment. Religious Freedom Restoration Act of 1993, S Rep No 103-111, 103d Cong, 1st Sess 13–14 (1993); Religious Freedom Restoration Act of 1993, HR Rep No 103-88, 103d Cong, 1st Sess at 9 (1993).

[10] 117 S Ct 2157 (1997).

public hearings. At the hearings, critics of *Smith* and *Flores* offered suggestions about how Congress might reenact RFRA in a new guise.[11]

* * *

RFRA was inspired by a surprisingly common view of the Supreme Court's religious liberty jurisprudence. In this account, *Smith* was preceded by a long constitutional tradition of excusing religious believers from compliance with laws that everyone else was obliged to obey. The five-Justice majority in *Smith* hijacked that tradition, a tradition upon which minority religious believers depended for their protection from indifferent or hostile majorities. This left only Congress to fill the breach, and RFRA was a modest and well-tailored vehicle by which Congress sought to restore the well-functioning status quo that *Smith* had disrupted. If one is in the grip of this account, it is natural to take a dim view of *Flores* in turn, as an instance of a churlish Supreme Court spurning the measured constitutional judgment of a concerned Congress, and so as a case which bodes poorly for the ability of Congress and the Court to work as partners in the project of securing constitutional justice.[12]

This picture of *Smith* and RFRA—and now *Flores* as well—has been widely accepted, and often repeated in congressional testi-

---

[11] House of Representatives Committee on the Judiciary, Subcommittee on the Constitution, Hearing on "Protecting Religious Freedom after Boerne v Flores," July 14, 1997. When this article was prepared, testimony from witnesses who appeared at the hearing was available on the Internet at http://www.house.gov/judiciary/222302.htm. The testimony is reported in Linda Greenhouse, *Laws Are Urged to Protect Religion*, New York Times A15 (July 15, 1997).

[12] Oliver Thomas, who is Special Counsel for Religious and Civil Liberties to the National Council of the Churches of Christ in the USA, offered Congress an especially extreme instance of this view. In testimony presented shortly after the Court decided *Flores*, Thomas said,

> The Supreme Court's decision to strike down the Religious Freedom Restoration Act (RFRA) is a blow not only to the sovereignty of the Congress but to the American people as well. As the *Dred Scott* decision of a century ago was for African-Americans, so *City of Boerne v. Flores* is for religious Americans today. But, as with *Dred Scott*, Americans working together will overcome this setback to freedom.

At the time this article was prepared, Thomas's testimony was available on-line at http://www.house.gov/judiciary/222305.htm. See also, e.g., Clarence Page, *Keeping the Faith: Religious Freedom Act Could Turn Into Worthy Amendment Scheme*, Chicago Tribune 19 (July 2, 1997).

mony, law review articles, and newspaper editorials.[13] It is also false at every turn. It misrepresents the Court's pre-*Smith* jurisprudence. It misrepresents what the Court held in *Smith* and its reasons for doing so. It misrepresents the meaning and effects of RFRA. It presupposes a novel, normatively unattractive, and practically unworkable conception of religious liberty. And, finally, it misrepresents the significance of *Flores* for congressional power.

This last point may be especially important. The jurisprudence of religious liberty has long been fraught with confusions of the sort that plague the defective conventional account of *Smith* and RFRA. Until *Flores*, however, these confusions were at least confined to religious liberty. For better or worse, *Flores* has raised the stakes. Significant though it may be as a religious liberty case, *Flores* looms even larger as a case about congressional power. Indeed, it may well be the most important statement by the Court about Congress's power under the Reconstruction Amendments since *Katzenbach v Morgan*[14] in 1966.

The questions are entwined, of course. *Flores* is above all a case about congressional excess. In the eyes of the *Flores* Court, Congress's sweeping deployment of the compelling interest test in RFRA was novel and dangerous. Where the Constitution's objective was to protect religious believers against unfair imposition of special disadvantages, RFRA privileged religious believers in a way that was both normatively unattractive and practically unworkable. When the *Flores* Court concluded that "[t]he stringent test RFRA demands of state laws reflects a lack of proportionality or congruence between the means adopted and the legitimate end to be achieved,"[15] it was renouncing a congressional vision of religious liberty that was at radical odds with its own. *Flores* is thus much more generous to reasonable congressional augmentations of civil liberties than its critics suppose. Further, as between the competing views of Congress and the Supreme Court, the Court has much the better of the matter: *Smith* was fundamentally correct in its

---

[13] For congressional testimony and newspaper articles, see, e.g., sources cited in nn 11 & 12. An influential law review article written from a similar perspective is Douglas Laycock, *The Religious Freedom Restoration Act*, 1993 BYU L Rev 221.

[14] 384 US 641 (1966).

[15] 117 S Ct at 2171.

rejection of a broad privilege for religiously motivated conduct.

These are our claims. We hope to make good on them in the pages that follow.

II. Reconstructing the Flores Court's Understanding of Congress's Section 5 Authority

A. FLORES, KATZENBACH, AND THE RIGHT/REMEDY DISTINCTION

Congress's authority to enact RFRA depends upon Section 5 of the Fourteenth Amendment. Section 5 authorizes Congress to enforce the other provisions of the Amendment; RFRA, accordingly, had to be understood as an attempt to enforce Free Exercise rights incorporated by the Due Process Clause of Section 1 of the Fourteenth Amendment. Since RFRA was founded on a view of Free Exercise that was at odds with the Court's announced view in *Smith*, the validity of RFRA depended on the idea that Congress, at least under some circumstances, could use its Section 5 authority to create statutory surrogates for rights the Court would not itself recognize.

The obvious starting point for this argument was *Katzenbach v Morgan*.[16] In *Katzenbach*, the Supreme Court upheld the constitutionality of Section 4(e) of the Voting Rights Act of 1965, which prohibited states from using English literacy tests to deny the franchise to graduates of Puerto Rican elementary schools. The Court found that Section 4(e) was a valid exercise of Congress's power to enforce the Fourteenth Amendment even though the Court itself had recently found that literacy tests did not violate the Constitution.[17] According to Justice Brennan, who authored the opinion of the Court, Congress enjoyed the power to act even in the absence of "a judicial determination that the enforcement of the state law precluded by Congress violated the [Fourteenth] Amendment."[18] Narrower constructions of Congress's power under Section 5 were unacceptable because they "would depreciate both congressional resourcefulness and congressional responsibility for implementing the Amendment."[19] *Katzenbach* thus made clear that

---

[16] 384 US 641 (1966).

[17] *Lassiter v Northampton Election Bd.*, 360 US 45 (1959).

[18] 384 US at 648.

[19] Id.

Congress could use Section 5 to regulate conduct and policies that were outside the scope of the judicially enforced amendment.

Katzenbach was famously unclear about why Congress had this power and what its limits were. Quoting *McCulloch v Maryland*,[20] the Court said that its job was to ask whether Congress had enacted a statute that was "plainly adapted" to the end of enforcing the Amendment and was "consistent with 'the letter and spirit of the Constitution.'"[21] The Court concluded that the ban on literacy tests at issue in *Katzenbach* met this test; Justice Brennan offered two conceptually distinct explanations for its result. One was broadly remedial: Congress might have intended to combat widespread-but-difficult-to-isolate discrimination against Puerto Ricans—for example, in the distribution of public services—by giving them more political clout with which to engage in self-help.[22] The other was more naturally understood as involving substantive deference by the Court to Congress's substantive constitutional judgment: Congress might have acted upon a reasonable but enlarged view of equal protection pursuant to which literacy tests in the circumstances of the growing Puerto Rican population resident in the United States were unconstitutional.[23]

Dissenting in *Katzenbach*, Justice Harlan worried that, by freeing Congress to pursue rights other than those the Court itself protected, the majority had effectively authorized Congress to make the Constitution mean whatever it liked and, in particular, to narrow or eliminate rights the Court had recognized. Justice Brennan answered with a footnote: "§5 grants Congress no power to restrict, abrogate, or dilute [the Fourteenth Amendment's] guarantees."[24]

This asymmetrical ability of Congress to broaden but not to narrow the Court's understanding of constitutional rights—sometimes referred to as "Brennan's Ratchet"—is part of what calls for explanation in *Katzenbach*. More generally, substantive deference to Congress on questions concerning the meaning of the liberty-bearing provisions of the Constitution is not a general feature of

---

[20] 17 US 316 (1819).

[21] 384 US at 650–51.

[22] Id at 652–53.

[23] Id at 653–54.

[24] Id at 651 n 10.

the constitutional landscape, and needs a justification that offers some guidance as to the shape of the deference it implicates.

A fractured decision four years later in *Oregon v Mitchell*[25] did not clarify matters. *Mitchell* dealt with the constitutionality of a federal law requiring the states to permit eighteen-year-olds to vote in both state and federal elections. Congress relied on Section 5 to justify both aspects of the law. Four justices, including Brennan, read *Katzenbach* broadly as including a substantial degree of deference to Congress's constitutional judgment, and would have upheld the statute in all respects.[26] Four other justices, including Harlan, read *Katzenbach* narrowly as an instance of Congress's power to provide remedies for constitutional rights that the Court itself recognized, and would have invalidated the statute.[27] Justice Black joined neither of these sides, and cast the deciding vote in the case on the basis of two idiosyncratic rationales. He upheld the statute as applied to federal elections, but on the basis of Congress's power to regulate voter qualifications under Article I, Section 4,[28] and he found the statute unconstitutional with regard to state elections, concluding that *Katzenbach*'s broad reading of congressional power was apt only to issues of racial discrimination.[29]

Justice Kennedy, writing for six Justices in *Flores*, adopted a view of Congress's Section 5 authority which combined Justice Brennan's spirit of generous deference to congressional judgment with Justice Harlan's insistence on the distinction between remedial and substantive deference.[30] So long as Congress could be understood as putting in place a scheme of remedies for recognized constitutional wrongs, the Court would broadly defer to congressional judgment.[31] On this basis, Congress could enact statutes that went considerably beyond judicially secured constitutional rights. Thus, *Katzenbach* and other prominent cases ceding wide authority to Congress were all correctly decided.[32] But Congress could not un-

---

[25] 400 US 112 (1970).

[26] Id at 141–44 (Douglas opinion); id at 248–49 (Brennan opinion).

[27] Id at 204–09 (Harlan opinion); id at 295–96 (Stewart opinion).

[28] Id at 123–24 (Black opinion).

[29] Id at 129 (Black opinion).

[30] 117 S Ct at 2164.

[31] Id at 2163–64.

[32] Id at 2170.

dertake to displace the Court's judgments about the content of constitutional rights themselves. This was the vice of RFRA: the "lack of proportionality or congruence between [its stringent test] and the legitimate end to be achieved"[33] disqualified RFRA as a plausible remedy for judicially recognizable rights.[34]

Remarkably, not a single Justice took issue with this understanding of Section 5. Justice O'Connor, while dissenting on the grounds that she thought *Smith* was wrongly decided, expressly supported the majority's discussion of Section 5, bringing to seven the number of Justices who embraced Justice Kennedy's rationale.[35] Justices Breyer and Souter felt the Court should have reconsidered *Smith*, and declined to consider the question of Congress's Section 5 authority.[36]

We will make three brief passes at the *Flores* Court's approach to the question of Congress's Section 5 authority. First, we will try to understand it on its own terms. Second, we will argue for an emendation to—or perhaps better, a gloss upon—the Court's approach which is more consistent with the historic partnership between the Court and Congress on matters of constitutional justice. Finally, we will situate our recommended understanding of *Flores* among other approaches to Section 5 authority.

B. RIGHTS, REMEDIES, AND RFRA

The distinction between rights and remedies—like the distinctions (to which it is obviously kin) between "ends" and "means" or between "substance" and "process"—is notoriously difficult to draw. The task of interpreting *Flores*—for commentators today, and for the Court itself in the future—will revolve around giving firm conceptual structure to a distinction that could easily dissolve into mush.

For *Flores* purposes, it would seem that the right/remedy distinction rests upon a view of the world more or less like this: rights attach to states of affairs which are required by the Constitution; remedies, in contrast, attach to states of affairs which are not re-

---

[33] Id at 2171.

[34] Id at 2171–72.

[35] Id at 2176 (O'Connor dissenting).

[36] Id at 2186 (Souter dissenting); id (Breyer dissenting).

quired by the Constitution, but which are instrumentally useful to achieving those states of affairs which are. Rights involve states of affairs that are desirable in themselves, while remedies may involve states of affairs that are desirable only as means of securing rights. From the vantage of the Constitution, accordingly, "rights" are mandatory constraints upon government; "remedies" are merely supportive, and government might reasonably choose among various remedial schemes useful to securing a particular right (indeed, government may have to make choices among schemes, since some schemes are likely to be inconsistent with others).

Thus, in the view of the *Flores* Court, Congress enjoys broad discretion to create remedies designed to help bridge the gap between the status quo and constitutionally required states of affairs, and likewise, to create prophylactic measures designed to prevent the status quo from deteriorating and sliding further away from a constitutionally required states of affairs. Some of these remedial or prophylactic measures will be considerably more demanding than the requirements of the Constitution they support—it is this which explains the Court's general willingness to welcome Section 5 legislation that enlarges upon constitutionally required states of affairs. But the Court is the ultimate arbiter of what the Constitution requires, and legislation which can only be understood as a disagreement with the Court's understanding of what the Constitution requires is outside the bounds of Congress's Section 5 authority. That is what makes RFRA unconstitutional.

C. COURT, CONGRESS, AND CONFLICT

For the *Flores* Court, Congress's Section 5 authority ends where disagreement over the substance of constitutional rights begins. We can better understand the functional scope of Congress's authority, therefore, by giving sharper edges to the idea of substantive disagreement. Suppose we begin with the simplest case: Congress enacts a remedy which is actually inconsistent with what the Court considers to be a constitutionally mandated state of affairs— which is, in other words, itself prohibited by the Constitution. This is the clearest case of a disagreement over the substance of constitutional rights. If Congress acts on its understanding of the Constitution under these circumstances, the resulting legislation will both violate the Bill of Rights and exceed Congress's Section

5 authority as well. If *Flores* stands for anything, it stands for the unexceptional proposition that the Court will enforce the liberty-bearing provisions of the Constitution according to its own best judgment of the content of those provisions. In our view,[37] and in the view of Justice Stevens (and perhaps other members of the Court),[38] RFRA is an instance of exactly this sort of radical disagreement, and violated the religion clauses of the Constitution.

Suppose we extend the theme of a conflict between the judgment of the Court and that of Congress, and imagine a case where Congress calls for a state of affairs which, though not itself prohibited by the Constitution, is considered by the Court to be counterproductive to the achievement of a state of affairs mandated by the Constitution. That too is an easy case of Congress's overstepping its remedial authority under Section 5, though not necessarily a substantive violation of the Constitution. Again, the insistence of the *Flores* Court that it judge for itself the meaning of the liberty-bearing provisions of the Constitution seems firmly in play, and the Court would understandably be unwilling to justify as remedial a congressional measure that undermined the constitutionally mandated state of affairs it purported to remedy.

Now we can go a step further and consider a somewhat more subtle form of conflict between the Court and Congress. Suppose that Congress calls for a state of affairs that is neither directly prohibited by the Constitution nor strictly counterproductive to the achievement of a state of affairs mandated by the Constitution, but which is nevertheless deeply at odds with the Court's best judgment in this sense: The measure in question is plainly ill-suited to the realization of a constitutionally mandated state of affairs.

We can distinguish three sorts of cases that might—at first blush, at least—be thought to fall within this category. First, Congress could set out to protect rights that, while not at odds with those the Court has recognized, are unrelated to them. Suppose, for example, that a conservative Congress repealed federal labor laws and sought to insulate employers against state legislation; suppose further that (for whatever reason) this legislation could not be defended under the Commerce Clause, and hence stood or fell

---

[37] Eisgruber and Sager, 69 NYU L Rev at 452–60 (cited in note 4).

[38] 117 S Ct at 2172 (Stevens concurring) (arguing that RFRA violated the Establishment Clause). No other Justice in the majority addressed the Establishment Clause issue.

as an effort by Congress to enforce the "liberty of contract" under the Fourteenth Amendment. Here, the *Flores* distinction between rights and remedies would clearly apply, as the congressional legislation would not support any liberty recognized by the modern Court. The measure in question would indeed be ill-suited to the realization of a constitutionally mandated state of affairs, and, per *Flores*, outside the bounds of Congress's Section 5 authority.

The second sort of case that could be thought to fall in the plainly ill-suited category is considerably more interesting and important. Congress might enact legislation which seems to have as its target a vision of constitutional justice more robust than the Court's own, but which is substantively close to commitments which underlie the Court's constitutional doctrine and is entirely consistent with those commitments. Suppose, for example, that Congress sought to fortify the laws against race discrimination by enabling people to bring disparate impact claims against state governments. In one sense, this law obviously supports rights the Court has deemed mandatory. Under the Court's reading of the Equal Protection Clause, facially neutral laws that combine a discriminatory purpose with a racially disparate impact are unconstitutional. Giving racial minorities a statutory claim against state governmental acts that produced a disparate impact would provide a legal filter which would undoubtedly trap some cases of unconstitutional conduct that would elude ordinary equal protection oversight. On the other hand, Congress might well have enacted the law because it construed the Constitution's fundamental equality norms more broadly than the Court did, or more likely still, the various members of Congress might hold very different views on the question of whether this legislation is best understood as substantive or remedial. In these circumstances, how carefully should the Court scrutinize the question of whether Congress has attempted to substitute its understanding of constitutional rights for that of the Court? Or, to continue our terminology, just how "plainly" ill-suited must legislation of this sort be before it falls outside Congress's Section 5 power?

It is at just this point that we want to argue for an important gloss on the *Flores* Court's analysis. We think the Court has very good reason to be exceptionally generous to Congress in a case of this sort. As the *Flores* Court itself acknowledged, "the line between measures that remedy or prevent unconstitutional actions and measures that make a substantive change in the governing law is not easy to discern."[39] In important part, this is because—as the disparate impact example suggests—reasonable efforts to prevent or remedy constitutional violations can spill well beyond the judicially specified terms of those violations. In equally important (and somewhat less obvious) part, it is because there is a gap between what the Court itself should recognize as the best possible way to effectuate the values protected by the Constitution, and what the Court constructs as constitutional doctrine.

The Court is institutionally situated in ways that quite properly shape its decisions. For example: it must articulate rules that offer clear guidance to lower courts and other governmental actors; it must defer broadly to legislative bodies when constitutional principles become thoroughly entwined with decisions of public policy that properly belong in such bodies; and its ability to fashion rules in service of constitutional values is often more limited than legislative bodies addressing comparable problems. These limitations on the capacity of the Court to enforce the Constitution do not map at all neatly onto the distinction between constitutional rights and remedies. It is this gap between judicial doctrine and a full realization of the values protected by the Constitution itself that presumably explains why the *Flores* Court is so welcoming of remedial efforts by Congress that go further than judicial doctrine. The same gap offers the Court a good reason to welcome reasonable efforts by Congress to help shape constitutional rights at the margins when the Court itself is unable to fully explore or clearly delineate those margins. Or, to put the point less provocatively, this gap offers the Court a good reason not to concern itself too closely with the largely unanswerable question of whether a sympathetic effort by Congress to help in the effort to fully realize the values protected by the Constitution is best characterized as enlarging upon the Court's structure of remedies or its understanding of the shape and scope of judicially enforceable rights.

We use the adjective "sympathetic" with a fairly precise meaning in mind. We mean to exclude from this claim for exceptional generosity toward congressional exercise of its Section 5 remedial authority the earlier cases we considered where Congress has acted

---

[39] Id at 2164.

in a way that puts constitutional rights in jeopardy, or where Congress has acted on a view of constitutional rights wholly foreign to the Court's best understanding. We also mean to exclude a third sort of case that comes to mind under the "plainly unsuited" rubric that we have most recently been exploring. The third sort of case involves congressional enactments that are essentially hostile to the Court's constitutional commitments, enactments which place the Court and Congress in conceptual conflict, even though they may not directly put constitutional rights in jeopardy. RFRA was precisely this third sort of enactment, and its demise at the hands of the *Flores* Court is entirely consistent with the generosity with which we urge the Court to approach cases of the second, sympathetic type. As we shall see, RFRA was indeed plainly unsuited to the realization of the what the *Flores* Court regarded as the state of affairs mandated by the Free Exercise Clause.

D. KATZENBACH REVISITED; FLORES RECONSIDERED

Before we defend this characterization of RFRA, we need to pause a moment and take stock. We have given firmer shape to the *Flores* Court's invocation of the rights/remedy distinction as the means of delineating Congress's Section 5 authority: Rights are best understood as emerging from constitutionally mandated states of affairs, and remedies as emerging from states of affairs that are not themselves constitutionally mandated but which are instrumentally supportive of those states that are. Where the constitutional judgment of Congress is in direct conflict with that of the Court, Congress will be unable to act on its judgment through the vehicle of Section 5 of the Fourteenth Amendment. This is most obviously true of legislation which—in the Court's eye—places constitutionally mandated states of affairs in jeopardy. It is also true of legislation that is wildly off-target in calling for states of affairs that bear no plausible relationship to constitutionally mandated states of affairs. And it is also true of legislation that is essentially hostile to the Court's constitutional understandings, even though such legislation may not necessarily place constitutionally mandated states of affairs in jeopardy. There remains, however, a category of legislation where Congress, broadly speaking, is acting in support of the Court's constitutional judgment, not in conflict. It will often be hard for the Court to know with any confidence whether legislation of this sort is better characterized as remedial or substantive; but the Court has good reason to welcome such legislation on either account, and no good reason to insist on distinguishing between these two possibilities.

The Court in *Flores* reviewed debates about Section 5 in the Reconstruction Congress,[40] but Justice Kennedy and the Court for whom he wrote seemed more moved by the consequences of a licentious reading of Section 5 for judicial authority and constitutional obduracy than by history. The Court worried that if Congress had "a substantive, non-remedial power under the Fourteenth Amendment," then "[s]hifting legislative majorities could change the Constitution and effectively circumvent the difficult and detailed amendment process contained in Article V."[41] Congress would be free to "define its own powers by altering the Fourteenth Amendment's meaning," and the Constitution would no longer be "superior paramount law, unchangeable by ordinary means."[42] Constitutional supremacy, the Court's authority to defend it, and limits on the authority of Congress would all be forfeit. The Court did itself a disservice by making such extreme and untenable assertions;[43] they provide convenient targets for unsympathetic critics. Rhetorical excesses aside, however, the Court's analysis of Section 5 legislation builds upon a sound insight: within our constitutional practice, the Supreme Court has the responsibility to act on its own judgment as to the content of the liberty-bearing provisions of the Constitution. As we shall see, Congress's misadventure with RFRA was an occasion which made that responsibility especially vivid and salutary.

Considerable commentary has been devoted to *Katzenbach* and its asymmetrical deference to congressional judgment. It may be helpful to place our reading of *Flores* alongside three other possible understandings of *Katzenbach*. One explanation that found great favor with the proponents of RFRA relies on the distinction between constitutional challenges based upon enumerated powers

---

[40] 117 S Ct at 2164–66.

[41] Id at 2167–68.

[42] Id (internal quotation marks omitted).

[43] There are a number of models which explain how Congress and the judiciary can share authority to interpret the Constitution without either endangering constitutional supremacy or losing the benefits of effective judicial review. Some of these theories are described in Laurence H. Tribe, *American Constitutional Law* 342–50 (2d ed 1988).

and those based upon the liberty-bearing provisions of the Constitution. The idea is this: when Congress is enlarging rights, typically the only objection sounds in enumerated powers, and the all but limitless deference traditionally granted Congress with regard to its enumerated powers should apply. When, in contrast, Congress is shrinking rights, the objection can be framed as a violation of a constitutional guarantee of liberty, with regard to which judicial deference is extremely limited.[44]

This view of *Katzenbach* is too facile: it suppresses the peculiar structure of Section 5, which makes the scope of Congress's authority depend on the liberty-bearing provisions of Section 1; and it likely overstates the deference that the contemporary Court is willing to pay to Congress in enumerated powers controversies. But all that is somewhat beside the point. Whatever else is true of this understanding of *Katzenbach*, it is not the view of the Court in *Flores*, and it is not the view we urge in our reconstruction of *Flores*. *Flores* emphatically does not give Congress the authority to act upon a view of constitutional substance that conflicts with the Court's own judgment in any of the ways that we have sketched; the powers/rights claim, in contrast, arguably does give Congress that authority.

A second explanation of *Katzenbach* turns on the increasingly popular idea that the Court sometimes quite legitimately "underenforces" important provisions—including liberty-bearing provisions—of the Constitution.[45] If this is true, then Congress should have the authority to fill in rights where the Court is forced to leave off on institutional grounds. This approach is fundamentally consistent with that taken by the *Flores* Court, since it agrees that the Court's own best judgment about the meaning of the Constitution should prevail in the event of a conflict with Congress's judgment as effectuated in Section 5 legislation. The underenforcement theory merely points out that some judicial outcomes are better attributed to the Court's institutional role than to its judgments of substance, and argues that the Court should especially

---

[44] This view is often associated with William Cohen, *Congressional Power to Interpret Due Process and Equal Protection*, 27 Stan L Rev 603 (1975).

[45] The theory was first articulated in Lawrence G. Sager, *Fair Measure: The Legal Status of Underenforced Constitutional Norms*, 91 Harv L Rev 1212 (1978). The theory is elaborated further in Lawrence G. Sager, *Justice in Plain Clothes: Reflections on the Thinness of Constitutional Law*, 88 Nw U L Rev 410 (1993).

welcome the collaboration of Congress in such cases. Underenforcement is one of the reasons for what we have described here as the gap between the best understanding of the substance of the Constitution and the Court's constitutional doctrine. The underenforcement understanding of *Katzenbach* is entirely consistent with (though not necessary to) our interpretation of *Flores*.

A third explanation of *Katzenbach* is one that we advanced in an earlier essay, where we argued that RFRA was unconstitutional on several grounds.[46] In that essay, we anticipated the Court's ruling in *Flores* and concluded that RFRA was outside the scope of Congress's Section 5 authority. We set forward a view of Section 5 that distinguished between Congress acting as the Court's partner, on the one hand, and as its adversary on the other.[47] Adversarial enactments, we argued, were outside the scope of Congress's Section 5 authority. We gestured toward the content of the idea of an adversarial enactment with a thought experiment: We imagined that a Justice of the Supreme Court who shared in the Court's prevailing view on the matter in question left the Court and found herself in Congress; if she could not support proposed legislation without changing her prior view of the appropriate judicial disposition of the matter, the legislation was adversarial.[48] This approach is largely consistent with our interpretation of *Flores*. Indeed, much that we have said here can be regarded as an attempt to flesh out our earlier argument. *Flores*, however, further refines the restrictions upon Congress in one respect: Under our earlier formulation, legislation—like our freedom of contract example—which secured rights wildly different from but not inconsistent with those that the Court would recognize might be thought to be in a third category; in such a case Congress is certainly not acting as the Court's partner, and it is unclear whether to regard it as the Court's adversary. But *Flores* not unreasonably places legislation of this sort outside of Congress's Section 5 authority.

Justice Kennedy's opinion on behalf of the Court in *Flores* may on first read seem Janus-faced. On the one hand, the opinion's emphasis on the distinction between remedial and rights-defining enactments by Congress was a self-conscious echo of Justice Har-

---

[46] Eisgruber and Sager, 69 NYU L Rev 437 (cited in note 4).

[47] Id at 462–64.

[48] Id at 462 & n 87.

lan—first in dissent in *Katzenbach* and then again in *Mitchell*; Harlan, like the *Flores* Court, believed that Congress's power under Section 5 had to be merely remedial if the Court were to preserve its own power to enforce constitutional limits against Congress.[49] Given Harlan's discomfort with the outcome in *Katzenbach*, the *Flores* Court's invalidation of RFRA, and that Court's silent neglect of theories or themes of the sort we have advanced here, one might think that the real point of the *Flores* opinion was to vindicate Harlan's *Katzenbach* dissent and sharply curtail the scope of congressional power.

But the *Flores* Court was at pains to endorse not just the outcome in *Katzenbach*, but those in *South Carolina v Katzenbach*,[50] *Fitzpatrick v Bitzer*,[51] and *City of Rome v United States*[52] as well.[53] True to its affirmation of this run of cases, the Court readily agreed that "Legislation which deters or remedies constitutional violations can fall within the sweep of Congress's enforcement power even if in the process it prohibits conduct which is not itself unconstitutional and intrudes into 'legislative spheres of autonomy previously reserved to the States.'"[54] Consistent with our emphasis here, the Court acknowledged that "the line between measures that remedy or prevent unconstitutional actions and measures that make a substantive change in the governing law is not easy to discern, and Congress must have wide latitude in determining where it lies. . . ."[55] Congress, in the eyes of the *Flores* Court, could direct its broad discretion not just to past violations of the Constitution but to future vulnerabilities as well.[56] And the *Flores* Court declined to insist that Congress generate an elaborate record in support of its constitutional impulses, noting that "[a]s a general matter, it is

---

[49] *Katzenbach*, 384 US at 668 (Harlan dissenting); *Mitchell*, 400 US at 204–05 & n 86 (Harlan opinion).

[50] 383 US 301 (1966).

[51] 427 US 445 (1976).

[52] 446 US 156 (1980).

[53] See 117 S Ct at 2170 (characterizing *South Carolina v Katzenbach* and *City of Rome v United States* as cases involving remedial legislation); see also id at 2163 (quoting, with approval, from *Fitzpatrick v Bitzer*). *South Carolina* and *Rome* are Fifteenth Amendment cases rather than Fourteenth Amendment cases; the *Flores* Court, like past courts, drew no important distinctions between the two lines of cases, and cited them interchangeably.

[54] Id at 2163 (quoting *Fitzpatrick*, 427 US at 455).

[55] Id at 2164.

[56] Id at 2169 ("preventive rules are sometimes appropriate remedial measures. . . .").

for Congress to decide the method by which it will reach a decision."[57] None of this reflects the crabbed view of congressional authority adopted by Justice Harlan or signals anything more than a modest clarification of extant doctrine. Where Justice Brennan in *Katzenbach* asked only that Section 5 legislation be "plainly adapted" to constitutional ends, and "consistent with the letter and spirit of the Constitution,"[58] Justice Kennedy in *Flores* called for "a congruence between the means used and the [constitutional] ends to be achieved."[59] On its face, hardly a revolution.

Understood in its best light, the rights/remedy distinction is not at all inconsistent with the spirit of sweeping deference to Congress with which the *Flores* opinion is laced. At the same time, as Justice Harlan's example reminds us, without firmer edges, a test which depends on that distinction can be put to many uses, including the advancement of views which are far less generous to congressional authority. It is a virtue of our interpretation of *Flores* that it provides such firmer edges and locates the *Flores* decision firmly within the deferential tradition to which the Court sees itself as heir.

Which leaves us, finally, with the result in *Flores*. RFRA, after all, was invalidated, and many readers of *Flores* will insist that the Court be understood to mean what it does, not what it says. It is at this point that the interpretation of *Flores* becomes heavily dependent on the Court's Free Exercise jurisprudence. On the conventional account of *Smith* and RFRA—the account repeated so often in the Committee reports accompanying RFRA—*Flores* appears to be grim news indeed for Congress. On that account, religious liberty means leaving religious believers unfettered by government regulations (including regulations every one else must obey); the Court, in *Smith*, decided that the compelling interest test provided more religious liberty than the Justices were willing to enforce in the name of the Constitution; and RFRA extended the Court's own, rather minimal, remedies for encroachments upon religious liberty. So, to RFRA's defenders, RFRA, like *Katzenbach*, occupied the hazy space in which rights and remedies are difficult to distinguish; like the Voting Rights Act, RFRA

---

[57] Id at 2170.

[58] 384 US at 651 (internal quotation marks omitted).

[59] 117 S Ct at 2169.

served a goal which the Court itself had recognized (in the case of the Voting Rights Act, political equality; in the case of RFRA, religious liberty), but supplemented the judicially enforceable Constitution with new rights that the Court had refused to endorse (in the case of the Voting Rights Act, a ban upon literacy tests; in the case of RFRA, a ban upon laws which burdened religious practice without compelling justification).

But this view of RFRA is not the Court's view, and it therefore misreads what *Flores* has to say about Section 5. Indeed, we do not know how many members of the *Flores* majority thought that RFRA disserved the Court's judgment in the rawest possible way, by violating the Establishment Clause; Justice Stevens said it did, and nobody contradicted him. We may assume, however, that some members of the *Flores* majority either rejected the Establishment Clause challenge to RFRA or were uncertain about its merits— otherwise, the Court should simply have decided the case on Establishment Clause grounds. What we do know is this: the *Flores* Court firmly endorsed the *Smith* Court's conclusion that application of the *Sherbert* test would have produced a "constitutional anomaly."[60] That is quite different, and far more severe, than saying that the compelling interest standard provided "too much" religious liberty. To call RFRA's test a "constitutional anomaly" suggests that it does not support religious liberty at all, and that even if it does not rise to the level of an Establishment Clause violation, it works at cross-purposes with the Court's understanding of religious liberty or other elements of constitutional justice. If we take the *Flores* Court's references to *Smith* and the substance of RFRA seriously, we can make full and attractive sense of all of Justice Kennedy's opinion for the Court: the generous rhetoric about deference to Congress, the approving references to *Katzenbach* and *Rome*, and the ultimate condemnation of RFRA. In the sections which follow we show not only that the *Flores* Court could reasonably hold this view of RFRA, but that it was entirely correct in so doing.

III. Sherbert's Troubled Legacy

In the judgment of the *Flores* Court, RFRA was outside the bounds of the generous deference owed Congress in the exercise

---

[60] *Smith*, 494 US at 886; see *Flores*, 117 S Ct at 2161 ("application of the *Sherbert* test would have produced an anomaly in the law").

of its Section 5 powers: "The stringent test RFRA demands of state law reflects a lack of proportionality or congruence between the means adopted and the legitimate end to be achieved."[61] For RFRA's defenders, this must be a bitter pill. In their view, after all, RFRA's "stringent test" sprung not from congressional imagination, but from the Court's own jurisprudence. RFRA's standard had for almost three decades been the Court's own—and, when the Court abandoned that test seven years ago, it did so by a slim one-vote margin. How could a test which the Supreme Court so recently *required* now fail to survive the deferential scrutiny which, according to Justice Kennedy's opinion for the *Flores* majority, was appropriate to congressional exercises of power under Section 5? But it is precisely this view of the confused strand of law that ran forward from the *Sherbert* decision which was rejected by the Court in *Smith;* and though the *Smith* opinion may have its flaws, its reappraisal of the meaning of *Sherbert* was long overdue.

Until 1963, the Supreme Court was consistently hostile to the possibility that religiously motivated persons were free to disobey otherwise valid laws. During this period, religious belief and expression were protected against some forms of governmental regulation, but only under circumstances where non-religious belief and expression would have enjoyed the same protection. But in 1963, the Supreme Court seemed to reverse itself in *Sherbert* and embrace the remarkable proposition that religiously motivated persons were exempt from otherwise valid laws unless the imposition of those laws was necessary to secure a compelling state interest.[62]

This would have been strong medicine indeed, but the Court abided by its prescription only on highly select occasions. Three other unemployment insurance cases followed *Sherbert;* in each, a non-mainstream religious believer who was generally available for work but barred by his religious scruples from taking a narrow range of jobs was held to be constitutionally entitled to receive unemployment insurance.[63] And in one case outside the unemploy-

---

[61] 117 S Ct at 2171.

[62] *Sherbert,* 374 US at 403.

[63] *Thomas v Review Board of the Indiana Employment Security Division,* 450 US 707 (1981); *Hobbie v Unemployment Appeals Commission of Florida,* 480 US 136 (1987); and *Frazee v Illinois Department of Employment Security,* 489 US 829 (1989).

The *Smith* Court maintained—and the *Flores* Court agreed—that *Sherbert* and the other three unemployment benefits cases stood for "the proposition that where the State has in

ment insurance context, the rhetoric of *Sherbert* seemed to prevail as well: in *Wisconsin v Yoder*,[64] the Court exempted some Amish parents from state laws requiring attendance at school through the age of sixteen. But outside the extraordinarily narrow precincts of the *Sherbert* quartet and *Yoder*, the Court consistently rejected religious motivation as an excuse for failures to comply with otherwise valid laws. In some cases, the Court created exceptions to *Sherbert*'s compelling interest test. In others, the Court nominally applied *Sherbert*'s test, but found the usually rigorous compelling state interest test rather easily satisfied in this context.

In many of the pre-*Smith* cases where the Supreme Court refused to find exemptions constitutionally required, the government's interests were diaphanous and its indifference to religious practice stark. In *Goldman v Weinberger*,[65] for example, the army had refused to permit an Orthodox Jew to wear a yarmulke with his uniform; the Court held that *Sherbert*'s "compelling state interest test" did not apply to military policies.[66] In *Lyng v Northwest Indian Cemetery Protective Association*,[67] the Forest Service had elected to build a road through an Indian burial ground that lay on federal property; although the road could have been located elsewhere, the Supreme Court declined to intervene, holding that the *Sherbert* test did not apply to government's decisions about how to use its own property.[68] In *United States v Lee*,[69] the Supreme Court reversed a Circuit Court decision exempting Amish workplaces from the Social Security program; the Court found that the integrity of the tax system amounted to a compelling state interest,[70] a judgment which seems incontestable in the abstract but was highly arguable on the facts of *Lee*, where, as Justice Stevens

---

place a system of individual exemptions, it may not refuse to extend that system to cases of religious hardship without compelling reason." *Smith*, 494 US at 884 (internal quotation marks omitted), quoted in *Flores*, 117 S Ct at 2161. We agree; see Eisgruber and Sager, 69 NYU L Rev at 450 n 49 (cited in note 4), and Eisgruber and Sager, 61 U Chi L Rev at 1287–89 (cited in note 4).

[64] 406 US 205.

[65] 475 US 503 (1986).

[66] Id at 506–07.

[67] 485 US 439 (1988).

[68] Id at 448–49.

[69] 455 US 252 (1982).

[70] Id at 258–60.

pointed out, the exemption demanded by the Amish might actually have *benefited* the national treasury.[71]

The marked collapsibility of the *Sherbert* "rule" in the Supreme Court was the norm in other courts as well.[72] The pattern was simple and constant: Free Exercise claimants seeking exemptions from generally applicable laws virtually never prevailed. In other constitutional contexts, the compelling state interest test was "strict in theory and fatal in fact";[73] in Free Exercise jurisprudence, it was strict in theory and notably feeble in fact.[74]

Whatever other lessons one might draw from the *Sherbert* doctrine's crooked path through American case law, this much is clear: RFRA's compelling state interest test could not be defended as a proven vehicle for vindicating Free Exercise Clause concerns. Its track record was neither extensive nor impressive. Ironically, if RFRA's compelling state interest test were to have any chance of consistent application, it had to be detached from the line of precedents that inspired it. As a result, one of the major questions that confronted courts as they began interpreting RFRA was whether the Religious Freedom Restoration Act in fact "restored" the vapid jurisprudence that existed prior to *Smith*, or whether it did something quite different.[75] RFRA's language itself seemed almost de-

---

[71] Id at 262 (Stevens concurring).

[72] See generally James E. Ryan, *Smith and the Religious Freedom Restoration Act: An Iconoclastic Assessment*, 78 Va L Rev 1407 (1992) (describing the poor track record of Free Exercise claims in the federal courts of appeals); see also *EEOC v Townley Engineering & Mfg Co.*, 859 F2d 610, 625–29 (9th Cir 1988) (Noonan dissenting) (surveying Free Exercise decisions by the federal courts).

[73] Gerald Gunther, *The Supreme Court, 1971 Term—Foreward: In Search of Evolving Doctrine on a Changing Court: A Model for a Newer Equal Protection*, 86 Harv L Rev 1, 8 (1972).

[74] Eisgruber and Sager, 61 U Chi L Rev at 1247 (cited in note 4).

[75] Many of RFRA's proponents hoped that the statute would generate a jurisprudence more vigorous than had existed before *Smith*. See, e.g., Thomas C. Berg, *What Hath Congress Wrought? An Interpretive Guide to the Religious Freedom Restoration Act*, 39 Vill L Rev 1, 26 (1994) ("RFRA does . . . more than wipe *Smith* itself off the books"); Michael Stokes Paulsen, *A RFRA Runs Through It: Religious Freedom and the U.S. Code*, 56 Mont L Rev 249, 256 (1995) ("RFRA does *not* 'codify' the late pre-*Smith* approach and is, in legal effect, far more than a mere restoration of pre-*Smith* case law").

Most RFRA courts, however, believed themselves bound by pre-*Smith* precedent. Several judges cited to the Senate Report on RFRA, which provided that "the compelling interest test generally should not be construed more stringently or more leniently than it was prior to *Smith*." S Rep No 103-111, 103d Cong, 1st Sess 9 (1993). *Smith v Fair Employment and Housing Commission*, 12 Cal 4th 1143, 1166, 913 P2d 909, 922 (Cal 1996); *American Life League, Inc. v Reno* 47 F3d 642, 655, n 6 (4th Cir 1995). But see *Smith v Fair Employment and Housing Commission*, 12 Cal 4th at 1231–32, 913 P2d at 966 (Baxter concurring and dissenting) (arguing that pre-*Smith* law was relevant only insofar as it was faithful to the spirit of *Sherbert* and *Yoder*). On the other hand, the *Flores* Court itself maintained that

liberately ambiguous. On the one hand, the Congress announced its intention to "restore the compelling interest test as set forth in *Sherbert* . . . and . . . *Yoder*";[76] on the other hand, Congress waffled on the other, more deferential, cases that had sapped the *Sherbert* test of its force and importance. Early on, the bill proposing RFRA referred only to *Sherbert* and *Yoder*, and did so twice over; a later amendment, however, substituted a reference in one instance to "prior Federal court rulings"—including, presumably, cases like *Lyng* and *Goldman* where the Supreme Court found creative ways to let the government off the hook.[77]

Whatever Congress intended, RFRA probably would have introduced a very different regime than the one it nominally "restored." The statute generated a tide of Free Exercise litigation in the federal courts. Landlords sought exemption from statutes prohibiting them from discriminating against unmarried couples.[78] Churches claimed that they were exempt from bankruptcy laws requiring charities to return gifts from the estates of bankrupt debtors.[79] Prisoners (who had been excluded from the scope of the *Sherbert* test by one of the Supreme Court's many decisions limiting the scope of that precedent) filed a raft of claims under RFRA, some

---

RFRA imposed "a least restrictive means requirement . . . that was not used in the pre-*Smith* jurisprudence RFRA purported to codify." 117 S Ct at 2171.

[76] 42 USC § 2000bb(b)(1).

[77] Compare 42 USC § 2000bb(a)(5) (1994) (referencing "prior Federal court rulings") with HR 2797, 102d Cong, 1st Sess § 2(a)(5) (June 26, 1991) (referencing *Sherbert* and *Yoder*) and S 2969, 102d Cong, 2d Sess § 2(a)(5) (July 2, 1992) (same). For further discussion, see Eisgruber and Sager, 69 NYU L Rev at 451 (cited in note 4).

[78] See, e.g., *Smith v Fair Employment and Housing Commission*, 12 Cal 4th 1143, 913 P2d 909 (Cal 1996). In *Smith*, a religiously motivated landlord sought an exemption from laws prohibiting housing discrimination against unmarried couples; the California Supreme Court, by a 4–3 vote, rejected the exemption claim. A three-judge plurality found no "substantial burden" on the landlord's exercise of religion, 12 Cal 4th at 1175–76, 913 P2d at 928–29. One judge found RFRA unconstitutional, 12 Cal 4th at 1179, 913 P2d at 931 (Mosk concurring). An intermediate appellate court had granted the claim. See also *Swanner v Anchorage Equal Rights Com'n*, 874 P2d 274, 279–80 (Alaska 1994), cert denied 115 S Ct 460 (denying a similar claim by a landlord on the ground that the state had a compelling interest in prohibiting discrimination). But see *Attorney General v Desilets*, 418 Mass 316, 330–32, 636 NE2d 233, 241 (Mass 1994) (requiring that the state either provide factual evidence of a compelling interest, or else excuse religiously motivated landlords from the obligation to rent to unmarried couples).

[79] See, e.g., *In re Young*, 82 F3d 1407 (8th Cir 1996) (granting exemption); *In Re Tessier*, 190 Bankr 396 (Bankr D Mont 1995) (interpreting RFRA to grant exemption, but holding RFRA unconstitutional); *In re Newman*, 183 Bankr 239 (Bankr D Kan 1995) (refusing, on statutory grounds, to grant the exemption).

sincere and others laughable.[80] Churches demanded exemptions from all variety of local zoning ordinances. Two recurring fact patterns involved churches that wished to open soup kitchens or homeless shelters in residential neighborhoods and churches that sought to escape the restrictions imposed by historic preservation ordinances.[81] A substantial number of these claims in fact prevailed under RFRA.[82]

Of course, *Sherbert* is not the only precedent to suffer from inconsistent and unprincipled application. And the rule of RFRA

---

[80] Prisoner complaints posed especially tricky questions about the relationship between pre-*Smith* and post-RFRA jurisprudence. On the one hand, RFRA's proponents had successfully rebuffed efforts to codify the rule of *O'Lone v Estate of Shabazz*, 482 US 342, 349 (1987), which had exempted prisons from the scope of *Sherbert*'s compelling interest standard. On the other hand, one might reconstruct *O'Lone* as an application of *Sherbert*'s stunningly flexible "compelling interest" standard: *O'Lone* might stand for the proposition that the state's interest in maintaining order in prison was, in all circumstances, "compelling." Confronted with the prospect of sorting through imaginative and numerous claims from prisoners, most courts were hestitant to abandon *O'Lone*'s deferential standard. Thus, for example, the Eighth Circuit purported to reconcile "heightened scrutiny" with "deference to prison officials": "both pre-*O'Lone* Supreme Court case law and the relevant legislative history indicate that a court applying RFRA must give due deference to the expertise of prison officials in establishing regulations to maintain prison safety and security, even when the court applies a "heightened standard of review." *Hamilton v Schriro*, 74 F3d 1545, 1554 (1996). The Congressional debate about *O'Lone* is summarized in Douglas Laycock and Oliver S. Thomas, *Interpreting the Religious Freedom Restoration Act*, 73 Tex L Rev 209, 239–43 (1994).

[81] Soup kitchen cases included *Stuart Circle Parish v Zoning Appeals*, 946 F Supp 1225 (ED Va 1996) (granting a temporary restraining order to prevent Richmond from enforcing its zoning ordinances against church-run feeding program); *Western Presbyterian Church v Board of Zoning Adjustment*, 862 F Supp 538, 546 (D DC 1994) (exempting church-run soup kitchen from Washington, DC, zoning ordinance); *Daytona Rescue Mission, Inc v City of Daytona Beach*, 885 F Supp 1554, 1560 (MD Fla 1995) (refusing to exempt church-run feeding program from Daytona zoning ordinance). The *Daytona Rescue Mission* court, unlike the other two courts, held that the zoning ordinances imposed no "substantial burden" on religious practice because churches could relocate their feeding programs to appropriately zoned neighborhoods. 885 F Supp at 1560.

Flores itself was, of course, among the historic preservation cases litigated under RFRA. In two other cases—*First United Methodist v Hearing Examiner*, 129 Wash 2d 238; 916 P2d 374 (Wash 1996), and *Keeler v Mayor & City Council of Cumberland*, 940 F Supp 879 (D Md 1996)—courts relied on post-*Smith* Free Exercise Clause doctrine, rather than RFRA, to grant churches relief from historic preservation statutes. The *Keeler* court had found RFRA unconstitutional in an earlier ruling in the same case. *Keeler v Mayor & City Council of Cumberland*, 928 F Supp 591 (D Md 1996).

[82] RFRA's impact appeared especially great in prison cases and zoning cases; see, e.g., cases cited in the two notes preceding this one. RFRA claims were, however, succeeding in other settings as well; see, e.g., *In re Young*, 82 F3d 1407 (bankruptcy case discussed in note 81 and accompanying text); *Cheema v Thompson*, 67 F3d 883, 886 (9th Cir 1995) (upholding injunction which permitted young Sikh children to wear ceremonial knives when attending school).

could be a good rule, even if the regime it purported to restore had never existed. But the *Smith* Court did not merely bring the news about *Sherbert*. It went considerably further, and made clear its judgment that application of the compelling state interest test to a case like *Smith* was both normatively unattractive and unworkable in practice. A rule that conditioned legal obligation "upon the law's coincidence with [one's] religious beliefs" would allow each individual "by virtue of his beliefs, 'to become a law unto himself,'" and would thereby "contradic[t] both constitutional tradition and common sense."[83] Any society that endorsed such a rule would be "courting anarchy," and that is especially so in a religiously diverse society like the United States.[84] According to the *Smith* Court, it would be "horrible to contemplate that federal judges will regularly balance against the importance of general laws the significance of religious practice"; judges have no standard by which to make the relevant judgments.[85] For the *Smith* Court, the application of *Sherbert* to facts of *Smith* would have produced a "constitutional anomaly."[86] This was a judgment shared by the *Flores* Court.[87] It is a judgment with which we agree.

IV. Exemptions and Subsidies

The *Smith* and *Flores* Courts are best understood as emphasizing a deep point about the *conceptual structure* of religious liberty, not simply a view about *how much* religious liberty is desirable or how it competes with other constitutional and political values. The point is this: the only sound conception of religious liberty is founded upon protecting religious exercise against persecution, discrimination, insensitivity, or hostility. There is no coherent normative basis for insisting that religious commitments receive better treatment than other, comparably serious commitments—and, as a result, it will be impossible to identify any principled stopping

---

[83] *Smith*, 494 US at 885.

[84] Id at 888.

[85] Id at 889 n 5.

[86] Id at 886.

[87] 117 S Ct at 2161 (reiterating *Smith*'s analysis).

point for the Free Exercise claims.[88] Indeed, if the Free Exercise Clause were understood as ensuring that religious commitments and practices flourish unimpaired by government policy, then Free Exercise rights will inevitably collide with equality principles—within and without the domain of religious liberty—essential to our notion of constitutional government. The result might not be literal "anarchy," but it would certainly be a "constitutional anomaly," and arguably a serious affront to the rule of law.

The facts of *Flores* provide a convenient avenue into the Court's concerns. At bottom, *Flores* is a case about money and convenience. If Boerne does not make an exception to its historic preservation ordinance, St. Peter's Catholic Church will either have to sell its building and buy or build a larger structure to house its swelling congregation, or split its congregation in two and buy or build a smaller church for the newly created congregation. These options may be quite expensive or inconvenient to the church, and perhaps to its parishioners as well, who may have additional travel burdens. On the other hand, the church is not claiming that St. Peter's rests on uniquely sacred ground or that it operates under a divine command not to relocate elsewhere. Indeed, under other quite plausible conditions—if, for example, St. Peter's occupied a lot too small to permit construction of a larger building—it is clear that the church would have moved or divided.

So, if either RFRA or the Free Exercise Clause were to exempt St. Peter's from the burdens imposed by Boerne's zoning scheme, it would have to do so on the ground that churches should be presumed exempt from financially burdensome—and possibly inconvenient—regulations. The logical scope of this claim is breathtaking. Suppose a church owns wetlands property. It could make a great deal of money by building homes on the property and renting them. Should it be exempt from environmental statutes prohibiting development? Suppose a church owns property in a residential neighborhood. It could make money by opening a restaurant in the neighborhood. Should it be exempt from statutes prohibiting a commercial use? A church could make more money

---

[88] We explored this point at length in Eisgruber and Sager, 61 U Chi L Rev 1245 (cited in note 4); the arguments that follow offer another path to the conclusions we proposed in our earlier argument.

if it were also exempt from the minimum wage law. Is it entitled to the exemption? Or, more sympathetically, but not conceptually at odds, suppose a church wanted to open a soup kitchen to feed the poor; is it constitutionally entitled to locate the kitchen anywhere it wants?[89] And if so, can a church that must slaughter animals locate its slaughterhouse anywhere it wants?

Elsewhere we have argued at length that there is no constitutional justification for favoring persons whose conduct is motivated by religious conviction, and further, that there is no attractive normative justification of any kind for so doing.[90] The Constitution singles out religious liberty for special attention, but that attention centers on the ideal of equal regard, pursuant to which the deep concerns of religious believers are protected against hostility, indifference, or a failure of comprehension, and assured equal stature with the deep concerns of other citizens.[91] The Constitution emphatically does not privilege religious concerns. In our view, the bald favoritism to religion contemplated in examples like those in the prior paragraph would be a patent breach of equal regard, and would undermine rather than fulfill the constitutional ideal of religious liberty.

But here we wish to highlight a point that we have not emphasized in the past: *Flores* and the examples of fiscal favoritism it inspires expose the incongruity of calling for exemptions on the one hand while renouncing subsidies on the other. Virtually everybody agrees that the Constitution prohibits the government from singling out churches for special subsidies. That portion of Establishment Clause jurisprudence is uncontroversial. Some commentators (and we are among them) believe that, at least until recently, the Supreme Court has been too reluctant to permit the government to include religious institutions, including religious schools, among the beneficiaries of neutrally defined, nonsectarian subsidies.[92] But almost nobody believes that government may choose to subsidize religious institutions exclusively. We do not see any way

---

[89] See cases cited in note 81.

[90] Eisgruber and Sager, 61 U Chi L Rev at 1254–82 (cited in note 4).

[91] Id at 1250–54, 1282–84.

[92] Eisgruber and Sager, 74 Tex L Rev at 586, 602, and 607–08 (cited in note 4); Christopher L. Eisgruber, *The Constitutional Value of Assimilation*, 96 Colum L Rev 87, 96–98 (1996).

to reconcile this uncontroversial axiom with the claim that churches should enjoy exemption from financially burdensome regulations.

We realize, of course, that government frequently must permit activities which it has no obligation to facilitate, much less fund. But that common feature of constitutional jurisprudence is different from the one at stake here. The government is not free to choose whether to subsidize religious activity specially; it is constitutionally prohibited from doing so. There is no sound reason to distinguish subsidies from exemptions that alleviate purely financial burdens (and thereby provide a financial benefit). If it is impermissible to prefer religion in one setting, it cannot be mandatory to prefer it in the other. That is the sense in which *Smith* and *Flores* depend upon a point about the *conceptual structure* of religious liberty, rather than about the *amount* of religious liberty that is desirable. It is not possible to privilege religious believers by exempting them, and them alone, from generally applicable laws without thereby running afoul of equality principles reflected in, among other things, the most basic axioms of Establishment Clause jurisprudence.

It would be a mistake to think that the patent fiscal favoritism of the RFRA claim in *Flores* is untypical. In many respects, *Flores* is a classic RFRA case. Zoning cases were a boom industry during RFRA's brief career on the federal statute books; indeed, aside from prisoner's rights cases, they were probably the largest source of RFRA claims.[93] Justice O'Connor put special emphasis on zoning cases in her *Flores* dissent,[94] as did Congress in the committee reports accompanying the passage of RFRA.[95]

In most, though certainly not all, zoning cases, the burdens upon religious exercise reduce to considerations of cost and convenience. *Smith*'s critics have generally made no effort to distinguish be-

---

[93] See, e.g., cases cited in note 81.

[94] 117 S Ct at 2177 (O'Connor dissenting) (citing zoning disputes as evidence of the need for RFRA).

[95] Id at 2169 (citing to House and Senate hearings). See also Simon J. Santiago, *Comment—Zoning and Religion: Will the Religious Freedom Restoration Act of 1993 Shift the Line Toward Religious Liberty*, 45 Am U L Rev 200, 201–02 (1995) (collecting evidence to show that zoning disputes involving churches were "often cited to muster congressional support for RFRA"); Berg, 39 Vill L Rev at 55 & nn 243–44 (arguing that RFRA's supporters were specially concerned with the impact of zoning restrictions upon churches) (cited in note 75).

tween cases in which the burden imposed was ultimately financial, and other cases in which the burden contained some irreducibly nonfinancial component. On the contrary, both Justice O'Connor and Congress singled out the St. Bartholomew's litigation in New York as an example of the problems which *Sherbert*'s compelling interest test might address.[96] As Justice O'Connor accurately reported in her *Flores* dissent, St. Bartholomew's demanded a constitutional exemption from New York City's landmarking ordinance because that law "'drastically restricted the Church's ability to raise revenue to carry out its various charitable and ministerial programs.'"[97] To be exact, St. Bart's wanted to raze its vestry and put up a high-rise office building in midtown Manhattan, which it could then lease at considerable financial benefit. Would it be any different if St. Bart's wanted to generate money by building a residential development on protected wetlands, or by operating a restaurant in a residential neighborhood?

For all of this, it would have been possible, in principle, to exclude mere financial burdens or inconveniences from the reach of RFRA, either by statutory provision or by judicial interpretation of RFRA's "substantial burden" trigger.[98] But remaking RFRA in some such way would merely shift the line between the statutory requirement of exemptions that strongly favor religion, on the one

---

[96] *Rector of St. Bartholomew's Church v City of New York*, 914 F2d 348 (2d Cir 1990). Justice O'Connor cites the case as evidence of the need for RFRA in her *Flores* dissent, 117 S Ct at 2177. The House Report on RFRA does likewise, HR Rep No 103-88, 103d Cong, 1st Sess 6 n 14 (1993).

[97] 117 S Ct at 2177 (O'Connor dissenting), quoting *St. Bart's*, 914 F2d at 355.

[98] See, e.g., *Goodall v Stafford County School Board*, 60 F3d 168, 171 (4th Cir 1995) ("[T]here is no substantial burden placed on an individual's free exercise of religion where a law or policy merely 'operates so as to make the practice of [the individual's] religious beliefs more expensive.'" (quoting *Braunfeld v Braun*, 366 US 599, 605 (1961) (plurality opinion)). In *Daytona Rescue Mission, Inc*, 885 F Supp at 1560, the court used reasoning of this kind to conclude that Daytona's zoning ordinance imposed no substantial burden on a church seeking to run a feeding program in a residential neighborhood; the church was free to open the program in another, more suitable neighborhood, even though doing so might be expensive or inconvenient for the church.

On the other hand, the Washington State Supreme Court has been especially frank about the fact that zoning cases often reduce to money, but that insight has not stopped the court from granting special exemptions for churches. *First Covenant Church v Seattle*, 120 Wash 2d 203, 220, 840 P2d 174, 184 (Wash 1992) ("Designation of First Covenant's church so grossly diminishes the value of the Church's principal asset that it impermissibly burdens First Covenant's right to free exercise of religion"); *First United Methodist*, 129 Wash 2d at 251, 916 P2d at 381 ("If United Methodist decides to sell its property in order to respond to the needs of its congregation, it has a right to do so without landmark restrictions creating administrative or financial burdens").

side, and a constitutional prohibition of subsidies precisely because they favor religion on the other side. There would still be such a line, and the result would still be genuinely anomalous. In, the end, it does not matter whether financial burden cases like *Flores* fall on the mandated exemption or prohibited subsidy side of the line: RFRA's proponents still have to explain to us all how it is that a strong favoritism and a strong antifavoritism principle can live side by side in a coherent regime of constitutional liberty.

V. The Constitutional Anomaly of Religious Privilege

It bears emphasis that the inescapable conceptual tension between subsidies and exemptions is not the ultimate reason for rejecting the compelling state interest test as the metric of Free Exercise. The tension is merely an illustration or a symptom of an important proposition at the heart of religious liberty: there is no good constitutional or other normative justification for conferring a sweeping privilege on religiously motivated conduct. Defenders of the compelling interest test have resisted this lesson in three ways. They have said that the distinction between exemptions and subsidies is simply written into the constitutional text or the history of its framing, so that history supplies the needed distinctions. Or they have said that government's basic obligation in the sphere of religious liberty is to leave religion alone. Or they have said that exemptions are in fact a kind of rough *quid pro quo* for special disadvantages the constitutional system imposes on religious believers. None of these arguments succeeds, and their failure lends strong support to the judgment of the *Smith* Court.

Begin with the brute argument from text and history. Commentators upon the Supreme Court's religious liberty jurisprudence have from time to time maintained that the Free Exercise and Establishment Clauses of the First Amendment are in tension with one another, or even that they conflict.[99] Some defenders of RFRA

---

[99] The Court once described itself as seeking "a neutral course between the two Religion Clauses, both of which are cast in absolute terms, and either of which, if expanded to a logical extreme, would tend to clash with the other." *Walz v Tax Commission*, 397 US 664, 668–69 (1970). See also, e.g., Jesse H. Choper, *The Religion Clauses of the First Amendment: Reconciling the Conflict*, 41 U Pitt L Rev 673, 673–74 (1980) (describing an "ineluctable tension" and "seemingly irreconcilable conflict" between the clauses); Suzanna Sherry, *Lee v Weisman: Paradox Redux*, 1992 Supreme Court Review 123, 148–49 (concluding that "what is needed is a *persuasive* justification for preferring one clause to the other" rather than further "attempts to reconcile the irreconcilable").

accordingly maintain that the odd conjunction of norms we are now examining—one norm demanding that government privilege religion with special exemptions, and another prohibiting government from aiding religion with special subsidies—is the result of the text's schizophrenia: the Free Exercise Clause, they say, by its terms, commands government to favor religion, but the Establishment Clause, by its terms, prohibits the government from doing so.[100] Certainly this result is not impossible; the best reading of the Constitution might involve the identification of two inconsistent principles within a single sentence. But this would be a surprising outcome, in any event, and especially in light of the modern history of the Establishment Clause. Until 1947, the Establishment Clause was often read more or less woodenly, as prohibiting the establishment of a government church; it was also utterly neglected, as the impulse to accomplish such a blatantly unconstitutional end had long been lost to history. The Supreme Court's decision in *Everson v Board of Education*[101] changed all that; it enlarged and revived the Establishment Clause as—in its essence— a general provision barring the state from favoring or supporting religious practice in a fashion inconsistent with the Constitution's commitment to religious liberty. That the Supreme Court should go out of its way in the fashion of *Everson* only to introduce a constitutional premise at stark odds with its extant commitment to religious liberty seems improbable in the extreme—certainly not a result to be arrived at lightly.

The Free Exercise Clause provides, "Congress shall make no law . . . prohibiting the Free Exercise [of religion]." So the obvious question: which laws prohibit the free exercise of religion? Put another way: what must religion be free from in order to be freely exercised? Consider the following interpretations: (1) "The exercise of religion is free so long as it is free from deliberate political persecution; hence, a law prohibits the free exercise of religion if

---

[100] This seems, for example, to be part of Justice O'Connor's view. In her *Smith* concurrence, she maintained that "the language of the [Free Exercise] Clause itself makes clear [that] an individual's free exercise of religion is a preferred constitutional activity." 494 US at 901–02. Professor Choper appears to hold a similar combination of views. He supports RFRA, but also espouses a complete ban on government subsidies for religion. Compare Jesse H. Choper, *Securing Religious Liberty: Principles for Judicial Interpretation of the Religion Clauses* 55–58 (1995) (criticizing *Smith* and praising RFRA) with id at 121–23 (arguing that government money may never be used for religious purposes).

[101] 330 US 1 (1947).

and only if it specifically singles out religious practice for unfavorable treatment"; (2) "The exercise of religion is free so long as it is free from burdens greater than those government places upon other, comparable activities; hence, a law prohibits the free exercise of religion if and only if it treats religion badly by comparison to other activities"; (3) "The exercise of religion is free only if it is free from all burdens except those justified by a state interest of the highest order; hence a law prohibits the free exercise of religion if and only if religious practices are exempt from most laws of general application"; (4) "The exercise of religion is free only if it is free from any cost at all; hence, a law prohibits the free exercise of religion if it imposes any costs upon religious practice (and, perhaps, if it impedes religion from defraying its costs)."

The first of these interpretations corresponds to the most narrow reading of the Supreme Court's doctrine in *Smith*, the second reflects our own position, the third is embodied in RFRA and the *Sherbert-Yoder* standard, and the fourth expresses a more absolute privilege for religion. Whatever might be said about the merits of these positions, one cannot choose among them by staring at the words of the Free Exercise Clause. It is a legitimate question what religion must be free from in order to be freely exercised—nobody believes that it must be free from every hindrance, as the fourth interpretation would suggest—and one cannot answer that question by repeating the words "free exercise" or "no law."

Sometimes, defenders of the *Sherbert* test supplement the words of the Free Exercise Clause with other textual arguments based on the structure of the First Amendment as a whole. For example, in her *Smith* concurrence, Justice O'Connor argued that *Sherbert's* compelling interest test, far from being a constitutional anomaly, would merely assimilate the Free Exercise Clause to the Free Speech Clause, to which, she said, the Court has regularly applied the compelling state interest test.[102] In fact, as Justice Scalia pointed out in *Smith*, this comparison between Free Exercise jurisprudence and traditional patterns of constitutional adjudication "supports, rather than undermines," the *Smith* decision.[103] When faced with laws that selectively burden religiously motivated conduct, the Supreme Court continues to apply the compelling inter-

---

[102] 494 US at 901–02 (O'Connor concurring in the judgment).

[103] Id at 886 n 3.

est test, just as it does under the Free Speech Clause with respect to laws that regulate activities on the basis of their communicative content.[104] Laws of this kind were not at issue in *Smith* or *Flores;* instead, the Court's decisions in those cases involved laws of general application which had an incidental impact upon religious activity.

In contrast, the Court does not apply the compelling interest test to laws which impact on speech in the same way that general, neutrally applied laws impact upon religiously motivated conduct. When a viewpoint-neutral rule imposes only incidental burdens upon communicative activity, the Court applies the much more deferential test derived from *United States v O'Brien*.[105] Two observations about the *O'Brien* test are in order. First, although the *O'Brien* test talks tough, it, like *Sherbert* itself, has proven tame in practice—as the *O'Brien* decision itself nicely illustrates.[106] Second, in the few instances when the Court has stricken rules under the *O'Brien* test, there is good reason to suppose that it has used the test to get at laws which, despite legislative protestations to the contrary, were in fact enacted in order to suppress unwanted communicative activity[107]—and, indeed, the law in *O'Brien* itself was almost certainly of that kind.[108]

In light of the Free Exercise Clause's patent ambiguity, some

---

[104] *Church of the Lukumi Babalu Aye v City of Hialeah*, 508 US 520 (1993) (holding unconstitutional a law prohibiting the ritual slaughter of animals).

[105] 391 US 367 (1968). The *O'Brien* test provides that a government policy having an incidental impact upon free speech will survive constitutional challenge only if it meets four conditions: it must be "within the constitutional power of the Government," it must "further[ ] an important or substantial governmental interest," the governmental interest must be "unrelated to the suppression of free expression," and "the incidental restriction on alleged First Amendment freedoms" must be "no greater than is essential to the furtherance of that interest." Id at 377.

[106] *O'Brien* dealt with a federal statute that made it a crime to burn a draft card. The Court upheld the conviction of a young man who had burned his card to protest the draft; the Court reasoned that the law was appropriately tailored to advance the government's "important or substantial" interest in preventing the destruction of draft cards. Id. For discussion, see Tribe, *American Constitutional Law* 983–84 (cited in note 43).

[107] For example, although the Court cited *O'Brien* in the course of an opinion that immunized an NAACP consumer boycott against criminal prosecution in *NAACP v Claiborne Hardware*, 458 US 886, 912 n 47 (1982), one might equally well treat a law that prohibits boycotts as one directed at communicative activity.

[108] In his analysis of *O'Brien*, Professor Tribe observes, "the publicly visible evidence quite clearly shows that [the law against burning draft cards] would not have been enacted but for the purpose of suppressing dissent . . . ." Tribe, *American Constitutional Law* at 825 (cited in note 43).

critics of *Smith* have turned to the Clause's history to explain their support for the compelling interest standard. In *Flores*, Justice O'Connor tried this strategy.[109] Justice Scalia answered O'Connor's historical argument at great length.[110] We think it sufficient to repeat—with minor qualifications—two of Scalia's most telling observations. First, "the most prominent scholarly critic of *Smith*, . . . after an extensive review of the historical record, was willing to venture no more than that 'constitutionally compelled exemptions [from generally applicable laws regulating conduct] were *within the contemplation* of the framers and ratifiers as a *possible interpretation* of the Free Exercise Clause.' "[111] Professor McConnell might be unhappy with this characterization of his view; he might think himself "willing to venture" a bit more than Scalia admits. McConnell treats Jefferson and Madison as the two crucial figures behind the Free Exercise Clause; according to McConnell, Jefferson was disdainful toward religion,[112] while Madison's attitude toward religious belief was "more affirmative."[113] According to McConnell, "Madison, with his more generous vision of religious liberty, more faithfully reflected the popular understanding of the free exercise provision that was to emerge both in state constitutions and the Bill of Rights."[114] McConnell's research is controversial,[115] but, as we have observed before,[116] one may concede McConnell's claim about Madison and Jefferson without thereby deciding the original meaning of the Free Exercise Clause. As McConnell describes it, Jefferson's "disdain" for religion is, by the standards of contemporary constitutional argument, an extreme position: it leaves ample room for a variety of "more generous" and "more affirmative" positions, some of them quite consistent

---

[109] 117 S Ct at 2178–85 (O'Connor dissenting).

[110] Id at 2172–76 (concurring in part).

[111] Id at 2172–73, quoting Michael McConnell, *The Origins and Historical Understanding of the Free Exercise of Religion*, 103 Harv L Rev 1409, 1415 (1990) (emphasis added by Justice Scalia).

[112] 103 Harv L Rev at 1452–53. He says Jefferson expressed "disdain . . . for the more intense manifestations of the religious spirit." Id at 1452.

[113] Id at 1453.

[114] Id at 1455.

[115] See, e.g., Philip A. Hamburger, *A Constitutional Right of Religious Exemption: An Historical Perspective*, 60 Geo Wash L Rev 915 (1992) (arguing that historical evidence supports *Smith*'s interpretation of the Free Exercise Clause).

[116] Eisgruber and Sager, 61 U Chi L Rev at 1272–73 (cited in note 4).

with the Court's decision in *Smith*. One might, for example, believe (as we do) that religious practices enjoy a dignity equal to other deep human convictions (such as the love parents feel for their children), and that the Constitution protects religious believers against the selective hostility or "disdain" which the government might otherwise show for some religious practices.

Scalia's basic point thus holds regardless of whether his description of McConnell's position is too blunt: nothing in McConnell's argument provides any ground for choosing among the competing interpretations of the Free Exercise Clause at issue in *Smith*. Scalia went on to make a second important observation about the historical record. He said that if indeed the original understanding of the Free Exercise Clause had required states to exempt religious practices from laws of general application, "it would be surprising not to find a single state or federal case refusing to enforce a generally applicable statute because of its failure to make accommodation. Yet the dissent cites none—and to my knowledge, and to the knowledge of the academic defenders of the dissent's position . . . none exists."[117] Again, O'Connor's "academic defenders" might quibble with Scalia's characterization of their view. But, again, Scalia's general point is correct regardless of whether one thinks him too bold with regard to the details. Even if *Smith*'s critics can identify *some* precedent to support their position,[118] they cannot point to an impressive string of legal precedent—on the contrary, they must contend, at a minimum, with the Supreme Court's hostility to exemptions for religiously motivated conduct in *Reynolds v United States*,[119] and with the absence of any Supreme Court squarely in favor of such exemptions before *Sherbert* in 1963.

The first strategy—the strategy dependent upon text and history—for explaining the relationship between the *Sherbert* doctrine and the Court's Establishment Clause doctrine thus fails. So the leading academic defenders of the *Sherbert* doctrine have tried a

---

[117] *Flores*, 117 S Ct at 2175 (Scalia concurring in part).

[118] Scalia himself mentions *People v Philips*, Court of General Sessions, City of New York (June 14, 1813), excerpted in *Privileged Communications to Clergymen*, 1 Cath Law 199 (1955), cited in *Flores*, 117 S Ct at 2175. *Philips* held that the New York Constitution required acknowledgement of a priest-penitent testimonial privilege. Scalia offers alternative rationales for the holding in *Philips*, 117 S Ct at 2175, but some of O'Connor's "academic defenders" would doubtless count this a case on their side.

[119] 98 US 145 (1878) (Mormon polygamy case).

more promising strategy . . . more promising, because this strategy depends upon a normative argument, not an invocation of purportedly arbitrary elements of constitutional justice. In various formulations, the normative claim is that the fundamental obligation of government with respect to religious freedom is to leave religion alone, or to be neutral in its impact upon religion, or to have no effect upon choices about religion. The *Sherbert-Yoder* doctrine and Establishment Clause jurisprudence reflect this obligation: exemptions from generally applicable laws are essential to preclude government from imposing burdens that make religion worse off, but subsidies for religion are equally impermissible because they would make religion better off than it would otherwise be. The commands of the Free Exercise and Establishment Clauses fit together, on this theory, by reflecting a principled preference in favor of the status quo that exists before the government interferes. The two clauses, in effect, converge on the status quo from opposite directions.

Professor Douglas Laycock, a prominent defender of the compelling interest test (indeed, Laycock helped push RFRA through Congress and then represented Archbishop Flores in the Supreme Court), makes one version of this argument. Laycock calls his position "substantive neutrality."[120] He writes that religion "should proceed as unaffected by government as possible," and he maintains that government policy must not provide persons with any incentive to change their religious convictions.[121] Professor Michael McConnell, another of the compelling interest test's most prominent defenders, has offered very similar arguments. Like Laycock, McConnell says that the state's obligation is to leave religion unaffected by government. McConnell contends that "the baseline . . . is the hypothetical world in which individuals make decisions about religion on the basis of their own religious conscience, without the influence of government."[122] He continues:

---

[120] Douglas Laycock, *The Underlying Unity of Separation and Neutrality*, 46 Emory L J 43, 68–73 (1997); Douglas Laycock, *Formal, Substantive, and Disaggregated Neutrality Toward Religion*, 39 DePaul L Rev 993, 1001 (1990); Douglas Laycock, *Equal Access and Moments of Silence: The Equal Status of Religious Speech by Private Speakers*, 81 Nw U L Rev 1, 3 (1986).

[121] Laycock, 39 DePaul L Rev at 1002 (cited in note 120).

[122] Michael W. McConnell, *Religious Freedom at a Crossroads*, 59 U Chi L Rev 115, 169 (1992).

"The underlying principle is that governmental action should have the minimum possible effect on religion, consistent with achievement of the government's legitimate purposes."[123]

In an article coauthored with Judge Richard Posner, McConnell characterizes this position as demanding "incentive neutrality": government must avoid enacting regulations which create "disincentives to religious choice."[124] In their jointly authored article, McConnell and Posner pay careful attention to the connection between exemptions and subsidies. Much of their analysis is consistent with our own. McConnell and Posner say that exempting religious institutions from a burdensome regulation is equivalent to exempting them from a tax,[125] and that tax exemptions are equivalent to subsidies.[126] They conclude, "Exemption from burdens and inclusion in benefits are indistinguishable in their economic effects."[127] McConnell and Posner recognize that these issues have to be handled by a single, consistent principle.[128] They believe that "incentive neutrality" is the principle of choice.

There are several serious difficulties with this school of positions, which has at its nominal center the idea of "neutrality."[129] The most important may be the confusion between two different norms, a confusion which these positions exploit and perpetuate. The first norm, which corresponds at least roughly to what we have here and elsewhere described as the principle of *equal regard*, is an antifavoritism principle, pursuant to which religious believers and religious beliefs are to be treated no worse and no better that other persons and their important personal commitments.[130] The second norm, which corresponds at least roughly to what we have elsewhere described as the principle of *unimpaired flourishing*, is a principle of selective insularity, pursuant to which religious believ-

---

[123] Id.

[124] Michael W. McConnell and Richard A. Posner, *An Economic Approach to Issues of Religious Freedom*, 56 U Chi L Rev 1, 37 (1989).

[125] Id at 33.

[126] Id at 12.

[127] Id.

[128] Id at 33.

[129] The beguiling concept of "neutrality" sets many traps in the field of religious liberty; we discuss some of them in Eisgruber and Sager, 74 Tex L Rev at 603–05, 606–08 (cited in note 4).

[130] Eisgruber and Sager, 61 U Chi L Rev at 1282–84 (cited in note 4).

ers are to be neither encouraged nor discouraged in the pursuit of their beliefs by anything the government might choose to do.[131] We can see the elision of these two principles quite vividly in the following quote from McConnell and Posner, which begins by trumpeting the principle of equal regard and then quite mysteriously slides into the principle of unimpaired flourishing:

> [T]he Establishment Clause forbids the government to use its power and fiscal resources to favor religion or religious institutions [and] the Free Exercise Clause forbids the government to use its power and resources to disfavor religion or religious institutions. The two provisions are complementary, together protecting religious choice from governmental interference whether in favor of a religion (or religion in general) or against it.[132]

The principle of equal regard has much to commend it, and we believe that it is the essence of our constitutional commitment to religious liberty.[133] But the principle of unimpaired flourishing is normatively unattractive and both conceptually and practically unworkable.[134] Unfortunately, both "substantive neutrality" and "incentive neutrality"—the operational bottom lines for Laycock and for McConnell and Posner, respectively—are variations on the principle of unimpaired flourishing, and suffer fully from that principle's difficulties.

To begin with, these approaches are emphatically not neutral with regard to religion, but rather, thinly disguised preferences for religion in the form of a cloak of functional immunity from the reach of state laws which the rest of us are fully obliged to obey. So compare, for example, these cases: in case one, an artist who has spent his entire creative career painting with acrylic paints of a certain sort is badly interfered with by a state law banning the production or sale of those paints on environmental grounds; in case two, the paints are required to fulfill the divinely defined mission of the monks of a religious order, who use those paints alone in the illustration of their manuscripts. (Other obvious case-pairs

---

[131] Id at 1254–56.

[132] McConnell and Posner, 56 U Chi L Rev at 32–33 (cited in note 124).

[133] Eisgruber and Sager, 61 U Chi L Rev at 1282–1301; Eisgruber and Sager, 74 Tex L Rev at 600–12 (both cited in note 4).

[134] Eisgruber and Sager, 61 U Chi L Rev at 1256–1273 (cited in note 4).

come to mind: the same-sex couple who wish to marry merely for love versus the same-sex couple under divine command to do so; the landlord who is morally repelled by the unmarried cavortings of her tenants versus her twin whose repugnance is driven by religious belief; the secular charitable group which wishes to run a thriving soup kitchen in a residential neighborhood versus a church group that wishes to do so. And so on.) Unimpaired flourishing (in any of its forms, including "substantive neutrality" and "incentive neutrality") radically favors religious motivation, by giving it and it alone a presumptive immunity from state regulation. It is precisely this favoritism which is normatively indefensible, and precisely this favoritism which makes exemption seem so much like subsidy. Redescribing it as neutrality does not solve the problem on either score.

Even if we somehow ignore this fundamental and threshold difficulty of these variations on unimpaired flourishing, fatal problems remain. Far from explaining why the Constitution should treat exemptions and subsidies differently, "incentive neutrality" (McConnell's and Posner's term) and "substantive neutrality" (Laycock's term) leave us utterly unable to pronounce upon the constitutionality of any particular exemption or subsidy. At the bottom of these practical problems is a fundamental conceptual problem. The standards proposed by McConnell and Laycock protect a status quo that existed before government enacted some policy which has now become the subject of a constitutional challenge. What constitutional reason is there to privilege the status quo? After all, that status quo is itself constituted by a multitude of other laws, most of which exert influence upon religious choices, and none of which can claim, merely because they came first, to have some special relation to religious freedom. According to McConnell and Laycock, the privilege they accord to the status quo is designed to leave choices "unaffected by government." What can they have in mind? Perhaps they suppose that "without government" churches would enjoy common law property rights, unaffected by, for example, landmark designation. So the argument might run, government cannot provide subsidies, because that would favor religion beyond the common law baseline, but nor can government impose regulatory burdens upon religion, for that, too, would torque religion away from this "natural" state of affairs. But surely there is no good reason to constitutionally favor the common law in this fashion. And how seriously would McConnell and Laycock have us take such an idea? Suppose a church *wanted* landmark designation, as sometimes happens: would such a church be denied that benefit on neutrality grounds?

Perhaps McConnell and Laycock mean to steer clear of such glaring mistakes; perhaps they mean to avoid treating the common law or the status quo as privileged under the silly pretense that these states of affairs are "unaffected by government." But what then could they mean to do? Presumably, they would have to repair conceptually to some prepolitical state of nature. But it is difficult even to state this view without lapsing into patent incoherence. It is all but impossible to imagine a world in which religious choice is "unaffected by government." Certainly St. Bart's could not sell its land in Manhattan for millions of dollars in such a world, since property law in general, and the Manhattan real estate market in particular, are exquisitely governmental creations. Indeed, St. Bart's is the beneficiary not only of neutral principles of property law, but of special zoning and tax exemptions that have often given churches preferred status. To take the advice of McConnell and Laycock seriously, we would have to imagine a world in which the Episcopal Church did not have the opportunity to make a small fortune by building an office tower in midtown Manhattan. Indeed, we would have to imagine a world in which the Church could not rely upon police forces and civil courts to enforce its claim to ownership of a particular parcel and a particular building. What would the Episcopal Church do in these circumstances? Hard to say: perhaps it would open a burger joint, since, in the absence of government, labor might be cheap and demand for food high. Or perhaps it would organize a private army to crusade on behalf of its rights (as it saw them). Or perhaps it would simply collapse; we suspect that, in the absence of government, the life of a religious institution is nasty, brutish, and short.

Nor are these difficulties in any way special to cases about zoning or economic disadvantage. Consider the facts of *Smith:* what choices about religion would Alfred Smith and Galen Black—the men who challenged Oregon's peyote law—have made in the absence of government? This seems a rather favorable case for the test McConnell and Laycock propose; after all, Native Americans were ingesting peyote without legal restriction before the United States government came into existence (although it would be intolerably ethnocentric to pretend that the Native Americans made their choices *in the absence of government* merely because they acted in the absence of *our* government). Certainly Smith and Black would not have to worry about a criminal prosecution—without government, there are no crimes and no police. But Smith and Black did not file their case because they had been prosecuted; they complained because they had been fired from their jobs (as drug counselors) and denied unemployment benefits.[135] In the absence of government, unemployment insurance schemes would either not exist or would be privately run; it is hard to speculate about their terms. In any event, Smith and Black might still lose their jobs by engaging in religiously motivated conduct: in the absence of government, their employer might fire them for any reason, because without government there are no antidiscrimination laws (and, indeed, to protect themselves against workplace discrimination on the basis of religious belief, Smith and Black would need not only government, but, indeed, a government that is, by historical standards, relatively aggressive). These observations seem sufficient to show the deficiencies of the standard McConnell and Laycock propose; if we wanted to pile on the evidence, we might speculate about whether, in light of the noxious side effects of peyote, Smith and Black might have acted differently in the absence of government-regulated medical care, or whether, in the absence of government police protection, Smith and Black might have feared violent persecution on account of their unusual religious practices.

The fact is that government inevitably, and quite desirably, influences choices about religion. It provides security, resources, and stability without which many forms of religious faith would be resoundingly difficult, if not impossible, to pursue. It inculcates and enforces principles of morality—such as, for example, the principle that persons enjoy equal status regardless of their race, faith, or sex, or the principle that speech should be free—which are more congenial to some religions than to others. It is sensible to de-

---

[135] *Smith*, 494 US at 874.

mand, as the *Smith* Court did, that government not affect religious choices out of hostility or insensitivity to the value of religious practice. But it is unjust, unwise, and conceptually incoherent to demand that religion, or choices about religion, should be "unaffected" by government.

So the second strategy for explaining the tension between the *Sherbert-Yoder* doctrine (which demands special privileges for religion) and Establishment Clause doctrine (which precludes them) fails. Consider a third possibility. Professor Abner Greene has attempted to explain the tension between these doctrines as the result of a rough *quid pro quo:* in Greene's view, government must exclude religious interests from political competition in order to avoid divisive controversies that would otherwise result; the *Sherbert-Yoder* doctrine balances this disadvantage by giving religious groups benefits which they might fairly seek if they were allowed to participate fully in political debates. On this view, the Free Exercise Clause gives back some of what the Establishment Clause takes away.[136]

Professor Greene's argument has not received the credit it deserves. Unlike the brute argument from text and/or history and the deeply confused argument from "neutrality," Greene's *quid pro quo* argument has the shape of a sensible and compelling normative claim for privileging religiously motivated conduct. We expect that diehard defenders of the RFRA approach will repair to some version of his claim with increasing frequency. But to get started, Greene's argument depends upon a view of the Establishment Clause which radically handicaps religious speech and religious participation in politics. That view is unsound in principle, inconsistent with recent Supreme Court decisions, and impossible to implement in practice. Greene believes, for example, that the Supreme Court should hold laws unconstitutional if legislators offered religious reasons for supporting them.[137] Greene thinks that these restrictions are necessary in order to ensure that citizens deliberate together on the basis of shared, mutually accessible rationales, rather than dividing on the basis of sectarian convictions that

---

[136] Abner S. Greene, *The Political Balance of the Religion Clauses*, 102 Yale L J 1611, 1634–35, 1643–44 (1993).

[137] Id at 1624.

depend for their cogency on contested theological truths.[138] We agree with Greene that public deliberations about policy and political justice should, ideally, relate back to a shared core of common premises, and that it is a matter of regret when public debate divides along sectarian lines.[139] But one cannot achieve the inclusiveness Greene favors by gagging religious persons and interests in the way that he proposes: on the contrary, doing so ensures that one group will feel itself excluded. Nor is there any reason to think that civic debate can proceed upon shared, secular premises only if religious institutions are excluded from the benefits of fairly administered public subsidies; on the contrary, like-minded citizens might choose to extend subsidies to religious institutions along with secular ones for various, entirely secular reasons (including the desire to facilitate intellectual and charitable activities of all kinds).

* * *

Scholars writing to defend the *Sherbert-Yoder*-RFRA application of the compelling interest standard and to reconcile its endorsement of religious privilege with the widely accepted view that religious subsidies would be flatly unconstitutional as a violation of the Establishment Clause have exercised great imagination and ingenuity. But they have undertaken the conceptually impossible. The unduckable inconsistency of demanding exemptions while barring subsidies is merely an artifact of a more general proposition: The privileging of religion is normatively indefensible whatever form the privilege assumes.[140] This is the instinct which led the Court in the nearly three decades between *Sherbert* and *Smith* to find reasons in one factual context after another to avoid giving religious believers immunity from the laws the rest of us were obliged to obey; it was this instinct and that experience which led the Court in *Smith* to reconstruct the *Sherbert* doctrine, and, which, in turn, led the Court in *Flores* to see Congress's enactment of RFRA as hostile rather than sympathetic to the Court's understanding of religious liberty.

---

[138] Id at 1621–24.

[139] We discuss the problem of religious division in Eisgruber and Sager, 74 Tex L Rev at 610–12 (cited in note 4).

[140] Eisgruber and Sager, 61 U Chi L Rev at 1260–70 (cited in note 4).

VI. Two Looks Forward

A. RELIGIOUS LIBERTY AFTER FLORES

In *Flores*, six Justices affirmed the rejection by the Court in *Smith* of the proposition that persons motivated by their deep religious beliefs enjoy a presumptive constitutional right to disregard otherwise valid laws of general application. One of those, Justice Stevens, would have gone further and held that the attempt to confer such a sweeping right was itself violative of the Establishment Clause. *Flores*, in this respect, is consistent with the general thrust of the current Court's revisionary jurisprudence of religious liberty. In both Establishment Clause and Free Exercise Clause cases, the Court has increasingly emphasized that government's fundamental obligation is to treat all deep personal commitments equally, regardless of whether those commitments are secular or religious, mainstream or unusual. The *Smith* Court's reformulation of *Sherbert* is an instance of this. So too are decisions in which the Court has relaxed restrictions it had previously imposed upon the government's freedom to include religious institutions among the beneficiaries of neutrally defined, nonpreferential subsidy programs[141]—and even found constitutional reasons to *insist* that a state-run college fund student religious activities along with comparable secular ones.[142] In effect, the Court is departing on the one side from its nominal commitment to exceptional privilege and departing on the other side from its wavering commitment to special disability, and converging toward a view that normalizes religion and sees equal regard as the essence of religious liberty.

Indeed, less than two weeks before it decided *Flores*, the Court handed down its decision in *Agostini v Felton*,[143] overruling a twelve-year-old restriction upon the means the states could use to

---

[141] See, e.g., *Witters v Washington Dept. of Services for the Blind*, 474 US 481 (1986) (upholding a state program which permitted college students pursuing religious training to share in an aid program subsidizing vocational education for all blind students); *Bowen v Kendrick*, 487 US 589 (1988) (upholding a program which allowed religious institutions to share in federal funding available to support pregnancy counseling); *Zobrest v Catalina Foothills School Dist.*, 509 US 1 (1993) (upholding the constitutionality of a program in which public funds were used to supply a sign-language interpreter for a deaf student attending Catholic school).

[142] *Rosenberger v Rector and Visitors of the University of Virginia*, 515 US 819 (1995).

[143] 117 S Ct 1997 (1997).

facilitate remedial education for disadvantaged students in parochial schools. *Agostini* was a literal rerun of *Aguilar v Felton*.[144] In
Aguilar, a five-Justice majority of the Court held that New York
violated the Establishment Clause when it sent remedial teachers
paid with federal funds into paraochial school classrooms (as well
as classrooms in public schools and nonreligious private schools).
The *Aguilar* majority relied on the controversial "*Lemon* test," pursuant to which a governmental act ran afoul of the Establishment
clause if it had a religious purpose, had the effect of advancing
religion, or entangled the government with religion.[145] New York's
attempt to avoid the advancement of religion by monitoring the
activities of the federally funded teachers was held to violate the
entanglement prong of *Lemon*.[146]

In *Agostini*, the Court revisited exactly the same facts. In the
interval, four cases had reflected the Court's mounting doubts
about the soundness of *Aguilar* and possibly of the *Lemon* test itself.
In *Bowen v Kendrick*,[147] the Court permitted the government to
subsidize counseling programs run by religious organizations. In
1993, the Court decided *Zobrest v Catalina Hills School District*.[148]
The facts of *Zobrest* resembled those of *Aguilar*: federal law required public school districts to aid handicapped students attending private schools; an Arizona school district provided a sign-
language interpreter to accompany a deaf student enrolled in a
local Catholic school. Unlike in *Aguilar*, the Justices held in *Zobrest*
that no establishment resulted from sending the publicly paid interpreter into the religious school; the Justices in the majority distinguished *Aguilar* on the ground that the interpreter, unlike the
teachers in *Zobrest*, was doing nothing more than translating messages originating from another speaker.[149] If anybody thought this
distinction might permit *Aguilar* to endure alongside *Zobrest*, their
expectations were dashed only one year later when, in *Kiryas Joel
v Grumet*,[150] five Justices made clear in dicta that they were ready

---

[144] 473 US 402 (1985).

[145] *Lemon v Kurtzman*, 403 US 602, 612–13 (1971).

[146] 473 US at 409.

[147] 487 US 589.

[148] 509 US 1.

[149] Id at 13.

[150] 512 US 687 (1994).

to overrule *Aguilar*.[151] In the Court's next term, those five Justices took a step in that direction when they decided *Rosenberger v Rector and Visitors of the University of Virginia*.[152] *Rosenberger* dealt with a University of Virginia policy which prohibited student religious groups from drawing upon the university's student activities fund. A student-run Christian newspaper challenged the rule on Free Exercise and Free Speech grounds; the university defended by citing Establishment Clause concerns. The Court agreed with the newspaper; its ruling had the obvious implication that educational institutions were sometimes not only constitutionally permitted, but indeed constitutionally obliged, to fund religious activities along with comparable secular activities.

Meanwhile, the New York City school system continued to operate under the injunction issued pursuant to *Aguilar*. Dismayed by the expense of creating "neutral sites"[153] and encouraged by the developments in *Kiryas Joel* and *Rosenberger*, the City filed a Rule 60(b)(5) motion seeking reconsideration of the constitutional question decided in *Aguilar*. After the Second Circuit ruled against the City on procedural grounds, the Court granted certiorari and reversed. In light of what had been said in *Kiryas Joel*, it was obvious that, if the Court reached the merits of the case, *Aguilar* would be overturned; the only question was how broadly the Court would rule. Justice O'Connor, writing for the Court, advanced both a broad and a narrow rationale for that outcome. The broad claim was that the aid program in *Aguilar* avoided Establishment Clause programs because it benefited religious institutions solely as the result of private choices rather than because of a public decision to do so. New York's program aided religious schools only to the

---

[151] See id at 717 (O' Connor concurring in part and in the judgment); id at 731 (Kennedy concurring in the judgment); and id at 750 (Scalia dissenting, joined by Rehnquist and Thomas).

[152] 515 US 819.

[153] The Court's ruling in *Aguilar* had the odd consequence that states could provide remedial services to students in religious schools only if the students left their schools and attended the remedial classes in a "neutral site." By putting the remedial classes in "neutral sites," public authorities could monitor teachers without risking unconstitutional entanglement in the affairs of the religious school. *Aguilar*, 473 US at 421 (O'Connor dissenting). In practice, the "neutral site" requirement meant that children received remedial education in trailers and vans parked outside their schools; the practice not only looked ridiculous but ate up large amounts of money that might otherwise have gone to pay for, e.g., more teachers. *Agostini*, 117 S Ct at 2005 (citing evidence that approximately $100 million had been spent to comply with *Aguilar* by equipping "neutral sites").

extent that parents chose to send their disadvantaged children to such schools. The New York program did not provide parents with any special incentive to send their children to religious rather secular schools. Therefore, Justice O'Connor said, the program neither advanced nor endorsed religion.[154] Justice O'Connor's opinion went on, however, to highlight an additional feature of New York's program with narrower implications: it did not contribute any dollars directly to the coffers of a religious school or organization. New York sent teachers, not money, and the teachers taught subjects that were "supplemental to the regular curricula"—and so did not necessarily " 'relieve sectarian schools of costs they would otherwise have borne. . . .' "[155]

This last point echoed the Court's opinion in *Rosenberger*, where Justice Kennedy emphasized that Virginia's activity fund sent checks directly to the creditors of student organizations, not to the organizations themselves—hence, as in *Agostini*, no state dollars flowed into the coffers of the religious beneficiary.[156] *Agostini*'s importance as a precedent depends upon whether the *Agostini* majority in fact regards this limitation as a crucial feature of its holding. Cases about tuition vouchers are percolating in the state courts: courts in both Ohio and Wisconsin have entertained challenges to programs offering tuition benefits to poor parents who wish to send their children to either religious or secular private schools.[157] Under the broadest principle O'Connor articulated in *Agostini*— pursuant to which no constitutional violation exists if public benefits flow to religious schools as a result of private choices—the tuition voucher programs from Wisconsin and Ohio would survive constitutional challenge, since parents decide whether to send their

---

[154] 117 S Ct at 2011–12.

[155] Id at 2013 (quoting *Zobrest*, 509 US at 12).

[156] *Rosenberger*, 515 US at 840.

[157] As of the writing of this article, the most recent Wisconsin court decision on point had held Milwaukee's school choice program unconstitutional under the Wisconsin state constitution, which contains rather specific language about the funding of religious schools. *Jackson v Benson*, 1997 WL 476290 (Wis App 1997); see Wis Const, Art I, § 18 (providing that no "money [shall] be drawn from the treasury for the benefit of religious societies, or religious or theological seminaries"). For discussions of the Wisconsin and Ohio controversies, see, e.g., Carol Innerst, *School Choice Given a Reprieve; Court Grants Stay to Cleveland to Appeal Adverse Verdict*, Washington Times (July 29, 1997) at A8; Richard P. Jones, *Religious School Vouchers Rejected; Appeals Court's Ruling to Be Appealed, Choice Program Supporters Say*, Milwaukee Journal Sentinel (August 23, 1997) at 1.

children to religious or secular schools. If, however, it matters whether state dollars reach religious coffers, the case would go the other way: unlike in *Agostini* and *Rosenberger*, there is no doubt that the voucher system adds public money to the accounts of religious educational programs.

Agostini and *Rosenberger* thus leave the Court with an "out"; it might retreat from its apparent embrace of egalitarian principles and reinvigorate *Lemon*'s skepticism about any program that includes religious institutions among its beneficiaries. We think that outcome unlikely, however; it is clear that equality norms are exerting a powerful pull upon the Justices. To be sure, the overlap between the majorities in the egalitarian Establishment Clause cases, *Agostini* and *Rosenberger*, and the egalitarian Free Exercise Clause cases, *Smith* and *Flores*, is not perfect. Justice Stevens joined the majorities in *Smith* and *Flores* but dissented in *Agostini* and *Rosenberger*, while Justice O'Connor did exactly the opposite. Justice Ginsburg, who was not on the Court when *Smith* was decided, joined the majority in *Flores* but dissented in both *Agostini* and *Rosenberger*.

Nevertheless, there is a solid four-vote coalition—consisting of Rehnquist, Kennedy, Scalia, and Thomas—driving both the *Smith-Flores* and *Rosenberger-Agostini* lines of cases. Other Justices on the Court have also endorsed the equality principles which, in our view, undergird the shifting face of the Court's doctrine. Indeed, the positions of Stevens and O'Connor are ironic, since they have been among the most vocal proponents of equality norms in religious liberty cases.[158] Any effort to construct a "view of the Court" when disparate majorities prevail by one- or two-vote margins is uncertain, but the Court's consistent emphasis upon equal treatment is unmistakable—and, we think, eminently sound.

Flores is the latest manifestation of that emphasis. The *Flores* Court plainly affirmed that part of *Smith* which rejected the sweeping exemption of religiously motivated persons from otherwise valid laws. *Flores* may thus become the occasion for a second round of misplaced despair. In the wake of *Smith*, extraordinary prognos-

---

[158] See, e.g., *Kiryas Joel*, 512 US at 715 (O'Connor concurring) (an "emphasis on equal treatment is, I think, an eminently sound approach"); *Lee*, 455 US at 263 n 2 (Stevens concurring) ("The risk that governmental approval of some [religious claims] and disapproval of others will be perceived as favoring one religion over another is an important risk the Establishment Clause was designed to preclude").

tications about the death of religious liberty were made. For example, Professor Douglas Laycock—who helped to draft RFRA, and then defended it before the Court in *Flores*—made the remarkable claim that, given *Smith*, "[t]he legal framework for persecution is in place" and only "the political will" is lacking.[159] In an article provocatively titled "The Remnants of Free Exercise" and published in this journal, Laycock speculated that, in light of *Smith*, the Court might well uphold the City of Hialeah's prohibition upon ritual sacrifice, an ordinance which he quite accurately described as an instance of religious persecution.[160] Less than one year later, Laycock helped lay his own worries to rest, arguing *Church of the Lukumi Babalu Aye v City of Hialeah* in the Supreme Court and emerging with a unanimous decision invalidating the ordinance.[161]

The emotional opposition to *Smith* may have been partly attributable to Justice Scalia's rhetoric. Toward the end of his opinion for the Court, Justice Scalia acknowledged that generally applicable laws may impose undesirable burdens on religious practices, but, he said, it was up to legislatures to do something about that problem—and then he conceded that legislatures would likely treat minority religions less well than mainstream ones.[162] Scalia's comments led some observers to think that, at least in the area of Free Exercise law, the Court had abandoned its commitment to the *Carolene Products* doctrine,[163] with its emphasis on solicitude for preferred freedoms and the interests of discrete and insular minorities.[164] These concerns have been compounded by the palpable injustice of some government policies, apparently immune

---

[159] Douglas Laycock, *The Remnants of Free Exercise*, 1990 Supreme Court Review 1, 60.

[160] Id at 65–68.

[161] 508 US 520.

[162] 494 US at 890 ("It may fairly be said that leaving accommodation to the political process will place at a relative disadvantage those religious practices that are not widely engaged in; but that unavoidable consequence of democratic government must be preferred to a system in which each conscience is a law unto itself or in which judges weigh the social importance of all laws against the centrality of all religious beliefs").

[163] *United States v Carolene Products*, 304 US 144, 152 n 4 (1938).

[164] For example, Laycock concluded his critique of *Smith* by observing, "One function of judicial review is to protect religious exercise against . . . hostile or indifferent consequences of the political process. The Court has abandoned that function, at least in substantial part, and perhaps entirely." Laycock, 1990 Supreme Court Review at 68 (cited in note 159).

from challenge under *Smith*, which impose senseless burdens on religious belief—for example, laws that require routine autopsies in the face of religiously motivated objections,[165] or laws that require Amish farmers to install strobe lights (rather than red lanterns) on the rear of their wagons.[166] Here, then, is proof of the bad consequences that follow when the Court refuses to bring religious minorities under the *Carolene Products* umbrella.

In fact, after *Smith* and *Flores*, religious minorities and religious practice continue to receive the kind of special judicial solicitude which the *Carolene Products* doctrine recommends. As we have already noticed, statutes that single out religious practices for special burdens are subjected to even harsher scrutiny than statutes that target communicative activity receive under the Free Speech Clause. Indeed, while any law specifically targeting ritual practice would receive strict scrutiny under *Lukumi Babalu Aye*, some laws singling out communicative behavior—such as, for example, time, place, and manner regulations—receive less demanding scrutiny.[167] In that respect, the post-*Smith* Court actually gives Free Exercise claims *better* treatment than it gives Free Speech claims. Religious discrimination is, moreover, no less suspect than racial discrimination. If anything, federal courts appear more willing to look for disparate impact discrimination under the Free Exercise Clause than they are in race discrimination cases under the Equal Protection Clause.[168] Consider: in *Keeler v Mayor and City Council of Cumberland*, a federal district court exempted a church from a local landmarking ordinance, claiming that the ordinance was constitutionally defective because it contained exemptions for financial hardship but not religious hardship;[169] in *Rader v Johnston*, a federal district court found evidence of discrimination when the University of Nebraska granted various freshmen the privilege of living

---

[165] *Yang v Sturner*, 750 F Supp 558 (D RI 1990).

[166] In *State v Hershberger*, 462 NW2d 393, 397–99 (Minn 1990), the Minnesota Supreme Court granted relief under Minnesota's state constitution.

[167] See generally Geoffrey R. Stone, *Content-Neutral Restrictions*, 54 U Chi L Rev 46 (1987).

[168] In *Washington v Davis*, 426 US 229 (1976), the Court construed the Equal Protection Clause to reach only intentional discrimination.

[169] 940 F Supp 879 (D Md 1996). The *Keeler* court found that Cumberland's historic preservation statute was not a "law of general application," and so was subject to strict scrutiny, even after *Smith*. Id at 885.

off campus but denied permission to a religious student who wished to live in a Christian residence;[170] in *Fraternal Order of Police v City of Newark*, a federal district court said that if the Newark police department permitted officers to wear beards to avoid skin rashes, then it must also permit officers to wear beards to satisfy religious obligations.[171]

Of course, Scalia is right that, after *Smith*, it will usually be up to legislatures to provide religious persons and institutions with relief from generally applicable laws that impose unnecessary incidental burdens upon their religiously motivated practices. But that is equally true of generally applicable laws that impose unnecessary incidental burdens upon communicative practices. And, in general, American legislatures are sensitive to this obligation because they respect the importance of individual liberty. Indeed, the reason we feel such a strong sense of injustice when confronted with the offensive stories about autopsies and fluorescent triangles is that we know that legislatures would usually provide exemptions to avoid such impositions on deeply held commitments—and we suspect that the legislature's failure (or some administrator's failure) to do so in these cases is the result of discrimination or hostility.

One might reasonably criticize *Smith* for failing to provide adequate constitutional protection against failures of equal regard that may occur under the guise of facially neutral, generally applicable laws—and, indeed, we have ourselves criticized *Smith* in exactly these terms. But these sorts of criticisms should not lead one to embrace the compelling interest standard, which is too blunt and too invasive to serve as a sensible vehicle for identifying instances of disparate impact or disparate treatment. Friends of religious liberty, whatever other views they might hold, ought not to lament the passing of that test. Indeed, the post-*Smith* decisions in *Keeler*, *Rader*, and *Fraternal Order of Police* are at least as favorable as what litigants would have received under *Sherbert*'s tough-talking but ultimately toothless regime. There is no evidence that the federal courts since *Smith* have become less kind to Free Exercise claims;

---

[170] 924 F Supp 1540 (D Neb 1996). The court found both that the university's policy did not amount to a rule of general application, and that the university had applied the rule in a discriminatory fashion. Id at 1553–54.

[171] No 97–2672 (D NJ, July 29, 1997).

it is even possible that they have become more sympathetic.[172] None of this is surprising. If taken seriously, *Sherbert*'s compelling interest standard would have made outrageous impositions upon the ability of the states to govern effectively. Given the unhappy choice between applying that standard or rejecting Free Exercise claims, courts took the latter option. *Smith* freed them to begin developing a jurisprudence that is at once more sensible and more sensitive to genuine claims of religious liberty. RFRA placed all this at jeopardy once again. *Flores*—at least as regards state law— has restored the opportunity for the development of a sensible and attractive jurisprudence of religious liberty.

B. THE FUTURE OF RFRA, "LITTLE RFRAS," AND MORE SENSIBLE FORMS OF RELIGIOUS ACCOMMODATION

RFRA applied to the federal government as well as to the states. Although Congress needed to invoke the Fourteenth Amendment's Enforcement Clause in order to justify RFRA's application to the states, Congress would presumably rely on other sources of authority with respect to federal applications. Exactly how this argument would be made is unclear; since RFRA slices through every sector of the federal code, Congress would probably have to rely upon *all* of its enumerated powers (RFRA makes exceptions to congressional statutes enacted under the Bankruptcy Power, the Commerce Power, the Post Roads Power, and so on; hence, Congress has power to enact RFRA under the Bankruptcy Power, the Commerce Power, the Post Roads Power, and so on).

The Supreme Court did not explicitly decide the fate of RFRA's federal applications. One case—*Sullivan v Sasnett*[173]—applying RFRA to federal law was pending when the Court decided *Flores;* the Court vacated the holding and remanded the case to the Seventh Circuit for reconsideration in light of its decision in *Flores*.[174] The Seventh Circuit will have to decide, among other things, whether the federal law applications of RFRA are severable from

---

[172] As we noted earlier, the federal courts were remarkably *unsympathetic* to Free Exercise claims under *Sherbert*. See note 72 and accompanying text.

[173] 91 F3d 1018 (7th Cir 1996).

[174] 117 S Ct 2502 (1997).

the state law applications. If so, that court, and others confronting RFRA's federal law applications, will have to address two constitutional questions left open by *Flores:* whether RFRA violates the Establishment Clause and whether it impermissibly encroaches upon judicial authority.[175] If state legislatures enact their own "little RFRAs," as some interest groups would like them to do, the Establishment Clause question will be on the table there as well.

Does the Court's position in *Smith* and *Flores* presage the conclusion that RFRA is unconstitutional under the Establishment Clause? Certainly there is pressure in that direction. The Court has already held, in *Texas Monthly, Inc. v Bullock*[176] and *Thornton v Caldor,*[177] that special exemptions for religious believers may violate the Establishment Clause. RFRA, however it is interpreted, creates some special privileges for religious believers. The remaining question is whether the "constitutional anomaly" of RFRA's stark privileging of religious believers rises to the level of an Establishment Clause violation.

For some of the Justices in the *Flores* majority, the answer to this question might depend upon how RFRA is interpreted. *Flores* involved a facial challenge to RFRA's constitutionality; neither the trial court nor the Court of Appeals for the Fifth Circuit had an opportunity to address any issues of statutory interpretation. As we have already discussed, some of those issues are quite important. For example, a narrowing construction of RFRA's "substantial burden" language could significantly reduce the statute's scope. In his *Flores* opinion, Justice Kennedy speculated that the "compelling interest standard" might perhaps be interpreted to require "intermediate scrutiny"—a delightful Alice-in-Wonderland-conclusion that would no doubt launch a thousand law review articles about the indeterminacy of legal language!—in which case he thought it possible that RFRA's greatest evil might be the imposition of "a heavy litigation burden" (rather than, we might suppose, the creation of special privileges that violate the Establish-

---

[175] We have previously argued that RFRA is unconstitutional on both of these grounds. Eisgruber and Sager, 69 NYU L Rev at 452–60 (Establishment Clause), 469–73 (judicial power) (cited in note 4).

[176] 489 US 1 (1989) (finding unconstitutional a Texas law that exempted religious publications from a sales tax applicable to other publications).

[177] 472 US 703 (1985) (finding unconstitutional a Connecticut law which gave all religious employees the right not to work on their Sabbath).

ment Clause).[178] Given a heroic narrowing construction, some of the Justices in the *Flores* majority might be willing to regard RFRA's special privileges as too minimal to deserve the Court's attention under the Establishment Clause.

This would be a mistake. The Court will find it impossible to draw a principled line between benefits for religion that are "small enough" and those that are "too big." Any application of an across-the-board exemptions doctrine, like the one RFRA and *Sherbert* prescribed, will be ad hoc and unpredictable—not because of judicial incompetence or shifting coalitions on the Court, but because there is simply no coherent, privilege-based view of religious liberty to guide its application. Under current Establishment Clause jurisprudence, any subsidy, no matter how small, directed *solely* to religious institutions would presumably be unconstitutional. There would be no way for the Court to explain why tiny favors were permissible when they took the form of exemptions but not when they took the form of subsidies. The Court would reinvent all the inconsistencies of *Sherbert* and *Lemon*, for exactly the same reasons, and with the same inevitable outcome—an incoherent hodgepodge of distinctions, doomed to eventual abandonment.

The only sensible way to review legislative accommodations for religious practice under the Establishment Clause is to ask whether they are reasonable prophylactic measures to guard against otherwise unreachable instances of discrimination, hostility, or insensitivity to religious belief. That is exactly the question Justice Kennedy asked when testing RFRA against the limits of Section 5.[179] He rightly concluded that RFRA sweeps too broadly to survive scrutiny. It defies common sense to presume that every incidental burden on religious liberty results from hostility or insensitivity to religious conviction. Indeed, in many areas of the law, religious interests are, if anything, specially favored. Zoning regulation, a specific target of RFRA and a likely focus of any state-enacted "little RFRAs," is a good example. Many zoning ordinances contain special exemptions available to all churches, but only to churches. Some of these benefits are, in our judgment, patent violations of

---

[178] 117 S Ct at 2171.

[179] Id ("RFRA's substantial burden test . . . is not . . . a discriminatory effects or disparate treatment test").

the Establishment Clause. No doubt zoning administrators sometimes abuse their authority to harm unpopular churches. But that
problem is not usefully attacked by extending all churches—no
matter how rich, how powerful, or how favored in the law—a
blanket writ to challenge the zoning ordinances which every other
citizen and institution must respect.

Whatever the fate of federal RFRA, nothing in *Flores* should
prevent either Congress or the states from enacting more nuanced
protections for religious commitments. Those protections might
include laws designed to alleviate disparate impact discrimination,
and specific prophylactic rules designed to prevent discrimination
not easily detected and proven. The Court's opinion in *Flores* is
quite clear that, from the standpoint of Congress's Section 5 authority, either of these alternatives would survive the objections
that proved fatal to RFRA.

Nor would such laws encounter Establishment Clause barriers.
That, we think, is the right lesson to draw from *Corporation of the
Presiding Bishop v Amos*,[180] where the Supreme Court upheld,
against an Establishment Clause challenge, provisions exempting
churches and other religious employers from the scope of federal
law prohibiting discrimination on the basis of religious belief. The
immunity extended to religious organizations by those provisions
is, we believe, in service of a more general constitutional right of
association enjoyed by secular and religious organizations alike.
Government may not prohibit citizens from forming predominantly noncommercial organizations, or from selecting leaders and
policy-makers within those organizations, on the basis of exclusive
principles.[181] As the facts of *Amos* illustrate,[182] Title VII's exemption reaches further than any constitutional right of privacy would
go; it permits churches to discriminate even with regard to employees who have no religiously significant role to play. Nevertheless, Congress might plausibly have concluded that collisions between Title VII and the organizational policy of churches would be
frequent; that these collisions would have been factually complex

---

[180] 483 US 327 (1987).

[181] We discuss this point in greater detail in Eisgruber and Sager, 61 U Chi L Rev at
1311–14 (cited in note 4).

[182] Amos worked as a "building engineer" at a gymnasium, open to the public, run by
the Church of Jesus Christ of Latter Day Saints. 483 US at 330.

because of the difficulty of figuring out which jobs have sacral significance within a particular religion; and, hence, that absent a sharp, bright-line rule, churches would be subject to litigation burdens and inconsistent decisions that other organizations would not have to bear. The rule in *Amos* is a plausible prophylactic rule, designed to avoid otherwise unreachable discrimination against churches, and that is the best way to explain the Court's decision in *Amos*.

It is also the best way to reconcile *Amos* with the Court's decisions in *Thornton* and *Texas Monthly*. Together, those three decisions suggest that the Court will uphold legislative accommodations for religion if they are reasonable prophylactic measures to guard against otherwise unreachable instances of discrimination, hostility, or insensitivity to religious belief. The power to enact such accommodations is quite important. When Congress has paid serious attention to religious liberty, rather than grandstanding in the way it did with RFRA, it has used narrow exemptions crafted to target probable instances of discrimination. Examples of such actions include a law passed to accommodate religious clothing in the military,[183] another passed to protect Native American peyote rituals against state and federal controlled substance laws,[184] and the withdrawl of funding for a Forest Service road that would have defiled an Indian burial ground.[185]

In addition to the Establishment Clause issues left unexamined in *Flores*, there remains the separation of powers issue. We and others have suggested that RFRA impermissibly prescribes a rule for decision by judges, directing them to interpret legal language in a fashion contrary to their own best judgment. In our hands, this argument builds upon the Court's old, and cryptic, decision in *United States v Klein*;[186] it requires, among other things, that one distinguish between the mere specification of a new statutory standard (which, obviously, Congress does every time it passes a law) and the imposition of a particular construction of other laws

---

[183] 10 USC § 774 (1994).

[184] 42 USC § 1996 (1994).

[185] House Committee on Appropriations, Department of the Interior and Related Agencies Appropriations Bill, 1989 HR Rep No 100–713, 100th Cong, 2d Sess 72 (1988).

[186] 80 US 128 (1871). We discuss the decision in Eisgruber and Sager, 69 NYU L Rev at 470–73 (cited in note 4).

(in this case, the Free Exercise Clause). Yet RFRA is obviously not an ordinary statute. The most formal account of RFRA's peculiarity would emphasize Congress's decision to foist upon the judiciary a test that it had deemed unworkable. Congress identified the "compelling interest" test as an artifact from the Court's past cases; implicitly acknowledged that the Court had rejected the test as unworkable; stipulated, by legislative fiat, that the test was "workable";[187] and forced it back upon the judiciary without any further elaboration of its meaning. In brief, Congress simply told the judiciary to do something it knew the judiciary had declared to be impossible. That is not the way Congress ordinarily legislates, and there is no justification for it to do so.

This formal and relatively narrow fault reflects a more fundamental defect in the statute. RFRA conscripts the federal judiciary in an elaborate constitutional charade. The judiciary is obliged to look for a traditional constitutional trigger, and when it is present to apply a traditional constitutional test. Not just any test, of course, but a test which it has found both normatively indefensible and utterly unworkable. This is not ordinary legislation but the enactment of a shadow constitution, with the judiciary obliged to play an unwilling supportive role.

VII. Conclusion

RFRA embraced one of the most striking notions in all of constitutional discourse: the idea that religiously motivated persons and groups are to a considerable degree sovereigns among us—that they enjoy the license to disregard legal restraints and burdens that other Americans must respect. Were this claim to succeed, it might be the case that religiously motivated parents were constitutionally entitled to educate their children at home, but that other parents were not; that religiously motivated landlords were entitled to discriminate among tenants on grounds of race, gender, or sexual orientation, while other landlords were not; that religiously motivated persons of the same sex could marry, but that others could not; or that churches or other religious organizations were free to disregard the historic preservation or zoning restrictions that bind everyone else in their communities.

---

[187] 42 USC § 2000bb(a)(5) (1994).

If it is possible at all to find a respectable pedigree for this idea, it may trace to the seductive if enigmatic idea that the Constitution erects a "wall of separation" between church and state.[188] The metaphor of separation suggested to some that religion ought to flourish or decline unimpaired by government policies or political values; hence the judiciary ought to enable religious actors to practice their faiths unconstrained even by democratically enacted laws that everybody else must obey. The idea of separation exerted a powerful pull on the Supreme Court's Establishment Clause jurisprudence, where it invited skepticism about any program that sent government aid to churches or, especially, religious schools: religion ought to grow or shrink uninfluenced by government largesse and political power.

Separation has always existed in uneasy tension with another powerful vision of religious liberty, one based upon the equality of persons. From the standpoint of equality, neither the Court's dogmatic opposition to aid for religious interests nor its occasional willingness to privilege believers with special exemptions made any sense. Why should the law privilege religious believers with exemptions unavailable for comparably serious secular commitments? The Supreme Court acknowledged the force of this point in various ways. For example, in *United States v Seeger*,[189] *Thornton*,[190] and *Texas Monthly*,[191] the Court either modified or struck down laws giving special privileges to religious believers. But the Court's most impressive, if tacit, acknowledgment of the equality principle was its toothless application of *Sherbert*'s compelling state interest. In one case after another, the Justices found ways to duck the test and deny exemptions to claimants who sought to cash in on *Sherbert*'s expansive promise.

---

[188] Thomas Jefferson used the "wall of separation" metaphor in his January 1, 1802, letter to the Danbury Baptist Association, and it appears in both the Court's first Free Exercise case, *Reynolds*, 98 US at 164, and the Court's first Establishment Clause case, *Everson*, 330 US at 16. In *Reynolds*, of course, the Court used the idea of "separation" to argue against religious privilege, rather than for it.

[189] 380 US 163 (1965) (holding, via artful statutory construction, that conscientious objector status was available to secular pacifists, even though the statute applied only to those who opposed war on the basis of "religious training and belief").

[190] 472 US 703 (finding unconstitutional a Connecticut law which gave all religious employees the right not to work on their Sabbath).

[191] 489 US 1 (finding unconstitutional a Texas law that exempted religious publications from a sales tax applicable to other publications).

Conversely, from the standpoint of equality, it was hard to see why churches should not be eligible for government benefits on the same terms as comparable secular enterprises, including, for example, private schools and secular charities. In *Everson v Ewing Township Bd. of Education*,[192] at the very outset of the Court's Establishment Clause jurisprudence, Justice Black noted that it would be unfair to deny churches and religious schools the benefit of publicly funded police and fire protection;[193] no opponent of public aid for religious education has ever been dogmatic enough to contest that point. Black's concession effectively foreshadowed the unhappy career of the *Lemon* test, in which the Court struggled to distinguish between invalid policies which "advanced religion" and permissible policies which merely made religious institutions incidental beneficiaries of subsidies aimed at some secular goal (such as police protection, fire safety, or cheap transportation).[194]

Since 1990, the Supreme Court's religious liberty jurisprudence has undergone a fundamental change. The unstable mix of separation and equality has given way to a jurisprudence emphatically centered upon equality. The transition is manifest in the demise of separation's two doctrinal avatars, the *Lemon* and *Sherbert* tests. *Lemon* has passed quietly, ignored rather than overruled in cases like *Rosenberger* and *Agostini*. *Sherbert*'s compelling state interest standard, in contrast, met an operatic end, dying loudly and at great length.

These developments have been widely noticed. Several scholars have called attention to the developing unity between the Court's Free Exercise and Establishment Clause jurisprudence; some have recognized that equality is beginning to achieve doctrinal primacy over separation.[195] Most of these treatments have, however, as-

---

[192] 330 US 1.

[193] Id at 17–18.

[194] The result, most commentators agree, has been a hash. Compare *Committee for Public Education v Nyquist*, 413 US 756 (1973) (holding unconstitutional a program that provided tax credits for educational expenses at any *private* school, including religious schools) with *Mueller v Allen*, 463 US 388 (1983) (holding constitutional a program that provided tax credits for educational expenses at any school, *public or private*, including religious schools). Compare also *Bd. of Education v Allen*, 392 US 236 (1968) (upholding the constitutionality of subsidies to religious schools for the purchase of textbooks) with *Meek v Pittenger*, 421 US 349 (1975) (holding unconstitutional subsidies to religious schools for the purchase of maps).

[195] For example, see generally Laycock, 46 Emory L J 43 (cited in note 120); Carl H. Esbeck, *A Constitutional Case for Governmental Cooperation with Faith-Based Social Services,*

sumed that the separation model was an attractive, or at least coherent, model for some portions of the Court's jurisprudence. That is a mistake, and a bad one. In this article, we have insisted upon two points. First, the Constitution's Free Exercise and Establishment Clauses are conceptually integrated. The Supreme Court's cases under the two clauses are converging upon a single principle neither because of methodological whim nor because of political choice, but rather because the two lines of cases raise the same issues. Second, the separation model was both normatively indefensible and practically unworkable. If the Court is ever to achieve a coherent doctrine in this troubled field, it has to reject that model and the doctrinal tests—*Lemon* and *Sherbert*—that go with it.

Congress took up the banner of RFRA much too quickly, and in so doing set itself on a collision course with a Supreme Court that had over the course of several decades worked itself slowly clear of a deeply misguided paradigm of religious liberty. *Flores* is the result. Seen in its best and most plausible light, *Flores*'s view of congressional authority under Section 5 of the Fourteenth Amendment is reasonable, and presages little if any meaningful change from the generous posture of deference that has prevailed since *Katzenbach*. Congress has an important role to play in policing state and federal conduct for instances of hostility or indifference to the important interests of religious believers. Until its misadventure with RFRA, Congress played that role with alacrity and good sense. There may be circumstances under which it will be necessary for Congress to go to war with the Court; but RFRA was the wrong fight to pick, and Congress would be well advised to let matters rest where they are, and to return to this far more attractive role with regard to religious liberty.

---

46 Emory L J 1 (1997); and Ira C. Lupu, *The Lingering Death of Separationism*, 62 Geo Wash L Rev 230 (1994).

EUGENE VOLOKH

FREEDOM OF SPEECH, SHIELDING CHILDREN, AND TRANSCENDING BALANCING

The government has a strong interest in shielding children from unsuitable—because sexually explicit or (perhaps) profane—speech. So says the Court, and so say even many who generally frown on the regulation of sexually explicit material.[1] At the same time, the Court has held, much speech of this sort is constitutionally valuable. How can these strong competing claims, the government interest and the constitutional right, be reconciled?

The Court's official answer is strict scrutiny: Speech to adults may be restricted to serve the compelling interest in shielding children, but only if the restriction is the least restrictive means of

Eugene Volokh is Acting Professor of Law, UCLA Law School.

AUTHOR'S NOTE: I would like to thank Tom Bell, Craig Bloom, Evan Caminker, Michael Kent Curtis, Stephen Gardbaum, Robert Goldstein, Jerry Kang, Kenneth Karst, Marty Lederman, Larry Lessig, Mark Lemley, Jonathan Mallamud, Declan McCullagh, David Post, David Sklansky, Geoffrey Stone, and William Van Alstyne for their helpful comments; the John M. Olin Foundation for their extremely generous research support; and, of course, my mother, Anne, and my father, Vladimir, who first taught me about computers.

[1] See, for example, *Sable Communications v FCC*, 492 US 115 (1989); *Reno v ACLU*, 117 S Ct 2329 (1997); *Ginsberg v New York*, 390 US 629, 649–50 (1968) (Stewart concurring) (distinguishing children's rights to access speech from adults' rights); *Paris Adult Theatre I v Slaton*, 413 US 49, 113 (1973) (Brennan dissenting, joined by Stewart and Marshall) (arguing that obscenity is constitutionally protected "at least in the absence of distribution to juveniles"); *Pope v Illinois*, 481 US 497, 513, 517 (1987) (Stevens dissenting, joined by Brennan and Marshall) ("government may not constitutionally criminalize mere possession or sale of obscene literature, absent some connection to minors"); *Sable Communications v FCC*, 492 US 115, 134 (1989) (Brennan dissenting in part, joined by Marshall and Stevens) ("To be sure, the Government has a strong interest in protecting children against exposure to pornographic material that might be harmful to them."). But see *Ginsberg*, 390 US at 650 (Douglas, joined by Black, dissenting) (arguing against any such restrictions).

doing so.[2] In *Reno v ACLU*,[3] the Court applied this framework to strike down the Communications Decency Act, a statute which pretty much banned not-for-pay online distribution of material containing "patently offensive" speech about "sexual or excretory activities." The decision was widely considered a great victory for free speech,[4] and I agree that it reached the right result.

Nonetheless, I believe that the logic of the *ACLU* opinion is deeply flawed, and that the flaws in the opinion reveal serious problems with the strict scrutiny framework. The opinion, I will argue, rests on a factually incorrect assertion. It fails to confront the critical normative judgment about the real sacrifice that free speech demands. The strict scrutiny framework that *ACLU* applies ultimately underprotects speech. And by following this framework, the opinion misses an opportunity to synthesize the cases into a different framework that's more accurate and more useful.

Below, I briefly describe the *ACLU* case (Part I), explain my criticism of the opinion (Parts II and III), present several alternative approaches to dealing with the problem (Part IV), and suggest how both the criticism and the alternatives might be generalized to other areas of free speech law (Part V).

I. Reno v ACLU

A. THE COMMUNICATIONS DECENCY ACT

In 1996, Congress passed the Communications Decency Act (CDA). Its most controversial provision—the only one I will focus on here—provided that

> (d) Whoever
> (1) in interstate or foreign communications knowingly . . .
> (B) uses any interactive computer service to display in a manner available to a person under 18 years of age, any comment, request, suggestion, proposal, image, or other communication

---

[2] See cases cited in Part III.A.

[3] 117 S Ct 2329 (1997).

[4] For example: "Senator Patrick J. Leahy . . . who was an opponent of the legislation, said, '. . . This is a victory for the First Amendment.' " *Supreme Court Strikes Down Communications Decency Act*, Facts on File World News Digest 473 A1 (July 3, 1997). "Free speech scored an important victory last week, when the U.S. Supreme Court ruled that freedom of expression applies to the Internet." Editorial, Denver Post E4 (July 6, 1997). See also Michael Loftin, *Victory for the First Amendment*, Chattanooga Times A8 (July 14, 1997).

that, in context, depicts or describes, in terms patently offensive
as measured by contemporary community standards, sexual or
excretory activities or organs . . .

shall be fined under Title 18, or imprisoned not more than
two years, or both.[5]

Most places on the Internet are generally open to everyone,
child or adult; there's no way to check readers' ages, short of the
expensive (and imperfect) proxy of demanding and verifying their
credit card numbers. Therefore, the CDA would have essentially
banned material that "depicts or describes, in terms patently offensive as measured by contemporary community standards, sexual or
excretory activities or organs"—which I will call "indecent" material for short[6]—from all parts of the Internet except those that
charge people for access using credit cards.[7] Because most of the
Internet is now available for free, and because this free access is

---

[5] Pub L No 104-104, 110 Stat 56 (1996), codified at 47 USC § 223(d). Two other provisions barred communicating indecency "knowing that the recipient of the communication
is under 18 years of age" and communicating indecency "to a specific person or persons
under 18 years of age." 47 USC §§ 223(a)(1)(B), (d)(1)(A). If these provisions were interpreted narrowly, to cover only speech to a particular person whom the speaker knows to
be a minor, they might well be constitutional, at least as applied to indecent speech that
is also "harmful-to-minors"; Justice O'Connor so argued in her dissent. *ACLU*, 117 S Ct
at 2354–55 (claiming that this was the best reading, and that even if the ban on indecent
speech was overbroad in including more than just "harmful-to-minors" speech, it was not
substantially overbroad); see Part IV.B.2.a.i (discussing distinction between "harmful-to-
minors" and "indecent"). The majority struck down the provisions because it thought they
could not be so narrowly read. Id at 2348–50.

[6] See *ACLU*, 117 S Ct at 2345 ("assum[ing] arguendo" that "indecent" was synonymous
with "patently offensive [depiction or description] of sexual or excretory activities or organs"); *FCC v Pacifica Foundation*, 438 US 726, 740–41 (1978) (accepting a similar FCC
definition of "indecent").

[7] Free sites can't practically use credit card numbers for verification because the verification costs money, apparently about $1 per transaction. *ACLU v Reno*, 929 F Supp 824, 846
finding of fact no. 99 (ED Pa 1996).

If there were a way in which a cyberspace speaker could, for free, check a would-be
listener's age—perhaps by checking some reliable "cyber ID" that the listener could cheaply
procure for himself—the matter might be different; a requirement that cyberspace speakers
check such IDs would still allow them to provide their speech without charge to adults.
The Court did not believe, however, that such a scheme was possible today, 117 S Ct at
2349–50, and from my knowledge of computer software, I'm not sure how it would be
possible any time in the foreseeable future.

The main proposal that I've heard—that adults pay a dollar or two for an "adult ID"
that they can later use, with no charge, to access any adult Web site—just won't work.
Even if speakers could check the listener's ID at no cost, the very absence of a charge means
that "free speech activists" could buy adult IDs and then widely post them, encouraging any
interested minors to use them. The only way to effectively deter such ID sharing is by
making sure that the ID owner gets charged every time the ID is used, the very thing that
adult IDs supposedly avoid.

widely considered one of the Internet's great strengths, this naturally struck many as a very broad restraint.

Moreover, as Justice Stevens's majority opinion[8] pointed out, the restraint was made broader by its vagueness. "Could a speaker confidently assume," the opinion asked, "that a serious discussion about birth control practices, homosexuality, the First Amendment issues raised by the Appendix to [*FCC v Pacifica Foundation*, the 'Seven Dirty Words' case], or the consequences of prison rape would not violate the CDA?" Justice Stevens was correct in thinking that the answer to this is "no"; while one might hope that prosecutors and juries wouldn't read the law this broadly, the text gives no such assurance. The statutory definition was potentially broad enough to cover such speech, with no safe harbor for speech that has substantial value, or for speech that doesn't appeal to prurient interests.

Thus, the Court faced a speech restriction that would have at least deterred, and quite possibly punished, a considerable amount of generally presumptively protected speech. At the same time, the restriction was said to be justified by a government interest to which the Court had paid considerable respect—the interest in shielding children from offensive material. Either the right or the interest had to at least partly yield.

B. THE COURT'S CHOICE OF LEVEL OF SCRUTINY

The Court could have avoided the full force of this conflict by fitting the CDA into one of the boxes where speech restrictions are more freely permitted than in other areas.

Low-value speech: If the CDA could have been seen as limited to "low-value" speech, the Court could have let the government prevail while theoretically imposing little sacrifice of free speech, because the burdened speech would be (by hypothesis) not very valuable. This wouldn't have entirely eliminated the free speech sacrifice—low value does not equal no value—but it would have made it seem less momentous.

But though Justice Stevens had in the past been the Court's

---

[8] Justice Stevens wrote for seven Justices; Justice O'Connor, joined by Chief Justice Rehnquist, concurred in the judgment on this point, and dissented on the question discussed in note 5.

leading proponent of this approach,[9] his opinion didn't even mention it. This might have been because the CDA covered much material that would be hard to call low value,[10] or because many of the other Justices are uncomfortable with the idea of treating "indecent" speech as low value.[11] In either event, the Court declined to take this escape route.

Secondary effects: The government urged the Court to treat the CDA as an essentially content-neutral law, justified not by the content of "indecent" speech, but by its supposed "secondary effects."[12] The Court correctly rejected this argument. Whatever the possible merits of the "secondary effects" doctrine in other contexts, the danger that speech will corrupt its listeners is a classic primary effect. "Listeners' reaction to speech is not a content-neutral basis for regulation";[13] a law "justified by the [government's] desire to prevent the psychological damage it felt was associated with viewing [indecency] [must be analyzed] as a content-based statute."[14]

The broadcasting analogy: The Court could also have concluded that online speech is entitled to the lesser constitutional protection afforded broadcast radio and television. For three decades, the Court has formally treated restrictions on broadcasting quite differently from similar restrictions on speech in other media.[15] The

---

[9] See *FCC v Pacifica Foundation*, 438 US 726 (1978) (Stevens plurality); *Young v American Mini Theatres, Inc.*, 427 US 50 (1976) (Stevens plurality).

[10] See 117 S Ct at 2344. But see *Pacifica*, 438 US at 745–46 (Stevens plurality) (suggesting that "patently offensive words dealing with sex and excretion" are of "slight social value").

[11] Compare *R.A.V. v City of St. Paul*, 505 US 377, 390 n 6 (1992) (stressing that the two opinions that most clearly urged different treatment for "low-value" speech—Justice Stevens's plurality opinions in *Young* and *Pacifica*—"did not command a majority of the Court").

[12] *City of Renton v Playtime Theatres, Inc.*, 475 US 41 (1986).

[13] *Forsyth County v Nationalist Movement*, 505 US 123, 134 (1992); see also *R.A.V. v City of St. Paul*, 505 US 377, 394 (1992); *Boos v Barry*, 485 US 312, 321 (plurality), 334 (concurrence) (1988); *ACLU*, 117 S Ct at 2342 ("the purpose of the CDA is to protect children from the primary effects of 'indecent' and 'patently offensive' speech, rather than any 'secondary' effect of such speech").

[14] *Boos v Barry*, 485 US 312, 321 (1988) (plurality).

[15] Thus, the interest in providing the public with a balanced presentation of the issues has been held to trump the free speech rights of broadcasters but not of newspaper publishers. Compare *Red Lion Broadcasting Co. v FCC*, 395 US 367 (1969) (broadcast radio and television) with *Miami Herald Pub. Co. v Tornillo*, 418 US 241 (1974) (newspapers). The interest in shielding people from unwanted exposure to profanity has been held to trump the free speech rights of broadcasters but not of people on the street. Compare *FCC v Pacifica Foundation*, 438 US 726 (1978) with *Cohen v California*, 403 US 15 (1971). See *FCC*

ACLU Court, though, refused to extend the broadcast test to the Internet. The Internet, the Court held, shares none of the "special justifications for regulation" that led to diminished protection for broadcast speakers: There is no "history of extensive government regulation of the . . . medium," no "scarcity of available frequencies at [the medium's] inception," and no specially " 'invasive' nature" to the medium that would make it easy for people to encounter offensive material by accident.[16] This holding was important but not surprising, because the broadcasting cases have generally had rather little gravitational force; in *Turner Broadcasting v FCC* (1994),[17] for example, the Court refused to extend them even to cable television.[18]

C. RECONCILING THE INTEREST AND THE RIGHT

Thus, the Court acknowledged that the CDA imposed a heavy burden on free speech: It restricted a great deal of presumptively fully protected speech based on its content, and did so in a fully protected medium.[19] But this cannot be the end of the inquiry, because orthodox free speech doctrine holds that even such a heavy burden may sometimes be imposed in the pursuit of a "compelling

---

v League of Women Voters, 468 US 364 (1984) (formally acknowledging that the broadcasting test is different from the test used for other media).

[16] 117 S Ct at 2343.

[17] 114 S Ct at 2445 (1994).

[18] A four-Justice plurality in *Denver Area Educ. Telecom. Consortium v FCC*, 116 S Ct 2374 (1996), did speak favorably of the broadcast indecency rules in the cable context; and the references in some *Denver Area* opinions to the supposed "novelty" of cable television and the concomitant need to take small steps seemed to foreshadow a similarly cautious decision about the Internet. See id at 2402 (Souter concurring) ("And as broadcast, cable, and the cyber-technology of the Internet and the World Wide Web approach the day of using a common receiver, we can hardly assume that standards for judging the regulation of one of them will not have immense, but now unknown and unknowable, effects on the others. . . . In my own ignorance I have to accept the real possibility that 'if we had to decide today . . . just what the First Amendment should mean in cyberspace, . . . we would get it fundamentally wrong,' " quoting Larry Lessig, *The Path of Cyberlaw*, 104 Yale L J 1743, 1745 (1995)); id at 2398 (Stevens concurring) ("it would be unwise to take a categorical approach to the resolution of novel First Amendment questions arising in an industry as dynamic as this"). Still, even if the *Denver Area* Court was in a cautious mood about new technologies, this mood had seemingly dissipated by the time of *ACLU*.

[19] As a general matter, the "free speech price"—the burden on constitutional rights imposed by a restriction—turns not only on the constitutional value of the restricted speech, but also on any collateral costs, such as the danger that the proposed restriction will be administered unfairly, *Grayned v City of Rockford*, 408 US 104 (1972), or that the restriction will skew public debate. For purposes of this discussion, though, I will focus primarily on the constitutional value of the lost speech.

governmental interest." Given the choice between sacrificing free speech and sacrificing the compelling interest, sometimes free speech will have to yield.[20]

One possible solution, of course, would be to say that shielding children from "patently offensive" descriptions of sex and excretion is not a compelling interest. Maybe such materials are somewhat harmful to children's upbringing; maybe children have no constitutional right to receive such material, and adults have no right to communicate it to them; but, the argument would go, the harm is not great enough to justify restraints on communication among adults. Better to sacrifice the shielding of children than to restrict speech.[21]

The Court, however, has not taken this view. In *Sable Communications v FCC*, the Court noted that "there is a compelling interest in protecting the physical and psychological well-being of minors . . . [by] . . . shielding minors from the influence of literature that is not obscene by adult standards,"[22] and *ACLU* did not contradict this.[23] One might still argue, of course, that this interest extends

---

[20] See, for example, *Burson v Freeman*, 504 US 191, 198 (1992) (plurality); *Austin v Michigan Chamber of Commerce*, 494 US 652, 655 (1990); *Boos v Barry*, 485 US 312, 334 (1988) (plurality); *Board of Airport Comm'rs v Jews for Jesus, Inc.*, 482 US 569, 573 (1987); *Cornelius v NAACP Legal Defense and Educ. Fund, Inc.*, 473 US 788, 800 (1985); *United States v Grace*, 461 US 171, 177 (1983); *Perry Educ. Ass'n v Perry Local Educators' Ass'n*, 460 US 37, 45 (1983).

Some readers have suggested that these cases do not truly represent the law, and that the Court's approach to content-based restrictions comes closer to an absolute ban, with a few narrow exceptions. I agree that the Court *should* follow that sort of more categorical approach, and that the Court in practice does sometimes seem to do so, paying only lip service to strict scrutiny. See Eugene Volokh, *Freedom of Speech, Permissible Tailoring and Transcending Strict Scrutiny*, 144 U Penn L Rev 2417 (1996). In fact, my goal in this article is to suggest that the Court should depart from strict scrutiny in cases such as *ACLU*. Nonetheless, the Court has repeatedly asserted that strict scrutiny is the official rule, and the *ACLU* opinion certainly speaks the language of strict scrutiny.

[21] Compare *Ginsberg v New York*, 390 US 629, 652–55 (1968) (Douglas dissenting) (denying the government's right to ban even knowing distribution of sexually explicit material to specific minors).

[22] *Sable*, 492 US at 126. Some have suggested that this statement may be dictum; I don't think it is, but even if it is, it's well-considered and forceful dictum, dictum that the Court seems to contemplate lower courts will follow, and that the lower courts have indeed followed. See *Dial Information Services Corp. v Thornburgh*, 938 F2d 1535 (2d Cir 1991); *Information Providers' Coalition v FCC*, 928 F2d 866 (9th Cir 1991).

[23] The opinion stresses that the Court has "repeatedly recognized the governmental interest in protecting children from harmful materials," and calls this an "important purpose." 117 S Ct at 2346. A footnote says that the law's challengers "do not dispute that the Government generally has a compelling interest in protecting minors from 'indecent' and 'patently offensive' speech," id at 2340 n 30; another part of the opinion says that the *Sable* Court "agreed that 'there is a compelling interest in protecting the physical and psychologi-

not to all patently offensive descriptions of sex and excretion, but only to extremely explicit ones, or only to those that appeal to prurient interests, or to some other narrow category; but *ACLU* did not rest on such an argument.[24]

So in some situations free speech to adults may be restricted in order to shield minors. But, the Court said, not here. Why?

D. APPLYING STRICT SCRUTINY

The CDA is invalid, the Court said, because it is possible to protect speech in this context without *any* sacrifice of shielding of children. The CDA is simply insufficiently "carefully drafted," simply lacks "precision."[25] The conflict that might require hard trade-offs between a precious constitutional right and a compelling government interest was, the Court said, in fact absent.

The Court explained that the burden on free speech "is unacceptable if less restrictive alternatives would be *at least as effective* in achieving the legitimate purpose that the statute was enacted to serve." Though the Court has "repeatedly recognized the governmental interest in protecting children from harmful materials," that interest "does not justify an *unnecessarily broad* suppression of speech addressed to adults." Congress must "desig[n] its statute to accomplish its purpose 'without imposing an *unnecessarily great* restriction on speech.'" The government bears a "heavy burden to explain why a less restrictive provision *would not be as effective* as the CDA." And given the "possible alternatives, such as requiring that indecent material be 'tagged' in a way that facilitates parental control of material coming into their homes, making exceptions for messages with artistic or educational value, providing some tolerance for parental choice, and regulating some portions of the Internet—such as commercial Web sites—differently than others, such as chat rooms," the government hasn't discharged this burden.[26]

---

cal well-being of minors' which extended to shielding them from indecent messages that are not obscene by adult standards," id at 2343.

[24] For a more detailed discussion of the uncertainty about exactly what speech the compelling interest covers, see Part IV.B.2.a.i.

[25] 117 S Ct at 2346.

[26] All quotes in this paragraph are from *Reno*, 117 S Ct at 2348 (emphasis added).

If the four phrases I italicized in the previous paragraph are correct, then Congress might have been able to have its cake and eat it too: It could have restricted speech *less* without sacrificing any shielding of children. The alternatives the Court identifies would be "at least as effective," and thus make the broader restraint imposed by the CDA "*un*necessarily broad" and not "*carefully* drafted." (If they would not have been as effective, then the CDA would have been a "[ ]necessarily broad suppression" and a "[ ]necessarily great restriction," because it would have been necessary in order for Congress to fully accomplish its purpose.[27])

Tastes great *and* less filling! If the Court is right, then there really was no excuse at all for the CDA being passed. If the Court is right.

II. The Court's Error

A. NO EQUALLY EFFECTIVE ALTERNATIVES

But the Court is wrong. None of the Court's proposed alternatives to the CDA—or any other alternatives I can imagine—would have been as effective as the CDA's more or less total ban.

1. Compulsory Tagging

Consider the Court's first proposed alternative—"requiring that indecent material be 'tagged' in a way that facilitates parental control of material coming into their homes." This is actually a pretty good alternative: Under it, parents who use special "filter" software can make their computers block access to any material that's tagged as indecent.[28] And it could be made better still if parents didn't have to spend time or money finding and buying the best filters, for instance, if the government made the software available for free, and service providers such as America Online had an op-

---

[27] Even if one reads "unnecessarily" more loosely, the other two quotes remain: The Court is suggesting that the test is whether there are alternatives that would be at least as effective.

[28] Of course, even this shielding will be ineffective if Internet speakers fail to properly rate their materials; but this risk of noncompliance would have been no less present with the CDA than with the self-rating scheme.

tion that easily turned it on.[29] Some parents still wouldn't use it, but perhaps one might say that they've chosen to let their children have unlimited access, so the government interest in shielding their children would then become less than compelling. (This latter view is controversial, but let's assume it for now.)

But even with this, compulsory tagging isn't "at least as effective" as the CDA in serving the CDA's "important purpose of protecting children from exposure to sexually explicit material." Filters work only on those computers on which they are installed and activated, and parents have little control over the computers used by their children's friends.

True, unusually conscientious parents may ask their children's friends' parents whether they have shielding software installed. But even conscientious parents often don't know every home that their teenagers might visit; and even for younger kids, what can one do when the other parent says, "Shielding software? Yeah, I think I have that option on, maybe"? Should one come over to check? What if the other parent says, "Yes, I definitely have the shielding software turned on," but turns out to be wrong? What if, unbeknownst to the other parent, his child has found some instructions for disarming the filter software, put on the World Wide Web by a helpful "anti-censorship" activist?[30]

And so long as even a significant minority of homes in a particular social circle don't use shielding software—whether intentionally or carelessly—most kids in the circle will be able to get access

---

[29] If need be, the government might mandate that service providers make such filtering easily available, though the market would probably do the same without government intervention.

[30] See *http://www.glr.com/nurse.html*, a Web page that purports to give this sort of information for various kinds of shielding software; see also Declan McCullagh, *The CyberSitter Diaper Change*, Netly News (Dec 20, 1996) (my thanks to Declan for pointing the *www.glr.com* Web page out to me). Putting such instructions online is not currently illegal; it is probably even constitutionally protected speech. See *Brandenburg v Ohio*, 395 US 444 (1969). Even if it is not constitutionally protected, it seems hard to stop, given the ease of anonymous communication online, and the possibility of people posting the instructions from foreign countries.

I don't know whether these instructions are still effective; I imagine that software manufacturers would try to change their software to prevent these disabling techniques from working. Nonetheless, my 12 years as a computer programmer lead me to believe that there will always be some way for a user to disable software that's installed on a computer that is under his control. Shielding software that's installed on a service provider's computer (e.g., shielding that's done through America Online) is harder to disable, but easier to avoid: One need only sign on to the service through the account of a friend whose parents have not turned on the shielding option.

to indecent material. They'll be able fairly quickly to find out who has the unshielded computer, and then come over to see what they want to see.[31] With online materials (unlike, say, with dial-a-porn), the kids don't even have to come over; a child who uses an un-shielded computer can pull down the material, remove the tag, and forward it to others.[32]

Congress might try to fight even this by (1) requiring tagging, (2) making it illegal for people—including children—to forward material with removed tags, and (3) making it illegal for people to let their unshielded computers be accessed by others' children. In theory, this might outlaw as much exposure of children to indecent material as the CDA would have.

But in practice, trying to deter Web site operators is much more effective than trying to deter kids from forwarding material to other kids, or trying to make parents police who is using their kids' unshielded computers.[33] Children are much less likely to know the law or to follow it, especially since the chances of a 12-year-old being prosecuted for e-mailing an indecent picture to another 12-year-old seem quite slim. And holding insufficiently watchful parents liable for access by their children's friends seems hardly fair or effective.[34]

---

[31] The interest in shielding children isn't just an interest in shielding them from uninten-tional exposure; it has always been understood as an interest in shielding children even from their own intentional attempts to get harmful material. See *Ginsberg v New York*, 390 US 629 (1968); *ACLU*, 117 S Ct at 2348 (listing proposed alternatives that aim to shield children against their own will).

[32] As I point out in Eugene Volokh, *Freedom of Speech in Cyberspace from the Listener's Perspective*, 1996 U Chi Legal F 377, 434, tagging might have a countervailing strength: People may be more willing to comply with a tagging requirement than with a general prohibition, because the personal cost of compliance to them is lower. Someone may be unwilling to refrain from indecent speech altogether (especially if he can't be punished because he's posting from abroad or is reliably anonymous), but might be happy to tag his speech so long as this still lets him communicate to adults. If this conjecture is correct, then maybe in the aggregate tagging would indeed be at least as effective as a ban. But this is quite speculative; the greater compliance with a tagging requirement may easily be outweighed by the ease with which minors can find and use unshielded computers. (Since writing the *Legal Forum* article in late 1995, I have come to believe that this ease of avoiding the filters will indeed be a very big factor.) In any event, the Court, the lower courts, and the briefs never even mentioned this argument.

[33] One could imagine the government doing both—going after both the Web site opera-tors and the private users, for instance, to keep kids from passing along materials they got from Web sites that are overseas and thus outside the CDA's reach. But even if the govern-ment prosecutes private users, a combined restraint on both operators and private users would be much more effective than going after private users alone.

[34] One reader suggested that the Court might be conceptualizing the interest not as shielding children from all indecency, but rather as returning the world to the way it was

Compulsory tagging would thus provide considerably less shielding than the CDA would. It may be fairly effective; it may be as effective as you can get without very greatly burdening speech; but it's not "at least as effective" as the CDA.[35]

2. Other Suggested Alternatives

What about the second alternative, "making exceptions for messages with artistic or educational value"? Well, *if* the government's

pre-cyberspace: a place where determined minors can find indecency, but where the task is hard enough that many minors will be dissuaded from it, or will at least realize that what they're doing is bad enough that adults have tried hard to stop it. But whether or not the Court was thinking this way, the opinion contains not a hint of this approach. Moreover, the compulsory tagging alternative would *not* return the world to its pre-cyberspace mode: As I discuss in the text, even with a tagging requirement, minors can access online indecency much more easily than they can access, say, dial-a-porn or print indecency, because online materials (unlike phone conversations or magazines) can easily be forwarded by one child to many others.

[35] The CDA's opponents also argued that "[b]ecause so much sexually explicit content originates overseas, . . . the CDA cannot be 'effective.' " See 117 S Ct at 2347 n 45 (citing Appellee American Library Ass'n et al. Brief, 1997 WL 74380 at *33–34); *ACLU v Reno*, 929 F Supp 824, 882 (ED Pa 1996) (separate opinion of Dalzell) (accepting this approach). The Court declined to reach this argument, and I believe the argument is unsound.

Few speech restrictions can eliminate all the harm at which they're aimed—consider, for instance, copyright law, libel law, and campaign contribution restrictions, all of which are in some measure underenforced and in some measure circumventable. But the Court has never held that "narrow tailoring" requires that the law entirely accomplish the interest it's trying to serve. The Court's cases that have upheld speech restrictions under strict scrutiny—*Burson v Freeman*, 504 US 191 (1992) (plurality), *Austin v Michigan Chamber of Commerce*, 494 US 562 (1990), and *Buckley v Valeo*, 424 US 1 (1976)—seem to suggest that it's enough that the law advance the interest to some degree, a sensible requirement. See Volokh, *Freedom of Speech, Permissible Tailoring and Transcending Strict Scrutiny*, 144 U Pa L Rev 2417, 2429 n 56 (cited in note 35) (discussing this point).

The CDA did indeed seem likely to reduce the amount of indecent material available to children. It would have deterred U.S. residents, and perhaps even foreign corporations that have American affiliates, from posting indecent material either on U.S. sites or foreign sites (merely putting the material off-shore wouldn't immunize someone who is subject to U.S. jurisdiction from CDA liability). See Daniel E. Troy and David J. Goldstone, *Foreign Entities Whose Web Sites Violate U.S. Laws Relating to Drug Advertising, Securities Offerings or Obscenity May Subject American Affiliates to Prosecution*, Nat'l L J (Nov 18, 1996), at B9. To avoid the CDA, an American would have to actually move overseas (and perhaps even sell all his U.S. property), something few people are willing to do.

Of course, where there's money to be made, foreign content providers might take up some of the slack caused by the decrease in U.S.-based supply. But precisely because this effect would be money driven, it would largely apply to for-sale material, which generally requires credit card payment and is thus less accessible to minors. (Some sellers of indecent material do put up free teasers, but in my limited experience these have tended to be—for obvious marketing reasons—rather tamer than the for-sale matter.) And the CDA might in the long term help reduce even entirely foreign indecency; implementing the CDA in the United States might make it easier for the U.S. government to lobby other countries to follow suit. See U.S. Reply Brief in *ACLU v Reno*, 1997 WL 106544, *16 ("Such a law sets an example for other countries and puts the United States in a position to urge them to establish effective controls.").

The reduction of the total amount of indecent material should reduce the amount of

interest in "protecting children from exposure to sexually explicit material" is sufficiently strong only when the material is artistically and educationally valueless, then this alternative would be as effective as the CDA at serving this limited interest. But the Court nowhere says that this is the relevant government interest, and nowhere explains why this would be so. Rather, the Court acknowledges the government interest in "protecting children from exposure to sexually explicit material" (or even "indecent material") with no qualifiers.[36] Maybe a CDA with an artistic/educational value exemption would not be dramatically less effective at serving this broader interest; but it certainly wouldn't be "at least as effective" as the CDA itself.

How about "providing some tolerance for parental choice"? Well, this sounds fine, but how exactly could this "tolerance" be implemented? If the Court is saying only that Congress must provide an exception for parents sending material directly to their children—and if the government interest is limited to protecting children from indecent material when their parents think the material is harmful—then that would indeed be a less restrictive and equally effective alternative. But if that's all the Court is saying, then the decision has been almost entirely for nought; Congress could tomorrow reenact a ban that's as broad as the CDA, and one that interferes as much with people's communications to consenting adults, subject to this one small exception. Surely that can't be all the Court is saying: Among other things, if it were, the statute couldn't be facially invalidated as *substantially* overbroad.[37]

More likely, the Court might be suggesting that Congress "pro-

---

material that's easily accessible to minors. Of course, determined and Net-skilled minors could still scour the Net search engines looking for all the indecency that's available without a credit card; it's hard to protect the highly motivated and intelligent from their own appetites. But less committed or knowledgeable minors might give up when their first few searches didn't find any free matter, or might end up seeing only a little indecent material rather than a lot. And by reducing the number of new free Web sites containing indecency, the CDA would help filter manufacturers keep up with newly created Web sites (see Part III.B.3), thus making the CDA-plus-filters a considerably better shield than filters alone.

This doesn't mean that the CDA would have been a perfect or even a terribly powerful tool for shielding children; wise parents would have had to rely on both the CDA and shielding software, and even that would have been imperfect. But the CDA, despite its imperfections, would have served the government interest to a considerable degree.

[36] See Part IV.B.2.a.i for a more thorough discussion of whether the interest extends only to sexually explicit "obscene-as-to-minors" material or to indecent materially more generally.

[37] See *New York v Ferber*, 458 US 747 (1982).

vide some tolerance for parental choice" by giving parents some means by which their children can freely surf the Web with no continuous intervention by parents—that parents should have some option by which they can free their children of the Act's burden. This assumes that the government has no sufficient interest in shielding children whose parents don't want the shielding, itself a contested proposition.[38] But even if the interest is so limited, no such option could be as effective as the Act in shielding the children whose parents *do* want the shielding. Any "electronic note from my mother" system is just too easy to evade.

Finally, "regulating some portions of the Internet—such as commercial Web sites—differently than others, such as chat rooms" would likewise be less effective than the CDA at shielding children. Wherever the regulations are less restrictive, they'll also be less effective. Again, they might be fairly effective, reasonably effective, not ineffective. But they won't be "at least as effective."

3. Fact Findings Below

Perhaps the Court's error would have been understandable if the Court had been led into it by erroneous fact findings at trial. But the district court never evaluated the supposed effectiveness of the Court's proposed alternatives.

The chief alternative dealt with at trial was filtering software: programs that, when run on a personal computer, block access from that computer to a list of "dirty" Internet locations. The list is maintained and frequently updated by the software manufacturers; the software can also block access to a range of locations (e.g., all Web pages at *http://www.playboy.com/*) or to materials that contain certain forbidden words. These filter programs could be modified to accommodate a mandatory tagging scheme, but the trial court findings focused only on filters as such, not on filters plus tagging.[39]

---

[38] See Part IV.2.a.ii.

[39] The trial court's opinion and the Supreme Court briefs did discuss "tagging," but in the context of a very different sort of tagging provision. The CDA provided a defense for content providers who used "reasonably effective" means of preventing minors from accessing their material; at trial, the government suggested that a provider's decision to tag its material might allow it to fit within that defense. The district court correctly rejected this contention: Tagging, standing alone, is not a reasonably effective way of preventing minors from accessing the page, because so many minors use computers that don't run filtering

And the three-judge district court was careful not to overstate the effectiveness of those alternatives that it considered. The court never found that any alternative would be "at least as effective" as the CDA; it found only that "a reasonably effective method . . . will soon be widely available"[40]—surely the word "reasonably" ought to be a clue that the alternative might not be "equally effective." None of the three separate opinions suggested that there were any equally effective alternatives. The three-judge district court in *Shea v Reno*, another case that struck down the CDA, and that was pending before the Court when *ACLU* was decided, likewise never said there were any equally effective alternatives.[41] Rather, *Shea* avoided reaching this question by holding that "[e]ven if . . . nothing short of a total ban on indecent communication could be as effective," the law would still be unconstitutional.[42]

The briefs before the Supreme Court likewise didn't focus on compulsory tagging as an alternative, probably because the party that had the most to gain from raising the matter—the ACLU—didn't want to be seen as endorsing compulsory tagging, which is itself a speech restriction (albeit one milder than the CDA).[43] Still, the government's opening brief did generally argue that "There Are No Alternatives That Would Be Equally Effective in Advancing the Government's Interests."[44] The government's reply brief likewise claimed that shielding software was "not effective," and that while it "could provide part of the answer to the problem of indecency of the Internet, it could not provide the full answer. The district court did not conclude otherwise."[45]

Three of the four amicus briefs filed on the government's side explicitly pointed out that filters alone would not be "as effective"

---

software. The district court never decided whether the different sort of tagging proposed by the Court—a compulsory tagging requirement—would be as effective as the CDA.

[40] *ACLU v Reno*, 929 F Supp 824, 842 finding of fact no. 73 (ED Pa 1996).

[41] *Shea v Reno*, 930 F Supp 916 (SDNY 1996).

[42] Id at 941.

[43] See, for example, Bill Pietrucha, *ACLU Wary of White House Censorship Goals*, Newsbytes (July 17, 1997), describing ACLU's hostility to even a noncompulsory universal self-rating system.

[44] U.S. Brief, 1997 WL 32931, *40; see also id at *23.

[45] U.S. Reply Brief, 1997 WL 106544, *13. See also Amicus Brief of Family Life Project, 1997 WL 22917, *19.

as filters plus the CDA because "children have access to many computers which will not employ software filtering devices such as in . . . neighbors' homes."[46] Even the ACLU's own brief said that the inquiry into whether "there are no 'equally effective' alternatives . . . misstates the relevant legal test. It is always true that only an 'absolute ban' on adult speech 'can offer certain protection against assault by a determined child.' "[47] Wherever the Court got the erroneous notion that the alternatives would be equally effective, it wasn't from the findings below or from any concessions by the government.

B. THE PROBLEMS CAUSED BY THE ERROR

The Court's error is more than just a harmless misstatement. To begin with, it's unfair to Congress. A Congress that restricts speech even though there are equally effective but less restrictive alternatives available—that implements a genuinely "unnecessary" restriction—is either incompetent or flagrantly unconcerned with the First Amendment: It's depriving us of free speech without getting us any benefit in return. In the Court's words, "[t]he CDA's burden on protected speech cannot be justified if it could be avoided by a more carefully drafted statute."[48] When the Court then says that the burden is indeed unjustified, it must be because Congress was the opposite of "careful"—either careless or uncaring.

In reality, Congress wasn't acting that badly. It did sacrifice some free speech, but this sacrifice was necessary to shield children as well as possible. Such a trade-off may be unconstitutional, and the Court's trade-off—sacrificing some shielding of children in order to more thoroughly protect free speech—may be better. But this assertion is much less damning than a claim that Congress actually bought nothing with the trade-off it made.

---

[46] Amicus Brief of Members of Congress (Coats et al), 1997 WL 22918, *22–23; see also Amicus Brief of Morality in Media, 1997 WL 22908, *25 ("Technology on home computers does not protect children or teens when they access computers elsewhere, for example, at a friend or relative's home"); Amicus Brief of Enough is Enough et al, 1997 WL 22958, *20 ("Children can reach the Internet in the homes of their friends and neighbors, where computers may have no filters installed.").

[47] ACLU Brief, 1997 WL 74378, *36. But see American Library Ass'n Brief, 1997 WL 74380, *34–35 (arguing that filtering was indeed at least as effective as the CDA).

[48] 117 S Ct at 2346.

Furthermore, as Part III.B.3 discusses in more detail, the Court's error makes *ACLU* a much less useful benchmark for future cases. The Court's First Amendment doctrine is "given meaning through the evolutionary process of common law adjudication,"[49] in which the facts of a case can be compared and contrasted with the facts of earlier ones. If the facts in the original case are incorrectly stated or analyzed, then the case will be of extremely limited precedential value.

But most importantly, the Court's stress on equal effectiveness risks dramatically *under*protecting speech in future cases. The pregnant negative in the Court's reasoning is that, had there really been no equally effective alternatives (as in fact there are not), the CDA should have been upheld.

Other cases have in fact stated this pregnant negative as a positive: Speech restrictions, these cases say, are valid if they are "necessary to serve a compelling state interest,"[50] and alternatives that "fall short of serving [the] compelling interest[ ]"[51] aren't enough to rebut the claim of necessity. After all, there are always alternatives that are less restrictive but ineffective, for instance, having no government action at all, or perhaps just having the government urge people to go along voluntarily. But only the equally effective alternatives show that the restriction is in fact unnecessary—not needed to accomplish the interest.[52] The Court has said

---

[49] *Bose Corp. v Consumers Union*, 466 US 485, 502 (1984); *Ornelas v United States*, 116 S Ct 1657, 1662 (1996) (same as to the Fourth Amendment); *Thompson v Keohane*, 116 S Ct 457, 466–67 (1995) (same as to *Miranda* cases).

[50] For example, *Burson v Freeman*, 504 US 191, 198 (1992) (plurality); *Simon & Schuster, Inc. v Members of the N.Y. State Crime Victims Board*, 502 US 105, 118 (1991); *Perry Education Ass'n v Perry Local Educators' Ass'n*, 460 US 37, 45 (1983). See *Board of Trustees v Fox*, 492 US 469, 476 (1989) ("If the word 'necessary' is interpreted strictly, [a requirement that restrictions may be no more expansive than 'necessary'] would translate into the 'least-restrictive-means' test").

[51] *Burson v Freeman*, 504 US 191, 206 (1992) (plurality); *Buckley v Valeo*, 424 US 1, 28 (1976) (disclosure of contributions is not an adequate means of preventing corruption or appearance of corruption because "Congress was surely entitled to conclude that disclosure was only a partial measure, and that contribution ceilings were a necessary legislative concomitant to deal with the reality or appearance of corruption").

[52] See, for example, *Information Providers' Coalition v FCC*, 928 F2d 866, 873 (9th Cir 1991) (concluding that a proposed alternative was inadequate because it "does not completely bar or totally impede" access by minors to indecency, and because it " 'would be insufficient to achieve realistically the goal of the statute: the protection of children' "); *Blount v SEC*, 61 F3d 938, 944 (DC Cir 1995) (speech restrictions are constitutional if they effectively advance a compelling interest, and are "narrowly tailored to advance the compelling interests asserted, i.e., . . . less restrictive alternatives to the rule would accomplish the government's goals equally or almost equally effectively").

similar things in other strict scrutiny contexts,[53] and lower court free speech decisions echo this view.[54]

As Part III will explain, these cases are somewhat ambiguous about just how effective the alternatives must be. One could read them as saying that a speech restriction is constitutional if there are no equally effective alternatives, or one could read them (and I think they are probably best read this way) as saying that the restriction is constitutional if there are no more or less equally effective alternatives.

But this ambiguity only makes *ACLU*'s emphasis on the alternatives being "at least *as* effective" particularly dangerous. A lower court, a legislator, or an executive official can easily read *ACLU*— coupled with the other cases—as choosing the "equally effective alternative" test: If none of the alternatives is "at least as effective" at serving the compelling interest, then the alternatives all "fall short of serving" the interest, the restriction is "necessary to serve" the interest, and therefore survives First Amendment scrutiny.

If this pregnant negative is accepted, then presumably Congress could just reenact the CDA whenever it gets enough evidence— which, for the reasons described above, should not be hard to do— that the alternatives would not be equally effective. Of course, in practice the Court may be unlikely to revisit the CDA's constitutionality simply in the face of more factual findings (though why

---

[53] *Maine v Taylor*, 477 US 131 (1986) (upholding state law that discriminated against interstate commerce under strict scrutiny because there was "no reason to believe that [a less restrictive alternative] would protect [the government interest] as effectively as a ban"); *American Party of Texas v White*, 415 US 767, 781 (1974) (upholding ballot access restriction under strict scrutiny because the law was a measure "taken in pursuit of vital state objectives that cannot be served equally well in significantly less burdensome ways"); see also *Hernandez v New York*, 500 US 352, 377 (1991) (Stevens dissenting) ("the State cannot make race-based distinctions if there are equally effective nondiscriminatory alternatives"); *Storer v Brown*, 415 US 724, 761 (1974) (Brennan dissenting) ("Naturally, the Constitution does not require the State to choose ineffective means to achieve its aims"; applying strict scrutiny to ballot access restriction); *Globe Newspaper Co. v Superior Court*, 457 US 596, 606–09 (1982) (holding that right of access to criminal trials may "not be restricted except where necessary to protect the State's interest," and striking down the law because the "interest could be served just as well" by a less restrictive alternative).

[54] See, for example, *Dial Information Services Corp. v Thornburgh*, 938 F2d 1535, 1541 (2d Cir 1991) ("in order for [challengers of a dial-a-porn restriction] to prevail, it must be determined that there are other approaches less restrictive than the [challenged law] but just as effective in achieving its goal of denying access by minors to indecent dial-a-porn messages"); *In re NBC v Cooperman*, 116 AD2d 287, 293, 501 NYS2d 405, 409 (1986) (prior restraints may not be imposed without "a determination that less restrictive alternatives would not be just as effective in assuring the defendant a fair trial").

shouldn't it, if constitutionality ultimately turns on a fact question?), but what about future bans, in cyberspace and out? They would be constitutional so long as there was no equally effective alternative for shielding children, a factual predicate that would almost always be met. As the Supreme Court has recognized, and as even the CDA's opponents acknowledged, only an "absolute ban" "can offer certain protection against assault by a determined child."[55] And yet surely this would be the wrong result, one that's inconsistent with the result in *ACLU* and with other cases, such as *Butler v Michigan* (which I discuss more below).[56]

III. Harmless Hyperbole?

A. THE "PRETTY MUCH EQUALLY EFFECTIVE ALTERNATIVE" TEST

I think it's not too much to ask that the Court's factual assertions be literally accurate,[57] but I recognize that many might fault me for being a bit too persnickety here. Maybe Justice Stevens was just engaging in harmless hyperbole: Maybe he meant that the burden on speech is unacceptable if "less restrictive alternatives would be at least *pretty much* equally effective"; that Congress hadn't proven that "a less restrictive provision would not be *more or less* as effective as the CDA."

In fact, the Court has seemed to suggest this sort of rule in some

---

[55] *Denver Area Educ. Telecom. Consortium v FCC*, 116 S Ct 2374, 2392 (1996); ACLU's Brief in *Reno v ACLU*, 1997 WL 74378, *36.

[56] 352 US 380 (1957); see Part III.E.

[57] One reader suggested that the *ACLU* opinion should be read not for its literal language, but for its general "mood": Put together with the opinions handed down the same week in *City of Boerne v Flores*, 117 S Ct 2157 (1997), and *Printz v United States*, 117 S Ct 2365 (1997), *ACLU* sends Congress a general signal to pay more attention to what it's doing, and to not pass popular but ill-considered feel-good legislation that jeopardizes important constitutional principles.

This, though, strikes me as an entirely unsound approach for the Court to take: I don't believe that anything in the Constitution gives the Court a license to strike down laws just because it thinks that Congress hasn't thought hard enough about them. Moreover, if the Court does this, it should at least explain that this is what it is doing, and give Congress some sense of just how much consideration and what kind of consideration Congress must give to statutes like this one. Even if Justice Stevens takes this sort of approach to constitutional adjudication, I would be amazed if all the other Justices in the majority—including Justices Scalia and Thomas—take the same view. Compare *Sable Communications v FCC*, 492 US 115, 133 (1989) (Scalia concurring) ("Neither due process nor the First Amendment requires legislation to be supported by committee reports, floor debates, or even consideration, but only by a vote.").

earlier child shielding cases, including *Sable Communications v FCC* and *Denver Area Educational Telecommunications Consortium v FCC;*[58] though the cases aren't entirely clear, this is probably the best way of putting the strict scrutiny test.[59] Maybe the Court meant to say only that some alternatives—perhaps the compelled tagging system—would probably be almost as effective as the CDA.

B. THE PROBLEMS WITH READING RENO V ACLU THIS WAY

1. Fostering Confusion among Lower Courts and Government Officials

There are, however, serious difficulties even with this reading of *ACLU.* To begin with, hyperbole makes bad caselaw. Lower courts might well think that they ought to read Supreme Court opinions literally, and that "at least as effective" means "at least as effective."[60] Quite likely some courts will read *ACLU* this way, while others impose a "pretty much equally effective alternative" standard; likewise for legislators and executive branch officials. This is hardly a recipe for coherent decision making.

2. Hiding the Normative Judgment

More importantly, the Court's factually erroneous claim that there are "*equally* effective" alternatives hides a significant and potentially controversial normative decision. By saying there are

---

[58] *Denver Area*, 116 S Ct at 2393. See also *Blount v SEC*, 61 F3d 938, 944 (DC Cir 1995) (speech restrictions are constitutional if they effectively advance a compelling interest, and are "narrowly tailored to advance the compelling interests asserted, i.e., . . . less restrictive alternatives to the rule would accomplish the government's goals equally or almost equally effectively"); and see, in another strict scrutiny context, *Wygant v Jackson Board of Educ.*, 476 US 267, 280 n 6 (1986) (interpreting "narrowly tailored" as mandating an inquiry into whether there are less restrictive means that "promote the substantial interest about as well and at tolerable administrative expense").

[59] See Volokh, *Freedom of Speech, Permissible Tailoring and Transcending Strict Scrutiny*, 144 U Pa L Rev at 2418–24 (cited in note 20), which cites more cases that establish this as the test and explains the test in more detail. See also id at 2438–40 (responding to the argument that strict scrutiny includes a "balancing" component).

[60] Compare *Dial Information Services Corp. v Thornburgh*, 938 F2d 1535, 1541 (2d Cir 1991) ("in order for [challengers of a dial-a-porn restriction] to prevail, it must be determined that there are other approaches less restrictive than the [challenged law] but just as effective in achieving its goal of denying access by minors to indecent dial-a-porn messages"); *In re NBC v Cooperman*, 116 AD2d 287, 293, 501 NYS2d 405, 409 (1986) (prior restraints may not be imposed without "a determination that less restrictive alternatives would not be just as effective in assuring the defendant a fair trial").

equally effective alternatives, alternatives that involve no loss of shielding for children, the Court could claim as a *descriptive* matter that the alternatives would be a win-win or at least a win-draw situation. But a requirement that the alternatives be merely "fairly effective," "almost as effective," or "pretty much equally effective" would mean some shielding of children would indeed be sacrificed. If the Court had to frankly admit that the alternatives would be a win for one side's concerns (free speech) at the expense of the other's (shielding children), then the Court would have had to give a *normative* explanation of why the losing side had to bear this loss.

The Justices would thus have had to say something like: "Any alternative to the CDA would sacrifice some shielding of children, and shielding children is a compelling government interest. But we think the benefits of protecting adults' access to free speech, even indecent speech, outweigh these costs. We realize Congress may have reached a different normative judgment, and concluded that even a small sacrifice of shielding was too high a price. But we disagree with Congress's normative judgment, for the following reasons. . . ."

There would have been nothing illegitimate about this frank substitution of the Court's own normative judgment for Congress's; I argue in Part IV that the Court should have done something quite like this. But the Court should acknowledge this normative disagreement, rather than trying to hide behind incorrect empirical claims.

3. Denying Lower Courts an Important Benchmark

The Court's decisions are supposed to give guidance to government officials and lower courts. Subjective standards that turn on differences in degree, such as a "pretty much equally effective alternative" standard, provide little constraint on their face.

To make such a standard useful, the Court must use each case to set a benchmark. Where "the content of the rule is not revealed simply by its literal text," it must be "given meaning through the evolutionary process of common law adjudication";[61] this requires the Court to confront the facts in each case, and explain why any particular alternative is or is not "pretty much equally effective."

---

[61] See note 49.

Consider the position in which Congress now finds itself. *ACLU* suggested that the CDA's goals might be accomplished by a compulsory tagging scheme, which "requir[es] that indecent material be 'tagged' in a way that facilitates parental control of material coming into their homes."[62] Some legislators have been considering such an alternative.[63] Should the legislators (and eventually the President and the courts) conclude that the proposal is constitutional?

The Court suggested that compulsory tagging might be a "less restrictive alternative" to the CDA, but didn't say it was a constitutional alternative. It is, after all, either a content-based speech restriction (you may not post material that's indecent but not tagged), compelled speech (you must tag), or a content-based burden on speech (indecent material is specially burdened by the tagging requirement). Under any of these views, the tagging requirement would be subject to strict scrutiny,[64] and would itself be unconstitutional if there's a still less restrictive alternative that would be pretty much equally effective.

The clearest candidate for a still less restrictive alternative is a pure filtering scheme: Parents would use filters on their computers—assume again that the government would provide them for free, or require service providers (such as America Online) to do so—and the filter manufacturers would monitor the Net, find indecent material, and program the filters to block access to this matter. Filters can indeed screen out a great deal of indecent material; but filters are less effective than filters coupled with compulsory tagging, because they rely exclusively on the filter manufacturers' thoroughness. Even the best filter producer can't check every Web page as soon as it's put up, and of course the producers

---

[62] 117 S Ct at 2348.

[63] See, for example, Thomas Goetz, *The CDA Next Time*, Village Voice 33 (July 8, 1997).

[64] *Riley v National Federation of the Blind*, 487 US 781 (1988). But see *Meese v Keene*, 481 US 465 (1987) (concluding, with no discussion of the compelled speech question, that a requirement that foreign-financed films be labeled "propaganda" does not violate the First Amendment). *Meese v Keene* seems to me to be an outlier. See Harry T. Edwards and Mitchell N. Berman, *Regulating Violence on Television*, 89 Nw U L Rev 1487, 1509–10 (1995) (suggesting that *Meese* is hard to square with the rest of compelled speech caselaw, and that it can best be read as a narrow support for "value-neutral and connotatively empty" tagging, which would not include ratings that "isolate and foreground one aspect or theme of a program"); Rodney A. Smolla, *Smolla and Nimmer on Freedom of Speech* § 19:7 (Clark Boardman Callaghan, 1994) (criticizing *Meese* as "deeply fraudulent").

can't screen individual newsgroup posts, chatroom conversations, and discussion list messages.[65]

So, given this, are filters a "pretty much equally effective alternative"? If *ACLU* had actually adopted this test, the Court would have had to describe the difference in effectiveness between the CDA and compulsory tagging (and the other alternatives), and to explain why this difference was so small as to be constitutionally insignificant. Then a legislator, President, or judge assessing the constitutionality of a compulsory tagging scheme could have used *ACLU* as a benchmark for determining whether the difference between tagging and pure filtering was likewise constitutionally insignificant.

But *ACLU* never acknowledged that the alternatives involved *any* sacrifice of effectiveness, so the Court didn't have to explain how much sacrifice of effectiveness was acceptable and how much would be too much. As a benchmark for judgments of "pretty much equal effectiveness," *ACLU* is largely useless. If "pretty much equal effectiveness" is the right test, then *ACLU* is an odd precedent for it: It neither properly sets forth the test, nor applies it in a way that provides a comparison point for future cases.

4. Neglecting to Show That the Alternatives Really Are Pretty Much as Effective

So far, I've argued that it was a bad idea for the Court to speak of "equally effective" if it meant "pretty much equally effective." But is the *ACLU* result right even under a "pretty much equally effective alternative" test?

---

[65] Some filters have options—which I call "clean-list filtering"—that allow access *only* to material that's been explicitly found to be clean, and can thus shield children from any material that hasn't yet been checked. See Response of Appellees ALA et al, No 96-511, at 23. But precisely because a child can see a page only if it's been certified clean, any such program will give children access to only a fraction of the clean material on the Web. Screeners almost certainly couldn't check even close to all the existing Web resources, and any new resources, including new pages at existing sites, might go unchecked for a long time. Clean-list filters thus may shield children better than compulsory tagging, but only at the price of rendering Internet access largely useless to them. I don't think the government must accept such an access-crippling alternative as being pretty much equally effective. See Volokh, *Freedom of Speech in Cyberspace from a Listener's Perspective*, 1996 U Chi Legal F at 431 and n 183 (cited in note 32) (giving more detailed argument). But compare *ACLU v Reno*, 929 F Supp 824, 883 (ED Pa 1996) (Dalzell concurring in the judgment) (suggesting that parents could, as an alternative to the CDA, just "deny their children the opportunity to participate in the medium until they reach an appropriate age").

The most credible of the alternatives that the Court suggested is tagging. If indecent material is tagged, then a computer with properly functioning filter software can block the tagged material. From the computer user's perspective, the material will be as inaccessible as if it had never been posted online. And compliance with the tagging requirement should, if anything, be at least as high as compliance with the CDA.

But, as Part II.A.1 shows, tagging doesn't stop children from seeing indecent material at the homes of friends whose parents don't use shielding software. So long as there's one such child in a social circle, the others can use his computer, or even have him e-mail them the indecent material. Of course, if he does the latter, he might be violating the law (assuming the compulsory tagging statute applies to private forwarders), but that's not going to much deter many children.

This is a pretty big loophole, considerably bigger than the one found tolerable in the dial-a-porn case (*Sable*). The proposed less restrictive alternatives in *Sable*—such as a credit card requirement or a requirement that a householder specifically ask the phone company to enable area code 900 phone calls[66]—would have been quite effective. Though children might get their hands on their parents' credit cards, or use a phone at the home of someone who has enabled 900 calls, they would be deterred by the fact that the parents or the phone subscriber would see the unauthorized charge and hold the child responsible for it. If parents did let their child have access, or if the child had his own credit card, he'd still be less likely to invite other children to use the card or the phone, because this would cost more money. A child who gets access to dial-a-porn at least can't forward it to many friends at the touch of a button.[67] Even if the alternatives in *Sable* were "extremely effective [so that] only a few of the most enterprising and disobedient young people would manage to secure access to such messages,"[68] the same is harder to say about the alternatives to the CDA.

---

[66] *Sable*, 492 US at 128 (mentioning credit card alternative); *Information Providers' Coalition v FCC*, 928 F2d 866 (9th Cir 1991) (discussing both alternatives in detail); *Dial Information Services Corp. v Thornburgh*, 938 F2d 1535 (2d Cir 1991) (same).

[67] Of course, one could tape-record a dial-a-porn conversation, make copies, and hand them out to friends, but compare to this the ease with which one can download an image and then instantly forward it by e-mail.

[68] *Sable*, 492 US at 130.

So tagging would probably provide considerably less shielding of children than the CDA would. How much less is impossible to measure, but there's reason to think it would be quite a bit less. According to some estimates, over 6 million children have access to the Internet today.[69] If even only half the children's parents would like them shielded, and if even only 20% of those will get access to indecent material under tagging but not under the CDA, the result is 600,000 children whose parents want shielding but who remain unshielded. It's not clear how, given this, compulsory tagging would be "pretty much equally effective."[70]

5. Failing to Explain *Butler v Michigan*

The final flaw with a "pretty much equally effective" standard is that it's inconsistent with the Court's first, and in some ways most important, ruling in this area: The 1957 holding in *Butler v Michigan*.[71]

Butler struck down a law that banned *all* distribution, to anyone, in any medium, of material deemed unsuitable for minors: The government, the Court held, may not "reduce the adult population to reading only what is fit for children."[72] I think this is right, for the reasons given by the Court in the various cases holding that sexually themed material—outside the narrow category of obscenity—is entitled to constitutional protection.

But under a "pretty much equally effective" alternative standard—"the Government may . . . regulate the content of constitu-

---

[69] The estimates vary, and are likely to change considerably over time. The estimate to which I refer puts the number at 6.7 million. *Kids Online: Evolving from a Niche*, Jupiter Communications Interactive Content (June 1, 1997) ("Currently, 6.7 million or 11 percent of all children between the ages of two and 17 access the Internet from home. Jupiter projects that this number will swell to more than 20.3 million or 31 percent by 2002."). The same research firm estimated the number at 4 million in 1996. Lawrie Mifflin, *New Guidelines on Net Ads for Children*, NY Times D5 (April 21, 1997); see also *Internet Working Group Meeting*, National Association of Attorneys General Consumer Protection Report (July 1996) (using estimate of 3.8 million); David Hayes, *Child-Friendly Internet Sites: Fine Fun, or Sly Salesmanship?* Kansas City Star A1 (March 29, 1996) ("as many as 4 million children have access to the Internet and 1 million use it regularly").

[70] This may only be a small fraction of all children, but the important point is that it's a high number: If the interest in shielding children is indeed compelling, then the fact that 600,000 children out of 6 million are unshielded is a serious problem, even if the 5.4 million other children are being shielded.

[71] 352 US 380 (1957).

[72] Id at 383.

tionally protected speech in order to promote a compelling interest [in shielding children] if it chooses the least restrictive means"[73] that are still "almost equally effective"[74]—the law in *Butler* would have been valid. It serves the same interest that the Court seemed to accept in *ACLU*, and did accept in *Sable:* shielding children from the supposedly harmful effects of indecent material. And no less restrictive alternative is even close to equally effective.

The obvious alternative to the total ban is a ban on distribution of the material to children,[75] but of course that's much less effective than a total prohibition. Once the material is allowed to adults, some of it will inevitably fall into the hands of minors. An underage teenager might stumble across material owned by an adult friend, or by a friend's parents; adults might easily sell it or give it to the teenager in private transactions that will be hard to discover.

If the material were totally banned, the government could seize it as contraband at the border, at the manufacturer, or at any place in the chain of distribution—a powerful tool for ensuring that the material will be kept away from minors. But so long as the material may lawfully be distributed to adults, it can be intercepted only when the government has concrete evidence that it's being distributed to children, evidence the government will only have for a tiny fraction of those materials that are actually falling into children's hands.

Allowing the distribution of indecent material to adults thus requires the government to make a significant sacrifice of its supposedly compelling interest in shielding children. *Butler* correctly concluded that it's better to pay this price than to pay the price of depriving adults of all access to indecent speech. But this is a judgment that the "pretty much equally effective alternatives" test doesn't accommodate.[76]

ACLU at times seemed to acknowledge *Butler*. "[T]he Government," the Court said (indirectly quoting *Butler*), "may not 'reduc[e] the adult population . . . to . . . only what is fit for chil-

---

[73] *Sable Communications v FCC*, 492 US 115, 126 (1989).

[74] For example, *Blount v SEC*, 61 F3d 938 (DC Cir 1995).

[75] 352 US at 383.

[76] *Butler* didn't have to ask whether there were pretty much equally effective alternatives, because it was decided before the Court began to apply the strict scrutiny framework to speech restrictions.

dren.'" "'Regardless of the strength of the government's interest' in protecting children, '[t]he level of discourse reaching a mailbox simply cannot be limited to that which would be suitable for a sandbox.'"[77]

But given this occasional acknowledgment, why the assertion in *Sable* that the government may indeed "regulate the content of constitutionally protected speech in order to promote a compelling interest [in shielding children] if it chooses the least restrictive means to further the . . . interest"?[78] Why the seeming pregnant negative in *ACLU* that the absence of equally effective alternatives would make the speech restriction valid?

IV. THE "BALANCING" METAPHOR AND FIVE CONCRETE DOCTRINAL OPTIONS

A. THE "BALANCING" METAPHOR

As I mentioned above, in most free speech controversies the question is about trade-offs. How much free speech should we be willing to sacrifice in order to shield children, or to achieve any other government interest? Conversely, how much shielding of children—or how much of any other important value—must we sacrifice in order to protect free speech? Behind every framework for scrutiny of speech regulations lurks a judgment about the trade-offs that must be paid.

One cliché response is that the Court must reach this judgment by "balancing," and in a certain (largely tautological) sense this is true: The judgment by definition requires deciding when the sacrifice of one value is "weightier" than the sacrifice of another. In a perfect world, we would "weigh" the value that would be lost by the burden on speech against the value that would be lost by the burden on the competing government interest.[79]

But this sort of "balancing" is not an answer; it's just a way of reframing the question. Balancing sounds manageable because the

---

[77] 117 S Ct at 2346.

[78] 492 US at 126. The "regulation" at issue in *Sable* was in fact a total ban on indecent speech in a particular medium.

[79] Of course, the value lost by the speech restriction includes not just the value of the lost speech itself, but also the risk of unfair application of the restriction, the risk that public debate will be skewed by the restriction, and various other costs. See note 19.

metaphor conjures up a familiar real-life device: a balance scale used for weighing two physical objects. The balance scale, though, works only because it uses a reliable physical process that unerringly compares a single, easily commensurable, attribute of two items.[80] No physical device can tell us whether some lump of government interest "weighs" more—is of greater "constitutional gravity"—than some chunk of free speech right. The statement "courts should balance" thus simply invites the question "How?"

Referring the matter to one's unarticulated intuitions—the scale in each judge's conscience—is, even if legitimate, simply impractical. The Supreme Court makes law for tens of thousands of legislative, executive, and judicial decision makers in American government. "Trust your instincts" is not a useful legal rule in such a system, especially (as the Court has repeatedly held) in free speech cases.[81]

Because of this, the Court has done its free speech "balancing" by creating relatively concrete doctrinal structures that help decide when a competing government interest "outweighs" the free speech value. Thus, for instance, under *Brandenburg v Ohio*, the need to prevent violence "outweighs" the right to advocate violence only when the speech is intended to lead to imminent injury, and is in fact likely to do so; otherwise, the speech right "outweighs" the government interest.[82] The Court had to reconcile— one might say balance—two competing concerns, but in doing so it produced a rule that says more than simply "Balance!"

The Court's task in child-shielding cases should likewise be to set forth a rule that reconciles the competing concerns in a way that other decision makers can adequately implement—to draw a more concretely applicable line that will still generally produce the right results.[83] There are five basic approaches to this problem.

---

[80] An oversimplification, but close enough for our purposes.

[81] See, for example, *Grayned v City of Rockford*, 408 US 104, 108 (1972) (condemning vague speech restrictions because they invite "arbitrary and discriminatory enforcement"); *Smith v Goguen*, 415 US 566, 574–76 (1974) (same).

[82] 395 US 444 (1969). Of course, the *Brandenburg* formula itself has some play in its joints; I claim only that it's more concrete than simple "balancing," not that it's mechanical.

[83] See Melville B. Nimmer, *Nimmer on Freedom of Speech: A Treatise on the First Amendment* § 2.02 (1984) (praising categorical balancing as a substitute for ad-hoc balancing in the First Amendment context); Kathleen M. Sullivan, *The Supreme Court 1991 Term, Foreword: The Justices of Rules and Standards*, 106 Harv L Rev 22, 69, 83–95 (1992) (noting how the Court translates mushy abstract principles into more administrable, even if somewhat less

B. FIVE CONCRETE DOCTRINAL OPTIONS

1. The Current Official Approach: "Compelling Interest Trumps"

The official strict scrutiny approach, set forth in *Sable*, is that the First Amendment tolerates the sacrifice of as much speech as it takes to shield children from indecency. True, the sacrifice must be genuinely "necessary"—there must be no alternatives that exact a lower free speech price without significantly sacrificing the government interest. But if the only way to really satisfy the interest is to restrict speech, then the government may do it.[84]

I call this the "compelling interest trumps" approach,[85] and as I argued above in Part III.B.5, I believe it is unsound. As *Butler* correctly holds, the government may not reduce adults to reading only what is fit for children. This is true even though letting adults access indecent material would necessarily sacrifice a great deal of shielding of children—even though a total ban would genuinely be the only means to effectively further the interest. For *Butler* and the result in *ACLU* to be right, the First Amendment must sometimes demand significant sacrifice of the government interest. But the "compelling interest trumps" approach does not reflect this principle.

It may seem odd to characterize this approach as government-friendly, because the conventional wisdom is that strict scrutiny in free speech cases is "fatal in fact."[86] But the test says that when

---

theoretically satisfying, categorical rules); Alex Kozinski and Eugene Volokh, *A Penumbra Too Far*, 106 Harv L Rev 1639, 1644–45, 1651–53 (1993) (same).

[84] See cases cited in Part II.B.

[85] This approach actually represents a family of possible tests, which differ in the degree to which they would tolerate some sacrifice of shielding. One possible test would say that any restriction is constitutional so long as there are no alternatives that are less restrictive but genuinely equally effective. Other tests may say that a restriction is constitutional only if all the alternatives are substantially less effective, with different definitions of "substantial." Likewise, the other approaches I describe below also represent families of possible tests.

[86] Gerald Gunther, *The Supreme Court, 1971 Term, Foreword: In Search of Evolving Doctrine on a Changing Court: A Model for a Newer Equal Protection*, 86 Harv L Rev 1, 8 (1972); compare *Bernal v Fainter*, 467 US 216, 219 n 6 (1984) (citing Gunther). See, for example, Geoffrey R. Stone, *Content-Neutral Restrictions*, 54 U Chi L Rev 46, 53 (1987) ("Strict scrutiny almost invariably results in invalidation of the challenged restriction."); Roger Pilon, *A Court Without a Compass*, 40 NY L Sch L Rev 999, 1006 (1996) ("strict scrutiny . . . lead[s] almost invariably to a finding of unconstitutionality"); Richard G. Wilkins, Richard Sherlock, and Steven Clark, *Mediating the Polar Extremes: A Guide to Post-Webster Abortion Policy*, 1991 BYU L Rev 403, 420–21 (" 'strict scrutiny' [in, among other things, free speech cases] almost always results in a finding of constitutional invalidity"); Book

there is no other comparably effective way of serving a compelling interest, the speech restriction should be upheld.[87] And the test includes no inquiry into the magnitude of the burden on speech; even serious burdens might thus pass strict scrutiny.[88]

And the Court has used strict scrutiny to uphold speech restrictions. In *Buckley v Valeo*, the Court upheld a restriction on campaign contributions, and a ban on speech (and not just contributions) that is coordinated with a candidate, advocates a candidate's election, and costs more than $1,000.[89] In *Austin v Michigan Chamber of Commerce*, the Court upheld a ban on speech by corporations in support or opposition to candidates.[90] A plurality in *Burson v Freeman* upheld a ban on campaign-related speech within 100 feet of a polling place.[91] In *Riley v National Federation for the Blind*, the Court said that a requirement that charity fundraisers make certain statements passed strict scrutiny.[92] And though the Court in *Sable* struck down a dial-a-porn ban, it did so on the grounds that other (presumably permissible) speech restrictions would be less burdensome.[93]

Lower courts have followed suit. Two courts of appeals upheld the post-*Sable* dial-a-porn restrictions.[94] The Washington Supreme Court upheld an injunction banning "the use of the words 'murder,' 'kill,' and their derivatives" in abortion clinic picketing, on

---

Note, *Freedom to Offend*, 105 Yale L J 1415, 1417 (1996) ("strict scrutiny, a process that is almost always fatal to the regulation").

[87] See Part III.A.

[88] Some suggest that strict scrutiny includes a "cost-benefit weighing" as part of the test itself, but I do not believe this is so. See Volokh, *Freedom of Speech, Permissible Tailoring and Transcending Strict Scrutiny*, 144 U Pa L Rev at 2438–40 (cited in note 20).

[89] 424 US 1, 25–28, 45 (1976). Of course, most effective speech to a mass audience, except perhaps some kinds of cyberspace speech, costs far more than $1,000.

[90] 494 US 652 (1990).

[91] 504 US 191 (1992).

[92] 487 US 781, 799 n 11 (1988) (dictum, but confident- and considered-sounding dictum, saying that it was permissible to compel fundraisers to disclose that they were professionals, though not permissible to compel them to disclose what fraction of the collected funds went to the charity). Compare id at 803–04 (Scalia concurring in part and in the judgment) (disagreeing with the Court's approval of such speech compulsions).

[93] 492 US 115, 128–31 (1989) (pointing out that a total ban was unnecessary because lesser speech restrictions would do a pretty much equally good job).

[94] *Dial Information Service Corp. v Thornburgh*, 938 F2d 1535 (2d Cir 1991) (upholding such restrictions under strict scrutiny); *Information Providers' Coalition v FCC*, 928 F2d 866 (9th Cir 1991) (same).

the theory that the ban was narrowly tailored to the "compelling State interest in preventing the [physical, emotional and psychological harm arising] when such words are heard by children."[95] Other cases have used strict scrutiny to uphold speech compulsions aimed at better informing would-be charitable contributors;[96] bans on anonymous political speech, aimed at better informing voters;[97] bans on all political speech within 600 feet of polls, including speech not related to items on the ballot;[98] restrictions on speech by judicial candidates, aimed at "protecting public confidence in the integrity of the judiciary";[99] and bans on public display of "obscene-as-to-minors" material.[100] Whether these decisions are right or wrong, they suggest that courts are willing to apply strict scrutiny in a way that upholds many restrictions.

As I have argued in another article, strict scrutiny still seems demanding largely because courts are often correctly unwilling to live by it.[101] *ACLU* is good evidence for that proposition.

---

[95] *Bering v Share*, 106 Wash 2d 212, 234, 241, 245, 721 P2d 918, 931, 935, 937 (1986), cert dismissed for want of jurisdiction, 479 US 1050 (1986).

[96] *State v Christian Action Network*, 491 SE2d 61 (W Va 1997) (upholding, despite *Riley*, a requirement that all printed solicitations include the statement "West Virginia residents may obtain a summary of the registration and financial documents from the Secretary of State, State Capitol, Charleston, West Virginia 25305. Registration does not imply endorsement.").

[97] *Griset v Fair Political Practices Comm'n*, 8 Cal 4th 851, 884 P2d 116, 35 Cal Rptr 2d 659 (1994) (upholding a ban on anonymous mailings by candidates to prospective voters, on the grounds that this serves the compelling interest in "a well-informed electorate"), cert denied, 514 US 1083 (1995). The case was held pending *McIntyre v Ohio Elections Comm'n*, 514 US 334 (1995)—a decision that struck down a ban on anonymous fliers related to ballot measures—but the Court then denied cert. Note that *Griset* was not justified as a means of avoiding corruption of candidates; it involved speech by the candidate's own committee, not an anonymous contribution to the candidate.

[98] *Schirmer v Edwards*, 2 F3d 117 (5th Cir 1993). *Burson v Freeman* upheld only a 100-foot buffer zone.

[99] *In re Kaiser*, 111 Wash 2d 275, 288–89, 759 P2d 392, 399–400 (1988) (compelling interests in preserving the "good reputation of the judiciary" and the "integrity of the judiciary" justify restricting a judicial candidate's "statements of party affiliation [and] statements regarding the motives of [an opponent's] attorney supporters"); *In re Complaint Against Harper*, 77 Ohio St 3d 211, 225, 673 NE2d 1253, 1265 (1996) (holding that "truthful criticism of the judiciary in a dignified manner" is protected but only "so long as the criticism is done fairly, accurately, and upon facts, not false representations").

[100] *American Booksellers v Webb*, 919 F2d 1493 (11th Cir 1990); *Crawford v Lungren*, 96 F3d 380 (9th Cir 1996).

[101] Volokh, *Freedom of Speech, Permissible Tailoring and Transcending Strict Scrutiny*, 144 U Pa L Rev 2417, especially 2441–43 (cited in note 20).

2. The "Substantial Burden Is Unconstitutional" Approach

What might substitute for the "compelling interest trumps" framework? One option is what I call the "substantial burden is unconstitutional" approach: If the law imposes a substantial burden on generally protected speech, then it is per se impermissible, even if this means we must sacrifice a significant amount of shielding of children.

The underlying principle is that the freedom of speech need not be just a presumption that can be rebutted by strong enough claims of countervailing government interest. The First Amendment may instead be seen as embodying a judgment that some speech must be protected even if it unavoidably causes harm.[102]

Under this view, the interest in shielding children might be seen as strong enough to justify modest restrictions on speech that's unsuitable for minors;[103] not every restriction need be considered an unconstitutional abridgement. Even relatively slight content-based restrictions are usually presumptively unconstitutional,[104] but such small prices may be worth paying when the strong government interest in shielding children is implicated. (As I discuss below, even *Ginsberg v New York*'s ban on distribution to children of obscene-as-to-minors material imposed some burden on protected speech among adults.) But if the proposed restriction imposes a substantial burden on the free speech right, then under this framework it cannot stand.

---

[102] Such rights are common in existing constitutional jurisprudence: The privilege against self-incrimination, the Double Jeopardy Clause, and the Ex Post Facto Clause, for instance, cannot be overcome by showing a compelling interest. Even if enforcing the Double Jeopardy Clause will set some murderers free to kill again, the judgment embodied in the Clause prevails: The release of some who might be guilty is a harm that must be accepted in order to get the benefits that the constitutional guarantee provides. See Volokh, *Freedom of Speech, Permissible Tailoring and Transcending Strict Scrutiny*, 144 U Pa L Rev at 2456 (cited in note 20).

[103] I intentionally say "unsuitable for minors," instead of "indecent" or "obscene as to minors," to refer to whatever definition of unsuitability the Court chooses to use. I argue in Part IV.B.2.a.i that indecent (but not obscene-as-to-minors) speech should not be seen as unsuitable for minors; but my general "substantial burden is unconstitutional" framework can work no matter where the Court draws the unsuitability line.

[104] See, for example, *Riley v National Federation of the Blind*, 487 US 781 (1988) (using strict scrutiny to strike down requirement—which the Court treated as equivalent to a content-based restriction—that charitable fundraisers reveal the fraction of collected funds that are actually given to the charity); *Carey v Brown*, 447 US 455 (1980) (using strict scrutiny to strike down content-based restriction on nonlabor picketing, though the restriction applied only to residential picketing). I agree these restrictions should be viewed with serious concern; I only suggest that these are fairly slight restrictions.

Of course, this view rests on a contested assumption—that avoiding substantial burdens on sexually themed or profane speech among adults is more important than shielding minors from such speech—but this is an assumption that the First Amendment itself supports. The First Amendment protects speech even when it causes significant harm, perhaps including eventual violence. The theory of the First Amendment is that restricting speech is in the long run presumptively more harmful than permitting the speech.[105] And all the speech that we're discussing here is not obscene as to adults, and is thus constitutionally valuable; as *ACLU* points out, some of it may well be related to significant political, artistic, and scientific matters.[106]

First Amendment doctrine does sometimes allow even substantial burdens on constitutionally valuable speech that is seen as too immediately harmful to tolerate. For instance, the government may sometimes ban newspapers from publishing certain military secrets, even if the publication is valuable to national debate;[107] the government may in narrow circumstances ban advocacy of violent conduct, even though the advocacy might contribute to political discussion.[108] The risk of imminent violence or death will always weigh heavily, even against the strongest of constitutional guarantees.[109]

---

[105] See Volokh, *Freedom of Speech, Permissible Tailoring and Transcending Strict Scrutiny*, 144 U Pa L Rev at 2444–52 (cited in note 20).

[106] 117 S Ct at 2344, 2347–48.

[107] See, for example, *Florida Star v B.J.F.*, 491 US 524, 532 (1989) (quoting *Near v Minnesota*, 283 US 697 (1931), for the proposition that "publication of the sailing dates of transports or the number and location of troops" might be unprotected); *Haig v Agee*, 453 US 280, 309 (1981) (revelation of the names of U.S. intelligence agents that has "the declared purpose of obstructing intelligence operations and the recruiting of intelligence personnel" is "clearly not protected by the Constitution"); *United States v Progressive, Inc.*, 467 F Supp 990 (WD Wis 1979) (holding that instructions for creating H-bombs may be restrained). But see *New York Times v United States*, 403 US 713 (1971), striking down an injunction against publication of *The Pentagon Papers*; though this case theoretically left open the possibility that the *Times* might be criminally punished for the publication, many now assume that publications such as this are constitutionally protected.

[108] See *Brandenburg v Ohio*, 395 US 444 (1969). One might argue that advocacy intended at producing imminent and likely unlawful conduct is constitutionally valueless, but I doubt it: It seems to me no less valuable in the abstract than advocacy aimed at producing unlawful conduct at some future date. The *Brandenburg* exception seems to me to be justified by the gravity of the harm the speech can produce, rather than by its perceived lack of value.

[109] Compare *City of Richmond v J.A. Croson Co.*, 488 US 469, 520 (1989) (Scalia concurring) (proposing near-absolute ban on race classifications, but suggesting that "a social emergency rising to the level of imminent danger to life and limb—for example, a prison race riot, requiring temporary segregation of inmates—can justify an exception to the [color-

But these provisions are very much exceptions (and narrow ones at that), and should require extremely powerful justifications, more powerful than the justifications needed for laws that don't substantially burden valuable speech.[110] They should not be lightly extended absent strong evidence of dramatic, imminent harm. While there is a broad intuitive consensus that sexually themed or profane speech may indeed be in some measure unsuitable for minors, such a general sense of long-term corruption strikes me as inadequate justification for allowing substantial burdens on valuable speech, especially when this supposed corruption is compared to the dangers that the First Amendment routinely demands that we run.[111]

Substantial burden tests are well known in constitutional law. In *Planned Parenthood v Casey*, for instance, the Court concluded that the government has a strong interest in protecting potential human life, but the woman's right to a pre-viability abortion must nonetheless prevail: Any substantial burdens on the right are per se invalid, though lesser burdens are presumptively constitutional.[112] Other doctrinal frameworks, such as those for religious freedom before *Employment Division v Smith*, freedom of expressive association, and the right to marry also include a substantial burden inquiry, though they at least theoretically allow even substantial burdens on the right so long as the law passes some form of heightened scrutiny.[113]

Even some of the Court's free speech tests fit well with a "substantial burden" framework, though they generally aren't explained this way. Libel law, for instance, rests on the notion that

---

blindness] principle"); *Lee v Washington*, 390 US 333, 334 (1968) (Black concurring) (taking a similar view).

[110] I refer here only to restrictions imposed by the government as sovereign, rather than the government acting as employer, K–12 educator, proprietor of a nonpublic forum, and so on. For the usual reasons, I think the government properly has more power to control its own money and its own property than to control the behavior of private persons.

[111] See *Pacifica*, 438 US at 767–75 (Brennan dissenting).

[112] 505 US 833 (1992). Under *Casey*'s substantial burden test, a law is unconstitutional if it has the effect of creating a substantial burden *or* if it was intended to create such a burden. I would not borrow the intent inquiry from *Casey*, because it seems both difficult to apply (perhaps even inherently indeterminate) and rarely dispositive.

[113] *Jimmy Swaggart Ministries v Board of Equalization*, 493 US 378 (1990) (religious freedom); *Roberts v U.S. Jaycees*, 468 US 609 (1984) (right of expressive association); *Zablocki v Redhail*, 434 US 374 (1978) (right to marry). But see Volokh, *Freedom of Speech, Permissible Tailoring and Transcending Strict Scrutiny*, 144 U Pa L Rev at 2449–50 (cited in note 20) (suggesting that in some religious freedom contexts, the Court applies a rule of per se invalidation, rather than strict scrutiny).

the important interest in protecting reputation justifies some speech restrictions, so long as they do not substantially restrain valuable speech. The Court has concluded that false statements of fact are generally constitutionally valueless,[114] so the impact of libel law on false statements is seen as a constitutionally insignificant burden; but the Court has recognized that libel rules can incidentally burden constitutionally valuable truthful speech, and has therefore often inquired into the magnitude of the burden created by various rules.[115] The "compelling interest trumps" approach is not used here: For instance, the actual malice test is a considerably less effective alternative to traditional strict liability when it comes to protecting public figures' reputations from false defamatory statements, but the Court has nonetheless rejected strict liability (and even a negligence test) because it would impose too great a burden on speech.[116]

To make this approach work for restrictions on material that's supposedly unsuitable for minors, the Court would have to do two things: (*a*) Identify what speech lacks substantial constitutional value when communicated to minors. Even a total ban on distributing such speech to minors would thus not create a substantial burden, so long as it's really limited to distribution to minors. (*b*) Determine when a burden on valuable speech (to adults or minors) qualifies as insubstantial.[117]

a) Identifying Speech That Lacks Value When Communicated to Minors

i) Indecent versus "obscene as to minors." As of 1975, the Court had concluded that (1) there is no constitutional value in communications to minors (except perhaps by or with the approval of

---

[114] See *Gertz v Robert Welch, Inc.*, 418 US 323, 340 (1974) ("there is no constitutional value in false statements of fact"). But see *New York Times Co. v Sullivan*, 376 US 254, 291–92 (1964) (suggesting that even knowing falsehoods about the government generally, rather than about a particular government official, might be constitutionally protected).

[115] See, for example, *Sullivan; Gertz*.

[116] *Sullivan*, 376 US at 254; see also *Gertz*, 418 US at 323 (requiring "actual malice" for punitive or presumed damages even when the plaintiff is a private figure).

[117] In this section, I assume that less-than-substantial burdens would be considered per se constitutional (or subjected to rational basis scrutiny, which if honestly applied is tantamount to the same thing). Nonetheless, the Court might also decide that even such slightly burdensome restrictions should be subjected to some serious scrutiny; this is explored in Part IV.B.3.

their parents) that are "obscene as to minors"—essentially communications that fit the three-prong obscenity test, but with a "for minors" qualifier on each prong[118]—but (2) there is value in communications to minors that fall outside this category.[119] This makes sense under the logic of obscenity law. Assume communicating obscenity to another person is generally constitutionally worthless as speech, because it appeals to prurient interests, is patently offensive, and lacks serious value.[120] Then communicating to a minor material that appeals to the minor's prurient interests, is patently offensive when distributed to minors, and lacks serious value for that minor would likewise be generally worthless. Even a total ban on such communications to people whom the speaker knows to be minors wouldn't substantially burden worthwhile speech, because it would ban only the speech that is, by assumption, valueless.[121]

In *FCC v Pacifica Foundation*, however, the Court went beyond this, holding that government may regulate speech even to shield minors from material that is merely indecent—that "refer[s] to excretory or sexual activities or organs" in a "patently offensive" way.[122] This includes material that doesn't appeal to the prurient interest, and may even cover material that has significant artistic,

---

[118] *Ginsberg v New York*, 390 US 629 (1968). *Ginsberg* involved a somewhat different formulation of the obscenity standard than is now the law after *Miller v California*, 413 US 15 (1973); however, it seems fair to assume that *Ginsberg* still stands, but with the three prongs modified to match the three-prong *Miller* test. See, for example, *ACLU*, 117 S Ct at 2356 (O'Connor dissenting in part); *Virginia v American Booksellers Ass'n, Inc.*, 484 US 383, 387 (1988) (discussing a state statute whose "definition of 'harmful to juveniles' is a modification of the *Miller* definition of obscenity, adapted for juveniles").

[119] *Erznoznik v City of Jacksonville*, 422 US 205, 213 and n 10 (1975).

[120] Right or wrong, that's what *Miller* held.

[121] Of course, the "obscene-as-to-minors" test poses formidable practical problems, because what's suitable for a 17-year-old may not be suitable for a 7-year-old. In theory, the proper approach would be to apply to each minor a test that's based on that minor's age: A bookseller selling to a 15-year-old would thus have to ask whether the material is "obscene as to 15-year-olds," and a Web page owner required to tag his page would have to tag it with something like "obscene as to 12-year-olds but permissible for 13-year-olds." Practically, though, such fine rating is extremely difficult, and imposes far too high a burden on speakers and distributors. An alternative is to have a uniform standard for all minors, but should the standard be what's suitable for 17-year-olds, which would underprotect younger children, or what's suitable for 7-year-olds, which would overrestrict speech to older children? These are difficult problems, and might counsel against having any sort of obscene-as-to-minors test. *Ginsberg*, though, seems to require us to muddle through with this inquiry as best we can.

[122] 438 US 726, 739 (1978).

literary, or scientific value, even for minors. *Sable* seemed to echo this, acknowledging that the government has a compelling interest in prohibiting "indecent" telephone communications to minors, or at least those that are sexually themed.[123] *ACLU* seemed to agree, though it was ambiguous on the point.[124]

This leaves much uncertain. Could the government, for instance, prohibit all indecent communications to minors, such as selling or even giving a 16-year-old a copy of Carlin's *Seven Dirty Words*? *Sable* and *Pacifica* suggest this might be constitutional,[125] while *Ginsberg* and *Erznoznik* suggest otherwise. Likewise, even if tagging schemes are generally constitutional, it's not clear whether Congress could constitutionally require tagging of indecent material or only of obscene-as-to-minors material. At some point, the Court will have to decide on the right standard.

"Obscene as to minors" seems to be the better solution. By definition, material that's "indecent" but not "obscene as to minors" either has serious artistic, literary, political, or scientific value for minors, or does not appeal to minors' prurient interests. If it has value for minors, then it ought to be protected. If it doesn't appeal to minors' prurient interests, then it's not clear why it should be treated differently than equally nonprurient material that deals with offensive topics other than sex or excretion.

More concretely, as *ACLU* pointed out, a lot of speech that might be considered "patently offensive"—"serious discussion about birth control practices, homosexuality, the First Amendment issues raised by [indecency itself], or the consequences of prison rape"[126]—does have considerable value. The one item the Court has held "indecent," the Carlin "Seven Dirty Words" monologue, is no less valuable than most humorous social commentary;[127] and

---

[123] *Sable*, 492 US at 125.

[124] Compare 117 S Ct at 2340 n 30 (stating that the CDA's challengers "do not dispute that the Government generally has a compelling interest in protecting minors from 'indecent' and 'patently offensive' speech") and id at 2343 (stating that *Sable* "agreed that 'there is a compelling interest in protecting the physical and psychological well-being of minors' which extended to shielding them from indecent messages that are not obscene by adult standards") with id at 2348 (neither accepting nor rejecting the argument that the First Amendment may tolerate "a blanket prohibition on all 'indecent' and 'patently offensive' messages communicated to a 17-year-old").

[125] See *Pacifica*, 438 US at 749 (Stevens plurality) ("Bookstores and motion picture theaters . . . may be prohibited from making indecent material available to children").

[126] 117 S Ct at 2344.

[127] See *Action for Children's Television v FCC*, 852 F2d 1332, 1340 n 13 (DC Cir 1988).

it's not clear why the government has a compelling interest in shielding children from it.

But even if one disagrees with my judgment, and concludes that the line should be drawn at indecency, my basic point remains: The Court must identify which speech is valueless as to minors, and use this definition in determining whether or not a restriction substantially burdens valuable speech.

ii) Rights of parents. The Court must also decide whether parents have a constitutional right to communicate—and to authorize others to communicate—"obscene-as-to-minors" material to their children. *Ginsberg* suggested as much,[128] as did *ACLU*.[129]

Doctrinally, this is not a trivial question; *Ginsberg* also suggested that the government has an interest in shielding children against the harmful effects of certain material, independent of the interest in protecting parental decisions about child-rearing.[130] If "obscene-as-to-minors" speech is indeed valueless to minors, one can argue that it remains valueless when it is communicated or tolerated by parents, and that parents should have no more right to expose their children to such speech than they would have with regard to simple obscenity.

Nonetheless, it is probably sounder to leave parents, rather than the government, with the ultimate decision here. Children of the same age vary widely in maturity, and parents usually know their child's maturity better than do prosecutors, judges, or juries. If parents believe there's educational value in giving their children access to supposedly "obscene-as-to-minors" material, there's good reason to defer to that judgment. And the notion that parents

---

[128] 390 US at 639 (stressing that "the prohibition against sales to minors does not bar parents who so desire from purchasing the [obscene-to-minors] magazines for their children").

[129] 117 S Ct at 2341 (stressing that "the statute upheld in *Ginsberg* was narrower than the CDA [in part because] 'the prohibition against sales to minors does not bar parents who so desire from purchasing the magazines for their children' "); id at 2348 (describing "possible alternatives such as requiring that indecent material be 'tagged' in a way that facilitates parental control of material coming into their homes" and "providing some tolerance for parental choice"). But see id at 2356–57 (O'Connor dissenting in part) (suggesting that there is "no support [in the record] for the legal proposition that [e-mail between family members is] absolutely immune from regulation").

[130] 390 US at 639–40. *ACLU* did not squarely confront this distinction, speaking generally of a "governmental interest in protecting children from harmful materials."

should, absent some powerful reason to the contrary, have discretion about how to raise their children buttresses this view.[131]

Of course, this deference to parents' views is only a presumption: Parents generally can't, for instance, make it legal for their 12-year-olds to have sex or to drop out of school, even if the parents think the children are mature enough to do so. But though exposure of children to "obscene-as-to-minors" material may be harmful, the harm seems considerably smaller than the possible harms of early sex or of lack of education. This relatively modest harm ought not be enough to rebut our normal deference to parental decisions, especially when free speech rights are also implicated.[132]

b) Identifying Insubstantial Burdens on Valuable Communications

Butler holds that banning all distribution of materials that are unsuitable for children is too great a burden on the free speech rights of adults, and surely this is correct. Though anything less than a total ban will increase the chances that some of the materials will leak out to children, that's a price the First Amendment requires us to pay.

But other burdens may not be so troublesome. Consider the law upheld in *Ginsberg*; though the law purports to ban only "knowing[ ]" sales to minors, it does in fact burden sales to at least some adults. Because the law essentially requires sellers to make "a reasonable bona fide attempt to ascertain the true age of such minor,"[133] many sellers are reluctant to sell to adults who look underage and who don't have proof of age handy. Those adults are therefore burdened in their access to constitutionally protected material.

Moreover, the law burdens the right of underage-looking adults to buy anonymously, because proof of age generally includes a per-

---

[131] *Meyer v Nebraska*, 262 US 390 (1923); *Pierce v Society of Sisters*, 268 US 510 (1925).

[132] This obviously involves a tough and subjective call about how harmful various behaviors are to children, but such calls are inevitable whenever one accepts the notion of broad but not unlimited parental rights. See, for example, *Meyer v State of Nebraska*, 262 US 390, 402–03 (1923); *Pierce v Society of Sisters*, 268 US 510, 534–35 (1925); *Prince v Massachusetts*, 321 US 158, 166–67 (1944). Compare Justice Holmes's thoughtful dissent in *Bartels v Iowa*, 262 US 404 (1923), a companion case to *Meyer*.

[133] *Ginsberg*, 390 US at 644.

son's name. The law also burdens sellers, who must take the time and effort to check the age of the young-looking adults; and it burdens publishers, who lose some adult potential readers as a result.

Finally, the *Ginsberg* statute burdens the rights of minors to receive material that's protected as to them, and the rights of writers, publishers, and sellers to communicate such material to them. The "obscene-as-to-minors" standard is vague, and as *Reno v ACLU* points out, even laws that are not vague enough to be unconstitutional tend to make speakers cautious.[134] A seller might well be reluctant to sell any sexually oriented material to a minor, even if a jury would ultimately conclude that this material wasn't "obscene as to minors." Minors might therefore find it hard to get material that they're theoretically entitled to read (though determined minors will probably find some store that will sell it to them).[135]

I don't want to overstate these burdens: They do seem relatively slight. In a sense they may be seen as incidental to a ban on only supposedly unprotected speech (distribution to minors of obscene-as-to-minors material). But the law explicitly applies whenever the distributor "[has] reason to know . . . or [has] a belief or ground for belief which warrants further inspection or inquiry of . . . the character and content of [the] material [and] the age of the minor,"[136] thus effectively requiring the distributor to investigate all borderline cases, including those where the material is ultimately found to be protected or the customer is found to be an adult. This is not merely a burden imposed by a general law that is not focused on speech (such as tax law or contract law);[137] the burden applies to a content-based category of speech, and necessarily interferes in some measure with the distribution of the speech to people who have a right to receive it.

Ginsberg thus shows that, while the most serious burdens on protected speech—such as a total ban—are unconstitutional, slighter

---

[134] 117 S Ct at 2344.

[135] Id at 2346 ("Given the vague contours of the coverage of the statute, it unquestionably silences some speakers whose messages would be entitled to constitutional protection.").

[136] *Ginsberg*, 390 US at 646, quoting N Y Pen L § 484-h(1)(g).

[137] See Stone, *Content-Neutral Restrictions*, 54 U Chi L Rev at 105–09 (cited in note 86) (distinguishing incidental restrictions that aim at broad classes of conduct from restrictions that target speech); *Arcara v Cloud Books, Inc.*, 478 US 697, 706–07 (1986) (same).

burdens may not be.[138] We might hesitate to ask courts to draw lines between slight burdens and substantial burdens, and I believe the Court is generally correct in avoiding such line-drawing for most content-based speech restrictions.[139] But so long as we are committed to allowing some restrictions on speech that's unsuitable for children, some such line-drawing is inevitable there.

Most hard cases involve burdens that are in between *Ginsberg* and *Butler*. In *Pacifica*, for instance, adult listeners were deprived of the opportunity to hear material for free during the day and evening,[140] and speakers were deprived of the opportunity to reach the normal radio audience. In *ACLU*, adult users were deprived of the opportunity to see material for free in cyberspace, and speakers were deprived of the opportunity to reach cyberspace users who didn't want to pay for the speech. In the compelled rating scheme suggested by *ACLU*, adult users would not be appreciably burdened, but speakers would have to take the time and effort to rate their material, and might suffer a hard-to-measure loss to the effectiveness of their message caused by the compelled statement.[141]

The Court's evaluation of these burdens must turn on its judgment as to (1) the value of the burdened speech, and (2) the significance of the interference with the size of the speaker's audience and with the adult listeners' ease of accessing the material.[142] It would be best if the Court could articulate some rules about this, but even if it can only make ad-hoc decisions, these decisions can

---

[138] See text accompanying note 150.

[139] See Geoffrey R. Stone, *Content Regulation and the First Amendment*, 25 Wm & Mary L Rev 189, 225–27 (1983).

[140] *Pacifica*, 438 US at 726, hinted that the rule might be different during the times of day when children are unlikely to be in the audience. *Action for Children's Television v FCC*, 932 F2d 1504 (DC Cir 1991), struck down a 24-hour ban on indecency; *Action for Children's Television v FCC*, 58 F3d 654 (DC Cir 1995) (en banc), held that it would be constitutional for the FCC to limit indecent broadcasts to the hours from 12 midnight to 6 A.M.

[141] See Edwards and Berman, *Regulating Violence on Television*, 89 Nw U L Rev at 1509–10 (cited in note 64).

[142] This general test should, I believe, be applicable to all media; nonetheless, it might play out somewhat differently in different contexts. Some media, for instance, might generally be less time sensitive than others, so certain delays may be substantial burdens in one medium but not in another. See, for example, the text accompanying note 150. Likewise, in some new media, predicting the effect of a regulation may be hard enough that the magnitude of the burden would be even more uncertain than it usually is. In these situations, a court might choose to err on the side of striking the regulation down unless it's fairly clear that it will not be substantially burdensome.

be used as benchmarks by other decision makers, so long as the facts in each case are candidly described.

I would suggest that any restriction that substantially reduces a speaker's audience—as the rules in *Pacifica* and *ACLU* would have—or that makes it substantially harder for adults to get the material they want should be seen as an impermissible substantial burden. Justice Powell was right that the FCC's action in *Pacifica* "[did] not prevent willing adults from purchasing Carlin's record [or] from attending his performances."[143] Likewise, the CDA would have allowed indecent speech so long as it was posted on sites that charged users through credit cards. Nonetheless, the *ACLU* Court was correct to stress the breadth of the restriction and to suggest that it "threaten[ed] to torch a large segment of the Internet community."[144] The CDA—like the regulation in *Pacifica*—substantially burdened listeners by making it considerably more expensive (and, in *Pacifica*, more time consuming) for them to get this information. As importantly, the laws substantially burdened speakers by requiring them to sell their speech rather than distributing it for free, thus dramatically reducing the size of their audience.[145]

Of course, others may want to draw the substantiality threshold higher. One court, for instance, has borrowed the "adequate alternative channels" test from the framework used for content-neutral time, place, or manner restrictions.[146] Under this view, burdens

---

[143] 438 US at 760. See also id at 750 n 28 (plurality) ("Adults who feel the need may purchase tapes and records or go to theaters and nightclubs to hear these words.").

[144] 117 S Ct at 2350.

[145] As this discussion suggests, I disagree with the *Pacifica* holding, and find it hard to reconcile with *ACLU*. Justice Stevens tried to distinguish *Pacifica* in *ACLU* by arguing that "The breadth of the CDA's coverage is wholly unprecedented. Unlike the regulations upheld in *Ginsberg* and *Pacifica*, the scope of the CDA is not limited to commercial speech or commercial entities," id at 2347, but this is just plain wrong. The *Ginsberg* law was not limited to commercial speech: Sales of magazines do not qualify as commercial speech; see *Virginia State Bd of Pharmacy v Virginia Citizens Consumer Council, Inc.*, 425 US 748, 761 (1976)). The *Pacifica* regulation was not limited either to commercial speech or commercial entities; in fact, the broadcast at issue in *Pacifica* was noncommercial speech carried by a nonprofit, noncommercial radio station. See *FCC v League of Women Voters*, 468 US 364, 370 (1984) ("Appellee Pacifica Foundation is a nonprofit corporation that owns and operates several noncommercial educational broadcasting stations"; I believe that Pacifica has been nonprofit since its founding, and know of no evidence that it changed character from 1978 to 1984)). Justice Stevens's other attempts to distinguish *Pacifica* from *ACLU*, 117 S Ct at 2342, are not as obviously factually wrong, but still strike me as unpersuasive.

[146] *American Booksellers v Webb*, 919 F2d 1493 (11th Cir 1990). See Alan Brownstein, *How Rights Are Infringed: The Role of Undue Burden Analysis in Constitutional Doctrine*, 45 Hastings

that leave open adequate alternative channels are deemed insubstantial, and therefore permissible. I don't agree: The adequate alternative channels test, at least as used by the Court, is generally quite tolerant of government regulation, even when the regulations significantly reduce the size of the audience and make it considerably harder for potential viewers to get the speech. This has been criticized even for content-neutral regulations,[147] but given the special concerns involved with content-based regulations,[148] it seems particularly inappropriate here.

In any event, though, even if some would draw the "substantial burden" line in a slightly different place than I would, I hope I have shown that the "substantial burden is unconstitutional" framework is generally the sounder one. Even when some restrictions on a certain category of speech (here speech that's unsuitable for minors) are allowed, the Court should recognize that some burdens are per se unconstitutional, even if they are genuinely necessary to maximally serve the compelling government interest.

c) Results the Rule Would Likely Yield

The "substantial burden is unconstitutional" framework would produce the following results:

i) Butler. The ban on all distribution of material that is unsuitable for minors would be unconstitutional, for a reason compatible with the Court's: The restriction greatly burdens constitutionally protected speech to adults.

ii) Ginsberg. The ban on sale of "obscene-as-to-minors" material to people the seller knows to be minors would be constitutional, for a reason again compatible with the Court's: The restriction bans only constitutionally valueless speech to minors, and imposes only a slight burden on valuable communications.

L J 867, 952 (1994); Gillian E. Metzger, Note, *Unburdening the Undue Burden Standard: Orienting Casey in Constitutional Jurisprudence*, 94 Colum L Rev 2025, 2064 (1994).

[147] Compare Susan H. Williams, *Content Discrimination and the First Amendment*, 139 U Pa L Rev 615, 716–17 (1991); see also id at 642 ("[T]he Court believes that if adequate alternative channels of communication remain, then a regulation restricting a particular alternative will have no more than a minimal effect on speech. This test can also have degrees of strictness. The Court has sometimes described the requirement as one of ample alternative channels, which appears to set a high standard. In practice, however, the Court has often applied an 'adequate' alternatives test, not an 'ample' alternatives test.").

[148] *ACLU*, 117 S Ct at 2348–49 (adequate alternative channels inquiry inapplicable to content-based restrictions); Stone, *Content Regulation*, 25 Wm & Mary L Rev 189 (cited in note 139).

iii)   Pacifica. The restriction on broadcasting "indecent" material would be unconstitutional, even if it is necessary to most fully serve the interest in shielding children, because it substantially burdens communications to adults.[149] And if profane speech has constitutional value even when the listener is a minor, then the restriction would also create a substantial burden on communications to children.

iv)   Sable. The dial-a-porn ban would be unconstitutional, not because there are less restrictive but pretty much equally effective alternatives, but because the ban substantially burdens communications to adults.

v)   Post-Sable dial-a-porn cases.[150] After *Sable*, Congress passed the Helms Amendment, which, as implemented by the FCC, prohibits access to dial-a-porn unless (*a*) the phone service subscriber specifically tells the phone company to allow area code 900 calls on his line, or (*b*) the dial-a-porn service asks for a credit card number. Such a law would be upheld—as it in fact was by the courts of appeals, though on least restrictive alternative grounds—because it doesn't substantially burden speakers or listeners. It does prevent dial-a-porn calls by people who don't have their own phone line and who don't have credit cards, but without a personal phone bill or a credit card, one generally lacks the mechanism to pay for the calls anyway. The only appreciable burden is a slight delay for

---

[149] Some commentators have suggested that a ban on broadcast indecency during afternoon hours would be permissible, on the grounds that "the public [is not] in any serious way restricted if the government requires that Carlin's monologue not be broadcast until after six o'clock or in the evening." C. Edwin Baker, *The Evening Hours During Pacifica Standard Time*, 3 Vill Sports & Ent L J 45, 54 (1996). But it seems to me that even if the burden on listeners of having to wait until 6 P.M. is seen as insubstantial, the burden on the broadcaster is substantial indeed: There are many more listeners tuned in during the morning and late-afternoon drive-time hours than there are after 6 P.M. See, for example, *A New Eastman Radio Study*, Mediaweek 8 (April 29, 1996) (77% of radio listeners tune in during morning drive time and 81% during the afternoon drive time, but only 57% listen between 7 P.M. and midnight). Professor Baker's conclusion that the burden is slight may be based on his view that broadcasters' rights are not particularly significant by themselves, and are properly seen as derivative of the listeners' rights, id at 53–54; I do not share this view, and it's not entirely clear where the Court stands on this question. Compare *Red Lion Broadcasting Co. v FCC*, 395 US 367, 390 (1969) ("It is the right of the viewers and listeners, not the right of the broadcasters, which is paramount") with *FCC v League of Women Voters*, 468 US 364, 378 (1984) ("Unlike common carriers, broadcasters are entitled under the First Amendment to exercise the widest journalistic freedom consistent with their public duties") (internal quotation marks omitted).

[150] *Dial Information Services Corp. v Thornburgh*, 938 F2d 1535 (2d Cir 1991) (upholding Helms Amendment, as implemented by FCC regulations); *Information Providers' Coalition v FCC*, 928 F2d 866 (9th Cir 1991) (same).

those who don't have credit cards, and who thus have to wait until the phone company unblocks their phone lines; but dial-a-porn seems not to be a particularly time-sensitive medium, so this delay is not a substantial burden.

vi) ACLU. The CDA would be unconstitutional because—as I discuss above—banning not-for-pay communications substantially burdens speech to adults, even if the material is still available for sale.[151]

vii) Hypothetical tagging requirement for "obscene-as-to-minors" material. Such a requirement would be constitutional because it does not impose a substantial burden. Its chief burdens are that it (*a*) requires people who put potentially obscene-as-to-minors material online to take the time and effort to rate it; (*b*) tempts people who put on borderline material to err on the safe side and rate it "obscene as to minors" even if it probably doesn't fit within the category; (*c*) risks depriving minors of such misrated-for-safety's-sake material; and (*d*) in some measure alters the speaker's message by compelling them to include the rating. The first three burdens, though, are no greater than what the Court upheld in *Ginsberg*, and they seem modest though not negligible. The fourth burden is harder to evaluate, but strikes me as likewise modest.[152]

viii) Hypothetical tagging requirement for "indecent" material. Such a requirement would be unconstitutional if the government's compelling interest extends only to shielding children from "obscene-as-to-minors" matter. Even slight content-based burdens, such as a tagging requirement, should be unconstitutional in the absence of a compelling interest.[153] If the compelling interest extends only to obscene-as-to-minors matter, then compelled ratings may be

---

[151] If cyberspace speakers could somehow automatically ask a would-be listener for a "cyber ID"—analogous to checking an ID under the *Ginsberg v New York* law—and this verification didn't cost any money, then the law might not substantially burden not-for-pay speech to adults. But to my knowledge no such scheme will be possible any time in the near future. See *ACLU*, 117 S Ct at 2349–50; note 7 above.

[152] Some have argued that a tagging requirement, even if not very burdensome for people who are in the business of distributing speech, is quite burdensome for others, such as individuals or nonprofit organizations distributing such material for free. Compare *ACLU*, 117 S Ct at 2347–48 (seeming to distinguish professional speakers from amateurs). I'm not sure this is true, but I agree that the substantial burden framework should at least in some measure be attentive to such nuances: A burden that's insubstantial in one medium or as to one class of speakers may well be substantial in other contexts.

[153] See, for example, *Riley v National Federation of the Blind*, 487 US 781 (1988). But see *Meese v Keene*, discussed above in note 64.

applied only to such material, not to indecent speech, violent speech, or other categories.

ix) Ban on public display and unattended sales of "obscene-as-to-minors" material. Many states bar public display and unattended sales, in places where minors might be present, of "obscene-as-to-minors" materials.[154] These restrictions have generally been upheld,[155] but they would probably be unconstitutional under the "substantial burden" analysis. Bans on public display—for instance, on murals, paintings hanging in restaurants, and the like—do substantially burden the displayer's ability to communicate to the public. Bans on unattended sales (or unattended browsing) are a lesser burden, but probably still a substantial one, because forcing the publications out of a newsrack and into a bookstore or an attended newsstand will probably substantially decrease their audience.

As the above shows, applying the "substantial burden is unconstitutional" approach would involve some hard calls. Setting the "substantiality" threshold higher might uphold bans on public display of "obscene-as-to-minors" matter, and perhaps even the *Pa-*

---

[154] For example, Ala Code §§ 13A-12-200.1(3), 13A-12-200.5 (1994) (probably prohibiting only display for sale); Ariz Rev Stat Ann § 13-3507 (West 1989) (prohibiting any display in any "place where minors are invited as part of the general public"); Fla Stat Ann § 847.0125 (West 1994) (prohibiting only display for sale); Ga Code Ann § 16-12-103(e) (Michie 1996) (prohibiting any display in any place "where minors are or may be invited as part of the general public"); Ind Code Ann § 35-49-3-3(2) (Burns 1994) (prohibiting any display "in an area to which minors have visual, auditory, or physical access"); Kan Stat Ann § 21-4301c(a)(1) (1995) (prohibiting display in commercial establishments only); La Rev Stat Ann § 14:91.11 (West 1995) (prohibiting any display "at a newsstand or any other commercial establishment which is open to persons under the age of seventeen years"); Minn Stat Ann § 617.293 (West 1987 & Supp 1996) (prohibiting commercial display); NM Stat Ann § 30-37-2.1 (1997) (prohibiting display only while offering for sale "in a retail establishment open to the general public," and "in such a way that it is on open display to, or within the convenient reach of, minors who may frequent the retail establishment"); NC Gen Stat § 14-190.14(a) (1993) (prohibiting display in commercial establishments only); 21 Okla Stat Ann §§ 1040.75, 1040.76 (West 1983 & Supp 1997) (prohibiting all display, "including but not limited to . . . commercial establishment[s]"); Tenn Code Ann § 39-17-914(a) (1991) (prohibiting display for sale or rent); Tex Penal Code Ann § 43.24 (Vernon 1994) (prohibiting all display, whenever person is "reckless about whether a minor is present who will be offended or alarmed by the display"); 13 Vt Stat Ann §§ 2801(8), 2804a (Equity 1974 & Supp 1997) (prohibiting display "for advertising purposes").

[155] See, for example, *Crawford v Lungren,* 96 F3d 380 (9th Cir 1996) (upholding ban on unattended coin-operated newsrack sales of "harmful to minors" material); *American Booksellers v Webb,* 919 F2d 1493 (11th Cir 1990) (upholding ban on display, in a place accessible to minors, of any material that's "harmful to minors"); *Davis-Kidd Booksellers, Inc. v McWherter,* 866 SW2d 520 (Tenn 1993) (same).

cifica regulation. Setting it lower might invalidate the hypothetical "obscene-as-to-minors" tagging requirement, and perhaps even the Helms Amendment and the law upheld in *Ginsberg*. Nonetheless, the rule creates a zone of fairly easy cases,[156] and in the hard cases focuses decision makers on the important question.

3. The "Substantial Burden/Less Restrictive Alternative Hybrid" Approach

The "substantial burden is unconstitutional" test would generally uphold any restriction on material unsuitable for minors (whether that is defined as indecent material or obscene-as-to-minors material) if the restriction imposes an insubstantial burden on free speech.[157] One might, however, argue that even minor burdens should be unconstitutional if they provide only slight marginal gains to the government interest—if there's a less restrictive but pretty much equally effective alternative. Even a small speech cost, the argument would go, can be justified only by a significant shielding benefit.

But whatever the merits of inquiries into "pretty much equally effective alternatives" in other strict scrutiny contexts, I doubt that such an inquiry would be particularly helpful here. Less restrictive alternatives will rarely be clearly pretty much as effective as more restrictive ones. This is particularly evident in *ACLU*, where few alternatives would work nearly as well as a total ban on free online material. Likewise, the alternative given in *Butler* to a total ban on the distribution of explicit material—a ban on distributing such material to children—is much less effective than the total ban. The alternatives to bans on broadcast indecency, such as restrictions on day and evening broadcasts, are likewise considerably less effective.[158]

---

[156] See Frederick Schauer, *Easy Cases*, 58 S Cal L Rev 399 (1985).

[157] I use the phrase "unsuitable for minors" advisedly here: Though I argue that the government should be able to burden—even insubstantially—only that speech which is "obscene as to minors," rather than merely "indecent," I recognize that others might take a different view. The "substantial burden" test is flexible enough to accommodate any definition of "unsuitability."

[158] The dial-a-porn ban struck down in *Sable* may have been something of an exception; the alternatives eventually upheld in *Information Providers' Coalition v FCC*, 928 F2d 866 (9th Cir 1991), and *Dial Information Services Corp. v Thornburgh*, 938 F2d 1535 (2d Cir 1991), did seem to be pretty much as effective as the ban. See the discussion in Part III.D.

These alternatives are less restrictive than a total ban because, unlike the ban, they aim to segregate two categories of people: (1) adults (and minors whose parents choose not to shield them), who should have access to the materials, and (2) all other minors, who shouldn't have access. But any such attempted segregation will also be less effective, because it will necessarily lump some minors from the second category together with the people in the first. Compelled tagging of online material (as opposed to a ban on free online indecency) protects the access rights of people who don't have filters running on their computer, but this class of people will necessarily include some minors who are visiting friends whose computers are unshielded. Channeling broadcast indecency to 10 P.M. through 6 A.M. (as opposed to totally banning it) protects the access rights of adults who are awake between 10 and 6, but also gives access to some minors who are up during those times. Allowing the distribution of explicit materials to adults (as opposed to totally banning such distribution) protects the access rights of adults, but also gives access to some minors who get the material from those adults.

Thus, while I think the substantial burden/less restrictive alternative hybrid approach is plausible, I suspect it would usually (if properly applied) reach the same results as the "substantial burden is unconstitutional" framework: Less restrictive means will almost always be less effective. I also suspect that the extra inquiry into less restrictive alternatives would be complicated and error prone, tending to lead courts into the same kinds of empirical mistakes that the *ACLU* Court fell into. These two points, I think, counsel in favor of the simpler "substantial burden is unconstitutional" framework. On the other hand, because the hybrid approach might at least theoretically protect speech more than a pure substantial burden framework would—without unduly sacrificing the government's ability to shield children—many free speech maximalists may support it.

4. The "Cost-Benefit Weighing" Approach

As I mentioned above, in theory the most appealing approach may be a sliding-scale one: If there is value in shielding children, then as a restriction provides more shielding (as compared to the next best alternative), we should be willing to tolerate a greater burden on the countervailing value of free speech. Thus, consider two examples:

A ban on unattended coin-operated newsracks containing obscene-as-to-minors (not just indecent) material. Striking down the ban would allow minors easy access to some hardcore matter. Upholding the ban would substantially interfere with distribution of the material to adults: Many publications are sold through newsracks precisely because newsracks make it easier for people to buy the publications, and thus substantially increase the publication's audience; requiring the material to be sold through attended newsstands would probably substantially decrease the audience. Nonetheless, while the burden is substantial, it is not a total ban, and perhaps is less substantial than the burden imposed by the CDA.[159]

Time restrictions on broadcast indecency. Here, at least before V-chip-like technology became available, there really were no less restrictive but pretty much equally effective alternatives to a total ban.[160] Striking down the ban would expose minors to whatever indecency people broadcast. Upholding the ban would substantially burden free speech, though not as much as the law in *Butler*, which applied to all media. Following some hints given by *Pacifica*, Congress and the FCC limited the indecency ban to 6 A.M. TO 10 P.M.,[161] which made it less burdensome but also less effective. Any even less burdensome restrictions would be less effective still.

My sense is that many people who generally favor strong free speech protections nonetheless support the newsrack ban and perhaps even some broadcast time restrictions:[162] The extra shielding

---

[159] Compare *Crawford v Lungren*, 96 F3d 380 (9th Cir 1996), which upheld such a newsrack restriction under a weighing approach.

[160] Though the D.C. Circuit has in fact struck down such a total ban, see note 140, it didn't suggest that there were any pretty much equally effective alternatives to the ban. Its conclusion was instead based on the proposition that the total ban was just too grave a burden.

[161] Actually, the new indecency restriction applied to the 6 A.M.–10 P.M. period for public broadcasters, and the 6 A.M.–12 midnight period for commercial broadcasters. The D.C. Circuit held this was impermissibly discriminatory, and that though a flat 6 A.M.–12 midnight ban would have been constitutional, the public broadcaster exemption had to be applied to all stations. *Action for Children's Television v FCC*, 58 F3d 654 (DC Cir 1995) (en banc).

[162] See, for example, C. Edwin Baker, *The Evening Hours During Pacifica Standard Time*, 3 Vill Sports & Ent L J 15 (1996) (suggesting that while the *Pacifica* ban swept too broadly, a ban on daytime broadcasts might be permissible); Arnold H. Loewy, *Obscenity, Pornography, and First Amendment Theory*, 2 Wm & Mary Bill Rts J 471, 491 (1993) (suggesting that "a more carefully tailored effort at channeling, such as a prohibition of scatological speech on Saturday morning television," might be appropriate).

of children seems enough to "outweigh" the substantial, but not very great, burden on free speech. Some lower court decisions dealing with newsrack restrictions, general restrictions on public display of obscene-as-to-minors material, and even the CDA itself in fact use something like this weighing approach.[163] Justice Scalia's *Sable* concurrence likewise argues that "the more pornographic"— and thus presumably the more harmful—the material, "the more reasonable it becomes to insist upon greater assurance of insulation from minors."[164]

One might therefore try to directly implement a "cost-benefit weighing" approach, in which the government decision maker (legislator, executive official, or judge) "weighs" the magnitude of the burden on speech against the magnitude of the extra shielding that the law would provide. Thus, under this test, the *ACLU* Court would have "weighed" the marginal speech burden imposed by the CDA (compared to that imposed by alternatives, such as a tagging requirement)—which is quite high, since a ban is much more burdensome than tagging—against the level of marginal shielding that the CDA provides relative to the alternatives, which the Court thought was minimal but which in fact was probably quite high.

But for the reasons I discussed above in Part IV.A, I don't believe this approach can be practically administered by the many judicial, legislative, and executive officials throughout the country. The "compelling interest trumps" and "substantial burden is unconstitutional" tests provide some definiteness because they involve the comparison of something, for instance, the degree of burden on speech, against a fixed benchmark that is similar in kind, such as a threshold burden: How large is the burden here relative to the burdens recognized as substantial or insubstantial by prior cases? Cost-benefit weighing, on the other hand, in each case demands a comparison of two things (the burden and the benefit) that are very different, a much harder proposition.

---

[163] See, for example, *Shea v Reno*, 930 F Supp 916, 941 (SDNY 1996) (asking whether "the benefits . . . achieved [by the CDA] would outweigh the burden . . . imposed on the First Amendment rights of adults"); *Carlin Communications, Inc. v FCC*, 837 F2d 546, 555 (2d Cir 1988) ("the State may not regulate at all if it turns out that even the least restrictive means of regulation is still unreasonable when its limitations on freedom of speech are balanced against the benefits gained from those limitations"); *American Booksellers v Webb*, 919 F2d 1493 (11th Cir 1990); *Crawford v Lungren*, 96 F3d 380 (9th Cir 1996).

[164] 492 US at 132.

The one free speech doctrine that explicitly tries to use cost-benefit weighing—the *Pickering* test for speech restrictions imposed by the government as employer—supports this skepticism. *Pickering* specifically calls for sliding-scale "balanc[ing]" of "the interests of the [employee], as a citizen, in commenting upon matters of public concern" against "the interest of the State, as an employer, in promoting the efficiency of the public services it performs through its employees."[165] The Court has acknowledged that "such particularized balancing is difficult,"[166] and this seems an understatement. From all I've seen of the lower court decisions, the test is essentially indeterminate in all but the easiest cases, cases that could well be resolved through more categorical rules. This indeterminacy is troubling even when the government is acting as employer, a context in which the Court properly accepts greater speech restrictions, but would be especially improper when evaluating laws imposed by the government acting as sovereign.[167]

Cost-benefit weighing in the child shielding context would also work only if the Court does what it has so far avoided doing: if it actually determines the extent of the harm caused by indecent or "obscene-as-to-minors" speech—rather than just the presence of some nontrivial harm—and thus the true benefit of shielding. There is something of a consensus that some such benefit exists, which is probably enough to justify trying to realize this benefit through less than substantially burdensome restrictions. But once one must "weigh" even substantial free speech burdens against the purported benefits of shielding, one can't avoid having to determine just how serious these benefits are. The relatively uncontroversial claim that the benefits exist will not be very helpful here: One will need some agreement on at least the rough magnitude of the benefits, compared to the magnitude of the speech burden, and such an agreement may be hard to achieve.[168]

---

[165] *Pickering v Board of Education*, 391 US 563, 568 (1968); see also *Rankin v McPherson*, 483 US 378, 388 (1987).

[166] *Connick v Myers*, 461 US 138, 150 (1983).

[167] See *Waters v Churchill*, 114 S Ct 1878, 1886–88 (1994) (plurality) (discussing differences in the First Amendment tests appropriate when the government is acting as sovereign and when the government is acting as employer).

[168] Compare *Ginsberg v New York*, 390 US 629, 641–43 (1968) (expressing uncertainty about whether "obscene-as-to-minors" speech is really harmful to minors, but concluding that a restriction on such speech is permissible because the speech is constitutionally valueless).

The weighing approach seems theoretically most satisfying, because it promises a full recognition and comparison of both the costs to free speech of regulation and the costs to minors of adult freedom. But for the reasons given above, it would probably be practically intractable, especially given the need for the Court to provide meaningful constraints to other government actors.

5. The "Multiple Speech Subclasses" Approach

We can avoid some of the administrative problems of a sliding-scale approach by trying to approximate it through a sort of graduated step-ladder—what I call the "multiple speech subclasses" framework, in which the Court sets up different levels of tolerable burden for different kinds of speech, based on perceived differences in harm. Applying this framework doesn't require direct comparison of burden and benefit, but only of burden against threshold burden.

For instance, the Court might say that merely indecent speech is fairly harmless, that any loss of shielding against indecent speech is thus of rather little consequence, and that any burden beyond the mildest should therefore be impermissible. This would be a "substantial burden is unconstitutional" approach, with a low threshold of substantiality. On the other hand, the Court might conclude that obscene-as-to-minors speech is more harmful (because it appeals to prurient interests), that the loss of shielding against that kind of speech is thus more important, and that even fairly substantial—but not very great—burdens on the speech should therefore be allowed. This would also be a "substantial burden is unconstitutional" approach, but with a higher substantiality threshold.[169]

This framework is less attentive than pure cost-benefit weighing to fine differences in weights on both sides, and is thus both theoretically less perfect and practically more administrable. It would require only a few up-front decisions about the price we should be willing to pay for the freedom to communicate various kinds

---

[169] In judging the sacrifice of shielding, the Court could also look at the efficacy of less restrictive alternatives: It might, for instance, say that if the less restrictive alternatives are equally effective, any burden is unconstitutional; if they are pretty much equally effective, substantial burdens are unconstitutional; and if they are not at all effective, only very large burdens (however defined) are unconstitutional. For the reasons explained in Part IV.B.3, though, I think this sort of framework will probably not be that useful.

of speech, rather than a fresh weighing in each case. A good analogy is the libel law framework, which sets up different tests for private concern speech, private figure/public concern speech, and public figure/public concern speech, each tolerating a different level of incidental burden on constitutionally protected expression.[170]

I suspect even this framework would probably be too complex to be workable; the "substantial burden is unconstitutional" approach discussed in Part IV.B.2 would be practically superior. Nonetheless, even some version of the "multiple speech subclasses" framework is better than the orthodox strict scrutiny "compelling interest trumps" test.

6. Summary

I have argued that, where speech that's supposedly unsuitable for children is concerned, the Court should focus primarily on the burden that the restriction imposes on valuable speech. The Court should draw benchmarks that distinguish permissible insubstantial burdens from impermissible substantial ones, benchmarks that government decision makers can consult in the future.

Laws that impose sufficiently substantial burdens, I've argued, are unconstitutional even if they're genuinely necessary to shield children; the "compelling interest trumps" framework is therefore unsound. And while it seems appealing to "weigh" the degree of the burden in each case against the benefit the law brings, such a "cost-benefit weighing" framework is practically unadministrable.

I've identified three alternatives to these frameworks: (*a*) "Substantial burden is unconstitutional," which strikes down all substantial burdens and allows all insubstantial ones. (*b*) "Substantial burden/less restrictive alternative hybrid," which strikes down all substantial burdens *and* those insubstantial burdens that are not genuinely necessary to shield children, and allows only those burdens that are both insubstantial and necessary. (*c*) "Multiple speech subclasses," which sets different levels of permissible burden for different subclasses of unsuitable-for-minors speech.

The "substantial burden is unconstitutional" framework is the

---

[170] See *Dun & Bradstreet, Inc. v Greenmoss Builders, Inc.*, 472 US 749 (1985) (private concern); *Gertz v Robert Welch, Inc.*, 418 US 323 (1974) (public concern/private figure); *New York Times Co. v Sullivan*, 376 US 254 (1964) (public concern/public figure).

simplest of the three, and I think the best. Though it's in some respects theoretically less satisfying than the others, because it seems to sometimes overprotect speech and sometimes underprotect it, it's probably practically more effective. "Less restrictive alternative" inquiries are, if done candidly, largely fruitless in this area; and defining one level of "unsuitability for minors" and one "substantiality" threshold seems hard enough that I doubt courts can effectively define multiple levels of unsuitability and multiple thresholds of substantiality.

Nonetheless, the choice between these three frameworks is a close call. They all recognize that some burdens are high enough to be impermissible even if the burdens are really necessary to shield children. They all accept, as the Court and much of the country seem to accept, that certain kinds of burdens on material that is unsuitable for minors are slight enough to be allowed. And because they require that burdens be compared against threshold burdens, rather than commanding an amorphous case-by-case weighing of burden on speech against increase of shielding, they are all relatively practically administrable. Each of them would have yielded a better—more honest and more precedentially valuable—opinion in *ACLU* than the Court produced using the orthodox "compelling interest trumps" framework.

V. Conclusion: Applications to Other Kinds of Speech Restrictions

This article has focused on one particular set of speech restrictions—restrictions on material that's supposedly unsuitable for minors. I have argued that:

1. *ACLU* reached the right result but erred in its reasoning.

2. This error sheds light on a deeper problem: The Court's official test in this area—strict scrutiny, with its "compelling interest trumps" approach—is unsound, and if applied candidly would lead to wrong results.

3. Instead of compensating for the unsound test's errors by misapplying it, the Court should design a test that's better suited to the concerns raised by the interest in shielding children.

4. Directly "weighing" the burden of a restriction against its benefits is not feasible in a system in which the Court must create administrable rules for a myriad other government actors.

5. Rather, the best solution is one that tolerates certain less-than-substantial burdens on a narrow class of speech, but that categorically invalidates any burdens that are substantial.

Much of this, I believe, is also applicable to other free speech contexts. *ACLU* is just one of many cases in which, as I have argued in a recent article,[171] the Court has fudged the facts in order to reach the right results under its strict scrutiny framework. This felt need to fudge strongly suggests that the strict scrutiny framework is itself unsound in these cases: Speech must often be protected even though protecting it unavoidably causes substantial costs to compelling government interests—even though there are *no* less restrictive but pretty much equally effective alternatives to speech suppression.[172] The line drawn by the "compelling interest trumps" test inadequately reconciles the values at stake in such cases.

I propose that instead the Court should return to the framework it generally followed as it was developing libel law, obscenity law, and various other major free speech doctrines:

1. A strong presumption that speech restrictions justified by the communicative impact of speech are unconstitutional.[173]

---

[171] Volokh, *Freedom of Speech, Permissible Tailoring and Transcending Strict Scrutiny*, 144 U Pa L Rev 2417 (cited in note 20).

[172] Thus, for instance, speech by political candidates in wartime is constitutionally protected even if it can gravely hurt the war effort, and even if banning it is the only effective way to win the war quickly and save soldiers' lives. Id at 2425–31. Speech that advocates violence is constitutionally protected even though it indeed tends to encourage future violence, and even though other means of preventing the future violence can't entirely, or even close to entirely, undo the damage that the speech has done. Id at 2432–36. Some kinds of disclosures by fundraisers cannot be compelled even though compelling them is the only effective way of preventing misperceptions on the contributors' part. Id at 2441–42. Independent expenditures advocating the election of a candidate are constitutionally protected despite the danger of corruption they unavoidably pose. Id at 2442. (Even those who disagree with *Buckley v Valeo* and conclude that the government should be able to restrict independent campaign-related expenditures would probably agree that *some* expenditures must be constitutionally protected despite their potential for causing corruption. Newspapers regularly spend many thousands of dollars in labor and newsprint explicitly endorsing candidates and sometimes quietly boosting them through favorable news coverage; and many politicians will think twice before saying no to a publisher whose efforts can mean so much in a future election. Nonetheless, I take it that a ban on endorsements by newspapers would be widely agreed to be unconstitutional, despite the risk of corruption that such assistance poses.) I don't want to repeat the entire explanation of my thesis here, but I hope my point about *ACLU* makes it more plausible: Strict scrutiny is a flawed approach for dealing with the constitutionality of content-based speech restrictions.

[173] I speak here of restrictions imposed by the government as sovereign. The presumption might be considerably weaker (or perhaps even nonexistent) when the government is acting

2. A recognition that certain classes of restrictions are constitutional, either because they do not substantially burden valuable speech, or (in rare situations) because, despite their substantial burden on valuable speech, they are genuinely so crucial that we must sometimes substantially sacrifice speech in their name.

3. Development of individual bodies of law to deal with these classes of restrictions.

Thus, libel law evolved from a conclusion that some restrictions on false and defamatory speech would serve an important interest without substantially burdening valuable expression.[174] Obscenity law evolved from a (controversial) judgment that restrictions on some sexually explicit material would likewise not substantially burden valuable speech. Incitement law recognized that some burdens even on core political advocacy might be needed to preserve life and limb, though even that most important of interests must often yield to free speech rights. Similar rules should be developed for those areas (which, I hope, will be relatively few) where—as with speech unsuitable for minors—the Court believes some additional restrictions are proper.

I am not particularly happy about the Court fragmenting First Amendment doctrine this way, and there certainly is great appeal to a simple, consistent Grand Principle that explains all free speech law. Perhaps one day such a principle may evolve from the Court's experience with the individual subtests;[175] in particular, I think versions of the substantial burden approach outlined above have promise in some (though not all) areas.[176] But so far the Court has not found a principle that is both broad and accurate.

---

in other contexts, for instance as employer, K–12 educator, proprietor of a nonpublic forum, speaker, and so on.

[174] *Gertz v Robert Welch, Inc.*, 418 US 323 (1974).

[175] Consider the expressive conduct test and the time/place/manner restriction test, which evolved separately, but have ultimately proven to be largely manifestations of the same principle. *Ward v Rock Against Racism*, 491 US 781 (1989).

[176] The substantial burden framework might help explain the *Buckley v Valeo* distinction between contributions and independent expenditures: A restriction on contributions, as *Buckley* pointed out, poses a relatively modest burden on speech, precisely because independent expenditures are available as an alternative. On the other hand, a restriction on independent expenditures as well as contributions would be a tremendous burden on a person's ability to communicate his views about a candidate. Even if banning expensive speech about candidates is necessary to minimize corruption, such a broad restraint on speech cannot be justified.

Likewise, the solution that I've proposed to the constitutional questions surrounding workplace harassment law, see Eugene Volokh, *Freedom of Speech and Workplace Harassment Law*, 39 UCLA L Rev 1791 (1992), may be best understood as focusing on the substantiality

For now, I would be satisfied with the Court jettisoning its current, unsound, Grand Principle, and reawakening to the need to look for better (even if more particularistic) approaches; and there's reason to think the Court is indeed prepared to do so. Justice Stevens himself has often criticized the strict scrutiny framework.[177] Justice Kennedy has at times explicitly urged that it be rejected and replaced by a more categorical approach similar to the one described above.[178] A recent opinion by Justice Thomas, while formally using strict scrutiny, in effect urged a substantial-burden-like test, one that would reject certain laws even if they are necessary to accomplish certain interests that the Court has found compelling.[179]

Believing as I do in rather strong free speech protection, I hope the Court will make the areas of permissible regulation as narrow as possible; and I recognize that discarding existing rules always poses a risk that the new rules will be worse. Nonetheless, the current situation is already not very good. The strict scrutiny test would on its face uphold certain restrictions that ought not be upheld; and though the Court has tended to avoid these results, it has done so only by creating precedents that, because of their lack of candor, make the law even murkier. Given this, there's much to be gained from rejecting strict scrutiny and confronting the important questions more openly and clearly.

---

of the burden on speech. Restrictions on unwanted one-to-one speech, I argue, are not substantially burdensome on valuable communications, because they still allow people to freely speak to colleagues other than the unwilling listener. (In my view, continued communication that is received *only* by unwilling listeners is of relatively slight constitutional value.) On the other hand, restricting one-to-many speech, such as posters or overheard lunchroom conversations or company newsletters or department-wide e-mail, does indeed substantially burden people's ability to communicate with potentially willing listeners.

[177] See, for example, *Eu v San Francisco County Democratic Central Comm.*, 489 US 214, 234 (1989) (Stevens concurring).

[178] *Simon & Schuster, Inc. v Members of the N.Y. State Crime Victims Board*, 502 US 105, 124–28 (1991) (Kennedy concurring in the judgment); *Burson v Freeman*, 504 US 191, 213 (1992) (Kennedy concurring). I disagree with Kennedy's ultimate conclusion in *Burson*, compare Eugene Volokh, *Freedom of Speech and the Constitutional Tension Method*, 3 U Chi Roundtable 223 (1996), but I generally agree with his overall framework.

[179] *Colorado Republican Fed. Campaign Comm. v FEC*, 116 S Ct 2309, 2329 (1996) (Thomas concurring in part and dissenting in part).

EVAN H. CAMINKER

PRINTZ, STATE SOVEREIGNTY, AND THE LIMITS OF FORMALISM

The latest in the recent spate of Supreme Court decisions reshaping American federalism,[1] *Printz v United States*[2] embodies the Court's most emphatic acclamation of state sovereignty since the New Deal. The Court had previously declared in *New York v United States*[3] that while Congress may preempt state regulation with federal regulation, and may encourage states to implement federal policy by offering them positive or negative incentives, Congress may not "commandee[r] the legislative processes of the States by directly compelling them to enact and enforce a federal regulatory program."[4] In *Printz*, the Court took a significant step further and held that Congress cannot conscript state executive officers to administer a federal statute. Invoking this principle, the Court invalidated provisions of the Brady Handgun Violence Prevention Act[5] that required state law enforcement officers to help administer a federal handgun control policy.

Evan H. Caminker is Professor of Law at the University of California, Los Angeles.

AUTHOR'S NOTE: I thank Vik Amar, Stephen Gardbaum, Craig Goldblatt, Marty Lederman, Michael Small, Jonathan Varat, and Eugene Volokh for their comments on an earlier draft, or for enriching conversation about the ideas contained herein. I also thank Peter Masaitis and Veronica Sanchez for their research and production assistance.

[1] See, for example, *United States v Lopez*, 514 US 549 (1995) (limiting the scope of the Commerce Clause power); *Seminole Tribe v Florida*, 116 S Ct 1114 (1996) (holding Congress cannot abrogate states' Eleventh Amendment immunity from suit in federal court pursuant to its Article I powers); *City of Boerne v Flores*, 117 S Ct 2157 (1997) (limiting scope of Fourteenth Amendment's Section 5 power).

[2] 117 S Ct 2365 (1997).

[3] 505 US 144 (1992).

[4] Id at 176 (citation omitted).

[5] 18 USC §§ 922, 924, 925A (1994).

Printz's holding is neither surprising nor implausible. And while it represents a decisive symbolic victory for state sovereignty, some would characterize its immediate practical impact as relatively minor.[6] But the decision is particularly striking because of the analytical route the Court took to its doctrinal destination; all but the most unreflective formalists should find its reasoning process troubling. More than any other decision in the recent antinationalist movement, *Printz* suggests that something is amiss in the way the Court justifies its vision of federal-state relations.

Justice Scalia's opinion for the Court is decidedly formalist in two distinct senses. First, the Court embraces "doctrinal formalism," by which I mean the Court takes a formalist approach to constructing a judicially enforceable doctrine. The Court announced a categorical anti-commandeering rule, one not subject to any case-by-case balancing of interests or measurement of burden. This doctrinal approach helps to send relatively clear signals to political actors, and courts applying the rule in future cases need

---

[6] The Court did invalidate key provisions of the Brady Act, which many thought an important weapon in the national fight against violent crime. But there are only a handful of other recent commandeering statutes that clearly fall within the decision's ambit. See Lead Contamination Control Act of 1988, 42 USC §§ 300j-21-26 (1994) (requiring states to assist local educational agencies in remedying lead contamination in drinking water coolers located in schools and day-care centers); Forest Resources Conservation and Shortage Relief Act of 1990, 16 USC §§ 620a–620J (1994) (requiring certain western states to promulgate regulations reducing their export of unprocessed timber harvested from state public lands). A plausible, though I think ultimately unpersuasive, commandeering claim has been made against the 1993 Indian Gaming Regulatory Act, 25 USC §§ 2701–21 (1994) (requiring, among other things, that states follow various procedures in negotiating with Native American tribes seeking to establish gaming ventures within the state). Furthermore, two district courts have used dubious reasoning to invalidate on commandeering grounds the Driver's Privacy Protection Act of 1994, 18 USC §§ 2721–25, see *Oklahoma v United States,* 1997 US Dist LEXIS 14455 (WD Ok); *Condon v Reno,* 972 F Supp 977 (DSC 1997), even though this federal statute merely restrains state action and does not impose affirmative obligations on state officials.

Various statutes require state officials to gather and report information to federal authorities. These include 15 USC § 2224 (1994) (states must report lists of places of public accommodation affecting interstate commerce); 15 USC § 2645 (1994) (governors must conduct certain reporting and approval activities with respect to local educational agencies); 20 USC § 4013 (1994) (governors must submit plans for asbestos abatement and follow certain reporting procedures); 42 USC § 5779(a) (1994) (state and local law enforcement agencies must report cases of missing children); 42 USC § 6933 (1994) (states must inventory hazardous waste sites); 42 USC § 6991(a) (1994) (governors must inventory underground storage tanks); 42 USC §§ 11001, 11003 (1994) (state must collect and report comprehensive data concerning the release of hazardous substances, and must create emergency response commissions). *Printz* purported not to decide whether such reporting requirements fall within the Court's anti-commandeering rule. 117 S Ct at 2376; see also id at 2385 (O'Connor concurring). I discuss this question at text and notes 108–15.

not directly assess and balance unavoidably contestable values. While some may have preferred the Court to announce a more deferential balancing test of sorts, I do not quarrel here with the Court's doctrinal formalism.

Justice Scalia's opinion also embraces "interpretive formalism," by which I mean the Court takes a formalist approach to interpreting the meaning of the Constitution. The Court's analysis is driven by its identification of various "essential postulates"[7] revealed by constitutional text and structure concerning both the vertical and horizontal separation of governmental powers. The Court constructed from these postulates both a formal model of a state as sovereign and a formal model of the federal executive as unitary, and then applied these models to deduce a prohibition against congressional commandeering of state executives. The Court eschewed a more "functionalist" approach to interpretation, in that it pointedly avoided a sensitive assessment of whether such commandeering undermines any of the diverse values or purposes thought to underlie our various divisions of governmental authority, either at its founding or today. This decision is about, not the values of federalism or executive unity, but the intrinsic nature of state sovereignty and the federal executive themselves.

Scholars and jurists have engaged in a long-standing debate concerning the general propriety of formalist and functionalist approaches to constitutional interpretation, with Justice Scalia ardently championing the former. My concern here is not with arbitrating this dispute at a high level of abstraction; indeed, I think that both interpretive approaches have an important role to play. My concern is rather with maintaining the integrity of each approach, which requires that each is both skillfully applied and invoked only when appropriate. Where foundational sources of text, structure, and history provide scant guidance, interpretive formalism can easily become an exercise in undirected choice from among competing conceptions and formulations—choice that seems arbitrary because it appears neither dictated by the underlying sources, nor counseled by articulated purposes, values, or consequences.

The constitutional question posed in *Printz* is not easily suscep-

---

[7] 117 S Ct at 2376.

tible to successful formalist reasoning. Interpretive formalism may, for example, be on firmer footing when employed to resolve certain horizontal separation of powers controversies; the Constitution says a great deal, both explicitly and implicitly, about certain specific questions concerning the organization and interaction of the three federal departments.[8] But there is a comparative dearth of textual, historical, structural, and conceptual guideposts with respect to the congressional regulation of state governmental activities. Thus, although the Court tried to surround its construction of state sovereignty and executive unity principles with an aura of inexorability, the interpretive enterprise inevitably rests on ad hoc judgments. At various points along the way, the Court bridged lacunae in its reasoning by choosing certain plausible premises and rejecting others, without persuasively grounding its choices in text, history, or structure. Nor did the Court offer and justify an affirmative constitutional vision of intergovernmental relations that might guide these choices. Even for those who agree with the result, the Court's opinion will likely feel strained and ultimately unpersuasive.

The Court's approach is unsettling in a second respect. Because the Court failed to articulate any normative constitutional vision concerning the proper federal-state balance of power driving its construction of state sovereignty, we are left in the dark as to the broader meaning of *Printz*. For example, the Court left open the possibility that particular constitutional provisions outside of Article I, Section 8 might still authorize congressional commandeering, but the Court provided little guidance for determining when this would be so. More ominously, the Court clearly forewarned that it might soon provide states with greater doctrinal protection against federal regulations that impose equivalent burdens on states and private entities alike. Indeed, the practical significance of *Printz* may lie as much or more in its potential doctrinal extensions than in the anti-commandeering rule itself. But whether the Court ultimately embraces or rejects these extensions will likely turn primarily on the Court's evaluation of various federalism norms, about which the *Printz* opinion itself pointedly provides no guidance.

---

[8] See, for example, *INS v Chadha*, 462 US 919 (1983) (enforcing bicameralism and presentment limitations on one-House legislative veto); *Freytag v Commissioner*, 501 US 868 (1991) (enforcing Appointments Clause limitations on organization of court systems).

Printz thus provides an illuminating case study of the limits of interpretive formalism. In Part I, I briefly describe the underlying case and the Court's opinion. In Part II, I examine the process by which the Court constructed the particular principles of state sovereignty and executive unity that led it to invalidate congressional commandeering of state executives. My assessment reveals that, even if the Court's destination is defensible, its methodological route is disquieting. In Part III, I first assess *Printz*'s doctrinal implications for Congress's continuing ability to commandeer state officials in various ways and contexts, as well as the decision's immediate practical implications for federal-state relations. I then assess *Printz*'s future doctrinal implications for generally applicable regulations imposed on both state and private actors.

I. The Printz Decision

The Gun Control Act of 1968[9] forbids dealers from selling certain types of guns to certain people, such as minors, nonresidents, convicted felons, fugitives from justice, and drug abusers. Congress amended the Act in 1993 by passing the Brady Handgun Violence Prevention Act.[10] This Act requires a prospective purchaser to give a gun dealer a written statement asserting her qualification for ownership under the federal criteria. The dealer must then submit the statement to the "chief law enforcement officer" (CLEO) in the jurisdiction, meaning a state police officer or sheriff. The CLEO must make a "reasonable effort" to determine in five days if the sale would comply with federal as well as state and local law; if it does not, the sale may not occur, and upon request the CLEO must explain why. This conscription of state officials is merely an interim provision, as the Act contemplates direct enforcement by gun dealers themselves through a national call-in background check system by the end of 1998.

The Supreme Court held in a five-four vote that the Brady Act's interim duties imposed on CLEOs violate the federal Constitution because "the Federal Government may not compel the States to implement, by legislation or executive action, federal regulatory

[9] 18 USC §§ 921 et seq (1994).
[10] 18 USC §§ 922, 924, 925A (1994).

programs."[11] Writing for the majority, Justice Scalia held that such commandeering violates a principle of state sovereignty that is grounded in historical understanding, constitutional structure, and precedent.[12]

The majority opinion first examined various historical data. After considering both early and more recent congressional experimentation with commandeering, and interpreting various passages in The Federalist that alluded to state administration of federal law, Justice Scalia dismissed the contention that the Constitution was originally understood to authorize congressional commandeering of executive officials. In his view, the scant record of commandeering efforts "tends to negate the existence of the congressional power asserted here . . . ."[13] Justice Scalia next invoked structural reasoning. He maintained that commandeering violates the concept of "dual sovereignty," according to which each state is entitled to freedom from congressional interference with its ability "to represent and remain accountable to its own citizens."[14] According to the majority, " '[t]he Framers explicitly chose a Constitution that confers upon Congress the power to regulate individuals, not States.' "[15] Finally, Justice Scalia argued that *Printz* cannot be fairly distinguished from *New York*. He rebuffed the federal government's proposed distinction between coerced lawmaking and mere assistance in law implementation, maintaining that the principle of state sovereignty underlying *New York* protects the autonomy of state officials who "execute" law as well as those who create it. The Court conceded that its categorical anti-commandeering rule may appear "formalist," but maintained that such a rule follows from the recognition that commandeering is "fundamentally incompatible with our constitutional system of dual sovereignty."[16]

---

[11] *Printz*, 117 S Ct at 2380.

[12] Justice Scalia's opinion was joined in full by Chief Justice Rehnquist and Justices O'Connor, Kennedy, and Thomas. Both Justices O'Connor and Thomas wrote brief concurring opinions.

[13] 117 S Ct at 2376.

[14] Id at 2377.

[15] Id, quoting *New York v United States*, 505 US 144, 166 (1992).

[16] *Printz*, 117 S Ct at 2384.

The majority opinion also concluded that commandeering of state executives violates Article II of the Constitution. According to the majority, this Article establishes a principle of executive unity, which demands that the President oversee the execution of all federal law. The Brady Act transgresses this principle, reasoned the majority, because the President lacks meaningful control over the thousands of state CLEOs instructed to implement the federal regulatory regime.[17]

Justice Stevens wrote the principal dissent. He first argued that the Necessary and Proper Clause supports the temporary enlistment of state officers to administer the Brady Act's regulation of commerce; the Tenth Amendment does not limit the scope or effectiveness of the powers delegated to Congress; and the Oath Clause confirms that federal laws establish policies for the states that their executive officers must respect. He then evaluated the same historical events and materials discussed by the Court, concluding that "the Court's ruling is strikingly lacking in affirmative support."[18] The Court's structural arguments, he contended, are insufficient to rebut the Act's presumption of constitutionality. In particular, the political safeguards of federalism work well to protect states from undue burdens, and commandeering administrative activity is not likely to confuse voters as to the responsibility for policy decisions. Finally, he distinguished New York as prohibiting only commandeering of legislative functions, and maintained that other precedents support the validity of executive as well as judicial conscription. He concluded that "[i]f Congress believes that such a statute will benefit the people of the Nation, and serve the interests of cooperative federalism better than an enlarged federal bureaucracy, we should respect both its policy judgment and its appraisal of its constitutional power."[19]

---

[17] See id at 2378.

[18] Id at 2389–94, 2393 (Stevens dissenting).

[19] Id at 2401 (Stevens dissenting).

Justice Stevens's dissent was joined by Justices Souter, Ginsburg, and Breyer. Justices Souter and Breyer (joined by Justice Stevens) contributed their own shorter dissents as well. Justice Souter suggested that Congress must reimburse states for the "fair value" of their services rendered. Id at 2404.

II. The Structural Constitution and State Administration of Federal Law

Printz holds that congressional commandeering of state administrative activity violates both of the central structural features of our Constitution, federalism and separation of powers. The Court's claim that its particular construction of state sovereignty and executive unity principles is *singularly* grounded in the Constitution, however, is unpersuasive.

A. THE PRINCIPLE OF STATE SOVEREIGNTY

1. *Competing constructs.* The essence of the majority's affirmative case against commandeering is its deduction, from the "essential postulates" of the constitutional structure, of a particular principle of state sovereignty—one that requires state executive autonomy from congressional direction. The Court began by observing (1) "[i]t is incontestible that the Constitution established a system of 'dual sovereignty,'"[20] in that the continued separate existence of states is presumed at various places throughout the constitutional text. At the very least this must mean (2) the states are sovereign within their realm of *exclusive* regulatory jurisdiction, which encompasses all subject matters not included within the limited delegation of authority to the federal government. Beyond that, Justice Scalia said, (3) states are also sovereign with respect to their autonomy of action within the *entirety* of their regulatory jurisdiction (whether exclusive of or concurrent with Congress). The majority then asserted that (4) the concept of "dual" sovereignty necessarily implies an equivalent stature, and hence a symmetrical relationship, between the federal and state sovereigns with respect to their autonomy. Because states cannot commandeer federal officials, it must be that Congress cannot commandeer state officials:

> It is an essential attribute of the States' retained sovereignty that they remain independent and autonomous within their proper sphere of authority. It is no more compatible with [the states'] independence and autonomy that their officers be "dragooned" . . . into administering federal law, than it would be compatible with the independence and autonomy of the United

---

[20] Id at 2376.

States that its officers be impressed into service for the execution of state laws.[21]

Thus "dual sovereignty" translates directly into an anti-commandeering rule.

This line of reasoning fails completely to take account of another "essential postulate" of the constitutional structure—federal supremacy.[22] All sovereigns are not created equal: "The United States is not a foreign sovereignty as regards the several States, but is a concurrent, and, within its jurisdiction, paramount sovereignty."[23] The difficult question is how to integrate the principles of dual sovereignty and federal supremacy properly. At a minimum, the latter postulate calls into question the claim that the two governments are coequal sovereigns with a purely symmetrical relationship. For example, Congress enjoys the unique (and hence asymmetrical) power to displace state laws through preemption whenever it regulates in the realm of concurrent federal and state jurisdiction.[24] Since symmetry does not follow automatically from dualism, the fact that states cannot conscript federal officials does not necessarily mean the converse is true.

There are at least three different understandings of "state sovereignty" that arguably reconcile the principles of dual sovereignty and federal supremacy.

a) Congress-state separation. Printz endorses this formulation, which posits that even within Congress's regulatory jurisdiction, states' sovereignty renders them immune from congressional direction—except where the Constitution specifically says otherwise. Unless Congress acts pursuant to a particular constitutional provision that authorizes it to commandeer particular state officials for particular tasks, such as the Judges Clause or the Extradition Clause,[25] Congress may not "direct the functioning of" state officers.[26] In the main, the federal and state governments operate only

---

[21] Id at 2381 (citation omitted).

[22] US Const, Art VI, § 2.

[23] *Claflin v Houseman*, 93 US 130, 136 (1876).

[24] See also *Tarble's Case*, 80 US 397 (1871), and *Ex parte Young*, 209 US 123 (1908) (together suggesting that state courts cannot issue injunctions against federal officials, even though federal courts can issue injunctions against state officials).

[25] See *Printz*, 117 S Ct at 2371–72.

[26] See id at 2383.

on the people, and not on each other.[27] According to this construct, commandeering of state officials is generally prohibited (though the permissibility of commandeering judicial activity certainly constitutes a significant exception to the rule).

b) States as subsidiaries. Under this formulation, federal supremacy means that Congress may regulate the national people directly, and regulate states and their officials directly. States are sovereign only in the sense that, where Congress either cannot or does not preempt state authority, states remain autonomous political units. But within Congress's subject matter jurisdiction, states might be viewed as subsidiaries of the national government. According to this construct, congressional commandeering of state officials is permissible.

c) Administrative supremacy. Under this formulation, federal supremacy means that Congress may both regulate the national people directly, and may also regulate state officials in their administrative (executive and judicial) capacities. This formulation, defended by Justice Stevens in his dissent, distinguishes between lawmaking and law enforcement: Congress may commandeer state officials to administer federal law, but not to engage in lawmaking.[28] States remain sovereign both in the sense that they are completely autonomous beyond Congress's exercise of its lawful jurisdiction, and in the sense that they retain autonomy over lawmaking even within Congress's jurisdiction (which, according to Justice Stevens, renders the formulation consistent with *New York v United States*).

The proper construction of "state sovereignty" is far from self-evident. Justice Scalia himself conceded that the constitutional text provides little help,[29] forcing reliance on ambiguous historical and

---

[27] The only constitutional provision that specifically authorizes state governments to direct federal government activity is Article V, which empowers two-thirds of the state legislatures to require Congress to call a convention for the purpose of considering constitutional amendments.

[28] See id at 2397 (Stevens dissenting).

[29] See id at 2370. The opinion later refers to various provisions in Articles III, IV, and V guaranteeing the separate existence of states, see id at 2376–77, but these provisions provide no assistance in choosing among the plausible constructs of state sovereignty. The Tenth Amendment does not itself define any limitation on congressional power. And the Necessary and Proper Clause provides no help. Even if the word "proper" excludes congressional means that violate the principle of state sovereignty, see id at 2379, that principle is not defined by this or any other clause. At most, therefore, the constitutional text confirms the existence of some implicit principle, but this begs the question of what that principle is.

structural clues. The *Printz* majority opted for the "Congress-state separation" formulation, but the affirmative case for this choice is underwhelming.

2. *Lessons from history.* Justice Scalia concluded that the history surrounding the Constitution's framing and early congressional practice "tends to negate the existence of the congressional power asserted here, but it is not conclusive."[30] In fact, the caveat is a vast understatement. The most that can be said for Justice Scalia's position is that history provides no clear affirmative sanction for congressional commandeering. History certainly does not confirm the Framers' rejection of such authority.

The majority first invoked the circumstances of the Constitution's birth as evidencing a rejection of commandeering authority:

> The Framers' experience under the Articles of Confederation had persuaded them that using the States as the instruments of federal governance was both ineffectual and provocative of federal-state conflict. Preservation of the States as independent political entities being the price of union, and "the practicality of making laws, with coercive sanctions, for the States as political bodies" having been, in Madison's words, "exploded on all hands," the Framers rejected the concept of a central government that would act upon and through the States, and instead designed a system in which the state and federal governments would exercise concurrent authority over the people—who were, in Hamilton's words, "the only proper objects of government."[31]

The majority is obviously correct that the Constitution was designed to empower Congress to regulate private activity directly, rather than having to use states as intermediaries.

But the relevant question is whether the new Constitution contemplated direct congressional regulation of private activity as a supplement to, rather than a complete substitute for, reliance on state administration. The two forms of congressional regulation are compatible; the Framers need not have made an either/or choice between them. So why, in a Constitution specifically designed to provide greater authority and practical vigor to the central government, would the Framers have denied Congress the

---

[30] Id at 2376.

[31] Id at 2377 (citations omitted).

earlier option? The Federalists likely would have continued to support the possibility of commandeering. The option of state administration of federal law might in certain circumstances reduce the cost of (and avoid potential hostility toward) a new federal bureaucracy, and would secure the advantage of having national policies implemented in various geographic regions by officers particularly attuned to local interests. And it is unclear at best that the Anti-Federalists would have opposed the possibility of commandeering. At least any time Congress chose to continue using state officials as administrative intermediaries, states would retain an extra measure of input into the workings of the federal government (and, as a practical matter, states could always continue to disobey any particular commands they found unduly burdensome). As Justice Stevens aptly observed, the commandeering-only design of the Articles of Confederation proved unacceptable "because it was cumbersome and inefficient" (quite an understatement), and "not because it demeaned the sovereign character of the several States."[32]

Justice Scalia sidestepped this obvious issue,[33] and suggested instead that separation of federal and state administration is designed to preserve liberty: "a healthy balance of power between the States and the Federal Government will reduce the risk of tyranny and abuse from either front."[34] But the Court did not explain why an anti-commandeering rule is an essential shield against federal tyranny. True, the mere separate existence of states diminishes the likelihood of federal abuses of power. States make theoretically possible the placement of boundaries on Congress's legislative jurisdiction (thus preventing federal omnicompetence), and they also provide political counterweights that can sound the alarm and mobilize the people against threatened congressional overreaching. But congressional commandeering authority hardly undermines these avenues for state opposition. Short of Congress's commandeering state executives so frequently and thoroughly that they have no time for purely "state" business—surely a politically in-

---

[32] 117 S Ct at 2389 (Stevens dissenting).

[33] Justice Scalia's only argument, that the Constitution would have expressly conferred commandeering authority had it meant to do so, is patently weak. Unless one has already determined that conscription of state officials is not a "proper" means for Congress to carry its enumerated powers into execution, see note 29, the Necessary and Proper Clause suffices to confer such authority.

[34] 117 S Ct at 2378 (citation omitted).

conceivable hypothetical—Congress cannot somehow dissolve the "double security" provided by the mere existence of states which, commandeering notwithstanding, retain a healthy measure of authority in exclusive fields of jurisdiction alone. Indeed, states arguably would retain greater force as a potential counterweight to congressional tyranny if Congress employed existing state officials rather than developed a massive federal police presence throughout the states.

The majority opinion also dismissed the claim that various passages from The Federalist showed that the Framers intended the Constitution to countenance commandeering of various state officials.[35] Some passages, the Court asserted, meant to endorse state administration of federal law only if the states so consented; others referred to something other than commandeering altogether.[36] But all of this interpretive work (some of it quite creative) does no more than attempt to rebut the contention that the Framers' original intent clearly supports the constitutionality of conscription; it does not purport to provide affirmative evidence supporting the contrary proposition.

The Court also rejected the federal government's claim that early Congresses required state officials to help implement federal statutes, a tradition that would provide "contemporaneous and weighty evidence" of the Constitution's meaning. The majority concluded that some early statutes presumed state consent and others commandeered only state judicial officials to perform only judicial functions, which is explicitly authorized by the Supremacy Clause and hence evidences no general commandeering authority over state executive officials. The only statute that clearly commandeered state executive officers was the Extradition Act of 1793, which was explicitly authorized by the Extradition Clause of the Constitution itself.[37]

---

[35] Id at 2372–75.

[36] See, for example, id at 2372, 2374. For discussion of the historical evidence, see Evan H. Caminker, *State Sovereignty and Subordinacy: May Congress Commandeer State Officers to Implement Federal Law?* 95 Colum L Rev 1001 (1995); Saikrishna B. Prakash, *Field Office Federalism,* 79 Va L Rev 1957 (1993); H. Jefferson Powell, *The Oldest Question of Constitutional Law,* 79 Va L Rev 633 (1993); Richard E. Levy, *New York v. United States: An Essay on the Uses and Misuses of Precedent, History, and Policy in Determining the Scope of Federal Power,* 41 U Kan L Rev 493 (1993).

[37] See *Printz,* 117 S Ct at 2370–72. Justice Scalia's characterization of the early statutes as commandeering judicial rather than executive activities is sometimes quite adventur-

Justice Scalia's opinion went further to suggest that the *absence* of such a congressional tradition provides "reason to believe that the power was thought not to exist."[38] The opinion focuses on three federal statutes, enacted over a span of 130 years, by which Congress assertedly sought state assistance in implementing various federal programs through noncoercive means.[39] But it seems quite unsound to claim that these three instances (or even a more general practice of commandeering-avoidance) *negate* the power to conscript such assistance—indeed, for reasons similar to those that have convinced Justice Scalia to eschew reliance on postenactment legislative silence when engaging in statutory construction.[40] Congress may have exercised its commandeering power very sparingly out of respect for state autonomy, or out of concern that state officers might refuse their duties or perform them poorly. And in any event, since when has novelty been an automatic strike against a congressional statute? Whether or not the history of the Framing and early congressional tradition affirmatively support congressional commandeering, they clearly provide no firm basis for choosing the "Congress-state separation" formulation over the alternatives.

3. *Constitutional text and structure.* The Court acknowledged that Congress has authority to commandeer state officials in certain specific circumstances, most commonly judicial officials. The majority suggested that such circumstances do not exemplify an unbounded commandeering power, however, because Congress's power to conscript state officials in these contexts is specifically

---

ous. See id at 2391 (Stevens dissenting) (arguing that the "majority's description of these early statutes is both incomplete and at times misleading").

[38] Id at 2370.

[39] Id at 2375–76. The majority's statutory interpretation is particularly forced here. For example, with respect to a World War I selective draft law, Justice Scalia claimed that "it is far from clear that the authorization [for the President] 'to utilize the service' of state officers was an authorization to *compel* the service of state officers." Id at 2375. But the statute clearly directs that "all officers and agents . . . of the several States . . . are hereby required to perform such duty as the President shall order or direct." Act of May 18, 1917, ch 15, § 6, 40 Stat 80.

[40] "[O]ne must ignore rudimentary principles of political science to draw any conclusions regarding [congressional] intent from the failure to enact legislation." *Johnson v Transportation Agency*, 480 US 616, 671–72 (1987) (Scalia dissenting). In *McIntyre v Ohio Elections Commission*, Justice Scalia acknowledged that a historical pattern of nonregulation provides strong evidence against the constitutionality of such regulation only if "there is ample evidence that the reason [the governmental regulation] was not engaged in is that it was thought to violate the [Constitution]." 514 US 334, 372 (1995) (Scalia dissenting).

granted by the constitutional text.[41] But this conclusion rests on a strained reading of that text, as well as an unjustified assumption that these particular grants of commandeering authority imply a more general anti-commandeering default rule.[42]

Superficially, the majority seems on solid ground when it focuses on the Supremacy Clause's explicit reference to state judges.[43] Why would this Clause single out state judges as responsible for federal law enforcement if state executives are similarly susceptible to congressional conscription? This rhetorical question has bite, however, only if the textual reference to judges really does the work of authorizing judicial commandeering. But this is not the only, and I believe not the best, reading of the Clause.

As Justice Stevens explained in dissent, the specific command that "the Judges in every State shall be bound" by federal law is neither historically nor analytically responsible for the rule, associated with *Testa v Katt*,[44] that state courts of appropriate jurisdiction generally cannot decline to entertain federal claims whenever a federal statute requires them to do so. Historically, *Testa* and its

---

[41] See *Printz*, 117 S Ct at 2371–72 (referring to the Extradition Clause, the Full Faith and Credit Clause, and the Supremacy Clause). One could certainly add to this list the Militia Clauses, US Const, Art I, § 8, cls 15 & 16, which specifically authorize Congress to conscript the states' primary military institutions for certain national purposes, including to "execute the Laws of the Union." Also, three courts of appeals have held that the National Voter Registration Act of 1993, 42 USC § 1973gg (1994), which requires state executive officials to take specific affirmative measures to facilitate voter registration in federal elections, is authorized pursuant to the Article I, § 4 congressional power to "alter" state election regulations. See *Association of Community Orgs. for Reform Now v Miller*, 129 F3d 833 (6th Cir 1997); *Voting Rights Coalition v Wilson*, 60 F3d 1411 (9th Cir 1995), cert denied, 116 S Ct 815 (1996); *Association of Community Orgs. for Reform Now v Edgar*, 56 F3d 791 (7th Cir 1995).

[42] The canon *expressio unius est exclusio alterius* does not necessarily apply here, as there is a plausible explanation of why the Constitution would sensibly include these specific commandeering provisions even if the Necessary and Proper Clause generally authorizes commandeering pursuant to Congress's Article I, Section 8 powers. Because the two Extradition Clauses define legal duties owed by states to one another and implicitly empower Congress to enforce those duties, they grant Congress regulatory authority beyond that already secured in Article I. The Militia Clauses specifically limit the federal commandeering power they grant by securing an enclave of state authority. The Article I provisions dictating state participation in the selection process for federal officials commandeer states to help establish the federal government, not to implement its regulatory goals. Each of these provisions has a special function, therefore, even assuming that Congress may commandeer states to implement its Article I regulatory objectives.

[43] US Const, Art VI, cl 2 (stating that all species of federal law "shall be the supreme Law of the Land; and the Judges in every State shall be bound thereby, any Thing in the Constitution or Laws of any State to the Contrary notwithstanding").

[44] 330 US 386 (1947).

predecessors grounded the duty to adjudicate federal claims in the general language of the Supremacy Clause ("[federal law] shall be the supreme Law of the Land"), which makes clear that federal law counts as state law just as if it were promulgated by the state rather than federal legislature.[45] Indeed, this entire line of cases never once drew any special significance from the Supremacy Clause's specific reference to judges.

"[T]he Clause's mention of judges was almost certainly meant as nothing more than a choice of law rule, informing the state courts that they were to apply federal law in the event of a *conflict* with state authority."[46] The phrase "any Thing in [state law] to the Contrary notwithstanding" refers to the possibility that federal and state law may conflict; in such a case, state judges are instructed that federal law prevails. Thus state courts must recognize federal defenses to state law causes of action, and may not apply state law defenses to defeat federal claims. But the Supremacy Clause's specific instruction to state judges does not answer the "commandeering" question of whether they must entertain federal causes of action, a question which of course can arise even when there is no "Thing in" state law "to the contrary."[47]

---

[45] See, for example, *Second Employers' Liability Cases*, 223 US 1, 57 (1912) ("When Congress, in the exertion of the power confided to it by the Constitution, adopted that [federal] act, it spoke for all the people and all the States, and thereby established a policy for all. That policy is as much the policy of Connecticut as if the act had emanated from its own legislature, and should be respected accordingly in the courts of the State.").

[46] *Printz*, 117 S Ct at 2400 n 31 (Stevens dissenting). For elaboration of this point, see Caminker, 95 Colum L Rev at 1036–38 (cited in note 36).

[47] This choice-of-law interpretation follows the text's historical derivation. The Clause emerged from a Convention dispute concerning the best mechanism for securing the supremacy of federal over state law. Originally, the Convention approved a congressional power "[t]o negative all laws, passed by the several States, contravening, in the opinion of the national legislature, the articles of union or any Treaties subsisting under the authority of the union." Max Farrand, ed, 1 *The Records of the Federal Convention of 1787* 47 (Yale Univ Press, 1966). The delegates later rejected this "congressional veto" approach in favor of a judicial alternative. 2 id at 27–28. Immediately thereafter, the Convention unanimously approved the following supremacy provision:

> that the Legislative acts of the U.S. made by virtue & in pursuance of the articles of Union, and all treaties made & ratified under the authority of the US shall be the supreme law of the respective States, as far as those acts or treaties shall relate to the said States, or their Citizens and inhabitants—& that the Judiciaries of the several States shall be bound thereby in their decisions, any thing in the respective laws of the individual States to the contrary notwithstanding.

2 id at 28–29. The first phrase affirmed the principle of federal supremacy, and the second phrase endorsed judicial rather than congressional authority to "guard against conflicts between State statutes and Federal laws." Charles Warren, *The Making of the Constitution* 322 (Little, Brown, 1928).

Rather, it is the *broader* principle of the Supremacy Clause—every congressional law establishes policy for the states no less than laws enacted by state legislatures—that is responsible for commandeering of state courts. This broader principle is equally applicable to state executive officers.

Moreover, only this broader principle can account for *FERC v Mississippi*,[48] in which the Court upheld a congressional directive that state public utility commissions implement federal regulations through their choice of several means, including "by resolving disputes [under the federal regulations] on a case-by-case basis."[49] The Court upheld this mandate as a straightforward application of the *Testa* principle, even though the commandeered "commissioners were unquestionably not 'judges' within the meaning of Art. VI, cl. 2."[50] The *Printz* majority acknowledged this point as "true enough," but continued:

> But the answer to the question of which state officers *must* apply federal law (only " 'judges' within the meaning of [the Supremacy Clause]") is different from the answer to the question of which state officers *may be required by statute* to apply federal law (officers who conduct adjudications similar to those traditionally performed by judges). It is within the power of the States . . . to transfer some adjudicatory functions to administrative agencies, with opportunity for subsequent judicial review. But it is also within the power of Congress to prescribe, explicitly or by implication (as in the legislation at issue in *FERC*), that those adjudications must take account of federal law.[51]

In other words, Congress may command state executive as well as judicial officers to implement federal law through adjudicatory functions. But this response gives up the game. This "adjudication-only" principle obviously goes beyond the "judges-only" principle that the majority claimed to be grounded in the constitutional text.

The majority's assertion that commandeering authority is cabined to adjudicatory contexts might be persuasive if there were good historical or structural reasons, or even functional reasons,

---

[48] 456 US 742 (1982).

[49] Id at 751. See also 16 USC § 824a (1994).

[50] *Printz*, 117 S Ct at 2401 (Stevens dissenting).

[51] Id at 2381–82 n 14 (citation omitted).

to differentiate between commandeering of judicial and executive functions. But such reasons are not self-evident. Indeed, at the time of the Founding, the distinctions between judges and executive magistrates, and between judicial and executive functions, were quite blurred.[52] This makes it unlikely that the Framers would have sharply discriminated between judicial and almost-identical executive functions for purposes of commandeering.

The majority did offer one explanation for treating courts as uniquely appropriate for conscription: "[U]nlike legislatures and executives, [courts] applied the law of other sovereigns all the time."[53] But the fact that courts have traditionally chosen to entertain claims created by another sovereign's laws cannot analytically account for a unique requirement that they do so. In any event, federal law is not the law of "another sovereign" that a state court may decide to consider as part of its judicial business. Rather, federal law is part of state law—this is the central lesson of *Testa*.[54] Justice Scalia himself recently explained this point: state courts enforce federal law "not because . . . their inherent powers permit them to entertain transitory causes of action arising under the laws of foreign sovereigns," but rather because federal laws "are laws in the several States, and just as much binding on the citizens and courts thereof as the State laws are."[55] Nothing in this principle of federal supremacy suggests that state officials performing adjudicative functions ought to be any more susceptible to imposition of congressional duties than are officials performing administrative functions. Moreover, state executive officials routinely do follow numerous congressional directives imposed on state and private actors alike. Finally, commandeering of state courts can interfere with a state's autonomy in the same ways as commandeering of its executive officials: judicial commandeering can force states to allow their courts to adjudicate claims that they would prefer to

---

[52] For example, two centuries ago, state judges (and associated judicial personnel) did many of the things that would today be performed by executive officers, including laying city streets and ensuring the seaworthiness of vessels. For discussion, see Caminker, 95 Colum L Rev at 1045 n 176 (cited in note 36).

[53] *Printz*, 117 S Ct at 2371.

[54] See *Testa v Katt*, 330 US 386, 390–91 (1947) ("repudiat[ing] the assumption that federal laws can be considered by the states as though they were laws emanating from a foreign sovereign").

[55] *Tafflin v Levitt*, 493 US 455, 469 (1990) (Scalia concurring) (citations omitted).

avoid because of distaste for the federal policies underlying the claims; and assuming limited resources, judicial commandeering can prevent states from ensuring that their courts can quickly adjudicate claims that the state wants to vindicate.

Commandeering legislative activity may raise different concerns. But the *Printz* majority expressly rejected Justice Souter's contention in dissent that state legislatures are uniquely protected from congressional commandeering by their peculiar function. Justice Souter asserted that "[t]he core power of a legislator acting within the legislature's subject-matter jurisdiction is to make a discretionary decision on what the law should be; that is why a legislator may not be legally ordered to exercise discretion a particular way without damaging the legislative power as such."[56] Justice Scalia responded that this "novel principle of political science . . . seems to us untrue":

> Perhaps legislatures are inherently uncommandable as to the outcome of their legislation, but they are commanded all the time as to what subjects they shall legislate upon—commanded, that is, by the people, in constitutional provisions that require, for example, the enactment of annual budgets or forbid the enactment of laws permitting gambling. We do not think that state legislatures would be betraying their very "essence" as legislatures (*as opposed to their nature as sovereigns, a nature they share with the other two branches of government*) if they obeyed a federal command to enact laws, for example, criminalizing the sale of marijuana.[57]

But if legislatures have no special "essence" that uniquely *protects* them from commandeering because their sovereign nature is shared equally with the judicial and executive branches, then Justice Scalia cannot persuasively turn around and maintain that courts have a special essence that uniquely makes them *vulnerable* to congressional conscription.

This internal tension highlights the fact that the majority's decision to treat adjudicatory functions as a special exemption from a general anti-commandeering rule reflects an ad hoc judgment, one not clearly flowing from constitutional text, history, or structure. Rather, the principles that permit judicial commandeering apply with equal force to executive commandeering as well.

---

[56] 117 S Ct at 2402 n 1 (Souter dissenting).

[57] Id at 2373–74 n 5 (emphasis added).

4. *The administrative supremacy construct.* The federal government maintained that the Constitution, as interpreted in *New York*, embraces the "administrative supremacy" formulation of state sovereignty according to which commandeering of state executive as well as judicial functions is permissible. This formulation rests on the intuitively plausible claim that the essence of a state's sovereignty is its law-creativity, that is, its authority to decide how to regulate private individuals within its territorial jurisdiction. The people (the true sovereign) establish the state to create a more efficient, effective, and deliberative mechanism of self-government; the state's decisions about how to govern the people on their behalf thus represent the core function of its assumed "sovereignty." As the Court has previously explained, "having the power to make decisions and to set policy is what gives the State its sovereign nature."[58] In contrast, implementing a chosen policy is not itself an exercise of political sovereignty. This distinction is mirrored within the tradition of judicial commandeering. While state courts may be required to implement federal law by entertaining federal causes of action, federal courts may not require a state court to reinterpret a state statute or modify state common law. And the distinction fits comfortably with *New York:* Congress may not compel states to regulate.

The *Printz* majority sidestepped this contention instead of confronting it. Justice Scalia first responded that a clean line cannot be discerned between " 'making' law and merely 'enforcing' it, between 'policymaking' and mere 'implementation.' "[59] Even CLEOs, the majority asserted, must make a policy decision in interpreting the Brady Act's requirement that they make "reasonable efforts" when conducting background checks.[60] Thus drawing a doctrinal line at "no policymaking" would not save the Act, and drawing a line at any other place is unacceptable because "an imprecise barrier against federal intrusion upon state authority is not likely to be an effective one."[61]

This response does not directly deny the conceptual point that sovereignty can be equated with lawmaking. The concern for easily

---

[58] *FERC v Mississippi*, 456 US 742, 761 (1982).

[59] *Printz*, 117 S Ct at 2380.

[60] Id at 2381.

[61] Id.

enforceable rules could be met by drawing a distinction between policymaking with respect to the content of primary rules governing private conduct, and policymaking with respect purely to internal bureaucratic operations. The Brady Act falls within the second category, because the primary duties governing the interface between government and individual are completely spelled out in the federal statute itself, and the discretion surrounding "reasonable efforts" merely concerns orders issued by CLEOs to subordinates concerning how they should administer the federally defined primary obligations.[62] In any event, it seems inappropriate to reject what might otherwise be the proper constitutional conception of sovereignty merely because its doctrinal protection requires courts to exercise some judgment.[63]

The majority's second reason for rejecting the "administrative supremacy" formulation is that congressional imposition of ministerial rather than policymaking burdens actually "worsens the intrusion upon state sovereignty" by "reducing [states] to puppets of a ventriloquist Congress."[64] But this colorful imagery begs the question: if the principle of state sovereignty protects lawmaking autonomy and nothing more, then congressional puppetry simply does not threaten this principle. The only evidence offered for the claim that ministerial duties constitute an affront to sovereignty is

---

[62] Leaving this potential bright-line distinction aside, even if there is a grey area along the spectrum between law creation and law enforcement, some congressional commands can easily be placed at one end or the other. The conclusion that the CLEOs' mandated duties are more properly characterized as "law implementation" rather than "lawmaking" seems hard to deny. The Brady Act does not require CLEOs to make general pronouncements about "reasonable efforts" at all; each CLEO can leave that decision up to each individual officer. And any CLEO pronouncement at most would establish policy only for a local jurisdiction, not the entire state. Finally, as just explained, the CLEO's discretion is not located at the intersection between government and the individual, since any pronouncement about "reasonable efforts" does not affect in any way gun purchasers' legal rights and disabilities under the Act. Rather, any CLEO pronouncement would merely dictate how subordinate executive officers perform their ministerial tasks of enforcing the Act's rules governing private conduct.

[63] The irony here is acute: the dissenters in *Garcia v San Antonio Metro. Transit Auth.* (including two members of the *Printz* majority) lambasted the Court in that case for eschewing the proper, though concededly difficult, task of linedrawing and balancing in favor of an assertedly improper categorical rule—one which happened to provide states no protection from congressional regulation at all. See 469 US 528, 561–63 (1985) (Powell dissenting), id at 588–89 (O'Connor dissenting).

Justice Scalia's own claim in *Printz* is also ironic, given his earlier reliance on a supposed historical but quite fuzzy distinction between commandeering of quasi-judicial and quasi-executive functions.

[64] 117 S Ct at 2381 (citation omitted).

that states may not commandeer federal officials. But as explained earlier, the principle of federal supremacy belies any requirement of symmetry here. Thus the majority again avoided rather than engaged the intrinsic merits of this formulation of state sovereignty.[65]

None of this is to say that one cannot plausibly oppose the "administrative supremacy" definition of state sovereignty. For example, one might challenge the claim that sovereignty inheres only (or at least distinctively) in the design of primary rules governing private conduct directly, and not in the design of secondary rules regulating the official conduct of state personnel. When the people of a state establish a system of representative government, the people may be equally concerned with the rules the representative agents establish to govern themselves, as well as the rules these agents establish to govern the people. But the majority opinion does not purport to undertake such an analysis, or consider any other argument against the plausibility of the "administrative supremacy" formulation in *Printz*. Without such an argument, the majority's claim that commandeering of state executive functions violates "an essential attribute of the States' retained sovereignty"[66] remains mere *ipse dixit*.

5. *Sovereignty and constitutional methodology*. Whatever the potential merits of interpretive formalist reasoning in other contexts, it does not fulfill its promise here. The majority is correct to start from the structural principle that the Constitution contemplates "dual sovereignty" in some sense. But as the Court has previously recognized, "to say that the Constitution assumes the continued role of the States is to say little about the nature of that role."[67]

---

[65] Justice Souter proposed a modified version of the administrative supremacy model. He distinguished between state legislatures on the one hand and executive and judicial officials on the other, contending that Congress may commandeer state executive and judicial officials, but may not compel legislators to enact legislation. This is because "[t]he core power of a legislator acting within the legislature's subject-matter jurisdiction is to make a discretionary decision on what the law should be; that is why a legislator may not be legally ordered to exercise discretion a particular way without damaging the legislative power as such." 117 S Ct at 2402 n 1 (Souter dissenting). This version is subtly different from that discussed in the text, in that it does not appear to deny Congress the authority to require nonlegislative officers to engage in lawmaking of sorts appropriate to their offices, e.g., through administrative rulemaking or adjudication. As explained earlier, see text at notes 56–57, Justice Scalia dismissed Justice Souter's proposed distinction by simply asserting that the distinction "seems to us untrue."

[66] See 117 S Ct at 2381.

[67] *Garcia*, 469 US at 550.

As Justice Scalia's argument progresses, he must select a path from among plausible alternative routes without clear constitutional signposts. In the end, while his formal construction of state sovereignty is surely a plausible one, his methodology does not persuasively demonstrate the "Congress-state separation" formulation to be superior to the competing formulations that differently integrate the notions of dual sovereignty and federal supremacy.

This is emphatically not to say that the Court's categorical anti-commandeering rule is indefensible; it is merely to say that a persuasive defense, if any, must rest on a sensitive evaluation of the ways in which the competing constructs of state sovereignty serve the normative values that underlie our constitutional scheme. Indeed, a number of normative or consequentialist arguments have been or might be raised in defense of an anti-commandeering rule. Some of these arguments cannot provide a principled basis for distinguishing between commandeering on the one hand, and preemption or accepted forms of congressional "encouragement" of state action on the other,[68] but other normative objections to commandeering appear more promising. One might argue that unfunded congressional commandeering of state officials confiscates state-owned administrative resources in a takings-like manner that essentially redistributes wealth from states to the federal government, and that this shift has regressive effects or violates some other standard of distributive justice.[69] Or one might argue that commandeering (unlike preemption) diverts state officials from their state law business to perform federal business, resulting in a net loss of combined federal plus state regulatory activity.[70] Or one might argue that commandeering is frequently an "improper" exercise of federal power because it is motivated by a congressional desire to avoid the political heat for making particular regulatory decisions or using federal resources to pay for them.[71] If

---

[68] See Caminker, 95 Colum L Rev at 1060–81 (cited in note 36) (evaluating normative claims that commandeering unfairly shifts political liability from federal to state officials, unduly constrains state autonomy, undermines the "double security" of opposing governments against each other, threatens to diminish local political participation, or undermines experimentation through diversification).

[69] See Roderick M. Hills, *The Political Economy of Cooperative Federalism: Why State Autonomy Makes Sense and "Dual Sovereignty" Doesn't*, 96 Mich L Rev (forthcoming 1998).

[70] See Deborah Jones Merritt, *Federalism as Empowerment*, 47 U Fla L Rev 541, 553–55 (1995).

[71] The *New York* decision emphasized a concern that commandeering might undermine political accountability, see 505 US at 168–69, while the *Printz* Court adverted to this

none of these or similar arguments ultimately proves persuasive (because the particular normative concern is either insufficiently grounded in the Constitution or fails convincingly to support an anti-commandeering edict), then the default rule remains, as always, to uphold Congress's selection of administrative means. But I believe that it is these kinds of arguments, not the Court's stolid formal reasoning, that provide the best possibility of justifying the result in *Printz*.

Of course, as is generally true with normative or consequentialist arguments, these concerns may prove to be triggered far more seriously by some acts of commandeering than by others, and perhaps by some not at all. Even so, one might defend the Court's decision to craft a categorical rule against nonjudicial commandeering. Rather than trust courts to police a nebulous line between acceptable and unacceptable infringements of normative constitutional values, or between trivial and serious burdens imposed on states, we might presume a categorical prohibition against even the first step to be the safest doctrinal response. As Justice Scalia has elsewhere observed:

> [T]he doctrine of separation of powers is a *structural safeguard* rather than a remedy to be applied only when specific harm, or risk of specific harm, can be identified. In its major features . . . it is a prophylactic device, establishing high walls and clear distinctions because low walls and vague distinctions will not be judicially defensible in the heat of interbranch conflict.[72]

In the federalism context, this zeal for fixed boundaries may underestimate the protections afforded states by the political safeguards of federalism, probably the best explanation for why thus far congressional commandeering has been limited to a handful of relatively benign circumstances (compared to the horribles often paraded).[73] Nevertheless, the combination of a strong normative basis for securing state autonomy over nonjudicial state personnel, coupled with the benefits of doctrinally formalist categorical rules,

---

concern only in passing to rebut a contrary claim. See 117 S Ct at 2382. See David L. Shapiro, *Federalism: A Dialogue* 111–13 (Northwestern Univ Press, 1995) (citing accountability problems and defending *New York* as maintaining states' "continued existence as politically functioning entities").

[72] *Plaut v Spendthrift Farm, Inc.*, 514 US 211, 239 (1995).

[73] For a contemporary version of how these political safeguards might operate, see Larry Kramer, *Understanding Federalism*, 47 Vand L Rev 1485 (1994).

can provide at least a plausible constitutional foundation for the Court's anti-commandeering rule. But this is decidedly not the line of defense offered in *Printz*.

B. THE PRINCIPLE OF EXECUTIVE UNITY

Justice Scalia's majority opinion illustrates the same pitfalls of interpretive formalism when it argues that the Brady Act violates, not just federalism principles, but separation of powers principles as well. The majority maintained that the coerced delegation of administrative responsibilities to state CLEOs precludes the President from meaningfully performing his constitutionally assigned duty to supervise all execution of federal law. This unprecedented argument, which threatens the legitimacy of many administrative agencies, comes in four simple sentences:

> The Constitution does not leave to speculation who is to administer the laws executed by Congress; the President, it says, "shall take Care that the Laws be faithfully executed," Art. II. § 3, personally and through officers whom he appoints (save for such inferior officers as Congress may authorize to be appointed by the "Courts of Law" or by "Heads of Departments" who are themselves presidential appointees), Art. II § 2. The Brady Act effectively transfers this responsibility to thousands of CLEOs in the 50 States, who are left to implement the program without meaningful Presidential control (if indeed meaningful Presidential control is possible without the power to appoint and remove). The insistence of the Framers upon unity in the Federal Executive—to insure both vigor and accountability—is well known. That unity would be shattered, and the power of the President would be subject to reduction, if Congress could act as effectively without the President as with him, by simply requiring state officers to execute its laws.[74]

This argument has three necessary premises: (1) Article II vests the power to execute federal law solely in the President, so that he must either execute federal statutes personally or supervise those persons who do; (2) such presidential supervision must extend to state as well as federal officers who implement federal law; and (3) the proper remedy for unsupervised state execution of the Brady Act is to invalidate the commandeering provision of the Act itself, rather than to extend the President's supervisory powers

---

[74] 117 S Ct at 2378 (citations omitted).

over CLEOs. The Court added, in a footnote, that Congress may nonetheless seek "voluntary state participation" in federal program administration.[75] While the majority once again reaches a plausible destination, it consistently fails to explain its adoption of certain formal constructs over plausible competitors. The cost is infusion of uncertainty over the breadth of the theory's potential future applications.[76]

1. *Article II and unitary executive theory.* A plausible defense of the first premise is certainly available:[77] The constitutional text recognizes only three types of power (legislative, executive, and judicial), and establishes only three institutions of government (Congress, the executive department, and the judiciary). No other type of power or governmental institution is mentioned, and the text is best interpreted as excluding the possibility of others.[78] According to Article II's Vesting Clause, "[t]he executive Power shall be vested in a President of the United States of America."[79] While some argue that this Clause merely designates the President as the recipient of powers elsewhere defined, there are several reasons why this Clause is better understood as actually conferring a general grant of "executive power," one that is more fully refined by the later enumerations in Article II, Sections 2 and 3.[80] Thus the

---

[75] See id at 2378 n 12.

[76] Parts of this section build upon a discussion in a symposium essay, see Evan H. Caminker, *The Unitary Executive and State Administration of Federal Law*, 45 U Kan L Rev 1075 (1997).

[77] For a full explication of the argument outlined in the text, see Steven G. Calabresi and Saikrishna B. Prakash, *The President's Power to Execute the Laws*, 104 Yale L J 541 (1994). For variations on the theme, see, for example, Steven G. Calabresi, *Some Normative Arguments for the Unitary Executive*, 48 Ark L Rev 23 (1995); Gary Lawson, *The Rise and Rise of the Administrative State*, 107 Harv L Rev 1231 (1994); Lee S. Liberman, *Morrison v. Olson: A Formalist Perspective on Why the Court Was Wrong*, 38 Am U L Rev 313 (1989).

[78] See, for example, Calabresi and Prakash, 104 Yale L J at 560–64, 566–68 (cited in note 77) (explaining why the maxim *expressio unius est exclusio alterius* applies to the trinity of powers and institutions).

[79] US Const, Art II, § 1, cl 1.

[80] For example, the Vesting Clauses of Articles II and III are linguistically and structurally similar to each other; the Article III Vesting Clause is necessarily the textual grant of the judicial power; and thus the Article II Vesting Clause should be understood analogously as the textual grant of the executive power. See Calabresi and Prakash, 104 Yale L J at 570–72 (cited in note 77).

The more detailed presidential powers and duties explicitly provided in Sections 2 and 3 qualify or constrain the general grant of executive power in Section 1. See id at 576–79.

entire executive power of the federal government devolves on the President. Whatever else this power may entail, it includes the power to execute the laws passed by Congress.[81] Of course, this does not mean that the President must execute all federal statutes personally; the Necessary and Proper Clause empowers Congress to establish an administrative bureaucracy and identify particular officials to assist the President. But such officials must always remain subject to the direction of the President, who is ultimately charged with the duty to take care that the laws be faithfully executed.[82]

There are also a number of powerful counterarguments to this unitarian thesis.[83] The theory's originalist grounding engenders much controversy,[84] and the proper "translation" of a unitarian originalist vision into the nation's third century presents further quandaries.[85] Moreover, if taken at face value, the majority's assertion of a unitary executive could call into question, at the least, the constitutionality of both "independent" agencies and various

---

[81] See 1 *Annals of Cong.* 481 (Gales ed, 1789) (James Madison) ("if any power whatsoever is in its nature executive, it is the power of appointing, overseeing, and controlling those who execute the laws").

[82] It is somewhat surprising that Justice Scalia referred to the Take Care Clause rather than the Vesting Clause as the font of the President's executive power. Compare *Morrison v Olson*, 487 US 654, 705 (1988) (Scalia dissenting) (invoking Vesting Clause). The predominant (and better) view is that the Take Care Clause does not grant any power but rather imposes a duty, prohibiting the President from ignoring or otherwise subverting statutory directives. See Calabresi and Prakash, 104 Yale L J at 583–84 (cited in note 77) (the Take Care Clause "mak[es] it clear that the President has no royal prerogative to suspend statutes"). While the President ultimately is responsible for all discretionary decisions concerning the implementation of federal law, the scope of that discretion, if any, turns on Congress's definition of the statutory duty.

It is also somewhat surprising that Justice Scalia did not mention the Appointments Clause; some unitary executive theorists believe this poses an additional constitutional obstacle to state administration of federal law.

[83] For scholarship both defending and challenging the unitarian position, see the articles cited in Calabresi and Prakash, 104 Yale L J at 545 nn 3–7 (cited in note 77).

[84] For arguments that unitary executive theory cannot be defended purely on originalist grounds, see, for example, Lawrence Lessig and Cass R. Sunstein, *The President and the Administration*, 94 Colum L Rev 1 (1994); Martin S. Flaherty, *The Most Dangerous Branch*, 105 Yale L J 1725 (1996).

[85] Compare Lessig and Sunstein, 94 Colum L Rev at 85–106 (cited in note 84) (outlining argument that, due to "changed circumstances," Article II might now be best interpreted as mandating a unitary executive), with Abner S. Greene, *Checks and Balances in an Era of Presidential Lawmaking*, 61 U Chi L Rev 123 (1994) (the Framers' separation of powers commitments, when best translated to account for present conditions, argue against a unitary executive), and Flaherty, 105 Yale L J at 1810–36 (cited in note 84) (same).

delegations of authority to private individuals and groups.[86] Perhaps Justice Scalia is willing to live with these implications; indeed, one might view *Printz* (perhaps along with *Lujan v Defenders of Wildlife*[87]) as an attempted end-run around the Court's rejection of his extreme unitarian position in *Morrison v Olson*.[88] But particularly given the potential consequences of the unitary theory, it is astonishing to see a five-member majority so casually embrace this controversial principle, without so much as a whisper of reservation or qualification. One therefore wonders about *Printz*'s precedential value on this point.[89]

2. *Presidential supervision of state administration.* The second premise—that the President must supervise even state officers when they administer federal law—is not logically entailed by the notion of a unitary executive. One can certainly imagine a construction of Article II unity according to which the President's supervisory duties extend only to federal law execution by subordinate *federal* officers. Such a bright-line limitation would better accord with widespread founding era practices, which cast doubt on the suggestion that presidential control reached either private

[86] See, for example, Harold J. Krent, *Fragmenting the Unitary Executive: Congressional Delegations of Administrative Authority Outside the Federal Government*, 85 Nw U L Rev 62, 84–93 (1990) (discussing private delegations).

[87] 504 US 555, 576–77 (1992) (opinion by Justice Scalia holding that congressional grant of standing to private parties lacking discrete injuries contravened the President's exclusive power to execute federal law on behalf of the public).

[88] 487 US 654 (1988).

[89] It is conceivable, of course, that Justice Scalia did not intend his Article II argument to constitute a truly independent basis for invalidating the Brady Act. Perhaps he intended this discussion merely as additional confirmation of his earlier surmise that the Framers would have considered commandeering to be an illegitimate means of congressional regulation; if so, had he earlier determined the Brady Act to be consistent with federalism principles, perhaps he would not have invalidated the Act on Article II grounds alone. Alternatively, even if Justice Scalia himself considered the Article II argument to constitute a fully independent basis for decision, perhaps some of his joining colleagues viewed the argument as supplementary if colorful musings that, if and when appropriate, could later be qualified or explained away as dicta unnecessary to the resolution of this case.

But whatever subjective intentions may explain its creation and subsequent joinder by a majority, the structure and language of Justice Scalia's argument do make it read like an alternative (if brusque) basis for decision. Certainly a statute's conformity with separation of powers requirements is typically thought to be independent of its conformity with federalism principles. And in any event, emphatic language such as this often takes on a doctrinal life of its own, driving both lower court deliberations and subsequent Supreme Court decision making as well. It therefore seems best to take the Article II discussion quite seriously, as meaning precisely what it says.

individuals or state officials.[90] Moreover, the normative justifications for executive unity do not appear to be equally triggered by
unsupervised state administration of federal law following the
Brady Act model. As Justice Scalia adverted in *Printz*, unity promotes executive "vigor and accountability," whereas a plural executive could encourage lethargy and finger-pointing. If Congress
delegated authority to implement national welfare policy to a tri-
umvirate composed of the Governors of California, New York, and
Florida, vigor and accountability might well be compromised. But
the Brady Act's style of commandeering does not implicate this
concern, as particular CLEOs are vested with authority over a discrete subject matter and geographic region. So long as administrative power is clearly divided rather than jointly shared, the threat
to executive vigor and accountability is averted.

A unitary executive is also, according to Hamilton, more likely
to represent the interests of the entire national people, rather than
one or more factions thereof which might periodically take control
of Congress.[91] Members of Congress are accountable primarily to
the states and districts that have elected them; particularly if they
sit on important committees, they can powerfully influence the implementation decisions of subordinate federal officials through legislative oversight hearings, the appropriations process, and the

---

[90] For example, early Congresses relied heavily on private *qui tam* actions to enforce a
wide variety of federal statutory duties. See Evan H. Caminker, *The Constitutionality of Qui
Tam Actions*, 99 Yale L J 341, 341–42 (1989). Moreover, as discussed previously, early
Congresses frequently required state officials to assist in the implementation of various
federal laws. See text at note 37 above; see also Harold J. Krent, *Executive Control Over
Criminal Law Enforcement: Some Lessons from History*, 38 Am U L Rev 275, 303–10 (1989).
Whether this tradition of unsupervised execution of federal law through private persons or
state officials is significant enough to cast doubt on the unitary executive theory in its
entirety, the tradition certainly raises questions concerning the theory's application beyond
subordinate federal officials.

Of course, to the extent that the early tradition of state administration involved judicial
rather than executive tasks, the requirement of presidential supervision would not have
applied. But whatever the merit of the majority's contention that the tasks were fairly characterized as judicial from the perspective of *state* separation of powers doctrine, see *Printz*,
117 S Ct at 2371 n 2, many of the tasks (such as prosecuting violations of federal law,
assessing vessels' seaworthiness, arresting and detaining fugitive seamen, and arresting and
returning slaves and fugitives from justice—the latter characterized by Scalia himself as
executive) certainly seem more fairly characterized as executive rather than judicial from
the perspective of *federal* separation of powers principles, which of course should dictate
the scope of presidential authority.

[91] *The Federalist* No 70, at 471 (Alexander Hamilton) (Jacob E. Cooke ed 1961).

confirmation process. A unitary president, some argue, is a necessary counterweight to this tendency toward regionalized capture of national programs by powerful members of Congress.[92]

This concern does not apply, however, to state administration of federal law in circumstances typified by the Brady Act. Federal officials drawing from the national treasury to enforce laws throughout the entire nation might, if "captured" by members of Congress promoting local interests, be well positioned to "siphon[ ] off national treasure to regional benefit."[93] In contrast, state officials making state-bounded enforcement decisions are not similarly positioned. They cannot impose the financial costs of aggressive enforcement on the people in other states by siphoning federal tax dollars. And discretionary implementation decisions by a particular state official are unlikely to impose appreciable nonfinancial externalities on persons outside the state.[94] In the typical situation, in which state enforcement decisions have only intrastate impacts, there is no reason to fear congressional pressure for parochial implementation. Nor is there an obvious mechanism for such pressure; state officials are not subject to the same avenues of congressional influence. Hence, there appears to be no need for unified presidential control to combat such a threat.

The Court could, therefore, have easily justified an interpretation of Article II that restricted the scope of mandatory presidential supervision to federal officials only. Justice Scalia might respond that adopting the broader categorical rule might serve unitary interests in a narrow range of cases, and that is enough to justify it. But this response would import an implicit judgment weighing the relative benefit of modestly furthering unitarian values through a far-reaching categorical rule against the cost of invalidating nu-

---

[92] See Calabresi, 48 Ark L Rev at 48–70 (cited in note 77).

[93] See id at 85.

[94] Unless the nature of the federal policy is such that underenforcement in a particular state allows that state's inhabitants to enjoy spillover benefits from more zealous enforcement in neighboring states, there should be no concern that the underenforcing state is in any appreciable sense warping the national policy through local (non)enforcement to serve its parochial interests. It is difficult to see, for example, how Montana or Arizona CLEOs could siphon significant benefits from the rest of the nation through their particular decision as to how (even whether) to enforce the Brady Act. And while underenforcement decisions by Montana or Arizona CLEOs might frustrate neighboring states (assuming residents of those states cross the border to purchase guns and return home), one cannot argue that this form of "externality" is caused by the Brady Act such that the neighboring states are any worse off than they were before.

merous benign state administrative programs. Here again, strictly formalist interpretation fails to determine the doctrinal conclusion.

3. *Remedying Article II violations to ensure "meaningful" presidential supervision.* A third essential premise of the majority's argument is that the proper way to remedy unsupervised state implementation is to nullify state officials' authority to execute federal law—rather than extending the President's supervisory authority to reach those officials. Professors Calabresi and Prakash, whose scholarship Justice Scalia cited in his Article II discussion,[95] maintain that the Court should not invalidate statutes such as the Brady Act, but instead should uphold them and declare that the designated state officials are subject to presidential supervision when they carry out their statutory duties.[96]

While some unitary theorists would appear to suggest that the President's formal authority to countermand and supersede CLEOs' discrete decisions alone would satisfy the requirements of Article II,[97] the predominant view would suggest that Article II requires a greater degree of presidential supervision: the President must be able to control, not just his subordinates' decisions, but also the subordinates themselves through the power of removal.[98] Time and resource constraints prevent the President from personally reviewing all of his subordinates' implementation decisions in order to countermand or supersede them when appropriate. In contrast, a credible threat of removal encourages subordinates to follow the President's policy directives and exercise competent judgment. When this threat fails to deter, the President's authority to replace obstinate or incompetent officers enhances his control over future implementation.

The President cannot, of course, remove state officials from their state offices. A President might withdraw a CLEO's authority to continue conducting background checks, but that is a mild penalty at best.[99] If one believes both that Article II requires mean-

---

[95] See *Printz*, 117 S Ct at 2378.

[96] See Calabresi and Prakash, 104 Yale L J at 639 (cited in note 77).

[97] See, for example, Lawson, 107 Harv L Rev at 1243 (cited in note 77); Liberman, 38 Am U L Rev at 353 (cited in note 77).

[98] See *Myers v United States*, 272 US 52, 132–35 (1926).

[99] Moreover, the possibility of supervision through judicial injunction provides no realistic alternative to a meaningful removal power. In theory, the President might sue particular CLEOs, seeking injunctive relief requiring those officers (under threat of contempt) to implement federal law consistent with the President's specific orders or general policy ob-

ingful presidential control and that meaningful control requires a removal power, then it follows that the Brady Act's Article II violation can be remedied only through invalidation of the commandeering provisions. Justice Scalia seems to agree with both premises, given his remark speculating whether "indeed meaningful Presidential control is possible without the power to appoint and remove."[100]

Justice Scalia's methodological problem, however, is that neither the requirement nor operative definition of "meaningful" control can fairly be derived from Article II's text, history, or structure. Rather, they necessarily rest on an essentially normative or consequentialist judgment concerning the degree and mechanisms of presidential control required to fulfill the values of unity and accountability, values which themselves must be instrumentally defined. Here again, the majority's construction of unitary executive theory follows one plausible path over another, without adequate explanation.

4. *Article II and voluntary state administration of federal law.* The majority's casual statement that Article II does not preclude Congress from seeking "voluntary state participation" in federal program administration is, at first glance, puzzling. The Court reaffirmed in *New York* that traditional "cooperative federalism" regimes, whereby Congress uses a combination of sticks (threatened preemption) and carrots (conditional monetary subsidies) to encourage states to participate in the implementation of federal regulatory programs, are consistent with principles of state sovereignty. But it is unclear why these regimes are consistent with the majority's interpretation of Article II. Arguably, the requirement of presidential supervision should run to *all* forms of state administration of federal programs, even when the state voluntarily enacts state regulations designed specifically to serve federal objectives or

---

jectives. But in practice, this avenue would prove unwieldy because a court could not easily fashion an appropriate injunction. A CLEO could be ordered to obey specific presidential policy directives, but then if the President wanted to change his directives, he'd have to seek judicial modification of the injunction. A CLEO could be ordered more broadly to obey "any policy directive articulated by the President," but such an injunction might be too broad and vague to be enforceable. Moreover, oversight-by-injunction would at the very least be very time consuming and ensure an ongoing adversarial relationship between President and CLEO.

[100] *Printz*, 117 S Ct at 2378.

satisfy federal standards.[101] When Congress encourages states to help implement a regulatory program by exercising some interstitial policymaking discretion, the implementation details may still affect significant national interests. Given the President's inability to exercise "meaningful control" over state officials' implementation decisions, the principle of executive unity would seem to invalidate all conventional joint federal-state programs. Indeed, Justice Stevens made precisely this point in his dissent, charging that the Court's Article II reasoning logically would invalidate the types of cooperative programs affirmed in *New York*.[102]

There is a partial answer to this challenge, one that flows directly from the majority's formalist approach to Article II—although it is one the majority did not give. The majority's approach seems to call for presidential supervision of all execution of "federal law" as this term is conventionally understood. This means statutes, regulations, or other rules whose content is prescribed by federal officials exercising powers granted by the federal Constitution. But state officials do not implement federal law as so defined when they participate in traditional joint federal-state programs of the sort Justice Stevens described. Instead, when Congress encourages states to regulate in pursuit of federal objectives, either through the promise of financial reward or the threat of preemption, the states accept the invitation by enacting interstitial *state law*. Although it is true in a colloquial sense that the volunteering states are "participating in a federal program" because the regulations they enact are intentionally tailored to meet federal objectives, it is also true in a formal sense that these discretionary regulations are components of state (not federal) law, and the states' subsequent enforcement activities merely implement their own state regulations. It follows that Article II does not require the President to control or supervise state officials' discretionary state law choices in achieving federally articulated objectives.[103]

---

[101] Indeed, Professor Harold Krent has suggested that the unitary executive theory applies broadly enough to include the entire range of "voluntary" joint federal-state programs. See Krent, 85 Nw U L Rev at 81 & n 56 (cited in note 86).

[102] *Printz*, 117 S Ct at 2396–97 (Stevens dissenting).

[103] Even this relatively clean dichotomy between federal and state laws raises some interesting questions of classification. For a suggestion that a particular federal statute might for some purposes "incorporate" state laws designed to satisfy federal criteria, see, for example, *Ashoff v City of Ukiah*, 130 F3d 409 (9th Cir 1997). For a discussion of whether interstate

This formalist justification for the majority's contention that co-erced but not voluntary state administration violates Article II is only a partial one. While it saves traditional cooperative federalism programs from Article II challenge, it cannot explain the majority's apparent willingness to countenance state officials' voluntary ad-ministration of purely federal laws such as the Brady Act itself.[104] And the majority's only proffered explanation raises more ques-tions than it answers.

Justice Scalia responded to Justice Stevens's challenge as follows:

> The dissent is correct that control by the unitary Federal Exec-utive is also sacrificed when States voluntarily administer fed-eral programs, but the condition of voluntary state participa-tion significantly reduces the ability of Congress to use this device as a means of reducing the power of the Presidency.[105]

This response does not purport to deny Justice Stevens's premise that voluntary state participation in federal programs qualifies as fed-eral law execution for purposes of Article II. How the response pur-ports to rebut Justice Stevens's conclusion, however, remains obscure.

The response might be read as follows: statutes inviting state enforcement pose a lesser threat to Article II values than do com-mandeering statutes, because the ex ante likelihood of disunified federal execution is lower when Congress invites than when it commands. But it is unclear why probabilities should matter. When a state chooses to accept a congressional invitation to en-force a federal statute, it would seem odd for the Court to accept the resulting diminution of executive power merely because, ex ante, there was some chance that the invitation would be declined. Moreover, this response imports a measure of balancing (distin-guishing between greater and lesser threats to presidential control), which rests in tension with the tenor of the majority's formalist reasoning.

---

compacts, which are treated as "federal law" for purposes of Article III jurisdiction, should similarly be treated as "federal law" for purposes of Article II superintendence, see Caminker, 45 Kan L Rev at 1103 n 115 (cited in note 76).

[104] The majority opinion refused to invalidate two provisions of the Brady Act because they "have conceivable application to a CLEO . . . only if he has chosen, voluntarily, to participate in administration of the federal scheme." *Printz*, 117 S Ct at 2384. Justice O'Connor declared more directly that "[s]tates and chief law enforcement officers may voluntarily continue to participate in the federal program." Id at 2385 (O'Connor concurring).

[105] Id at 2378 n 12.

An alternative reading of the majority's response focuses on the motive for, rather than effect of, Congress's reliance on state implementation. The reference to Congress's ability "to *use* this device as a means of reducing" the President's power might suggest that an Article II violation is triggered by Congress's desire to circumvent the unitary executive. But why? When evaluating separation of powers challenges to congressional action, the Court traditionally asks two questions: Has Congress acted in a manner that unduly arrogates power to itself? and, Has Congress interfered with another branch's ability to fulfill its assigned constitutional duties?[106] With respect to the second question, the Court generally does not ask whether Congress specifically intended to impede another department's assigned responsibilities; indeed, Congress cannot interfere "for even the *very best* of reasons."[107] To the extent that Justice Scalia's response focuses on congressional motive, therefore, it raises further questions about the grounding and formulation of the majority's cryptic Article II claim in the first place.

The majority's failure to provide a lucid response to Justice Stevens's charge creates uncertainty as to whether and why the professed boundary of *Printz*'s Article II argument is consistent with its rationale. More generally, the majority's implicit choices among various plausible constructions of executive unity, as with competing state sovereignty formulations, either reflect ad hoc judgments or turn on a deeper yet unspecified normative vision.

III. The Future of State Executive Immunity: Where Does Printz Lead?

The formalistic reasoning of *Printz* raises questions about the scope and effect of the anti-commandeering rule itself. It also raises a much broader question concerning states' immunity from generally applicable federal burdens.

A. THE SCOPE AND EFFECT OF THE COURT'S ANTI-COMMANDEERING RULE

1. *What constitutes "commandeering" of state executive officials?* The Court used a variety of similar phrases to explain that Congress

---

[106] See, for example, *INS v Chadha*, 462 US 919, 963 (1983).

[107] *Plaut v Spendthrift Farm, Inc.*, 514 US 211, 228 (1995).

may not coerce state participation in the "actual administration of a federal program,"[108] but it never defined just what "administration" might entail. Both the majority and Justice O'Connor's concurring opinions purported to hold open the question whether Congress may impose "reporting requirements" on state or local authorities, whereby state officials must provide information on various topics to specified federal officials. As the majority put it, federal statutes "which require only the provision of information to the Federal Government, do not involve the precise issue here before us, which is the forced participation of the State's executive in the actual administration of a federal program."[109]

It is unclear, however, on what basis reporting requirements can meaningfully be distinguished from "actual administration of a federal program." As Justice O'Connor pointed out, some existing reporting requirements might be called "purely ministerial."[110] But any categorical distinction between "reporting" and "administration" based on some conception of the former's ministerial or even de minimis character appears both difficult to define and strikingly inconsistent with the Court's disdain elsewhere for similar distinctions (e.g., between "policymaking" and "implementation" requirements). As Justice Scalia continually insists, "an imprecise barrier against federal intrusion upon state authority is not likely to be an effective one."[111] And the Court also clearly eschewed any noncategorical balancing test that might lead to an exception for what might be characterized as "de minimis" violations.[112]

---

[108] See *Printz*, 117 S Ct at 2376; see also, for example, id at 2381 ("administering federal law"); id at 2383 ("direct the functioning of the state executive"); id at 2384 ("administer or enforce a federal regulatory program").

[109] Id at 2376; id at 2385 (O'Connor concurring).

[110] Id at 2385 (O'Connor concurring) (referring specifically to 42 USC § 5779(a), which requires state and local law enforcement officials to report cases of missing children to the Department of Justice).

[111] Id at 2381.

[112] Id at 2383, 2384. For the same reasons, the Court's approach would also seem to reject any attempt to draw distinctions among the various reporting requirements based on the varying extent of the burdens they impose. For example, some so-called reporting requirements do not merely require state officials to disclose information they already possess to the federal government; in some cases, state officials must first gather, create, and/or structure the information in a manner prescribed by federal law. See note 6 above.

Moreover, the fact that states might be better situated than the federal government to gather certain types of data fails to distinguish pure reporting requirements from the Brady Act itself, which was defended in part on this very ground. See 117 S Ct at 2383 (rejecting relevance of claim that the Brady Act "is most efficiently administered by CLEOs during the interim period").

Moreover, the primary duty imposed by the Brady Act itself is a "reporting" requirement of sorts; CLEOs are required to retrieve and report specific data concerning prospective gun purchasers. Should it matter that the CLEOs are required to provide that information directly to private individuals (dealers or purchasers) rather than federal officials, so that the Brady Act nominally regulates state-citizen relations rather than merely state-federal relations? If "actual administration of a federal program" entails direct interaction with private citizens, then Congress apparently could save the Brady Act simply by requiring CLEOs to provide their requested information to the local United States Attorney, who would then pass the information along to dealers and purchasers. Surely the Court would reject this definitional limitation.

The rationale for the Court's suggestion that its anti-commandeering rule might not apply to reporting requirements thus remains obscure. As a result, the Court's rationale might well extend to encompass *any* burden imposed uniquely on state officials that commands their attention and resources to serve federal objectives. Indeed, the *New York* Court seemed to employ an expansive definition of commandeering when invalidating one aspect of the "take-title provision"—a definition that apparently encompassed a burden whose implementation required little if any affirmative activity by state executives. The statutory provision "required States either to enact legislation providing for the disposal of radioactive waste generated within their borders, or to take title to, and possession of the waste . . . ."[113] Various members of the Court have characterized the obligation of taking title to waste as a requirement affirmatively to implement a legislative or administrative response to the federally defined problem.[114] But the requirement that states take title to privately produced waste can be enforced without affirmative administrative action. If a state failed to enact conforming legislation providing for waste disposal, an individual injured through exposure to privately produced waste could sue the state for compensatory damages on the ground that

---

[113] See *Printz*, 117 S Ct at 2380.

[114] For example, in *Printz*, the Court characterized the take-title provision as "effectively requiring the States either to legislate pursuant to Congress's directions, or to implement an administrative solution." Id at 2380; see id at 2398 (Stevens dissenting) (provision operates as a compelled subsidy, which is "almost certainly a legislative act" or perhaps an act of "purely executive policymaking").

the take-title provision made the state the new owner of the waste and hence the proper defendant. In this manner, the take-title provision would essentially be self-executing, without need for any affirmative legislative or administrative action on the part of the state. Yet the *New York* Court still characterized this provision as a type of "compelled subsidy" which qualified as "commandeering."[115]

The fact that the Court in both *New York* and *Printz* described the take-title provision as an example of coerced legislative or administrative action might reveal a too-casual misapplication of the Court's own anti-commandeering theory—or it might reveal that the Court's understanding of what it means for Congress to "direct the functioning of the state executive" is quite capacious, so as to include the mere payment of liability judgments. The latter would suggest that any targeted burden imposed on states alone runs afoul of the *Printz* principle, whether or not the burden requires "administration" of federal law in a conventional sense.

To be sure, I do not mean to doubt the Court's sincerity in suggesting that the prohibition against coerced "actual administration" of federal programs might not encompass reporting requirements and, by inference, perhaps other burdens imposed uniquely on states as well. But once again, the Court leaves us in the dark as to the possible formalist rationales for such distinctions, and it expressly rejects any functionalist rationales. The ultimate breadth of the Court's anti-commandeering rule, then, necessarily awaits definition in future cases.

2. *Which particular constitutional provisions authorize commandeering?* Both *Printz* and *New York* involved statutes enacted pursuant to the Commerce Clause. In both cases, the Court said that other provisions of the Constitution might authorize commandeering. Not only did the *Printz* Court suggest that early statutes obligating state judges to enforce federal prescriptions were authorized by the Supremacy Clause,[116] but the Court approved Congress's long-standing conscription of state executives to extradite fugitives from justice as a "direct implementation . . . of the Extradition Clause of the Constitution itself, see Art. IV, § 2."[117] The

---

[115] *New York*, 505 US at 175.

[116] See 117 S Ct at 2370–71, 2380.

[117] Id at 2371–72 (footnote omitted).

Court did not mention the Militia Clauses, but they too clearly authorize Congress to conscript the states' primary military institutions for certain national purposes—including to "execute the Laws of the Union."[118] At least two other clauses are of pressing interest today: the Article I, Section 4 power to regulate state elections of federal officials, and the Section 5 power to enforce the Fourteenth Amendment.

Both of these provisions have recently been invoked in defense of the National Voter Registration Act of 1993,[119] which aims to encourage citizen participation in federal elections by ordering state officials to take specific measures to facilitate easy voter registration: states requiring pre-vote registration must provide registration materials through the mail and at various state and local government offices, including those where driver's license applications and renewals are processed (hence the colloquial designation "Motor Voter Act"). The Constitution provides that:

> The Times, Places and Manner of holding Elections for Senators and Representatives, shall be prescribed in each State by the Legislature thereof; but the Congress may at any time by Law make or alter such Regulations, except as to the Places of chusing Senators.[120]

Thus, while states design federal election systems and implement them through state election officers, Congress may "make" its own regulations—superseding conflicting state regulations under the Supremacy Clause—and Congress may also "alter" the existing state regulations. A fair reading of this text suggests that Congress may still require the same state election officers to implement the federally altered scheme, unless Congress chooses instead to replace them by authorizing the appointment of federal election officials.[121] On this basis, federal appellate courts have rebuffed

---

[118] US Const, Art I, § 8, cls 15 & 16.

[119] 42 USC § 1973gg (1994).

[120] US Const, Art I, § 4, cl 1.

[121] See *Ex parte Siebold*, 100 US 371, 388–91 (1879) (affirming Congress's power to leave in place a state election scheme while creating additional sanctions for state officials who violate that scheme, based on the view that "the [state] officers of election, in elections for [federal] representatives, owe a duty to the United States, and are amenable to that government as well as to the State. . . .").

claims that the Motor Voter Act violates the anti-commandeering rule announced in *New York*.[122]

A similar question, with potentially far broader consequences, is whether Congress's Section 5 power to "enforce, by appropriate legislation, the provisions" of the Fourteenth Amendment also authorizes Congress to conscript state officials to implement federal mandates.[123] As a purely textual matter, one might initially assume that Section 5 precisely mirrors the scope of Article I's Necessary and Proper Clause. But the Supreme Court has held and recently confirmed that Section 5 authorizes Congress to override states' Eleventh Amendment sovereign immunity (sometimes articulated as implicit in Article III) and empower private individuals to bring suits against unconsenting states in federal court—something Congress may not do under its Article I powers. In *Fitzpatrick v Bitzer*, the Court reasoned that Section 1 of the Fourteenth Amendment specifically reallocated power from the states to the federal government, and hence states waived their erstwhile immu-

---

[122] As Judge Posner concluded:

Congress could have established a separate system of voter registration for federal elections, manned by federal officers . . . . If Congress had done that, however, the burden would fall on the federal fisc alone. . . . But Article I section Four does not authorize Congress only to establish a system of federal voter registration. The first sentence, remember, requires the states to create and operate such a system and the second authorizes Congress to alter the state's system—but it is still the state's system, manned by state officers and hence paid for by the state.

Association of Community Orgs. for Reform Now v Edgar, 56 F3d 791, 795 (7th Cir 1995); see also *Association of Community Orgs. for Reform Now v Miller*, 129 F3d 833 (6th Cir 1997); *Voting Rights Coalition v Wilson*, 60 F3d 1411 (9th Cir 1995), cert denied, 116 S Ct 815 (1996).

[123] The Motor Voter Act was also defended on this ground, with proponents arguing that Congress's effort to encourage voter registration was designed to protect the fundamental right to vote and to remedy subtle forms of racial discrimination perpetuated by existing state registration schemes. See *Association of Community Orgs. for Reform Now v Edgar*, 800 F Supp 1215 (ND Ill 1995) (holding Act authorized pursuant to Congress's Section 5 as well as Article I, § 4 powers), aff'd on Section 4 grounds, 56 F3d 791 (7th Cir 1995). Similarly, the United States has invoked Congress's Section 5 power to defend the Driver's Privacy Protection Act of 1994, 18 USC §§ 2721–25 (1994), which regulates the dissemination and use of certain information contained in state motor vehicle records in order to protect privacy rights purportedly secured by the Fourteenth Amendment. But see *Condon v Reno*, 972 F Supp 977 (DSC 1995) (rejecting the Section 5 defense on the ground that the disclosure of this particular information does not implicate Fourteenth Amendment privacy rights; and rejecting the Commerce Clause defense on anti-commandeering grounds).

While I focus here on Congress's Section 5 power, the same question arises with respect to Congress's Section 2 powers to enforce the Thirteenth and Fifteenth Amendments. Indeed, the latter has also been invoked to defend the Motor Voter Act.

nity from congressionally authorized suits to enforce Section 1's new restrictions on their residual sovereign authority.[124] More generally, the Court has explained that "principles of federalism that might otherwise be an obstacle to congressional authority are necessarily overridden by the power to enforce the Civil War Amendments 'by appropriate legislation.' "[125]

This reasoning seems every bit as applicable to commandeering of state officials as to overriding state immunity from suit. Both might be appropriate means in particular contexts of ensuring state fidelity to Fourteenth Amendment norms. The text of Section 5 does not specifically override federalism objections to private suits against states any more than to commandeering; no clear intent of the Fourteenth Amendment's framers could be marshaled to support any distinction between the two;[126] and with reference to the federalism values at stake, it is unclear why the default anti-commandeering rule should be considered any more fixed or fundamental than the default anti-suit rule. Thus, so long as it is "appropriate" for Congress to enforce a particular Section 1 restriction on states by affirmatively dictating state executive officials' activity, *Bitzer*'s reasoning suggests that Congress may abrogate states' immunity from commandeering.[127]

Before concluding that either or both Article I, Section 4 and

---

[124] See 427 US 445, 452–56 (1976); see also *Seminole Tribe v Florida*, 116 S Ct 1114 (1996) (reaffirming Section 5 power to override Eleventh Amendment immunity even while holding that the Commerce Clause does not similarly authorize Congress to override such immunity).

[125] *City of Rome v United States*, 446 US 156, 179 (1980); see also, for example, *Gregory v Ashcroft*, 501 US 452, 468 (1991); *EEOC v Wyoming*, 460 US 226, 243 n 18 (1983); *South Carolina v Katzenbach*, 383 US 301, 324 (1966).

[126] Indeed, if anything, it is more likely that the Framers contemplated the question whether Section 5 would override an anti-commandeering principle, because at least such a principle had been previously mentioned by Justices of the Court. See *Kentucky v Dennison*, 65 US 66 (1861); *Prigg v Pennsylvania*, 41 US 539 (1842). By contrast, the Court did not clearly suggest that the Eleventh Amendment generally barred federal question suits against states until *Louisiana v Jumel*, 107 US 711 (1883), and *Hans v Louisiana*, 134 US 1 (1890), well after Section 5 was enacted.

[127] Of course, even if commandeering is a legitimate means of congressional regulation under Section 5, any such statute must still "enforce . . . the provisions" of the Fourteenth Amendment with respect to its subject matter. The Supreme Court's decision in *City of Boerne v Flores*, 117 S Ct 2157 (1997), issued the same week as *Printz*, made clear that in this respect, the scope of Congress's Section 5 power is limited to measures designed to "remedy or prevent" Fourteenth Amendment violations as defined by the judiciary (rather than Congress). The Motor Voter Act and Driver's Privacy Protection Act aside, other existing commandeering statutes (including the Brady Act) may raise questions under *Boerne*'s subject matter limitation.

the Fourteenth Amendment's Section 5 override the constitutional impediments to commandeering, however, we must consider the implications of *Printz*'s Article II discussion as well. Assuming that the Court intended this argument to constitute an independent basis for decision, at first glance it would appear that congressional commandeering pursuant to any grant of power would still violate the unitary executive requirement. But this conclusion is too quick: the *Printz* majority approved the Extradition Act of 1793 and its successors, which conscript state executive officials to administer a particular federal policy of interstate comity. Why wouldn't this Act equally run afoul of Article II?[128]

The Court failed to acknowledge, let alone address, this question. Its answer must be that, if the Constitution specially authorizes congressional commandeering of state officials in a discrete context, such authority must be understood to override the inherent unitary executive constraints, just as it overrides general federalism constraints. For example, if Article I provided that "Congress shall have power to direct state executive officials to print a national currency," surely congressional exercise of this power could not reasonably be constrained by a robust conception of Article II's unitary executive mandate, else this express power would be rendered completely nugatory.[129]

How clear must the constitutional authority to commandeer state officials be in order for it to qualify for an automatic override of erstwhile Article II constraints? It cannot be that comman-

---

[128] One might argue that the Extradition Act does not implicate Article II concerns by conceptualizing the obligation imposed on the asylum state as a duty to aid in the execution of a sister state's laws, rather than a duty to aid in the execution of federal law. If so, then state compliance does not implicate the principles underlying the unitary executive, mirroring my proposal that congressionally induced state administration of state law designed to secure federal objectives should not be held to violate Article II. See text at note 103 above. But I find this conceptualization unpersuasive. The asylum state's duty to respect the demanding state's extradition request is imposed by the congressional statute to give effect to a federal principle of interstate comity—even if the ultimate goal of such comity is to help the demanding state enforce its own criminal laws. Thus, asylum state officials are required to implement federal law, which would seem to trigger the unitary executive requirement.

[129] Of course, Article II's requirement of presidential supervision might still apply to the extent that specific supervisory means are not inherently inconsistent with the very notion of conscripting state officials. For example, while the President could not assert removal power over state officials implementing federal law, Article II might still empower the President to issue directives to those state officials in an effort to guide their administrative decision making.

deering is permissible only when the Constitution itself imposes affirmative mandates on state officials, because the Extradition Clause is not self-executing, and consequently state officials are legally bound to comply only when Congress implements the described duty via statute.[130] The Court must believe, therefore, that Article II permits commandeering even when the Constitution does not itself impose mandates but grants Congress a power that specifically encompasses the authority to commandeer state officials.

The tricky task here, of course, is to define what counts as a sufficiently "specific" authorization of commandeering power for this purpose.[131] This standard should certainly be met when the Constitution grants Congress a power whose exercise inherently requires conscription of state officials, such that a requirement of robust presidential supervision would render the power grant completely devoid of operative significance. Extradition commandeering satisfies this test, for any congressional implementation of the Extradition Clause necessarily entails state execution. Similarly, this approach justifies Article I, Section 4 commandeering, for any congressional "alter[ation]" of a state's federal election scheme necessarily entails state execution as well. But Section 5 commandeering falls outside of this category, for not all means of enforcing the Fourteenth Amendment necessarily require conscription of state officials.

Of course, one could imagine a more capacious definition of "specific" commandeering authorization for present purposes. Suppose a particular grant of power is such that its exercise does not functionally entail commandeering of state officials. Perhaps Article II constraints should still be considered overridden if it were clear, from other interpretive indicia (e.g., text, Framers' intent), that the power grant specifically extended Congress the *option* of exercising that power through commandeering. Whether Section 5 would qualify for an Article II override under this more expansive test strikes me as a complicated and difficult question.

---

[130] See *California v Superior Court*, 482 US 400, 406–08 (1987).

[131] The standard cannot be so lax that *any* authority to commandeer is considered specific enough to escape Article II scrutiny. Otherwise, Article II would cease to operate as an independent ground for decision in *Printz*, contrary to my assumption here. For the Article II argument to have any bite at all, there must be some commandeering that is authorized notwithstanding any federalism objections, and yet not be so "specifically authorized" as to merit automatic exemption from Article II constraints.

In the end, Justice Scalia's opinion in *Printz* invites future courts to consider whether the general anti-commandeering rule is overridden by particular constitutional provisions other than the two he mentioned, the Supremacy and Extradition Clauses. Persuasive arguments can be made that both Article I, Section 4 and Section 5 of the Fourteenth Amendment are best interpreted as also authorizing Congress to conscript state officials in certain contexts. As a result, at least the Motor Voter Act does, and some future commandeering statutes might also, still comply with the Constitution's federal design.

Erection of an apparently independent Article II barrier to commandeering, however, seemingly casts an even broader shadow than the federalism obstacle. Because the Court's opinion did not explain the interplay between the two constraints, the precise outline of this shadow remains quite hazy.

3. *How will the anti-commandeering rule practically affect intergovernmental relations?* However broadly *Printz*'s commandeering disability is ultimately defined, Congress may still invite and persuade states to lend their services to federal program administration. First, Congress may assert its Spending Clause power to offer states substantial monetary subsidies, on the condition that the states then regulate private activity according to federal standards.[132] Second, Congress may force states to choose between administering federal programs or having their laws preempted and replaced with either a federally enforced policy or even a regulatory void.[133] The availability of these inducement strategies substantially minimizes the practical constraint of *Printz*, as well as those erected by other recent federalism decisions such as *Seminole Tribe*—which is why the next major battle over federalism doctrine may well erupt over the constitutional constraints properly imposed on these strategies. A decision by the Supreme Court to constrict Congress's power to encourage state activity through these means could have a far greater practical impact on inter-

---

[132] See *New York v United States*, 505 US 144, 167 (1992); see also *Printz*, 117 S Ct at 2385 (O'Connor concurring).

[133] See *New York*, 505 US at 167–68. For example, assuming this would be a valid exercise of its Commerce Clause power, Congress could enact a law preempting any and all state regulations of gun purchases unless CLEOs enforced the Brady Act. Or, Congress could do precisely the opposite (if allowed by the Second Amendment) and enact a law prohibiting the sale of guns within a state unless its CLEOs enforced the Brady Act.

governmental relations than any recent skirmish over federalism doctrine.

Of course, Congress's desire to negotiate around the anti-commandeering rule through such inducement strategies will be tempered by the financial and political costs they entail. And in certain circumstances these means might not provide a workable substitute for commandeering. Negotiation between states and the federal government may fail; and Justice Stevens is surely correct to observe that a commandeering power might still be extremely important to protect national interests in an emergency.[134] Thus any claim that the anti-commandeering rule will have *no* effect on the likelihood of state administration of federal law is overstated.

Equally overstated, however, is the majority opinion's single consequentialist assertion that "[t]he power of the Federal Government would be augmented immeasurably if it were able to impress [state officers] into its service—and at no cost to itself."[135] Theoretically this may be true, but as a practical matter it is an exaggeration to say that commandeering authority would work an enormous realignment in federal-state relations. *Printz* does not appear to curtail prior nationalist assertions of power in a significant manner, as Congress has heretofore enacted only a handful of statutes that require state executive officials to implement federal programs in the same direct manner as does the Brady Act. And we can only conjecture whether, but for *Printz*, Congress would have increasingly turned to commandeering in the years ahead, or whether the political safeguards of federalism would have continued to hold commandeering to a minimum.

B. STATE IMMUNITY FROM GENERALLY APPLICABLE BURDENS

One very significant doctrinal implication of *Printz* is not found in its holding, but rather in its ominous signals portending a more far-reaching change to its treatment of generally applicable federal regulations that burden states along with private citizens. The Court's historical flip-flopping on this issue is well known. In *Na-*

---

[134] See *Printz*, 117 S Ct at 2387 (Stevens dissenting). For a further discussion of the ways in which commandeering can serve legitimate federal interests not easily achievable through the use of incentives, see Caminker, 95 Colum L Rev at 1083–86 (cited in note 36).

[135] *Printz*, 117 S Ct at 2378.

tional League of Cities v Usery,[136] the Court overruled *Maryland v Wirtz*[137] and held that certain generally applicable laws—those that directly impair states' ability to structure their internal operating processes in areas of traditional governmental functions—violate principles of state sovereignty unless they are justified by an overriding federal interest.[138] A decade later, the Court overruled *National League of Cities* in *Garcia v San Antonio Metropolitan Transit Authority*,[139] determining that the only constitutional protection afforded states to be free from such generally applicable laws is that created by the "political safeguards of federalism." But the two dissenters in *Garcia* who remain on the Court today vowed that *National League of Cities* would prevail again[140]—and another decade has gone by.

On the surface, *Printz* contains signals that *National League of Cities*'s resurrection is at hand. As the majority defined state sovereignty, it seems equally obstructed by a federal law regulating the functioning of state executives whether or not the law visits the same burden upon private parties. Because the Court refused to inquire whether the burden is weighty or involves policymaking,[141] generally applicable burdens such as those imposed by the Fair Labor Standards Act or the Clean Water Act appear to pose the same threat to state sovereignty as does the Brady Act. Indeed, the "unfunded mandates" generating fierce state and local complaints in recent years have almost entirely been imposed via generally applicable legislation. And it is unclear why such mandates would not qualify as "forced participation of the States' executive in the actual administration of a federal program."[142]

Moreover, the Court nowhere endorsed the political safeguards reasoning underlying *Garcia*. The Court curtly rejected the federal government's claim that the Brady Act does not threaten to blur the lines of political accountability between federal and state

---

[136] 426 US 833 (1976).

[137] 392 US 183 (1968).

[138] See 426 US at 845, 852–55.

[139] 469 US 528 (1985).

[140] See id at 580 (Rehnquist dissenting); id at 589 (O'Connor dissenting).

[141] See *Printz*, 117 S Ct at 2384.

[142] Id at 2376. The majority did not rely—at least explicitly—on a governmental/proprietary distinction that might purport to save generally applicable burdens from its anti-commandeering rule. Such a distinction is notoriously difficult to draw and defend.

actors, but the Court carefully avoided implying that the absence of such risk would constitute a sufficient reason to abjure judicial protection of state sovereignty.[143]

Most directly, the Court expressly questioned the vitality of *Garcia* when explaining why the Brady Act violates its constructed principle of state sovereignty:

> Finally, the Government puts forward a cluster of arguments that can be grouped under the heading: "The Brady Act serves very important purposes, is most efficiently administered by CLEOs during the interim period, and places a minimal and only temporary burden upon state officers." There is considerable disagreement over the extent of the burden, but we need not pause over that detail. Assuming *all* the mentioned factors were true, they might be relevant if we were evaluating whether the incidental application to the States of a federal law of general applicability excessively interfered with the functioning of state governments . . . [citing, inter alia, *National League of Cities*]. But where, as here, it is the whole object of the law to direct the functioning of the state executive, and hence to compromise the structural framework of dual sovereignty, such a "balancing" analysis is inappropriate. It is the very *principle* of separate state sovereignty that such a law offends, and no comparative assessment of the various interests can overcome that fundamental defect.[144]

Without more, then, it would appear that *National League of Cities* redux is just around the corner.

Having said all of this, it is precisely Justice Scalia's devotion to doctrinal formalism that makes prediction hazardous here. Justice Scalia has consistently maintained that courts should avoid open-ended balancing tests such as that applied in *National League of Cities*,[145] and his reference to this case may have been intended

---

[143] See id at 2382.

[144] Id at 2383 (footnote omitted). In footnote 17, the Court responded to Justice Stevens's claim that if the Brady Act had imposed a similar burden on both police officers and private persons, the burden on the former would have been permissible. Although the Court conceded "[t]hat is undoubtedly true," the Court might have agreed with the dissent not because the hypothesized law was generally applicable, but instead because it burdened police officers only in their individual rather than official capacities. Id at 2383 n 17. Accordingly, the burden would not run afoul of any resurrected *National League of Cities*-like balancing test.

[145] Indeed, four days before *Printz*, Justice Scalia refused to join Justice Kennedy's lead opinion reformulating the doctrine of *Ex parte Young*, 209 US 123 (1908), into a case-by-case balancing test concerning the particular need for federal court control of state officials through injunctive relief. See *Idaho v Coeur d'Alene Tribe*, 117 S Ct 2028 (1997). Justice Scalia instead joined Justice O'Connor's concurring opinion, which preserved the traditional

merely to appease others in the majority. The more difficult question is this: What categorical test might he endorse in its stead? Minimal scrutiny of generally applicable burdens, or an absolute state immunity from such burdens?

It is conceivable that Justice Scalia would adhere to *Garcia*'s conclusion that generally applicable regulations should not receive special judicial scrutiny. Although Justice Scalia surely recognizes that generally applicable laws can impose the same type of burden on state executives as state-targeted commandeering statutes, his focus above on the "whole object of the law" suggests that only laws that *particularly* target state executives violate the "very principle of separate state sovereignty" he has constructed. On this view, the states' sovereign status provides them with a right not to be singled out by Congress on the basis of their statehood, and nothing more.[146]

Indeed, the precise language and structure of Justice Scalia's argument call to mind his First Amendment jurisprudence. He distinguishes doctrinally between generally applicable regulations that incidentally burden free speech or religious exercise, which receive no special scrutiny, and regulations whose very object is to burden speech or religious activity, which receive strict scrutiny.[147] This distinction is not based on a concern about lawmakers' subjective motives; rather, Justice Scalia simply interprets the First Amend-

---

bright-line rule that federal courts may enjoin state officials with regard to prospective but not retrospective relief. Id at 2045–47.

[146] If this is Justice Scalia's view, it is somewhat surprising that he did not attempt to draw support from the mid-century *New York v United States* decision concerning the doctrine of intergovernmental tax immunity. See 326 US 572 (1946). There the Supreme Court upheld a nondiscriminatory federal tax on the sale of mineral waters as applied to New York, which engaged in the bottling and sale of such waters. Various Justices suggested, however, that a federal tax targeting "state activities and state-owned property that partake of uniqueness" (such as state taxation and owning a Statehouse) would be invalid as "taxing the State as a State." Id at 582 (opinion of Frankfurter); see also id at 586 (Stone concurring). This first *New York* case seems a natural precursor of the second; perhaps it goes unmentioned because the relevant discussion is dicta.

[147] See, for example, *Employment Div., Ore. Dept. of Human Resources v Smith*, 494 US 872, 878 (1990) ("[I]f prohibiting the exercise of religion (or burdening the activity of printing) is not the object of the tax but merely the incidental effect of a generally applicable and otherwise valid provision, the First Amendment has not been offended."); *Barnes v Glen Theatre, Inc.*, 501 US 560, 577 (1991) (Scalia concurring in the judgment) ("In each of the foregoing cases [invalidating regulations on First Amendment grounds], we explicitly found that suppressing communication was the object of the regulation of conduct. Where that has not been the case, however—where suppression of communicative use of the conduct was merely the incidental effect of forbidding the conduct for other reasons—we have allowed the regulation to stand.").

ment to establish a right to be free of regulations whose object is to suppress speech or religious practice.[148] Justice Scalia might analogously understand state sovereignty to entail a right to be free from laws that target that very sovereignty, but not from laws that incidentally interfere with internal functions. Certainly the former category, in which states are truly regulated "as states" rather than as a subset of employers or proprietors or anything else, bespeaks a greater and more visible federal insensitivity to state sovereignty than does the latter.

On the other hand, it is also possible that Justice Scalia would instead opt for an absolute state immunity from being forced to serve federal objectives through executive activity, even when the burden extends to nonstate entities as well. He does appear solicitous of the states' interest in "remain[ing] independent and autonomous within their proper sphere of authority," an interest threatened by generally applicable as well as targeted legislation. And it would be easy enough doctrinally to apply a categorical state immunity without threatening Congress's authority to regulate in the private sphere.[149]

Justice Scalia's formalist approach in *Printz* makes it hard to foretell his next move. While the majority clearly regards *Garcia* as fair game rather than fixed precedent, Justice Scalia's commitment to doctrinal formalism suggests that he might shun a return to the *National League of Cities* balancing test in favor of a categorical rule. But because Justice Scalia's opinion eschews explicit discussion of the normative values underlying various definitions of state sovereignty, he provides no clear guidance concerning why or how important he believes it is to protect state autonomy. Thus his commitment to interpretive formalism makes it difficult to divine whether he would mirror his First Amendment jurisprudence by embracing a no-scrutiny rule, or whether he would protect

---

[148] See *Church of the Lukumi Babalu Aye, Inc. v Hialeah*, 508 US 520, 558–59 (1993) (Scalia concurring in part) (distinguishing between improper focus on "subjective motivation of the lawmakers" and proper focus on "object of the laws").

[149] This distinguishes the sovereignty context from the First Amendment context. In the latter arena, Justice Scalia has expressed concern that, if the Court allowed any individual claiming to engage in conduct for religious or expressive reasons to be exempt from (or demand special judicial scrutiny for) generally applicable laws, government's ability to prohibit socially harmful conduct would be substantially obstructed. See, for example, *Barnes*, 501 US at 579. In contrast, it would not be administratively difficult to exempt states from general regulations.

states significantly through an absolute immunity rule—perhaps the most momentous question affecting federal-state relations posed by the resolution of this case.

IV. Conclusion

Printz does not stand out within the series of recent antinationalist decisions for its immediate doctrinal effect, both because Congress heretofore has only infrequently conscripted state executive services, and because Congress can generally induce state administration of federal law through noncoercive means (albeit at some additional cost). Rather, *Printz* stands out both for its resounding celebrations of the principles of state sovereignty and executive unity—and its lack of constitutional grounding therefor. The Court's anti-commandeering rule might be defensible along a variety of normative avenues. But the majority fails to prove its case here, because its chosen methodology is simply not up to the task. As this case study illuminates, where constitutional text, structure, and history provide few clear guideposts, interpretive formalism easily devolves into a sequence of choices from among plausible but competing constructs and principles. And these choices appear capricious, as they are neither dictated by text or structure, nor guided by articulated constitutional values, consequences, or purposes. Even opponents of commandeering, I suspect, will find the Court's route to its doctrinal destination contrived.

Perhaps the Court believed that its reasoning was less important than its resoluteness. There may be something intuitively offensive about the commandeering of one government's services by another, and perhaps this offense cries out for a responsive judicial proclamation of the centrality of sovereignty in our federal regime. And an opinion-crafting formula of "emphatically proclaimed, plausibly maintained" may serve a number of proper functions for a Court desiring to communicate with its public. But this aspiration is too modest for the Court's far broader set of public responsibilities—and quite brazen for a Court that purports to care that its decisions invalidating democratically enacted legislation are properly grounded in our Constitution.

VICTOR BRUDNEY

O'HAGAN'S PROBLEMS

A problem that has bedeviled the courts in litigation under Section 10(b) of the Securities Exchange Act of 1934 and Rule 10b-5 promulgated thereunder by the Securities and Exchange Commission[1] is to determine under what circumstances a person who buys or sells securities is required to disclose to the opposite party to the transaction material non-public information about the securities that he has, but that the opposite party does not have. A recently addressed form of the problem engages the question whether, if A acquires such information from C (to whom he is a fiduciary) by a form of deceit, and uses the information in trading with B, A's misappropriation and use of the information constitutes a "deceptive device or contrivance" that operates "as a fraud or

---

Victor Brudney is Weld Professor of Law, Emeritus, Harvard Law School.

AUTHOR'S NOTE: I am indebted to Lucian A. Bebchuk and Reinier Kraakman for probing—and unsettling—inquiries, but they do not bear responsibility for the views expressed herein.

[1] Section 10(b) provides:

> It shall be unlawful for any person . . .
> (b) To use or employ, in connection with the purchase or sale of any security . . . any manipulative or deceptive device or contrivance in contravention of such rules and regulations as the [Securities and Exchange] Commission may prescribe as necessary or appropriate in the public interest or for the protection of investors.

Securities Exchange Act of 1934, Pub L No 291, 48 Stat 891 (1934), codified at 15 USC § 78j (1997).

> Rule 10b-5 provides:
> It shall be unlaw for any person . . .
> (a) To employ any device, scheme, or artifice to defraud [or] . . .
> (b) To engage in any act, practice or course of business which operates or would operate as a fraud or deceit upon any person. . . .
> in connection with the purchase or sale of any security.

17 CFR § 240.10b-5 (1996).

deceit" "in connection with the purchase or sale of any security." The Supreme Court, in answering that question in the affirmative,[2] shed some light on the problem. But shadows remain that obscure the import and reach of its conclusion.

I

When B sells a security to (or buys one from) A in reasonable reliance upon information affecting the value of that security that A gives to B, which information is (and A knows to be) materially false, no one would dispute that A has engaged in a "deceptive device or contrivance" that operates "as a fraud or deceit" upon B in violation of Section 10(b) and Rule 10b-5.[3]

A problem arises if A's information advantage over B in the transaction stems not from A's false statements to B, but from A's possessing material non-public information about the value of the security that B does not have, and that A knows B does not have. A's trading advantage over B is equally potent in the latter case as in the former. But the question is whether in the latter case A's trading with B constitutes "a deceptive device or contrivance" that operates "as a fraud or deceit."

The premises of efficient exchange in a free market generally imply a categorical denial of all informational trading advantages to all persons who gain the advantage by false statement. But the same premises preclude a categorical denial of information advantages that A has over B that do not rest upon such falsehoods by A. Some such information advantages—for example, those derived

---

[2] *United States v O'Hagan*, 117 S Ct 2199 (1997), which involved the indictment of O'Hagan, a partner in a law firm that represented a potential takeover bidder, for purchasing stock in the target prior to the bid. In addition to ruling that Section 10(b) and Rule 10b-5 could validly reach O'Hagan's behavior, the Court held that Rule 14e-3(a) (17 CFR § 240.14e-3(a) (1996)) was a valid implementation by the SEC of § 14(e) of the Exchange Act (15 USC § 78n(e)), which proscribes fraudulent or deceptive behavior in connection with tender offers—notwithstanding the Rule's failure to require that the prohibited trading entail a breach of fiduciary duty. The Court also upheld the Government's argument in support of O'Hagan's conviction for violation of the mail fraud statute (18 USC § 1341). Justice Ginsburg wrote for a majority of six. Justice Thomas, who was joined by the Chief Justice, concurred in the mail fraud ruling, but dissented from the Court's rulings on Rules 10b-5 and 14e-3(a). Justice Scalia concurred in the Court's rulings on mail fraud and Rule 14e-3(a), but dissented separately from the Court's holding on Rule 10b-5.

[3] In this Comment, possible questions of reliance or causality and questions of intent are pretermitted by assuming for the former that A's behavior reasonably induces B's response, and for the latter that A intends to induce B to act.

from A's exercise of intelligence, diligence, wealth, skill, experience, or simply luck that A possesses but B does not—induce pursuit of information and produce exchanges that can generate considerable value for society as well as considerable gain to A. The added value to society from discovery and use of new information presumably justifies imposing upon B the risk (and upon society the cost) of such trading advantage by A. But trading advantages that A has over B by reason of information acquired from B or C or others by fraud or force or other unlawful conduct do not carry quite the same justification. The added social cost of trading advantages so acquired must be weighed against the benefit from their use.

The common law recognized the need to interdict some, but not all, of A's information advantages in trading with B that were not produced by A's express falsehoods. It treated trading on some such advantages as effectively "deception" or "fraud," but others as not involving deception or fraud or other wrongdoing. Thus, in transactions between a trustee and a beneficiary or a principal and an agent involving the subject matter of the trust or agency, information advantages about the transaction possessed by the trustee or agent without any false statement being involved were interdicted by requiring the trustee or the agent to disclose the information before the transaction could be valid.[4] On the other hand, in exchanges made at arms length between strangers—such as merchants or normal investors—deception was not often found by reason simply of a trader's superior information; and a requirement of disclosure of information was not likely to be imposed unless A possessed information advantages over B that in some strong sense could be characterized as undeserved or "unfair."[5]

---

[4] See Restatement (Second) of Trusts §§ 170 (comment w), 216, 222 (1959); Austin Wakeman Scott and William Franklin Fratcher, *The Law of Trusts* §§ 170.9, 222, 222.3 (Little, Brown, 4th ed 1987). Restatement (Second) of Agency §§ 387 (comments a and b), 390 (comment a) (1957).

[5] See Restatement (Second) of Contracts § 161(d) and comments (1981); Restatement (Second) of Torts § 551 and comments (1977); E. Allan Farnsworth, 1 *Contracts*, 406–10 (Little, Brown, 1990); W. Page Keeton, Dan B. Dobbs, Robert E. Keeton, and David G. Owen, *Prosser and Keeton on the Law of Torts* (West, 5th ed 1984) § 106 at 736–39; Stuart M. Speiser, Charles F. Krause, and Alfred W. Gans, 9 *The American Law of Torts* §§ 32.60–32.70, at 321–53 (Clark, Boardman & Callaghan, 1992); see also *Model Penal Code and Commentaries*, Part II, § 223.3(f), pp 197–200 (1980); Wayne R. LaFave and Austin W. Scott, Jr., 1 *Substantive Criminal Law* § 8.7(b)3 at 385–86 (West, 1986). For an insightful examination of the complexities of the common law "rules" on disclosure obligations, see

That Section 10(b) and Rule 10b-5 do not confine the notions "deceptive device or contrivance" or "fraud or deceit" to behavior that consists of false statements, but under some circumstances include A's failure to disclose to B material non-public information that B does not possess, when A trades with B, is conceded by all.[6] If A's failure to disclose *some* information in trading with B is thus included in the concepts "deceptive device or contrivance" and "fraud or deceit," but considerations of efficiency preclude interdiction of A's use of *all* his undisclosed material information, the problem is to identify criteria for delineating the *some* kinds of information advantages that A is to be denied by requiring disclosure of that kind of information. That problem is not solved by the facile formula that finds a culpable failure to disclose "where there is a duty to disclose." The questions remain: What is that duty, and what are its source and rationale? Answers to those questions require focusing on Congressional purposes in regulating the securities markets in the 1933 and 1934 Acts.

Both the 1933 and 1934 Acts contain provisions requiring many persons who buy or sell securities to disclose information to the public in specified circumstances,[7] and imposing particular duties, including disclosure, on specified professionals in dealing with clients and on corporate insiders in dealing with their stockholders.[8] Section 10(b) of the 1934 Act is a catch-all clause to cover use of deceptive devices, primarily by traders, that may not be covered

---

Deborah A. DeMott, *Do You Have the Right to Remain Silent? Duties of Disclosure in Business Transactions,* 19 Del J Corp L 65 (1994). Compare Anthony T. Kronman, *Mistake, Disclosure, Information and the Law of Contracts* 7 J Legal Stud 1 (1978).

[6] With little or no disagreement, those provisions have been so construed by the lower federal courts at least since 1968 (*SEC v Texas Gulf Sulphur Co,* 401 F2d 833 (2d Cir 1968)) and by the Supreme Court several times (see *Affiliated Ute Citizens of Utah v United States,* 406 US 128 (1972); *Chiarella v United States,* 445 US 222 (1980), and *Dirks v SEC,* 463 US 646 (1983)), and indeed by all the Justices in *O'Hagan* except possibly Justice Scalia, see 117 S Ct at 2220.

[7] For example, mandated disclosure under the 1933 Act and implementing Rules by issuers and controllers with respect to securities that they sell or offer to sell to the public, and the disclosure required under §§ 12 and 17 in order that the seller avoid engaging in fraudulent behavior. Securities Act of 1933, 48 Stat 84–85 (1933), codified at 15 USC § 77l and § 77q (1997), respectively. Similarly, disclosure is mandated under §§ 12, 13, 14, and 16 of the Exchange Act and implementing Rules and is required under §§ 10, 15, and 18 and implementing Rules of that Act in order that a party avoid engaging in fraudulent behavior. Securities Exchange Act of 1934, codified at 15 USC §§ 78j, 78l–p, 78r (1997).

[8] For example, §§ 15 and 16 of the Exchange Act (codified at 15 USC §§ 78o and 78p).

by those provisions,[9] even if it also may reach behavior that is covered by those provisions.[10]

Section 10(b) could, in theory, have been construed to deny *all* information advantages to *all* traders, by making failure to disclose any and all material information to the opposite party a deceptive device or contrivance that operates as a fraud or deceit on that party. But that would have imposed costs upon society that there is no evidence that Congress sought to impose. As the Court pointed out in *Chiarella*, Section 10(b) does not impose "a general duty between all participants in market transactions to forgo actions based on material, non-public information."[11]

Another construction of Section 10(b) and the concept of a "practice . . . which operates . . . as a fraud or deceit" could limit the use of information advantages held only by some kinds of traders vis-à-vis other traders, by making their failure to disclose material information a fraud on the opposite party—for example, corporate insiders vis-à-vis their corporation's security holders, brokers vis-à-vis clients, professionals vis-à-vis nonprofessionals, or other persons in a fiduciary or special confidential relationship to the opposite party to the trade.[12] The breadth of the statutory prohibition of fraudulent behavior by "any person" suggests that Section 10(b) is addressed to some other mode of limiting required disclosure of information than by focusing on the special relationship of the parties. That conclusion is supported by negative inference from other provisions of the statute that specifically address and restrain the behavior of parties in many such kinds of special relationships, such as corporate insider-stockholder or broker-

---

[9] Section 9 of the original Bill, the predecessor of Section 10(b), was said to be designed to catch "any other cunning devices" (see Stock Exchange Regulation, Hearings on HR 7852 and 8720 before House Committee on Interstate and Foreign Commerce, 73d Cong, 2d Sess 115 (1934) (testimony of Thomas G. Corcoran)) that fulfill no useful function in transactions in impersonal securities markets that deal in what had earlier been described to Congress as "intricate merchandise" (see HR Rep No 85, 73d Cong, 1st Sess 8 (1933)). It was acknowledged by the Court to be such a "catch-all" provision (see *Ernst & Ernst v Hochfelder*, 425 US 185 at 203–05 (1976)).

[10] See, for example, *Herman & MacLean v Huddleston*, 459 US 375 at 385–87 (1983); Louis Loss and Joel Seligman, IX *Securities Regulation* at 4409–39 (Little, Brown, 3rd ed 1991).

[11] 117 S Ct at 2211, citing *Chiarella*, 445 US 222 at 233 (1980).

[12] This construction was suggested by the Court in *Chiarella*, 445 US 222. The theme was embroidered in *Dirks*, 463 US 646, and countless lower court decisions.

client.[13] In the 1934 Act, Congress was addressing the operation of the nation's securities markets, and in that context seeking to regulate the behavior of all kinds of players in those markets (including unscrupulous market operators who could not conceivably be deemed fiduciaries), not simply focusing on the agency obligations of corporate insiders.[14]

For Congress to have incorporated only state common law in authorizing prescription of the duty to disclose would entail attempting to solve a national problem by reference to episodic, widely varying and loose state standards. But among the evils that Congress aimed to cure in the Exchange Act were the porosity as well as the extreme unevenness of state standards, including disclosure obligations in securities exchange transactions, whether governing the behavior of corporate fiduciaries,[15] or market profes-

---

[13] Sections 15 and 16 of the Exchange Act, 15 USC § 78o, § 78p (1997); compare §§ 204A, 206–08 of the Investment Advisers Act of 1940, 15 USC §§ 80b-4a, 6–8 (1988).

[14] Section 2 of that Act recites that it is "necessary to provide for regulation and control" of "transactions in securities as commonly conducted upon securities exchanges and the over-the-counter markets" "and of practices and matters related thereto, including transactions by officers, directors and principal security holders, . . . in order to . . . insure the maintenance of fair and honest markets in such transactions." 15 USC § 78b (1997). See Alison Grey Anderson, *The Disclosure Process in Federal Securities Regulation: A Brief Review*, 25 Hastings L J 311, 316–20 (1974); Steve Thel, *The Original Conception of Section 10(b) of the Securities Exchange Act*, 42 Stan L Rev 385 (1990); Dennis J. Karjala, *Federalism, Full Disclosure and the National Markets in the Interpretation of Federal Securities Laws*, 80 Nw U L Rev 1473, 1515–25 (1986).

[15] Prevailing state law (in terms of the number of states imposing fiduciary duties and their commercial importance) did not interdict insider trading in 1934, and even the few states that did appeared to limit the interdiction to face-to-face dealings. See cases collected in *Chenery Corp. v SEC*, 128 F2d 303 at 307 (DC Cir 1942), remanded 318 US 80 (1942); William K. S. Wang and Marc I. Steinberg, *Insider Trading* §§ 16.1 and 16.2, pp 1106–33 (Little, Brown, 1996). A persuasive case can be made for the proposition that corporate management and controllers have fiduciary obligations either to "the corporation" or to public security holders or to both that require them to disclose material non-public corporate information, if not also market information, when buying or selling their corporation's securities—or to abstain from transacting. The common law may have been gestating such a case for disclosure to stockholders, but had not yet made it when the federal securities laws addressed (and came to dominate) the matter (Wang and Steinberg, supra). There have been common law intimations of insiders' fiduciary obligations to the "corporation" that may be satisfied by denying gain to the insiders from transactions involving use of corporate information that they did not, or could not, lawfully disclose—even though the corporation might not be able so to use it (compare, e.g., *Diamond v Oreamuno*, 248 NE2d 910 (NY 1969) with *Freeman v Decio*, 584 F2d 186 (7th Cir 1978)). Those obligations may also support obligations to the victims of the trades. Finally, a case might even be cobbled together for imposing such obligations on "the corporation" when it trades in its own stock (compare *Wood v MacLean Drug Co.*, 266 Ill App 5 (1932); *Ward La France Truck Corp.*, 13 SEC 373 (1943), and compare § 13(e) of the Exchange Act), although the common law was no more sympathetic to that case than to imposing fiduciary disclosure obligations on management or controllers

sionals,[16] or persons dealing at arms length.[17] To restrict the reach of Section 10(b) (the "catch-all" provision) to such episodic and varying state strictures on fiduciaries would thus be incongruous in seeking a uniform solution for a national problem, and at odds with the effort to make the securities markets safer for investors than did the common law.

In setting federal standards for the meaning of the concept "deceptive device or contrivance," Congress was creating a *federal* duty to disclose that was not confined to the disclosure obligations entailed in the state law concepts of fiduciary obligations or fraud or deceit.[18] If limiting market players' information advantages and imposing the corresponding duty to disclose by reference only to the parties' special relationship, as at common law in some states, is inadequate for the Congressional purpose as the statute suggests, some other frame of reference is necessary. One such frame of reference that is more consonant with Congressional purposes would deny to *all* traders in the securities markets *some* kinds of information advantages (by requiring disclosure to the opposite party of such information), but not *all* the information or trading

---

(see *Gladstone v Murray Co.*, 50 NE2d 958 (Mass 1943); *Steven v Hale-Haas Corp.*, 23 NW2d 620, 632 (Wis 1946)). It is not without a certain irony that the Supreme Court, in its efforts to narrow the scope of the disclosure requirements of Section 10(b), assumed, and in some sense may have furthered, broad local law fiduciary disclosure obligations of management and controllers (*Chiarella*, 445 US 222, and *Dirks*, 463 US 646) and possibly even of "the corporation"—notwithstanding its bizarre insistence that the fiduciary under Section 10(b) could only violate his duty if, like a person committing arms-length fraud, he acted intentionally.

[16] See, for example, development of the "shingle" theory under § 17(a) of the Securities Act (15 USC § 77q) and Rule 15 c1-2 (17 CFR § 240.15c1-2 (1996)) under the Exchange Act to prevent excessive charges by broker-dealers in transactions with clients that were formally denominated "sales" or "purchases." See Louis Loss and Joel Seligman, VIII *Securities Regulation* 3772–98 (Little, Brown, 3rd ed 1991).

[17] The prohibition of false statements certainly covers transactions between strangers. And, as we have seen, even at common law in exchange transactions between strangers, disclosure was occasionally required by contract or tort doctrine. See note 5. Congress sought and gave the SEC discretion to effect restrictions on dealings between strangers (both nominal and real), including imposing disclosure obligations that went beyond the occasional common law strictures. See note 18.

[18] See note 14; Louis Loss, III *Securities Regulation* 1421–44 (Little, Brown, 2d ed 1961); Loss and Seligman, VII *Securities Regulation* 3421–48 (Little, Brown, 3rd ed 1991). Compare mail fraud statute (18 USC § 1341 (1994)), which has been interpreted to create a federal standard of fraud. See, for example, *Durland v United States*, 161 US 306 at 314 (1896); Peter J. Henning, *Just Maybe It Should Be Called Federal Fraud: The Changing Nature of the Mail Fraud Statute*, 36 BC L Rev 435 (1995). Compare *Virginia Bankshares, Inc. v Sandberg*, 501 US 1083 (1991), construing (in a private action) antifraud provisions of Rule 14a-9 under the Exchange Act more narrowly than common law fraud.

advantages that the trader possessed. One kind of information advantage for traders that Congress might reasonably have thought it appropriate to interdict in removing pot holes in a rutted securities market by prohibiting "any deceptive device or contrivance" would be the use by A in trading with B of material non-public information that A misappropriated—that is, information that A acquired unlawfully, whether or not acting as a fiduciary.[19] The underlying principle would also interdict A's use of some kinds of lawfully acquired information that B could not lawfully have discovered, purchased, or otherwise acquired—as is likely to be the case for an A whose incentive to produce the information does not rest on expected securities trading gains.[20] In trading with B in impersonal securities markets, A's failure to disclose information unlawfully, or indeed wrongfully, acquired entails use of a deceptive device or contrivance that gives A information advantages over B. It operates as a fraud or deceit upon B as much as does a similar failure to disclose by a fiduciary or other person in a special confidential relationship, or indeed a false statement by a stranger in direct dealing. B could more properly, and possibly at less cost to society, be asked to attempt to overcome the information disparity

---

[19] Compare W. Page Keeton, *Fraud-Concealment and Non-Disclosure* 15 Tex L Rev 1, 25–26 (1936).

A corporate officer's use of non-public corporate information to trade with a stockholder entails the officer unlawfully "taking" the information that "belongs" to the corporation, for whose functions it was generated. The information does *not* "belong" to the insider, certainly as against B the stockholder, and not less significantly as against other security holders. To be sure, B could, in theory, inquire of the corporation for the information that A has or might have, but apart from information that the corporation has already presumably disclosed pursuant to statutory mandates, B is not entitled to be given the information. Often the corporation is entitled (or even required) to decline to give it—as when release of the information would injure the enterprise. Where that is not so, the corporation has discretion to release the information publicly, but not the obligation or even the authority to do so discriminatorily only to B (even though she is a stockholder) or to individual bondholders unless covenanted for.

[20] Consider, for example, whether the sellers in *Walton v Morgan Stanley & Co., Inc.*, 623 F2d 796 (2d Cir 1980), and *Frigitemp Corp. v Financial Dynamics Fund Inc.*, 524 F2d 275 (2d Cir 1975) (who were not the plaintiffs in those cases), could lawfully have obtained from their corporations the information that the defendants had acquired. See note 19. Whether the corporate plaintiffs were (or should have been held to have been) unlawfully treated by the sly mutual funds and investment bankers in those cases is another matter. Consider also whether if Polaroid effects a research breakthrough in the production of a new camera that gives it a substantial commercial advantage over Kodak, it should be able to sell Kodak stock short in the market without disclosure—notwithstanding the doubtful role of trading gains over Kodak investors in Polaroid's incentive structure to engage in the research. See generally Victor Brudney, *Insiders, Outsiders and Information Advantages Under the Federal Securities Laws* 93 Harv L Rev 322, 353–76 (1979).

in the latter cases (i.e., without giving her the legal assistance of imposition of a disclosure obligation on A) than in the first case, because in order to acquire A's information in the first case, B would be required to act unlawfully considerably more frequently than in the latter cases. But current legal doctrine relieves B of all need to make that effort in the latter cases. There is less reason to fail to relieve B of the need to make such effort (i.e., to fail to require disclosure) in the first case than in the latter cases.[21]

To include use of such an information advantage by A in the concept "deceptive device or contrivance" would effect the Congressional aspiration to make the securities markets user-friendly without incurring a prohibitive social cost. An efficient securities market does not require investors to compete with one another in pursuing the search for information unlawfully. Nor does the lawful originator of non-public useful information (e.g., about products, services, businesses, or markets) that underlies values of particular securities require as an incentive to pursue such information that he be able to use it for securities trading purposes[22]—except as he is in the business of trading in securities or advising others on trading. In such cases, generally his acquisition and advantageous use or dissemination of information are lawful;[23] and public investors are not precluded from lawfully acquiring such information by research or purchase from those in the business of selling it. Including in the meaning of "deceptive device or contrivance" failure to disclose material non-public information that A acquired unlawfully or B was precluded from lawfully acquiring discourages illegitimate search for information even as it leaves investors, analysts, advisors, and others free to engage in legitimate search.

---

[21] Possibly liability of a putative violator in circumstances comparable to those referred to in note 20 should turn on whether he "should know" that investors with whom he transacts are not lawfully entitled to the information that advantages him.

[22] A somewhat different problem is raised by the tension between the needs of takeover aspirants, who legitimately acquire an information advantage over public investors, and the needs of the latter, who cannot lawfully erode that advantage. The Williams Act (embedded in portions of 15 USC §§ 78m and 78n) is an effort to strike some balance between those conflicting needs by requiring modest disclosures by, and some process restraints on, the bidder to offset his temptation to manipulate his information and bargaining advantages so as to distort investors' choices. Whether the gains from a nonmanipulated market are worth the cost of curtailing some of the bidder's information advantage is not readily determinable.

[23] Except possibly for practices like trading against or front-running his customers or advisees.

Moreover, it relieves investors of concern about trading with those who acquire such information unlawfully and the attendant wasteful social cost of refraining from trading, or guarding against trading, with such persons. In short, investors are not to be encouraged to engage in unlawful search for information or be required to incur the risk of trading with those who do so, and society is spared the cost of that risk if the law denies traders such information advantages.

Such a delineation of "deceptive device or contrivance" or of "fraud or deceit" does not include or imply a requirement of disclosure of information that will enable all investors to have equal information (i.e., parity) before trading. Nor does it require all investors to have equal access to all the information that some can, but others cannot, obtain by legitimate efforts in pursuing information for purposes of securities trading gains. It covers only information which the culpable trader acquires by means that are unlawful, or which the trading victim may be precluded from purchasing or otherwise acquiring lawfully, particularly from a source who acquired the information for non-trading purposes.

To be sure, a rule holding B to be the victim of a "deceptive device or contrivance" by reason of A's use in trading with B of any material non-public information that A acquires "unlawfully" or that the law thus precludes B from acquiring is not limned in bright lines. Such a federal interdiction derives in part from state prohibitions against many different modes of taking or appropriating to oneself another person's property. But those prohibitions, unlike the episodic and widely varying fiduciary obligations fashioned by common law or equity courts for corporate insiders or professional market transactors, rest upon an array of state statutory strictures as well as common law notions that exist in almost all states and whose content is substantially the same in those states.[24] Declining to confine the concept "unlawfully" to technical definitions of terms used in each state's statutory or common law and asserting a federal standard of culpable failure to disclose will inevitably generate ambiguities at the edges of the stricture.[25] So

---

[24] For example, laws against embezzlement, larceny, or the compendious notion, "theft." See *Model Penal Code and Commentaries*, Part II, § 223, at 122 et seq (1980); Wayne R. LaFave and Austin W. Scott, Jr., 1 *Substantive Criminal Law* §§ 8.1–8.8, at 325–416 (West, 1986).

[25] See note 20.

too do the ambiguities stirred by the current interpretation of Section 10(b) that invokes the elastic fiduciary notion,[26] or indeed by the spacious concept of fraud as used in state laws or in other federal statutes. Such ambiguities are endemic to any prescription of disclosure as part of a proscription of fraud or deception in an exchange transaction. The severity of their impact is substantially diluted by their place in a legal structure that contemplates a rule of disclose or abstain.[27]

On the above analysis, the "deceit" practiced upon the opposite party to the transaction is indisputably practiced "in connection with the purchase or sale of any security." Moreover, on that analysis, the culpable "connection" reaches the purchase or sale of *any* security, including debt securities or derivatives, not merely stock.[28]

II

The Court in *O'Hagan* adverted to the possibility of the above analysis in relating the so-called "misappropriation theory" to the content of "deceptive device or contrivance" and "fraud or

---

[26] The elasticity of the notion was stretched to cover "special confidential relationship [with outsiders] in the conduct of the business of the enterprise" in *Dirks*, 463 US 646 at 655 n 14 (1983); and its ambiguity is aptly illustrated in *United States v Chestman*, 947 F2d 551 (2d Cir 1991) and cases collected in Donald C. Langevoort, *Insider Trading: Regulation, Enforcement and Prevention* § 3.02[3] and [4] at 3-8 to 3-15 (Clark, Boardman & Callaghan, 1995) and Loss and Seligman, VIII *Securities Regulation* (cited in note 10) at 3593–98. It is not irrelevant to note that the Supreme Court is hostile to the idea of federal courts importing into Section 10(b) *federal* fiduciary notions because such concepts are so open-ended (*Santa Fe Industries, Inc. v Green*, 430 US 462 (1977))—even though *state* fiduciary notions seem not to be too open-ended to preclude their importation into Section 10(b).

[27] The disclosure obligations of a corporation that is not transacting in its securities, and therefore may have no option to abstain, should be (and are) narrower than those of a trader. See Victor Brudney, *A Note on Materiality and Soft Information Under the Federal Securities Laws*, 75 Va L Rev 723 (1989).

[28] As the Court noted in *O'Hagan* (117 S Ct 2199 at 2212), its prior opinions do not preclude liability under Section 10(b) for failure to disclose by nonfiduciary insiders; but its teaching that rests the disclosure obligation of A to B under Section 10(b) and the Rule in fiduciary ground (*Chiarella*, 445 US 222; *Dirks*, 463 US 646) does not, at least formally, extend A's obligation to disclose to those to whom he is not a fiduciary insider—for example, bondholders or optionholders. See Loss and Seligman, VIII *Securities Regulation* at 3598–3602 (cited in note 10); Richard M. Phillips and Robert E. Kohn, *Applying the Insider Trading Doctrine to Debt Securities*, 6 Insights No. 11 at 18 (Nov 1992). Compare § 20(d) of the Exchange Act enacted in 1984 (15 USC § 78t(d) (1984 Supp)), which effectively eliminated the requirement that breach of a fiduciary duty is a necessary condition for violating Section 10(b) in transactions in options of various kinds.

deceit." But that analysis was not urged by the Government, nor is it prominent in the tangled jurisprudence of Section 10(b) and the Rule.[29] Instead, the Court placed its emphasis on the Government's argument that a trader engages in a "deceptive device or contrivance" when as a fiduciary to a third party he acquires material non-public information deceitfully from the third party (by false statement or by nondisclosure), and uses the information to trade with others to whom he is not a fiduciary without disclosing it. The focus is on the deceit of the third person by his fiduciary rather than on any deception of (or, possibly, any wrongdoing to) the opposite party to the transaction to whom the trader has no fiduciary obligations. That focus generates—and obscures—several troublesome questions.

One difficult question, which the Court answered in the affirmative, is whether the "deceit" which is practiced upon the third person, but not otherwise upon the opposite party to the transaction, occurs "in connection with the purchase or sale of any security."

The "connection" between "deceit" and the securities transaction can, in theory, span widely separated poles of behavior. At one extreme, the "connection" can be effected by a trader who deceives a third person into giving him necessary funds or equipment (e.g., a telephone) and using those funds or equipment to engage in a securities transaction with the opposite party. At the other extreme, the "connection" exists when the trader induces the opposite party voluntarily to make an exchange that is deceptive as to her by reason of the trader's materially false statements or impermissible failure to disclose material non-public information. In between is, inter alia, a trader's use of material non-public information that he acquires by "deceiving" a third party (to whom he is a fiduciary) to turn over to him information about the value of a security that enables him to take advantage of the ignorant oppo-

---

[29] Except for the dissent of Chief Justice Burger and the dissent of Justice Blackmun in *Chiarella*, 445 US 222 at 240 and 245, respectively, and the concurrence of Justice Brennan, 445 US at 239–40. For discussion of the courts' melange of interpretive analyses of the Section and the Rule over a half century, see Edward A. Fallone, *Section 10(B) and the Vagaries of Federal Common Law: The Merits of Codifying the Private Cause of Action Under a Structuralist Approach*, 1997 U Ill L Rev 71; Theresa A. Gabaldon, *State Answers to Federal Questions: The Common Law of Federal Securities Regulation*, 20 J Corp L 155 (1995); Lawrence E. Mitchell, *The Jurisprudence of the Misappropriation Theory and the New Insider Trading Legislation: From Fairness to Efficiency and Back*, 52 Albany L Rev 775 (1988).

site party to the trade. All of the Justices in *O'Hagan* apparently agreed that the first possible "connection" between deceit and the trade is not "in connection with the purchase or sale of any security." The majority in *O'Hagan* ruled that the third possible transaction entailed a sufficient "connection" between "deceit" and the "purchase or sale of any security" to make the trader a violator of Section 10(b), notwithstanding that the trader's conduct might also violate other laws that protect the third party from expropriation of his property and not violate any other laws that protect the opposite party to the trade. Justice Thomas's dissent saw no difference between the first and the third transaction so far as concerns the necessary "connection" between the "deceit" and "the purchase or sale of any security," and therefore would have held that the requisite "connection" was lacking in *O'Hagan*, whose facts more or less match the pattern of the third transaction.

The dissent's objection to the legitimacy of the "connection" that the majority found between the deceit of the third party and the information advantage that the deceit gave to the malefactor in purchasing the security from the opposite party to the transaction is misplaced. It appears to argue that the logic of the "connection" that the majority found sufficient proves too much, because it would apply equally to deceitful acquisition by the malefactor from the third party of funds or apparatus that the former needed and used in order to communicate and trade with the opposite party. But the majority's "connection" ties the malefactor's misbehavior to the third person to the information advantage that it thus acquires over the opposite party; and it is that information advantage that Congress was seeking in the Exchange Act to deny to the malefactor—not the advantage of funds or other mechanisms that he needed (and obtained by deceit) in order to communicate and trade with the opposite party. In short, the potentially incongruous breadth or "incoherence" of the "connection" that Justice Thomas's dissent claims for the majority's decision is eliminated by reading the term in its statutory context rather than as an abstraction. The "connection" that fits the Congressional effort to regulate the flow of information in the interest of enhancing efficiency and honesty in the securities markets is limited to the relationship of "deceptive device or contrivance" to the acquisition of information to be used in trading in the securities markets. The incoherent "connection" that the dissent sees is neither required nor made by the language or logic of the statute or the majority opinion.[30] On the other hand, the majority's analysis is supported by Congressional aspirations in the Exchange Act and is permitted by the language of Section 10(b) and the Rule.[31]

It is not a minor consequence of thus "connecting" the trade with the opposite party to the deceit of the third person that it makes the trader a violator of the Section and the Rule, even though he has no fiduciary relationship to the opposite party. That view which is faithful to the Congressional concerns with protecting investors who trade in *any* security substantially eliminates the principal obstacle to according bondholders and holders of derivatives some of the protection of the Section and the Rule.

III

The Court's decision generates several additional problems that are more difficult to solve than the "in connection with" problem.

A

The first set of such problems derives from uncertainties about the meaning that the Court's opinion suggests for the concepts "deceptive device or contrivance" and "fraud or deceit," and the delineation of the conduct to be included in the concepts. Those problems also implicate the question whether it is rational, and consistent with the policy of the statute, to require disclosure of information obtained from a third party only by "deceit" rather than by other unlawful means.

Both the majority and Justice Thomas's dissent recognize that the "deceit" or misappropriation thus practiced on third persons includes a failure by the malefactor (at least if he is a fiduciary) to disclose to the third person his appropriation of the latter's property (i.e., the information) to use for his own benefit in trading with others. That conception of "deceit" of the third person is

---

[30] It is not clear, but the dissent may also entail a broader attack on the "connection" that the majority upheld. See note 34.

[31] It is also suggested by the Court's prior decision in *Superintendent of Insurance of New York v Bankers Life and Casualty Co.*, 404 US 6 (1971), a case which enjoys little currency with the present Court.

not rationally limited to conduct only by fiduciaries toward the third person, or indeed only by persons like embezzlers whom he is deemed to have trusted in giving them possession of his property. Presumably it also covers making false statements to induce a third person stranger to give information to the trader. It rests on the premise that a person is deceived if his consent to give up property or a thing of value is obtained by any person who knowingly lies to him or fails to give him material information that he is *entitled* to have in deciding whether to give up the property. His entitlement may rest upon the notion that he appropriately trusted the malefactor to deal fairly with him, and the latter did not admonish him in advance. But it may no less appropriately rest on the notion that the malefactor took for his own use, *without the third party's consent*, property that belonged to the latter.

On that view, much unilateral taking of non-public information from a third person (by a fiduciary, or by a stranger by embezzlement or theft or possibly by overhearing it in an airplane or a restaurant or the like) can be characterized as fraud or deceit, because it is taken without the third person's consent, and the failure to give such consent is, at least in part, the result of a failure to disclose to the third person that one is taking the other's non-public information for one's own use. The failure to disclose and obtain consent is what permits such unilateral wrongdoing to be characterized as fraud or deceit. The duty to disclose in such circumstances may be said to exist not because disclosure ex ante is essential to validate a voluntary exchange, but because the taking is independently wrongful; and it can only be made rightful by the consent of the third person after adequate disclosure.[32] Indeed, such a premise is at the heart of the "deceit" attributed to a fiduciary in insider trading. The fiduciary is misappropriating information that "belongs" to the corporation and possibly the trading

---

[32] See *SEC v Cherif*, 933 F2d 403 (7th Cir 1991), involving stealing by an ex-employee who used confidential information obtained as employee to obtain access to secrets. Similar reasoning seems to underpin decisions under the mail fraud statute (18 USC § 1341) which, as the Court noted in *O'Hagan* (117 S Ct at 2208, quoting its earlier opinions), find fraud in "the fraudulent appropriation to one's own use of the money or goods entrusted to one's care by another." In *Carpenter v United States*, 484 US 19 at 27 (1987), the Court interpreted the words "to defraud" in that statute to "have the common understanding" of " 'wronging one in his property rights by dishonest methods or schemes' and 'usually signify the deprivation of something of value by trick, deceit, chicane or overreaching.' " See Langevoort (cited in note 26), § 603[1] at 6-10 to 6-14.

beneficiary, and in trading with her while failing to disclose to her (that misappropriation and) the content of the information misappropriated, the fiduciary deceives her.[33] Analogously, according to the Court, when a trader is a fiduciary to a third person and "takes" information from the third person without disclosing his taking or his (intended) use of the information, he may be said to deceive the third person.[34]

That conclusion, which appears to underlie both the majority opinion and the dissent in finding "deceit" in *O'Hagan*, raises a number of subsidiary questions. Is the misappropriation deceitful *only* when the taking is by a fiduciary, or is it also deceitful when it is effected by nonfiduciaries but by any form of stealth such as embezzlement? Or is it deceitful when unilaterally acquired, as in larceny or by force? In any event, is the taking *always* deceitful if the third party could or would conceivably have consented to it, but never if the third party could or would not have consented?[35]

The difficulties in delineating the concept of "deceit" thus invoked by the Court also underpin the problem in limiting the trader's information advantage over the opposite party to information that he misappropriated only by deceit as a fiduciary rather than by embezzlement or other form of theft or appropriation, if in all

---

[33] See note 19. See also Frank H. Easterbrook, *Insider Trading, Secret Agents, and the Production of Information*, 1981 Supreme Court Review 309 at 314–39 (1981).

[34] However, the analogy is not entirely apposite. When the fiduciary trades with the beneficiary, the information required to be disclosed to the beneficiary is information (about the value of the security) that effectively belongs to the beneficiary (see note 19) and is taken or appropriated by the fiduciary without the beneficiary's consent; the beneficiary, who is, by definition, unaware of the content of the information, must be informed of it so that she may consent in trading with the fiduciary. In contrast, the information to be disclosed by the fiduciary to the third-party beneficiary when the former takes or appropriates the latter's property (i.e., information) for his own use in trading is more the fact of taking the information for the fiduciary's use than the trading import of the information for another trader. However apposite or inapposite may be the analogy to "deceit" between a fiduciary's obligation to disclose to a beneficiary who is the opposite party to a trade and his obligation to a nontrading third party, it is apparently accepted by both the majority and the dissent in *O'Hagen*. Its possible inappositeness and the consequent difference between deceiving the trading victim and deceiving the third person and the differing materiality of the undisclosed information (compare Langevoort (cited in note 26), § 6.03[2] at 6-14 to 6-15) and the different consequences of disclosure in the two cases may underlie the dissent's argument about the lack of the requisite "connection."

[35] What evidence is necessary to show that the third party could, or would, not have consented? Would the principals in *Carpenter v United States*, 484 US 19 (1987) (the Wall Street Journal) and *United States v Bryan*, 58 F3d 933 (4th Cir 1995) (a government agency) have consented to the malefactors trading on the undisclosed information? Could either of those principals lawfully have given such consent?

the cases the third party would not knowingly have consented. Such trading advantages are not differently "connected" to the necessary trade with, or to their impact on, the opposite party than those acquired by deceiving the third party. To deny the trader an information advantage only in the latter case appears irrationally to rely on the notion of *idem sonans*. Nothing in the fulfillment of the Congressional policy of creating a market in which public investors are neither to be discouraged from trading nor stimulated to unlawful behavior requires that a culpable trader have been a fiduciary to a third party or to have deceived rather than robbed the third party. Nor does anything in the policy or language of Section 10(b) or the Rule so require. The statutory culpability of misappropriation so viewed rests less on the character than on the fact of the unlawfulness by which the trader acquires the information from the third person and on the inability of the opposite party to the trade to acquire the information lawfully. It is A's use of the information so acquired to take advantage of B that is the deceptive device or contrivance that can be cured only by disclosure to B, not A's particular unlawful manner of acquiring the information from C.

To be sure, if A discloses his misappropriation to C and C authorizes A's use of the information to trade with B, Section 10(b) and the Rule would not be violated by A's trading unless C was required to disclose before trading. The possibility of C's consent suggests the question whether in order for the misappropriator's use of the information that is deceitfully acquired from the third person to violate the statute it must be information that the third person himself was unable to have used lawfully[36] or was unwilling to use[37] in trading. Or is the statute violated by the fact of the malefactor's misappropriation and use of the third party's information even though the information could have been used lawfully (without disclosure) by the third person in trading?[38] The Congressional purpose to fashion a user-friendly securities market sug-

---

[36] For example, if the trader using the information about a pending ruling is a judge's clerk or a Federal Reserve employee.

[37] See note 35.

[38] For example, *Chiarella*, 445 US 222 (use by the bidder), in contrast to the trading insider's corporation's possible disability from using such information. See notes 15 and 19.

gests a negative answer to the former and an affirmative answer to the latter question.

That the third person could or would have used the information lawfully does not excuse the trader's use of his unlawfully acquired information in the public market without the third person's consent. To be sure, the particular trading victim is no worse off if the trader uses the information that the third person could or would lawfully have used without disclosure in trading. But the risk to which the trading victim and traders generally are exposed when the lawful possessor of the information uses it lawfully is one that an efficient market contemplates. On the other hand, the risk created when such information is unlawfully taken from the third person and used by a trader is one that would improperly taint the efficient and honest market that Congress sought; that risk imposes unnecessary costs on both public investors and on society.

B

A second set of problems that is implicit, and more or less deliberately left unanswered, in the Court's opinion derives from the question whether the violation of Section 10(b) and the Rule found by the Court will underpin a private suit for damages or other relief, or will only underpin government action—criminal or civil. *O'Hagan* was a criminal prosecution, and the court was careful to emphasize that its analysis of the statutory violation entailed a criminal prosecution. It did not say that the violation found could underpin a civil suit by the government—either for injunction or for disgorgement of profits or for other disciplinary action. But it is difficult, if not indeed impossible, to see why conduct that violates Section 10(b) and Rule 10b-5 that the statute authorizes the government to prosecute[39] is not also subject to the language and policy of the statute providing for other sanctions by government action.[40] More significant in the politics of Section 10(b) and Rule 10b-5 is the court's avoidance of any reference to civil suits by private plaintiffs seeking damages or other remedies.

As the Court has repeatedly pointed out, such actions are not expressly authorized by the statute. They are created by judicial

---

[39] Section 32 of the Exchange Act, 15 USC § 78ff (1997).

[40] For example, §§ 21 and 21A–21C of the Exchange Act, 15 USC §§ 78u–78u-3.

inference from the statutory provisions. The question is, how free is the judiciary, that claims to have nurtured a "judicial oak . . . from little more than a legislative acorn" that is the private action under Section 10(b),[41] to determine the contours of that "oak." Does fidelity to the Congressional delineation (explicitly and by judicial inference) of behavior prohibited in Section 10(b) permit the judiciary to fashion in private actions a different meaning for that prohibited behavior than it does in criminal prosecutions or government enforcement proceedings?

Arguably, fidelity imposes stricter limits on courts in interpreting the substance of Congressional prohibitions than in inferring that Congress did (or did not) authorize a private action as a sanction for violating its prohibition[42]—notwithstanding an occasional claim of large freedom to determine the contours of a violation in private actions.[43] In any event, larger interpretive freedom fairly characterizes the Court's role in developing constraints on the qualifications of a person to be a plaintiff in a private action that the judiciary inferred to be implicitly authorized by Congress,[44] or the permissible personal defenses against such a plaintiff's claim, or the right to contribution on such claims.[45] But nothing in the Court's claim to foster-parenthood of the private action under Section 10(b) relieves it of the obligation to respect the legislative origins of the cause of action[46] and abide by the legislative delineation of the misbehavior to be sanctioned.

To be sure, the vagaries of judicial interpretation of statutes

---

[41] *Blue Chip Stamps v Manor Drug Stores*, 421 US 723, 737 (1975).

[42] Compare *Central Bank of Denver NA v First International Bank of Denver NA*, 511 US 164 (1994).

[43] Compare *Virginia Bankshares, Inc. v Sandberg*, 501 US 1083 (1991), particularly opinion of Scalia, J, at 1110.

[44] *Blue Chip Stamps v Manor Drug Stores*, 421 US 723 (1975); see also *SEC v Rana Research, Inc.*, 8 F3d 1358, 1363–64 (9th Cir 1993).

[45] Compare *Bateman Eichler, Hill Richards, Inc. v Berner*, 472 US 299 (1985), with *Pinter v Dahl*, 486 US 622 (1988) (pari delicto defense); see *Musick, Peeler & Garrett v Employers Ins. Co. of Wausau*, 508 US 286 (1993) (contribution); see also *Lampf, Pleva, Lipkind, Prupis & Pettigrow v Gilbertson*, 501 US 350 (1991) (statute of limitations).

[46] There is no doubt that the Court must defer to a legislative scheme of regulation in determining whether a private action may be inferred from the scheme, but there is considerable uncertainty about the making of the inference. Compare the varied rationales and results in the cases discussed in Loss and Seligman, IX *Securities Regulation* 4312–39 (cited in note 10); and Richard W. Jennings, Harold Marsh, Jr., and John C. Coffee, Jr., *Securities Regulation* 784–842 (Foundation Press, 7th ed 1992).

may, at times, relieve a person of civil liability to victims of behavior for which he has been convicted of violating a statute specially designed to protect those victims.[47] But that result can hardly be reached when cognate violations of the same statutory prohibition have long been held to justify a private action as a sanction.[48] That the lower court judiciary can validate such an incongruity in interpreting Section 10(b) has been demonstrated.[49] The question is not without difficulty if the culpable behavior is regarded as being practiced only on, and the only victim is seen to be, the third party. But once the "connection" is established between the "deceit" of the third person and the "purchase or sale of any security," it is hard to see why the trader should escape liability to the opposite party to the trade, whether or not he should also be deemed civilly liable to the third party for violating the statute or for violating local law or otherwise.[50] The opposite party was injured[51] by use

---

[47] See authorities cited in note 46.

[48] Particular statutory schemes may permit the judicial inference that Congress contemplated only government enforcement of its commands, and precluded private remedies. See note 46. But when courts properly infer that Congress has authorized (or required) private actions as an enforcement mechanism against violators of its prohibition, as in Section 10(b), strong justification or explicit Congressional language is needed to permit courts to conclude that behavior that is found to violate "the text" of a specific Congressional prohibition will not support the private remedy that has long been held to be available against cognate behavior that violates that same prohibition. Neither such justification nor Congressional language can be found here.

[49] For example, *Moss v Morgan Stanley, Inc.*, 719 F2d 5 (2d Cir 1983); see *SEC v Clark*, 915 F2d 439, 445 nn 8–10 (9th Cir 1990); see Mitchell, 52 Albany L Rev 775 (cited in note 29), for discussion of the tensions among the premises that might underlie Section 10(b) and the resulting incongruous interpretations.

[50] That a person who has been injured by a malefactor's behavior that violates more than one statutory prohibition (whether imposed by the same or different sovereigns) may have a separate cause of action for violation of each statute against a single malefactor is not a novel notion. Similarly, if two persons are injured in different ways by behavior by a single person that violates a single statutory prohibition, the need to determine the injury to, and damages to be paid to, each does not preclude each (i.e., both) from asserting valid causes of action against the malefactor. Thus, the person from whom a trader deceitfully acquired information may have suffered one injury (e.g., in not being able to keep the information secret, whether or not he intended to use it to buy securities "cheaply"), while the innocently ignorant person who sold the securities "cheaply" to the trader suffered another injury. Determining the amount of compensation to which each is entitled may present difficult problems, but those difficulties do not preclude each victim from asserting a valid cause of action against the trader.

[51] The injury resulted from the opposite party trading at a price (1) that did not, and could not, reflect the value that the security would have when the trader's deceitfully acquired information became public, and (2) at which the opposite party would not have traded if the latter had the information that she did not in fact have and could not lawfully acquire.

by the trader of information deceitfully acquired from a third party, and that deceit is "connected" with a "purchase or sale of any security" only by reason of the transaction with the opposite party.[52]

Finally, it should be noted that the Exchange Act was amended in 1988 to authorize, if not indeed to confirm, the availability of private actions for limited recoveries by contemporaneous traders for violation of Section 10(b) and the Rule in circumstances like those in *O'Hagan*.[53] The Court's interpretation of the reach of Section 10(b) and Rule 10b-5 as they existed before the Exchange Act was amended in 1988 upheld the Government's claim in *O'Hagan*, and made it unnecessary to consider the Government's additional arguments based upon that amendment, or to express any views on its import for the availability of private actions for conduct occurring either before or subsequent to its enactment.

---

[52] There are problems with allowing a private action to the third party, for deceiving whom Section 10(b) authorizes sending the malefactor to jail, particularly if the third party is not a purchaser or seller; and in any particular case there may be no injury to and no recovery by the third party. See Wang and Steinberg, *Insider Trading* (cited in note 15) § 6.10.3 at 492–506. If such a cause of action *is* available to the third party, it certainly should be available to the trading victim. Otherwise the securities laws are given a special deterrent effect against deceiving the third party, even though he does not engage in a purchase or sale of a security, but not the trading victim who does engage in the purchase or sale of a security and is the very person whom it is an essential objective of the securities laws to protect. Moreover, even if such a cause of action by the third person is deemed not to be made available by Congress, the injured trading victim should not be denied a private remedy against the deceiver under the statute. Otherwise the private remedy that Congress authorized the injured trading victim to assert against the trader (for violating Section 10(b) and the Rule) who deceives her directly becomes unavailable because she was injured by reason of a deceit that violates the same statutory provision but is imposed upon her derivatively—notwithstanding that the statutory provision is violated only if the deceit is thus imposed upon her derivatively. See generally Langevoort (cited in note 26) § 9.03 at 9-17 to 9-27.

[53] Section 20A of the Exchange Act, 15 USC § 78t (1997); Langevoort (cited in note 26), § 9.02[4] at 6-33 and 9-16 to 9-17. The 1984 amendment (see note 28) and the 1988 amendment and the House Committees' explanations for them (see HR Rep No 98-355 (98th Cong, 1st Sess 1983), 3–5, 13–15; HR Rep No 100-910 (100th Cong, 2d Sess 1988) at 10–11, 26–27, 35) suggest that the Congresses enacting the amendments understood the meaning of the pre-amendment language of Section 10(b) and the Rule to be in accord with the Court's opinion in *O'Hagan*, and that the statute could be violated by persons who misappropriated information even if the misappropriator was not a fiduciary of the opposite party to the trade.

DAVID A. SKLANSKY

TRAFFIC STOPS, MINORITY
MOTORISTS, AND THE FUTURE OF
THE FOURTH AMENDMENT

Most Americans never have been arrested or had their homes searched by the police, but almost everyone has been pulled over. Traffic enforcement is so common it can seem humdrum. Notwithstanding the occasional murder suspect caught following a fortuitous vehicle code violation,[1] even the police tend to view traffic enforcement as "peripheral to 'crime fighting.'"[2]

Fourth Amendment decisions about traffic enforcement can seem peripheral, too. Every criminal lawyer knows that the Supreme Court treats the highway as a special case. Motorists receive reduced protection against searches and seizures, in part because

David A. Sklansky is Acting Professor of Law, UCLA School of Law.

AUTHOR'S NOTE: I received helpful criticism from Peter Arenella, Ann Carlson, Steven Clymer, Robert Goldstein, Pamela Karlan, Deborah Lambe, Jeff Sklansky, Carol Steiker, William Stuntz, and Eugene Volokh, financial support from the UCLA Chancellor's Office, and research assistance from the Hugh & Hazel Darling Law Library.

[1] See, for example, Stephen Braun, *Trooper's Vigilance Led to Arrest of Blast Suspect*, LA Times A1 (Apr 22, 1995) (describing arrest of Oklahoma City bomber Timothy McVeigh following traffic stop); Richard Simon, *Traffic Stops—Tickets to Surprises*, LA Times B1 (May 15, 1995) (noting that serial killers Ted Bundy and Randy Kraft were caught during traffic stops).

[2] David H. Bayley, *Police for the Future* 29 (Oxford, 1994). Not surprisingly, traffic officers take a different view. See id; Simon, *Traffic Stops*, LA Times at B1 (quoting California Highway Patrol Sgt. Mike Teixiera's assertion that "[w]e probably get more murderers stopping them for speeding than we do by looking for them").

of law enforcement necessities,[3] and in part because the Supreme Court simply finds it unrealistic in this day and age for people to expect much privacy in their cars.[4] Doctrinally as well as practically, constitutional restrictions on traffic enforcement thus can appear of marginal consequence.

This is deceptive. Despite its unglamorous reputation, traffic enforcement is perilous work, and law enforcement administrators increasingly view it as integral to effective crime control. For many motorists, particularly those who are not white, traffic stops can be not just inconvenient, but frightening, humiliating, and dangerous. And for the scholar, the Supreme Court's application of the Fourth Amendment to traffic stops can offer important clues to the overall status and future of search and seizure law. It is not just that doctrines crafted for the highway can later turn up elsewhere, although this certainly happens.[5] More important is that the way the Court handles controversies over vehicle stops—what it says and what it does not say—has a good deal to tell us about its broader understandings of the role of the Fourth Amendment.

This is particularly true today, because in the past two terms the Court has given vehicle stops an unusual amount of attention. In the ten-month period from May 1996 to February 1997, the

---

[3] See, for example, *Chambers v Maroney*, 399 US 42, 51 (1970) (explaining that "a search warrant [is] unnecessary where there is probable cause to search an automobile stopped on the highway," because "the car is movable, the occupants are alerted, and the car's contents may never be found again if a warrant must be obtained"); *Michigan Dep't of State Police v Sitz*, 496 US 444, 451 (1990) (upholding sobriety checkpoint in part because of "the magnitude of the drunken driving problem").

[4] See *South Dakota v Opperman*, 428 US 364, 367–68 (1976) (reasoning that "the expectation of privacy with respect to one's automobile is significantly less than that relating to one's home or office," because cars "are subjected to pervasive and continuing governmental regulation" and "periodic inspection," police stop and examine cars for vehicle code violations "[a]s an everyday occurrence," highway travel is "obviously public" because it subjects the occupants and contents of cars to "plain view," and cars "are frequently taken into police custody" as part of "community caretaking"). To similar effect is *United States v Chadwick*, 433 US 1, 12–13 (1977).

[5] Warrantless inventory searches, initially predicated on the reduced expectation of privacy in a motor vehicle, see *South Dakota v Opperman*, 428 US 364 (1976), in time were extended to booking searches of arrestees, see *Illinois v Lafayette*, 462 US 640 (1983). Similarly, "protective sweeps" were approved first for cars, see *Michigan v Long*, 463 US 1032 (1983), then for houses, see *Maryland v Buie*, 494 US 325 (1990); and the Court's lenient approach to sobriety checkpoints, see *Michigan Dep't of State Police v Sitz*, 496 US 444 (1990), ultimately formed part of the basis for its approval of drug testing for student athletes, see *Vernonia School District 47J v Acton*, 115 S Ct 2386, 2391 (1995).

Court held that the legality of a traffic stop based on probable cause does not depend on the officer's intent,[6] used a case involving a vehicle stop to decide the standard of review for findings regarding the existence of probable cause or reasonable suspicion,[7] authorized an officer conducting a traffic stop to ask permission to search the car without first making clear the driver is free to leave,[8] and ruled that passengers as well as the driver can be ordered out of the car.[9]

Since virtually everyone violates traffic laws at least occasionally, the upshot of these decisions is that police officers, if they are patient, can eventually pull over almost anyone they choose, order the driver and all passengers out of the car, and then ask for permission to search the vehicle without first making clear the detention is over. For reasons I hope to make clear, this is a discomforting state of affairs. My principal focus here, however, is less on the wisdom of the Court's recent decisions than on the lessons these decisions teach about the general state of Fourth Amendment law. I argue that the four cases reveal a strong degree of consensus on the Court about the proper application of the Fourth Amendment, and that the consensus results not from a settled body of doctrine but rather from shared, largely unspoken understandings. These understandings strongly favor law enforcement and, more troublingly, disregard the distinctive grievances and concerns of minority motorists stopped by the police. In ways the vehicle stop cases help to illustrate, this disregard is deeply embedded in the structure of current Fourth Amendment law, and over the long term it limits the protection the Amendment provides to all of us.

In Part I of this essay I briefly describe the four cases, after first reviewing even more summarily the doctrinal background against which they were decided. Part II discusses the striking degree of unanimity the Court has displayed in the vehicle stop decisions and in recent Fourth Amendment cases generally. Part III inquires whether this lack of discord is the product of a stable body of doctrine and determines that it is not. I argue in Part IV that the

---

[6] *Whren v United States*, 116 S Ct 1769 (1996).

[7] *Ornelas v United States*, 116 S Ct 1657 (1996).

[8] *Ohio v Robinette*, 117 S Ct 417 (1996).

[9] *Maryland v Wilson*, 117 S Ct 882 (1997).

unanimity instead results from shared understandings that are decidedly pro-government, and in Part V that these understandings
systematically ignore the ways in which roadside stops of minority
motorists tend to differ from those of whites. Part VI explores the
implications of this disregard for searches and seizures generally
and suggests that the vehicle stop cases illustrate several ways in
which a systematic disregard for the distinctive concerns of racial
minorities has become embedded in the structure of Fourth
Amendment doctrine and constrains the doctrine's growth. Finally, in Part VII, I ask whether the minority concerns ignored by
search and seizure law are adequately addressed elsewhere, I conclude that they are not, and I offer some tentative thoughts about
how the problems I have identified can best be addressed.

I. THE CASES

The basic Fourth Amendment rules regarding vehicle stops
can be stated simply. When the police pull a car over, they take
hold, temporarily, of both the car and the driver. The Fourth
Amendment guarantees "[t]he right of the people to be secure in
their persons, houses, papers, and effects, against unreasonable
searches and seizures," so vehicle stops, like other "seizures," must
be "reasonable."[10] Although a full-scale arrest is reasonable only
if based on probable cause to believe the suspect has committed
a crime,[11] a car stop or other detention falling short of an arrest
need only be "justified at its inception" and "reasonably related
in scope to the circumstances which justified the interference."[12]
Such a detention is "justified at its inception" if it is supported
by probable cause that the driver has violated traffic laws, or by
"reasonable suspicion, based on objective facts, that the individual
is involved in criminal activity."[13]

---

[10] See, for example, *Delaware v Prouse*, 440 US 648, 653 (1979).

[11] See, for example, *United States v Watson*, 423 US 411 (1976). Probable cause consists
of "facts and circumstances" sufficient to lead a reasonable officer to believe that the suspect
is committing or has committed an offense. *Draper v United States*, 358 US 307 (1959).
The Court has resolutely refused to define the term with any further precision. See, for
example, *Illinois v Gates*, 462 US 213, 232 (1983) (stressing that "probable cause is a fluid
concept . . . not readily, or even usefully, reduced to a neat set of legal rules").

[12] *Terry v Ohio*, 392 US 1, 20 (1968).

[13] *Brown v Texas*, 443 US 47, 51 (1979). The Court has never made clear whether a traffic
stop may be justified by reasonable suspicion, falling short of probable cause, that the driver

An officer who has pulled a car over may order the driver out.[14] If the officer reasonably suspects that the driver is armed and dangerous, a patdown is allowed,[15] and the passenger compartment may be searched for weapons if the officer reasonably believes the driver "is dangerous and . . . may gain immediate control of weapons."[16] In either case, the officer's concern must be objectively reasonable, based on "specific and articulable facts."[17] Beyond this, there are few sharp rules restricting the "scope" of roadside stops and other investigatory detentions; the duration of such a detention, for example, is limited only by the general requirement of reasonableness.[18]

If before or during the detention the officer develops probable cause to believe the car contains contraband or evidence of a crime, the car may be searched without a warrant.[19] The car also may be searched if the officer receives consent that appears "voluntary" in view of "all the circumstances"[20] from someone the officer reasonably believes has sole or shared authority over the vehicle.[21]

All these rules were in place five years ago; most of them have been settled for more than two decades. They provided the backdrop for the four car stop cases the Court decided in the past two terms. *Ornelas v United States*[22] and *Whren v United States*[23] were handed down during the 1995 Term, *Ohio v Robinette*[24] and *Maryland v Wilson*[25] during the 1996 Term. Before discussing what these

---

has committed a noncriminal traffic offense. See Wayne R. LaFave, 4 *Search and Seizure* § 9.2(c) (West, 3d ed 1996). In practice the question rarely arises, because most stops for traffic violations follow the officer's direct observation of the violation.

[14] See *Pennsylvania v Mimms*, 434 US 106 (1977).

[15] See *Terry*, 392 US at 27.

[16] *Michigan v Long*, 463 US 1032, 1049–50 (1983).

[17] Id at 1049; *Terry*, 392 US at 21.

[18] See *United States v Sharpe*, 470 US 675 (1985).

[19] See *Pennsylvania v Labron*, 116 S Ct 2485, 2487 (1996); *California v Acevedo*, 500 US 565, 569–70 (1991); *Chambers v Maroney*, 399 US 42 (1970).

[20] *Schneckloth v Bustamonte*, 412 US 218, 233 (1973).

[21] See *Illinois v Rodriguez*, 497 US 177 (1990).

[22] 116 S Ct 1657 (1996).

[23] Id at 1769.

[24] 117 S Ct 417 (1996).

[25] Id at 882.

cases mean collectively, it will help to examine each individually.

A. ORNELAS V UNITED STATES

Unlike the other three cases, *Ornelas*, although it arose from the detention of a motorist and his passenger, did not involve the substantive limits on traffic stops. Rather, it focused on the standard of appellate review for findings of probable cause or reasonable suspicion. The decision merits our attention, however, because it illuminates the significance of the other three cases.

Saul Ornelas and Ismael Ornelas-Ledesma were stopped by officers of the Milwaukee County Sheriff's Department as they were about to drive out of a motel parking lot in downtown Milwaukee. The officers suspected the men were trafficking in narcotics.[26] After speaking briefly with the defendants, the officers searched the car and found two kilograms of cocaine hidden behind a door panel. The district court found that facts known to the officers gave them reasonable suspicion for the initial stop and probable cause for the search.[27] The court of appeals affirmed, concluding that the district court's findings did not constitute "clear error."[28]

The question addressed by the Supreme Court was whether the trial court's findings of reasonable suspicion and probable cause were properly reviewed de novo or for "abuse of discretion"—the

---

[26] One of the officers later explained that his suspicions initially were aroused by the car itself: an older model, two-door General Motors vehicle, "a favorite with drug couriers because it is easy to hide things in them," bearing license plates from California, "a 'source State' for drugs." *Ornelas*, 116 S Ct at 1659. The officers determined from a check of registration records that the car was owned by "either Miguel Ledesma Ornelas or Miguel Ornelas Ledesma from San Jose, California," and the motel registry revealed "Ismael Ornelas," accompanied by another man, had checked in at 4:00 in the morning without a reservation. Id. The officers then had the Drug Enforcement Administration check the Narcotics and Dangerous Drugs Information System (NADDIS)—"a federal database of known and suspected drug dealers"—for the names Miguel Ledesma Ornelas and Ismael Ornelas; both names turned up, one as a heroin dealer and one as a cocaine dealer. Id.

[27] The district court also found that the defendants had consented to a search of the car. Under Seventh Circuit precedent, however, the consent search could not include removing the door panel, without probable cause to believe it concealed contraband or evidence. See *United States v Garcia*, 897 F2d 1413, 1419–20 (7th Cir 1990). The Supreme Court in *Ornelas* "assume[d] correct the Circuit's limitation on the scope of consent only for purposes of this decision." 116 S Ct at 1660 n 1.

[28] *United States v Ornelas-Ledesma*, 16 F3d 714, 719 (7th Cir 1994), rev'd, 116 S Ct 1657 (1996).

Court's preferred term for the deferential standard of review applied by the court of appeals.[29] The justices voted 8–1 for de novo review and remanded the case to the court of appeals.

Chief Justice Rehnquist wrote for the majority. Assessments of probable cause and reasonable suspicion, he explained, should be reviewed searchingly, in order to promote consistency of results, to give appellate courts control of the legal principles they propound, and to allow progressive clarification of the law.[30] The Court "hasten[ed] to point out," however, "that a reviewing court should take care both to review findings of historical fact for clear error and to give due weight to inferences drawn from those facts by resident judges and local law enforcement officers."[31] Such inferences, the Court explained, included those drawn by an officer "through the lens of his police experience and expertise."[32] More particularly, they included both the officer's inference in the case before the Court that a loose door panel he discovered might conceal illegal narcotics, and "the trial court's finding that the officer was credible and the inference was reasonable."[33]

Justice Scalia, the sole dissenter, argued for deference to the expertise of district judges, and suggested that determinations of probable cause and reasonable suspicion were so fact-intensive that appellate review in particular cases would do little to clarify the law.[34] He also accused the majority of lacking "the courage of its conclusions," because "in *de novo* review, the 'weight due' to a trial court's finding is zero."[35]

B. WHREN V UNITED STATES

The three roadside detention cases decided after *Ornelas* all involved what the police described as routine traffic stops. Each of

---

[29] The Court explained that " '[c]lear error' is a term of art derived from Rule 52(a) of the Federal Rules of Civil Procedure, and applies when reviewing questions of fact." 116 S Ct at 1661 n 3.

[30] See id at 1662.

[31] Id at 1663.

[32] Id.

[33] Id. Given these broad hints, it should come as no surprise that on remand the court of appeals, applying the nominally more demanding standard of review prescribed by the Supreme Court, once again reaffirmed the district court's finding of reasonable suspicion. See *United States v Ornelas*, 96 F3d 1450, 1996 WL 508569 (7th Cir 1996).

[34] Id at 1663–65 (Scalia dissenting).

[35] Id at 1666.

these concerned, in a sense, what counts as "routine" for purposes of the Fourth Amendment.

Whren v United States[36] arose when police in Washington, D.C., pulled over a Nissan Pathfinder and saw two bags of crack cocaine in the hands of Michael Whren, the front-seat passenger. This evidence was used to convict Whren and the driver of federal narcotics offenses. Both defendants challenged their convictions on the ground that the stop leading to the discovery of the cocaine violated the Fourth Amendment. The police claimed they had stopped the car because the driver had broken several traffic laws; specifically, he had paused at a stop sign "for what seemed an unusually long time—more than 20 seconds," he had turned without signaling, and he had "sped off at an 'unreasonable' speed."[37] The defendants contended they had been stopped "because the sight of two young black men in a Nissan Pathfinder with temporary tags, pausing at stop sign in Southeast Washington," had struck the police as suspicious.[38]

There was some circumstantial evidence for the defendants' version. They had been pulled over and ultimately arrested not by traffic officers but by plainclothes vice-squad officers patrolling a "high drug area" of the city in an unmarked car—officers who were actually prohibited, as a matter of departmental policy, from making routine traffic stops.[39] But the Supreme Court sided with the police. In a unanimous opinion authored by Justice Scalia, the Court held that "the constitutional reasonableness of traffic stops"

---

[36] 116 S Ct 1769 (1996).

[37] Id at 1772. District of Columbia traffic laws prohibited turning without signaling, driving at "a speed greater than is reasonable and prudent under the conditions," and failing to "give full time and attention to the operation of the vehicle." Id at 1772–73 (quoting 18 DC Mun Regs §§ 2204.3, 2200.3, 2213.4 (1995)).

[38] Brief for the Petitioners at 2. Lower courts generally have held that "racial incongruity" may provide part but not all of the basis for reasonable suspicion. LaFave, 4 *Search and Seizure* § 9.4(f) at 183 n 220 (cited in note 13). See also *United States v Brignoni-Ponce*, 422 US 873, 885–87 (1975) (holding that "Mexican appearance" is a "relevant factor" but on its own cannot justify car stops by roving border patrol agents). For thoughtful criticism of permitting even this limited use of race, see Sheri Lynn Johnson, *Race and the Decision to Detain a Suspect*, 93 Yale L J 214 (1983); *Developments in the Law—Race and the Criminal Process*, 101 Harv L Rev 1472, 1500–20 (1988). The officers in *Whren* claimed that race had played no role in their decision to stop the Pathfinder. See *United States v Whren*, 53 F3d 371, 373 (DC Cir 1995), aff'd, 116 S Ct 1769 (1996).

[39] 116 S Ct at 1772, 1775.

does not depend "on the actual motivations of the individual offi-cers involved."[40] Because the police had probable cause to believe the driver of the Pathfinder had violated traffic laws—they saw the violations themselves—the stop was lawful, regardless of their ac-tual motivation. "Subjective intentions," Justice Scalia explained, "play no role in ordinary, probable-cause Fourth Amendment analysis."[41]

C. OHIO V ROBINETTE

The controversy in *Ohio v Robinette*[42] had to do not with the initiation of a traffic stop, but with its aftermath. Robert Robinette was stopped for speeding and received a warning. Deputy Sheriff Roger Newsome then asked him "[o]ne question before you get gone: [A]re you carrying any illegal contraband in your car? Any weapons of any kind, drugs, anything like that?"[43] When Robinette said he was not, Newsome, apparently as a matter of routine, asked for permission to search the car.[44] Robinette agreed. The search turned up a small amount of marijuana and a methamphetamine pill. Robinette was convicted of possession of a controlled sub-stance, but the Ohio Supreme Court threw the conviction out.

The Ohio court reasoned that, once the basis for the stop had terminated, Newsome was required to tell Robinette that he was free to leave. Otherwise, the subsequent interactions between Rob-inette and Newsome could not be deemed consensual:

> Most people believe that they are validly in a police officer's custody as long as the officer continues to interrogate them. The police officer retains the upper hand and the accouter-

---

[40] Id at 1774.

[41] Id.

[42] 117 S Ct 417 (1986).

[43] Id at 419.

[44] Like the officers in *Whren*, Newsome "was on drug interdiction patrol at the time." *State v Robinette*, 653 NE2d 695, 696 (Ohio 1995), rev'd, 117 S Ct 417 (1996). He testified that he routinely asked permission to search cars that he stopped for traffic violations. See id. As Justice Ginsburg noted in her concurring opinion, Newsome testified in another case that "he requested consent to search in 786 traffic stops in 1992, the year of Robinette's arrest." 117 S Ct at 422 (citing *State v Rutherford*, 639 NE2d 498, 503 n 3 (Ohio Ct App), dism'd, 635 NE2d 43 (Ohio 1994)).

ments of authority. That the officer lacks legal license to continue to detain them is unknown to most citizens, and a reasonable person would not feel free to walk away as the officer
continues to address him.[45]

By a vote of 8–1, however, the Supreme Court of the United
States rejected the Ohio court's "bright-line" rule, reasoning that
the only "Fourth Amendment test for a valid consent to search is
that the consent be voluntary,"[46] and reaffirming that voluntariness
must be determined "from all the circumstances."[47] Writing for
the majority, Chief Justice Rehnquist added that it would be "unrealistic to require police officers to always inform detainees that
they are free to go before a consent to search may be deemed
voluntary."[48]

Concurring in the judgment, Justice Ginsburg agreed that the
requirement imposed by the Ohio court could not be found in
the Fourth Amendment, but she strongly suggested that the Ohio
Supreme Court might appropriately ground such a requirement in
state constitutional law.[49] Justice Stevens, the lone dissenter, also
agreed that "[t]he Federal Constitution does not require that a
lawfully seized person be advised that he is 'free to go' before his
consent to search will be recognized as voluntary," but he argued
that "the prophylactic rule announced [by the Ohio Supreme
Court] . . . was intended as a guide to the decision of future cases
rather than as an explanation of the decision in this case."[50]

D. MARYLAND V WILSON

Whereas *Whren* involved the justification for a routine traffic
stop, and *Robinette* addressed its aftermath, *Maryland v Wilson*[51] fo-

---

[45] 653 NE2d 695, 698.

[46] 117 S Ct at 421.

[47] Id (quoting *Schneckloth v Bustamonte*, 412 US 218, 248–49 (1973)).

[48] 117 S Ct at 421.

[49] Id at 421–24. Justice Ginsburg agreed with the majority that "[t]he Ohio Supreme
Court invoked both the Federal Constitution and the Ohio Constitution without clearly
indicating whether state law, standing alone, independently justified the court's rule," and
that this ambiguity rendered appropriate the Court's exercise of jurisdiction under *Michigan
v Long*, 463 US 1032 (1983). Id at 422.

[50] Id at 424.

[51] 117 S Ct 882 (1997).

cused on what may happen *during* the stop. Specifically, the case concerned whether a police officer carrying out a lawful traffic stop has blanket authority to order passengers out of the car. Jerry Wilson, the front-seat passenger in a car pulled over for speeding, dropped some crack cocaine when he was directed to leave the vehicle. The Maryland courts ruled the cocaine inadmissible against Wilson, on the ground that ordering Wilson out of the car was unreasonable and therefore in violation of the Fourth Amendment. Although the Supreme Court had earlier held that the *driver* may be ordered out of the car during a lawful traffic stop,[52] the Maryland courts reasoned that passengers were different.

By a vote of 7–2, the Supreme Court disagreed. Writing once again for the majority, Chief Justice Rehnquist acknowledged that "there is not the same basis for ordering the passengers out of the car as there is for ordering the driver out," because "[t]here is probable cause to believe that the driver has committed a minor vehicular offense, but there is no such reason to stop or detain the passengers."[53] Nonetheless, "the additional intrusion on the passenger is minimal," and "the same weighty interest in officer safety is present regardless whether the occupant of the stopped car is a driver or passenger."[54] Indeed, the Chief Justice noted, "the fact that there is more than one occupant of the vehicle increases the possible sources of harm to the officer."[55]

Justices Stevens and Kennedy dissented. Justice Stevens argued that a police officer carrying out a traffic stop should be authorized to order passengers out only if the officer "has an articulable suspicion of possible danger."[56] Justice Kennedy called for a more open-ended approach, permitting such a command whenever "there are

---

[52] See *Pennsylvania v Mimms*, 434 US 106 (1977).

[53] 117 S Ct at 886.

[54] Id. "In 1994 alone, there were 5,762 officer assaults and 11 officers killed during traffic pursuits and stops." Id at 885 (citing Federal Bureau of Investigation, *Uniform Crime Reports: Law Enforcement Officers Killed and Assaulted* (1994)). See also Lisa A. Regini, *Extending the Mimms Rule to Include Passengers*, FBI Law Enforcement Bull 27 (June 1997) (suggesting these dangers may make "routine traffic stops" the "most misnamed activity in law enforcement").

[55] 117 S Ct at 885.

[56] Id at 887 (Stevens dissenting).

objective circumstances making it reasonable for the officer to issue the order."[57]

II. The New Consensus

To anyone familiar with the Supreme Court's writings on the Fourth Amendment over the past several decades, probably the most striking thing about *Ornelas, Whren, Robinette,* and *Wilson* was not the results reached—none of which, taken individually, came as a great surprise—but the lack of discord within the Court. In the four decisions combined, there was a total of only four dissenting votes, and only one separate concurring opinion.

Even these numbers overstate the degree of disagreement. Justice Scalia, the lone dissenter in *Ornelas,* agreed with the majority that trial courts deserve deference on questions of probable cause and reasonable suspicion; what he wanted was less a different rule than a rule worded more clearly. Justice Stevens, the only dissenting vote in *Robinette,* explicitly approved the Court's substantive holding, and disagreed only about whether the lower court had applied a contrary rule in the case under review. Justice Ginsburg, who concurred separately in *Robinette,* expressly embraced the Court's holding, and wrote separately only because it seemed to her "improbable that the Ohio Supreme Court understood its first-tell-then-ask rule to be the Federal Constitution's mandate for the Nation as a whole."[58] Similarly, although Justices Stevens and Kennedy dissented in *Wilson,* the rules they proposed differed only modestly from the one adopted by the Court.[59]

---

[57] Id at 890 (Kennedy dissenting). Justice Kennedy ascribed this conclusion to Justice Stevens, whose dissent he also joined. Justice Stevens apparently recognized that Justice Kennedy's approach was less circumscribed than his own; he did not join Justice Kennedy's dissent.

[58] Id at 422 (Ginsburg concurring).

[59] The rule proposed by Justice Stevens—requiring an officer to have "an articulable suspicion of possible danger" before ordering a passenger out of a car, 117 S Ct at 887 (Stevens dissenting)—may even have been satisfied in the case before the Court. The officer who ordered Wilson out of the car testified that he did so because "movement in the vehicle" suggested to him that "there could be a handgun in the vehicle," and gave him concern for his safety. *State v Wilson,* 664 A2d 1, 2 (Md 1995), rev'd, 117 S Ct 882 (1997). For reasons the record does not disclose, the Maryland Court of Special Appeals nonetheless upheld the trial judge's finding that the officer did not act out of any "sense of heightened caution or apprehensiveness." Id at 15.

Justice Kennedy joined Justice Stevens's opinion and also wrote a separate opinion sug-

The institutional harmony displayed in these cases is typical of the Court's recent Fourth Amendment decisions. This is a new phenomenon. As recently as five or ten years ago, an important search or seizure commonly produced four or more sharply divergent opinions. Often no single opinion spoke for the Court.[60]

Although the Court still splinters today on some other subjects—voting rights[61] and freedom of speech[62] are two good examples—it increasingly speaks with a clear and united voice when it

---

gesting that "the command to exit ought not to be given unless there are objective circumstances making it reasonable for the officer to issue the order." Id at 890 (Kennedy dissenting). Although Justice Kennedy apparently saw no divergence between his standard and the rule advocated by Justice Stevens, the difference could in fact prove significant. By tying the legality of an exit command to what is "reasonable" under the circumstances, the test proposed by Justice Kennedy might disallow the command in some situations in which the per se rule endorsed by Justice Stevens would allow it: situations involving a small amount of possible danger, outweighed perhaps by the burden that leaving the car would impose on the passenger. Of greater importance, Justice Kennedy's open-ended test might allow passengers to be ordered out of cars in some situations lacking any indications of danger to the officer: "objective circumstances" making the order reasonable, Justice Kennedy suggested, could include not only indications of possible danger, but also "any circumstance justifying the order . . . to facilitate a lawful search or investigation." Id.

"Since a myriad of circumstances will give a cautious officer reasonable grounds for commanding passengers to leave the vehicle," Justice Kennedy acknowledged that "it might be thought the rule the Court adopts today will be little different in its operation than the rule offered in dissent." Id at 890–91. He did not quarrel with that conclusion, suggesting only that "[i]t does no disservice to police officers . . . to insist upon exercise of reasoned judgment." Id at 891.

[60] See, for example, *California v Acevedo*, 500 US 565 (1991) (four opinions); *Michigan Dep't of State Police v Sitz*, 496 US 444 (1990) (four opinions); *Minnesota v Olsen*, 495 US 91 (1990) (four opinions); *Florida v Wells*, 495 US 1 (1990) (four opinions); *Maryland v Buie*, 494 US 325 (1990) (four opinions); *United States v Verdugo-Urquidez*, 494 US 259 (1990) (five opinions); *Florida v Riley*, 488 US 445 (1989) (four opinions, no majority opinion); *Arizona v Hicks*, 480 US 321 (1987) (four opinions); *Illinois v Gates*, 462 US 213 (1983) (four opinions); *Florida v Royer*, 460 US 491 (1983) (five opinions, no majority opinion); *Schneckloth v Bustamonte*, 412 US 218 (1973) (six opinions); *Coolidge v New Hampshire*, 403 US 443 (1971) (five opinions, partial majority opinion); *United States v White*, 401 US 745 (1971) (five opinions and a "statement," no majority opinion); Roger B. Dworkin, *Fact Style Adjudication and the Fourth Amendment: The Limits of Lawyering*, 48 Ind L J 329 (1973) (observing that "the Supreme Court can seldom muster a majority on any important fourth amendment issue"); Wayne R. LaFave, *"Case-by-Case Adjudication" versus "Standardized Procedures": The Robinson Dilemma*, 1974 Supreme Court Review 127, 127–28 & n 2 (noting multiple opinions and closely divided votes in Fourth Amendment cases decided in 1972 and 1973 Terms).

[61] See, for example, *Bush v Vera*, 116 S Ct 1941 (1996) (six opinions, no majority); *Miller v Johnson*, 115 S Ct 2475 (1995) (four opinions).

[62] See, for example, *Turner Broadcasting System, Inc v FCC*, 117 S Ct 1174 (1997) (four opinions, partial majority); *Denver Area Educ Telecom Consortium v FCC*, 116 S Ct 2374 (1996) (six opinions, partial majority); *Colorado Republican Campaign Comm v FEC*, 116 S Ct 2309 (1996) (four opinions, no majority).

addresses constitutional restrictions on searches and seizures by the police.[63] Usually the opinion is authored by Chief Justice Rehnquist or a more conservative member of the Court.[64]

Nothing illustrates this new consensus on the Fourth Amendment more clearly than Justice Scalia's unanimous opinion for the

---

[63] In addition to the cases discussed in the text, see *Richards v Wisconsin*, 117 S Ct 1416 (1997) (unanimous ruling that "no knock" searches may be "unreasonable" even in a drug case, although not in the case before the Court); *Pennsylvania v Labron*, 116 S Ct 2485 (1996) (per curiam holding that "automobile exception" to the warrant requirement does not require exigency); *Wilson v Arkansas*, 115 S Ct 1914, 1915 (1995) (unanimous ruling that the "common-law 'knock and announce' principle forms part of the reasonableness inquiry under the Fourth Amendment"); *United States v Padilla*, 508 US 77 (1993) (per curiam holding that criminal defendants lack standing to object to violations of the Fourth Amendment rights of their coconspirators).

The Court can still divide noticeably when asked how the Fourth Amendment applies to government agencies other than the police. See *Vernonia School District 47J v Acton*, 115 S Ct 2386 (1995); *Arizona v Evans*, 115 S Ct 1185 (1995). The majority in *Acton*, led by Justice Scalia, upheld a school district's program of mass, suspicionless drug testing of student athletes. Justice O'Connor, joined by Justices Stevens and Souter, dissented vehemently from the decision, and Justice Ginsburg, who joined the majority opinion, also wrote separately in an effort to limit the ruling. In *Evans*, the Court held that the Fourth Amendment does not require suppression of evidence seized during an illegal arrest resulting from a clerical mistake by court personnel. Chief Justice Rehnquist wrote for the majority, Justice O'Connor and Justice Souter each filed concurring opinions seeking to limit the scope of the ruling, and Justice Stevens and Justice Ginsburg each wrote dissents. The Court was less divided in *Chandler v Miller*, 117 S Ct 1295 (1977), when it struck down, over Chief Justice Rehnquist's lone dissent, a Georgia statute requiring candidates for certain elected positions to take urinalysis drug tests. As I discuss later, this may have had to do with the fact that among those Georgians subjected to drug testing were candidates for seats on the state supreme court, court of appeals, and superior courts. See note 151 and accompanying text.

[64] In addition to the cases discussed in text, see *Vernonia School District 47J v Acton*, 115 S Ct 2386 (1995) (Scalia); *Arizona v Evans*, 115 S Ct 1185 (1995) (Rehnquist); *Wilson v Arkansas*, 115 S Ct 1914 (1995) (Thomas). An exception is *Richards v Wisconsin*, 117 S Ct 1416 (1997) (Stevens).

Justice Thomas and Chief Justice Rehnquist have been in the majority of all but three of the Fourth Amendment cases the Court has decided since Thomas joined the Court in 1993. The exceptions are *Minnesota v Dickerson*, 508 US 366 (1993), *Powell v Nevada*, 511 US 79 (1994), and *Chandler v Miller*, 117 S Ct 1295 (1997). The holding in *Powell* was relatively technical: the Court ruled that *County of Riverside v McLaughlin*, 500 US 44 (1991), which found the Fourth Amendment to require that suspects arrested without warrant ordinarily receive a judicial determination of probable cause within 48 hours, applied retroactively. The Chief Justice joined Justice Thomas's dissent. In *Dickerson*, the Chief Justice wrote the dissent, joined by Justice Thomas and Justice Blackmun. The principle holding in that case, with which all nine justice agreed, was that the Minnesota Supreme Court had erred in ruling that officers may not seize nonthreatening contraband detected during a protective patdown search. The majority, led by Justice White, nonetheless affirmed the Minnesota court's reversal of Dickerson's conviction, reasoning that the patdown exceeded permissible limits; the dissenters would have remanded that issue. In *Chandler*, a majority of eight, led by Justice Ginsburg, struck down a Georgia statute requiring candidates for a wide range of executive and judicial positions to take drug tests; Chief Justice Rehnquist was the lone dissenter.

Court rejecting the pretext claim in *Whren*. *Whren* touched on an issue of persistent ambiguity in constitutional criminal procedure—the relevance of a police officer's motivations. On the one hand, the Court has long expressed a strong preference, at least in theory, for tying the legality of law enforcement measures to objective circumstances, rather than to officers' intentions.[65] On the other hand, some doctrines of criminal procedure hinge explicitly on police intent,[66] and even when applying doctrines that do not, the Court often has seemed influenced, sometimes heavily, by suppositions about why the police acted as they did.[67]

Had the Supreme Court decided *Whren* twenty-five years ago, it is difficult to say what the result would have been. Ten years ago, the government probably would have won, but one suspects there would have been a strong dissent, and perhaps one or two opinions concurring only in the result. Very possibly no opinion would have spoken for a majority of the Court; if one did, it likely would have emphasized the particular facts before the Court and left "for another day" the question whether, in different circum-

---

[65] See, for example, *Stansbury v California*, 114 S Ct 1526, 1529–30 (1994); *Illinois v Rodriguez*, 497 US 177, 185–86 (1990); *New York v Quarles*, 467 US 649, 656 & n 6 (1984). At times the Court has even said things like "the fact that the officer does not have the state of mind which is hypothecated by the reasons which provide the legal justification for the officer's action does not invalidate the action taken as long as the circumstances, viewed objectively, justify that action." *Scott v United States*, 436 US 128, 138 (1978) (Rehnquist).

[66] See, for example, *South Dakota v Opperman*, 428 US 364, 375–76 (1976) (upholding warrantless inventory searches of impounded automobiles for "caretaking" purposes) (followed in *Colorado v Bertine*, 479 US 367, 372 (1987) and *Florida v Wells*, 495 US 1, 4 (1990)); *United States v Massiah*, 377 US 201 (1964) (holding that Sixth Amendment barred use against defendant of statements "deliberately elicited from him after he had been indicted and in the absence of his counsel") (followed in *Brewer v Williams*, 430 US 387 (1977), and *United States v Henry*, 447 US 264 (1980)); *United States v Lefkowitz*, 285 US 452, 467 (1932) (holding that "[a]n arrest may not be used as a pretext to search for evidence").

[67] See, for example, *New York v Burger*, 482 US 691, 716 n 27 (1987) (upholding warrantless administrative inspection in part because neither legislature nor officers appeared to have used the inspection as a "pretext" to search for evidence of crime); *Arizona v Mauro*, 481 US 520, 528 (1987) (finding *Miranda* warnings unnecessary in part because police did not appear to have acted "for the purpose of eliciting incriminating statements"); *Jones v United States*, 357 US 493, 500 (1958) (invalidating search in part because "[t]he testimony of the federal officers makes clear beyond dispute that their purpose in entering was to search for distilling equipment, not to arrest petitioner").

Justice Scalia correctly pointed out that both *Burger* and *Opperman* involved searches made without probable cause. See *Whren*, 116 S Ct at 1773. The same could be said of *Jones*. What he did not explain was why this distinction should make all the difference.

stances, an officer's subjective intent could ever invalidate an otherwise lawful traffic stop.[68] The dissent would have stressed that to allow pretextual stops for traffic violations is to license arbitrary exercises of official discretion similar to those notoriously authorized in the eighteenth century by general warrants and writs of assistance,[69] and that a "paramount purpose of the fourth amendment is to prohibit arbitrary searches and seizures as well as unjustified searches and seizures."[70] The principal opinion presumably would have disclaimed giving police the broad authority

---

[68] See, for example, *Skinner v Railway Labor Executives' Ass'n*, 489 US 602, 621 n 25 (1989) ("leav[ing] for another day the question whether routine use in criminal prosecutions of evidence obtained pursuant to the [Federal Railway Administration's drug testing program] would give rise to an inference of pretext, or otherwise impugn the administrative nature of the FRA's program"); *O'Connor v Ortega*, 480 US 709, 723 (1987) ("leav[ing] for another day" application of the Fourth Amendment to workplace searches by government employers for purposes unrelated to work); *United States v Robinson*, 414 US 218 (1973) ("leav[ing] for another day questions which would arise" if the arrest giving rise to a search was "a departure from established police department practices").

[69] See, for example, LaFave, 1974 Supreme Court Review at 152–53 (cited in note 60); Barbara C. Salken, *The General Warrant of the Twentieth Century? A Fourth Amendment Solution to Unchecked Discretion to Arrest for Traffic Offenses*, 62 Temple L Rev 221, 254–58 (1989).

For concise accounts of the resentments provoked by general warrants and writs of assistance, and the key role these resentments played in the drafting and adoption of the Fourth Amendment, the classic sources are Nelson B. Lasson, *The History and Development of the Fourth Amendment to the United States Constitution* 43–78 (Johns Hopkins, 1937), and Telford Taylor, *Search, Seizure, and Surveillance*, in *Two Studies in Constitutional Interpretation* 19, 24–38 (Ohio State, 1969). Essentially, general warrants were broad grants of authority from the executive to crown officers to search for and to arrest certain offenders, generally printers and publishers of seditious libel, and to search for and seize their papers. In the 1760s, Lord Camden and Lord Mansfield struck down these warrants in a series of decisions well known and widely applauded in the colonies. Writs of assistance were legislative acts empowering colonial revenue agents to search for smuggled goods. In 1761, James Otis argued famously but unsuccessfully against renewal of the writs in Massachusetts. General warrants were disfavored partly because they authorized broadscale seizure of all the offenders' papers, and partly because they gave crown officers wide discretion in determining who the offenders were. Writs of assistance were resented because of the virtually unlimited discretion they gave revenue agents to decide when, where, and how to search for contraband. This history recently has been placed in wider context by William Cuddihy's unpublished 1990 Ph.D. thesis, *The Fourth Amendment: Origins and Original Meaning, 1602–1791*. For a useful summary of that "exhaustive" and "exhausting" work, see Morgan Cloud, *Searching through History; Searching for History*, 63 U Chi L Rev 1707, 1713 (1996).

[70] Anthony G. Amsterdam, *Perspectives on the Fourth Amendment*, 58 Minn L Rev 349, 417 (1974). See also, for example, *Camara v Municipal Court*, 387 US 523, 528 (1967) (noting that "the basic purpose" of the Fourth Amendment, "as recognized in countless decisions of this Court, is to safeguard the privacy and security of individuals against arbitrary invasions by governmental officials"); Tracey Maclin, *The Central Meaning of the Fourth Amendment*, 35 Wm & Mary L Rev 197, 201 (1993) (arguing that "the central meaning of the Fourth Amendment is distrust of police power and discretion").

decried by the dissent. Law professors and lower courts would have been left to speculate how broad the holding really was.[71]

No such speculation is necessary now. All nine justices joined Justice Scalia's opinion in *Whren*, and whatever else may be said about that opinion, it is not equivocal. Not only did Justice Scalia refuse to inquire why the District of Columbia police had pulled over the Pathfinder, he declared flatly that the Court's prior cases "foreclose any argument that the constitutional reasonableness of traffic stops depends on the actual motivations of the individual officers involved"—or even on whether "the officer's conduct deviated materially from usual police practices, so that a reasonable officer in the same circumstances would not have made the stop for the reasons given."[72]

Although the latter inquiry had been favored by a leading scholar of the Fourth Amendment and by a growing minority of lower courts,[73] Justice Scalia made short work of it. This nominally

---

[71] Debate continued for two decades, for example, about what sense to make of the Supreme Court's statement in *United States v Scott*, 436 US 128, 138 (1978), that "the fact that the officer does not have the state of mind which is hypothecated by the reasons which provide the legal justification for the officer's action does not invalidate the action taken as long as the circumstances, viewed objectively, justify that action"—and, in particular, about whether the Supreme Court adopted the government's broad claim in that case that "subjective intent alone . . . does not make otherwise lawful conduct illegal or unconstitutional." See, for example, LaFave, 1 *Search and Seizure* § 1.4(e) at 105 (cited in note 13) (arguing that *Scott* "can hardly be read as a definitive analysis settling that in *all* circumstances Fourth Amendment suppression issues are to be resolved without assaying 'the underlying intent or motivation of the officers involved,'" but that "this is precisely what the rule ought to be"); id at 102–25 & nn 61, 62, & 70 (summarizing and citing cases); John M. Burkoff, *The Pretext Search Doctrine Returns after Never Leaving*, 66 U Detroit L Rev 363, 372 (1989) (contending that "Supreme Court decisions handed down both before and after the *Scott* decision have neither uniformly adopted nor applied an objective fourth amendment test as was seemingly dictated by *Scott*"); John M. Burkoff, *Bad Faith Searches*, 57 NYU L Rev 70, 74–75 (1982) (calling the broad language of *Scott* "mere dicta," and arguing that "[r]easons of policy as well as doctrinal consistency require that the case be read more narrowly"); James B. Haddad, *Pretextual Fourth Amendment Activity: Another Viewpoint*, 18 U Mich J L Ref 639, 674 (1989) (noting that "*Scott* did not involve a pretext claim," but arguing that the Supreme Court, properly, has never invalidated an otherwise valid search or seizure on the ground that the officers lacked the proper motive).

[72] 116 S Ct at 1774.

[73] See, for example, *United States v Cannon*, 29 F3d 472 (9th Cir 1994); *United States v Smith*, 799 F2d 704 (11th Cir 1986); *State v Daniel*, 665 So2d 1040 (Fla 1995); *State v Haskell*, 645 A2d 619 (Me 1994); *Alejandre v State*, 903 P2d 794 (Nev 1995); *State v French*, 663 NE2d 367 (Ohio Ct App 1995); *State v Blumenthal*, 895 P2d 430 (Wash Ct App 1995); LaFave, 1 *Search and Seizure* § 1.4(e) at 119–20 & nn 55–59 (cited in note 13) (citing cases). None of the scholarly and judicial support for the defendants' position was noted in the Court's opinion.

objective test, he explained, actually was "driven by subjective considerations," because "[i]ts whole purpose is to prevent the police from doing under the guise of enforcing the traffic code what they would like to do for different reasons."[74] In addition, Justice Scalia stressed the difficulty of "plumb[ing] the collective consciousness of law enforcement in order to determine whether a 'reasonable officer' would have been moved to act upon the traffic violation."[75] He conceded that "police manuals and standard procedures may sometimes provide objective assistance," but suggested that "ordinarily one would be reduced to speculating about the hypothetical reaction of a hypothetical constable—an exercise that might be called virtual subjectivity."[76] Finally, even if the test could be applied, Justice Scalia pointed out that it would make the protections of the Fourth Amendment turn on police practices that "vary from place to place and from time to time," a prospect the Court found simply unacceptable.[77]

These arguments were all of the cavalier sort one tends to encounter in opinions not tested by a dissent. No competent criminal lawyer could be expected to believe that past cases flatly "foreclose[d]" a direct inquiry into the purpose of a traffic stop; anyone familiar with the cases knew they were far murkier.[78] And Justice

---

[74] 116 S Ct at 1774.

[75] Id at 1775.

[76] Id.

[77] Id.

[78] For example, in a footnote to its per curiam affirmance of the conviction in *Colorado v Bannister*, 449 US 1 (1980), the Court had noted "[t]here was no evidence whatsoever that the officer's presence to issue a traffic citation was a pretext to confirm any other previous suspicion about the occupants." Id at 4 n 4. Justice Scalia quite properly treated the footnote as inconclusive: the most it demonstrated was "that the Court in *Bannister* found no need to inquire into the question now under discussion." *Whren*, 116 S Ct at 1773.

With other cases, though, Justice Scalia was less careful. For example, he described *United States v Robinson*, 414 US 218 (1973), as having "held that a traffic-violation arrest (of the sort here) would not be rendered invalid by the fact that it was 'a mere pretext for a narcotics search,'" and *Scott v United States*, 436 US 128 (1978), as having "said that '[s]ubjective intent alone . . . does not make otherwise lawful conduct illegal or unconstitutional.'" 116 S Ct 1774. The actual import of those cases was less clear. After noting in a footnote in *Robinson* that the defendant claimed his arrest for a traffic offense was pretextual and that the officer denied it, the Court said only this: "We think it is sufficient for purposes of our decision that respondent was lawfully arrested for an offense, and that [his placement] in custody following that arrest was not a departure from established police department practice. We leave for another day questions which would arise on facts different from these." 414 US at 221 n 1. In *Scott*, the Court recounted the *government's* position that "[s]ubjective intent alone . . . does not make otherwise lawful conduct illegal or unconstitutional," endorsed this position for purposes of assessing compliance with the statutory re-

Scalia's objections to the "reasonable officer" test were unlikely to sway any careful reader. To begin with, it is not at all clear that the purpose of the test must be "to prevent the police from doing under the guise of enforcing the traffic code what they would like to do for different reasons." Professor LaFave, for one, had argued that "it is the *fact* of the departure from the accepted way of handling such cases which makes the officer's conduct arbitrary, and it is the arbitrariness which in this context constitutes the Fourth Amendment violation."[79] More fundamentally, it is hard to see why even someone opposed to probing for pretext in particular cases should object to objective rules simply on the ground that they are "driven by subjective considerations"; indeed, a strong case can be made that much of Fourth Amendment law is "driven" by concerns about improperly motivated searches and seizures.[80]

At the level of application, police manuals and standard procedures surely could provide—and had provided—far more assistance than Justice Scalia acknowledged in assessing the objective reasonableness of traffic stops; the suggestion that the "reasonable officer" test could not be applied was belied by the experience of the lower courts that had in fact applied it.[81] (Indeed, one of the

quirement that wiretaps minimize the interception of conversations not the focus of the surveillance, and then opined more broadly that "the fact that the officer does not have the state of mind which is hypothecated by the reasons which provide the legal justification for the officer's action does not invalidate the action." 436 US at 138. Given the context of the broad language in *Scott*, even scholars unsympathetic to pretext claims have treated the case as questionable authority for their position. See note 71.

Justice Scalia also cited *United States v Villamonte-Marquez*, 462 US 579 (1983), which upheld the warrantless boarding of a sailboat by customs officers to inspect documents; in a footnote, the Court rejected an argument that the action was unlawful because it was prompted by a tip that a vessel in the vicinity was carrying marijuana. See id at 584 n 3. The rejected claim, however, appeared to be statutory rather than constitutional, see id, and, as in *Scott*, was not truly an allegation of pretext: as the Court pointed out, among the "vital" purposes of shipboard document inspections was "the need to deter or apprehend smugglers" in order to "preven[t] the entry into this country of controlled substances" and other contraband. See id at 591, 593.

[79] LaFave, 1 *Search & Seizure* § 1.4(e) at 120–21 (cited in note 13).

[80] This is precisely the case made by Professor Haddad. See Haddad, 18 U Mich J L Ref at 653–73 (cited in note 71).

[81] See Janet Koven Levit, *Pretextual Traffic Stops: United States v Whren and the Death of Terry v Ohio*, 28 Loyola U Chi L J 145, 178–80 (1996). Despite the gradual spread of the "reasonable officer" test in the lower courts (see note 73), the Tenth Circuit, which had adopted the test in 1988, see *United States v Guzman*, 864 F2d 1512 (10th Cir 1988), abandoned it as "unworkable" in 1995, see *United States v Botero-Ospina*, 71 F3d 783, 786 (10th Cir 1995). The court reached that conclusion largely because it found its own application of the rule "inconsistent" and because the rule had rarely caused the court to "reverse an order denying suppression." Id. As I discuss later (see notes 184–89 and accompanying text), the inconsistencies identified by the Tenth Circuit were the normal, transitional results of

side benefits of the test may have been the encouragement it provided police departments to spell out their standard procedures
more clearly, thereby minimizing litigation over the reasonableness of particular traffic stops, and in the bargain protecting against
improper exercises of discretion.[82]) The business in *Whren* about
"virtual subjectivity" was hard to take seriously: criminal procedure is chock full of rules that call precisely for "speculating about
the hypothetical reaction of a hypothetical constable."[83] And although police practices certainly do vary, why this made them improper predicates for Fourth Amendment restrictions (Justice
Scalia called them "trivialities"[84]) was largely unexplained.[85]

---

refining a new rule case by case; in any event, as the dissent pointed out, the obvious remedy
for inconsistent application was to "clarify the standard rather than abandon it altogether."
Id at 792 n 2 (Seymour dissenting). As for the fact that the test rarely resulted in appellate
reversal of an order denying suppression, this showed the rule was "unworkable" only if
law enforcement officers, prosecutors, and trial judges all were assumed incapable of following it, and if weak protection was thought worse than none.

[82] See, for example, Amsterdam, 58 Minn L Rev at 423–28 (cited in note 70) (discussing
the advantages of constraining police discretion through departmental rules).

[83] See, for example, *Florida v Jimeno*, 500 US 248, 252 (1991) (authorizing police to open
a closed container found while searching a car pursuant to consent if the "consent would
reasonably be understood" to extend to the container); *Illinois v Rodriguez*, 497 US 177,
188–89 (1990) (holding that valid consent may be given by anyone a reasonable officer
would believe exercised "common authority over the premises"); *United States v Sharpe*,
470 US 675 (1985) (holding that an investigative stop may last as long as is reasonable
under all the circumstances); *United States v Leon*, 468 US 897, 919 & n 20 (1984) (holding
that the exclusionary rule does not apply where an officer relies in "objective good faith"
on a search warrant issued by a judge or magistrate); *New York v Quarles*, 467 US 649, 656
(1984) (holding that *Miranda* warnings need not be given before police questioning that,
regardless of its actual motivation, could have been "reasonably prompted by a concern
for the public safety"); *Rhode Island v Innis*, 446 US 291, 301–02 (1980) (holding that "the
definition of interrogation" for purposes of triggering the *Miranda* rule "can extend only
to words or actions on the part of police officers that they *should have known* were reasonably
likely to elicit an incriminating response"); *Terry v Ohio*, 392 US 1, 21–22 (1968) (noting
generally that application of Fourth Amendment requires asking whether "the facts available
to the officer at the moment of the seizure or the search" would " 'warrant a man of
reasonable caution in the belief' that the action taken was appropriate") (quoting *Carroll
v United States*, 267 US 132, 162 (1925)).

[84] *Whren*, 116 S Ct at 1775.

[85] The Court supported this point with "cf" citations to *Gustafson v Florida*, 414 US 260
(1973) and *United States v Caceres*, 440 US 741 (1979). *Gustafson* was a search-incident-to-
arrest case in which the Court noted, in passing, that although local regulations neither
required the defendant's arrest nor set conditions for his body search, these facts were not
"determinative of the constitutional issue." 414 US at 265. *Caceres* "decline[d] to adopt any
rigid rule" requiring the suppression of evidence obtained in violation of IRS regulations
concerning electronic surveillance. 440 US at 755. Neither case suggested that the variable
nature of local police regulations rendered them entirely irrelevant to the reasonableness
of a search or seizure under the Fourth Amendment. On the other hand, *Gustafson* certainly
did provide a particularly striking illustration of the Supreme Court's general lack of interest

None of this is to say that the result in *Whren* was plainly wrong. The "reasonable officer" rule has much to recommend it, but Justice Scalia was probably right to suggest that it would give rise to difficult problems of application. Whether those problems justified the holding in *Whren* is a question I will take up later. The important point for now is not the answer the Supreme Court gave, but how unanimous and unqualified the answer was. The justices were able in *Whren* to resolve a difficult and persistent ambiguity of criminal procedure in a decisive manner that ten or twenty years ago would have been impossible.[86] The Supreme Court's Fourth Amendment jurisprudence has begun to settle down. It is worth asking how this has been accomplished.

III. The New Consensus and the Old "Mess"

Complaints about the disarray of Fourth Amendment law have long been a staple of legal scholarship. It now has been thirty-five years since Roger Dworkin first called Fourth Amendment cases "a mess"[87] and Anthony Amsterdam said this was an understatement.[88] Nearly two decades ago, Silas Wasserstrom and Louis Michael Seidman found "virtual unanimity" that "the Court simply has made a mess of search and seizure law."[89] More recently Akhil Amar has described Fourth Amendment law as "jumble[d]," "contradictory," and—of course—a "mess."[90] As Morgan Cloud

---

in constraining police discretion by compelling, or even encouraging, departmental rule-making. See Amsterdam, 58 Minn L Rev at 416 (cited in note 70).

[86] The only potential limit to the sweep of the holding in *Whren* is the weight the Court placed on the fact that the Fourth Amendment action there was supported by probable cause; possibly a different result might be reached for stops based only on reasonable suspicion. The Court acknowledged that "in principle every Fourth Amendment case, since it turns upon a 'reasonableness' determination, involves a balancing of all relevant factors," but it concluded that "[w]ith rare exceptions not applicable here . . . the result of that balancing is not in doubt where the search or seizure is based upon probable cause." 116 S Ct at 1776; see also note 67. This of course includes almost all lawful stops for traffic violations. See note 13.

[87] Dworkin, 48 Ind L J at 329 (cited in note 60).

[88] See Amsterdam, 58 Minn L Rev at 349 (cited in note 70). Even earlier, Professor LaFave had noted that "[n]o area of the law has more bedeviled the judiciary, from the Justices of the Supreme Court down to the magistrate." Wayne LaFave, *Search and Seizure: "The Course of True Law . . . Has Not . . . Run Smooth,"* 1966 U Ill L F 255.

[89] Silas J. Wasserstrom and Louis Michael Seidman, *The Fourth Amendment as Constitutional Theory*, 77 Georgetown L J 19, 20 (1988).

[90] Akhil Reed Amar, *Fourth Amendment First Principles*, 107 Harv L Rev 757, 758, 761 (1994).

has noted, "[c]ritics of the Supreme Court's contemporary Fourth Amendment jurisprudence regularly complain that the Court's decisions are," among other things, "illogical, inconsistent, . . . and theoretically incoherent."[91]

The harmony the Court displayed in the recent vehicle stop cases may at first suggest that these criticisms are now obsolete. On closer inspection, though, the recent cases show all the inconsistency for which Fourth Amendment law has become famous. Whatever accounts for the Court's broad consensus in these cases, it is not newfound doctrinal coherence.

Start with *Ornelas*, in which the Court held that "as a general matter determinations of reasonable suspicion and probable cause should be reviewed *de novo* on appeal."[92] Despite this holding, the Court instructed the appellate court on remand to give "due weight" to the trial court's finding that the officers' determinations had been reasonable. I will argue later that these two directives can be reconciled in spirit, but as a matter of simple logic it is hard to argue with Justice Scalia's characterization of the Court's opinion as "contradictory."[93]

It is not much easier to square the concluding remarks of *Ornelas* with the Court's reasoning two weeks later in *Whren*. In explaining the "due weight" that reviewing courts should give to the inferences of law enforcement officers and trial judges, the Court in *Ornelas* emphasized that determinations of probable cause and reasonable suspicion must be made "in the light of the distinctive features and events of the community."[94] For example, the Court explained, "what may not amount to reasonable suspicion at a motel located alongside a transcontinental highway at the height of the summer tourist season may rise to that level in December in Milwaukee."[95] In *Whren*, however, the Court rejected not only an examination of the actual motivations underlying a roadside stop, but also any inquiry whether reasonable police practices called for the stop. It did so in part because "police enforcement practices,

---

[91] Morgan Cloud, *Pragmatism, Positivism, and Principles in Fourth Amendment Theory*, 41 UCLA L Rev 199, 204 (1993).

[92] 116 S Ct at 1663.

[93] Id at 1666 (Scalia dissenting).

[94] 116 US at 1663.

[95] Id.

even if they could be practicably assessed by a judge, vary from place to place and from time to time," and the Court could not "accept that the search and seizure protections of the Fourth Amendment are so variable."[96]

Particularly given that *Ornelas* and *Whren* were decided only days apart, it seems fair to ask why it is "more problematic to determine whether a police officer acted according to local practices in making a traffic stop than to determine whether an investigative stop is rooted in reasonable suspicion."[97] This question may well have answers. The local circumstances deemed significant by the Court in *Ornelas* were factual; they concerned matters such as geography, climate, and population patterns.[98] It is at least arguable that ignoring *this* sort of local variation in assessing reasonableness would press the limits of logic, whereas variations in local *laws* can more sensibly be ignored, and indeed *should* be ignored, in determining whether the Fourth Amendment prohibits a particular search or seizure as "unreasonable."[99]

But this is by no means obvious. If "the basic purpose" of the Fourth Amendment "is to safeguard the privacy and security of individuals against arbitrary invasions by governmental officials,"[100] a great deal can be said, and has been said, in favor of the view that

---

[96] 116 S Ct at 1775.

[97] Levit, 28 Loyola U Chi L J at 180 (cited in note 81).

[98] By way of illustration, the majority opinion in *Ornelas* noted that Milwaukee:

is unlikely to have been an overnight stop selected at the last minute by a traveler coming from California to points east. The 85-mile width of Lake Michigan blocks any further eastward progress. And while the city's salubrious summer climate and seasonal attractions bring many tourists at that time of year, the same is not true in December. Milwaukee's average daily high temperature in that month is 31 degrees and its average daily low is 17 degrees; the percentage of possible sunshine is only 38 percent. It is a reasonable inference that a Californian stopping Milwaukee in December is either there to transact business or to visit family or friends.

Ornelas, 116 US at 1663.

[99] See *California v Greenwood*, 486 US 35, 43 (1988) ("We have never intimated . . . that whether or not a search is reasonable within the meaning of the Fourth Amendment depends on the law of the particular State in which the search occurs."). There is a sense, of course, in which "the meaning of the Fourth Amendment" inevitably does depend on local laws—not local laws explicitly addressing police procedure, but local laws defining what conduct is criminal, and thereby determining, albeit indirectly, what sets of circumstances constitute "probable cause" and "reasonable suspicion." See William J. Stuntz, *Substance, Procedure, and the Civil-Criminal Line*, 7 J Contemp L Issues 1 (1996). This point received no attention in *Whren*.

[100] *Camara v Municipal Court*, 387 US 523, 528 (1967). See also notes 69–70 and accompanying text.

"reasonable" searches and seizures must be carried out pursuant to standardized procedures—and that searches and seizures that affirmatively violate established procedures are a fortiori unconstitutional.[101] The Supreme Court has never shown great enthusiasm for this view,[102] but neither has the Court rejected it across the board.[103] My point at present is not that local laws must play as large a role as other local circumstances in Fourth Amendment doctrine. It is rather that the case for drawing a sharp distinction here is far from plain, and that, without further explanation, the Court's instructions at the conclusion of *Ornelas* sit uncomfortably with the Court's insistence in *Whren* that Fourth Amendment protections should not "vary from place to place and from time to time."

Nor were these the only incongruities created by *Ornelas*. Three days after deciding *Whren*, the Court held unanimously in *Koon v United States*[104]—the federal criminal case arising out of the infamous beating of Rodney King—that a trial court's decision to depart from the federal sentencing guidelines should be reviewed not de novo but merely for "abuse of discretion."[105] Part of the reason was that trial courts need "flexibility to resolve questions involving 'multifarious, fleeting, special, narrow facts that utterly resist generalization,'" that departure decisions involve "'the consideration of unique factors that are "little susceptible . . . of useful generalization,"'" and that, "as a consequence, *de novo* review is 'unlikely to establish clear guidelines for lower courts.'"[106] All of this, of course, could be said equally well of determinations of probable

---

[101] See, for example, Kenneth Culp Davis, *Discretionary Justice: A Preliminary Inquiry* 80–96 (Louisiana State, 1969); LaFave, 1 *Search and Seizure* § 1.4(e) at 124–25 (cited in note 13); Amsterdam, 58 Minn L Rev at 409–39 (cited in note 70); LaFave, 1974 S Ct Rev at 161 (cited in note 60); Carl McGowan, *Rule-Making and the Police*, 70 Mich L Rev 659 (1972).

[102] See note 85.

[103] See, for example, *Illinois v Lafayette*, 462 US 640, 647 (1983) (upholding searches of arrested suspect pursuant to "standardized inventory procedures" before incarceration); *South Dakota v Opperman*, 428 US 364, 372 (1976) (approving inventory searches of lawfully seized automobiles "pursuant to standard police procedures").

[104] 116 S Ct 2035 (1996).

[105] Id at 2047. Although all nine justices agreed on the proper standard of review, the Court split on the proper application of that standard to the facts before it. Steven Clymer pointed out to me the tension between *Koon* and *Ornelas*.

[106] Id (quoting *Cooter & Gell v Hartmarx Corp.*, 496 US 384, 404–05 (1990) (in turn quoting *Pierce v Underwood*, 487 US 552, 561–62 (1988))).

cause and reasonable suspicion. Justice Scalia had pointed out as much in his *Ornelas* dissent, and the majority in that case had all but conceded the point. But none of the opinions in *Koon* so much as mentioned *Ornelas*.[107]

Now consider *Robinette*. The crux of the Court's reasons for rejecting a "first-tell-then-ask rule"[108] was its disavowal of *"per se* rule[s]" in applying the Fourth Amendment.[109] No member of the Court found fault with the Ohio Supreme Court's premise that "[m]ost people believe that they are validly in a police officer's custody as long as the officer continues to interrogate them."[110] The majority left that claim unchallenged; Justice Ginsburg, concurring separately, quoted it with evident approval;[111] and Justice Stevens, in dissent, called it "surely correct."[112] The basis for the holding in *Robinette*—a holding that even Justices Ginsburg and Stevens expressly endorsed—was the Court's wholesale rejection of any fixed, categorical approach to determining whether a search or seizure is "unreasonable" within the meaning of the Fourth Amendment.

"Reasonableness," Chief Justice Rehnquist explained for the majority, depends upon "the totality of the circumstances," and "[i]n applying this test we have consistently eschewed bright-line rules, instead emphasizing the fact-specific nature of the reasonableness inquiry."[113] Eschewing bright-line rules is indeed a well established principle of Fourth Amendment jurisprudence, and the Chief Justice had no difficulty collecting examples of its application.[114] Repetition, though, is not the same thing as constancy, par-

---

[107] In other contexts, the Supreme Court sometimes has reasoned that a more probing standard of review should be applied to the application of rules that protect important constitutional values. See, for example, *Bose Corp. v Consumers Union*, 466 US 485, 501–02 (1984). This might seem a promising basis for distinguishing *Ornelas*, which involved constitutional determinations, from *Koon*, which did not. But the opinions in *Ornelas* and *Koon* paid no attention to this factor, and the "due weight" that *Ornelas* instructed reviewing courts to give to the inferences of trial judges and law enforcement officers is difficult to reconcile with the exercise of "independent judgment" required by decisions like *Bose Corp*.

[108] *Robinette*, 117 S Ct at 422 (Ginsburg concurring).

[109] Id at 421.

[110] 653 NE2d at 698.

[111] 117 S Ct at 422 (Ginsburg concurring).

[112] Id at 425 (Stevens dissenting).

[113] Id at 421.

[114] See id (citing *Florida v Bostick*, 501 US 429 (1991) (rejecting flat prohibition of suspicionless questioning of passengers on board intercity buses); *Michigan v Chestnut*, 486 US

ticularly in Fourth Amendment law, and the suggestion that the Court has "consistently" avoided bright-line rules for searches and seizures borders on the comic.

Anyone with the vaguest awareness of Fourth Amendment law knows it is full of bright-line rules. Homes may not be entered without a warrant except in an emergency,[115] cars may be searched without a warrant if there is probable cause,[116] warrantless arrests for felonies are permissible in public based on probable cause,[117] an arrested suspect may be searched without a warrant,[118] if a suspect is arrested in a car the interior of the car is automatically subject to search[119]—this hardly begins to exhaust the list. And it does not include two bright-line rules the Court invoked in *Robinette* itself—only a paragraph before proclaiming that reasonableness is simply a matter of "the totality of the circumstances."

The first of these rules led the Court to conclude there was "no question that, in light of the admitted probable cause to stop Robinette for speeding, [the officer] was objectively justified in asking Robinette to get out of the car."[120] The basis for this judgment was *Pennsylvania v Mimms*,[121] in which the Court had held "that once a motor vehicle has been lawfully detained for a traffic violation, the police officers may order the driver to get out of the vehicle without violating the Fourth Amendment's prohibition of unreasonable searches and seizures."[122] *Mimms*, of course, was the ruling the Court extended in *Maryland v Wilson* to apply to passen-

---

567 (1988) (rejecting "bright-line" rule that any investigatory pursuit amounts to a seizure); *Florida v Royer*, 460 US 491 (1983) (declining to rule that "drug courier profile" alone cannot provide basis for investigatory stop); *Schneckloth v Bustamonte*, 412 US 218 (1973) (rejecting rule that valid consent to search can be given only by a suspect who knows that he or she has the right to refuse consent).

The Chief Justice could also have cited, for example, *United States v Sharpe*, 470 US 675 (1985) (refusing to create *per se* rule regarding how long an investigative detention justified only by reasonable suspicion may last). Were *Robinette* decided today, he could add *Richards v Wisconsin*, 117 S Ct 1416 (1997). See note 148.

[115] *Payton v New York*, 445 US 573 (1980).

[116] See, for example, *Pennsylvania v Labron*, 116 S Ct 2485 (1996); *California v Acevedo*, 500 US 565 (1991).

[117] See *United States v Watson*, 423 US 411 (1976).

[118] See *United States v Robinson*, 414 US 218 (1973).

[119] See *New York v Belton*, 453 US 454 (1981).

[120] 117 S Ct at 421.

[121] 434 US 106 (1977).

[122] Id at 111 n 6.

gers as well as the driver. Writing for the Court in *Wilson*, how did Chief Justice Rehnquist reconcile *Robinette* with the reaffirmation and expansion of *Mimms*? By sheer fiat. Certainly, the Chief Justice acknowledged, "we typically avoid *per se* rules concerning searches and seizures," but that "does not mean that we have always done so; *Mimms* itself drew a bright line, and we believe the principles that underlay that decision apply to passengers as well."[123] So much for consistent eschewal.

The second bright-line rule invoked by the Court in *Robinette* was less blatant than the *Mimms* rule, but it ultimately was no more consistent with the Court's purported commitment to open-ended assessments of reasonableness. Despite strong reason to believe that Robinette was not actually stopped to enforce the speed limit,[124] the Court had no trouble concluding that the fact that Robinette was speeding made his initial stop lawful. The Court reached that conclusion, of course, based on its ruling five months earlier in *Whren* that the subjective intentions of an officer making an objectively justifiable traffic stop are irrelevant. Even granting the wisdom of *Whren*, the decision on its face affirmatively *prohibits* an analysis of reasonableness of a search or seizure based on "all the circumstances surrounding the encounter."[125] It does so by cordoning off an entire category of "circumstances" that might ordinarily be thought pertinent to the reasonableness of an officer's actions, and making them irrelevant as a matter of law.[126]

One can try to put a good face on this by recasting "the totality of the circumstances" as "the totality of objective circumstances." The Court in *Robinette* did essentially that, explaining that "[r]easonableness . . . is measured in *objective* terms by examining the totality of the circumstances."[127] But this does not wash. Once we allow bright lines to circumscribe the factors that can be taken into account in determining reasonableness, it becomes harder to

---

[123] 117 S Ct at 885 n 1. There was no sign in *Maryland v Wilson* that the Court was simply bowing to precedent, no sign that the Court felt bound by or in any way disagreed with its earlier decision in *Mimms*.

[124] See note 44.

[125] *Florida v Bostick*, 501 US 429, 439 (1991).

[126] Actually, the decision went further than that, declaring that "as a general matter, the decision to stop an automobile is reasonable where the police have probable cause to believe that a traffic violation has occurred." 116 S Ct at 1772. See also note 86.

[127] 117 S Ct at 421.

explain why we should not allow bright lines to mark off certain prohibited police behavior. It will no longer do to say simply that per se rules are "consistently eschewed," in "recognition of the 'endless variations in the facts and circumstances' implicating the Fourth Amendment."[128] Certain per se rules, including the major one set forth in *Whren* and the more minor one extended in *Wilson*, are found desirable; certain facts and circumstances are addressed in advance. There may be good grounds for distinguishing between the bright-line rules embraced in *Whren* and *Wilson* and the one rejected in *Robinette*, but the Court in *Robinette* did not even acknowledge the need to draw the distinction.

IV. Behind the New Consensus

What made the recent vehicle stop cases straightforward for the Court plainly was not the doctrinal inevitability of the results. What then explains the striking lack of discord? Can any common theme explain the Court's ease in deciding these cases? Setting *Ornelas* aside for the moment, what unites the other three cases is obvious. *Whren*, *Robinette*, and *Wilson* all gave significant latitude to law enforcement. In *Robinette* and *Wilson* this was the Court's stated intent: the Court explained in *Robinette* that it would be "unrealistic to require police officers to always inform detainees that they are free to go before a consent to search may be deemed voluntary,"[129] and, in *Wilson*, the Court focused heavily on the "weighty interest in officer safety."[130] And although there was no similar reference to law enforcement exigencies in *Whren*,[131] the Court's decision in that case obviously gave a large boost to law enforcement by allowing officers to use traffic violations to justify investigatory stops for any purpose whatsoever. Because almost everyone violates traffic rules sometimes, this means that the police, if they are patient, can eventually pull over anyone they are inter-

---

[128] Id (quoting *Florida v Royer*, 460 US 491, 506 (1983)).

[129] 117 S Ct at 421.

[130] 117 S Ct at 885. See also id at 886.

[131] The practical concerns articulated in *Whren* had to do with justiciability, not policing. See *Whren*, 116 S Ct at 1775–77. See also *Wilson*, 117 S Ct at 890 (Kennedy dissenting) (justifying *Whren* on the ground that "[w]e could discern no other, workable rule").

ested in questioning; this is why traffic enforcement has been called "the general warrant of the twentieth century."[132] After *Robinette* and *Wilson* they can also order all the occupants out and question them without ever telling them they are free to leave.[133]

The consequences for everyday police practices are substantial. Even before *Robinette* and *Wilson*, "savvy police administrators" were "rediscover[ing] the value of traffic enforcement" as "an integral part of both criminal interdiction and community policing."[134] In Grand Prairie, Texas, for example, "traffic enforcement personnel" made 37% of all arrests in 1994, and only "slightly more than half the arrests made by the traffic officers were made for traffic-related offenses."[135] Nationwide, the Drug Enforcement Administration estimates that 40% of all drug arrests begin with a traffic stop.[136]

The Court in *Whren* plainly was not blind to the practical implications of the case for law enforcement. Part of the defendants' argument in *Whren* was precisely that driving today "is so heavily and minutely regulated that total compliance with traffic and safety rules is nearly impossible," and that "a police officer will almost invariably be able to catch any given motorist in a technical viola-

---

[132] Salken, 62 Temple L Rev at 221 (cited in note 69). The trial judge in *Maryland v Wilson*, for example, noted that in his opinion "no one goes 55 m.p.h" on the stretch of Interstate 95 where the car in that case was pulled over for traveling 64 m.p.h. in a 55 m.p.h. zone. *State v Wilson*, No. 94 CR 01201 (Md Cir Ct Jan 10, 1995), aff'd, 664 A2d 1 (Md Ct Spec App 1995), rev'd, 117 S Ct 882 (1997). Similarly, statisticians observing cars on the New Jersey Turnpike in 1993 concluded that "virtually everyone on the Turnpike was driving faster than the speed limit." Joseph B. Kadane and Norma Terrin, *Missing Data in the Forensic Context* 3 (on file with author).

[133] Justice Kennedy drew attention to the combined effects of *Whren* and *Wilson* in his dissent from the latter ruling: "The practical effect of our ruling in *Whren*, of course, is to allow the police to stop vehicles in almost countless circumstances. When *Whren* is coupled with today's holding, the Court puts tens of millions of passengers at risk of arbitrary control by the police." *Wilson*, 117 S Ct at 890 (Kennedy dissenting).

[134] Earl M. Sweeney, *Traffic Enforcement: New Uses for an Old Tool*, Police Chief 45 (July 1996). Sweeney directs the New Hampshire Police Standards and Training Council. His article stressed that "an alert police officer who 'looks beyond the traffic ticket' and uses the motor vehicle stop to 'sniff out' possible criminal behavior may be our most effective tool for interdicting criminals," and pointed out that "[m]any cities that are plagued by gang activity, illegal guns, open-air drug markets and drive-by shootings have discovered that saturating an area with traffic patrol shuts down these illegal operations." Id.

[135] Garrett Morford, J. Michael Sheehan, Jr., and Jack Stuster, *Traffic Enforcement's Role in the War on Crime*, Police Chief 48 (July 1996).

[136] Highway Safety Comm., Int'l Ass'n of Chiefs of Police, *Top 10 Lies in Traffic Enforcement*, Police Chief 30 (July 1997).

tion."[137] After describing this contention, Justice Scalia made no effort to dispute it, or even to cast it into doubt. Much as in *Robinette*, the Court appeared to concede the defendants' empirical claim, at least for the sake of argument, but treated the claim as irrelevant in applying the Fourth Amendment.

At first glance, *Ornelas* may appear to break this pattern of progovernment decisions. Ornelas and his co-defendant won in the Supreme Court, and the case was widely reported as a victory for criminal defendants.[138] But the matter is not so simple. It is revealing that the government in *Ornelas* joined the defendants in requesting reversal.[139] Moreover, the opinion on remand consisted of a single paragraph reaffirming the district court's findings and upholding the search.[140] The fact is, of course, that de novo review helps whichever side lost below, and government appeals of suppression orders are far from uncommon. And although rulings on suppression motions are challenged in appellate courts more often by the defense than by the prosecution, there are reasons to believe that *Ornelas* will wind up helping the government more than criminal defendants.

The first of these is the contradiction pointed out in dissent by Justice Scalia. Immediately after holding that determinations of probable cause and reasonable suspicion should generally receive de novo review, the Court in *Ornelas* "hasten[ed] to point out" that appellate courts "should take care . . . to give due weight to the inferences drawn . . . by resident judges and local law enforcement officers." This instruction is not simply inconsistent with true de novo review; it is inconsistent in a way that gives the prosecution a leg up. A deferential standard of review like "clear error,"

---

[137] 116 S Ct at 1773.

[138] See, for example, Joan Biskupic, *Greater 4th Amendment Scrutiny Ordered*, Wash Post A12 (May 29, 1996) (noting the case "enhances the ability of defendants to challenge a conviction before an appeals court"); David G. Savage, *Supreme Court Orders Review of Police Search*, LA Times A16 (May 29, 1996) (describing the decision as "a rare victory for convicted drug dealers and other criminals"). But see Linda Greenhouse, *Supreme Court Roundup*, NY Times A14 (May 29, 1996) (pointing out that "the standard of appellate review is an issue that can cut in either direction").

[139] Because the United States agreed with the petitioners that determinations of probable cause and reasonable suspicion should be reviewed de novo, the Supreme Court was forced to appoint an amicus curiae to defend the judgment below. See *Ornelas*, 116 S Ct at 1661 n 4.

[140] *United States v Ornelas*, 93 F3d 1450, 1996 WL 508569 (7th Cir 1996).

the standard initially applied by the court of appeals in *Ornelas*, gives weight to the judgments of the trial court, but not to those of the officers involved in the case. By rejecting a "clear error" standard in favor of a "de novo with due weight" standard, the Court in effect declared that police officers should receive as much deference as trial judges. Taken as a whole, then, *Ornelas* may make appellate review of suppression rulings appreciably more hospitable to law enforcement.

Given the practicalities of criminal adjudication, moreover, *Ornelas* would likely help the prosecution more than the defense even without the language at the end about giving "due weight." For a range of familiar reasons, federal judges on average are more apt to sympathize with and to believe law enforcement witnesses than criminal defendants.[141] Far more often than not, federal judges find the inferences drawn and actions taken by law enforcement officers reasonable, and deny suppression motions challenging those inferences and actions. Decisions in the other direction are departures from the norm. Strictly as a statistical matter, therefore, one might expect it to be less likely for two out of three appellate judges to find a Fourth Amendment violation than for a single trial judge to do so.

None of this is spelled out in *Ornelas*, and there is no reason to believe it was the principal focus of the Court's concern. But it cannot entirely have escaped the Court's awareness that a "clear error" standard threatened to protect aberrational rulings suppressing key evidence in criminal cases. This is particularly so given the timing of the decision. Two months before *Ornelas* was argued, District Judge Harold Baer drew nationwide criticism for finding that police in Washington Heights lacked reasonable suspicion to stop a car that turned out to carry eighty pounds of cocaine and heroin.[142] Judge Baer reversed himself the week after the Court

---

[141] See, for example, Paul Brest, *Who Decides?* 88 S Cal L Rev 661 (1985) (discussing the "demography of the judiciary"); William J. Stuntz, *Warrants and Fourth Amendment Remedies*, 77 Va L Rev 881, 912–13 (1991) (suggesting that "the character of the claimant in an exclusionary rule proceeding tends to exacerbate the bias that is naturally present in all after-the-fact proceedings").

[142] See *United States v Bayless*, 913 F Supp 232, vacated, 921 F Supp 211 (SDNY 1996); Don Van Natta, Jr., *Judge Finds Wit Tested by Criticism*, NY Times B1 (Feb 7, 1996). The police claimed their suspicions had been aroused when, among other things, four men threw a duffel bag in the trunk of the car and then, after noticing police officers watching them, ran away. 913 F Supp at 234–35. Judge Baer called the police testimony "at best suspect," id at 239, and commented, in the most controversial part of his ruling, that given the well-

heard argument in *Ornelas*[143]—but not before 150 members of the House of Representatives had petitioned President Clinton to request the judge's resignation,[144] and the White House had signaled receptivity.[145] The Court's consideration of *Ornelas* thus was vividly informed by the prospect of errant district judges sabotaging both the drug war and judicial independence by finding that the police lacked probable cause or reasonable suspicion.

For all these reasons, *Ornelas* is consistent with the pro-government pattern evident in *Whren, Robinette,* and *Wilson.*[146] Together, these decisions suggest that Fourth Amendment cases may have become easier for the Court because the justices now share a set of underlying understandings that are markedly more favorable to law enforcement than to criminal suspects, particularly those suspected of trafficking in narcotics.[147] The traffic stop cases are not

---

publicized police corruption in the neighborhood, "had the men not run when the cops began to stare at them, it would have been unusual," id at 242.

[143] See *United States v Bayless*, 921 F Supp 211 (SDNY 1996). Judge Baer based his second ruling on new evidence bolstering the credibility of the police officers involved in the stop and undermining the credibility of the defendant. Id at 213–16. He also lamented that "the hyperbole (dicta) in my initial decision not only obscured the true focus of my analysis, but regretfully may have demeaned the law-abiding men and women who make Washington Heights their home and the vast majority of the dedicated men and women in blue who patrol the streets of our great City." Id at 217. The following month Judge Baer denied a defense motion for his recusal, but recused himself anyway to avoid "several unnecessary and otherwise avoidable problems and attendant delay." See *United States v Bayless*, 926 F Supp 405 (SDNY 1996).

[144] See John M. Goshko, *Accusations of Coddling Criminals Aimed at Two Judges in New York*, Wash Post A3 (Mar 1, 1996). Nor was the Senate silent. See, for example, 142 Cong Rec S539 (daily ed Jan 26, 1996) (remarks of Sen. Dole); id at S1162 (daily ed Feb 9, 1996) (remarks of Sen. Hatch); Van Natta, NY Times at B1 (reporting that Senator Moynihan, who had recommended Baer's appointment to the federal bench, now expressed regret for the endorsement).

[145] See Alison Mitchell, *Clinton Pressing Judge to Relent*, Wash Post A1 (Mar 22, 1996).

[146] *Ornelas* is also consistent with Carol Steiker's recent argument that the Burger and Rehnquist Courts have retreated from the Warren Court's approach to constitutional criminal procedure less by explicitly loosening the restrictions on police conduct than by limiting the extent to which violations of those restrictions result in the exclusion of evidence or reversals of convictions. See Carol S. Steiker, *Counter-Revolution in Constitutional Criminal Procedure? Two Audiences, Two Answers*, 94 Mich L Rev 2466 (1996). *Whren, Robinette,* and *Wilson* fit Professor Steiker's thesis less well, but then she acknowledges that "the Court's Fourth Amendment police-conduct norms . . . have changed much more over the past twenty-five years than have its Fifth or Sixth Amendment norms." Id at 2503.

[147] Of course, the defendants in *Ornelas, Whren,* and *Robinette* were not just suspects: they had been convicted of narcotics offenses. Jerry Wilson had not been convicted, but that was only because the trial court suppressed the crack cocaine he dropped when stepping out of the car. The fact that the defendants in these cases were for all practical purposes proven criminals obviously undercut the visceral appeal of their Fourth Amendment claims; this is a familiar consequence of enforcing the Fourth Amendment through the exclusion of evidence in criminal prosecutions. See, for example, Amar, 107 Harv L Rev at 796, 799

the only evidence of this phenomenon. In seven of the ten Fourth Amendment cases decided in the last three terms, the Court ruled for the government.[148] The only exceptions were *Ornelas, Chandler v Miller,*[149] and *Wilson v Arkansas.*[150] *Chandler* was not a criminal case; it concerned the constitutionality of a Georgia statute imposing drug tests on candidates for a wide range of executive, legislative, and judicial offices[151]—a class of people with whom the Court could be expected to empathize. *Wilson v Arkansas was* a criminal case, but even more clearly than *Ornelas,* it was a government victory in all but name. The reasons for this are worth a brief detour, because *Wilson v Arkansas* both presaged the recent traffic stop cases and helps to explain them.

Sharlene Wilson challenged her narcotics convictions in part on the ground that much of the evidence against her had been found in a search of her home, and that the officers conducting the search, although armed with a warrant, had failed to knock and to announce their presence before entering. The Arkansas Supreme Court affirmed, finding "no authority for Ms. Wilson's theory that the knock and announce principle is required by the Fourth Amendment."[152] In a unanimous opinion by Justice

---

(cited in note 90); Stuntz, 77 Va L Rev at 912–13 (cited in note 141); John Kaplan, *The Limits of the Exclusionary Rule,* 26 Stan L Rev 1027, 1036–39 (1974). But the exclusionary rule was not the entire explanation for the Court's pronounced sympathy for law enforcement in the traffic stop cases. The opinions in those cases make clear that the justices did not simply have more sympathy for law enforcement than for the particular defendants before the Court; they had more sympathy for law enforcement than for criminal suspects in general.

[148] In addition to *Whren, Robinette,* and *Wilson,* see *Richards v Wisconsin,* 117 S Ct 1416 (1997); *Pennsylvania v Labron,* 116 S Ct 2485 (1996); *Vernonia School District 47J v Acton,* 115 S Ct 2386 (1995); *Arizona v Evans,* 115 S Ct 1185 (1995). *Richards* rejected a "blanket" exception in felony drug cases to the "knock and announce" principle set forth in *Wilson v Arkansas,* 115 S Ct 1914 (1995), but held that under the circumstances before the Court the failure to knock and announce was reasonable. *Labron* reaffirmed the per se rule that automobiles may be searched without a warrant whenever there is probable cause to believe that contraband, criminal proceeds, or evidence will be found. For brief descriptions of *Acton* and *Evans,* see note 63.

[149] 117 S Ct 1295 (1997).

[150] 115 S Ct 1914 (1995).

[151] The state offices covered by the law were "the Governor, Lieutenant Governor, Secretary of State, Attorney General, State School Superintendent, Commissioner of Insurance, Commissioner of Agriculture, Commissioner of Labor, Justices of the Supreme Court, Judges of the Court of Appeals, judges of the superior courts, district attorneys, members of the General Assembly, and members of the Public Service Commission." Ga Code Ann § 21-2-140(a)(4) (1987), quoted in *Chandler,* 117 S Ct at 1299.

[152] *Wilson v Arkansas,* 878 SW2d 755, 758 (1994), rev'd, 115 S Ct 1914 (1995).

Thomas, the Supreme Court reversed and remanded, holding that the traditional common law rule requiring officers to knock and announce "forms part of the reasonableness inquiry."[153]

But not too stringent a part: the Court held only that "*in some circumstances* an officer's unannounced entry into a home might be unreasonable under the Fourth Amendment."[154] Justice Thomas explained that "[t]he Fourth Amendment's flexible requirement of reasonableness should not be read to mandate a rigid rule," and that "although a search or seizure of a dwelling *might* be constitutionally defective if police officers enter without prior announcement, law enforcement interests may also establish the reasonableness of an unannounced entry."[155] In particular, Justice Thomas noted with approval that English and American courts had upheld unannounced entry where there was "a threat of physical violence," where an arrested suspect escaped and fled into his house, or where officers had "reason to believe that evidence would likely be destroyed if advance warning were given."[156] The Court remanded for a determination whether such considerations provided "the necessary justification for the unannounced entry in this case."[157]

That amounted to little more than a formality. Affidavits and testimony presented to the trial court indicated that Wilson's housemate had convictions for arson and firebombing, and that Wilson herself had waved a semiautomatic pistol in the face of an informant, "threatening to kill her if she turned out to be working for the police."[158] In addition, the police argued plausibly that announcing their presence would have given Wilson and her housemate an opportunity to dispose of some or all of the narcotics evidence the police had hoped to find.[159] "These considerations," Justice Thomas noted, "may well" have justified the decision by the police to refrain from knocking.[160] No one who read the

---

[153] 115 US at 1915.

[154] Id at 1918 (emphasis added).

[155] Id at 1918–19 (emphasis added).

[156] Id.

[157] Id at 1919.

[158] Id at 1915.

[159] See id at 1919.

[160] Id.

Court's decision could seriously expect it to benefit Sharlene Wilson.[161]

Whom then did it benefit? What did *Wilson v Arkansas* accomplish? Not a meaningful expansion of Fourth Amendment protections. As in *Ornelas*, it is worth noticing the position taken by the United States. Arguing as *amicus curiae* in support of Arkansas, the Solicitor General's office asked the Court to hold "that the manner of entry in executing a search warrant is a component of the reasonableness analysis under the Fourth Amendment and that knock and announce is a component of that analysis"—precisely what the Court later held.[162] What the Court held, essentially, is that a "no knock" search is "unreasonable" under the Fourth Amendment when it is unreasonable not to knock. This is hardly a resounding blow for civil liberties.[163]

The greatest significance of *Wilson v Arkansas*, however, may lie not in its holding but in its reasoning. To support the Court's

---

[161] In fact, the justification for failing to knock was never even litigated on remand, because the one-year sentence Wilson received on the count of conviction vacated by the Supreme Court ran concurrent with longer sentences imposed on counts unaffected by the legality of the search. Telephone Interview with John Wesley Hall, counsel for Sharlene Wilson (Sept 12, 1996); Telephone Interview with Kent Holt, Assistant Attorney General, State of Arkansas (Apr 18, 1997).

[162] Official Transcript, 1995 WL 243487, at *43 (argument of Michael R. Dreeben, Assistant to the Solicitor General). The United States suggested that a remand was unnecessary because the evidence before the trial court clearly established that dispensing with knock and announce was reasonable in this case. See id at *44.

[163] It could of course assist criminal defendants and constitutional tort plaintiffs in jurisdictions that previously thought that even an unreasonable failure to knock before entering could not violate the Fourth Amendment, but Arkansas itself may not have been such a jurisdiction. The Arkansas Supreme Court described Wilson's argument as asserting, based solely on *Miller v United States*, 357 US 301 (1958), "that the Fourth Amendment requires officers to knock and announce prior to entering the residence." The court noted, correctly, that *Miller* was a statutory case, involving 18 USC § 3109, which specifies when federal officers are allowed to break open doors, but has no application to state officers. The court further opined that there was "no authority for Ms. Wilson's theory that the knock and announce principle is required by the Fourth Amendment," but it did not explain what it meant by "the knock and announce principle." Perhaps the Arkansas court meant to say what Justice Thomas took it to say: that a failure to knock, no matter how unreasonable, could never render a search unconstitutional. Just as likely, however, the court meant simply to reject a flat rule requiring prior announcement in all circumstances. Compare *Dodson v State*, 626 SW2d 624, 628 (Ark App) (holding that "[a]lthough the mere failure of police to announce their authority and purpose does not per se violate the constitution, it may influence whether the subsequent entry to arrest or search is constitutionally reasonable"); *United States v Nolan*, 718 F2d 589, 601–02 (3d Cir 1983) (suggesting that the Fourth Amendment does not impose "a knock and announce requirement with precise and narrowly defined exceptions," but that "a failure by police to knock and announce could, depending on the circumstances, violate the more general Fourth Amendment reasonableness requirement").

judgment that "the reasonableness of a search of a dwelling may depend in part on whether law enforcement officers announced their presence and authority prior to entering,"[164] Justice Thomas reviewed common law decisions dating from the early seventeenth century.[165] The purpose of this inquiry, he explained, was to determine whether "the Framers of the Fourth Amendment thought that the method of an officer's entry into a dwelling was among the factors to be considered in assessing the reasonableness of a search or seizure";[166] he concluded that they did. Perhaps the most noteworthy fact about *Wilson v Arkansas* is that no justice objected to the suggestion that in assessing whether a search or seizure is "unreasonable," the Court should focus exclusively, or at least principally, on those factors deemed important at the time of the adoption of the Fourth Amendment.

This has broad consequence. Although the constitutional prohibition of "unreasonable" searches and seizures may be understood merely as shorthand for a bar against specific practices feared by the drafters,[167] the Fourth Amendment can also be viewed, and has more often been viewed, as banning searches and seizures that are "unreasonable" in light of "all the circumstances"—including circumstances that have changed since the adoption of the Bill of Rights.[168] The difference is important, because many things have

---

[164] 115 S Ct at 1916.

[165] See id at 1916–19.

[166] Id at 1918.

[167] See, for example, *Minnesota v Dickerson*, 508 US 366, 380 (1993) (suggesting that the Fourth Amendment aims "to preserve that degree of respect for privacy of persons and the inviolability of their property that existed when the provision was adopted").

[168] Indeed, as Peter Arenella has observed, the Supreme Court has seldom turned to the "Framers' intent" to resolve any of the central questions of Fourth Amendment jurisprudence: "Instead, the Court's fundamental interpretative strategy is to identify and balance the competing values implicated by this restraint on governmental power." Peter Arenella, *Fourth Amendment*, in Leonard Levy, Kenneth Karst, and Dennis Mahoney, eds, 2 *Encyclopedia of the American Constitution* 223 (Prentice-Hall, 1987). See also, for example, *Tennessee v Garner*, 471 US 1 (1985) (concluding that "sweeping change in the legal and technological context" renders the common law rule allowing deadly force against all fleeing felons no longer consistent with the Fourth Amendment); *Katz v United States*, 389 US 347, 352 (1967) (reasoning that the Fourth Amendment must be read in light of "the vital role that the public telephone has come to play in private communication"); Amsterdam, 58 Minn L Rev at 399 (cited in note 70) (calling implausible the supposition that the framers of the Fourth Amendment "meant to preserve to their posterity by guarantees of liberty written with the broadest latitude nothing more than hedges against the recurrence of particular forms of evil suffered at the hands of a monarch beyond the seas").

Even those who have urged paying more attention to the intent underlying the Fourth Amendment generally have not suggested that "reasonableness" should depend only on

changed radically. In particular, we now have urban police forces that are professional and quasi-military, and inner cities that typically are impoverished and racially segregated.[169] These developments have suggested to some that the reasonableness of a search or seizure today may depend heavily on factors not widely thought important in the eighteenth century, such as any indications that the action was motivated by the suspect's race, or the extent to which, regardless of motivation, the action unnecessarily widens social divides.[170]

Wilson v Arkansas suggested that all this may be irrelevant under the Fourth Amendment. And much of what *Wilson v Arkansas* suggested, *Whren* made explicit. Part of the defendants' argument in *Whren* was that pretextual traffic stops are used disproportionately against black suspects; Whren and his co-defendant had themselves aroused suspicion, they suggested, largely because they were two young black men in a new sports utility vehicle.[171] Justice Scalia's answer for the Court was short and simple: "the constitutional basis for objecting to intentionally discriminatory application of laws is the Equal Protection Clause, not the Fourth Amendment."[172]

I will suggest later that requiring all claims of racial unfairness to be brought under the Equal Protection Clause is in fact unwise,[173] but for now the important point is that this requirement heavily burdens those who raise such claims. The Supreme Court has construed the Equal Protection Clause to permit almost any government action that avoids explicit discrimination, unless it can

those factors thought important in the eighteenth century. See, for example, Amar, 107 Harv L Rev at 800–11, 818 (cited in note 90) (arguing that the history and text of the Fourth Amendment call for a "broad and powerful" inquiry into the reasonableness of searches and seizures, including consideration of issues of race, class, and gender). In the terms made familiar by Ronald Dworkin, the Fourth Amendment has commonly been understood to embody a "concept," not a "conception." Ronald Dworkin, *Taking Rights Seriously* 134–37 (Harvard, 1977). Compare Alexander M. Bickel, *The Original Understanding and the Segregation Decision*, 69 Harv L Rev 1, 63 (1955) (arguing that "an awareness on the part of [the] framers [of the Fourteenth Amendment] that it was *a constitution* they were writing . . . led to a choice of language open to growth").

[169] See Carol S. Steiker, *Second Thoughts about First Principles*, 107 Harv L Rev 820, 830–44 (1994); Amsterdam, 58 Minn L Rev at 401, 416 (cited in note 70).

[170] See, for example, Amar, 107 Harv L Rev at 808 (cited in note 90); Amsterdam, 58 Minn L Rev at 405–06 (cited in note 70).

[171] See note 38 and accompanying text.

[172] *Whren*, 116 S Ct at 1774.

[173] See notes 250–55 and accompanying text.

be shown to be based on outright hostility to a racial or ethnic group.[174] As a consequence, the Clause provides no protection against what is probably the most widespread cause today of discriminatory policing: unconscious bias on the part of generally well-intentioned officers.[175] And even when a police officer *does* act out of racial animus—pulling over a black motorist, for example, simply because the officer does not like blacks—*demonstrating* that typically proves impossible. Even the least imaginative officers almost always can find, or invent, racially neutral grounds for their suspicions.[176]

The Court's recent decisions on vehicle stops thus share three characteristics with the Court's recent Fourth Amendment cases more broadly: a lack of institutional discord, continued doctrinal inconsistency, and a pronounced pattern of ruling in favor of the government. The last of these offers an explanation for the first: the reason Fourth Amendment cases tend not to generate much conflict within the Court is not that Fourth Amendment law has become more coherent, but because the justices now share a set of underlying understandings that heavily favor law enforcement.

V. MINORITY MOTORISTS AND THE COURT

For judicial decisions to be guided by half-articulated understandings is hardly alarming, nor is it necessarily improper for

---

[174] See, for example, *United States v Armstrong*, 116 S Ct 1480, 1486–87 (1996); *McCleskey v Kemp*, 481 US 279, 298 (1987).

[175] See, for example, Sheri Lynn Johnson, *Unconscious Racism and the Criminal Law*, 73 Cornell L Rev 1016 (1988); Kenneth L. Karst, *Foreword: Equal Citizenship Under the 14th Amendment*, 91 Harv L Rev 1, 51 (1977); Randall L. Kennedy, *McClesky v Kemp: Race, Capital Punishment, and the Supreme Court*, 101 Harv L Rev 1388, 1419 (1988); Charles R. Lawrence III, *The Id, the Ego, and Equal Protection: Reckoning with Unconscious Racism*, 39 Stan L Rev 317 (1987).

[176] Sheri Johnson, among others, has noted the "amazing variety of behavior" that law enforcement agents have reported finding suspicious:

> Police have inferred an attempt to conceal both from a traffic violator's reach toward the dashboard or floor of a car, and from his alighting from his car and walking toward the police. [Narcotics] officers have inferred a desire to avoid detection both from a traveler's being the last passenger to get off a plane, and from his being the first. Immigration and Naturalization Service agents have argued both that it was suspicious that the occupants of a vehicle reacted nervously when a patrol car passed, and that it was suspicious that the occupants failed to look at the patrol car. Finally, the government has argued in a customs case that "excessive" calmness is suspicious.

Johnson, 93 Yale L J at 219–20 (cited in note 38).

the Court to give more weight to the interests of police officers than to the interests of criminal suspects and detained motorists. What makes the recent vehicle stop decisions troubling is not what is there but what is missing: a recognition that car stops and similar police actions may raise special concerns for Americans who are not white.

Once more it helps to return to *Whren*. The defendants in *Whren* argued that traffic stops, because of their great potential for abuse, require a kind of review that might not be necessary for other kinds of searches and seizures. Specifically, they argued that traffic stops should be deemed unreasonable if they deviate "materially from the usual police practices, so that a reasonable officer in the same circumstances would not have made the stop for the reasons given."[177] Writing for a unanimous Court, Justice Scalia found this proposal not only at odds with precedent, but also unworkable, for two separate reasons. First, as discussed earlier, he suggested that the requested inquiry simply could not be carried out; it amounted to a futile effort to "plumb the collective unconscious of law enforcement."[178] Second, Justice Scalia thought the limitation to traffic offenses arbitrary and ultimately unstable. He took no issue with the defendants' claim that vehicle codes were "so large and so difficult to obey perfectly that virtually everyone is guilty of violation, permitting the police to single out almost whomever they wish for a stop."[179] But what principle, he asked, would allow the Court "to decide at what point a code of law becomes so expansive and so commonly violated that infraction itself can no longer be the ordinary measure of the lawfulness of enforcement"?[180] And even if such codes could be identified, "by what standard (or what right)" could the Court determine "which particular provisions are sufficiently important to merit enforcement"?[181]

There was a good deal of hyperbole here. Inquiring into the objective reasonableness of a traffic stop is not nearly so daunting as Justice Scalia suggested,[182] and a line between vehicle code en-

---

[177] *Whren*, 116 S Ct at 1774.

[178] Id at 1775. See text accompanying notes 75–76.

[179] Id at 1777.

[180] Id.

[181] Id.

[182] See notes 79–83 and accompanying text.

forcement and ordinary criminal enforcement would hardly be the fuzziest distinction drawn in criminal procedure—nor would it be entirely novel.[183] Still, Justice Scalia had grounds to fear that prohibiting pretextual traffic stops, either by inquiring into the actual motivations of the officers involved or by asking whether a reasonable officer would have made the stop, inevitably would embroil the Court in a potentially interminable job of line drawing. This has happened with the rule allowing warrantless searches incident to arrest,[184] with the rule allowing the warrantless search of automobiles,[185] and, more broadly, with the rule prohibiting warrantless searches except in "exceptional circumstances."[186] It has happened with the *Miranda* rule.[187] It has happened with the application of the Fourth Amendment to all intrusions into "reasonable expectations of privacy."[188] It has happened, in short, whenever the Court has determined that the Constitution requires judges to conduct an inquiry they previously had bypassed. It could hardly be avoided were the Court to announce that cars may be stopped for "vehicle code violations" only when "reasonable" in light of local circumstances and procedures. Doubtless there would be later cases, some of them difficult, about what counts as "vehicle code violations," and what should be taken into consideration for purposes of determining "reasonableness."[189]

[183] See *Berkemer v McCarty*, 468 US 420, 435 (1984) (holding that *Miranda* warnings are unnecessary before "roadside questioning of a motorist detained pursuant to a routine traffic stop").

[184] See, for example, *Maryland v Buie*, 494 US 325 (1990); *New York v Belton*, 453 US 454 (1981); *United States v Edwards*, 415 US 800 (1974); *Cupp v Murphy*, 412 US 291 (1973); *Chimel v California*, 395 US 752, 755–68 (1969) (reviewing cases).

[185] See, for example, *California v Acevedo*, 500 US 565, 569–79 (1991) (reviewing cases); *California v Carney*, 471 US 386 (1985).

[186] *Johnson v United States*, 333 US 10, 14 (1948). As Justice Scalia himself recently pointed out, the "exceptions to the warrant requirement are innumerable." Official Transcript, *Richards v Wisconsin*, 1997 WL 143822, at *8 (US Mar 24, 1997).

[187] *Miranda v Arizona*, 384 US 436 (1966). See, for example, *Davis v United States*, 512 US 452 (1994); *Minnick v Mississippi*, 498 US 146 (1990); *Illinois v Perkins*, 496 US 292 (1990); *Arizona v Roberson*, 486 US 675 (1988); *New York v Quarles*, 467 US 649 (1984); *Rhode Island v Innis*, 446 US 291 (1980); *Edwards v Arizona*, 451 US 477 (1981); *Michigan v Mosley*, 423 US 96 (1975).

[188] See, for example, *Minnesota v Olson*, 495 US 91 (1990); *Florida v Riley*, 488 US 445 (1989); *California v Greenwood*, 486 US 35, 41 (1988) (reviewing cases); id at 46–49 (Brennan dissenting) (same).

[189] Some of this had already happened in lower court decisions applying the "reasonable officer" test for pretextual traffic stops. There was confusion regarding the proper reference group for determining "reasonable" police conduct—the entire police force or the officer's unit?—and there was uncertainty regarding the relevance of the officer's own general prac-

The question, always, should be whether the costs of elaborating and applying a new rule are worth the benefits. This in turn requires an assessment of the need for the rule, and it is here that the *Whren* opinion is most strikingly deficient. Other than a dismissive reference to "the perceived 'danger' of the pretextual stop,"[190] and a suggestion that complaints about racial unfairness be left for the Equal Protection Clause, Justice Scalia has nothing to say about the concerns that have led many to conclude that, notwithstanding the jurisprudential difficulties, some sort of Fourth Amendment protection must be provided against pretextual traffic stops.

One reason the Court felt comfortable dismissing these concerns may have been that it viewed the burdens imposed by traffic stops as trifling.[191] *Maryland v Wilson,* for example, described ordering passengers out of the car as only a "minimal" additional intrusion.[192] "As a practical matter," Chief Justice Rehnquist explained for the majority, "the passengers are already stopped," and "[t]he only change in their circumstances which will result from ordering them out of the car is that they will be outside of, rather than inside of, the stopped car."[193] As Justice Stevens suggested in

---

tices. See Levit, 28 Loyola U Chi L J at 178–80 (cited in note 81). Six months before *Whren,* the Tenth Circuit had pointed to its own inconsistent answers to these questions as evidence that the test was "unworkable." *United States v Botero-Ospino,* 71 F3d 783, 786 (10th Cir 1995). See note 81. Of course, courts have faced similar questions, and similar confusion, in applying the "reasonable person" standard in other contexts. How the new test could best be clarified is open to dispute. Professor Levit argues that the test should turn on "local practices" rather than "a particular officer's past history." Levit, 28 Loyola U Chi L J at 180. My own preference would be to allow consideration of any evidence bearing on the question whether a reasonable person in the officer's position, lacking any other purpose, would have stopped the motorist because of traffic violations; in some cases this would include the officer's own conduct, because what a reasonable person would do can be illuminated by what the officer in fact has done. The important point, though, is that the inconsistency and uncertainty created by the new test for pretext—the test the Supreme Court unanimously rejected out of hand in *Whren*—are the kind of inconsistency and uncertainty widely thought acceptable if not inevitable in the application of new legal rules. See generally S. F. C. Milsom, *Reason in the Development of the Common Law,* 81 Law Q Rev 496, 513 (1965) (concluding that case-by-case adjudication typically produces "great logical strength in detail and great overall disorder").

[190] 116 S Ct at 1774.

[191] Compare *United States v Martinez-Fuerte,* 428 US 543, 563 (1976) (approving selective referrals of motorists to secondary inspection at Border Patrol checkpoint away from the border, "even if it be assumed that such referrals are made largely on the basis of apparent Mexican ancestry," because "the intrusion here is sufficiently minimal that no particularized reason need to exist to justify it").

[192] 117 S Ct at 886.

[193] Id.

dissent, these remarks were consistent with the earlier suggestion of then-Justice Rehnquist that even random vehicle stops infringed on "only the most diaphanous of citizen interests."[194]

For many Americans, though, traffic stops are much more than occasional inconveniences. Blacks, in particular, tend to see such stops as a systematic, humiliating, and often frightening form of police harassment. What the *Whren* Court termed "the perceived 'danger' of the pretextual stop"[195] is almost universally described by African Americans as an everyday reality—the familiar roadside detention for "Driving While Black."[196] Although precise numbers

---

[194] Id at 890 n 12 (Stevens dissenting) (quoting *Delaware v Prouse*, 440 US 648, 666 (Rehnquist dissenting)). Justice Stevens noted that although the burden imposed on passengers by ordering them out of cars "may well be 'minimal' in individual cases," it could be considered significant by "countless citizens who cherish individual liberty and are offended, embarrassed, and sometimes provoked by arbitrary official commands." 117 S Ct at 888 (Stevens dissenting). But even Justice Stevens wound up making the burden seem of only middling consequence. "Wholly innocent passengers," he argued, "have a constitutionally protected right to decide whether to remain comfortably seated within the vehicle rather than exposing themselves to the elements and to the observation of curious bystanders." Id at 889. Discomfort, inclement weather, and nosy onlookers are surely unpleasant, but a casual reader of the opinions in *Maryland v Wilson* could be excused for wondering what the fuss was about.

[195] 116 US at 1774.

[196] See, for example, 143 Cong Rec E 10 (daily ed Jan 7, 1997) (remarks of Rep. Conyers) (asserting "[t]here are virtually no African-American males—including Congressmen, actors, athletes, and office workers—who have not been stopped at one time or another for an alleged traffic violation, namely driving while black"); Michael A. Fletcher, *Driven to Extremes: Black Men Take Steps to Avoid Police Stops*, Wash Post A1 (Mar 29, 1996) (noting that "[m]any African American men suspect that police single them out for stops and searches" and that "many law-abiding black motorists . . . find themselves scheming to avoid the police"); Andrea Ford, *United by Anger*, LA Times B1 (Nov 6, 1996) (reporting that "black men ranging from everyday workers to prosperous professionals and celebrities agree . . . that police indiscriminately detain them because of . . . an unwritten traffic offense—DWB, Driving While Black"); Henry L. Gates, Jr., *Thirteen Ways of Looking at a Black Man*, New Yorker 59 (Oct 23, 1995) (explaining that "[t]here's a moving violation that many African-Americans know as D.W.B.: Driving While Black"); David A. Harris, *Driving While Black: Unequal Protection Under the Law*, Chi Tribune 19 (Mar 11, 1997) (noting that, when pulled over by police, "African-Americans in Illinois and around the country ask . . . 'Is this driving while black again?' "); Pat Schneider, *"A Lot Deeper Than a Ticket": Cop Stops Burn Black Drivers*, Capital Times (Madison, Wis) 1A (Oct 23, 1996) (describing reports of "common wisdom" among African Americans: "Don't get caught 'DWB'—Driving While Black").

Echoing the reports of many black male professionals, former Assistant Attorney General Deval Patrick has explained, "I still get stopped if I'm driving a nice car in the 'wrong' neighborhood." Deval Patrick, *Have Americans Forgotten Who They Are?* LA Times B5 (Sept 2, 1996). See also, for example, Christopher Darden, *In Contempt* 110 (Harper Collins, 1996) ("I always seem to get pulled over by some cop who is suspicious of a black man driving a Mercedes"); Elizabeth A. Gaynes, *The Urban Criminal Justice System: Where Young + Black + Male = Probable Cause*, 20 Ford U L J 621, 625 (1993) ("Most black professionals can recount at least one incident of being stopped, roughed up, questioned, or degraded by white police officers"); *Washington v Lambert*, 98 F3d 1181, 1182 (9th Cir 1996) (describing

are hard to come by, the few available empirical studies confirm what anecdotal evidence has long suggested: minority motorists are pulled over far more frequently than whites.[197]

And the experience of being pulled over is often distinctly different for minority motorists. Of course there is a "distinctive sense in which police discrimination injures citizens" all by itself, by sending a message of official hostility and suspicion.[198] But the difference goes beyond that. Los Angeles police, for example, "do not use the chokehold on middle-class white people, nor make them lie down on their faces in the pavement," but a "police officer told the Christopher Commission that the use of the prone-out technique in minority communities was 'pretty routine,' that police had been taught 'that aggression and force are the only things these people respond to.'"[199] Most incidents of police abuse go unreported, but the Los Angeles police repeatedly have been embarrassed by their treatment of black motorists who turn out to have ready access to the media. Last year the Court of Appeals for the Ninth Circuit summarized several of these incidents:

---

detentions of innocent persons based largely on race as "all too familiar"). For additional accounts, see Angela J. Davis, *Race, Cops, and Traffic Stops*, 51 U Miami L Rev 425, 425, 438–40 (1997); David Harris, *Factors for Reasonable Suspicion: When Black and Poor Means Stopped and Frisked*, 69 Ind L J 659, 679–81 (1994); Tracey Maclin, *"Black and Blue Encounters"—Some Preliminary Thoughts About Fourth Amendment Seizures: Should Race Matter?* 26 Valp U L Rev 243, 251–53 (1991).

[197] In 1992, for example, reporters in Florida reviewed videotapes of more than 1,000 vehicle stops on Interstate 95. They found "almost 70 percent of the motorists stopped were black or Hispanic," and that "[m]ore than 80% of the cars that were searched were driven by blacks and Hispanics," despite the fact that "the vast majority of interstate drivers are white." Jeff Brazil and Steve Berry, *Color of Driver Is Key to Stops in I-95 Videos*, Orlando Sentinel Tribune A1 (Aug 23, 1992). Less than 1% of the drivers stopped received traffic tickets. See id. Similarly, a 1993 study concluded that 13.5% of cars on the New Jersey Turnpike had black occupants, but police records indicated that 46% of motorists stopped on the turnpike between April 1988 and May 1991 were black. See Robert D. McFadden, *Police Singled Out Black Drivers in Drug Crackdown, Judge Says*, NY Times A33 (Mar 10, 1996). An ACLU study in 1996 concluded that 17% of motorists on Interstate 95 in Maryland were black, although state police reported that blacks were 73% of the motorists stopped. See Kris Antonelli, *State Police Deny Searches Are Race-Based*, Baltimore Sun 1B (Nov 16, 1996); Davis, 51 U Miami L Rev at 441.

[198] *Developments*, 101 Harv L Rev at 1515 (cited in note 38). See also *United States v Martinez-Fuerte*, 428 US 543, 573 (1976) (Brennan dissenting) (warning that selective referral of Mexican American motorists for secondary inspection at immigration checkpoints inside the United States is likely to stir "deep resentment" because of "a sense of unfair discrimination"); *Memphis v Greene*, 451 US 100, 147 (1981) (Marshall dissenting) (noting that closing street in white neighborhood to principally black through-traffic injured black motorists in part by sending them "a clear, though sophisticated, message that because of their race, they are to stay out of the all-white enclave").

[199] Paul Chevigny, *Edge of the Knife: Police Violence in the Americas* 45 (New Press, 1995).

The police . . . erroneously stopped businessman and former Los Angeles Laker star Jamaal Wilkes in his car and handcuffed him, and stopped 1984 Olympic gold medalist Al Joyner twice in the space of twenty minutes, once forcing him out of his car, handcuffing him and making him lie spread-eagled on the ground at gunpoint. Similarly, actor Wesley Snipes was taken from his car at gunpoint, handcuffed, and forced to lie on the ground while a policeman kneeled on his neck and held a gun to his head. Actor Blair Underwood was also stopped in his car and detained at gunpoint. We do not know exactly how often this happens to African-American men and women who are not celebrities and whose brushes with the police are not deemed newsworthy.[200]

The problem is not confined to Los Angeles. Based on hearings held in six cities across the country, a 1995 study by the National Association for the Advancement of Colored People concluded that "[p]olice officers have increasingly come to rely on race as the primary indicator of both suspicious conduct and dangerousness,"[201] and that "[v]erbal abuse and harassment seem to occur almost every time a minority citizen is stopped by a police officer."[202] Understandably, blacks at all income levels feel differently than whites about encounters with the police. The NAACP found that law-abiding black parents "war[n] their children about the police," and that "[a]verage African-American families do not know whether they should call the police, stop for the police, or help the police—all for fear of becoming a target of police misconduct themselves."[203]

This should ring familiar. Police practices, including investigatory stops, topped the list of grievances the Kerner Commission

---

[200] *Washington v Lambert*, 98 F3d 1181, 1182 n 1 (9th Cir 1996).

[201] Charles J. Ogletree et al, *Beyond the Rodney King Story: An Investigation of Police Conduct in Minority Communities* 23 (Northeastern, 1995).

[202] Id at 40. Representative Conyers has suggested that "this kind of harassment is even more serious than police brutality," because "no one hears about this, no one does anything about it." 143 Cong Rec E 10 (daily ed Jan 7, 1997).

[203] Ogletree et al, *Beyond the Rodney King Story* at 103. Survey data confirm the broad gulf between views of the police among whites and those among blacks and other minorities. When asked how much confidence they have in the police, 26% of blacks and 23% of racial minorities more broadly say "very little" or "none," compared to only 9% of whites. See US Dep't of Justice, Bureau of Justice Statistics, *Sourcebook of Criminal Justice Statistics— 1995* 133 (GPO, 1996). Thirty-two percent of blacks and 30% of all nonwhites rate the honesty and ethical standards of police officers as "low" or "very low," compared to only 11% of whites. See id at 140.

concluded had led to the urban riots of 1967.[204] Three months after the Kerner Commission Report, when the Supreme Court laid down rules for brief investigatory detentions in *Terry v Ohio*,[205] the majority referred explicitly to "[t]he wholesale harassment by certain elements of the police community of which minority groups, particularly Negroes, frequently complain,"[206] and stressed that patdown searches "may inflict great indignity and arouse strong resentment."[207] The Court's awareness of those resentments doubtless contributed to its refusal to treat investigatory stops as negligible intrusions outside the scope of the Fourth Amendment. Writing for the majority, Chief Justice Warren labeled "simply fantastic" the suggestion that stopping and frisking a suspect—"while the citizen stands helpless, perhaps facing a wall with his hands raised"—amounts only to a "petty indignity."[208] The very term "stop and frisk," he wrote, was a "euphemis[m]"[209] for "a serious intrusion upon the sanctity of the person," which was "not to be undertaken lightly."[210]

How effectively *Terry* protected against this intrusion, and others like it, is a matter of dispute.[211] But at least the decision ex-

---

[204] *Report of the National Advisory Commission on Civil Disorders* 143–44, 302–04 (Dutton, 1968).

[205] 392 US 1 (1968).

[206] Id at 14.

[207] Id at 17.

[208] Id at 16–17. Few readers in 1968 needed to be told the race of the "citizen stand[ing] helpless, perhaps facing a wall with his hands raised," any more than pop music listeners in 1971 needed to be told the color of "frightened faces to the wall." Sly and the Family Stone, *Brave & Strong*, on *There's a Riot Goin' On* (Epic Records, 1971). See also Greil Marcus, *Mystery Train: Images of America in Rock 'n' Roll Music* 79 (Penguin, 3d ed 1990).

[209] 392 US at 10.

[210] Id at 11.

[211] The decision was a conscious compromise, refusing either to exempt investigatory stops from Fourth Amendment scrutiny or to subject them to the traditional requirement of a warrant issued by a judge or magistrate based on a showing of probable cause. Chief Justice Warren seemed aware that the intermediate requirements he imposed—reasonable suspicion of criminality for a stop, reasonable suspicion of danger for a frisk—left room for a large amount of abuse. Presumably that is why he prefaced his analysis by pointing out the limited usefulness of the exclusionary rule "where the police either have no interest in prosecuting or are willing to forego successful prosecution in the interest of serving some other goal." Id at 14.

It was in this context that the Chief Justice mentioned the "wholesale harassment" of minority groups; such harassment, he pointed out, "will not be stopped by the exclusion of any evidence from any criminal trial." Id at 14–15. For a thoughtful argument that "the Warren Court's world-weary realism . . . was, in fact, highly unrealistic," see Adina Schwartz, *"Just Take Away Their Guns": The Hidden Racism of Terry v Ohio*, 23 Fordham Urban L J 317, 325, 347–59 (1996). Schwartz also contends that the pessimism in *Terry*

pressly recognized the problem of police harassment, took note that the problem appeared particularly acute from the vantage point of black Americans, acknowledged the role that investigatory stops can play in patterns of police abuse—and kept these "difficult and troublesome" realities in mind when interpreting and applying the Fourth Amendment.[212] There is no sign of similar awareness in the recent vehicle stop decisions. That is a major reason these cases seemed easier than they should have to the Court.

VI. The Lost Subtext

Thus far I have argued that the Supreme Court's recent decisions regarding vehicle stops show a striking degree of consensus, that this consensus can be seen in the Court's recent Fourth Amendment cases more generally, that the consensus results less from doctrinal coherence than from a shared set of understandings, and that these understandings include not only a firm appreciation for the difficulties of law enforcement but also a sense that brief roadside detentions are relatively unintrusive and unproblematic. I also have suggested that car stops seem unintrusive and unproblematic to the Court in part because it tends to neglect the ways in which everyday life in America, including the experience of being pulled over by the police, remains strongly affected by race.

It is almost commonplace by now that much of the Court's criminal procedure jurisprudence during the middle part of this century was a form of race jurisprudence, prompted largely by the treatment of black suspects and black defendants in the South.[213] The Court's concern with race relations served as the unspoken subtext of many of its significant criminal procedure decisions; oc-

---

about the effectiveness of the exclusionary rule amounted to a determination that "facts about racial impact provide no reason for legal limits on police discretion to stop and frisk." See id at 346. I think this misreads the decision. The *Terry* Court made clear that where "overbearing or harassing" conduct by the police is identified, "it must be condemned by the judiciary and its fruits must be excluded from evidence in criminal trials." 392 US at 15. Moreover, as I have argued in the text, the view the majority took of investigatory stops seems to have been strongly influenced by its awareness of how these stops were experienced in minority neighborhoods.

[212] 392 US at 9.

[213] See, for example, Robert M. Cover, *The Origins of Judicial Activism in the Protection of Minorities*, 91 Yale L J 1287, 1305–06 (1982); Steiker, 107 Harv L Rev at 841–44 (cited in note 169); A. Kenneth Pye, *The Warren Court and Criminal Procedure*, 67 Mich L Rev 249, 256 (1968).

casionally, as in *Terry*, the concern was made more explicit. The recent vehicle stop cases serve as a reminder that this theme has largely disappeared from Fourth Amendment law. Not only do these cases show little concern for the intangible, insidious damage done when minority motorists know, or suspect with good reason, that they are routinely stopped and hassled because of their race; they also display scant awareness of the evidence that more tangible forms of abuse are experienced far more commonly by minority motorists than by whites.

The disregard of racial problems in the Court's recent vehicle stop decisions obviously has implications for all of Fourth Amendment law, not just for the rules governing roadside detentions. I have already suggested one of those implications: the Court's willingness, signaled in *Wilson v Arkansas* and made explicit in *Whren*, to treat racial issues as essentially irrelevant to the determination of "reasonableness" under the Fourth Amendment. The broader ways in which insensitivity to minority and particularly black experience has stunted the development of Fourth Amendment law is beyond the scope of this essay and the subject of a growing body of scholarship.[214] Two aspects of the problem need mention, however, because both are illustrated by the recent vehicle stop cases.

The first is the almost exclusive emphasis modern Fourth Amendment law has placed on protecting a certain kind of privacy. For three decades now, the Court has understood the chief mission of the Fourth Amendment to be to guard against violations of "reasonable expectations of privacy."[215] By "privacy," the Court means, in essence, freedom from prying eyes and ears.[216] This understanding of the Amendment replaced, at least as a matter of form, an earlier view that had focussed more on the protection of property.[217] The change was understandable and on the whole beneficial, given advances in technology and the concerns raised

---

[214] See, for example, Johnson, 73 Cornell L Rev at 1016 (cited in note 175); Maclin, 26 Valp U L Rev at 243 (cited in note 196); Schwartz, 23 Fordham Urban L J at 317 (cited in note 211); *Developments*, 101 Harv L Rev at 1500–20 (cited in note 38).

[215] *Alderman v United States*, 394 US 165, 179 n 11 (1969); *Terry v Ohio*, 392 US 1, 8 (1968); *Katz v United States*, 389 US 347, 360 (1967) (Harlan concurring).

[216] See William J. Stuntz, *Privacy's Problem and the Law of Criminal Procedure*, 93 Mich L Rev 1016, 1020–24 (1995); *Robinette*, 117 S Ct at 425 (Stevens dissenting) (noting that even innocent motorists "have an interest in preserving the privacy of their vehicles and possessions from the prying eyes of a curious stranger").

[217] See, for example, Stuntz, 93 Mich L Rev at 1049–54.

in the 1960s and 1970s about widespread government snooping.[218]

As William Stuntz has recently reminded us, however, a focus on "informational privacy" tends to obscure the degree to which investigative procedures inflict injuries other than the disclosure of facts an individual wishes to keep secret.[219] As a consequence, the Court has underestimated the objections that might reasonably be made, for example, to a dog sniff search, finding this intrusion too slight to trigger Fourth Amendment protections.[220] As another consequence, decisions since 1968 have rarely paid as much attention as *Terry* to the humiliation and subjugation that can accompany investigatory detentions. This in turn makes it harder to see why roadside stops deserve much concern. As Professor Stuntz has noted, "car stops involve much less private disclosure" than house searches and electronic surveillance, but "they also involve other sorts of harm that may not be captured by the law's focus on informational privacy."[221]

Decisions such as *Whren, Robinette,* and *Maryland v Wilson* thus can be understood in part as the product of the Court's relative disregard of the ways in which searches and seizures can cause grievances unrelated to assaults on confidentiality. Because these other grievances by and large are the ones disproportionately suffered by blacks and members of other racial minorities, the focus on informational privacy can take some of the blame for the Court's insensitivity to race matters in the vehicle stop cases. But it works the other way, too. By failing to consider the special objections raised by nonwhites against traffic stops and other police actions, the Court has blinded itself to the most egregious shortcomings of a Fourth Amendment jurisprudence overwhelmingly focussed on the protection of confidentiality.

Insensitivity to the racial aspects of policing probably has contributed to another serious weakness of modern Fourth Amendment law: the Court's reliance on the fiction of consensual encounters with the police. Like the law of interrogations and confessions,

---

[218] See, for example, Amsterdam, 58 Minn L Rev at 407–08 (cited in note 70).

[219] Stuntz, 93 Mich L Rev at 1021.

[220] See *United States v Place*, 462 US 696 (1983).

[221] Stuntz, 93 Mich L Rev at 1062.

Fourth Amendment law places considerable weight on the notion that there is such a thing as a wholly noncoercive encounter with a police officer, and that such encounters are the norm rather than the exception. Anyone who has ever been stopped by the police knows this is nonsense: every encounter with a uniformed officer necessarily involves some amount of apprehension, and hence some amount of psychological if not physical coercion. Nor is this state of affairs entirely regrettable; few of us would want to deprive the police of the ability to get people to do things they would prefer not to do. The key questions are how much and what kinds of coercion are appropriate, and under what circumstances.[222]

These are precisely the questions *not* asked in *Robinette*—or in the two earlier decisions on which it relied, *Schneckloth v Bustamonte*[223] and *Florida v Bostick*.[224] Analogizing to confession law, *Bustamonte* announced the Court's willingness to deem a search of a suspect's property "consensual," and hence automatically constitutional, as long as the suspect's agreement to the procedure was not "coerced, by explicit or implicit means, by implied threat or covert force."[225] As in the interrogation context, the Court made clear in *Bustamonte* that separating valid consent from invalid consent would, in practice, require balancing "competing concerns."[226] Also as in the interrogation context, the Court chose to clothe that balance in the fiction that some requests from police officers—the ones it would deem acceptable—are wholly free from any "implied threat" or "subtl[e] . . . coercion."[227] The Court made clear in

---

[222] Professor Stuntz has made much the same point: "The question should not be whether the officer had the suspect's permission to look at something. Permission will always be more fictive than real anyway. Rather, the question should be whether the officer's behavior was too coercive given the reason for the encounter." Stuntz, 93 Mich L Rev at 1064.

[223] 412 US 218 (1973).

[224] 501 US 429 (1991). Carol Steiker has plausibly characterized *Schneckloth* and *Bostick* as the modern Fourth Amendment decisions "that are most out of sync with the spirit (if not the letter) of the Warren Court's criminal procedure." See Steiker, 94 Mich L Rev at 2491 (cited in note 146).

[225] 412 US at 228.

[226] Id at 227. Compare *Moran v Burbine*, 475 US 412, 424 (1986) (explaining that the rules set forth in *Miranda v Arizona*, 384 US 436 (1966), strike "the proper balance between society's legitimate law enforcement interests and the protection of the defendant's Fifth Amendment rights").

[227] *Bustamonte*, 412 US at 228. Much of Chief Justice Warren's majority opinion in *Miranda v Arizona*, 384 US 436 (1966), was taken up with a detailed explication of how a suspect questioned in custody is "subjugate[d] . . . to the will of his examiner." Id at 457. Ultimately, however, *Miranda* suggested that "adequate protective devices"—notably the famous series of warnings—could entirely "dispel the compulsion inherent in custodial

Bustamonte just how seriously it was willing to treat this fiction by twice reciting the arresting officer's "uncontradicted testimony" that the roadside encounter leading to the search was "very congenial."[228]

What *Bustamonte* said for searches, *Bostick* said for investigatory questioning. Whether the police need justification for such questioning, the Court explained, depends on whether the encounter is "voluntary" and "consensual," and that depends on whether "a reasonable person would feel free to decline the officers' requests or otherwise terminate the encounter."[229] But as in *Bustamonte*, the very facts of the case before the Court made clear that the standard it announced was not to be taken too literally. Terrance Bostick was approached on board an intercity bus by two raid-jacketed narcotics officers, one carrying a pistol in a zipper pouch. This quite plainly is not a setting in which people can sensibly be expected to feel unpressured. By selectively invoking its principle against per se rules and rejecting the Florida Supreme Court's suggestion that bus interrogations of this kind are necessarily nonconsensual, the Court again served notice that prohibitions against police coercion should be applied with an eye toward practicality rather than linguistic precision.[230] It made clear, that is to say, that "consent"

---

surroundings." Id at 458. Two decades later the Court made this explicit: "full comprehension of the rights to remain silent and request an attorney are sufficient to dispel whatever coercion is inherent in the interrogation process." *Moran v Burbine*, 475 US 412, 427 (1986). The utter falsity of this assumption is readily apparent to anyone who has ever practiced criminal law—or for that matter watched an episode of *NYPD Blue*. The Court has also held that *Miranda* warnings need not be given before questioning at a routine traffic stop, because that setting does not impose pressures on a suspect "that sufficiently impair his free exercise of his privilege against self-incrimination to require that he be warned of his constitutional rights." *Berkemer v McCarty*, 468 US 420, 437 (1984).

[228] 412 US at 220–21.

[229] 501 US at 436.

[230] The point was underscored by the Court's response to the argument that the situation must have been coercive, because otherwise Bostick would never have agreed, as he ultimately did, to the search of his luggage, which turned out to contain cocaine. Writing for the majority, Justice O'Connor instructed the Florida Supreme Court to reject this argument on remand, "because the 'reasonable person' test presupposes an *innocent* person." 501 US at 438.

As a matter of logic, this made no sense; Bostick's argument was that his own behavior suggested most people in his situation, regardless whether they had anything hide, would feel pressure to cooperate. The real reason the Court could not accept Bostick's argument was that it proved too much: treat consenting against one's interest as evidence of coercion, and the whole fiction of "consent" becomes impossible to sustain.

and "voluntariness" are, in the context of constitutional criminal procedure, legal fictions.[231]

Robinette made this even clearer. The Court in that case dealt with motorists who have been pulled over by police officers and have not been told they are free to leave. It is fanciful to suppose that reasonable people in such circumstances will feel free from any implied threat or subtle coercion; as Justice Stevens suggested, these predictable effects are precisely why officers like Deputy Newsome bother to ask so often for consent.[232] Chief Justice Rehnquist's opinion for the Court disputed none of this, but nonetheless insisted that the voluntariness of any consent in such settings would have to be determined case by case, "from all the circumstances."[233] The Court explained that a more rigid rule, requiring police officers "to always inform detainees that they are free to go before a consent to search may be deemed voluntary," would be "unrealistic."[234]

Why unrealistic? Not, obviously, because it would be impossible or even difficult to administer. "Tell them they're free to go before you ask to search their cars" is not a complicated instruction. The rule is "unrealistic" only because it can be expected to reduce the number of drivers who consent to searches, by dispelling some, although certainly not all, of the coercion attendant to roadside detentions. Once again, the Court made clear that "consent" is to be defined practically rather than literally—in other words, that it is a fiction.

Fictions have their uses, and not all those uses are to be deplored. This is one of the central lessons of Lon Fuller's classic work on legal fictions.[235] It is well enough to say that the legality of police coercion must ultimately be a question of how much,

---

[231] The Florida Supreme Court took the hint on remand and found the encounter in *Bostick* "consensual" and hence fully constitutional. See *Bostick v State*, 593 So2d 494 (Fla 1992).

[232] See 117 S Ct at 425 (Stevens dissenting). In *Ornelas* the supposition proved too fanciful even for the government, which "conceded . . . that when the officers approached petitioners in the parking lot, a reasonable person would not have felt free to leave." 116 S Ct at 1660. The concession seems sensible, although it is unclear what if anything made the encounter more coercive than a typical traffic stop.

[233] 117 S Ct at 421.

[234] Id.

[235] Lon Fuller, *Legal Fictions* (Stanford, 1967).

what type, and under what circumstances. But how should we begin to answer that question? One way is to proceed by use of a legal fiction: some sorts of coercion, we will say, are legally uncognizable; we will call decisions made under those kinds of coercion "uncoerced" and "voluntary." We know that these decisions really are not "uncoerced" and "voluntary" in the ordinary sense in which those words are used, but we will give the words a new meaning, in order to use them as a kind of shorthand. And not just any, arbitrary shorthand, but a shorthand with a useful resonance; for part of what we want to guide our determination whether to call a decision "uncoerced" and "voluntary" in the fictional, legal sense is how far the decision is from being *truly* uncoerced and voluntary.

This is fine so long as no one is fooled. But even Fuller stressed that "[a] fiction taken seriously, i.e., 'believed,' becomes dangerous and loses its utility."[236] A fiction is "wholly safe," he noted, only "when it is used with a complete consciousness of its falsity."[237] Unfortunately, the fiction of consent in criminal procedure is used by the Supreme Court with something far short of "a complete consciousness of its falsity." One consequence is that the fiction has made it easier for the Court to disregard the special fears and forms of intimidation that can lead nonwhites—like the defendants in *Bustamonte* and *Bostick*[238]—to agree to cooperate with the police. The pressures placed on these suspects, after all, are in a sense simply extreme variants of pressures felt by virtually everyone pulled over by the police, precisely the pressures that the fiction of consent instructs us to ignore.

Here, too, the causation likely runs both ways. While the fiction of consent may have made it easier for the Court to disregard the special circumstances of minority suspects, that disregard, in turn, probably has helped to sustain the fiction. Were the Court more attentive to the pressures routinely experienced by minority sus-

---

[236] Id at 9–10.

[237] Id.

[238] Bustamonte and his companions appear to have been hispanic. See *Schneckloth v Bustamonte*, 412 US 218, 220 (1973). Terrance Bostick was black. Telephone interview with Kenneth P. Speiller, counsel for Terrance Bostick (Aug 19, 1994). For a provocative discussion of the significance of Bostick's race, see Dwight L. Greene, *Justice Scalia and Tonto, Judicial Pluralistic Ignorance, and the Myth of Colorless Individualism in Bostick v Florida*, 67 Tulane L Rev 1979, 2022–43 (1993).

pects stopped by the police, it might find it more difficult to overlook the similar but less extreme pressures routinely experienced
by all suspects.[239] It surely is no accident that when the Court invalidated consent granted after an assertion of authority to search,
and proclaimed that "where there is coercion there cannot be consent," it did so in a case with racial aspects the Court expressly
recognized.[240] In contrast, the Court took no notice of race in *Bustamonte* or *Bostick*, and this made the fiction of consent at least
somewhat less fanciful and easier to defend in those cases—and
consequently also in *Robinette*.[241]

VII. THE FUTURE OF THE FOURTH AMENDMENT

The Court's recent decisions about vehicle stops thus are
part of a general pattern in Fourth Amendment cases of overlook-
ing the special grievances of blacks and other racial minorities. Ignoring those grievances makes it easier for the Court to define
"reasonableness" in a manner that largely excludes considerations
of racial equity, to keep Fourth Amendment law focused principally on the protection of informational privacy, and to sustain the
fiction that encounters with the police can be, and typically are,
free of coercion. These features of Fourth Amendment law in turn
make it easier for the Court to disregard the aspects of police conduct that most frequently give rise to minority complaints.

None of this might matter greatly if those complaints were addressed elsewhere. If, as the Court suggested in *Whren*, complaints
about racial unfairness in police practices could safely be left to
equal protection law, it might not be important to take them into
account under the Fourth Amendment. Similarly, concerns about
police harassment might properly be disregarded in formulating
rules for vehicle stops if police abuse could adequately be con-

---

[239] This is not to say that without the fiction of consent all such pressure would be deemed
unlawful. Some investigative procedures currently sustained as "consensual" would doubtless still be allowed on the ground that they involve only "reasonable" coercion, or coercion
so slight as to render the Fourth Amendment inapplicable—but probably not procedures
the whole point of which is to take advantage of those ignorant of their rights.

[240] *Bumper v North Carolina*, 391 US 543, 550 (1968).

[241] Unlike Bustamonte and Bostick, Robert Robinette was white. Telephone interview
with Carley J. Ingram, Assistant Prosecuting Attorney, Montgomery County, Ohio (Apr
16, 1997).

trolled through prohibitions of unjustified force and intentional humiliation. In both cases, Fourth Amendment restrictions on roadside detentions would seem a clumsy, roundabout way of addressing conduct—racial discrimination or police abuse—more sensibly controlled through direct prohibitions. Unfortunately, neither sort of direct prohibition is likely to prove effective.

Consider first the problem of harassment. A plausible argument can be made that if one is concerned with police abuse, and in particular with police violence and threats of police violence, one should address those concerns head-on, either through rules regulating, for example, the use of force by law enforcement officers, or through a case-by-case application of the general Fourth Amendment prohibition of "unreasonable" searches and seizures. The Court has recognized that excessive force can make a search or seizure "unreasonable";[242] this reasoning could perhaps be extended to things like verbal harassment.

For several reasons, however, the problem of police abuse is unlikely to be solved by rules prohibiting specific forms of abuse. Part of the difficulty is administrative: it is too easy for officers who engage in harassment or unnecessary violence simply to deny it.[243] An equally important set of difficulties is institutional. Elected officials tend not to champion significant restrictions on law enforcement, because the victims of police abuse typically belong to groups with minimal political clout.[244] The judiciary, moreover, has shied away from detailed regulation of police officers' use of force, partly because it fears hampering law enforcement, and partly because rules of this kind inevitably involve the drawing of

---

[242] See *Graham v Connor*, 490 US 386 (1989); *Tennessee v Garner*, 471 US 1 (1985).

[243] It has grown more difficult in recent years because of the spread of video cameras—both those in the hands of bystanders, and those that a growing number of police departments install in their patrol cars. But cameras in patrol cars need to be turned on, and bystanders with video cameras are not always present.

[244] See Donald A. Dripps, *Criminal Procedure, Footnote Four, and the Theory of Public Choice; Or, Why Don't Legislatures Give a Damn About the Rights of the Accused?* 44 Syracuse L Rev 1079 (1993). The isolated exceptions tend to prove the rule. For example, when debating the Exclusionary Rule Reform Act of 1995, HR 666, 104th Cong, 1st Sess (1995), which purported to bar the exclusion in federal criminal case of any evidence obtained by a search or seizure "carried out in circumstances justifying an objectively reasonable belief that it was in conformity with the Fourth Amendment," the House of Representatives approved amendments exempting searches and seizures carried out by the Internal Revenue Service and by the Bureau of Alcohol, Tobacco, and Firearms, but quickly and overwhelmingly rejected a similar amendment exempting searches and seizures carried out by the Immigration and Naturalization Service. See 141 Cong Rec H 1386–98 (daily ed Feb 8, 1995).

more or less arbitrary lines.[245] A final set of problems is procedural. The exclusionary rule works awkwardly to enforce rules against police harassment, because harassment typically does not lead to the discovery of evidence and is not intended to do so.[246] Victims of police harassment can file civil suits or administrative or criminal complaints, but these face a range of familiar obstacles,[247] and are particularly ineffective as a remedy for the kind of low-level harassment unlikely to result in large damage awards even when the plaintiffs prevail.[248]

It therefore remains important for courts to impose sensible restrictions on when officers may pull over a car, what they may require occupants to do once the car is pulled over, and when and

---

[245] These concerns led Justice O'Connor, joined by Chief Justice Burger and Justice Rehnquist, to dissent even from the Court's ruling in *Tennessee v Garner*, 471 US 1 (1985), imposing Fourth Amendment restrictions on the use of deadly force against fleeing felons. See id at 22–33 (1985) (O'Connor dissenting).

[246] See Stuntz, 93 Mich L Rev at 1072 (cited in note 216). While acknowledging that suppression is better suited "to rules about evidence gathering" than to "regulating police violence," Professor Stuntz suggests that "the causal connection between the police misconduct and finding the evidence is convenient, but it need not be crucial." See id. But given the controversy already generated by the suppression of evidence that would not have been discovered but for police illegality, it seems unlikely that courts or legislatures will expand the rule to exclude evidence that would have been discovered in any event. Indeed, the trend in the caselaw is in the other direction. See *Nix v Williams*, 467 US 431, 444 (1984) (holding that even illegally obtained evidence is admissible if it "ultimately or inevitably would have been discovered by lawful means"); *New York v Harris*, 495 US 14, 21 (1990) (holding that "where the police have probable cause to arrest a suspect, the exclusionary rule does not bar the State's use of a statement made by the defendant outside of his home, even though the statement is taken after an arrest made in the home in violation of [*Payton v New York*, 445 US 573 (1980)]").

[247] See, for example, Amsterdam, 58 Minn L Rev at 429–30 (cited in note 70); *Developments*, 101 Harv L Rev at 1497 n 19 (cited in note 38). The "obvious futility of relegating the Fourth Amendment to the protection of other remedies" was at the heart of the Supreme Court's decision to extend the exclusionary rule to state criminal cases. *Mapp v Ohio*, 367 US 643, 653 (1961). Despite perennial calls for "refurbishing the traditional civil-enforcement model," Amar, 107 Harv L Rev at 811 (cited in note 90), the futility remains obvious. The central difficulty is that truly effective civil remedies overdeter if levied against individual officers, see Peter H. Schuck, *Suing Government* 71–73 (Yale, 1983); Stuntz, 93 Mich L Rev at 1073 n 203 (cited in note 216), and have proven too expensive either for the public to assume voluntarily, or for the courts to impose on the public, see, for example, *Monell v Dep't of Social Servs*, 436 US 658 (1978) (holding that municipalities are liable under USC § 1983 only for civil rights violations resulting from official policy), followed in *Board of County Comm'rs v Brown*, 117 S Ct 1382 (1997) (holding municipality not liable for excessive force employed by officer hired in negligent disregard of his history of violence).

[248] This last problem would be less important, obviously, had the Court's standing decisions not put injunctions beyond the reach of most plaintiffs alleging police misconduct. See *City of Los Angeles v Lyons*, 461 US 95 (1983); *Rizzo v Goode*, 423 US 362 (1976); *O'Shea v Littleton*, 414 US 488 (1974).

how the detention must terminate. Much as restricting the opportunities for crime is a critical component of any meaningful effort to control crime, so restricting the opportunities for police harassment is a critical component of any meaningful effort to minimize harassment. And, of course, if the judiciary chooses *not* to restrict these opportunities, it should at the very least avoid "whitewashing" reality in a way that tells some Americans their experiences do not count, and that "conveys the wrong message to other officials who could potentially provide alternative remedial responses."[249]

A related point can be made about equal protection. In theory there is no problem with relying on the Equal Protection Clause to protect against racial unfairness in law enforcement. The problem is that equal protection doctrine, precisely because it attempts to address all constitutional claims of inequity, has developed in ways that poorly equip it to address the problems of discriminatory police conduct. Equal protection doctrine treats claims of inequitable policing the same as any other claim of inequity; it gives no recognition to the special reasons to insist on evenhanded law enforcement,[250] or to the distinctive concerns with arbitrariness underlying the Fourth Amendment.[251] As a result, challenges to discriminatory police practices will fail without proof of conscious racial animus on the part of the police. For reasons discussed earlier, this amounts to saying that they will almost always fail.[252]

Unless and until equal protection law become more attentive to the factual contexts giving rise to claims of unfairness, it thus will remain of limited help to the victims of police discrimination. In the meantime, the "reasonableness" requirement of the Fourth Amendment, particularly when coupled with the aim of the Amendment's framers to protect against the arbitrary exercise of

---

[249] Kennedy, 101 Harv L Rev at 1416 (cited in note 175).

[250] See, for example, David A. Sklansky, *Cocaine, Race, and Equal Protection*, 47 Stan L Rev 1283, 1309–11, 1316 (1995). As the Supreme Court itself has recognized, apparent inequity within the criminal justice system does more than deny the victim, in the most basic sense, equal protection of the law, it also powerfully undermines "public confidence in the fairness of our system of justice," and can seriously exacerbate racial divisions. *Batson v Kentucky*, 476 US 79, 87–88 (1986). See also *Rose v Mitchell*, 443 US 545, 555 (1979) ("Discrimination on the basis of race, odious in all aspects, is especially pernicious in the administration of justice"); notes 203–07 and accompanying text.

[251] See notes 69–70 and accompanying text.

[252] See notes 175–76 and accompanying text.

power by officers in the field, could and should provide a strong alternative basis for addressing a particular form of inequality: discretionary law enforcement practices that "unreasonably" burden blacks and members of other racial minorities.

To be sure, Fourth Amendment inquiries of this kind would theoretically duplicate those under the Equal Protection Clause, and might generate results inconsistent with those reached under equal protection analysis. But there is nothing new in the suggestion that equality is the proper concern of more than one provision of the Constitution,[253] and for reasons I have addressed at greater length elsewhere,[254] a little messiness in legal doctrines aimed at securing equitable treatment can be a good thing. Because the Fourth Amendment is narrowly focused on searches and seizures, it could provide an opportunity to develop specialized doctrines of equality that, if they proved workable and successful, could later be considered for wider application under the Equal Protection Clause. And regardless of whether this kind of cross-fertilization would ultimately prove beneficial for equal protection law, it certainly would allow the courts to confront the problem of discriminatory policing without the need to devise doctrines that could also be applied to utility rates and bus fares.[255]

I am not suggesting that the Constitution should restrict searches and seizures of minority suspects more stringently than those of whites. There may be something to be said for bringing affirmative action of this kind to Fourth Amendment doctrine, particularly as a way to combat conscious or unconscious bias on the part of police, prosecutors, and judges. But separate Fourth Amendment rules for minority suspects probably would offend most Americans' sense of justice, far more than affirmative action

---

[253] See generally Kenneth L. Karst, *Belonging to America: Equal Citizenship and the Constitution* (Yale, 1989). Regarding, for example, the role of equality in freedom of speech, see Kenneth L. Karst, *Equality as a Central Principle in the First Amendment*, 43 U Chi L Rev 20 (1975); Geoffrey R. Stone, *Content Regulation and the First Amendment*, 25 Wm & Mary L Rev 189, 201–07, 247–48 (1983).

[254] See Sklansky, 47 Stan L Rev at 1312–15, 1320–22 (cited in note 250).

[255] The Eighth Amendment ban on "cruel and unusual punishments" offers a similar opportunity for a context-specific exploration of equitable treatment. To date, unfortunately, the Supreme Court has largely passed up this opportunity as well. See *Harmelin v Michigan*, 501 US 957 (1991) (finding proportionality of prison sentences largely irrelevant under the Eighth Amendment); *McCleskey v Kemp*, 481 US 279, 312–21 (1987) (concluding that racial disparities in the application of the death penalty do not violate the Eighth Amendment).

in employment decisions and academic admissions, because of the widespread feeling, which I share, that individualized fairness is especially important in the criminal justice system.[256] Then, too, the administrative difficulties of an affirmative-action Fourth Amendment, both for the police and for the courts, could easily make the rules rejected as unworkable in *Whren* and *Robinette* seem like child's play by comparison.

Nor am I arguing that the Fourth Amendment should automatically impose some form of heightened scrutiny on any practices shown disproportionately to disadvantage blacks or other members of other racial minorities. This approach has some attraction, for the same reason it has some appeal as a proposed rule of equal protection: democratic processes tend to provide less reliable protection against unfair burdens when those burdens fall disproportionately on members of a traditionally disempowered minority.[257] But the principal drawback to disparate impact as a trigger for heightened equal protection review—overinclusiveness—weighs even more heavily against its categorical use in search and seizure law. Because minority neighborhoods tend to be poorer and more crime-ridden, *most* police practices disproportionately burden minority suspects. For the same reason, however, minorities as a whole are disproportionately burdened by crime itself, and therefore might not benefit from an across-the-board tightening of Fourth Amendment rules.

What the recent vehicle stop cases suggest that Fourth Amendment law needs is not a special rule to protect minority groups, but more attention to the special concerns of minority groups in the formulation and application of all Fourth Amendment rules. Precisely what rules such attention would generate is uncertain, but with regard to traffic stops, we can make some reasonable conjectures.

---

[256] There obviously are limits to this sentiment. In different ways, both the exclusionary rule and the recent trend toward fixed, mandatory sentences may reflect a willingness to sacrifice some degree of individualized fairness in the interest of improving criminal justice overall. Significantly, though, both these compromises have been supported in part by appeals to individualized justice, and neither has been promoted as means for redressing inequalities between groups.

[257] See John Hart Ely, *Democracy and Distrust: A Theory of Judicial Review* 135–79 (Harvard, 1980); Sklansky, 47 Stan L Rev at 1298–99, 1307–08 (cited in note 250). Regarding the implications of this phenomenon for free speech law, see Geoffrey R. Stone, *Content-Neutral Restrictions*, 54 U Chi L Rev 46, 72–77 (1987).

To begin with, a Fourth Amendment jurisprudence more alert to minority interests and experiences probably would find room for a rule disallowing pretextual detentions for traffic violations: the burdens the rule placed on the judiciary would be outweighed by the need to minimize the opportunities for arbitrary and discriminatory police harassment. It might also accommodate a "first-tell-then-ask" rule, because it likely would *not* indulge the fiction of consensual encounters with the police: the benefit the fiction provides to the judiciary would be outweighed by the abuses it helps to mask. In the interest of officer safety and judicial economy, a more minority-sensitive law of search and seizure might still declare flatly that the police may order passengers out of any lawfully stopped car. But it would do so only after full consideration and frank acknowledgement of the fear and humiliation that orders of this kind can cause, particularly when made selectively on the basis of race.

The "touchstone" of the Fourth Amendment, the Court keeps repeating, "is reasonableness,"[258] and reasonableness must be assessed under "all the circumstances."[259] Like many cliches, this one is worth heeding. What is most troubling about the recent vehicle stop decisions are "all the circumstances"—including the continuing and destructive role of race in American policing, the injuries other than forced disclosures suffered at roadside detentions, and the shortcomings of direct restrictions on police abuse and generalized guarantees of equality—that the Supreme Court overlooked.

---

[258] *Ohio v Robinette*, 117 S Ct at 421; *Florida v Jimeno*, 500 US 248, 250 (1991); *Pennsylvania v Mimms*, 434 US 106, 108–09 (1977); *Terry v Ohio*, 392 US 1, 19 (1968).

[259] *Maryland v Wilson*, 117 S Ct at 884. See also *Robinette*, 117 S Ct at 421; *Whren*, 116 S Ct at 1776; *Ornelas v United States*, 116 S Ct at 1661.

RICHARD L. HASEN

ENTRENCHING THE DUOPOLY: WHY THE SUPREME COURT SHOULD NOT ALLOW THE STATES TO PROTECT THE DEMOCRATS AND REPUBLICANS FROM POLITICAL COMPETITION

INTRODUCTION

For the first time, a majority of the Supreme Court has upheld an election law against First Amendment challenge on grounds that the law permissibly favors the "two-party system." In *Timmons v Twin Cities Area New Party*,[1] the Court upheld Minnesota's ban on fusion, "the electoral support of a single set of candidates by two or more parties,"[2] that a minor party had hoped to use to build electoral support. *Timmons* follows earlier cases in which various Justices in dissenting and concurring opinions had accepted a similar two-party argument.[3]

Richard L. Hasen is Visiting Associate Professor, Loyola Law School (Fall 1997), Visiting Professor, UCLA School of Law (Spring 1998), Assistant Professor of Law, Chicago–Kent College of Law.

AUTHOR'S NOTE: Thanks to Anita Bernstein, Mike Fitts, Hal Krent, Dan Lowenstein, Brad Smith, participants at Loyola Law School and UCLA School of Law workshops, and participants at the *Stanford Law Review* symposium on Law and the Political Process for useful comments and suggestions. Thanks also to Scott Dauscher and Denise Lohmann for research assistance.

[1] 117 S Ct 1364 (1997).

[2] Peter H. Argersinger, *"A Place on the Ballot": Fusion Politics and Antifusion Laws*, 85 Am Hist Rev 287, 288 (1980).

[3] See Part I.

Timmons's significance rests not so much on the Court's approval of antifusion laws—for reasons explained below,[4] fusion likely would not affect the outcome of the vast majority of elections in which it is used—but instead on the Court's holding that a state has a legitimate interest in favoring the Democratic-Republican duopoly. Such a holding could affect how the Court decides future ballot access cases, political patronage cases, and other election law cases in which a state defends a law infringing on First Amendment rights. But *Timmons* and the earlier opinions extolling the virtues of the two-party system have not examined with care the premise that the two-party system is worthy of protection, nor have they discussed whether Supreme Court protection of the two-party system is necessary.

The Court's omission on the first score seems to reflect an uncritical reliance on a substantial normative political science literature, the "responsible party government" position, that argues for protection of the two-party system. Scholars in this camp contend that the two-party system promotes political stability, cures the mischiefs of faction, and provides a valuable voting cue. The first two claims—stability and antifactionalism—are unproven and perhaps unprovable. The voting cue claim has greater empirical validity, although the importance of the cue no doubt has declined over the last decades. But the continued existence of the voting cue does not depend upon Supreme Court protection of the two-party system; indeed, it appears likely that less protection of the two-party system will enhance the voting cue by increasing the salience of differences among parties and candidates. Thus, none of the reasons that might be put forth to justify Supreme Court protection of the two-party system are persuasive, especially when measured against the social costs of such a system.

Part I of this article briefly describes the cases, with a focus on *Timmons*, in which the Court or dissenting or concurring Justices have extolled the virtues of the two-party system. Part II describes the responsible party government position and argues that, in the modern party system, there are good reasons to doubt that two-party duopoly promotes political stability, reduces the influence of factions, or enhances the voting cue. Part III demonstrates that

---

[4] See Part III.

even if the two-party system is a valuable institution, the Supreme Court need not uphold laws like those at issue in *Timmons* in order to preserve the two-party system. Alternative rulings by the Supreme Court would not, as others have suggested,[5] lead to the creation of a multiparty system in the United States: short of eliminating winner-take-all elections or single-member districts[6]— something that would not be required by Supreme Court rejection of the two-party argument[7]—the United States is likely to continue to be dominated by two major political parties.[8]

I. From Damnation to Praise of Duopoly: The Road From Williams to Timmons

A. AGAINST DUOPOLY

Until *Timmons*, the Court had never squarely addressed whether it was permissible for a state to favor the two-party system in crafting its election laws. But the Court came very close to rejecting the idea in a 1968 case, *Williams v Rhodes*.[9]

In *Williams*, two minor political parties challenged Ohio's extremely restrictive ballot access laws that "made it virtually impossible for a new political party, even though it has hundreds of thousands of members, or an old party, which has a very small number of members, to be placed on the state ballot to choose electors" for presidential candidates.[10] Ohio sought to justify these laws on

---

[5] John B. Anderson and Jeffrey L. Freeman, *Taking the First Steps Towards a Multiparty System in the United States*, 21 Fletcher Forum World Affairs 73, 81 (Spring 1997) (affirmance of 8th Circuit decision in *Timmons* "would offer encouragement to those who view [fusion] as a practical solution to the problem of fostering the coalition-building capacity of a new party"); Richard Winger, *How Ballot Access Laws Affect the U.S. Party System*, 16 Am Rev Pol 321, 346 (1995) (blaming restrictive ballot access laws and the Supreme Court's decisions in the ballot access area for preventing the emergence of "substantial nationwide third parties in the U.S.").

[6] Not that the ideas lack academic proponents. See, for example, Douglas J. Amy, *Real Choices/New Voices: The Case for Proportional Representation Elections in the United States* 188– 90 (Columbia, 1993) (advocating use of proportional representation and multimember districts to choose members of the House of Representatives). The single-member district requirement for the House of Representatives is statutory, not constitutional. See 2 USC § 2c (1994).

[7] See note 77.

[8] See Part III.B (discussing Duverger's law).

[9] 393 US 23 (1968).

[10] Id at 24. Among other provisions, the law required that new parties desiring a place on the ballot obtain petitions signed by voters totaling 15% of the number of ballots cast in the preceding gubernatorial election. Id at 24–25. In contrast, the Democratic and Re-

grounds that "the State may validly promote a two-party system in order to encourage compromise and political stability."[11] The Supreme Court rejected the argument and ultimately all of Ohio's arguments for the ballot-access restrictions:

> The fact is, however, that the Ohio system does not merely favor a "two-party system"; it favors two particular parties— the Republicans and the Democrats—and in effect tends to give them a complete monopoly. There is, of course, no reason why two parties should retain a permanent monopoly on the right to have people vote for or against them. Competition in ideas and governmental policies is at the core of our electoral process and of the First Amendment freedoms.[12]

Though the Court in *Williams* did not reject the idea that a state in theory could defend an election law on grounds that it promoted the "two-party system" rather than the Democratic-Republican duopoly, it is difficult to imagine how a court in fact would separate the two interests.[13]

The Court again rejected protection of the Democratic-Republican duopoly in *Anderson v Celebrezze*.[14] There, the Court considered independent presidential candidate John Anderson's challenge to Ohio's early filing deadline for independent presidential candi-

---

publican parties were allowed to retain their positions on the ballot simply by obtaining 10% of the votes in the last gubernatorial election and did not need to obtain any signature petitions. In addition, Ohio laws made "no provision for ballot position for independent candidates as distinguished from political parties." Id at 25–26. Ohio also placed other burdens in front of minor party candidacies. Id at 27. The Ohio American Independent Party, founded by supporters of former Alabama governor George C. Wallace, obtained more than the required number of signatures, though not in the time limits set by the state. Id at 26–27.

[11] Id at 31–32.

[12] Id at 32.

[13] Perhaps the court would understand the question as one of legislative intent: if the legislature (made up predominantly, if not exclusively, of Democrats and Republicans in all states, see notes 188–89 and accompanying text) enacts a law with an intention to discriminate against third parties or independent candidates, the practice should be barred. But if the legislature intends to promote a stable two-party political system, the practice should be allowed despite the resulting discrimination against third parties or independent candidates. See *Mobile v Bolden*, 446 US 55 (1980) (Constitution prohibits only intentional discrimination against minority voters, and not the discriminatory results of a law passed to further legitimate state interests); see also Michael J. Klarman, *Majoritarian Judicial Review: The Entrenchment Problem*, 85 Georgetown L J 491, 528–30, 535–36 (1997) (arguing that courts should void ballot access restrictions unless the legislature would have enacted the restriction at issue in the absence of entrenchment considerations). But proving or disproving such intent would be difficult indeed.

[14] 460 US 780 (1983).

dates. The Court characterized *Williams* as concluding that "First Amendment values outweighed the State's interest in protecting the two major political parties,"[15] but it recognized, consistent with the intervening case of *Storer v Brown*,[16] that the State had a legitimate interest in preventing "splintered parties and unrestrained factionalism."[17] Reconciling the two cases, the *Anderson* court rejected the idea "that a political party could invoke the powers of the State to assure monolithic control over its own members and supporters."[18] It struck down Ohio's law preventing candidate Anderson from appearing on Ohio's ballot.

B. PRECURSORS TO TIMMONS

In the various patronage cases and in a case involving political gerrymandering, *Davis v Bandemer*,[19] dissenting and concurring Justices endorsed the concept that the state could promote the two-party system.

In the patronage cases, the debate centered upon whether patronage practices helped the two-party system and not upon whether preservation of the two-party system itself is a legitimate (or compelling) state goal that trumps individual First Amendment rights. The plurality expressly refused to address the latter question in the first patronage case, *Elrod v Burns*.[20] But Justice Powell wrote for himself and two other Justices in dissent that "patronage hiring practices have contributed to American democracy by stimulating political activity and by strengthening parties, thereby helping to make government accountable."[21] In the next patronage

---

[15] Id at 802.

[16] 415 US 724 (1974).

[17] *Anderson*, 460 US at 803, quoting *Storer*, 415 US at 736.

[18] *Anderson*, 460 US at 803.

[19] 478 US 109 (1986).

[20] 427 US 347, 368–69 (1976) (plurality opinion) ("[H]owever important preservation of the two-party system or any system involving a fixed number of parties may or may not be, . . . we are not persuaded that the elimination of patronage practice . . . will bring about the demise of party politics" (citation omitted)). For a discussion of whether patronage practices help the two-party system, and for a look at the patronage cases generally, see Cynthia Grant Bowman, *The Law of Patronage at a Crossroads*, 12 J L & Pol 341 (1996); Richard L. Hasen, *An Enriched Economic Model of Political Patronage and Campaign Contributions: Reformulating Supreme Court Jurisprudence*, 14 Cardozo L Rev 1311 (1993); and Cynthia Grant Bowman, *"We Don't Want Anybody Anybody Sent": The Death of Patronage Hiring in Chicago*, 86 Nw U L Rev 57, 83–89 (1991) (Bowman, *Anybody Anybody*).

[21] *Elrod*, 427 US at 382 (Powell dissenting).

case, *Branti v Finkel*,[22] Justice Powell, again in dissent and joined by one other Justice, expanded on his view of the importance of political parties in the two-party system. He argued that political parties: (1) allow political candidates "to muster donations of time and money necessary to capture the attention of the electorate";[23] (2) provide for government accountability, apparently through use of political patronage;[24] (3) facilitate cooperation between the executive and legislative branches of government, at least when the leaders of both branches are from the same party;[25] and (4) provide a voting cue for uninformed voters.[26]

Justice Scalia, dissenting along with three other Justices in the next patronage case, *Rutan v Republican Party of Illinois*,[27] carried on Justice Powell's fight over the virtues of patronage, and spent much of his dissent arguing that patronage practices help the two-party system. In *Rutan*, Justice Scalia explained, albeit briefly, his belief that the two-party system has "obvious" stabilizing effects as the two parties moderate toward the political center.[28]

Finally, in the political gerrymandering case, *Davis v Bandemer*, Justice O'Connor, writing for herself and two other Justices in a concurring opinion, stated that "[t]here can be little doubt that the emergence of a strong and stable two-party system in this country has contributed enormously to sound and effective government."[29] Justice O'Connor further remarked that the two-party system "permits both stability and measured change."[30]

---

[22] 445 US 507, 528 (1980) (Powell dissenting).

[23] Id. This interest corresponds with my discussion of how parties solve collective action problems for politicians. In Part III, I argue that Supreme Court protection of the two major parties is unnecessary to preserve this benefit for politicians.

[24] 445 US 507, 529 (Powell dissenting).

[25] Id at 530–31. This interest corresponds with the desire to curb government gridlock, discussed in note 150.

[26] 445 US 531. See Parts II.A.3 and II.C.3 (discussing the voting cue).

[27] 497 US 62, 92 (1990) (Scalia dissenting).

[28] Id at 107. On political stability, see Parts II.A.1 and II.C.1. In the most recent pair of patronage cases, *Board of County Commissioners v Umbehr*, 116 S Ct 2342 (1996), and *O'Hare Truck Service v City of Northlake*, 116 S Ct 2353 (1996), Justice Scalia, writing for himself and one other Justice, dissented from the Court's decision to extend patronage prohibitions to independent contractors, but he did not reiterate his reasons for favoring the two-party system.

[29] *Davis*, 478 US at 144–45 (O'Connor concurring).

[30] Id at 145. One other pre-*Timmons* case deserves mention: in *Buckley v Valeo*, 424 US 1 (1976), the Court considered a challenge by minor political parties to provisions of the Federal Elections Campaign Act that favored major political parties. See id at 93–108 (per

Significantly, in none of these cases did the Justices who were endorsing the benefits of the two-party system engage in a detailed analysis of empirical evidence supporting or refuting such claims. Justice Powell's dissent in *Branti* and Justice Scalia's dissent in *Rutan* cite a smattering of scholarly sources;[31] the other opinions cited none. This unfortunate tradition continued in *Timmons v Twin Cities Area New Party*,[32] where a majority for the first time endorsed a state's defense of its election law against First Amendment challenge on the grounds that it promoted the two-party system. As supporting authority for recognizing the two-party interest, the Court cited only three sources: Justice Scalia's dissent in *Rutan*, Justice O'Connor's concurrence in *Bandemer*, and Justice Powell's dissent in *Branti*.[33]

C. THE TIMMONS EMBRACE OF DUOPOLY

In *Timmons*,[34] the Twin Cities Area New Party, a chartered chapter of a nascent national political party, wished to nominate Andy Dawkins as its candidate for state representative. Dawkins was already the candidate of the Democratic-Farmer-Labor party

---

curiam). The Court first rejected the challenge to the formula for public financing of presidential campaigns that favored major political parties. It held that Congress need not subsidize the proliferation of splinter parties, id at 98, and in any case the voluntary spending limits on major parties could enhance the relative position of minor parties, id at 99. It then applied similar logic to public funding of major party nominating conventions, id at 104–05, and to the minor parties' challenge to primary election campaign financing, id at 105–08. The Court did not discuss whether the public financing provisions could be justified on grounds that they favored the two-party system.

[31] In support of his argument that the two-party system deserves special protection (as opposed to the argument that patronage furthers the interest in promoting the two-party system—though separating the two in his opinions is quite difficult), Justice Powell cited the following scholarly sources: Edward N. Costikyan, *Behind Closed Doors: Politics in the Public Interest* 253–54 (Harcourt, Brace & World, 1966); Richard Murray and Arnold Vedlitz, *Party Voting in Lower-Level Electoral Contests*, 59 Soc Sci Q 752, 756 (1979); and Martin Tolchin and Susan Tolchin, *To the Victor . . .* 19 (Random House, 1971). He also cited a few newspaper articles and a book by a journalist, David Broder, *The Party's Over: The Failure of Politics in America* 239–40 (Harper Collins, 1972). See *Branti*, 445 US at 528–31. In support of the same argument in *Rutan*, Justice Scalia cited the following scholarly sources: Marie-France Toinet and Ian Glenn, *Clientelism and Corruption in the "Open" Society: The Case of the United States*, in Christopher Clapham, ed, *Private Patronage and Public Power* 193, 208 (St. Martin's, 1982); and Michael A. Fitts, *The Vices of Virtue: A Political Party Perspective on Civic Virtue Reforms of the Legislative Process*, 136 U Pa L Rev 1567, 1603–07 (1988). See *Rutan*, 497 US at 107.

[32] 117 S Ct 1364 (1997).

[33] Id at 1374.

[34] 117 S Ct 1364 (1997).

(DFL) for that office.[35] Although neither Dawkins nor the DFL objected to the fusion candidacy,[36] Minnesota officials refused to accept the New Party's nominating petition because Minnesota law prohibits such a practice.[37]

The New Party challenged Minnesota's antifusion statutes under the First and Fourteenth Amendments.[38] The district court granted summary judgment for the state defendants, but the Eighth Circuit reversed, holding that the ban severely burdened the party's associational rights and therefore was unconstitutional.[39]

The Supreme Court reversed the judgment of the Eighth Circuit, holding that the burden on the New Party's associational rights was not severe[40] and that Minnesota advanced three "sufficiently weighty" regulatory interests to justify the limitation imposed on the party's rights.[41] First, the Court accepted the state's argument that "a candidate or party could easily exploit fusion as a way of associating his or its name with popular slogans and catchphrases," such as by creating the "No New Taxes" party.[42] Second, the Court agreed that permitting fusion would allow "minor par-

---

[35] Id at 1367–68. "The DFL is the product of a 1944 merger between Minnesota's Farmer-Labor Party and the Democratic Party, and is a 'major party' under Minnesota Law." Id at 1367 n 2.

[36] Id at 1368. Fusion is also called "cross-filing" or "multiple-party nomination." Id at 1367 n 1. To be fair to the DFL, there would be no reason for the party to have objected given that the practice violated state law. Nor was there any procedure in place for the DFL to lodge a formal objection. The Court's opinion does not reveal whether DFL officials objected in any informal way to Dawkins's fusion candidacy. The DFL was not a party to the litigation.

[37] Id at 1368 n 3, citing Minn Stat §§ 204B.04(2), 204B.06(1)(b) (1996).

[38] *Twin Cities Area New Party v McKenna*, 863 F Supp 988, 990 (D Minn 1994).

[39] *Twin Cities Area New Party v McKenna*, 73 F3d 196, 200 (8th Cir 1996).

[40] *Timmons*, 117 S Ct at 1372. The Court held the burden was not severe because

Minnesota's laws do not restrict the ability of the New Party and its members to endorse, support, or vote for anyone they like. The laws do not directly limit the Party's access to the ballot. They are silent on parties' internal structure, governance, and policy-making. Instead, these provisions reduce the universe of potential candidates who may appear on the ballot as the Party's nominee only by ruling out those few individuals who both have already agreed to be another party's candidate and also, if forced to choose, themselves prefer that other party. They also limit, slightly, the Party's ability to send a message to the voters and to its preferred candidates.

[41] Id.

[42] Id at 1373.

ties to capitalize on the popularity of another party's candidate, rather than on their own appeal to the voters, in order to secure access to the ballot."[43] Finally, the Court agreed that the states "have a strong interest in the stability of their political systems" and therefore they may "enact reasonable election regulations that may, in practice, favor the traditional two-party system."[44]

It is difficult to accept the first or second of these arguments as "sufficiently" weighty to overcome even a relatively minor burden on the New Party's associational rights. As for the first interest, reasonable ballot access laws can prevent the formation of many sham parties,[45] and the Court expressly denied that it was relying on any "alleged paternalistic interest in 'avoiding voter confusion.'"[46] The second argument quickly disappears upon understanding that the state could simply list candidates on the ballots once under each party and then count only the votes cast for the candidate under the minor party label to meet that minor party's ballot access requirements.[47]

---

[43] Id.

[44] Id at 1374.

[45] The Court called the New Party's argument along these lines ironic because it amounted to a minor party calling for more demanding ballot access requirements. Id at 1373. Current Minnesota law makes it quite easy to set up such a sham party. Candidates not from a major political party need only collect signatures from 2,000 voters (or 1% of the number of voters voting in the state in the election, whichever is less) to run for state-wide office. See Minn Stat § 204B.08(3)(a) (1996); see also § 204B.03 (requiring non-major party candidates to collect signatures to appear on ballot); § 200.02(6) and (7) (defining, respectively, "political party" and "major political party").

The dissent considered Minnesota's concern over sham parties "entirely hypothetical." 117 S Ct at 1378 (Stevens dissenting). But in New York, a state that permits fusion, the "Tax Cut Now Party" served as the alter ego of the Republican party in the 1994 election. See Ian Fisher, *Minor Parties File Petitions for Pataki and Rosenbaum*, NY Times B6 (Aug 24, 1994). Republican officials "said the new party was aimed at Democrats who opposed Gov Mario M. Cuomo but might still be reluctant to pull the lever for a Republican." Id. Over 50,000 voters voted for now-Governor George Pataki, the Republican candidate, on the Tax Cut Now Party line, entitling the party, renamed the "Freedom Party," to a spot on the New York state ballot for five years. *Drive By*, The Hotline (Apr 27, 1995). The party had only 419 members, however. Id.

[46] 117 S Ct at 1375 n 13. According to the Court, the problem with sham parties is that they would "undermine the ballot's purpose by transforming it from a means of choosing candidates to a billboard for political advertising." Id at 1373. But that problem does not seem "sufficiently weighty" when measured against the burden on third parties' associational rights, and, as noted above, it can be solved by reasonable ballot access requirements.

[47] A recent student note convincingly argues that the most important benefit of fusion to the third party is not the election of the multiparty candidates, but rather use of some of the multiparty votes to meet future ballot access requirements for the minor party. Note, *Fusion Candidacies, Disaggregation, and Freedom of Association*, 109 Harv L Rev 1302, 1305 (1996).

This leaves the state's interest in promoting the two-party system, which, as Justice Stevens remarked in his dissent, "appears to be the true basis for the Court's holding."[48] After noting that the state may not "completely insulate the two-party system from minor parties' or independent candidates' competition and influence,"[49] and may not enact "unreasonably exclusionary restrictions,"[50] the Court held it was permissible for Minnesota "to decide that political stability is best served through a healthy two-party system."[51] According to the Court, the "traditional two-party system . . . temper[s] the destabilizing effects of party-splintering and excessive factionalism."[52] The Court simply seemed to assume that the antifusion law indeed would benefit the two-party system, an assumption that is at least debatable: for example, fusion could strengthen the two-party system by causing the two major political parties to become ideologically distinct, and ideological distinction could cause more voters to identify with political parties.[53]

Although three Justices dissented, only two of them rejected on the merits the state's argument regarding the two-party system. Justice Stevens, along with Justice Ginsburg, found the risk to political stability engendered by fusion politics "speculative at best."[54] But Justice Souter rejected the two-party system argument only on the ground that the state failed to raise it.[55] According to Justice Souter, "[i]f it could be shown that the disappearance of the two party system would undermine [the state's interest in the stability of its political system], and that permitting fusion candidacies poses a substantial threat to the two-party scheme, there might well be a sufficient predicate for recognizing the constitutionality" of the

---

[48] 117 S Ct at 1379 (Stevens dissenting).

[49] Id at 1374.

[50] Id, citing *Williams v Rhodes*, 393 US 23, 31–32 (1968).

[51] Id.

[52] 117 S Ct at 1374.

[53] See Brief Amici Curiae of Twelve University Professors and Center for a New Democracy in Support of Respondent Twin Cities Area New Party, 1996 WL 496827, *14 (Aug 30, 1996) (*CND Amicus Brief*); see also Argersinger, 85 Am Hist Rev at 303 (cited in note 2) (arguing that antifusion laws at the end of the nineteenth century brought an end to "the importance and even existence of significant third parties").

[54] 117 S Ct at 1380 (Stevens dissenting).

[55] Id at 1381 (Souter dissenting); see also id at 1379 (Stevens dissenting). The majority disagreed. See id at 1374 n 10.

fusion ban.[56] Thus, six Justices agreed that it is legitimate for the state to enact election laws aimed at preserving the two-party system, and one Justice was willing to entertain the argument upon proof of a link between the two-party system and political stability.[57]

Timmons of course does not authorize states to favor the Republican and Democratic parties in any way they like. But *Timmons* establishes that a state may "decide that political stability is best served through a healthy two-party system"[58] and that this "interest in securing the perceived benefits of a stable two party system"[59] justifies measures that restrict, to some degree, the exercise of First Amendment rights. This makes it much more likely that courts will uphold ballot access laws imposing onerous requirements on third parties seeking a place on the electoral ballot.

Beyond the ballot access cases, *Timmons* will make it easier for states to entrench the two-party duopoly through campaign finance laws, policies regulating access to public television,[60] patronage practices, partisan gerrymandering, and potentially a wide variety of other measures. Indeed, the Supreme Court recently denied certiorari in a Florida case in which the state supreme court upheld a state law subsidizing the filing fees of only major party candidates on grounds that the law "is reasonably related to the state's important interest in strengthening and encouraging major parties, and thereby discouraging minor parties, as a means of preventing factionalism and the multiplicity of splinter groups."[61]

---

[56] Id at 1382 (Souter dissenting).

[57] The remaining two Justices, Stevens and Ginsburg, also appear to agree that a state may enact laws that disadvantage third parties if there is a sufficiently strong showing that the law promotes political stability, at least so long as the laws do not infringe on the First Amendment rights of third parties. Id at 1378 (Stevens dissenting).

[58] Id at 1374.

[59] Id.

[60] *Libertarian Party of Florida v Smith*, 687 S2d 1292, 1295 (Fla 1996), cert denied, 118 S Ct 57 (1997).

[61] Currently pending before the Supreme Court is a case involving a public television station's decision to exclude from a televised debate for a Congressional seat all candidates besides the Democratic and Republican candidates. The Eighth Circuit held that the debate was a limited public forum and that a government-employed journalist could not decide to exclude a third-party candidate on grounds that the candidacy was not "viable." *Forbes v Arkansas Educational Television Comm'n*, 93 F3d 497, 505 (8th Cir 1996), cert granted, 117 S Ct 1243 (1997).

II. The Unconvincing Case That the Two-Party System Deserves Protection

Although the Court has never engaged in any detailed analysis of the importance of the two-party system, perhaps members of the Court thought such an analysis was unnecessary because the proposition is uncontroversial.[62] The leading advocates of that proposition, the responsible party government scholars, have argued that the two-party system promotes political stability, combats factionalism, and provides a valuable voting cue. As I show in this part, however, these scholars have not proven that the two-party system, especially the modern system since the advent of capital-intensive, candidate-centered campaigns, actually has these effects.

One might answer my arguments below and in Part III, where I argue that protection of the two-party system is unnecessary even if desirable, by asserting that the empirical evidence of the benefits of the two-party system is sufficiently murky that states should be allowed to make a reasoned choice about whether to favor the two-party system. For example, Minnesota can choose to ban fusion while New York can choose to allow it.

But laws infringing on citizens' First Amendment rights require (or should require) more than a rational basis unsupported by any evidence. The Court in *Timmons* explained that "[r]egulations imposing severe burdens on plaintiffs' rights must be narrowly tailored and advance a compelling state interest."[63] And even those that impose lesser burdens should require a close look: a state still must show "important regulatory interests"[64] to justify "reasonable, nondiscriminatory restrictions."[65] As the Court explained in *Anderson v Celebrezze:*

> [A court] must identify and evaluate the precise interests put forward by the State as justifications for the burden imposed by its rule. In passing judgment, the Court must not only determine the legitimacy and strength of each of those interests; it

---

[62] See *Branti*, 445 US at 528 (Powell dissenting) ("Until today, I would have believed that the importance of political parties was self-evident.").

[63] 117 S Ct at 1370.

[64] Id, quoting *Burdick v Takushi*, 504 US 428, 434 (1991).

[65] 117 S Ct at 1370, quoting *Burdick v Takushi*, 504 US at 434.

also must consider the extent to which those interests make it necessary to burden the plaintiff's rights.[66]

For at least three good reasons the Court should be skeptical of speculative empirical claims made in support of legislation favoring the two-party system. First, there is a severe agency problem here: virtually all of the legislators who will make these decisions are members of one of the two major political parties,[67] and the choice may be less the product of reason than of self-interest.[68]

Second, there are informational losses associated with restrictions on third parties. As Justice Marshall explained in his dissent in *Munro v Socialist Workers Party*,[69] a "minor party's often unconventional positions broaden political debate, expand the range of issues with which the electorate is concerned, and influence the positions of the majority, in some instances ultimately becoming majority positions."[70] Ross Perot's 1992 and 1996 candidacies, with their focus on deficit reduction, are prime examples of Justice Marshall's argument.

Favoring the two-party system ultimately provides voters with less information about the choices available to them in terms of candidates, parties, and issues. If more information about political choices is better than less,[71] restrictions that limit the availability of information should be justified on grounds supported by empirical evidence, not speculative appeals to preserve the two-party system. Indeed, we need look no further than *Williams v Rhodes* to recognize that "[t]here is, of course, no reason why two parties should retain a permanent monopoly on the right to have people vote for or against them. Competition in ideas and governmental policies is at the core of our electoral process and of the First Amendment freedoms."[72]

---

[66] 460 US 780, 789 (1983).

[67] See notes 188–89.

[68] See Samuel Issacharoff and Richard H. Pildes, *Politics as Markets: Partisan Lockups of the Democratic Process*, 50 Stan L Rev (forthcoming 1998); Hasen, 14 Cardozo L Rev at 1331 (cited in note 20).

[69] 479 US 189 (1986).

[70] Id at 200 (Marshall dissenting).

[71] But see Michael A. Fitts, *Can Ignorance Be Bliss? Imperfect Information as a Positive Influence in Political Institutions*, 88 Mich L Rev 917, 920–23 (1990) (arguing in favor of centralized political institutions to disseminate information to the public).

[72] 393 US 23, 32 (1968).

Finally, the lack of a competitive political market may have other costs as well. In an economic duopoly, absence of market competition leads to social inefficiencies. The inefficiencies may be greatest when there is collusion among the two firms,[73] but even absent collusion, some models of duopolistic competition predict prices above the competitive rate.[74] By analogy, duopolistic political competition, even given "natural monopolies,"[75] may lead to similar inefficiencies. Though Supreme Court opinions rejecting state protection of the two-party system will not lead to the creations of viable third parties,[76] the extra protections for the Democratic and Republican parties that *Timmons* allows could further retard development of a competitive political market. Without third parties to challenge the positions of the two major parties and their candidates, the major parties are likely to become (some would say, remain) complacent and unresponsive to social pressures and movements. A strong duopoly could make it less likely that the Democrats and Republicans will feel pressure to become the encompassing parties that responsible party government theorists hope they will become. By the same token, protecting the preeminent position of the two major parties could exacerbate interest-group rent-seeking in the political process. A more competitive political market makes it difficult for party leaders to credibly promise to deliver votes in deals with rent seekers.

When a state adopts a law that has these adverse effects on important interests, it has to provide at least a strong justification. But it is doubtful that the responsible party government position that the Court uncritically accepted in *Timmons* can provide any justification for legislation designed to maintain the two-party system—much less the kind of justification needed to warrant inflicting these burdens on First Amendment interests.[77]

---

[73] See David M. Kreps, *A Course in Microeconomic Theory* 524–31 (Princeton, 1990) (discussing collusion by duopolists and difficulty in predicting when collusion will be sustained).

[74] Id at 326–28 (presenting Cournot model in which duopolists set prices above the competitive price but below the monopoly price); but see id at 330–35 (presenting Bertrand model in which duopolists set price equal to the competitive price).

[75] Issacharoff and Pildes, 50 Stan L Rev (cited in note 68).

[76] See Part III.

[77] In the absence of any burdens on the First Amendment, I believe rational basis review of election laws that favor the two-party system should be sufficient. Thus, the Court would not need to apply heightened scrutiny to an argument that the use of single-member districts or plurality elections are unconstitutional. Though these laws more than any others tend to dictate the number of viable political parties, see Part III below, they do not explic-

A. THE THEORY OF RESPONSIBLE PARTY GOVERNMENT[78]

Before Woodrow Wilson became U.S. president, he served as president of the American Political Science Association (APSA). As APSA president, Wilson used his bully pulpit, such as it was, to advocate the theory that came to be known as "responsible party government."[79] According to this theory, the health of American democracy depends upon a strong two-party system, and government and the parties should take steps to strengthen the system. The model was that of the British party system, "supposedly disciplined and cohesive, and unhampered by constitutional barriers in their governing function."[80]

Other APSA presidents following Wilson continued to push the point. E. E. Schattschneider, writing in 1942, made the oft-quoted

---

itly restrict the exercise of rights protected by the First Amendment, as antifusion laws, ballot access laws, and patronage practices do. Under a rational basis review, single-member districts and plurality elections may be upheld on the ground that the state must make a choice among numerous possible electoral systems, and there is no a priori reason to choose one over the other; to hold otherwise would require the Court not only to choose between the current system and more proportional systems, but to choose among a huge variety of proportional systems. In addition, a state reasonably could prefer single-member districts and plurality elections because they may be easier or cheaper to administer than multimember or multiround elections.

[78] For a detailed history of early responsible party government scholarship, see Austin Ranney, *The Doctrine of Responsible Party Government* (Illinois, 1962). Ranney characterized the position as follows:

> There must exist at least two (and preferably only two) unified, disciplined political parties. Each has its conception of what the people want and a program of various measures designed to satisfy those wants. In a pre-election campaign each attempts to convince a majority of the people that its program will best do what the people want done. In the election each voter votes for a particular candidate in his district, primarily because that candidate is a member of the party which the voter wants to take power, and only secondarily because he prefers the individual qualities of one candidate to those of the other. The party which secures a majority of the offices of government in the election then takes over the entire power of the government and the entire responsibility for what the government does. It then proceeds to put its program into effect. Or perhaps unforeseen circumstances arise which make the party decide to alter or even abandon its program. In any event, at the next election the people decide whether, on the whole, they approve of the general direction that the party in power has been taking—in short, whether their wants are being satisfied. If the answer is yes, they return that party to power; if the answer is no, they replace it with the opposition party.

Id at 12.

[79] Id at 25–47 (summarizing Wilson's views).

[80] David E. Price, *Bringing Back the Parties* 103 (Congressional Quarterly, 1984). There is considerable controversy over whether the British party system ever lived up to this ideal. For a summary of the arguments, see Evron M. Kirkpatrick, *"Toward a More Responsible, Two-Party System": Political Science, Policy Science, or Pseudo-Science?* 65 Am Pol Sci Rev 965, 974–76 (1971).

claim that "modern democracy is unthinkable save in terms of the parties."[81] V. O. Key remarked that parties "perform the function of the articulation of the interests and aspirations of a substantial segment of the citizenry, usually in ways contended to be promotive of the national weal."[82]

The effort reached its zenith in 1950 with the publication of *Toward a More Responsible Two-Party System* by the APSA's Committee on Political Parties.[83] The report contained detailed proposals for strengthening the two-party system, also "based on a particular reading of British experience."[84] Some of the proposals concerned steps political parties could take themselves, such as setting up party councils that included elected officials to set party policy.[85] Other proposals concerned changes in election laws, such as lengthening the Congressional House term to four years.[86] The *APSA Report* declared the two parties to be "indispensable instruments of government" aimed at providing the electorate "with a proper range of choice between alternatives of action."[87] It has been roundly criticized for its failure to provide empirical justification for its normative program.[88]

A number of political scientists, including members of a loose-knit group of about 500 political scientists called the Committee on Party Renewal,[89] continue to push the responsible party govern-

[81] E. E. Schattschneider, *Party Government* 1 (Holt, Rinehart & Winston, 1942).

[82] V. O. Key, *Politics, Parties, & Pressure Groups* 9 (Thomas Y. Crowell, 5th ed 1964).

[83] *Toward a More Responsible Two-Party System: A Report of the Committee on Political Parties American Political Science Association* (Rinehart, 1950) (*APSA Report*). The report originally was published as a supplement to volume 44, number 3, 1950, of *The American Political Science Review*.

[84] Kirkpatrick, 65 Am Pol Sci Rev at 967 (cited in note 80).

[85] *APSA Report* at 43 (cited in note 83); see also Larry J. Sabato, *The Party's Just Begun: Shaping Political Parties for America's Future* 176–99 (Scott, Foresman, 1988).

[86] *APSA Report* at 75 (cited in note 83).

[87] Id at 15 (emphasis omitted). The report does not detail the reasons for supporting a two-party system, on grounds that "[t]he two party system is so strongly rooted in the political traditions of this country and public preference for it is so well established that consideration of other possibilities seems entirely academic." Id at 18.

[88] See, for example, Kirkpatrick, 65 Am Pol Sci Rev at 978 (cited in note 80) ("It is interesting that, as normative political science, no effort whatsoever was made to clarify or justify this norm. Apparently its benefits were presumed to be self-evident and perhaps they were and are so for most Americans. But what is commonly acceptable is not necessarily good scholarship.").

[89] The Committee's Declaration of Principles, Principles of Strong Party Organization, and Statement on Campaign Finance appear as Appendixes A–C in the committee's amicus brief in the case of *Colorado Republican Fed. Campaign Comm. v Fed. Elect Comm'n*, 116 S

ment position, in part through a litigation strategy.[90] Much of the focus of litigation has been to preserve and strengthen the rights of political party organizations to conduct their internal affairs without state regulation.[91] The group did not file an amicus brief in *Timmons*, perhaps because some committee members believe that third-party challenges to the two major parties actually strengthen the two-party system.[92]

Although responsible party government scholars have advanced a number of arguments as to why a strong two-party system promotes democracy, the arguments fit into three broad categories: political stability, antifactionalism, and voting cue.

1. *Political stability.* Perhaps the greatest perceived benefit of a two-party system is political stability, an attribute that *Timmons* and earlier opinions cited specifically as flowing from a strong two-party system.[93] According to the theory, the two-party system promotes political stability by creating extremely large coalitions, called encompassing coalitions by some.[94] The party, as an encompassing coalition, is able to accommodate a large number of diverse groups and viewpoints, giving each group a stake in the outcome of the election. The party therefore discourages politics divided

---

Ct 2309 (1996). Brief Amicus Curiae Committee for Party Renewal et al, 1996 WL 75770, *1a–16a (*CPR Amicus Brief*).

[90] See Daniel Hays Lowenstein, *Associational Rights of Major Political Parties: A Skeptical Inquiry*, 71 Tex L Rev 1741, 1791 (1993) (criticizing party renewal advocates' focus on litigation and arguing in favor of taking the case to the American people).

[91] For a sampling of views of responsible party government scholars on the association cases, see Mark E. Rush, *Voters' Rights and the Legal Status of American Political Parties*, 9 J L & Pol 487 (1993); Brian L. Porto, *The Constitution and Political Parties: Supreme Court Jurisprudence and Its Implications for Partybuilding*, 8 Const Comm 433 (1991); Roy Christman and Barbara Norrander, *A Reflection on Political Party Deregulation Via the Courts: The Case of California*, 6 J L & Pol 723 (1990); Leon D. Epstein, *Will American Political Parties Be Privatized?* 5 J L & Pol 239 (1989); Clifton McCleskey, *Parties at the Bar: Equal Protection, Freedom of Association, and the Rights of Political Organizations*, 46 J Pol 346 (1984). For a skeptical inquiry into political parties' rights of association, see Lowenstein, 71 Tex L Rev 1741 (cited in note 90).

[92] An amicus brief in *Timmons* signed by a number of responsible party government scholars, including Walter Dean Burnham, opposed the fusion ban, stating that "a two-party system that actively hinders minor parties tends to discourage meaningful electoral competition between issue-oriented political parties." *CND Amicus Brief* at *14 (cited in note 52).

[93] *Timmons*, 117 S Ct at 1374; *Rutan*, 497 US at 107 (Scalia dissenting); *Davis*, 478 US at 144–45 (O'Connor concurring); *Branti*, 445 US at 527–28 (Powell dissenting).

[94] Fitts characterizes political parties as encompassing coalitions, relying upon Mancur Olson's work in *The Rise and Decline of Nations* (Yale, 1982). See Fitts, 136 U Pa L Rev at 1607 (cited in note 31).

by group or ideological viewpoints. This in turn fosters political stability.[95]

Strong parties also encourage stability by making government more accountable. Cohesive majority parties can take the credit for positive governmental output and take the blame for negative governmental output.[96] Absent strong parties, elected officials may simply lack the backbone or organization necessary to make difficult decisions.[97]

Stability also results as both political parties gravitate toward the political center.[98] Using an early spatial model of voting, Anthony Downs found that in a two-party system both parties "will try to be similar and to equivocate."[99] Ideological campaigns are rare,[100] and the lack of ideology also promotes political stability by keeping existing social cleavages latent. According to responsible party government scholars, political parties exert influence over individual elected officials to tend toward the political center, which these scholars implicitly correlate with acting for the "public good."[101]

---

[95] See Xandra Kayden and Eddie Mahe, Jr., *The Party Goes On: The Persistence of the Two-Party System in the United States* 207 (Basic Books, 1985) (arguing that a weak party system "cannot provide focus for political debate, cannot generate commitment to the political system by the public at large. It cannot bring the interests together for compromise and cannot promote consensus").

[96] As Schattschneider put it, "A major party mobilizes a majority in order to take control of the government and accepts responsibility for the whole conduct of public policy." Schattschneider, *Party Government* at 63 (cited in note 81).

[97] See Price, *Bringing Back the Parties* at 114–16 (cited in note 80).

[98] Schattschneider, *Party Government* at 85 (cited in note 81) (stating that two-party system produces "moderate" parties).

[99] Anthony Downs, *An Economic Theory of Democracy* 137 (Harper Collins, 1957). More complex models have challenged this conclusion. See note 147.

[100] See Downs, *Economic Theory of Democracy* at 115 (cited in note 99) ("Parties in a two-party system deliberately change their platforms so that they resemble one another . . . ").

[101] For example, the *APSA Report* warned that weakened political parties "might . . . set in motion more extreme tendencies to the political left and the political right. This, again, would represent a condition to which neither our political institutions nor our civic habits are adapted." *APSA Report* at 95 (cited in note 83) (emphasis omitted); see also Price, *Bringing Back the Parties* at 111 (cited in note 80) (Parties "help offset the biases of pluralism, balancing the demands of society's best-organized and best-financed groups with appeals that are more directly responsive to broader public interests."); Key, *Politics* at 167 (cited in note 82) ("[P]arties must do more than combine interests for the satisfaction of mutually compatible greed: they must . . . implant a widespread belief that their policies promote the common weal."); Schattschneider, *Party Government* at 85 (cited in note 81) ("[I]t is difficult to imagine anything more important than the tendency of the parties to avoid extreme politics.").

2. *Antifactionalism.* The second great perceived benefit of the two-party system is its tendency to minimize the power of factions or special interest groups.[102] In the absence of strong parties, elected officials are more likely to be swayed by interest groups pursuing a narrow agenda who may offer or threaten to withdraw political support, campaign contributions, or other political items necessary for the politician's reelection.[103]

When elected officials are swayed by special interests, they fail to act in the public good. Not only does this defeat the purposes of democratic politics (according to these scholars), but it undermines political stability, leads to gridlock, and causes the voters to lose confidence in their elected officials and in the democratic system generally.[104]

3. *Voting cue.* The final perceived benefit of the two-party system is the presence of a voting cue for voters.[105] Voters often do not

---

[102] See David K. Ryden, *Representation in Crisis: The Constitution, Interest Groups, and Political Parties* 119 (SUNY, 1996) ("Parties are uniquely positioned to dampen the factional tendencies of intensified group participation."); Sabato, *Party's Just Begun* at 5 (cited in note 85) ("[T]he two parties serve as vital, umbrellalike, consensus-forming institutions that help counteract the powerful centrifugal forces in a country teeming with hundreds of racial, economic, social, religious, and political groups."); Walter Dean Burnham, *Critical Elections and the Mainsprings of American Politics* 133 (W.W. Norton, 1970) ("[P]olitical parties, with all their well-known human and structural shortcomings, are the only devices thus far invented by the wit of Western man which with some effectiveness can generate countervailing collective power on behalf of the many individually powerless against the relatively few who are individually—or organizationally—powerful."); *APSA Report* at 19 (cited in note 83) (calling for a reinforced party system to cope with the *"multiplied organized pressures"*); Schattschneider, *Party Government* at 85 (cited in note 81) ("[P]arty managers *need not meet every demand made by every interest."*); but see id at 192 ("If the parties exercised the power to govern effectively, *they would shut out the pressure groups."*).

[103] See Sabato, *Party's Just Begun* at 20–21 (cited in note 85); Price, *Bringing Back the Parties* at 110–11 (cited in note 80) (parties balance demands of special interests "against broader public interests"); *CPR Amicus Brief* at *14 (cited in note 89) ("Single-issue groups lead to fragmented government, the neglect of broader policy needs, and the neglect of needs of citizens not represented by groups."); Schattschneider, *Party Government* at 196 (cited in note 81) (pressure group tries to "alarm [a member of Congress] and threatens him with defeat.").

[104] Schattschneider, *Party Government* at 208 (cited in note 81) (arguing that only strong parties, and not pressure groups can handle the "planning, . . . integration, and over-all management of public affairs for the protection of the great interests of the nation").

[105] Sabato, *Party's Just Begun* at 8 (cited in note 85) ("party affiliation provides a useful cue for voters, particularly the least informed and interested, who can use party as a shortcut or substitute for interpreting issues and events they may little comprehend"); Price, *Bringing Back the Parties* at 109 (cited in note 80) ("By helping voters make rational and consistent electoral choices, parties link the popular base of the political order and the institutions of government.").

have the time or the inclination to invest in information about whom to vote for; indeed, most information voters acquire about political candidates they acquire fortuitously, without any effort.[106] The party affiliation of the candidate provides an informational shortcut. Voters may not know anything personal about the candidates, but if a particular voter knows whether she prefers the Democratic or Republican ideological position, and she knows the party affiliations of the candidate, she may use that information to choose a candidate closer to her own ideological position. Studies consistently have shown that Democratic politicians are more "liberal" and Republican politicians are more "conservative" on a host of issues,[107] making the party cue, if not infallible, a good first cut for the voter.

The voting cue argument for political parties certainly is in tension with the argument that the two-party system produces nonideological parties tending toward the political center.[108] After all, if both parties tend toward centrist politics, the cues ultimately are irrelevant for making a meaningful electoral choice. Some responsible party government scholars have recognized this tension but have ostensibly resolved it by noting that enough debate exists about the location of the political center to allow for some tame ideological competition. Thus the *APSA Report* called for the two major parties to differentiate themselves from one another but said such differentiation "will not cause the parties to differ more fundamentally or more sharply than they have in the past" or lead to the erection of "an ideological wall" between the parties.[109]

B. THE MODERN TRANSFORMATION OF THE U.S. PARTY SYSTEM

For more than three decades, scholars and other political observers have debated whether the two major American political parties are in a state of decline, stasis, or resurgence. We have been

---

[106] See Downs, *Economic Theory of Democracy* at 221–25 (cited in note 99).

[107] For a summary of some of the evidence, see John H. Aldrich, *Why Parties? The Origin and Transformation of Political Parties in America* 169–78 (Chicago, 1995).

[108] See Frank J. Sorauf and Paul Allen Beck, *Party Politics in America* 393 (Harper Collins, 6th ed 1988) (noting that critics of the responsible party government position have concentrated on "one insistent theme: the nonideological, heterogeneous, and pragmatic nature of the American parties").

[109] *APSA Report* at 2 (cited in note 83).

told that *The Party's Over*,[110] *The Party Goes On*,[111] and *The Party's Just Begun*.[112] The apparent conflict among the three positions stems, at least in part, from conflicting definitions of what constitutes the political party. V. O. Key conceived of political parties as composed of at least three distinct elements: the party organization, the party-in-government, and the party-in-the-electorate.[113] To speak of resurgence or decline of parties, therefore, requires a greater degree of specificity.

In recent years party organizations have shown remarkable resurgence. But the party-in-the-electorate has all but collapsed.[114] These changes have transformed the fundamental nature of American political parties and diminished the importance of political parties to the maintenance of American democracy.

Both the resurgence of party organizations and the demise of the party-in-the-electorate can be traced to changes in the nature of campaigning, especially in the 1960s. In brief, changes in the technology of campaigning, most importantly the rise of television, and various party reforms, most importantly changes in the presidential nomination process, have transformed campaigns for major offices from party-centered, labor-intensive campaigns to candidate-centered, capital-intensive campaigns.[115]

Through the late 1800s, elections were party-centered affairs. Before 1889 parties printed up ballots for individuals to cast. Each party used a different color ballot, making it easy to determine the party allegiance of each voter and making voting for any combination of candidates other than a straight party ticket exceedingly difficult.[116] Bribery and intimidation were common.[117] Not until

---

[110] Broder (cited in note 31).

[111] Kayden and Mahe (cited in note 95).

[112] Sabato (cited in note 85).

[113] Key, *Politics* at 163–65 (cited in note 82) (describing meanings of "party").

[114] As I explain in Part III.A, the "party-in-government," as measured by the percentage of legislators from one of the two major political parties and by party unity scores, appears to have strengthened moderately since World War II.

[115] For a public choice history of the transformation, see Joseph D. Reid, Jr. and Michael M. Kurth, *Public Employees in Political Firms: Part A. The Patronage Era*, 59 Pub Choice 253 (1988), and Joseph D. Reid, Jr. and Michael M. Kurth, *Public Employees in Political Firms: Part B. Civil Service and Militancy*, 60 Pub Choice 41 (1989).

[116] Burnham, *Critical Elections* at 74–75 (cited in note 102); see also Argersinger, 85 Am Hist Rev at 290–91 (cited in note 2).

[117] Burnham, *Critical Elections* at 73 (cited in note 102); Key, *Politics* at 639 (cited in note 82).

1889 did Massachusetts first introduce the Australian (or secret) ballot for elections; other states quickly followed suit.[118] Voter turnout declined with the secret ballot's arrival.[119]

Even after the rise of the secret ballot, campaigns remained party-centered and labor-intensive. Get-out-the-vote drives in major cities often depended upon the workings of political machines. Party bosses doled out favors (most importantly, government jobs) in exchange for party work. In the first Mayor Daley's Chicago, for example, the Democratic Organization took a 2% deduction from each city employee's paycheck and required city workers to work for the election of the party's candidates.[120]

Though some significant changes in the nature of parties may be traced to party reform beginning in the Progressive era,[121] the most drastic changes in party structure coincide with the arrival of television. Television provided a method by which candidates could take their message directly and easily to voters.[122] It also challenged the parties' ability to lay exclusive claim to political legitimacy.[123] Voters no longer needed to rely upon a party cue to know whether they agreed with the candidate's views.[124]

Television advertising became a major method for conducting state-wide and many national campaigns.[125] Advertising was (and

---

[118] Burnham, *Critical Elections* at 74 (cited in note 102).

[119] Jac C. Heckelman, *The Effect of the Secret Ballot on Voter Turnout Rates*, 82 Pub Choice 107, 119 (1995). Heckelman found that the introduction of the secret ballot in various states at the beginning of the century accounted for an average drop in turnout of 6.9%, a fact he attributes to the elimination of effective bribery.

[120] See Bowman, *Anybody Anybody*, 86 Nw U L Rev at 84 (cited in note 20).

[121] See Austin Ranney, *Curing the Mischiefs of Faction: Party Reform in America* 17–19 (California, 1975).

[122] For an extensive discussion, see William Crotty, *American Parties in Decline* 75–89 (Little, Brown, 2d ed 1984).

[123] Joel H. Silbey, *The Rise and Fall of American Political Parties 1790–1993*, in L. Sandy Maisel, ed, *The Parties Respond: Changes in American Parties and Campaigns* 3, 14 (Westview, 2d ed 1994) (*The Parties Respond*).

[124] Polsby has compared mounting a modern presidential campaign to the production of a Broadway show: "A company is newly created. It sells tickets, books theaters, writes a script (frequently known as 'the speech'), and advertises the star. Individual contributions are solicited through the mail." Nelson W. Polsby, *Consequences of Party Reform* 72 (Oxford, 1983).

[125] "Usually, only serious candidates for major offices—presidential, senatorial, and gubernatorial make substantial use of television advertisements. Probably only about one-half of the House candidates purchase television time, and its cost often represents just a small portion of their campaign spending." Herbert E. Alexander and Anthony Corrado, *Financing the 1992 Election* 233–34 (M.E. Sharpe, 1995). But House candidates spend their money on direct mail advertising, another expensive medium.

remains) expensive. As candidates began having a greater need to
raise funds and a lesser need for party faithful (including patronage
employees) to get out the vote, the mass political party declined.[126]
New Deal legislation that provided financial support for individuals who had previously relied upon political machine patronage for
such support also precipitated the decline.[127]

Reforms of internal party electoral processes, particularly the
presidential nomination processes, also have changed the orientation of campaigns away from the party and toward the candidate.[128]
"Since 1968, presidential primaries have become the dominant
method for selecting delegates to the national nominating conventions, and they are now utilized in over half of the states, including
most of the largest."[129] These changes moved power to choose the
major parties' nominees from the hands of local bosses into the
hands of party-affiliated voters, the party-in-the-electorate,
thereby weakening the link between the party-in-the-electorate
and the party organization and strengthening the direct relationship between candidate and voter.

With the demise of most patronage positions and with the pre-
dominance of mass media advertising, there is less of a need for
a mass political party. The decline in demand has been coupled
with a decline in party identification by the voters.[130] It is not so
much that voters have negative attitudes toward parties as that they
find the parties irrelevant to their political lives.[131] It is therefore
no longer correct to conceive of a "party-in-the-electorate." As

---

[126] Silbey in *The Parties Respond* at 17 (cited in note 123) (after the 1940s, candidates no
longer ran for office "primarily by mobilizing the party faithful, if they did so at all.").

[127] Aldrich, *Why Parties?* at 268–69 (cited in note 107).

[128] For a summary of the post-1968 reforms, see William Crotty, *Party Reform* (Longman,
1983).

[129] Sorauf and Beck, *Party Politics in America* at 314 (cited in note 108). The move to the
direct primary below the presidential level began as a progressive reform in 1903 and was
adopted by most states by the 1920s. See Burnham, *Critical Elections* at 75 (cited in note
102).

[130] Scholars have debated the extent to which partisan identification is a social-psychologi-
cal attachment as opposed to a rational affiliation. For a summary of the debate, see Aldrich,
Why Parties? at 165–69 (cited in note 107), and for a spirited defense of the social-psycho-
logical theory that "party identification is a long-term predisposition, largely exogenous to
the vote decisions within a given election campaign," see Warren E. Miller and J. Merrill
Shanks, *The New American Voter* 149 (Harvard, 1996).

[131] See Martin P. Wattenberg, *The Decline of American Political Parties 1952–1984* (Harvard, 1986); see also Aldrich, *Why Parties?* at 248–52 (cited in note 107).

Aldrich has put it, the "party-in-the-electorate" has been transformed simply into the "parties-in-elections."[132]

Although some expected this change in the nature of American political campaigns to spell the demise of formal party organizations, this has not been the case. As Aldrich explains, party organizations play an increasingly important role as "party in service to its candidates."[133] The capital-intensive, television-driven campaign requires both fundraising expertise and media savvy. Party organizations have filled this role, revitalizing their role in campaigns. Parties provide the tools for candidates to run successfully under the party's banner, providing the needed expertise and cash.[134]

The national Democratic and Republican party organizations surely are at their height of power, with larger staffs and more money than ever before.[135] Counting both hard and soft money,[136]

---

[132] Aldrich, *Why Parties?* at 260 (cited in note 107); see also Polsby, *Consequences of Party Reform* at 132–33 (cited in note 124) ("Party is increasingly a label for masses of individual voters who pick among various candidates in primary elections as they would among any alternatives marketed by the mass media.").

[133] Aldrich, *Why Parties?* at 269 (cited in note 107).

[134] Frank J. Sorauf and Scott A. Wilson, *Political Parties and Campaign Finance: Adaptation and Accommodation Toward a Changing Role*, in *The Parties Respond* at 235, 248 (cited in note 123) (The parties' "ability to raise money and to direct the raising of money from others, as well as their ability to provide campaign technologies and services, has won the parties an active role in campaign politics that they did not have in the 1960s and 1970s."); Kayden and Mahe, *The Party Goes On* at 191 (cited in note 95) ("Today, campaigns are run by professionals (and even volunteers) who are trained in their tasks and who rely on advice and assistance from the national and state parties and the private consulting firms they employ to do their advertising, fund raising, and general campaigning."); but see Crotty, *American Parties in Decline* at 75 (cited in note 122) ("Television allows those candidates who can command the necessary financial resources to mount impressive challenges to incumbents at all levels. Such candidates are not dependent on the political party to sponsor their careers.").

[135] Aldrich, *Why Parties?* at 256–60 (cited in note 107); see also Schattschneider, *Party Government* at 129–69 (cited in note 81) (describing weakness of national political parties as of 1942). Of course, some of that power is a shift from local to national political power, but probably not all of it.

[136]

> Soft money is used to pay a portion of the overhead expenses of party organizations, as well as other shared expenses that benefit both federal and non-federal elections. It is used for issue advocacy, as well as generic party advertising. A portion is transferred from national committees to state and local party committees, while some is contributed directly to candidates in non-federal races. It also supports construction and maintenance of party headquarters.

Federal Election Commission News Release dated March 19, 1997, FEC Reports Major Increase in Party Activity for 1995–96 2 (available on the Internet at http://www.fec.gov).

the national, state, and local party committees of the Democrats
and Republicans together raised $900.2 million[137] and spent $894.3
million[138] in the 1995–96 election cycle. In contrast, the total
amount of public financing provided to presidential candidates
Clinton, Dole, and Perot during that period was $154.5 million.[139]

Despite this new-found national power and despite technological innovation making it easier than ever to target and communicate with large numbers of voters, revitalized party organizations
have not increased the feelings of partisan intensity among the
electorate, as Kayden and Mahe had predicted.[140] Party organizations have grown immensely, but their growth has not revived the
party-in-the-electorate.

C. THE DUBIOUS BENEFITS OF DUOPOLY IN THE POST-1960s ERA

I now consider whether parties can provide the benefits described by responsible party government scholars, given the fundamental transformation of American political parties. Is it still true,
as Kayden and Mahe claim, that "[t]he system has been designed
for the benefit of the major political parties and most of us would
not want it any other way"?[141]

1. *The uncertain link between the two-party system and political stability.* Assessing the modern parties' role in promoting political stability is a difficult empirical question, one that depends not only
upon how stability is measured but also upon how much political
stability that exists may be attributed to the major political parties.

---

[137] Republicans raised $416.5 million in hard money and $138.2 million in soft money.
Democrats raised $221.6 million in hard money and $123.9 million in soft money. Id at
1–2.

[138] Republicans spent $408.5 million in hard money and $149.7 million in soft money.
Democrats spent $214.3 million in hard money and $121.8 million in soft money. Id at
1–2. This money does not include the over $24 million provided to both parties to help
pay for their national nominating conventions. See Federal Election Commission, Financing
the 1996 Presidential Campaign (available on the internet at http://www.fec.gov/pres96/
presgen1.htm).

[139] As major party nominees, Clinton and Dole each received $61.8 million. As a minor
party candidate receiving 19% of the vote in the 1992 election, Perot received $29 million.
Federal Election Commission, Financing the 1996 Presidential Campaign at 2 (cited in
note 138).

[140] Kayden and Mahe, *The Party Goes On* at 199–200 (cited in note 95). Of course, rational
party leaders may not want to increase feelings of partisan intensity unless they believe that
their party will benefit from it.

[141] Id at 8.

If we measure political stability by the number of viable political parties, things have remained especially stable: we still have only two. The most recent challenge to the two-party system came from the 1992 and 1996 candidacies of H. Ross Perot and the formation of Perot's Reform Party. But despite millions of Perot's own dollars in the 1992 race and $29 million in federal public financing in the 1996 race, Perot did not manage to capture a single electoral vote in either election.[142]

Measuring political stability by counting the number of parties, however, removes political stability as a rationale for protecting the two-party system. In other words, one cannot defend protecting the two-party system on grounds that such protection leads to a system dominated by two parties. There must be some benefit apart from the number of parties that constitutes "stability" worthy of protection.

We could instead measure political stability by voter confidence in the government. By 1992 nearly three-quarters of all Americans believed that the government was "pretty much run by a few big interests looking out for themselves" rather than "for the benefit of all people." Fewer than one-third of all Americans believed that in 1964.[143] We may quibble over whether this measure demonstrates political instability, lack of government legitimacy, political alienation, something else, or nothing at all. But even if all agreed that these data measure growing political instability, we cannot show that the changing nature of political parties has been responsible for causing or checking instability. The evidence, however, does tend to negate the concept of American political parties serving as "encompassing coalitions" representing vast interests in American society;[144] widespread dissatisfaction is inconsistent with a view of political parties as representing broad social interests.

Nor does proof of political instability in countries with numer-

---

[142] Much of that is to blame the electoral college and simply illustrates the mechanical effect of Duverger's Law. See Part III.B. Perot captured about 19% of the vote in 1992 and 8.6% of the vote in 1996. Robert Famighetti, ed, *The World Almanac and Book of Facts 1997* at 108 (World Almanac Books, 1996).

[143] Richard L. Hasen, *Clipping Coupons for Democracy: An Egalitarian/Public Choice Defense of Campaign Finance Vouchers*, 84 Cal L Rev 1, 3 nn 3–4 (1996), citing unpublished data from the University of Michigan Center for Political Studies, American National Election Studies 1952–1996, Table 4.13.

[144] See note 94 and accompanying text.

ous parties indicate that multipartism *causes* instability. The causal relationship could be nonexistent, causality could run in the opposite direction, or both instability and multipartism could both be caused by another factor or factors. The conventional wisdom in the United States is that proportional representation (PR) leads to multipartism and that this multipartism leads to governments, like those of Israel, that are dangerously unstable.[145] This is only half right. As I explain in Part III, plurality systems tend to be much more likely than PR to develop into two-party, rather than multiparty, systems.

But Rogowski has made a convincing argument that parliamentary systems using PR "best guarantees the *stability* of democratic policy."[146] After explaining the theoretical reasons why PR could promote greater stability than the U.S. electoral system based upon plurality,[147] Rogowski turned to the empirical evidence:

> Empirically, too, the supposed connection between plurality election and stability rests on overgeneralization or faulty recall to a surprising degree. Despite a widespread belief to the contrary, for example, the French Third Republic never used PR; indeed, according to some eminent historians, the regime's shifting parliamentary majorities were artifacts of its two-ballot majority system, reflecting only minuscule changes in popular sentiment. The ill-fated Spanish Republic . . . also elected its parliaments by plurality. Interwar Germany and Italy employed PR; but so, in those same years, did the extremely stable Swiss, Swedes, Norwegians, Danes, Belgians, and Dutch (who frequently attributed their "low-voltage politics" to the proportional system). Overall Rae concludes that it is "clearly silly" to hold that PR encourages insurgent parties or destabilizes regimes.[148]

---

[145] For an argument that the Israeli electoral system is not typical of most systems of proportional representation, and is therefore a misleading example, see Amy, *Real Choices/New Voices* at 169–70 (cited in note 6).

[146] Ronald Rogowski, *Trade and the Variety of Democratic Institutions*, 41 Intl Org 203, 209 (1987).

[147] For example, Rogowski notes that Downs's argument that plurality systems tend toward two parties in the political center, see text accompanying note 99, depends entirely on Downs's assumption that parties compete along a single ideological dimension. Rogowski, 41 Int Org at 209 (cited in note 146). Where there is multidimensional conflict, the model predicts plurality elections leading to high turnover and extreme instability of policy. Id.

[148] Id at 209–10 (footnotes omitted).

Rogowski instead attributes political stability or instability to social, ideological, or ethnic cleavages in society.[149]

In short, it is difficult to make a case for or against the argument that the modern two-party system is necessary for, or successful at, maintaining political stability, once we define political stability as more than the mere existence of only two viable political parties. I therefore reject premising an argument for Supreme Court protection of the two-party system on the unproven conjecture that the system maintains political stability.[150]

2. *Facilitating the mischiefs of faction?* The antifactionalist nature of modern two-party duopoly also is open to serious question. Indeed, far from being bulwarks against special interests, the major parties are increasingly the means by which interest groups accomplish their objectives. This development is a natural outgrowth of the shift from the classic party organization to the party-in-service-to-the-candidate. The classic party organization, especially strong local political machines, could command the loyalty of voters through granting or withholding government benefits, like patronage jobs. In such a system, interest groups had little that parties would need in order to deliver votes to the parties' candidates.

In contrast, the modern party-in-service-to-the-candidate has no mass political party and few government benefits to grant or with-

---

[149] Id at 210–12.

[150] According to responsible party government scholars, the decline in parties also has meant a decline in voter turnout and eras of divided government, where one party controls the presidency and the other party controls one or both houses of Congress. On the voter turnout point, see Paul R. Abramson and John H. Aldrich, *The Decline of Electoral Participation in America*, 76 Am Pol Sci Rev 502, 510 (1982) (finding that the decline in partisanship explains between 25% and 30% of the decline in voter turnout among white Americans). The correlation, however, does not prove causation, and it is possible that both turnout and decline in partisan identification are both effects of some other cause, such as a declining norm of voting. For a discussion, see Richard L. Hasen, *Voting Without Law?* 144 U Pa L Rev 2135, 2156–64 (1996). In any case, we do not know whether the decline in voter turnout has undermined political stability. See Stephen E. Bennet and David Resnick, *The Implications of Nonvoting for Democracy in the United States*, 34 Am J Pol Sci 771, 773–76 (1990) (arguing that widespread voting is essential to the survival of democratic government).

Some have blamed divided government for government gridlock. But Mayhew found that Congress was just as likely to enact major legislation during periods of divided government as during periods of unified government. See generally David R. Mayhew, *Divided We Govern: Party Control, Lawmaking, and Investigations, 1946–1990* (Yale, 1990). For a citation of other relevant authority on this debate, see Daniel Hays Lowenstein, *Election Law: Cases and Materials* 315–16 (Carolina Academic Press, 1995). In any case, we do not know if government gridlock has undermined political stability, or even whether gridlock exists.

hold. Instead, the modern party organization is the fundraiser and media handler of the candidate. It depends upon infusions of cash. In this system, interest groups have much that parties need in order to deliver votes to the parties' candidates.[151]

It is now common for candidates (and elected officials) to meet with those willing to donate money to the parties; party fundraising has been both the key to access and the source of recent scandal.[152] The current federal system of campaign finance has exacerbated this trend. Though individuals are limited to donating $1,000 to federal candidates during each election[153] and labor unions and corporations are barred from contributing directly to candidates,[154] soft money given to political parties for the general purpose of promoting the parties' candidates is not subject to these limits. Moreover, four Justices recently indicated their belief that parties may have a constitutional right to engage in unlimited spending in coordination with their candidates,[155] and a fifth vote may be close.[156] Recognition of such a right will more firmly entrench the parties as conduits between elected officials and interest groups seeking access.

Good circumstantial evidence indicates that sale of access to politicians by political parties has worked. As Richard Briffault notes,

> between January 1, 1995 and June 30, 1996—that is, well before the peak months of the 1996 presidential campaign—national Republican committees received $1.6 million from Philip Morris Co., $970,000 from RJR Nabisco, $448,000 from US Tobacco, $400,000 from Brown & Williamson Tobacco Co., and $300,000 from the Tobacco Institute. These are pretty large sums to be "diffused"—and there is at least anec-

---

[151] Parties cannot raise the money as well as interest groups because of the problem of collective action: interest groups are smaller and more focused than parties. They therefore can more easily extract contributions from their members. See generally Mancur Olson, *The Logic of Collective Action* (Harvard, 1971).

[152] For a concise summary of current scandals, see David E. Rosenbaum, *Campaign Finance: Developments So Far*, NY Times 9 (Apr 3, 1996).

[153] See 2 USC § 441a(a)(1)(A) (1996). Multicandidate political committees (commonly known as "political action committees" or "PACs") may contribute up to $5,000 per candidate per election. 2 USC § 441a(2)(A) (1996).

[154] See 2 USC § 441b(a) (1996).

[155] *Colorado Republican Fed. Campaign Comm. v Fed. Elect. Comm'n*, 116 S Ct 2309 (1996).

[156] Justices Breyer, O'Connor, and Souter did not reach the issue on "prudential" grounds, id at 2311 (plurality opinion), and they failed to express an opinion on how the issue should be decided.

dotal evidence of national Republican officials seeking to make state officeholders more attentive to the tobacco industry's interests.[157]

Recent evidence demonstrates that the Democratic party similarly has been exchanging tobacco money for access to members of Congress controlling tobacco-related legislation.[158]

Although I agree with critics who would say that this analysis fails to make an ironclad case that parties now facilitate the mischiefs of faction, I believe there is enough evidence here to call into serious question the contrary idea that modern parties serve antifactionalist goals. The circumstantial evidence and underlying theory point in the opposite direction. In short, neither political stability nor antifactionalism justifies the Supreme Court's decision to favor the two-party system.

3. *The missing link between the voting cue and the two-party system.* Given the candidate-based nature of modern political campaigns, the party voting cue has become less relevant in elections. As far back as 1979, Nie, Verba, and Petrocik explained that party affiliation no longer predicts behavior very well: "[F]ewer have such affiliation and fewer of those with affiliation follow it. The individual voter evaluates candidates on the basis of information and impressions conveyed by the mass media, and then votes on that basis."[159]

One strong piece of evidence that the party cue is less valuable to voters in high-salience races is the percentage of voters who engage in ticket splitting, voting for one major party for the president and another major party for their representative in Congress. Although only about 3% of voters split their votes in 1900, on average since the 1960s one-third of all voters have done so.[160] But the cue remains especially relevant in low-salience elections, such as the election of county coroner, where the alternative voting cues

---

[157] Richard Briffault, *Campaign Finance, the Parties, and the Court: A Comment on Colorado Republican Federal Campaign Committee v Federal Elections Commission,* 14 Const Comm 91, 115 (1997) (footnote omitted). Briffault presents an excellent overview of the case and its implications.

[158] See *Tobacco Lobby Dines with Dems* (AP story dated July 9, 1997, on file with author).

[159] Norman H. Nie, et al, *The Changing American Voter* 346 (Harvard, enlarged ed 1979).

[160] See Morris P. Fiorina, *The Electorate at the Polls in the 1990s,* in *The Parties Respond* 123, 125–26 (cited in note 123).

relied upon by voters include gender, ethnic surname, occupation, or even use of a nickname.[161]

To be sure, the voting cue retains some vitality even in high-salience elections; Lowenstein argues that we would not see parties engaged in such pitched battles over partisan gerrymandering unless the party label retained some predictive power for voting.[162] And, after all, two-thirds of voters still do not split their tickets.[163]

It does not follow, however, that the Supreme Court is justified, in cases like *Timmons*, in allowing states to enact legislation for the purpose of protecting the voting cue by protecting the two-party system. In fact, *Timmons* illustrates precisely the opposite point: a strong two-party system is unnecessary to enhance the voting cue. Fusion could actually strengthen the voting cue by differentiating those Democratic and Republican candidates who become more issue-driven or ideological from those who reject such a position.[164] Thus, voters in New York can separate not only Democrats from Republicans, but also Liberal Democrats from Democrats and Conservative Republicans from Republicans.[165] A Democrat without the Liberal endorsement or a Republican without the Conservative endorsement is likely to be more centrist than those candidates with the competing endorsements.[166] Similarly, had Minnesota allowed Representative Dawkins to run as

---

[161] For the classic study of low-salience elections, see Gary C. Byrne and J. Kristian Pueschel, *But Who Should I Vote for for County Coroner?* 36 J Pol 778 (1974). I examine the voting cue related to the election of judges in Richard L. Hasen, *"High Court Wrongly Elected": A Public Choice Model of Judging and Its Implications for the Voting Rights Act,* 75 NC L Rev 1305, 1315–17 (1997).

[162] Daniel Hays Lowenstein, *American Political Parties* 63, 65, in Gillian Peele et al, eds, *Developments in American Politics* (St. Martin's, 1992).

[163] For a nuanced view on the decline of party identification among the electorate, see Leon D. Epstein, *Political Parties in the American Mold* 239–71 (Wisconsin, 1989).

[164] New York, which has had fusion politics since the 1840s, still sees 100% of its state legislators affiliating with the Democrats or the Republicans. See *The Book of the States 1996–97* 68 table 3.3 (Council on State Governments, 1997); Peter Field, *Fusionism,* in Kenneth T. Jackson, ed, *The Encyclopedia of New York City* 446 (Yale, 1995). For a detailed analysis and criticism of New York's fusion laws, see Howard A. Scarrow, *Parties, Elections and Representation in the State of New York* (New York Univ Press, 1983).

[165] And for that matter, voters could differentiate the occasional Liberal Republicans and Conservative Democrats from the others.

[166] See Scarrow, *Parties in New York* at 70 (cited in note 164) (presenting evidence that Liberal and Conservative parties tend to endorse Democratic and Republican candidates of appropriate ideological leanings).

both a Democrat and a New Party candidate, voters would receive more information about Dawkins's beliefs, assuming voters had an idea that the New Party is to the left of the Democrats.

The Supreme Court dismissed this reasoning in *Timmons* as an impermissible attempt to use the ballot as a means of expressing messages (as opposed to the permissible purpose of aggregating preferences and choosing candidates).[167] But this misunderstands the argument. The point is not that the New Party should be allowed to express itself on the ballot; it is that fusion provides more information and thereby enhances the voting cue for voters trying to choose among various candidates—one of the interests that the two-party system supposedly serves.

Ballot access restrictions also limit information available to candidates, thereby limiting the voting cue. By allowing third parties and independent candidates greater access to the ballot, more information will be available to voters on the range of ideological or other political choices that may be available to them. Of course, a crowded ballot could in some instances lead to voter confusion, and voter confusion could be a legitimate reason to limit the ballot in an appropriate circumstance.[168] But that reason is independent from a desire to preserve the voting cue. In sum, there is good reason to believe that the voting cue would be enhanced by loosening the hold of the two major parties on the electoral process.

III. The Unconvincing Case That the Two-Party System Needs Protection

All democratic nations have political parties,[169] even nations like the United States, whose constitution fails to mention political parties. In this part, I discuss recent work in political science showing that it is in the rational self-interest of politicians[170] to establish

---

[167] *Timmons*, 117 S Ct at 1372 ("Ballots serve primarily to elect candidates, not as fora for political expression.").

[168] Unlike the Court in *Munro v Socialist Workers Party*, 479 US 189, 195 (1986), in cases where First Amendment rights are burdened, I think it prudent to require actual proof that voters are likely to be confused, rather than assuming this fact without empirical evidence.

[169] Aldrich, *Why Parties?* at 3 (cited in note 107).

[170] I assume that politicians are vote maximizers. Election translates into utility gained by the politician in terms of power, popularity, the ability to impose values, or some combination of these benefits. See Hasen, 75 NC L Rev at 1315 (cited in note 161).

and maintain political parties and that two-party equilibrium in the United States remains stable. The two-party system is virtually certain to survive even if the Supreme Court does not permit states to limit First Amendment rights in order to protect it.

A. THE RATIONAL BIRTH AND LONGEVITY OF PARTIES

Whatever political parties are, they are groups of individuals, not unitary rational actors who can be understood as engaging in goal-maximizing behavior. Accordingly, to understand political parties in terms of maximizing behavior, I begin at the level of the individual, in particular, the politician who chooses whether to affiliate with a political party in running for office, and if so, with which party to affiliate. Parties are endogenous institutions shaped by rational, ambitious politicians.[171] "These politicians do not have partisan goals per se. Rather, they have more fundamental goals, and the party is only the instrument for achieving them."[172] Although politicians turn to political parties only when the parties are useful for solving problems that cannot be solved, or solved as well, through other means,[173] political parties traditionally have been quite useful for American politicians.

Political parties solve collective action problems for politicians. Parties provide important organizational advantages to a candidate, including economies of scale in campaigning.[174] A party label provides a shorthand way for voters, who have little incentive to invest time into learning about the positions of candidates,[175] to identify at least some of the candidate's beliefs. It provides the candidate with a "brand name."[176]

Perhaps most importantly, parties provide a rational method for groups of legislators to maximize their individual preferences. Thomas Schwartz offers an elegant example of the principle.[177]

---

[171] See Aldrich, *Why Parties?* at 4 (cited in note 107).

[172] Id.

[173] Id at 5.

[174] Id at 49; see also Sabato, *Party's Just Begun* at 8–9 (cited in note 85).

[175] See note 106 and accompanying text.

[176] Aldrich, *Why Parties?* at 49 (cited in note 107).

[177] Thomas Schwartz, "Why Parties?" 1–3 (unpublished research memorandum, UCLA, July 1989) (on file with the author). John Aldrich provides an extended discussion of this example. See Aldrich, *Why Parties?* at 29–39 (cited in note 107).

Three legislators, 1, 2, and 3, are voting on three bills, a, b, and c, with the following expected payoffs for each legislator:

Bill	Legislator 1	Legislator 2	Legislator 3
a	4	4	−9
b	4	−9	4
c	−9	4	4

As Schwartz explains, each bill passes in the absence of a prior agreement among the legislators because each bill benefits a majority. But with all three bills passed, each legislator nets −1 (4 + 4 − 9), a Pareto inefficient solution; each legislator would have been better off if all three bills could be defeated, netting each legislator 0.[178]

As an alternative to independent voting by each legislator or to universal agreement among all legislators to defeat the three bills, suppose legislators 1 and 2 (but not legislator 3) form a party, agreeing to vote together on all three bills. Under this agreement, legislators 1 and 2 would choose to vote for bill a and against bills b and c, yielding Legislators 1 and 2 each a payoff of 4;[179] legislator 3 would receive a payoff of −9. Legislators 1 and 2 are better off being in the "party" than either voting independently (with an outcome of −1 each), or voting against all three bills (with an outcome of 0 each). The formation of parties therefore is both individually rational and rational for groups of legislators, though it is not necessarily a socially efficient outcome.[180]

Besides solving these various collective action problems, political parties solve social choice problems for legislators, that is, problems that emerge from the possibility of cyclical voting and unstable majorities.[181] To illustrate, suppose that legislators 1 and 2 are not part of a political party, but are only temporary allies. Legislator 3 could make a deal with legislator 1 to vote against bills a

---

[178] Schwartz, "Why Parties?" at 2 (cited in note 177).

[179] Id at 3.

[180] Assume that the payoffs in the matrix represent payoffs to the legislators' respective constituencies. From a social standpoint, formation of the Legislator 1–2 party yields a total social cost of −1 (4 + 4 − 9), while a vote against all three bills yields a total social cost of 0, a socially superior result.

[181] For a good introduction to the social choice literature, see Maxwell L. Stearns, *The Misguided Renaissance of Social Choice*, 103 Yale L J 1219 (1994).

and c and for bill b, with a side payment to legislator 1 of 1 unit. Legislator 1 would be better off with the deal, because the result yields an outcome of 5 (4 + 1), and legislator 3 is better off, moving from an expected payoff of −9 to a payoff of 3 (4 − 1). Legislator 2 would then end up with a −9 payoff. But this result is unstable. Legislator 2 could make a deal with legislator 3 to vote against bills a and b, and for bill c. Legislator 2 moves from an expected payoff of −9 to an expected payoff of 4, and Legislator 3 moves from an expected payoff of 3 to an expected payoff of 4. And so on, with no end to the cycle.[182] A long-term agreement to vote together (rather than defect and form new alliances) solves the cycling problem. This long-term agreement itself is a "political party."[183]

Even absent strong ideological cohesion or social pressure among legislative party members to remain in the party,[184] parties survive because most legislators recognize the collective and social action problems inherent in politics and recognize that defection from the party is unlikely to yield higher individual benefits. Parties are not the only means by which politicians may solve these sorts of problems, but parties historically have done well at it.

Moreover, once parties exist, they become the easiest method by which to gain higher office, a point rational vote-maximizing politicians[185] almost universally recognize.[186] Thus, despite the fact

---

[182] For a slight variation on the numerical example, but reaching the same result, see Aldrich, *Why Parties?* at 42–43 (cited in note 107).

[183] Schwartz, "Why Parties?" at 3 (cited in note 177). As Aldrich explains, "the value of the party would be to institutionalize for the long haul (and over issues) and reduce uncertainty, ensuring each member some benefits for being in this party, such as here in avoiding the worst outcome." Aldrich, *Why Parties?* at 42 (cited in note 107).

[184] See Aldrich, *Why Parties?* at 26 (cited in note 107). That is not to say these forces are irrelevant. See Schwartz, "Why Parties?" at 8 (cited in note 177) ("In a group blessed with the small size, intimacy, longevity, and organizational resources of a legislature, it is in general not too hard for subgroups—especially sovereign majorities—to solve their collective-action problems and prevent defections."). It is only to say that parties should survive even in the absence of ideological cohesion and social pressure.

[185] A politician who is not vote-maximizing may rationally choose not to run with a political party or a major political party. For example, a politician who wishes to promote a particular unpopular ideological viewpoint may find it rational to run as an independent candidate, without a challenge from party members or leaders.

[186] Ross Perot's 1992 bid for the presidency is a good counterexample. There, Perot's vast wealth and his strategy to run as a Washington outsider may have made it rational for him to run without the benefits of a political party. However, by 1996 Perot formed and ran under the banner of a new party, the Reform Party. This move may have been motivated, at least in part, to qualify Perot for $29 million in public financing. See Mimi

that personal staffs, district offices, travel and communications budgets, and other office perks have transformed House incumbents into "435 political machines,"[187] members of Congress continue to find it rational to associate with a party. The 105th Congress had only one representative out of 435 who was neither a Democrat nor a Republican, down from 2 in the 104th Congress.[188] In neither the 104th nor 105th Congress were there any independent Senators. The situation is much the same in state legislatures. Only 18 of 7,375 (0.24%) of current state legislators elected in partisan elections were neither Democrats nor Republicans.[189]

Affiliation has meant more than simply a convenient label: members of the same political parties tend to vote together. Indeed, members of Congress have become increasingly more likely to vote together. In the House of Representatives, the voting cohesion of the majority House Democrats before the Republicans gained the majority in 1994 reached levels "unprecedented in the post–World War II era."[190] Similarly, on party votes in the 1980s and early 1990s, the Senate's majority party (alternatively Democrats and Republicans) maintained high party cohesion.[191] Party unity scores have hovered around 80% or more in the 1980s and early 1990s for both parties and in both chambers.[192]

Hall, *Perot Accepts Taxpayer Funding, Asks Supporters to Match the $29M*, USA Today 4A (Aug 20, 1996).

[187] Morris P. Fiorina, *The Electorate at the Polls in the 1990s*, in *The Parties Respond* 123, 130 (cited in note 123).

[188] See *Congressional Yellow Book: 105th Congress Roster* 11 (Leadership Directories, Inc, special ed Jan 1997).

[189] I calculated these figures using data from *Book of the States 1996–97* 68 table 3.3 (cited in note 164). I omitted Nebraska's 49 legislative members from the calculations because they are elected on a nonpartisan basis.

[190] Barbara Sinclair, *Parties in Congress: New Roles and Leadership Trends*, in *The Parties Respond* 299, 303 (cited in note 123) ("For the period 1951 through 1970, House Democrats' average party unity score was 78 percent; this fell to 74 percent for the period 1971–1982. After the 1982 election, the scores began rising and averaged 86 percent for the period 1983–1992.").

[191] Id at 315 ("Republicans voted with their party 81.2 percent of the time on average from 1981 through 1986, the period they controlled the Senate, compared with 71.9 percent during the 1969–1980 period. From 1987 through 1992, Senate Democrats supported their party's position on 83 percent of the roll calls on average—compared with 74.3 percent for 1969–1980 and 76.2 percent for 1981–1986.").

[192] See Aldrich, *Why Parties?* at 176 (cited in note 107).

B. THE TWO-PARTY EQUILIBRIUM IN THE UNITED STATES

The durability of the American party system depends, at least in part, on the fact that it is a two-party, rather than multiparty, system. For the last 150 years, two parties have dominated the political process. The Democrats competed first with the Whigs and, since the 1850s, with the Republicans, as the Whigs left the scene.[193] And there is every reason to believe the two-party system will thrive for the indefinite future.

To explain the two-party system's longevity, consider why two-party or multiparty systems emerge. Although some scholars writing earlier this century argued that the American two-party system is the product of an essential dualism of American politics[194] or of a particular political culture,[195] much of the modern work in this area traces to an important analysis of Maurice Duverger in 1951 focusing on the structure of the American electoral process, in particular, the first-past-the-post, or plurality voting feature, of the American system.[196] Under this system, the winner is the candidate getting the most votes in a single-round election.[197]

Although Duverger was not the first observer to associate plurality voting with the two-party system,[198] Duverger was the first to say that the association "approaches the most nearly perhaps to a true sociological law."[199] He attributed the law to two factors, a "mechanical" one and a "psychological" one.[200] "The mechanical

---

[193] Sorauf and Beck, *Party Politics* at 35 (cited in note 108).

[194] See Key, *Politics* at 207–10 (cited in note 82).

[195] For a summary of the different explanations for the number of political parties, see Sorauf and Beck, *Party Politics* at 43–47 (cited in note 108).

[196] Maurice Duverger, *Political Parties: Their Organization and Activity in the Modern State*, trans Barbara North and Robert North (Wiley, 2d English rev ed, 1959).

[197] Duverger called this a "simple-majority single-ballot" system, see id at 217, but that term is misleading because it implies a majority requirement: "With two or fewer candidates, the winner has a simple majority of the votes cast; with three or more candidates, the winner may have only a plurality." William H. Riker, *The Two-Party System and Duverger's Law: An Essay on the History of Political Science*, 76 Am Pol Sci Rev 753, 754 (1982).

[198] For an intellectual history of the idea before Duverger, see Riker, 76 Am Pol Sci Rev at 754–58 (cited in note 197).

[199] Duverger, *Political Parties* at 217 (cited in note 196). He also stated in less strong terms the hypothesis "the simple-majority system with second ballot and proportional representation favour multi-partism." Id at 239 (emphasis omitted). Riker termed this second idea "Duverger's hypothesis," in contrast to "Duverger's law." Riker, 76 Am Pol Sci Rev at 754 (cited in note 197).

[200] Duverger, *Political Parties* at 224 (cited in note 196).

factor consists in the 'under-representation' of the third, i.e. the weakest party, its percentage of seats being inferior to its percentage of the poll."[201] Thus, the third most popular party receiving 20% of the votes gets nothing under a plurality system but gains a percentage of the seats in a more proportional system; under a pure proportional representation scheme, the third party receives 20% of the seats. The psychological factor affects voters: "In cases where there are three parties operating under the simple-majority single-ballot system the electors soon realize that their votes are wasted if they continue to give them to the third party: whence their natural tendency to transfer their vote to the less evil of its two adversaries in order to prevent the success of the greater evil."[202]

Duverger's law has received great scrutiny in the years since the publication of his book. Duverger himself recognized that certain countries such as Canada (a plurality system with more than two viable parties) did not fit his pattern, and he qualified his argument to note that the identity of the two parties that compete effectively under plurality rule may differ in different parts of the country.[203] Some scholars have claimed that the prevalence of single-member districts, rather than plurality voting, is more responsible for the emergence of two parties.[204] Others have argued that a single, undivided office of the presidency drives the two-party system in the United States.[205]

Other authors who accept that the plurality rule drives Duver-

---

[201] Id.

[202] Id at 226.

[203] Id at 223. Riker set forth his own revision to take into account the Canadian and Indian electoral systems. See Riker, 76 Am Pol Sci Rev at 760–61 (cited in note 197).

[204] For a statistical analysis reaching the conclusion that district magnitude (M), "the number of seats filled at an election in a district, is a most important feature of electoral systems," see Rein Taagepera and Matthew Soberg Shugart, *Seats and Votes: The Effects and Determinants of Electoral Systems* 19 (Yale, 1989). The authors state what they call a "generalized Duverger's Rule" that "[t]he effective number of electoral parties [N] is usually within ± 1 unit from $N = 1.25 (2 + \log M)$." Id at 145. In contrast, Aldrich claims that "Duverger's law does not depend on single-member districts, but it is clear that having single-member districts instead of at-large elections or multimember districts accentuates the pressures plurality elections impose toward two-party systems." Aldrich, *Why Parties?* at 56, 303 n 24 (cited in note 107). Of course, the United States has both a prevalence of single-member districts and plurality voting, so it does not provide a good case for testing the alternative theories.

[205] See Gerald M. Pomper, with Susan S. Lederman, *Elections in America: Control and Influence in Democratic Politics* 38–40 (Longman, 2d ed 1980).

ger's law have noted that the psychological factor that Duverger described does not fit well into a rational choice model of politics.[206] Nonetheless, as Schattschneider observed, politicians have long successfully argued to voters that "people who vote for minor opposition parties dissipate the opposition, that the supporters of the minor parties *waste their votes.*"[207] Empirical studies indicate that at least some people engage in this type of sophisticated voting.[208] And no doubt there are instances where the aggregate effects of voting for a third party candidate (the "spoiler" candidate) have led to the election of a candidate least preferred by a majority of voters,[209] thereby reinforcing the perceived need for sophisticated voting.

Regardless of the extent to which the psychological factor explains Duverger's law, the mechanical factor—the persistent underrepresentation of third parties in a plurality system—certainly explains some of the two-party system's durability. Using what Aldrich terms an elite-based rational choice explanation for Duver-

---

[206] See Aldrich, *Why Parties?* at 57 (cited in note 107) (the wasted vote logic "rests on the problematic assumption that voters base their decisions on the probability of making or breaking ties"). To speak of "wasting" a vote on a third party candidate implies that there is such a thing as a vote that is not wasted. As Riker has observed: "If the chance to influence is negligible, then energy spent on a calculus and sophisticated voting is wasted and irrational." Riker, 76 Am Pol Sci Rev at 764 (cited in note 197); see also Paul E. Meehl, *The Selfish Voter Paradox and the Thrown-Away Vote Argument*, 71 Am Pol Sci Rev 11 (1977).

The rationality of sophisticated voting is best understood as part of the voters' illusion, whereby voters believe that their decision to vote affects whether many others decide to vote as well. On the voters' illusion, see George A. Quattrone and Amos Tversky, *Contrasting Rational and Psychological Analyses of Political Choice*, 82 Am Pol Sci Rev 719, 733 (1988). Given the (nonrational) voters' illusion, voting (and, by extension, sophisticated voting) is rational. See Hasen, 144 U Pa L Rev at 2164 (cited in note 150).

[207] Schattschneider, *Party Government* at 82 (cited in note 81).

[208] See, for example, Paul R. Abramson et al, *"Sophisticated" Voting in the 1988 Presidential Primaries*, 86 Am Pol Sci Rev 55 (1992); Jerome H. Black, *The Multicandidate Calculus of Voting: Application to Canadian Federal Elections*, 22 Am J Pol Sci 609 (1978); Bruce E. Cain, *Strategic Voting in Britain*, 22 Am J Pol Sci 639 (1978).

[209] Amy gives the example of the 1980 U.S. Senate Race in New York:

That year three candidates ran—Alphonse D'Amato (Republican party), Elizabeth Holtzman (Democratic party) and Jacob Javits (Liberal party). Eleven percent of the voters opted for Javits, which took votes away from the other liberal candidate, Holtzman. She lost to D'Amato by one percentage point—45 percent to 44 percent—largely because probable supporters defected to Javits. Polls indicated that most of Javits's votes would have gone to Holtzman in a two-way race between she and D'Amato. But in a plurality system those votes for the Liberal party candidate simply ensured that the most conservative candidate won.

Amy, *Real Choices/New Voices* at 85 (cited in note 6).

ger's law,[210] Riker explained the relationship between the mechanical effect and rationally based elite behavior:

> The interesting question about [third] parties is not why they begin, but why they fail. I believe the answer is that donors and leaders disappear. A donor buys future influence and access, and many donors are willing to buy from any party that has a chance to win. (In the United States, at least, many donors give to *both* parties.) But as rational purchasers they are not likely to donate to a party with a tiny chance of winning, and in a plurality system, most third parties have only that chance, because plurality rules give large parties a large relative advantage over small parties. . . . Similarly a potential leader buys a career, and as a rational purchaser he has no interest in a party that may lose throughout his lifetime.[211]

Likewise, Aldrich and Bianco have explained that Duverger's law persists in an established two-party system because most politicians desire a long and successful career. The two-party system provides duopoly-like barriers to entry; rational politicians recognize the "importance of affiliating with a party with a high probability of success for current and future contests," which in the United States is the Democratic or Republican party.[212]

The two-party system in the United States may be at its strongest point in history. In the past there were large areas of single-party rule. "The South was solidly Democratic for a century, machines ruled in many cities and rural areas, and in such areas of one-party dominance there was for long periods effectively no competition for office by the opposing party. . . . Today both parties can seriously imagine competing effectively—and possibly winning—in every region of the nation."[213]

Given this evidence, it is difficult to imagine election laws that do less than eliminate plurality voting or single-member districts

---

[210] See Aldrich, *Why Parties?* at 57 (cited in note 107).

[211] Riker, 76 Am Pol Sci Rev at 765 (cited in note 197) (citation omitted).

[212] John H. Aldrich and William T. Bianco, *A Game-Theoretic Model of Party Affiliation of Candidates and Office Holders*, 16 Mathematical Computer Modeling 103, 116 (1992). The choice of parties matters to politicians primarily during a time of party realignment, as when the Republican party challenged the Whigs to be the main competitor with the Democrats. See id at 114–15; see also Aldrich, *Why Parties?* at 126–56 (cited in note 107) (describing Whig-Republican competition).

[213] Aldrich, *Why Parties?* at 12 (cited in note 107).

seriously undermining the two-party duopoly.[214] Short of such drastic changes in a state's election law, the Court should reject, as implausible, state claims that election laws arguably burdening third-party rights, such as antifusion laws, are necessary to preserve the two-party system. The *Timmons* case proceeded under the assumption that the survival of the two-party system depended in part upon a relatively minor election law: Minnesota's decision to ban fusion. Justice Stevens in dissent stated that the assumption "demeans the strength of the two-party system."[215] The Court did not require empirical support for its assumption, and for good reason: there appears little to suggest that the pressures and incentives that lead almost all state and federal elected officials to affiliate with the Democrats or the Republicans would change in the presence of fusion.

CONCLUSION

Timmons itself will cause only limited changes to our political system. But Supreme Court imprimatur of the two-party system is unjustifiable and dangerous. Responsible party government adherents have not shown that the two-party system promotes either political stability or antifactionalism. Nor can duopoly be premised on preserving of the voting cue, assuming that such a cue retains vitality. The Supreme Court need not uphold laws like the antifusion law in *Timmons* in order to preserve either the voting cue or the two-party system. When First Amendment interests are involved, a state seeking to shield Democrats and Republicans from competition should have a better reason than protection of the two-party system.

---

[214] Cox indicates that elimination of single member districts and plurality elections would indeed affect the number of parties in the United States: "Does anyone believe that the United States would remain a two-party system, even if it adopted the Israeli electoral system?" Gary W. Cox, *Making Votes Count: Strategic Coordination in the World's Electoral Systems* 19 (Cambridge, 1997).

[215] *Timmons*, 117 S Ct at 1381 (Stevens dissenting). In a sense, the Court majority was correct that successful fusion politics, as in New York, leads to a party system with more than two parties. But even in New York, the two parties still dominate: the Republican and Democratic candidates remain the only viable candidates. See Cox, *Making Votes Count* at 91–92 (cited in note 214).

DENNIS J. HUTCHINSON

"THE IDEAL NEW FRONTIER JUDGE"

For an administration which had appointed more than 100 federal judges in little more than one year in office, John and Robert Kennedy were remarkably unprepared for the first vacancy on the Supreme Court of the United States that occurred during their watch. There had been rumors at the end of the previous term of the Court, in the summer of 1961, that Hugo L. Black, 75, might soon retire, and that Felix Frankfurter, 78, known to be in ailing health, was considering retirement as well. A Chattanooga newspaper even speculated that Estes Kefauver, the senior Senator from Tennessee, would be named to replace Black, a baseless rumor that embarrassed both men and prompted Kefauver to issue a public denial. The first vacancy for the Kennedys turned out to be neither Black nor Frankfurter but the most obscure member of the Court, Charles E. Whittaker, who in 1958 had been President Eisenhower's third appointment to the Court.

How the vacancy was filled is a story that has been told many times,[1] with many taking credit for influencing the out-

Dennis J. Hutchinson is Professor in the College and Senior Lecturer in Law, The University of Chicago.

AUTHOR'S NOTE: This article is an adaptation from a larger work, *The Man Who Once Was Whizzer White: A Portrait*, forthcoming from The Free Press. Some quotations are rendered in italics, because the statements were made long enough ago that I deem exact quotation unreliable. I thank the Seeley G. Mudd Manuscript Library, Princeton University, for permission to quote from the transcript of the Walter Murphy–William O. Douglas interview conducted in March, 1962.

[1] The principal accounts are James E. Clayton, *The Making of Justice* 50–52 (Dutton, 1964) (cited below as "Clayton"); Arthur M. Schlesinger, Jr., *Robert Kennedy and His Times* 377–78 (Houghton Mifflin, 1978) (cited below as "Schlesinger"); Nicholas Katzenbach Oral History 56–71 (John F. Kennedy Library, 1964, 1969); Nicholas deB. Katzenbach, *Byron White's Appointment to the Supreme Court*, 58 U Colo L Rev 429, 430 (1987) (cited below as "Katzenbach"); Randy Lee Sowell, *Judicial Vigor: The Warren Court and the Kennedy Administration* (Ph.D. dissertation, U Kansas, 1992).

come,[2] and several taking credit for suggesting the final nominee.[3] Robert Kennedy provided different accounts[4] to favored journalists at the time and then later for the Kennedy Library Oral History Project. What in fact happened is now reasonably clear and differs in two principal respects from the standard accounts. First, the Kennedys had more than three weeks, not just a few days, to consider their options; there was ample time for research and deliberation. But second, for all of the energy expended in two offices of the Department of Justice—the Deputy Attorney General's Office and the Office of Legal Counsel—the President knew his own mind from the outset, and the only question was whether any information or argument would dislodge him from his initial preference. Both Kennedys would later discuss lists of candidates considered, but only Robert Kennedy thought seriously of more than one candidate, and the accounts of lists and debates have suggested more deliberation, at least in the White House, than in fact occurred. In the words of Myer (Mike) Feldman, Deputy Counsel to the President, "Byron White was a foregone conclusion. For the second vacancy [Arthur Goldberg in place of Frankfurter], we actually generated a list, which the Department [of Justice] went over, and then we worked it over again."[5] For the first vacancy, "The President had one name in mind from day one."

* * *

Charles Evans Whittaker was a Kansas City, Missouri, Republican whom President Eisenhower had appointed, largely on his brother Arthur's recommendation, first to the federal district court, then to the Court of Appeals for the Eighth Circuit. In

---

[2] Katzenbach (Katzenbach Oral History at 70–71; Katzenbach at 430); William O. Douglas, *The Court Years* 122–27 (Random House, 1980) (cited below as "Douglas, *Court Years*") (compare William O. Douglas Oral History, interviewed by Walter F. Murphy, Cassette No 7b, transcript p 152, Seeley G. Mudd Library, Princeton University (cited below as "Princeton interview"); Joe Dolan (interview with author, Nov 11, 1995, Englewood, Colorado, cited below as "Dolan interview"; Duquesne University Conference, April 12, 1996, cited below as "Dolan, Duquesne"); Clark Clifford with Richard Holbrooke, *Counsel to the President* 374–75 (Anchor, 1992) (cited below as "Clifford").

[3] Katzenbach Oral History 62 (Katzenbach); Dolan, Duquesne (Dolan); Victor S. Navasky, *Kennedy Justice* 265 (Bernard Segal) (Atheneum, 1971) (cited below as "Navasky").

[4] Compare Clayton, at 50–52, and New York Times, April 1, 1962, with Edwin O. Gutman and Jeffrey Shulman, eds, *Robert F. Kennedy: In His Own Words* 115–18 (Bantam, 1988) (cited below as "Guthman & Shulman").

[5] Myer Feldman, interview with the author, June 23, 1996, Washington, D.C. (cited below as "Feldman interview").

1957, when Stanley F. Reed retired after two decades on the Court, Eisenhower promoted Whittaker again. He turned out to be one of the most unprepossessing members of the Court during the modern era. His opinion output was annually the lowest on the Court and his work the most labored. On March 6, 1962, a few weeks after his sixty-first birthday, he checked in to Walter Reed Army Hospital, suffering from physical and mental exhaustion. He had done no Court work since February 1.[6] The press was unaware of Whittaker's condition or hospitalization, but Robert Kennedy, fresh from an extended overseas trip, had visited Justice William O. Douglas at the Supreme Court on March 5 and probably learned of Whittaker's plight then. Within days, the Attorney General contacted Emanuel Celler and James O. Eastland, chairmen of the House and Senate judiciary committees, to confer on the situation. Both had strong views on Supreme Court vacancies. Celler had recommended Robert C. Weaver, the black administrator whom the President had been unable to appoint to a cabinet-level housing post he wished to establish. Eastland had been one of the leaders in the token but menacing fight by Southern segregationists against Potter Stewart's confirmation to the Court in 1958 and could be expected to resist, by muscle or guile, a nomination he deemed too liberal. The nomination of Thurgood Marshall to the Second Circuit Court of Appeals, which began with a recess appointment in September of 1961, had not yet been calendared for a hearing before Eastland's committee (and would not be for another six months).

On March 15, a few days after Robert Kennedy spoke simultaneously with Celler and Eastland, Chief Justice Earl Warren called on Whittaker at Walter Reed to assess his condition.[7] Warren knew immediately that Whittaker was incapacitated and began steps to accomplish his formal retirement on grounds of disability. The first step was to convene a medical board at the hospital to advise the Chief Justice as to Whittaker's capacity to continue his duties. The second step, assuming that the Board found Whittaker incapacitated, was to prepare a letter from the Justice to the Presi-

---

[6] Warren to Conference (except Frankfurter), April 25, 1962, Box 124, Tom C. Clark Papers, Jamail Research Center, University of Texas at Austin School of Law.

[7] Warren Schedule, Box 32, Earl Warren Papers, Library of Congress (Manuscript Division) (cited below as "EWLC").

dent, with a covering letter of confirmation from the Chief Justice, formally retiring pursuant to section 372(a) of the Judicial Code.[8] Once the three-man board's anticipated conclusion had been approved by the chief medical officer of the hospital, Warren telephoned the White House to inform the President. The agreed effective date of the retirement was April 1, which gave the President up to two weeks to pick a successor before Whittaker's letter needed to be publicly acknowledged. Whittaker's state of mind is captured not in the formal documents sent to the President but in a draft statement which Whittaker dictated but which, undoubtedly thanks to Warren's counsel, was not used:[9]

> Having become overtired from continued concentration on the Court work, I entered Walter Reed Hospital on March 6th for rest, observation and tests.
>
> The doctors have found no organic trouble, but advise me that my return to the Court would unduly jeopardize my future health. Accordingly, I have advised the President that I wish to retire from active service on the Supreme Court in accordance with the provisions of the law.

No statement—from Whittaker, Warren, or anyone else—was issued at the time.

Now that Whittaker's retirement was official, the scramble was on within the White House and the Department of Justice to advise the President. There were no prefabricated lists, long or short.

---

[8] Section 372(a) of Title 28, USC (1958), provided:

> Any justice or judge of the United States appointed to hold office during good behavior who becomes permanently disabled from performing his duties may retire from regular active service, and the President shall, by and with the advice and consent of the Senate, appoint a successor.
>
> Any justice or judge of the United States desiring to retire under this section shall certify to the President his disability in writing.
>
> Whenever an associate justice of the Supreme Court . . . desires to retire under this section, he shall furnish to the President a certificate of disability signed by the Chief Justice of the United States.

At age 61, with eight years of active service as a federal judge, Whittaker was not eligible to retire at full pay on the basis of age and service under § 371 (age 70 and 10 years service, or age 65 and 15 years service). Under another provision of § 372, Whittaker was entitled to retire on disability at "one-half the salary of the office" "during the remainder of his lifetime." He did so for three years until he was retained by General Motors Corporation as a legal consultant; he then resigned his judicial office and forfeited his half-pension. He later became an outspoken critic of the Court and of civil disobedience. See Charles E. Whittaker and William Sloane Coffin, Jr., *Law, Order and Civil Disobedience* (American Enterprise Institute, 1967).

[9] Draft statement, "Dictated March 16, 1962, not used," Box 358, EWLC.

The President met with Ted Sorensen, the counsel to the president, and Mike Feldman, Sorensen's deputy, and it was agreed that Sorensen would generate a list of possible nominees to be reviewed later. Shortly after the meeting, Abraham Ribicoff (Secretary of Health, Education and Welfare), having seen the Supreme Court up close and the Cabinet from the inside, took himself out of contention and refocused his ambitions on elective politics.[10]

At the Department of Justice, the advisory process ran along two channels. In the formal channel, Robert Kennedy directed Byron White (then Deputy Attorney General) to have his office prepare a comprehensive list of candidates with detailed evaluations. White told his principal aide, Joe Dolan, to scour every category— federal appellate and trial judges, state Supreme Court justices, bar leaders, and political figures; in due course, Dolan was expected to discuss the project with Bernard Segal, still the chairman of the American Bar Association's Standing Committee on the judiciary, which would expect to issue a formal rating of the final nominee. White assigned Nicholas Katzenbach's Office of Legal Counsel the labor-intensive job of reading and critically evaluating the written opinions of any judge who made the short list. The second channel was personal to Robert Kennedy, who was making his own inquiries and keeping his own counsel. The two channels would merge when necessary.

Although later oral histories suggest that the Department's review process did not begin until late March, Nicholas Katzenbach was ready to report directly to the Attorney General on March 18,[11] two days after Whittaker's letter was sent to the President, and coincidentally, a day after the Chief Justice and the Attorney General had been featured guests at the annual white-tie dinner of the Gridiron Club at the Statler Hilton Hotel. Katzenbach's nine-page memo to Robert Kennedy focused on one candidate, William H. Hastie, who was Robert Kennedy's provisional preference to replace Whittaker. Hastie, age 57, was a Phi Beta Kappa graduate of Amherst College and an editor of the *Harvard Law Review*, Class of 1930. He spent his early career as a government lawyer and law school teacher and dean. In 1946 he was appointed

---

[10] Princeton interview at 155.

[11] Log of closed Presidential Office Files, Departments and Agencies, Justice, John F. Kennedy Library (cited below as "JFKL").

Governor of the Virgin Islands, and in 1948, after actively campaigning for Harry Truman, was appointed to the Court of Appeals for the Third Circuit—the first black ever named to an Article III judgeship. With impeccable academic credentials and more than a decade on a respected federal appellate court, Hastie was a compelling candidate for the Supreme Court.

Hastie's name had been urged on John F. Kennedy even before the inauguration. Harris Wofford, who with Sargent Shriver had been Kennedy's principal campaign aide on civil rights, sent the President-elect a 31-page memorandum on December 30, 1960, detailing 16 initiatives for the administration to undertake in 1961. Under "14. *Breakthrough in Government Employment of Negroes*," Wofford stated: "A Negro should also get an early Federal District Judgeship in New York City. When the time comes Judge William Hastie of the Third Circuit Court of Appeals should get most serious consideration for appointment to the Supreme Court."[12] Katzenbach was much less enthusiastic. Although his memo to Robert Kennedy is not available for research, his views are not in doubt. He recalled in 1964 that "most of the work we [OLC] did was with respect to Hastie," although others suggested by more than one source were Roger Traynor (California Supreme Court, age 62), Walter V. Schaefer (Illinois Supreme Court, age 57), and Paul Freund, age 54, a chaired professor of constitutional law at Harvard Law School:

> We made a whole review of every opinion that Hastie had written. . . . [W]e went through [Hastie's opinions], and then we wrote a long memorandum with respect to Hastie [only]. There had been some—Byron had been concerned about some left-wing connections that Hastie had had in his early career, and these really ended up being nothing of any importance at all. A review of the opinions indicated a somewhat pedestrian turn of mind. They were good, competent opinions, there was very little that you could find in them, in my judgment that was brilliant at all. And this was possibly in part the problem of the circuit he was in. There were no interesting opinions, by and large.

Katzenbach was clearly unimpressed with Hastie's work product, but he was extremely impressed with Traynor's, and that presented

<hr />

its own problem. Traynor's opinions, in Katzenbach's view, were "right in the tradition of Justice Black,"[13] that is, manifesting an aggressive concept of the judicial role and generous solicitude for freedom of speech, including for those of suspect loyalty.[14] The problem for the President would be that he would be identified with Traynor's views and assumed to be endorsing them[15]—a serious political issue in the eyes of red-baiters in the Senate, of whom Eastland was *primus inter pares.*

The day after Katzenbach sent his memo to Kennedy, the Attorney General scheduled an impromptu appointment with Chief Justice Warren to solicit advice on the nomination in general and on Hastie in particular. The interview left Kennedy surprised by what he heard and chastened over consulting the Chief Justice. Warren "was violently opposed to having Hastie on the Court," Kennedy later recalled.[16] "He said, 'He's not a liberal, and he'll be opposed to all the measures that we are interested in, and he just would be completely unsatisfactory.'" Kennedy also asked about Paul Freund, and Warren opposed him as well. Kennedy then spoke with his old friend Justice Douglas by telephone, and Douglas declared that Hastie would be "just one more vote for Frankfurter."[17]

While Robert Kennedy was taking soundings on Hastie, at the other end of Pennsylvania Avenue his brother was doing the same with his own staff. Ted Sorensen, the President's Special Counsel, produced a list of 19 names on March 21. Six were "Members of

---

[13] Katzenbach Oral History at 57, 59–60.

[14] See generally John W. Poulos, *The Judicial Philosophy of Roger Traynor* 46 Hastings L J 643 (1995).

[15] Katzenbach Oral History at 61.

[16] Guthman & Shulman at 115.

[17] Schlesinger at 377. Douglas provided three different accounts of his role in the Whittaker vacancy. In 1962, he told Walter Murphy that "Bobby Kennedy, an old, old friend of mine, came to see me about the vacancy" and suggested Hastie, who Douglas said was "pedestrian." Princeton interview at 155. In 1967, he told an interviewer for the Kennedy Library that he had not been contacted by the Attorney General, Douglas Oral History at 25–26, JFKL. In the second volume of his memoirs, published in 1980, he claimed that the President asked his advice on the vacancy and that he recommended J. Skelly Wright, a "district judge . . . in Louisiana," but that Kennedy concluded he could not "never get Wright by" Senator Eastland's Judiciary Committee. Douglas, *Court Years* at 122, 127. Douglas was incapacitated at the time he finished his memoirs and may have forgotten that Wright had already "gotten by" Eastland Feb 28, 1962, for a seat on the Court of Appeals for the District of Columbia, a position he had enjoyed under a recess appointment since Dec 15, 1961—news conveyed to him by the Deputy Attorney General, Byron White. Liva Baker, *The Second Battle of New Orleans* 464 (Harper Collins, 1996).

the Administration and the Senate":[18] Goldberg (age 53), Katzenbach (40), White (44), Stevenson (62), H. H. Fowler (53), and Cox
(49). Four were federal judges (Hastie; Henry J. Friendly, 58, of
New York; George T. Washington, 53, and David Bazelon, 52—
both of the Court of Appeals for the District of Columbia) and
three were state court judges (Roger Traynor, 62, of California;
Stanley Fuld, 59, of New York; and Walter V. Schaefer, 57, of
Illinois). Paul Freund topped the list of "Members of the Bar and
Academic Community." Others were Bethuel M. Webster (61),
Clark Clifford (55), Herbert Wechsler (52), "Edward Levi (University of Chicago Dean) [50]," and Whitney North Seymour (61).
Most were Democrats—and so identified on the list; the exceptions were Friendly, Traynor, Webster, Seymour, and Levi. (The
list also included ages: Traynor was the oldest at 62, Katzenbach
the youngest at 40.) Regardless of the list, Hastie remained the
focus of staff attention at both ends of Pennsylvania Avenue.

The White House staff worried that appointing a black was politically "too obvious."[19] The President asked one of the listed candidates, Washington lawyer Clark M. Clifford, for advice, hoping
to learn from the mistakes that caused Clifford's mentor, Harry
Truman, to make undistinguished appointments to the Court;
Clifford seconded the White House staff. "I thought it would be
a mistake for him to reach out just to put a Negro on the bench,"
Clifford later said.[20] When the brothers met to compare their
findings, Robert Kennedy argued against the "obviousness" point,
but Katzenbach's memo had already tainted Hastie with the
President.

The question then was whether there was an alternative. The
President kept White's name out of the discussion as his hole card
while other names began to be killed off along with Hastie. Clifford and Katzenbach both liked Paul Freund, but Freund had
turned down the President when asked to be Solicitor General,
and Robert Kennedy did not like the symbolism of yet another
Harvard faculty member in high office—along with Archibald Cox

---

[18] Sorensen to JFK, March 21, 1962, Box 88A, Presidential Office Files ("Supreme
Court"), JFKL.

[19] Schlesinger at 377.

[20] Id. Clifford later wrote in his memoirs that he thought Hastie's opinions were "shaky"
and that "it would demean both the Court and the civil rights movement if he made an
appointment which appeared to be based solely on the grounds of race." Clifford at 374.

at Justice, McGeorge Bundy as National Security Adviser, and Arthur M. Schlesinger, Jr., as special assistant to the President. Two strikes, and to the President, Freund was out. Arthur Goldberg was a possibility, but the President felt he needed him more in the cabinet now than on the Supreme Court, especially with the steel contract negotiations still up in the air. The President also believed that there would be time for Goldberg and others—perhaps four appointments—if he served two full terms. None of the others on the emerging final list from the Department generated any interest in either of the Kennedys—Traynor, Schaefer, Leon Jaworski (Houston lawyer, age 56),[21] Edward Levi (a Katzenbach suggestion).

Time was now beginning to run against the President. Too many people knew that Whittaker's resignation was in the President's hands, and the President himself had other issues weighing down his mind. On March 22, he sat through a punishing four-hour lunch in the White House with J. Edgar Hoover, the Director of the Federal Bureau of Investigation, who revealed in lurid detail how much the Bureau knew about the President's sexual liaison with Judith E. Campbell, whom a FBI memo archly designated as an "Associate of Hoodlums"[22] because she doubled as a mistress for Sam Giancana, a Chicago mobster. That afternoon, Kennedy placed the last of 70 telephone calls to Campbell through the White House switchboard. Publicly, the issue of the day was whether the steel industry would reach a new contract with labor and avert what was predicted to be an economically debilitating strike. Goldberg was effectively on call to mediate if the parties came to impasse. To fortify himself for the impending week during which the Court question would be resolved and other issues would probably not—such as his stalled Medicare Bill and the steel negotiations—the President flew to Palm Springs, California, for the weekend.

Byron White had been the President's first choice all along and now became the focal point of the search. Propitiously, he left

---

[21] Jaworski told Joe Dolan that he *did not want to leave Texas* and did not wish to be considered for the appointment. Dolan interview.

[22] Federal Bureau of Investigation Memo, March 20, 1962, J. Edgar Hoover Official and Confidential File 96 (John F. Kennedy), quoted in Richard Reeves, *President Kennedy* 289 (Simon and Schuster, 1993).

town for his long-planned trip to Colorado. His absence allowed Katzenbach, who now favored White, to move White's name more formally into the deliberations at both ends of Pennsylvania Avenue. The problem was Robert Kennedy. He did not think of White—the muscular, energetic man of action with whom he went skiing and played basketball—as a judge in a cloister; and, whether he would admit it or not, Kennedy had come to rely on White so implicitly to run the Department in his absence that it would be literally unthinkable for White to be gone. As it turned out, portraying White as a crutch to Robert Kennedy was precisely the reverse psychology necessary to cancel his resistance to White's candidacy. Katzenbach later recalled his telephone call to White in Colorado inquiring about his interest in Whittaker's seat. Katzenbach

> said we had a lot of people on the list and we haven't got you and I'd like to put you on the list. There was a long pause, and he said, "Well, I think the President can do much better than that." And I said, "Well, the geography is very good." And he said, "Well, I think the President can do much better than this, and I would rather not be put on the list." I said, "Do you really want me to scratch you off entirely?" And he said, "Well, I wouldn't be unhappy if you scratched me off entirely. Go ahead."[23]

Receiving this "slightly ambiguous answer," Katzenbach "left him on. I think if I had pushed him any further, he would have said, 'Yes, scratch me off entirely.' So I didn't want to do that because at that point he had become my candidate."[24]

White was now not only on the Department's list but at the top. The question, made pressing by his equivocal response to Katzenbach, was whether he would accept the nomination if it were offered. On March 27, after taking an urgent telephone call from the President, Robert Kennedy called White in Colorado and was surprised by White's reaction:

> And he was not very enthusiastic about it, really. I don't remember specifically his words, but they were rather interesting: I don't think he liked to retire from active life so quickly. But I talked to him on the basis of the fact that who knew

---

[23] Katzenbach Oral History at 63.

[24] Id.

what was going to happen in the future? If you knew definitely
that he could be around for five years and then be appointed
in 1967, then that was fine. But you never knew that. The time
to do it was at the time you could. It was really on that basis
that he accepted the appointment.[25]

White spoke to the President from Denver late afternoon on
March 28 after presiding over the Social Science Foundation board
meeting and cleared the way for the President to go forward.
White's mind now needed to turn to his schedule for the balance
of the week—meeting with the U.S. Attorney for Colorado and
receiving the Pueblo Sertoma Club's "American Way of Life
Award" Thursday, then addressing the Manufacturers Association
of Colorado on Friday morning before a final meeting of the
Foundation board. In between appointments, he granted an interview to the *Denver Post* in which he defended the administration's
controversial wire-tapping bill on the ground, in part, that "the
right of citizens to freedom from organized crime is a right that
champions of civil rights sometimes overlook."[26]

On Thursday, March 29, the President held a 30-minute press
conference at midday at which he announced Justice Whittaker's
retirement, promised a prompt nomination, and evaded questions
as to what qualifications he would use in making the decision. He
refused to comment on speculation that Ribicoff would be named.
In the afternoon, Chief Justice Warren issued a statement reporting that Whittaker "has advised us that he has worked to the
point of physical exhaustion, and that any further resumption of
his rigorous duties here would seriously impair his health."[27] A
modified version of Justice Whittaker's prepared statement, first
drafted two weeks earlier, was also released to the press. That
night, White accepted the Sertoma Club award and told his audience, "Washington, D.C. is not America. It is here."[28] He also
said, "Our real gold reserve is not Ft. Knox. It is our people. In
America's struggle between tyranny and freedom, it is the courage
and ability of the people and their activities that will win the battle." In addition to the plaque memorializing the club's award,

---

[25] Guthman & Shulman at 16.

[26] Denver Post, March 29, 1962.

[27] Los Angeles Times, March 30, 1962.

[28] Pueblo Chieftain, March 30, 1962.

White was given a miniature gold frying pan, which symbolized the Fryingpan-Arkansas Reclamation Project—vital to agricultural development interests in the area and currently in jeopardy before the House Rules Committee. White said he supported the project and expected its passage.

The next morning, the question of Justice Whittaker's successor seemed to be wide open to the public, but in fact it was reaching closure at the White House. White, interviewed by both Denver newspapers, denied any inside knowledge of the search, including rumors published by the Associated Press that he was on a short list (along with Hastie, Freund, Thurgood Marshall, and Eugene V. Rostow of Yale). "About all I can say," White told the *Denver Post,* "is that it will be filled by a lawyer and by a man."[29] UPI speculated that Goldberg, Cox, Freund, and Ralph Bunche at the United Nations were the principal candidates. In the *Washington Post,* James E. Clayton identified the top four candidates as Freund, Friendly, Schaefer, and Traynor. The second tier was White, Cox, Goldberg, Hastie, Erwin N. Griswold (Dean of Harvard Law School, age 57), and Rostow. In the *New York Times,* Anthony Lewis implicitly handicapped the field in the following order: Hastie, Freund, Goldberg, White, Ribicoff, Levi, Cox, and Kefauver. James Reston's *Times* editorial-page column, after reviewing the record of the Warren Court and its frequently controversial and close decisions, recommended "a distinguished, detached, personally unprovocative scholar who can help minimize the personal and philosophical divisions that have developed in the court during the past few years." His models were Charles Evans Hughes and "Cardoza.[sic]"[30]

While speculation boiled in the press, the President was holding a final meeting in the Oval Office to discuss the appointment, which he was now eager to make at once. Senator Richard B. Russell of Georgia had telephoned the President and advised him that any nominee other than an acceptable conservative would prompt a conspicuous visit from a delegation of southern Senators, which he would lead, to make their case.[31] Against the backdrop of intensifying press speculation and Russell's warning, Kennedy prepared

---

[29] Denver Post, March 30, 1962.

[30] New York Times, March 30, 1962.

[31] Schlesinger at 377.

to listen to the presentation from—sitting across from him left to right—the Attorney General, Joe Dolan, and Katzenbach. Robert Kennedy still took Hastie seriously, still believed that a black on the Supreme Court would help the country immeasurably overseas, but had cooled on him due to criticism in every quarter he encountered—the Department, the White House, and even the Court itself. The Attorney General had also been convinced by Katzenbach that the ABA would give White its highest rating, which was a definite advantage. Finally, Katzenbach had used Robert Kennedy's vanity against itself with the following argument:

> "I really think Byron White would be the best person to appoint to this job, but you have just lost John Seigenthaler as Administrative Assistant [to a newspaper editorship], and I think it would be very, very tough on you to lose Byron White just a couple of weeks later, because these are really two people closest to you and the Justice Department to lose. And I think that's a legitimate consideration, and you ought to consider it before recommending Byron." I think that was the argument that probably got Byron the job because he said, "I'm not going to stand in Byron's way. I can handle the Justice Department without Byron White."[32]

By the end of the week, among the White House staff, Hastie had faded and nominally reappeared, and Freund had enjoyed a brief reemergence thanks to Sorensen and McGeorge Bundy. The morning of the final meeting, Sorensen produced a hasty, one-page memorandum advocating Freund's nomination. The memo, in its entirety, read:

> The ages of the eight remaining judges are 71, 76, 79, 63, 62, 62, 56 and 47. (Whittaker, at 61, was the third-youngest member).
> Of the three oldest members two are liberal politicians (Warren and Black) and could be more easily replaced by same. One is a Jew and former Harvard professor (Frankfurter). Warren, of course, is Chief Justice.
> You cannot appoint both Hastie and Weaver to HEW without appearing to be guilty of reverse racism.
> The first appointment should be hailed by all for his judicial mien—not known primarily as a politician—not subject to confirmation delays because of controversial associations.

---

[32] Katzenbach Oral History at 71. See also Navasky at 255; Katzenbach at 430.

If a politician is to be chosen, Goldberg is the ablest; and George Meany could accept Leonard Woodcock with at least as much grace as he accepted Goldberg.

Recommendation: Appoint the highly respected Freund from St. Louis;* save Goldberg for the vacancy of Chief Justice; save Hastie for the next vacancy before 1964.

*Also a Jew and Harvard Professor, but one [who] will presumably retire.[33]

Hand-printed across the top of the memo, Sorensen added: "Note: I put Byron's name on the attached list,[34] too. It did not come up among any of those consulted. When Clark Clifford saw it on the list, he opposed, saying bar would regard Byron as primarily political, too brief in his present job." Bundy simultaneously pressed Freund's case more urgently in his memorandum for the President:

The best and most confidential advice from Cambridge is that Paul Freund would have voted with the *majority* in the Tennessee reapportionment case, and might even have carried Frankfurter with him.

Freund is a great scholar—but not a closet scholar; a Brandeis in conviction, but a Cardozo in temperament.

He is a deeply amusing as well as a cultivated man—a genuine wit—he could become a close personal help to you, with his detachment, his high personal style, and his regard for you.

Of all the men you might choose, he is the most likely to be a great judge—and he is ripe for appointment now.

Sorensen and Bundy were obviously coming to the same conclusion from different angles. To Sorensen, Freund was unexceptionably distinguished, politically costless, and probably fireproof in the Senate. To Bundy, who in another contemporary memo to the President referred to Frankfurter as "a man I love,"[35] Freund was the modern Frankfurter and a model judge (although his speculation about Freund's influence on Frankfurter in *Baker v Carr*,[36] the

---

[33] Sorensen, Memorandum for the President, March 29, 1962, Box 88A, Presidential Office Files ("Supreme Court"), JFKL. Bundy's memorandum, dated a day later, is also contained in the same file.

[34] The list, dated March 21, 1962, and summarized above in text at note 18.

[35] Bundy, Memorandum for the President, July 26, 1962, Box 88A, Presidential Office Files ("Supreme Court"), JFKL (reviewed by the National Archives and Records Service Oct 22, 1996, and opened for research).

[36] 369 US 186 (1962).

Tennessee reapportionment case, was probably wishful thinking at best). Both of the President's men were projecting their own priorities onto the President, who privately had not swerved from his first inclination—to name someone he knew well, admired enormously, and trusted at a level of friendship that surpassed abstract philosophy.

In any event, Sorensen and Bundy did not have the last word: the final staff presentation to the President was being made by the Department of Justice and not by Sorensen or anyone else in the White House. The Attorney General and Katzenbach were now both on White's side, and Dolan was White's original and least inhibited cheerleader. Dolan's function at the final meeting with the President—whether Dolan himself fully realized it or not—was to provide emphasis for the developing consensus[37] and for the choice the President personally desired all along.

The meeting began, and the now-familiar bidding was reviewed. (The night before, Dolan had impishly confided to White by telephone that the decision *was down to a black or white choice*.[38]) The President decided to provoke Dolan: "Joe, I understand you want Byron White." "No, that's not right, I just think he should be seriously considered." "Maybe," the President tested, "I should name Hastie." "You can't do that," Dolan protested energetically. "You'll blow everything we have going on the Hill. Hastie would be an absolute political disaster!" The President smiled thinly and said he would decide "today—It will be Hastie or White."[39]

After returning to the Department, Katzenbach left Washington for a promised weekend in Williamsburg with his son. The President decided after lunch to name White, preferably that day. He

---

[37] The only holdout in the President's inner circle was Kenny O'Donnell, the Appointments Secretary, whose objections were more "sarcastic" than substantive. See Kenneth P. O'Donnell and David F. Powers, *"Johnny, We Hardly Knew Ye"* 280 (Pocket Books, 1972): "I had no objections to White's nomination, but I reminded the President that he had been getting a hard time from Bobby and his friends in the Justice Department whenever we tried to reward a nice young man, who had helped us politically, with an appointment to a federal judgeship. The Justice people always complained that our nominee was either too young, too inexperienced, had not served as a judge, or had not attended Harvard Law School. 'And now Bobby wants to put Whizzer White on the Supreme Court,' I said to the President. 'I'm sure Whizzer will be fine on the Court, but it seems to me he doesn't have any of that Oliver Wendell Holmes background that the Justice Department is always demanding when we try to give somebody a judge's job.' "

[38] Dolan interview.

[39] Id.

telephoned Dolan in Katzenbach's absence and told him to contact
Bernard Segal to obtain, if possible, an on-the-spot commitment
to rate White Exceptionally Well Qualified. Segal, jealous of his
prerogatives, especially with Kennedy's first appointment to the
Supreme Court, initially resisted, and even suggested that the
President change his mind until the Standing Committee could
meet to advise him formally. He was in a weak position, however,
and he knew it. There was no formal agreement or understanding
that Supreme Court nominees would be screened by his committee, and in any event Segal himself had suggested White as "a
strong candidate"[40] to Dolan during one lengthy telephone call
earlier in the week that had lasted until 3 A.M. as candidates were
reviewed in chatty detail. The Attorney General now pressed Segal
and agreed to delay the announcement of the nomination for only
two hours so that the Committee could "meet" by conference call.
In return for the brief concession, by 6 P.M. eastern time the Kennedys had secured the rating they wanted,[41] plus a warm official
endorsement to boot. The press release from the ABA Committee,
issued simultaneously with the President's announcement, was
strong, if also a bit clubby and defensive at the margins:

> Ordinarily our committee might hesitate to accord this rat-
> ing to a lawyer of Mr. White's comparative youth when ap-
> pointment to the Supreme Court of the United States is con-
> cerned. However, our committee has worked closely with Mr.
> White for more than a year and we have had an unusual oppor-
> tunity to observe him under a variety of circumstances. We
> have developed a high regard for his rugged adherence to prin-
> ciple, his sense of fairness, his intellectual capacity, his even
> temperament, his soundness as a lawyer.[42]

All that was left was to locate White and receive his assent to
the nomination. He had driven much of the night through a blind-
ing snow storm, but arrived only thirty minutes late for his break-
fast talk to the business group, who had unfriendly views of the
Administration's antitrust policy. He then went to Denver Univer-

---

[40] See also Navasky at 264–65.

[41] Joel Grossman, *Lawyers and Judges* 134–35 (John Wiley and Sons, 1965); Navasky at
264–65.

[42] Associated Press, March 31, 1962; Statement of Bernard G. Segal, Chairman, Standing
Committee on the Federal Judiciary of the American Bar Association, Archives of the ABA,
courtesy of Irene Emsellem, Governmental Affairs Office, ABA.

sity for the meeting of the Foundation board. At approximately 4 P.M. mountain time, a university secretary "peeked around a door, tip-toed past a crowded table and handed a piece of paper" to White which read "Telephone call. Urgent."[43] At the other end was Ted Sorensen. Minutes later, the President was on the line. Arthur Schlesinger recalled the exchange:

> "Well, Byron," Kennedy said, "we've decided to go ahead on you." There was a moment's silence, and the President said, "We want to get the announcement out in twenty minutes, so we need an answer right away." Another silence, and the President said, "All right, we'll go ahead."[44]

Kennedy privately told Ben Bradlee of *Newsweek* the next day that White "wasn't very enthusiastic" about the offer, because "he honestly hated to leave the Justice Department."[45] For the President, that reluctance was "another plus in his favor. He's the ideal New Frontier judge."[46]

The President then turned to Schlesinger and told him to draft a statement explaining his choice. The Attorney General told Schlesinger to emphasize "that White was no mere professor or scholar but had actually seen 'life'—in the Navy, in private practice, in politics, even on the football field."[47] Schlesinger's statement accordingly underscored that White had "excelled in everything he has attempted—in his academic life, in his military service, in his career before the Bar, and in the federal government."[48] The announcement of the nomination, hastily called and delivered to only a handful of reporters, lasted exactly three minutes. Marion White, who had stayed behind in Washington while her husband was in Colorado, telephoned the President at 7:15 to thank him after talking to her husband. At approximately the same moment, Martin Luther King and Wyatt Tee Walker—who had not heard of the nomination—conferred by telephone to decide whether they should mount a public campaign in support of Judge Hastie for the Whittaker vacancy; their conversation, overheard

---

[43] Associated Press, March 30, 1962.

[44] Schlesinger at 378.

[45] Benjamin C. Bradlee, *Conversations with Kennedy* 67 (Norton, 1975).

[46] Id.

[47] Schlesinger at 378.

[48] Associated Press and numerous newspapers, March 31, 1962.

by an FBI wiretap, was transcribed and forwarded to the White House.[49] After dinner, the President directed an aide at 10:50 P.M. to obtain a copy of an early edition of the *Washington Post* to see how the nomination played.

The Post's banner headline coverage must have satisfied the President, especially the second subhead, which noted "Kennedy's Choice Widely Praised by Lawmakers."[50] Senator Eastland predicted that White would be "an able Supreme Court justice"[51] and declared his support for the nomination. Senator Mike Mansfield, the majority leader from Montana, praised White somewhat parochially as "the right man in the right place for the right job and from the right section of the country." Senator Everett Dirksen of Illinois, the minority leader, doubted White would have any confirmation problem and called him "one of those solid people who takes a very good look before reaching a decision and then stands by it."[52] Chief Justice Warren, apparently unconcerned over intervening at the margins of a political issue, decided to make his own statement. He called the appointment "splendid," and said: "It was a very fine appointment. He is a man of great ability. He has a wonderful background for this post and is a fine man."[53] The newspaper headlines, pointing to football and the Navy as well as to the Justice Department, highlighted the glamour of the nomination. The Associated Press photo library provided dashing pictures of White playing college football, riding the bicycle at Oxford in cap and gown, and clad in pith helmet under a South Pacific jungle canopy.[54] Editorial page cartoonists immediately depicted footballs flying toward the front entrance to the Supreme Court building.[55]

Most editorials applauded the nomination. The *New York Herald-Tribune* praised a "truly first-rate choice,"[56] and the *Washington*

---

[49] Taylor Branch, *Parting the Waters* 583–84 (Simon and Schuster, 1988).

[50] Washington Post, March 31, 1962.

[51] United Press International, March 30, 1962.

[52] New York Herald-Tribune, March 31, 1962.

[53] Associated Press, March 31, 1962.

[54] The most comprehensive gallery was the Denver Post Sunday pictorial page, April 1, 1962.

[55] For example, Los Angeles Times, April 3, 1962; Washingon Evening Star, April 1, 1962.

[56] New York Herald-Tribune, April 1, 1962.

Star thought White "excellent,"[57] but there were off-key notes as well, particularly from syndicated columnists. David Lawrence lashed the President for passing over experienced judges to appoint a "political henchman and a friend of long standing" with "no judicial experience whatsoever,"[58] and for not consulting Congress or bar leaders. Lawrence also criticized the ABA Committee for short-circuiting its own evaluation process. Doris Fleeson, a columnist for the *Washington Star* for two decades, saw the nomination of the "cautious and plodding" White as "strictly personal" to the President—evidence that he "was simply not ready to remake the Court in his political image."[59] James Reston, writing from Washington in the *New York Times*, speculated that White would be more "liberal" than Whittaker and would be inclined to vote with the "Warren-Black-Douglas-Brennan group," but "beyond that nobody here is willing to guess very much about what either Mr. White or Mr. Kennedy will do in the future."

Reston's newspaper was the only major one that was sharply critical of White's nomination. Declaring that "the ideal justice should be a student of life as well as of the law, a man of intellect and compassion and—because the Court must be a teacher—ability to articulate," the *Times* decided, "[o]n the basis of his public life and career," that White "has not yet measured up to these standards." With experience limited mainly to private practice, "he has not yet achieved the scholarly legal distinction that would justify hailing his appointment as a great and inevitable one." Conceding his ability and the respect of his colleagues, the *Times* concluded, with seeming resignation, that "He embarks on one of the loneliest and most exacting of jobs."[60] The *New Republic* was unimpressed, leading its editorial with the observation that "The appointment of a Supreme Court Justice is always something of a shot in the dark."[61] After reviewing his career, the magazine quoted a "colleague" (probably Frankfurter) as predicting "that Mr. White is likely to be found 'a bit to the left of Mr. Justice

---

[57] Washington Evening Star, April 1, 1942.

[58] Id, April 2, 1962.

[59] Id.

[60] New York Times, April 1, 1962.

[61] The New Republic, April 9, 1962, at 7.

Potter.' "[62] With no "[sic]," it is unclear whether the magazine was embarrassing White's unnamed colleague or itself. The editorial concluded that White "fits thoroughly adequate traditions."[63] The President had succeeded in securing widespread popular and political approval for his nomination, and the captiousness of the intellectual class was both to be expected and discounted. John Kennedy had a friend whom he trusted and who was emblematic of the vigorous tone of his administration, and nothing else really mattered to him.

Local coverage in Colorado newspapers, with one unsurprising exception, hailed the appointment with pride and, in some quarters, as manifest destiny. White's father-in-law, Robert L. Stearns, the retired president of the University of Colorado and of the Boettcher Foundation, said, "It's the logical outcome of his own ability and legal training"[64]—a sentiment that infected many of the stories and editorials published in the state over the weekend in which the nomination was announced. Asked if he was proud of his son, Al White, the Justice-designate's 82-year-old father, was no more tolerant of obvious questions from reporters than he had been 25 years earlier when his son was an all-American football player: "You shouldn't have to ask that. Of course I am."[65] A reporter for the *Rocky Mountain News* tried to determine, in 650 words, the shaping influences on Byron White's life, but his parents responded too matter-of-factly for dramatic effect. Al White attributed his sons' success to their "industriousness."[66] Religious influence? Connection with organized religion was said to be "practically non existent," but " 'We read Unity (a magazine of religious thoughts and Bible texts) and we read the Bible each day,' the father said." Books? "I can't remember him doing much reading until he got into college," reflected his mother. Reporters looking for background color on the new Justice found a richer lode in the Justice's brother, now Director of Research for the Lovelace Foundation for Medical Education and Research in Albuquerque, New Mexico. He rehearsed tales of brotherly sugar-beet-

---

[62] Id.

[63] Id.

[64] Denver Post, March 31, 1962.

[65] Rocky Mountain News, March 31, 1962.

[66] Id, April 1, 1962.

raising projects, field-hand work, and the like. The contrast between the "rich boy" President and the Horatio Alger of the beet
fields was irresistible to columnists such as Roscoe Fleming[67] in
the *Denver Post* and others.

The only cool note locally came predictably from Gene Cervi,
the iconoclastic Colorado editor who had locked horns with White
more than once in state Democratic Party politics. Acknowledging
that "[m]ost of Colorado is bursting with pride at the appointment," Cervi's signed editorial in his business journal declared,

> As professional dissenters, particularly in the wake of the
> praise heaped on the new justice, we tried to think of some-
> thing that would knock his halo at least slightly askew. We
> couldn't do it. . . .
>
> We believe on one hand that he will be a qualified or limited
> Liberal in its modern sense, that is, in the sense that President
> Kennedy is a Liberal. His unique position of being the swing
> man on 4-to-4 decisions is not lost on him even for a moment.
> They say he is fair—whatever that means. We know he is
> tough. Nonetheless, we could believe on the other hand, that
> he will interpret the Constitution coldly, dispassionately, ever
> mindful of the separation of governmental powers. This, of
> course, would place him with the Conservatives, and it's possi-
> ble he may one day give his former boss, the President, some
> unexpected decisions. Let's face it. At this point he's an enigma
> in these terms. . . .
>
> In the much publicized list of his many accomplishments,
> there is one thing he hasn't done. He hasn't been a conspicuous
> loser on any significant issue and the time to decide whether
> he could be a good loser is past. His climb to the citadel has
> ended in joyous triumph. He's inside—for life. Now, the true
> measure of the man will be taken by history.
>
> Will he be celebrated for majority opinions or will he be
> distinguished for stirring dissents?[68]

Ever since the White-Dolan forces overwhelmed the residual support for Adlai Stevenson in the Democratic state convention in
1960, Cervi—a faithful Stevenson man—had viewed White as
"vindictive," a "lousy winner," and Kennedy a conservative collab-
orator.[69] Cervi's editorial, fueled to some extent by a grudge but

---

[67] Denver Post, April 5, 1962.

[68] Cervi's Rocky Mountain Journal, April 4, 1962.

[69] Carl Bakal, *New Man on the Big Bench* 99 TRUE, July 1962.

perspicacious all the same, prevented the Colorado press coverage from being an unqualified celebration.

Byron White's nomination formally arrived at the Senate on April 4, 1962, and confirmation hearings were scheduled for April 11. Between the announcement of his nomination and the Senate hearings and vote, two puzzles—one visible, the other hidden—attached to the President's decision. The public puzzle was fore-shadowed in the Fleeson and Reston columns: what were White's philosophical views of the judicial role and the place of the Court in the American polity, or, put much more crudely in the popular fashion of journalists of the day, was he a "liberal"—at least in the Warren-Black-Douglas-Brennan mold? Two reporters asked the nominee directly and learned as much as anyone who had ever asked the question of him in terms. Miriam Ottenberg, who put the question to White shortly after he became Deputy Attorney General, repeated the question in the judicial context by telephone the night of his nomination and was told: "The proof will be in the judging."[70] The *Fort Collins Coloradoan*, functionally White's hometown newspaper, did no better. Asked whether he would classify himself as a "liberal or a conservative," he replied: "I guess we'll just have to let the record speak for itself."[71] Tom Gavin, now of the *Denver Post*, had the luxury of interviewing White in person. He was told more, but not much. Gavin, a blunt and wise-cracking writer who was also a determined reporter, asked White if "he will be a liberal or conservative justice."[72]

> "I never know what people mean by those words," he said.
> Well, then, which Supreme Court justices have you particularly admired?
> "There have been a lot of good justices. Mr. Justice (Oliver Wendell) Holmes was a great justice. He was a great student of the law." (There's no hint there. While Holmes wrote a number of opinions considered liberal, he authored as many others which could be termed conservative.)
> Did President Kennedy discuss your mutual views on the high court before announcing your nomination?
> "We had a good talk."
> Yes, but did he say anything in particular?

---

[70] Washington Evening Star, March 31, 1962.

[71] Fort Collins Coloradoan, April 1, 1962.

[72] Denver Post, April 1, 1962.

"I won't quote the President. You'll have to ask him."

What about the Court's recent ruling on legislative reapportionment? Did you agree with the majority opinion?

"I really can't comment on any question relating to the
Court," White said.[73]

Gavin observed that White's "reserve made him almost an oddity
in the administration of President Kennedy, where compulsive
rhetoric flourishes as a new art form."[74]

Byron White was indulging in the luxury of necessity. He never
had any use for the reductionistic categorization and "thinking by
labels," as he sometimes called it, manifested in the journalists'
questions. Now, the political deference to the confirmation process
and the dignity of the Court allowed him to be evasive or silent
as he wished. The question remains to what extent President Kennedy considered White's legal views and indeed to what extent he
cared. Nicholas Katzenbach later said that Kennedy took a personal interest in his Supreme Court appointments, not because he
worried about their judicial philosophy but because they would be
more personally identified with him than lower court appointees
would. That made White a natural in the eyes of Katzenbach, who
suspected that there would be more public attention and scrutiny
of Kennedy's first appointment than of any subsequent ones.
Therefore, Katzenbach thought that the first appointment:

> ought to be somebody who in some way was identified with
> the President's views. On most of these issues, I don't think
> the President really had a view very strongly, and I don't think
> Byron had a view very strongly on most of these issues. But I
> felt that, were that true, it ought to be somebody, then, closely
> identified with the President.[75]

On that ground—which Sorensen had raised in his last-minute
memo—the White House counsel's office agreed with Katzenbach
that White was a very sensible choice.

Both the White House and the Justice Department made sure
the press got the point, as the *New York Times*' explanation of the
appointment three days after it was made demonstrates: "In picking" between White and Freund, "President Kennedy took the

---

[73] Id.

[74] Id.

[75] Katzenbach Oral History at 64.

man he knew better. White House aides said the basic reason for the President's choice was his intimate knowledge of Mr. White's philosophy and abilities, and his respect for them."[76] How precisely were White's judicial views, as opposed to his political views, considered? "Not in any detail," according to Sorensen much later.[77] "Look," Mike Feldman also explained much later, "He was with us in the campaign, he had a good relationship with the President, and we just assumed that took care of the matter."[78] Burke Marshall is more pointed. "I can only remember one judicial appointment where the question of judicial philosophy was raised at all," Marshall later recalled. "Bob worried that Frank Shea might be soft on criminals if he became a judge. Outside of the Southern judges and civil rights, that was the extent of discussions about future behavior. Absolutely."[79]

Two strands of the Kennedy brothers' thinking intertwined to shut off sustained consideration of a potential nominee's judicial views. The President, in Katzenbach's phrase, did not see "the Supreme Court as being a really co-equal branch" of government.[80] John Kennedy paid little attention to the work of the Court, did not see its decisions as a major factor in the nation's political economy, and did not wish to tarry over niceties of judicial philosophy. Desegregation of public schools, First Amendment protection for suspected Communists, and prayer in public school were all political problems to President Kennedy more than products of philosophical division within the Court. The only legal issue that seems to have stirred him personally during his first year plus in office— in terms of contemplating a legislative or legal initiative—was government financial aid to parochial schools, which he flirted with, but abandoned for political reasons.[81] The other strand was the

---

[76] New York Times, April 2, 1962.

[77] Theodore C. Sorensen interview, Sept 19, 1996, New York City.

[78] Feldman interview.

[79] Burke Marshall interview, April 24, 1996, New Haven, Connecticut.

[80] Katzenbach Oral History at 78.

[81] Within a month of the inauguration, Presidential aides sought advice from the Department of Justice on the feasibility of providing federal funds to students attending parochial schools, an initiative prompted by "Cuban refugee children in Miami" and plans by Governor Nelson A. Rockefeller of New York to provide similar state aid there. Frederick G. Dutton to Archibald Cox, Feb 23, 1961, Box 66, Attorney General's General Correspondence, JFKL. Even before Cox could respond, Theodore C. Sorensen, Special Counsel to the President, detailed the legal and political arguments against a federal program and closed with his "personal conviction that the first Catholic President, under fire from the

Kennedys' mutual hostility to dogmatic thinking and their impatience with theory and abstraction. They derided what they saw as overheated partisans of both right and left, in the administration slang of the day, of "reactionaries" and "honkers." Robert Kennedy complimented Byron White's steady navigation between extremes to Katzenbach after the nomination: "He said, 'Well, Byron ought to be good because he's got so much sense,' which I think Bobby generally use[d] in the sense of blunting doctrinaire ideas with some kind of practical pragmatism."[82] Harris Wofford, who qualified as one of the administration's "honkers," put the President's nonideological tastes in a less admiring light, but one which White found both admirable and compatible: "I think John Kennedy's central principle in politics, as far as I was able to distill it, was his desire to see the maximum intelligence brought to bear on public problems. He had no ideology and, if anything was put off by too far-reaching ideas."[83] The remark to Ben Bradlee—that White's hesitancy to join the Court made him the "ideal New Frontier judge"—bespeaks the President's taste for irony and his admiration for diffidence toward judicial as opposed to political power.

Byron White's reluctance was no pose. The private puzzle prompted by the nomination is why White wanted the job in the first place. When Robert Kennedy first called him in Denver a few days before the nomination to see if he really wanted the position, his immediate response was, *Now why would the President want to do something like that?*[84] His hesitance with the President when the offer was actually made was equally authentic. Almost as soon as he had accepted the nomination he suffered a case of buyer's remorse. When he returned to Washington on April Fool's Day, 1962, he dropped in on William Geoghegan, another close aide, in his office. To enthusiastic congratulations, White responded:

Catholic Hierarchy, cannot now reverse his vote on the Morse Amendment in 1960 when he was a candidate to support the first aid-to-parochial schools Bill." Sorensen Memorandum ("—In answer to questions—"), March 7, 1961, Box 66, id. Morse proposed an amendment to Kennedy's 1959 federal aid to education bill which would have allowed funds for non-public schools, but Kennedy called Morse's proposal "unconstitutional." Sorensen, *Kennedy* 111 (Harper and Row, 1965).

[82] Katzenbach Oral History at 77.

[83] Wofford Oral History at 16, JFKL.

[84] Dolan interview.

I guess they want to put me out to pasture early.[85] Geoghegan still remembers vividly a tableau between nomination and confirmation: "Byron's back was acting up and he would just lie on the long couch in my office, on his back, flipping a football up in the air—perfect vertical spirals—asking, more to himself than to me, *should I be doing this? Is this really the right decision? Can I really contribute?*"[86]

The same man who felt that he could be elected to office in Colorado only "once" now wondered whether he was suited by temperament and comparative advantage to be effective and satisfied in a world he knew only too well from his days as a law clerk to Chief Justice Vinson. He would be sitting with two Justices his friends had clerked for 15 years before—Hugo L. Black and William O. Douglas; a third, Felix Frankfurter, was ill, and doubts were growing daily that he would return to the bench. Unlike the Department of Justice, whose teamwork and camaraderie he relished, the Supreme Court was a collection of nine individuals answering only to themselves and defining their own philosophical and institutional objectives. He knew from his clerkship that the skilled and rapid writers, such as Black and Douglas, could have greater impact than otherwise able lawyers, and his writing was neither fluid nor elegant. "He wrote a lot like he played," according to his former partner Donald Hoagland, who knew him well and admired him deeply. "Not pretty, not graceful, but he got the job done and didn't leave anything standing in his wake." One of his closest friends thought at the time that White never would have sought the appointment on his own, that if pushed by Katzenbach would have issued a Sherman statement, but that once the process began to focus on him, *He was flattered and, like most lawyers, he just couldn't resist. I mean, it was the Supreme Court after all.*

White did not permit himself to muse for very long. On Monday, April 2, he paid a call on Chief Justice Warren at Warren's invitation and spent a half hour with him.[87] That day, the Court, apparently confident of White's confirmation, restored a dozen previously argued cases to its calendar for reargument the follow-

---

[85] See also Jim Mann, Los Angeles Times, Aug 7, 1978.

[86] Geoghegan interview, June 10, 1996, Washington, D.C.

[87] Calendar of the Chief Justice, Box 32, EWLC.

ing term, only three with enduring interest—*Kennedy v Mendoza-Martinez*, *Gibson v Florida Legislative Investigation Committee*, and *Townsend v Sain*. A day later, the Court entertained two visitors whose presence prompted small headlines. Marion White, whom the *Post* had so far denominated "Mrs. 'Whizzer' "[88] in the "for and about Women" section of the paper, was spotted in the box seats reserved for guests of Justices, sitting behind none other than Mr. Justice Whittaker, who had been discharged from Walter Reed March 26 and was making his first appearance at the Court in a month as well as his first since his retirement took effect.

While the confirmation hearings were pending, newspaper columnists across the country dug into their morgue files and rehearsed memories of White's glorious past or interviewed middle-aged football warriors whose playing days suddenly acquired a new luster. Arthur J. Rooney, still the owner of the Pittsburgh professional football franchise for whom White had played in 1938, said "President Kennedy couldn't have appointed a greater man."[89] Rooney had seen White less than a month before in Philadelphia at the banquet of the Maxwell Club, which had selected Clint Frank over White as its outstanding college player of the year in 1937. Columnists tended to extol White's dual success in classroom and playing field or bask in White's reflected glory. For example: "Over here in the all brawn and no brains section of the newspaper, which is the sports department, there is a new kind of respectability prevailing" (John Steadman of the *Baltimore American*).[90] Shirley Povich of the *Washington Post*, who had covered White in the National Football League, said it better: "For every professional football player whose nose has been ground into the dirt or whose calling has been scorned as primitive by politer society, there now must be a glow of pride. One of their boys has made it all the way to the Supreme Court of the United States."[91] Arthur Daley of the *New York Times*, whom White had privately rebuked for popularizing a favorable but fanciful story about White's war record, wrote a column echoing Povich two weeks later. This time he omitted the phony tale of the South Pacific.

---

[88] Washington Post, March 31, 1962.

[89] Pittsburgh Post-Gazette, March 31, 1962.

[90] Baltimore American, April 22, 1962.

[91] Washington Post, April 17, 1962.

The stack of clippings was testimony to the durable purchase of the alliterative nickname that Daley conceded the "painfully modest hero grew to dislike. He may have trouble living it down, however. He was no fringe performer. He was a great star, a real Whizzer."[92]

Byron White's confirmation hearings were held April 11, and over time their light-hearted expeditiousness became a source of fond nostalgia for many, especially the journalist David Brinkley, who often recalled how quickly White's hearings were completed. The entire proceedings before the Senate Judiciary Committee lasted only 90 minutes, although most of the time was consumed with Bernard Segal's oral presentation of the ABA Committee's report, extended by Senator Sam J. Ervin's complaint that the ABA awarded its highest ratings without insisting on any judicial service. "Frankly," Ervin told Segal, "I would be just a little bit happier if he had been a judge for about 10 years."[93] White was accompanied at the hearing by Joe Dolan and by Ethel Kennedy, wife of the Attorney General. The *Washington Post* noted that before he began his own testimony, "White, a reticent man, sat quietly, doodling on a pad and smoking cigarettes as Senators and lawyers praised his ability."[94] There was no written record to review, since White had given only six speeches as Deputy Attorney General and none touched on judicial review or allied issues.

The gravity of the hearings was evidenced by the fact that Chairman Eastland attended for only five minutes before leaving and turning the gavel over to Senator Carroll from Colorado until the final two minutes and the brief executive session. The tone is captured by the statement of Senator Phillip Hart—the conscience of the Senate, or at least of the Committee—that "this is the first appointment of a player of the Detroit Lions to the Supreme Court."[95] In addition to Segal, a presentation was made on behalf of the Colorado Bar Association, which, like the ABA, considered White "exceptionally well qualified."[96] The CBA report was pre-

---

[92] New York Times, May 1, 1962.

[93] Hearings before the Committee on the Judiciary, US Senate, April 11, 1962: Nomination of Byron R. White, 87th Cong, 2d Sess at 15 (cited below as "Hearings").

[94] Washington Post, April 12, 1962.

[95] Hearings, p 20.

[96] Id.

sented by Hugh A. Burns, whom White had tried to recruit for
the University of Colorado football program 15 years earlier.
Burns, now a prominent Denver lawyer, was in Washington on
other business and was asked by the president of the state bar to
present its report.

Almost lost in the perfunctory hearing were a pair of statements
by White—one on the record, the other not—which sounded innocuous but which stemmed from deeply earnest convictions.
Halfway through White's brief appearance, which lasted, as Brinkley always insisted, exactly 11 minutes, Senator Edward V. Long
of Missouri asked the nominee on the record to comment on the
notion that the Supreme Court "legislate[s]."[97] White replied:

> I think it is clear under the Constitution that legislative
> power is not vested in the Supreme Court. It is vested in the
> Congress; and I feel the major instrument for changing the
> laws in this country is the Congress of the United States.
> The business of the Congress is that of changing the law.[98]

Off the hearing record, after the proceedings were adjourned, a
Washington journalist approached White and asked him to define
the constitutional role of the Supreme Court. According to Burns,
who was standing next to him, White replied coldly, "To decide
cases."[99] Burns later said that he would never forget the exchange:
"The statement was both a brush-off and a statement of philosophy; you could tell by the way he said it that it carried a fundamental belief for him."[100] After a five-minute executive session,[101] the
Committee unanimously approved White's nomination.

The nomination moved to the floor that afternoon. Senator
Richard B. Russell made a brief speech, saying that he supported
the nomination, but urged the President to fill the next vacancy
on the Court with a "genuine conservative constitutionalist," because there were 40 to 50 million "conservatives" in the country
who deserved representation on the Court.[102] Under Senate Rules,
the nomination should have lain over for 24 hours after the hear-

[97] Id at 23.

[98] Id.

[99] Hugh A. Burns interview, April 18, 1996, Denver, Colorado.

[100] Id.

[101] Washington Evening Star, April 12, 1962.

[102] New York Times, April 12, 1962.

ing, but Senator John Carroll of Colorado successfully moved for unanimous consent to suspend the Rules and the Senate then proceeded to confirm White by voice vote as the ninety-third man to sit on the Supreme Court of the United States.

When Byron White retired 31 years later at the conclusion of October Term 1992, his tenure was longer than all but nine justices in the Court's history.[103] One of the most curious aspects of the journalistic coverage of White's decision to retire was the empty investigation into the nature of White's "liberalism." Had he been appointed by Dwight Eisenhower or Lyndon Johnson, the question never would have been raised, but White was the last connective tissue to John Kennedy, the New Frontier, and its optimism about the capacity of government which energized many during the early 1960s. One journalist wrote that John Kennedy "nominated Byron White, thinking he was a Warren Court liberal,"[104] only to be disappointed. Even Justice Lewis F. Powell, Jr., who served with White for 16 terms, assumed in 1987 that White's "conservative drift" would have "disappointed President Kennedy."[105] The comments ignore the political context of White's appointment and forget the priorities of the appointing President. Robert Kennedy spoke proudly in 1964 of White's appointment;[106] there is no record of President's Kennedy's view of White's early performance, or whether he formed a view at all.

---

[103] Justice John McLean served one month longer than White.

[104] Christian Science Monitor, Oct 29, 1996; compare Charles Roos in Rocky Mountain News, March 31, 1996.

[105] John C. Jeffries, Jr., *Justice Lewis F. Powell, Jr.* 541 (Scribners, 1994).

[106] Guthman & Schulman at 118.

GREGORY A. MARK

THE COURT AND THE CORPORATION: JURISPRUDENCE, LOCALISM, AND FEDERALISM

The most conspicuous attribute of American corporate law, especially when compared to the law of virtually every other country,
is that it is the product not of the national government but of
the state governments.[1] For much of this century, this feature of
American constitutional federalism was held to be a pernicious
one, whether the author of the critique was journalist, justice, or
legal academic.[2] In the past few years, however, the legal academic
and judicial, if not the popular, conception has dramatically altered.[3] Whereas the traditional critics saw the federal structure re-

Gregory A. Mark is an Associate Professor of Law, Rutgers Law School, Newark.

AUTHOR'S NOTE: I am grateful for the helpful comments I received when presenting this
paper at the American Society for Legal History (where James Ely was especially generous
with his criticisms) and for the spirited discussion of issues raised by this paper when I
presented it at the University of Chicago Legal History Workshop. I also thank Amy L.
Miller and Sharyn Fiske for their assistance in preparing the paper.

[1] See Alfred F. Conard, *Corporations in Perspective* § 3 (Foundation Press, 1976).

[2] See, for example, William L. Cary, *Federalism and Corporate Law: Reflections Upon Delaware*, 83 Yale L J 663 (1974); *Liggett v Lee*, 288 US 517, 549 (1933) (Brandeis, J, dissenting);
Lincoln Steffens, *New Jersey: A Traitor State, Part II—How She Sold Out the United States*,
25 McClure's Magazine 41 (1905).

[3] The claim that the competition inherent in a federal system is beneficial is most fully
developed in the realm of public economics. It has been elaborated in a number of settings
and deployed by legal academics in many contexts, though none of them to my knowledge
historical, except in debates over charter competition. The economics that lies behind such
claims is, however, more complicated and leads to more problematic conclusions than most
legal academics have acknowledged. See William W. Bratton and Joseph A. McCahery, *The
New Economics of Jurisdictional Competition: Devolutionary Federalism in a Second-Best World*, 86
Georgetown L J 201 (1997). This is not the place to apply Bratton's and McCahery's conclusion. Rather, this essay suggests that the reason corporate charter competition is the

sulting in a "race to the bottom" in which shareholders and the public were subject to ever greater exploitation as states loosened their corporate codes in a competition to attract charter revenues, the revisionists saw such competition as a "race to the top," resulting in more efficient rules of corporate governance which redounded to the benefit of shareholders in the first instance and then to the political economy more generally.[4] Indeed, one of the leading scholars in the field has singled out competitive federalism as the key to the success of American corporate law, arguing, "The genius of American corporate law is in its federalist organization."[5]

Few of the proponents of the race to the top have explored the history of charter competition,[6] whereas it is an explicit theme of most of the race to the bottom literature. Neither proponents nor opponents of the race have, however, asked why a system of competitive federalism exists in the first place. Indeed, opponents of the race might well concede the claim that the system is one of genius, though they would recharactarize it as an evil genius rather than a beneficent one. Nonetheless, proponents and opponents appear to take the genius as given. Moreover, with some exceptions, the focus of inquiries into competitive federalism, whether historical or not, is on corporate codes, rather than systems of corporate law which include the codes as well as the work of the courts, both

---

paradigmatic example of successful competition is inadvertent and owes a great deal to the ways in which competitive choices were foreclosed by the universalizing jurisprudence of early Supreme Court cases.

[4] The seminal article in what has become a rich literature was authored by then professor, now judge, Ralph Winter. See Ralph K. Winter, *State Law, Shareholder Protection, and the Theory of the Corporation*, 6 J Legal Stud 251 (1977).

[5] Roberta Romano, *The Genius of American Corporate Law* 1 (AEI Press, 1993). Professor Romano's claim is itself historically contingent, based on, or at least facilitated and legitimated by, other phenomena. Perhaps the corporate product of America's governmental structures appears to be the work of genius because it is, for all intents and purposes, unique among the important economies of the world. More likely, however, American corporate law appeared in 1993, and appears today, in a flattering light because the American economy is comparatively successful, both when compared with the relatively stagnant economies of the other great market powers, Japan and Germany, and with the collapsed economies of the formerly centrally planned economies, especially the Soviet Union. Perhaps also the federalist organization appears to have been a factor in the resurgence of America's economy following the relative doldrums of the 1970s. Certainly the vision of devolutionary genius more than coincides with the scholarly attention (in the form of the public choice school) to the beneficial effects of a governmental regime in which units of government are said to compete with one another for the attention, affection, and capital of individual human beings.

[6] A conspicuous exception is Henry A. Butler, *Nineteenth-Century Jurisdictional Competition in the Granting of Corporate Privileges*, 14 J Legal Stud 129 (1985).

in corporate common law and in the interpretation of corporate codes. Thus, while the origins of the American business corporation have been extensively explored, almost no one has asked, much less answered, questions about the origins of this key attribute of corporate law, nor have the forces that shaped the competition into the system that Professors Cary and Romano, and Judge Winter and Justice Brandeis, and many others, variously described been much explored.

The closest thing to an explanation in the literature is Professor Conard's of some twenty years ago, and it is limited to only one aspect of the systems of corporate law. He claimed, "The historical reasons for the extreme multiplicity of corporate codes in the United States are not difficult to discover."[7] He rightly observed that the Constitution "says nothing" concerning corporations, which were "a very minor business of government in 1787."[8] He also asserted that if the Founders thought about corporations at all they would have assumed that both levels of government could and would charter them, but that "the effect of . . . saying nothing was to permit the states to continue granting corporate status under the doctrine of reserved powers."[9] Unfortunately, the Founders did think about corporations; not a lot, to be sure, but enough so that we know that the power to charter was contested ground. And, while business corporations—or corporations more generally—were not a central concern of the Founders, they were a growing concern, one which quickly became much more important. Finally, in a system in which both state and federal governments could charter corporations, the assumption that the power was reserved to the states, especially in the face of what turns out to have been a mixed historical practice and countervailing claims, is itself problematic.

Examination of the historical record suggests something quite different from Conard's explanation. Rather than being easy to discover as integral to the federal plan, or even as a logical outgrowth of a federal system, the historical reasons for a multiplicity of corporate law regimes are fairly difficult to discern. Indeed, corporate federalism seems almost to be a product of sheer accident—less

---

[7] See Conard § 4 at 6 (cited in note 1).

[8] Id.

[9] Id.

politely put, dumb luck, perhaps good, perhaps bad, but luck nonetheless. That we accidentally have a system of state corporate law
in which states compete in producing corporate law regimes is not
to mean that the accident must be viewed negatively, as we might
view an airplane crash, but rather that we must try to understand
that the competition for corporate charters is neither part of the
plan of our federal system nor a necessary result of federalism, but
rather is the result of an amalgam of actions and inactions that
left the potential governance structure of the corporate economy
up for grabs for a considerable period. That amalgam included a
legacy of localism where both business and corporate entities were
concerned, a legacy that warred with the commercial and nationalist ambitions of a certain sector of society, one prominently embodied in the Supreme Court.

This essay suggests that our understanding of the history of corporate federalism should be informed by four distinct phenomena.
First, corporations were not a particularly important business entity at the time of the Revolution, the Constitution, or for a few
years after. They did, however, quickly grow in importance. Moreover, they were conceived as an important legal phenomenon in
many other areas of social organization. Thus, the federal structure
of corporate law is based not so much on corporations as business
entities but on corporations as entities created for business as well
as for other functions. In making this claim, I am obviously not
saying anything very new either to the historical or the legal communities about the importance of the corporation as an organizational form, though I believe the observation that it has an impact
on our understanding of the federal character of our law is novel.
Second, corporations were perceived as local phenomena. Again,
I do not think the observation itself is new. Nonetheless, no explanation currently exists for why Americans should have had that
perception, nor does one exist for why it should have continued,
especially in the face of a nationalizing economy. I believe the perception derives from at least two phenomena, probably more. In
the aftermath of the Revolution centralized political authority was
distrusted by the people, and thus the states were seen as the most
legitimate focus of political authority. Also, localism was reinforced
by the nature of the business corporations that actually became
part of the national economy in the early nineteenth century.
Third, in trying to understand the history of corporate law it is a

mistake to focus solely on corporate codes. We must also look to the role of the courts,[10] which decided what the appropriate jurisprudential vision of the corporation should be, what the rules for interpreting corporate charters should be, and what terms should fill the gaps in corporate charters. Thus, fourth, to the extent that nationalists manifested an understanding of the growing integration of the nation's economy, their efforts ran counter to the competition supposedly inherent in the federal structure. Since Congress never assumed its potential role in corporate law, what action took place took place in the courts.[11] The only national court was the Supreme Court, and its efforts to understand the business corporation in a federal structure manifested a desire not just for legitimating the national power to incorporate, but also for uniformity in the governance of corporations, especially in managerial conduct and in the interpretation of charters. In this effort the nationalist justices carefully juxtaposed the rhetoric of localism with ingenious claims involving the universalism of corporate law. It is the Court's role in the nascent period of America's corporate law that, ultimately, narrows and focuses the competitive realm of state charter competition. Using its powers under the Contracts Clause, as well as other powers, the Court defined what corporations were, then explained how to interpret corporate charters, and finally set about to create rules of corporate governance themselves.

In this essay, I wish to make several claims about the origins and early development of corporate federalism. First, corporate chartering is not a power allocated either to the federal government or to the states. Second, the attention paid to incorporation by the Founders reinforces the view that neither the federal government nor the states could lay sole claim to the power to incor-

---

[10] In exploring the role courts played, we should avoid anachronism. While the federal courts today play a small role in formulating corporate law (except for securities law, of course), their historical role is of much greater significance.

[11] Willard Hurst made this claim more generally some years ago, arguing "There were institutional reasons why the Court, rather than Congress, led in protecting multi-state areas of economic maneuver. It was a bold step when the Court originally seized the initiative to define public policy of such scope. But once it had done this, the Court was better adapted than the Congress for the detailed protection of private freedom." James Willard Hurst, *Law and the Conditions of Freedom in the Nineteenth-Century United States* 50 (University of Wisconsin Press, 1956). Though many of Hurst's claims in that classic work have been subject to criticism and revision, this claim about the governmental preferences of Americans has not been one of them.

porate. The actual record of incorporation before the nineteenth century doubly reinforces that view. Third, to the extent that the existence of corporations themselves suggests that incorporation was a state and not a national function, their creation by states was dictated not by the existence of federalism, but by the role played by corporations in the political economy of the United States (as opposed to England). They served local, not national, ends, and national ends seemed not to require corporations—with, of course, a notable exception. Finally, despite the localism of enterprise in America, the Supreme Court, while paying lip service to localism, strove at every opportunity to legitimate national incorporation, to protect corporations created by states from subsequent attacks by their creators, and to universalize corporate law to counteract the seeming perversities of local interpretation which might threaten corporate, hence economic, development. Under Chief Justice Marshall, the impetus was nationalist and mercantile. Under Chief Justice Taney, the impetus was market liberalism, a market liberalism contained within the nationalizing framework set up by Marshall's Court. The Court thus narrowed the range of choices available for corporate law by limiting what states could do with charters, by insisting that charters be interpreted uniformly and in a certain way, and by expanding and universalizing the common law of corporate governance.

I. Options

Apparently, very little thought was given to the question of incorporation at the time of the Revolution or in the years leading up to the Constitution. At least we have few records suggesting much thought was given to incorporation. Rather, assumptions were carried forward. Those assumptions were, however, weakly grounded in both the theory of state sovereignty and the practice of incorporation. Moreover, they were carried forward with a casualness that seems, in retrospect, astonishing.

When the colonies separated from England they became states, states that already conceived of themselves as sovereign in virtually every sense and whose sovereignty was embodied in each state's legislature. As Gordon Wood put it, "[W]hen the Americans came in 1776 to erect their own confederated empire, most did so with an overwhelming conviction, as Samuel Adams told the Carlisle

Commission in 1778, 'that in every kingdom, state, or empire there must be, from the necessity of the thing, one supreme legislative power, with authority to bind every part in all cases the proper object of human laws.' "[12] Creation of bodies corporate and politic had, of course, been a sovereign legal prerogative since time immemorial. The sovereign power to create corporations thus devolved from England to the former colonies, not in their confederated form, but to each of the former colonies specifically, and within the structures of the new state governments, to the legislatures. This devolution was so uncontroversial that one strains to find anyone who even bothers to comment that it had happened. Indeed, the best evidence that it happened is that the state legislatures immediately took over where the crown had left off, granting charters to corporations of all varieties. Chief Justice Marshall seemed to confirm—under the circumstances to say that he legitimated it would be going too far—such a transfer of authority with as much casualness as the devolution itself in speaking for the Court in *Dartmouth College*.[13] In announcing that the charter of the college was a contract between the crown and the trustees of the college, he addressed New Hampshire's role as successor to the crown *in a parenthetical* to the Court's conclusion, noting, "This is plainly a contract to which the donors, the trustees and the crown (to whose rights and obligations New Hampshire succeeds) were the original parties."[14]

While Revolutionary belief in the states and in their legislatures certainly fixed a vision of state legislative sovereignty in the Revolutionary mind, colonial experience may have abetted the belief that the states would be the creators of corporations. Even though the ultimate sovereign power had resided with the crown, the practice in colonial America had been that, in many instances, the crown's power, including the power to charter corporations, was delegated to colonial authorities. Moreover, the delegations were such that colonists were in all likelihood only seldom reminded that the ultimate authority to incorporate lay with the crown, for as one of the earliest historians of American corporations has noted, "The delegation of the right to incorporate was seldom ex-

---

[12] Gordon S. Wood, *The Creation of the American Republic, 1776–1787* 353 (Norton, 1969).

[13] *Dartmouth College v Woodward*, 17 US 518 (1819).

[14] Id at 643–44.

plicit and practically never comprehensive in terms. As a rule it had to be inferred from more or less general grants or relationships."[15] Thus, at the time of the Revolution colonists who had any experience with the creation of corporations would have witnessed either the local creation of the corporation with only a vague connection with central English authority or would have assumed that the powers of the crown passed to the new states.

With that legacy and with the theoretical understanding of sovereignty prevalent at the time of the Revolution, one might think that no one could suggest that the confederation congress itself had the sovereign power to create corporations. After all, even had the colonial legacy been one of clear English central authority, the Revolution had made central national authority suspect. The Articles of Confederation, in turn, reflected that suspicion. Thus, the Articles of Confederation, with the language of Article II reserving sovereignty to the states and limiting the implied powers of the United States, would seem to have made an interpretation that the confederation congress had the power to incorporate problematic at best.[16] Nonetheless, reality sometimes plays havoc with theory. Before the adoption of the Constitution, the confederation congress did grant a charter of incorporation. While at first glance a single grant may seem unexceptional, it is important to keep in mind that from 1781 until 1790 only thirty-three charters were granted to business corporations at all.[17] Indeed, the congress made the grant in 1781, and from 1781 until 1785 only eleven charters, including the one by the confederation congress, were conferred upon business corporations in the entire country.[18]

More importantly, the power of the confederation congress to undertake such a grant, to a bank, was the source of some debate and concern on more than one occasion in the congress, James Wilson going so far as to suggest that the act of incorporation for a national bank by the congress could not be within the sovereign powers of the states at all and thus was within the confederation's

---

[15] Joseph Stancliffe Davis, 1 *Essays in the Earlier History of American Corporations* 8 (Harvard, 1917; reprint ed, Russell & Russell, 1965) (footnote omitted).

[16] Articles of Confederation, Art II ("Each State retains its sovereignty, freedom and independence, and every power, jurisdiction and right, which is not by this confederation expressly delegated to the United States, in Congress assembled.").

[17] See Davis, 2 *Essays* at 24 (Table I) (cited in note 15).

[18] Id.

powers, despite the lack of delegated authority.[19] Nonetheless, and despite the reservations of others, even those of so weighty a figure as Madison (who liked the idea of a bank but felt the congress powerless to create it),[20] the charter was granted. With no mechanism available under the Articles to countermand the incorporation, the bank came into existence. In an abundance of caution, however, and at the urging of the congress, it sought and received state charters to augment its federal charter.[21] Nonetheless, whatever the stated or unstated federal power, the federal authority had acted to grant a charter.

The ambiguity of the federal power notwithstanding, we ought to look to the state constitutions in the confederation period for the explicit assertion of their sovereign power to create corporations. Even in those constitutions, however, the power was not usually explicit. Of the state constitutions that antedated the federal Constitution, only Pennsylvania's 1776[22] and Vermont's 1786[23] constitutions explicitly mentioned the power to create corporations. As a rule, the power to create corporations was considered implicit in the general power to legislate, since charters were acts of legislation. As a sovereign power, however, incorporation was not so integral to state legislative sovereignty then that it had to be specially claimed in the constitutive documents of the states.

Though not explicitly claimed, the power was being increasingly used. Whether directly from English authority, or indirectly in the colonies themselves, only seven businesses were chartered in America before the Revolution.[24] By comparison with the colonial period, however, the confederation period was a hotbed of incorporation. No business corporations were chartered by the state legislatures during the war, although thirty-two were chartered thereafter and before 1790. To the extent that one can extrapolate

---

[19] James Wilson, II *The Works of James Wilson* 824–47 (R. G. McCloskey, ed, Harvard, 1967).

[20] James Madison to Edmund Pendleton, January 8, 1782, in Gaillard Hunt, ed, 1 *The Writings of James Madison* 167–69 (Putnam, 1900).

[21] Id.

[22] *Pa Const of 1776, Plan or Frame of Government for the Commonwealth or State of Pennsylvania*, § 9, in Francis Newton Thorpe, V *The Federal and State Constitutions, Colonial Charters, and Other Organic Laws of the States, Territories, and Colonies Now or Heretofore Forming the United States of America* 3081, 3084–85 (Government Printing Office, 1909).

[23] *Vt Const of 1786, Chapter II, § IX*, in Thorpe, VI *Constitutions* at 3749, 3755.

[24] See Davis, 2 *Essays* at 24 (Table I) (cited in note 15).

from such a small sample, it also appears that the pace of incorporation was quickening. In the four years from 1786 until 1790,
two-thirds of the thirty-two state charters were granted;[25] thus the
rate of incorporation was twice that of the prior four years.

Despite the quickening pace of business incorporations and notwithstanding the debates over the power of the confederation to
charter corporations, as well as the amity with which such important players as Madison viewed institutions such as a national bank,
incorporation was not a topic which commanded much attention
in the summer of 1787. Which is not to say that it commanded no
attention at all. The convention had an Incorporation Committee,
chaired by Rufus King. King, evidently, did almost nothing.[26] Incorporation was also briefly discussed at the convention itself. The
debate over incorporation, if Madison's notes are good and sufficient evidence, revolved around a motion by Madison to amend a
motion by Franklin to provide the federal government with the
power to cut canals.[27] It reflected the ambiguity of earlier debates
in the confederation as the early congresses were to reflect the
ambiguity in practice. Madison's amendment provided for the
power "to grant charters of incorporation where the interest of
the U.S. might require & the legislative provisions of the individual States may be incompetent."[28] Rufus King "thought the power
unnecessary" while also suggesting that the states "will be preju-
diced and divided into parties" were the federal government to
have the power.[29] Interestingly, Wilson presaged a vision of the
race to the bottom (and the role of the Supreme Court in the first
half of the nineteenth century), claiming, "It is necessary to prevent *a State* from obstructing the *general welfare*."[30] The amendment died nonetheless, receiving the votes of only three states,
with eight others voting against it.[31] The death of federal incorpo-

---

[25] Id.

[26] Ronald E. Seavoy, *The Origins of the American Business Corporation, 1784–1855: Broadening the Concept of Public Service During Industrialization* 113 n 20 (Greenwood, 1982).

[27] Charles C. Tansill, ed, *Documents Illustrative of the Formation of the United States* 724
(Government Printing Office, 1927) (Madison's notes).

[28] Id.

[29] Id. The notion that states would be divided, that they would compete for federally
incorporated businesses, is apparent in his remarks that follow, in which he noted the "contention" between Philadelphia and New York for a bank.

[30] Id (emphasis in original).

[31] Id at 725.

ration was, however, greatly exaggerated. The first federal Congress, following Hamilton's request for a national bank,[32] Jefferson's opinion that it was unconstitutional,[33] and Hamilton's rejoinder that the power was implicit insofar as it was a means to achieve a specified constitutional end,[34] created a national bank.[35]

This, then, was the pattern that would mark debates about incorporation for some time to come. Claims of the illegitimacy of federal power were met with claims of necessity, and necessity triumphed, at least for a few decades. Assumptions of the legitimacy of state incorporation were met with the reality of constantly shifting state attitudes toward corporations. Thus, a pattern of back and forth, premised on the one hand in visions of the legitimate extent of federal power and on the other in the nature of needed incorporations, was to characterize the understanding of incorporation for decades.

It is a commonplace that the early business corporations were essentially utilities—road and canal companies, for example—or business entities with similar characteristics—banks and insurance companies. The usual understanding has been that almost all business corporations were thus, to borrow a phrase of later importance, businesses affected with the public interest. There is another way of viewing the vast majority, though not all, of the businesses. It is an understanding, however, that would grow as the number of corporate businesses grew and the range of their objects came to include everyday manufacturing and commercial activities. That view held that businesses were essentially local. Of the 317 business corporation charters granted from the colonial period through 1800, almost 80 percent were for highways and local public services.[36] Of the remaining 20 percent, it is not unreasonable to suppose that many, if not most, contemplated local operations only, given the objects for which they were chartered. Of those that did

---

[32] Report on a National Bank, Dec. 13, 1790, in Samuel McKee, Jr., ed, *Papers on Public Credit, Commerce and Finance by Alexander Hamilton* 53 (Columbia, 1934).

[33] Opinion on the Constitutionality of a Bill for Establishing a National Bank, Feb. 15, 1791, in Julian P. Boyd, ed, 19 *Papers of Thomas Jefferson* 275 (Princeton, 1974).

[34] Final Version of an Opinion on the Constitutionality of an Act to Establish a Bank, Feb. 23, 1791, in Harold C. Syrett, ed, 8 *Papers of Alexander Hamilton* 97 (Columbia, 1965).

[35] See Bray Hammond, *Banks and Politics in America from the Revolution to the Civil War* 118 (Princeton, 1957).

[36] See Davis, 2 *Essays* at 24 (Table I) (cited in note 15).

not contemplate local operation, only the largest financial institutions could be said in any meaningful sense to be anything but
local. What was true of that period was almost equally true of the
first half of the nineteenth century, at least until the integration
of railroads came to be a common phenomenon. The vastest majority of business corporations were local. Their physical facilities
were usually concentrated in a single place, their employees lived
in a limited area, their managers were usually their owners and
both owners and employees lived in close proximity to the facilities, and their objects contemplated limited activities and sometimes specified that the activities were to take place in certain
locations. They were chartered by states to invigorate local
economies.[37]

Simply because states granted corporate charters and no one
questioned the legitimacy of state incorporation did not mean that
the role of the states was uncontroversial. State incorporation was
controversial not simply because incorporation carried with it a
legacy, if not of monopoly, then at least of protections from competition.[38] State incorporation was also controversial because, to
the extent that charters were seen to carry such favors, they were
objects of jealousy in the commercial community, whether favors
had been granted or not.[39] Moreover, with the grant of favors came
the claims of corruption, from mere favoritism to bribery.[40] And,
finally, of course, despite the fact that charters resembled one another far more than they differed, many—both inside and outside
the legislatures—complained that the legislatures were being overwhelmed with petitions for incorporation, their resources of time
and energy diverted from more useful enterprises in the face of
the insistent pleas of potential corporators.[41]

Legislative reaction was predictable. When forces favoring cor-

---

[37] See, for example, Seavoy at 39–76, 255–74 (cited in note 26) (discussing New York
business corporations); John W. Cadman, Jr., *The Corporation in New Jersey: Business and
Politics 1791–1875* 205–39 (Harvard, 1949) (noting in particular that "the manufacturing
operations of nearly all the companies were to be carried on in New Jersey," id at 216).

[38] See James Willard Hurst, *The Legitimacy of the Business Corporation in the Law of the
United States 1780–1920* 31, 38 (University Press of Virginia, 1970).

[39] Id at 42.

[40] See Lawrence M. Friedman, *A History of American Law* 196 (Simon & Schuster, 2d ed
1985).

[41] Id at 194–95.

porate expansion held power, special charters were granted aplenty.[42] Where reaction set in, sometimes special chartering was simply curtailed, but more often limited forms of general corporate chartering statutes were enacted.[43] Embodied in the reaction, however, were restrictions on corporations—usually concerning capital or longevity—or other regulatory measures, that made incorporation under the statutes less attractive than special incorporation.[44] And, it took some time before states, Ulysses-like, tied legislatures to the mast to avoid returning to regimes of special charters by barring special charters in state constitutions.[45]

Even corporate localism, however, was countered with a contending national vision. The debates over the national banks, among other things, demonstrated that there were those who believed that the country needed business institutions that would operate not just interstate, but on a national scale. Many, Hamilton most notably, also believed in the integration and commercialization of the economy more generally, and sought active intervention by the government on behalf of those goals, in the mercantilist spirit. Still, few thought much about the corporation operating as the engine for such an economy. For example, one reads Hamilton's *Report on Manufactures* and discovers not so much as the first word on the corporate form.[46]

The result of all of these factors—the relative rarity of business corporations juxtaposed with the increasing resort to the corporate form for business operations, the conception of business enterprise as essentially a local phenomenon contrasted with the cosmopolitan desire of some to integrate and commercialize the economy, and, of course, the ambiguities of theories and prejudices concerning the relative powers of the states and the federal government being overborne in cases of perceived necessity, such as in the chartering of national banks—left unclear just what courts should do when confronted with questions of the governance of corporate enterprises. Unsurprisingly, then, rather than setting out clearly

---

[42] See, for example, Cadman at 72–74 (cited in note 37).

[43] See, for example, id at 16–17, 25–26, 75–83 & n 211.

[44] See, for example, id.

[45] See Butler at 153 (Table 1) (cited in note 6).

[46] Report on Manufactures, Dec. 5, 1791, in Saul K. Padover, ed, *The Mind of Alexander Hamilton* 300 (Harper & Brothers, 1958).

what the relative roles of the states and the federal government should be, the courts replicated the conflicts. In the Supreme Court, the only organ of the federal government to play a substantial role in this controversy in the period (since, apart from the bank controversy, the congress and the executive did so little), the nationalists were thus confronted with the ambiguous legacy of localism and nationalism that theory and practice had handed to it. Lacking a clear constitutional allocation of power, the Justices generally strained to leave open the possibility of something other than a constricted local vision of enterprise where corporations were concerned.[47]

As I have noted, the power of incorporation was not given in so many terms to the federal government. In fact, given the choice, the Founders refused to include the power. On the other hand, they did not expressly reserve the power to the states. Moreover, their refusal to include the power in the Constitution was grounded not in a deeply considered and informed debate, but rather in quite the opposite—inaction by those charged to consider the matter and an (apparently) abbreviated exchange of views. Nor can it be said that the states jealously staked out incorporation as a sovereign power to be defended against federal encroachment. No one advanced any argument that incorporation was inherently within or was necessarily a state power. Indeed, few states claimed it as a power in their constitutions. Rather, it was a power inferred from the legislative capacity of a government. Incorporation was thus a power coextensive with legislative power. It was, in that sense, simply a constitutionally unallocated power of government.

The theoretical ambiguity of incorporation accompanied an almost equally ambiguous practical legacy. The Articles of Confederation, surely more than the Constitution, appeared to have created a government incapable of chartering a corporation. Nonetheless, faced with the apparent necessity for a national bank, one was chartered by the confederation congress. About a decade later, with a similar, albeit lesser, ambiguity concerning power and legitimacy, the first federal Congress did the same thing.

The necessity of national incorporation simply did not present

---

[47] The Court, of course, was unable to grant charters itself. What it could, and did, do was to legitimate the exercise of national power and limit the capacity of states to restrict corporate functioning.

itself in very many cases in the early years of the republic. America's mercantilist impulses, best expressed by Hamilton, were insular. That is, unlike England, whose imperial expansion was based on quasi-governmental chartered bodies and whose economic reach was facilitated by chartered trading companies, as America expanded westward, its businesses followed acquisition of new territory and did not facilitate expansion. Even as notoriously commercial as America's agricultural communities were, their trading patterns were segmented and localized. While that meant, as Tony Freyer has so convincingly shown, that the country needed a national commercial law,[48] its need for a national corporate law, absent much apparent need for national corporations, was much less clear.

The localism of the law governing business corporations was also a product of the development of corporate law more generally, that is, the law governing public corporations as well as private nonprofit corporations. While the distinctions between public and private corporations were reasonably clear, and became more so, arguments—apparently quite serious arguments—continued to be made through 1850 concerning whether government ownership imparted a public character to business entities, and similarly that certain functions were necessarily so governmental in character as to render the business corporation a public corporation. Because public corporations created by states were, by definition, local entities, the confluence of a state charter, state ownership, and seemingly government function reinforced an assumption of localism in corporate jurisprudence more generally. Similarly, the eleemosynary corporation seemed to be a peculiarly local enterprise—and it generally was. Hospitals and religious institutions served their localities, as did most other charities, including even educational institutions. Thus, the local focus of public and charitable corporations was reflected in their charters and the law governing their management. While distinctions were drawn between the law governing public and private corporations, they were fewer and narrower than one might expect. Those drawn between charitable and business corporations were almost nonexistent.

But for the occasional federal charter, usually for an eleemosy-

---

[48] Tony Allan Freyer, *Forums of Order: The Federal Courts and Business in American History* (JAI, 1979).

nary institution, Congress took no steps to nationalize corporate law or to create national companies, other than the bank. There was little demand that it do so. Thus, the localism of American corporate chartering, a relatively weak force at the founding, especially in the face of perceived necessity, grew in strength through inertia. Paradoxically, the Supreme Court, even in its nationalist guise, countenanced that form of localism, though its intent was to facilitate both commerce and corporate actors by trying to protect corporations from their state creators.

II. Materials

The Supreme Court, of course, could only work with the materials it was given. Insofar as corporate law is concerned, its diet was especially meager.[49] Prior to 1850, the Court was faced with only thirty-eight cases in which the word corporation or its derivatives were even mentioned.[50] Nonetheless, the Court seized nearly every opportunity to pronounce on the nature of a corporation, the interpretation of charters, and the governance of the entities.

Before 1850, the first of these cases that the Court heard was decided in 1804, the last in 1849. Unsurprisingly, the number of corporate law cases grew as corporations grew more important in the political economy, with thirty-one of the thirty-eight decided in the last thirty of the fifty-year period. Nevertheless, the most important cases arose throughout the Marshall Court and early in the Taney Court, setting into sharp relief the tension between localism and jurisprudential nationalism.

Of the thirty-eight cases, two dealt with public corporations and thirty-six with private. Of the cases dealing with private entities, thirty-two were ones involving business corporations. Of those, twenty dealt with banks, three dealt with insurance companies,

---

[49] The Court's nationalist impulses were, of course, constrained not just by the nature and number of cases involving corporations which were appealed to it. Other phenomena, notably slavery, may have limited the Court's efforts to nationalize what were perceived as traditional state functions by many, no matter how weakly those functions were in fact grounded at the state level.

[50] Conducting a search for cases using the word incorporation and its derivatives yields many more cases, most of which are irrelevant, as the word is used as a verb, as when one "incorporates by reference." I thus treat the cases using corporation and its derivatives as the definitive sample.

seven dealt with transportation companies, and two dealt with commercial or manufacturing entities. The Court thus had a limited range of cases in which it could advance rules of law that might facilitate economic nationalism.

Because business entities were conceived of as local, the competitive dynamic of modern federalism was still nascent. To the extent that states competed at all, they competed for corporations in their entirety. What competition there was was relatively rare, occurring (generally later than this period) between states which bordered each other, such as New York and New Jersey.[51] Furthermore, rather than a regime of competition, state corporate codes embodied a regime of emulation. The usual pattern was that internal pressures within a jurisdiction—entrepreneurs seeking particular charter terms such as unlimited life or, much more often, legislators seeking relief from the burden of the petitions for corporate charters or, most often, insurgent legislators making an issue of bribery or monopoly terms in charters—would lead to a quasi-general law of incorporation, usually for certain types of enterprises, such as mining companies, or turnpike companies, or banks, or some limited range of business corporations. Neighboring legislatures then simply copied such statutes, not to attract corporations across borders, but to satisfy their own internal demands.[52]

This dynamic was of an entirely different order than the modern regime of competitive federalism. That is, the internal impulses in the states did not always lead to looser or more facilitative terms of incorporation. To the contrary, they often provided for stricter terms than would have been available under individual legislative charters because they responded to multiple political pressures, sometimes pro-corporate and sometimes restrictive or regulatory. Thus, localism did not necessarily lead to codes and charters more facilitative of a competitive and integrated economy. The Supreme Court Justices who believed the law facilitated, or ought to facilitate, the economic integration of the nation decided their cases with this ever-shifting state law background.

With no clear constitutional allocation of the power to incorporate, the Supreme Court was neither directed to nor barred from taking jurisdiction over cases involving corporate law. For

---

[51] See Cadman at 177–81 (cited in note 37).

[52] See Hurst, *Legitimacy* at 146 (cited in note 38).

the Court to hear such a case, however, corporate law had to involve an issue on which the Court could take jurisdiction, and such
issues were generally constitutional. A twentieth-century lawyer
might expect such issues to arise under the Commerce Clause.[53]
Nineteenth-century lawyers, however, knew that the Contracts
Clause was key.[54] Thus most, though not all, of the litigation concerning corporate law came before the Court via the Contracts
Clause.

III. Outcomes

Given that corporate law is today state law, turning to the
Supreme Court for insight into corporate jurisprudence would
generally be error. That for the first fifty years of the nineteenth
century the Court was a major expositor of corporate jurisprudence alone suggests just how much things have changed and how
tentative our assumptions about the naturalness of state domination of corporate law ought to be. In fact, the Court pronounced
on topics that would appear to be purely the concern of state corporate law, namely, the theory of the corporation, the rules governing charter interpretation, and the law of corporate objects and
managerial conduct. While each of these categories may be distinctly stated, in practice they overlap a great deal and are difficult
analytically to separate. Nevertheless, they serve as a sufficient
basis through which to analyze what the Court did in the early
development of American corporate law. Each category of cases
demonstrates that the Court recognized the dominance of state
chartering, but each also suggests ways in which the Court sought
to limit state interference with corporations in order to facilitate
economic development. And, while the Marshall and Taney
Courts differed in their approaches, each used appeals to supposedly universal law to counteract state law tendencies to retard the
use of corporations for business enterprise. The relative merits of
the Marshall and Taney Court approaches to property and development have been well analyzed by others, especially Stanley

---

[53] US Const, Art I, § 8, cl 3.

[54] US Const, Art I, § 10, cl 1.

Kutler,[55] and I do not propose to cover that ground again. Rather, this essay will suggest that the efforts of both Courts resulted in a highly bounded sphere of discretion for state experimentation with what we now regard as the foundations of corporate law. That legacy, while not dictating the outcome of charter competition when it did develop, did point it in the direction of facilitating, rather than regulating, corporate action through corporate law.

A. THEORY OF THE CORPORATION

In the first important corporate case heard by the Court, *Head & Amory v Providence Insurance Co.*, Chief Justice Marshall took the opportunity to point out that while corporations were creatures of the acts that created them, they were equally creatures of the common law that governed them.[56] In making that announcement, Marshall said nothing particularly controversial. By giving the common law a place in the law governing corporations, however, Marshall necessarily left open the use of English precedents to inform American common law and, more importantly, left the Court's role in determining the common law of corporate governance dependant on the Court's own common law role. The Court soon took advantage of both vehicles to comment on the nature of corporations.

Some five years later, Marshall took advantage of the assumptions embodied in *Head & Amory. Bank of United States v Deveaux*,[57] while holding that corporations were not citizens for purposes of establishing the jurisdiction of federal courts, nonetheless held that corporations were aggregates of citizens who did not lose their access to federal courts simply by joining together under corporate name.[58] The Court knew that that was how to understand corporate entities because "our ideas of a corporation, its privileges and its disabilities, are derived entirely from the English books, [and] we resort to them for aid, in ascertaining its character."[59] Rather than looking to American cases, and they did exist, which might

---

[55] Stanley Kutler, *Privilege and Creative Destruction: The Charles River Bridge Case* (Johns Hopkins, paperback ed 1990; J.B. Lippincott, 1971).

[56] 2 Cranch 127, 167 (1804).

[57] 5 Cranch 61 (1809).

[58] Id at 65.

[59] Id at 64.

have suggested state-by-state variations in the conception of the corporation, Marshall looked to English cases. The corporate party in the case, the Bank of the United States, was, of course, federally chartered, and that might have been the basis on which he looked to English rather than American state cases, though he never said so, whether out of political sensitivity or for any other reason. But, of course, the Bank of the United States was also chartered by several states. Marshall did not even mention those charters, though in so doing he was only following the counsel who argued the case, insofar as the record reveals what they argued. The Court thus casually adopted a single, universal understanding of what constituted a corporation, rather than allowing the states to define the entity. That it would do so, and do so casually, with few questions about the propriety of such a juridical role, suggests how subtly the Court would define the structure of corporate law in the United States.

A decade passed before *McCulloch v Maryland*[60] and *Dartmouth College v Woodward*[61] gave the Marshall Court another chance to theorize on the corporation, though the wait only seemed to allow the Court a chance to build up to extended consideration of the topic in both cases. Briefly, *McCulloch* held, among other things, that Congress had the power to charter corporations as a means to achieve otherwise constitutionally permissible ends.[62] While the power to charter a corporation was not specifically granted to Congress, neither was it denied. Furthermore, nothing in the Constitution by implication reserved the power to the states, not even the Tenth Amendment. In construing the legislative power of Congress, while the Court must notice the bounds of Congress's authority, within those bounds Congress had the authority to pick means it deemed appropriate to the legislative ends, including the incorporation of business entities to achieve them.[63] The Necessary

---

[60] 4 Wheat 316 (1819).

[61] 4 Wheat 518 (1819).

[62] Id at 325.

[63] Though Congress failed to exercise its legislative imagination, the European, and especially the English, tradition of trading companies, the mercantilist plans of Hamilton and others, and a multitude of textual references, including the powers to create the post office and postal roads, to grant patent and other rights, to maintain the military, and, of course, to regulate commerce, among other powers—all could have served as the basis for further federal incorporations. The Court's invitation to Congress to act could hardly have been more explicit: "That a corporation must be considered as a means not less usual, not of higher dignity, not more requiring a particular specification than other means, has been

and Proper Clause was thus not to be read as constraining, but facilitating Congress's legislative authority.[64] While it was true that the extant examples of business corporations were both local in character and state incorporated,[65] that demonstrated not that incorporation was solely a state function but rather that the corporation was becoming a normal means by which to conduct economic activity. Indeed, so normal that even the confederation congress had thought that incorporation was appropriate.[66] And, of course, where necessity required federal action, it would be unwise to leave the federal government dependent upon a state or the states.[67] Left unsaid, though clearly implicit, was the coda, "even where state authority is clear."

For many reasons, Congress did not pursue the opportunity granted to it by the Court. Many years would pass before a federal charter was again issued for a business corporation, though the Court made clear its willingness not only to sanction federal chartering as a means to legitimate constitutional ends, but also to sanction a host of ancillary activities that those corporations might engage in, even when not directly connected to those ends. *Osborne v Bank of the United States*[68] presented the question of the constitutionality of the provisions of the bank's charter authorizing it to conduct normal banking functions, the argument for their unconstitutionality being that they were not embodied in the constitutional end of currency regulation. Justice Marshall's rhetoric[69] re-

---

sufficiently proved. If we look to the origin of corporations, to the manner in which they have been framed in that government from which we have derived most of our legal principles and ideas, or to the uses to which they have been applied, we find no reason to suppose, that a constitution, omitting, and wisely omitting, to enumerate all the means for carrying into execution the great powers vested in government, ought to have specified this. . . . If a corporation may be employed, indiscriminately with other means, to carry into execution the powers of the government, no particular reason can be assigned for excluding the use of a bank, if required for its fiscal operations." 4 Wheat at 421–22.

[64] Id at 406–12.

[65] Id at 411, 435 (discussing, respectively, exercise of sovereign power in creating corporations and the capacity of states to tax their own creations).

[66] Id at 423.

[67] Id at 424.

[68] 9 Wheat 738 (1824).

[69] The argument that Marshall's rhetoric and jurisprudence are inseparable has been most ably voiced recently. See Christopher L. Eisgruber, *John Marshall's Judicial Rhetoric*, 1996 Supreme Court Review 439, 440–41 ("Marshall . . . had to address the legitimacy of American law in general, including statutory law. The early judiciary's claim to speak for the American people was contested, but so too were the claims of Congress and the state legislatures. Marshall accordingly approached the legitimacy of judicial review from a different

jecting the argument appears narrow at first glance: "Can this instrument, on any rational calculation, effect its object, unless it be endowed with that faculty of lending and dealing in money, which is conferred by its charter? . . . Those operations give its value to the currency in which all the transactions of the government are conducted. They are, therefore, inseparably connected with those transactions."[70] Were one to emphasize the requirement of "inseparable connection," then the limits would indeed have been tight. But that was not what Marshall wrote. The connection only required that the operations "give value" to the currency, a much looser connection. The Marshall Court was in reality prepared to authorize a wide range of business activity in national corporations, so long as they could plausibly be connected to constitutional ends.

The Court, however, faced no such issues because Congress chartered no other national business corporations. Thus, the Court also faced the parallel problem of the protections available to corporations chartered by the states, and just how to universalize such protections.

Dartmouth College, at first glance, appears to run against the nationalist grain. Not only is it the case in which Marshall famously announces that a corporation is an artificial and intangible entity, and in so doing clearly establishes the distinction between public and private entities, it is also the case that announces that a corporation is nothing more than what the law that creates it makes of it (and it is usually state law that does the creating). But, of course, the very statement embodied in the case defining what a corporation is, is an effort at creating a uniform understanding for the very purpose of protecting the entities created by the states from their creators. Moreover, the holding is brilliantly circular. After all, the case holds that under the Contracts Clause of the federal Constitution, states may not interfere in their creations because those creations are contracts, not something else, but con-

---

perspective than the one adopted by modern judges: rather than trying to convince people that the judiciary posed no threat to majoritarian institutions, Marshall tried to convince people that national institutions, including the federal judiciary, would govern well."). I am wholly in accord with Eisgruber's view. Marshall's conception of the nation and his views of political economy were inextricably linked, and his rhetorical tactics were always in service to the larger strategic vision.

[70] 9 Wheat at 861–63.

tracts.[71] With one stroke, the Marshall Court thus uniformly defined what corporations were, and in so doing, brought them within the sphere of the Court's subject matter jurisdiction. As if to underline the point, Marshall explicitly noted that one of the vices of the confederation was that the confederation congress was powerless to protect corporate entities from the vagaries of the states.[72] Even Justice Story's concurrence, in which he provides the famous "out" for the states, that is, their power to insert a reservations clause into corporate charters,[73] takes away with one hand what it has just given with the other, for not only does it reduce the state to a contracting party from a sovereign entity, it also creates a presumption against the state—the reservation must be affirmatively stated, it will not be inferred. While *Dartmouth College* therefore acknowledges that corporations are only what a state makes of them and that a state may create corporations for various purposes—and one should remember, those purposes were overwhelmingly local—it also says that it is the Court that gets to define what corporations are and in so doing circumscribe the very localism of the imperatives that created them.

Following the cases of 1819, a handful of other cases also elaborated at the edges on the contributions of the earlier cases to corporate theory, though in the main they changed nothing of substance. Only one deserves serious mention, and that only briefly. In *Briscoe v Bank of the Commonwealth of Kentucky*,[74] the Court held that ownership by the state of a corporate entity did not reconstitute its character from private to public. No doubt to Story's consternation—he dissented—the Court used the distinction propounded in *Dartmouth College* to allow states to charter banks with impunity and thereby evade the constitutional restriction on state currency. Even here, however, the Court arrogated to itself—implicitly via the Contracts Clause one supposes—the power to de-

---

[71] Marshall's definition of corporations was problematic for another reason. Even were it clear that corporations were and had been considered contracts, whether such contracts were covered by the Contracts Clause is itself debatable. At least one historian has recently surveyed both the primary literature and secondary interpretations and has concluded that "Federalists and Antifederalists held a wide range of opinions about the meaning of the clause." See Steven R. Boyd, *The Contracts Clause and the Evolution of American Federalism, 1789–1815*, 44 Wm & Mary Q 529, 531 (1987).

[72] 4 Wheat at 651.

[73] Id at 675.

[74] 11 Pet 257 (1837).

fine what a corporate entity was in order to facilitate the activity of the corporation, albeit not for nationalist purposes, for the Court had moved into the Taney era, but nonetheless for purposes thought to facilitate economic activity. In that sense, then, though the vision of what was appropriate judicial facilitation had changed, the underlying claim of the Marshall era, that the Court could define what a local corporate entity was for the purpose of facilitating its activity, remained.

B. CHARTER INTERPRETATION

Interpreting charters was one thing, the rules about how to interpret charters—the meta rules—another. Charters were local, meta rules were universal. *Head & Amory* and *Deveaux* are, once again, the starting places. Though the former announces that the "general" rule is that a corporation may only act in the manner prescribed in the act of incorporation,[75] the latter provides the first exception to the "general" rule. Application of the general rule and its exception, however, meant that the Court did not ask first how states interpreted their own charters. While *Head & Amory* merely affirms a universal rule of interpretation, *Deveaux* goes a step further, creating a universal exception to a general rule. Some things, *Deveaux* announces, are implicit in all charters. They are attributes of corporate existence which need not, therefore, be spelled out. Among such attributes are the right to sue and be sued.[76] One year later the Court gave the "general" rule its complete twist. In *Korn & Wisemiller v Mutual Assurance Society*[77] the Court said that the "general principles" of interpretation could be aided by the words of the charter. Thus, the rules of interpretation to be applied to the charters issued by the states were universal and those rules included general understandings of what constituted corporations and corporate action. Again, the presumption was a nationalizing one in the face of state particularisms, and rather than trying to harmonize the general rules to the specific jurisdiction, the Court worked the other way, harmonizing state law to universal principles. So subtle and so pervasive was this nationaliz-

---

[75] 2 Cranch at 166.

[76] 5 Cranch at 80.

[77] 6 Cranch 192 (1810).

ing impulse that, at least in corporate law cases, the record reflects only one case in which state rules of interpretation are even mentioned, and that is in the innocuous and tertiary opinion of Justice Baldwin in *Charles River Bridge v Warren Bridge*.[78] What is more, Baldwin only notices Massachusetts rules of construction after he has noted that all corporations are in need of protection from the state and that they should all be "governed by the same rules of law, as to the construction and the obligation of the instrument by which the incorporation is made."[79] In that case, the Massachusetts rules comported with the universal, mooting the point.

In the cases that followed the three early cases, more and more attributes of the corporation came to be seen as universal, that is, implicit in all charters, including such attributes as limited liability.[80] After several cases had named some of the specific attributes, *Bank of the United States v Dandridge*[81] articulated the general position, noting that certain powers come by implication to all corporations. They included not just those of legal standing, but also the power to act within the political economy and to govern itself. As the Court put it, "To corporations, however erected, there are said to be certain incidents attached, without any express words or authority for this purpose; such as the power to plead and be impleaded, to purchase and alien, to make a common seal, and to pass by-laws."[82] That the Supreme Court would be the agency that might continue to define what corporate powers were, however, still awaited articulation. It was not long in coming. Justice Baldwin's concurring opinion in *Briscoe*,[83] while by definition not the position of the Court, set the stage. He argued that terms could be defined in only one way, regardless of whether one was construing common law, statutory law, or the law of nations, and in this sense there was no localism in the common law.[84]

Briscoe was decided in the same term as *Charles River Bridge*. The latter case, famous for its developmental bias in the face of *rentier*

---

[78] 11 Pet 420, 583 (1837).

[79] Id.

[80] See *Bank of the United States v Planters' Bank of Georgia*, 9 Wheat 904, 907 (1824).

[81] 12 Wheat 64 (1827).

[82] Id at 67 (footnote omitted).

[83] 11 Pet 257 (1837).

[84] Id at 328.

property rights, also made a clear statement about the Court's role, rather than the states', in applying the rules for interpreting charters. Indeed, at its heart, that is what the case is about. Taney's position was clear. In interpreting charters, the Court would not read in exclusive powers. In other words, if a state wanted to create a monopoly or an exclusive privilege, it would have to do so explicitly. He grounded this interpretive position in the public interest. Since exclusive grants restrict individual rights, they must be strictly construed.[85] Furthermore, this rule of construction was also to be applied universally because of the public interest, the public interest in dynamic property.[86] While Taney's opinion can be read to say that the Court would not read any implied powers into corporate charters, even though it had previously done exactly that in discovering a host of implied terms, that was not the thrust of the opinion. Nor was it the way future courts would understand *Charles River Bridge*.

Justice Baldwin reiterated his position from *Briscoe* in his concurring opinion in *Charles River Bridge*, with even greater emphasis on its application to corporate law.[87] He argued that corporations of whatever kind, whether public or private, ". . . are all governed by the same rules of law, as to the construction and the obligation of the instrument by which the incorporation is made. . . . No new principle was adopted in prohibiting the passage of a law by a state which should impair the obligation of a contract; it was merely affirming a fundamental principle of law . . . by putting contracts under the protection of the constitution[.]"[88] That Baldwin's universal understanding of legal language was to be the position of the Court, and that Taney's strict construction did not mean that the Court would not continue to imply terms into corporate contracts was made clear by Justice Woodbury, writing for the Court in *Planter's Bank v Sharp*.[89] It meant, in the end, the opposite. The Court would not sanction monopoly by implying terms. It would, however, imply terms where that would encourage entrepreneurialism. Woodbury's opinion essentially limited

---

[85] Id at 544–47.

[86] Id at 544–48.

[87] Id at 583.

[88] Id.

[89] 6 How 301 (1848).

Charles River Bridge to an antimonopoly rationale. Woodbury wrote that corporate charters should be interpreted not so that only incidental powers were implied, but that whatever might be deemed necessary by the managers and which was not forbidden was also implied.[90] Indeed, it was the role of the judiciary to review corporators' contracts with the state for incorrectly narrow interpretations. As he put it, "The rights of a party under a contract might improperly be narrowed or denied by a State court, without any redress, if their decision on the extent of them cannot be reviewed and overruled here in cases of this kind[.]"[91] From this Taney and McLean dissented, but not nearly so sharply as might have been expected after *Charles River Bridge*. Their dissent admitted that some implication was inevitable, but that the Court should limit itself to necessary implications.[92] Taney thus recognized that his strict constructionism was simply an act of line-drawing. He might not give entrepreneurs as much freedom as Baldwin and others on the Court, but he would give some. Thus, *Charles River Bridge* deployed the rhetoric of strict construction to kill any inferences of monopoly, but that rhetoric was sharply limited where entrepreneurial freedom would be infringed. Both positions, however, could be harmonized in a universalist and pro-entrepreneurial stand. That Taney did not protest more severely in *Planter's Bank* suggests two things. First, Taney believed that businesses were still local community concerns, created in the interests of the community. Second, Taney believed that entrepreneurs should, in the dynamic and technologically driven economy he championed in *Charles River Bridge*, be given freedom in order that their businesses might best serve those communities.

What was implicit in Taney's opinion was the same universalizing tendency in every other opinion that had preceded it. The Court was acting like a super common law court, universalizing implications within the contracts that created corporations and universalizing the rules for interpreting the contracts themselves. The Court never retreated from its acknowledgment that corporations were creatures of the states that created them; indeed, that phrase was endlessly repeated. The Court nonetheless progres-

---

[90] Id at 322–23.

[91] Id at 327.

[92] Id at 338.

sively narrowed its deference to the states' expression of their wills, insisting that if a state wanted something in a corporate charter it had better write it in explicitly, state common law governing corporations, charter interpretation, and contract law notwithstanding.

C. CORPORATE AND MANAGERIAL CONDUCT

The law governing corporate and managerial conduct would appear to have been the area of the law most insulated from the Court's nationalizing impetus, and in some respects that turns out to be true. Nonetheless, even where the internal workings of the corporate enterprise were concerned, the Court created rules of conduct that were both designed to facilitate corporate enterprise and that displayed the same penchant for uniformity exhibited in the more general realms of corporate theory and charter interpretation. I will not attempt to review every case with such attributes but simply pick a few examples.

To begin, again, with *Head & Amory*, the Court held that while corporate acts must be done as prescribed in the charter, the charters must be read as enabling legislation within the realm of the objects for which the charter was granted.[93] Justice Story took the first step in *Bank of Columbia v Patterson's Adm'r*, affirming that corporations could act through agents and that corporations need not act always under seal.[94] It was not long before the acts of the agents themselves thus came under the scrutiny of the Court.

Dartmouth College, while acknowledging that the objects for which corporations are created are likely to be local in character, nonetheless held that where private corporations are concerned, the objects of the corporators may be somewhat more expansive than those of the state granting the charter. In the case of Dartmouth College that was especially true. While located in New Hampshire, its location was a fortuity, the donors and founder having more universal aims for the educational institution created by the charter than those that concerned New Hampshire alone.[95] Thus, the Contracts Clause could be invoked to protect a degree

---

[93] 2 Cranch at 168–69.

[94] 7 Cranch 299, 306.

[95] 4 Wheat at 640–41.

of managerial discretion in the pursuit of the aims of the founders, for the Court recognized that a change in the structure and composition of the governing structure of the college (which is what, after all, New Hampshire was attempting) necessarily altered the managerial role.[96] In other words, the donors and founders, the corporators, contracted for a particular managerial system and were entitled to the fruits of the bargain.[97] Justice Washington was even more explicit, suggesting that the government had little business interfering with that discretion.[98] Justice Story explicitly applied those considerations to the business corporation.[99]

After that, the only limit to the Court's involvement was the fact that few cases arose in which the exercise of managerial discretion was challenged. Several cases hint at expressions of a nascent duty of care and duty of loyalty, but the ownership structure of most corporations made it unlikely that managerial decisions would often be challenged by dissident shareholders; there were too few publicly held corporations, and share ownership was not widely dispersed. When corporate and managerial action was questioned, however, the Court did not hesitate to step in and define, usually expansively, the extent of managerial freedom. Questions arose concerning the discretion of managers in grading roads,[100] the power of directors to ratify the actions of bank officers,[101] corporate liability for the acts of its agents,[102] and concerning similar questions of managerial conduct. In each case the Court looked to a general law of corporations and provided an answer, even when the case arose within a specific jurisdiction and did not involve a federally chartered entity. Moreover, in each case the Court delved deeply into the legitimacy of managerial authority.

---

[96] Id at 663.

[97] Id at 665 ("They contracted for a system, which should, so far as human foresight can provide, retain forever the government of the literary institution they had formed, in the hands of persons approved by themselves.").

[98] Id at 662.

[99] Id at 681. Justice Story was not about to leave managers unsupervised. He feared state legislative interference with managers. He did not fear other forms of supervision, especially judicial supervision. Not only did he note the "visitorial" power of the state to check managerial abuse of discretion, id at 673–74, he also explicitly affirmed the chancery power of the courts in the superintendence of managers, id at 676.

[100] *Gozsler v Corporation of Georgetown*, 6 Wheat 593 (1821).

[101] *Fleckner v Bank of the United States*, 8 Wheat 338 (1823).

[102] *Bank of Metropolis v Guttschlick*, 14 Pet 19 (1840).

In the case involving road grading, for example, the question was whether a public corporate charter explicitly authorized the road grading. If it did not, was the act a public corporate version of an *ultra vires* act?[103] The Court dispatched the case quickly. It held that the officers of the corporation had implicit authority to decide on road grading even though no such power was remotely mentioned in the charter.[104] It is worth emphasizing just how much this pre–*Charles River Bridge* case meant. Strictly construed, of course, a charter that did not specify a power could not contain it. After all, in this era, often charters were specifically granted for no other purpose than to build a road. To read in such a power was problematic. To say, on the other hand, that the exercise of such a power was implicit in the authority of the managers to facilitate the aims of the public corporation was quite another thing.

And such managerial freedom was not limited to public corporations. In *Fleckner*, the Court made detailed inquiry into the actual duties of bankers in order to discover what might be read into the corporate contract. The Court sought to discover how bank officers defined their discretion[105] and how that discretion, when exercised in cases at the margin, might be ratified by the bank's directors.[106] To reiterate, in a regime of strict construction, exercise of certain forms of discretion by bank officers, as opposed to bank directors, would be impermissible. In a regime of charter construction designed to insulate entrepreneurs from the vagaries of legislatures, however, the Court was generous in defining the realm of managerial powers implicit or necessary to the objects for which the corporation was chartered. Having recognized the need for such discretion in the corporate contracts with the state, the Court protected it.

Some five years later, the Court again made an inquiry into the discretion of a bank's officers. In *Minor v Mechanics' Bank of Alexandria*,[107] the issue again was the implicit authority of bank officers

---

[103] 6 Wheat at 597–98.

[104] Id at 595 ("Like all power, it is susceptible of abuse. But it is trusted to the inhabitants themselves, who elect the corporate body, and who may therefore be expected to consult the interests of the town.").

[105] 8 Wheat at 358–60.

[106] Id at 362.

[107] 1 Pet 299 (1828).

in the face of charter provisions. Underlying the case were conflicting visions of the public interest in banks.[108] The Court noted
that protection of the public was usually provided for through cap-
italization limits. Notwithstanding such a protection, however, the
Court noted that rules governing fraud also applied to protect
stockholders,[109] not just for their protection alone but also for the
protection of the public—customers and others—who had a right
to rely on the expected integrity of bank officers in the conduct
of banking affairs.[110] The Court then proceeded to fashion a duty
of care to govern bank officers. In doing so, the Court cited no
holdings of its own or of other courts, but rather created the duty
out of the charter itself. If the Court had in other cases read an
implicit degree of managerial discretion into the corporator's contract with the state, it now had begun to read in limits to that
discretion. Moreover, it did so on the same grounds as it read in
the discretion in the first place, the public interest. And how were
the public interest limits of discretion defined? Did the Court actually formulate a standard? Not exactly. The Court looked to the
ordinary practice of bankers, how they ordinarily held themselves
out to the public, in order to ascertain their legitimate sphere of
discretion.[111] But, the Court limited the discretion, though in a
completely unsurprising manner. Should an officer engage in a
fraud, any attempt by the directors to ratify the act would be disal-
lowed as unjust.[112]

Though much has been written about the problem of foreign
corporations and jurisdiction,[113] and it is largely outside of my concern here, it is nonetheless relevant in at least one respect. The
rule that a corporation could act in the federal courts because of
the citizenship of its corporators assumed that all (or most) of the

---

[108] Id at 69.

[109] Id at 71.

[110] Id at 70.

[111] Id at 69–73.

[112] The common law role of the Court is, at first glance, surprising, until one remembers
that before the Civil War Alexandria was part of the District of Columbia. Thus, the local
courts were federal courts, and, though the bank had received a federal charter, it was as
a local bank. Nonetheless, the Court did not distinguish its common law role in this case
from its role in any cases involving national banks or locally chartered banks. See, for
example, id at 70 (comparing the case to *Bank of United States v Dandridge*).

[113] Still the best work is Gerard Carl Henderson, *The Position of Foreign Corporations in
American Constitutional Law* (Harvard, 1918).

corporators resided in the same jurisdiction. In other words, for diversity purposes, the Court assumed a degree of localism in the ownership of corporations. That assumption was based in fact: corporations were locally owned, for the most part. But only for the most part. The exceptions began to undermine the rule until finally, in *Louisville, Cincinnati & Charleston Railroad Co. v Letson*,[114] the Court abandoned the fiction, setting the situs of the corporation in the incorporating jurisdiction. In either case, however, it was the ability of the Court to fix a corporation's location locally that gave it access to the federal (that is, the national) courts. Similarly, in *Bank of Augusta v Earle*,[115] the Court explicitly acknowledged local power to exclude foreign corporations[116] while creating a presumption that unless specifically excluded, a corporation was free to operate in every state in which it was authorized by its charter to do business. In both instances localism was acknowledged as the underlying premise of corporate law, and in both cases the effects of localism were minimized.

Bank of Augusta is also important in other respects, though. In understanding how the Court thought about the phenomenon of the growing use of the corporate form, it is an especially useful case. Chief Justice Taney authored the opinion in the case, which was decided two years after *Charles River Bridge*. His opinion, when read in conjunction with the earlier case, demonstrates not just that *Charles River Bridge*'s strict construction rhetoric should itself be read narrowly, as instrumentally facilitative of entrepreneurialism rather than as a doctrinaire attitude toward charters, but also as indicative of how the Court would deal with corporate and managerial conduct. The Chief Justice was even more overtly consequentialist in *Bank of Augusta* than he was in *Charles River Bridge*.

Early in Taney's opinion for the Court, he noted that not only did the United States have a large and growing number of corporate entities, but that they had come to play an important role in the economy. He went out of his way to suggest that the Court should be careful about the consequences of its holdings for the future of these enterprises. In discussing *Deveaux*, Taney laid the groundwork for abandoning its rationale for corporate access to

---

[114] 2 How 497 (1844).

[115] 13 Pet 519 (1839).

[116] Id at 589.

federal courts, and they were purely consequentialist. He hypothesized carrying *Deveaux* to its logical extreme. Abandoning *Deveaux*'s willingness to "look to the character of the persons com-
posing a corporation"[117] for purposes of establishing jurisdiction,
he promptly, and logically, abandoned the willingness for other
purposes as well, especially contract. He wrote that the principle
"has never been supposed to extend to contracts made by a corporation; especially in another jurisdiction."[118] Why not? Before answering, it is important to repeat that Taney never considered
abandoning *Deveaux*'s fiction and depriving federal courts of jurisdiction. His extension of *Deveaux* to the realm of contract was
purely hypothesized, done solely to illustrate the dangers inherent
in the fiction. Given that he still had paramount regard for the
states' capacity to control their own economies,[119] such a move was,
at least in theory, however, conceivable for him. Nonetheless, Taney noted just what an extension of the logic of *Deveaux* would
mean if carried beyond jurisdiction. "The result of this would be
to make a corporation a mere partnership in business, in which
each stockholder would be liable to the whole extent of his property for the debts of the corporation[.]"[120] The *Deveaux* fiction
consumed itself, in Taney's understanding, and he would have
none of it. The price for access to federal court could not be that
of wiping out limited liability.

Implicit in the reasoning was just how much the Supreme Court
had come to define corporations and adjust itself to their operations. Having given them access to federal court on a fiction, having defined corporations as local contractual relationships but then
having brought those relationships within the jurisdiction of federal courts on the basis of that definition, the Court proceeded to
use the jurisdiction to define the role of the corporation in the
political economy and the role of managers within the corporation.
For example, having decided that limited liability was essentially
an inherent component of corporate existence, and having granted
access to federal court on the fiction of complete local ownership
to protect the rights of the corporators, the Court could not then

---

[117] Id at 586.

[118] Id.

[119] Id at 586–87.

[120] Id at 586.

deny an inherent component of corporate existence to the corporators when the fiction was exposed.

Taney, however, could not bring himself, or the Court, to give a limited liability corporation unfettered access to every state in the union, including those engaging in an activity for which the foreign state had refused to charter a corporation to operate within its borders. Such would be to "exempt them from the liabilities which the exercise of such privileges would bring upon individuals who were citizens of the state."[121] This, Taney argued, would lead to a pernicious end, the race to the bottom: "[I]t would deprive every state of all control over the extent of corporate franchises proper to be granted in the state; and corporations would be chartered in one, to carry on their operations in another. It is impossible upon any sound principle to give such a construction to the article in question."[122] Taney, and the Court, thus emphatically rejected the idea that corporations ought to shop for charters.

Bank of Augusta, despite that reservation in favor of localism, in reality ended up giving free reign to interstate operations without countenancing charter shopping. To operate beyond state boundaries, a charter had to authorize the activity, but given comity, unless a state barred the activity of a foreign corporation, it was presumed to be allowed. Thus, even the Taney Court continued the tradition of the Marshall Court: a bow to localism, then the exercise of national power with the intent to facilitate corporate activity, all the while federalizing and universalizing corporate law through Supreme Court pronouncement.

IV. Localism and Nationalism

That the Court attempted to facilitate commerce comes as no surprise. That it may have acted to facilitate the actions of the vehicles of commerce is also not much of a surprise. That the federal structure that we today take for granted as the defining characteristic of American corporate law was honored largely in the breach by the Court in the early years of the country is, I believe, somewhat more surprising. By so acting, the Court also set the parameters for what acceptable changes in the law might be. As

---

[121] Id.

[122] Id.

those changes were facilitative of corporate and managerial free-dom, the Court limited the range of options that would become available by setting out certain paths for the judicial policing of managerial conduct. Thus, when charter competition actually be-gan, the competition had already been channeled and given a definite direction. States were not completely free to engage in experimentation, for behind every potential tinkering with their creations lay the Supreme Court—with the other federal courts operating under its guidance—always ready to deploy the Con-tracts Clause and its other powers to limit those experiments. It is thus not surprising that the ensuing competition among the states would be in the direction of ever looser or more facilitative corporate law.

GERALD N. ROSENBERG
AND JOHN M. WILLIAMS

DO NOT GO GENTLY INTO THAT
GOOD RIGHT: THE FIRST
AMENDMENT IN THE HIGH COURT
OF AUSTRALIA

I. Introduction

Democracy and free speech go hand in hand. In the United States and abroad, the guarantee of freedom of speech in the First Amendment of the U.S. Constitution is celebrated as the hallmark of a free and democratic people. In the late twentieth century, new democracies, striving to overcome histories of nondemocratic rule, look to the free speech guarantees of the U.S. Constitution. As one British scholar notes, "exporting the First Amendment may

Gerald N. Rosenberg is Associate Professor of Political Science and Lecturer in Law, University of Chicago. He was Visiting Fellow, Research School of Social Sciences, Australian National University, 1995–1996. John M. Williams is Lecturer, Law School, University of Adelaide, South Australia.

AUTHORS' NOTE: The authors gratefully acknowledge helpful comments from John Braithwaite, Nancy Crowe, Charles Epp, Jacob Gersen, Jon Gould, Mark Graber, John Mark Hansen, Sir Anthony Mason, Brian Opeskin, Philip Pettit, Lynn Sanders, Anne-Marie Slaughter, Adrienne Stone, David Tucker, Fiona Wheeler, Leslie Zines, and participants in the Law Program/Law School Seminar Series at the Research School of Social Sciences, Australian National University, and at the American Politics Workshop, University of Chicago.

well be the most significant contribution the United States makes to international legal culture towards the end of the twentieth century."[1]

The relationship between democracy and free speech, however, is not straightforward. In particular, the use of the electronic media (television) for political advertisements in election campaigns raises issues about the effects of political advertising, and the immense sums of money such advertising requires, on democracy. With the United States as the major leading exception, many democracies around the world have regulated television campaign advertisements out of concern about these issues.[2] But even in the U.S. concern has been raised about the effects of political advertisements on democracy.[3] As President Clinton stated, "Candidates should be able to talk to voters based on the strength of their ideas, not the size of their pocketbooks. . . . "[4]

This article examines the relationship between democracy, paid political advertisements on television, and constitutional rights to free speech. In particular, it focuses on the influence of the First Amendment on a 1992 decision of the Australian High Court, *Australian Capital Television Pty. Ltd. v The Commonwealth*[5] (hereafter "*ACTV*"). In *ACTV*, the High Court found an implied right of political communication in the Australian Constitution.[6] Relying

---

[1] Eric Barendt, *Free Speech in Australia: A Comparative Perspective*, in *Symposium: Constitutional Rights for Australia?* 16 Sydney L R 149 (1994).

[2] See, generally, Linda Lee Kaid and Christinia Holtz-Bacha, eds, *Political Advertising in Western Democracies: Parties & Candidates on Television* (Sage, 1995); Herbert E. Alexander and Rei Shiratori, eds, *Comparative Political Finance Among the Democracies* (Westview, 1994).

[3] See pages 465–71.

[4] Remarks by the President in Address to the Conference on Free TV and Political Reform, The National Press Club, Washington, DC (March 11, 1997), p 6. See also James Bennet, *Clinton Suggests Licensing Deal for Free TV Time in Campaigns*, New York Times, national ed (March 12, 1997), p 1.

[5] 177 C.L.R. 106 (1992). A companion case was *Nationwide News Pty. Ltd. v Wills* (1992) 177 C.L.R. 1.

[6] The implied right to political communications was further developed in *Theophanous v Herald & Weekly Times* (1994) 182 C.L.R. 104, finding a qualified immunity against prosecution under defamation laws; and in *Stephens v Western Australian Newspapers Ltd.* (1994) 182 C.L.R. 221, extending the implied right to public discussion of the performance and conduct of members of State legislatures. The scope of the protection has been further considered in *Lange v Australian Broadcasting Corporation* (1997) 145 A.L.R. 96, which reaffirmed the implied right but emphasized the relationship between the Constitution and the common law in determining the validity of a defense to a defamation action; and *Levy v Victoria*

on that speech right, it found constitutionally invalid federal legislation prohibiting paid television and radio campaign advertising during election campaigns and creating a scheme of free time in its place. Borrowing implicitly, if not explicitly, from U.S. First Amendment jurisprudence, the Australian High Court adopted a "free-market" notion of speech and applied it in a way familiar to any student of U.S. constitutional law.

In the analysis that follows we ask whether the interpretation of the relationship between democracy, paid political advertisements on television, and constitutional rights to free speech provided in *ACTV* is persuasive. Is it a decision that other constitutional courts should follow? In answering these questions in the negative, we make three main points. First, constitutional courts, including the Australian High Court, ought not necessarily embrace the First Amendment to the U.S. Constitution and U.S. judicial interpretations of it. Australia, as well as many other democracies, lacks the equivalent of First Amendment protections of speech, and its parliamentarians and judges should not be uncritically swayed by U.S. understandings that may hinder rather than promote the practice of democracy. Second, in applying the constitutional guarantee of political communication, constitutional courts ought to reject the prevalent U.S. notion that political communication is best understood as a "free market" of ideas. This is primarily because a "free-market" understanding mistakenly sees virtually any government regulation as interference with constitutional rights. Third, the political practice to which constitutional principles apply must be analyzed. In asking whether legislation furthers the constitutional principles of free speech and democracy, courts must examine empirically current practice. Thus, because the Australian High Court too closely followed current U.S. Supreme Court understandings of the relationship between democracy and free speech, mistakenly understood political communication as operating in an unregulated "free market," and did not analyze empirically current political

---

(1997) 146 A.L.R. 248, upholding hunting season regulations as appropriate and adapted to the protection of the implied political free speech guarantee. The impled right was limited in *McGinty v Western Australia* (1996) 186 C.L.R. 140, holding that democracy and the right of free speech implied by it does not require one person, one vote, and *Langer v The Commonwealth* (1996) 186 C.L.R. 302, upholding a Commonwealth law prohibiting the encouraging of voters to fill in a ballot paper otherwise than in the legally prescribed manner and imposing a penalty of imprisonment for six months for violations.

practice, its decision in *ACTV* was mistaken[7] and should not be followed by other constitutional courts.

Although we focus on a decision of the Australian High Court, our analysis is applicable more broadly. If we are correct, then there is good reason to believe that the First Amendment does not prevent Congress from regulating paid television and radio campaign advertising during election campaigns, or from requiring television stations to provide candidates with free time. Our argument shifts the focus on the regulation of speech from a "free-market" analysis to a question of what type of regulation best furthers the constitutional goals of a robust democracy. Further, our emphasis on the application of constitutional principles to the "real world" of democracy applies powerfully to the United States, where the constitutional barriers the Supreme Court has put in the way of governmental regulation of campaigns[8] may have limited, rather than enhanced, the democratic process.

II. Background

A. THE AUSTRALIAN JUDICIAL SYSTEM

Before proceeding further, some institutional background may be useful. The Australian and U.S. constitutional systems contain much that is common and much that is different. Importantly, both countries are governed by constitutions and both have constitutional courts of last resort with the power of judicial review.[9]

---

[7] The High Court's decisions in *ACTV*, *Theophanous*, and *Stephens* created a good deal of controversy. For some, these decisions represent a newfound activism by the High Court that is an unwarranted and illegitimate incursion into the democratic realm of the Parliament. See T. D. Campbell, *Democracy, Human Rights, and Positive Law*, in (1994) Sydney L R 16 (2) 195. Others have praised the Court's decisions and welcomed them as the first steps in "righting" the Australian Constitution. P. Bailey, *"Righting" the Constitution without a Bill of Rights*, in (1995) 23 (1) FL Rev 1 at 2. From a U.S. perspective, Anthony Lewis has argued that the decisions indicate the Warren Court's "radiating influence in the world," and concluded that decisions like *Theophanous* are "an important further step in the internationalizing of the law of freedom." Anthony Lewis, *Abroad at Home: A Widening Freedom*, New York Times (Oct 21, 1994), p 31.

[8] In particular, *Buckley v Valeo*, 424 US 1 (1976) (invalidating that part of the Federal Election Campaign Act of 1971 that limited campaign expenditures); *National Bank of Boston v Bellotti*, 435 US 765 (1978) (invalidating state law prohibiting corporations from spending money to influence the vote on any issue not materially affecting the corporation).

[9] Interestingly, in neither Chapter III of the Australian Constitution (on the judiciary) nor in Article III of the U.S. Constitution is the power of judicial review expressly granted. However, the Australian High Court has taken the view that "in our system the principle of Marbury v. Madison is accepted as axiomatic." *Australian Communist Party v The Com-*

However, the Australian Constitution contains no Bill of Rights.[10] The guarantee of free speech in the First Amendment to the U.S. Constitution, for example, has no explicit corollary in the Australian Constitution. Following the Westminster system, judicial deference to Parliament is more firmly established in Australia than is judicial deference to Congress in the United States.[11] The result is a greater emphasis on common law as the means by which rights are protected in Australia. It is also the norm for each of the seven members of the High Court to write a separate opinion in each decision. This can make it difficult to understand the reasoning behind High Court decisions. It also imposes a burden on authors (and their readers): it is often the case that most, if not all, of the seven opinions must be discussed in detail. The reason is that under a seriatim system of issuing opinions, the law is not the function of a majority opinion but instead of the highest common factor among the opinions supporting the judgment.

B. THE LEGISLATION

At issue in *ACTV* was the constitutionality of the Political Broadcasts and Political Disclosures Act 1991 (Cth)[12] (hereafter the "Act").[13] The legislation banned political advertisements on television or radio during an election period.[14] In their place, the Act

---

monwealth (1951) 83 C.L.R. 1 at 262 per Fullagar J. For a discussion of the origins and the politics of judicial review in Australia, see B. Galligan, *Politics of the High Court* (1987).

[10] A number of guarantees based on the U.S. Bill of Rights did find their way into the Australian Constitution, although the High Court has generally read them narrowly. They are §§ 41 (right to vote), 51(xxxi) (acquisition of property by the Commonwealth shall be on "just terms"), 80 (trial by jury), 116 (freedom of religion), and 117 (prohibition against discrimination of residents of another state).

[11] See Sir Anthony Mason, *The Role of a Constitutional Court in a Federation: A Comparison of the Australian and the United States Experience* (1986) 16 FL Rev 1 at 6–8; L. F. Crisp, *Australian National Government* 75–78 (Longman Cheshire, 5th ed 1983).

[12] Acts of the Federal Parliament are formally referred to as Commonwealth Acts and are abbreviated "Cth."

[13] The Act introduced a new Part IIID into the Broadcasting Act 1942 (Cth). The Act also amended certain other Acts, including the Broadcasting Act 1942, the Commonwealth Electoral Act 1918, the Radiocommunications Act 1983, the Referendum (Machinery Provisions) Act 1984, and the Income Tax Assessment Act 1936.

[14] The ban covered what was described as "political matter" (§ 95B(6)) or "prescribed material" (§ 95B(6)). However, the Act made clear that the prohibition did not apply to the broadcasting of news, current affairs, or comment (§ 95A(1)(a)), talkback radio (§ 95A(1)(b)), and some material for the visually handicapped (§ 95A(2)), charities (§ 95A(3)), and public health (§ 95A(4)).

established a system of "free time" to be provided to political participants by broadcasters. Additionally, the Act mandated that policy launches[15] be broadcast free of charge, once,[16] provided that they were no longer than 30 minutes in duration.[17]

The allocation of free time under the Act was carefully set out. It was determined by the Australian Broadcasting Tribunal, an independent statutory body, in accordance with a formula under which 90%[18] of the total time was allocated to political parties with members in the previous parliament and which were contesting the current election.[19] The division of the 90% of the total time between the parties was based on the proportion of first preference votes they received in the previous election.[20] The remaining 10% of the total time was divided between two categories. The first contained Senators who had previously been members of a party which had a "free-time" allocation.[21] The second category was composed of individuals or parties that made application to the tribunal for "free time."[22] This category included interest groups.

The Act also specified the format that free-time broadcasts must take. In the case of television, the Act required that all campaign advertisements present only the so-called "talking head"[23] with a static background[24] and "without dramatic enactment or impersonation."[25] Such broadcasts were required to run for two minutes in the case of television[26] and one minute in the case of radio.[27]

---

[15] Section 95S. A policy launch was defined by § 5 of the Act as "a single spoken or written statement of all or any of the party's policies. . . . "

[16] Section 95S(5).

[17] Section 95S(4).

[18] Section 95H(2).

[19] Section 95H(1)(a)–(b).

[20] Section 95H(3). Australian voters list candidates in order of preference, ranking them from 1 to N (where N is the number of candidates).

[21] Section 95L.

[22] Section 95M(1)–(2).

[23] Section 95G(a) described the image to consist of "the head and shoulders of the speaker."

[24] Section 95G(b).

[25] Section 95G(a).

[26] Section 95G(f)(i).

[27] Section 95G(f)(ii).

The Act was premised on two major concerns,[28] neither of which is unique to Australia. First, there was a growing concern that the explosion in the cost of campaign financing in the media age, and the dependence of political parties on raising the large sums of money electronic campaign advertising requires, would lead to corruption. This concern was amply supported by a series of political corruption scandals in the years preceding the Act.[29] The Act was designed to meet this concern by prohibiting paid political advertisements during election periods. As the Report of the Senate Select Committee on the Act put it, "A stated objective of the Government in bringing forward a bill of this nature, was to safeguard the integrity of the political system by taking the pressure off political parties to raise increasing amounts of money for election campaigning."[30] In parliamentary debate, the Hon. Kim Beazley, then Minister for Transport and Communications, explained the Act as an attempt "to repel the threat of corruption to public order in Australia."[31] Senator Nick Bolkus, then Minister for Administrative Services, was even more direct, suggesting that the government's objective was "very clear . . . to tackle the corruptive influence of the corporate dollar on the electoral process."[32]

The second concern on which the Act was premised was that

---

[28] Some critics of the Act charged that the "real" aim of the bill was "to reduce the cost of the next federal election campaign to a Labor Party which is financially embarrassed." (Dissenting Report—Senators John Olsen & Rod Kemp, in The Political Broadcasts and Political Disclosures Bill 1991, Report by the Senate Select Committee on Political Broadcasts and Political Disclosures (Canberra: Australia Government Publishing Service, 1993) at 78 (hereafter "Senate Report")). Without taking a position on the truth of this claim, we do show that the effect of the Act would have been to *lessen* the overall percentage of television campaign advertising on behalf of the Labor Party.

[29] In addition to the Senate Report, see, for example, Who Pays the Piper Calls the Tune—Minimising the Risks of Funding Political Campaigns: Inquiry into the Conduct of the 1987 Federal Election and 1988 Referendums, Rep No 4, Joint Standing Committee on Electoral Matters, Parliament of the Commonwealth of Australia, June 1989; Commission of Inquiry Into Possible Illegal Activities and Associated Police Misconduct (Brisbane: Hampson, Government Printer, 1989) (The "Fitzgerald Report"—Queensland); Independent Commission Against Corruption, Report on Investigation into North Coast Land Development (Sydney: The Commission, 1990) (New South Wales); Report of the Royal Commission Into an Attempt to Bribe a Member of the House of Assembly, and other Matters (Hobart: Government Printer, 1991) (finding an attempted bribery of a member of the Tasmanian Parliament).

[30] Senate Report at 5.

[31] Mr. K. Beazley, Second Reading Speech, H Rep 3478 (May 9, 1991).

[32] Senator N. Bolkus, Second Reading Speech, Senate 61 (August 13, 1991).

electronic campaign advertising contributed little to the practice of democracy. The Senate Report on the Act, for example, noted the "debased nature of most political advertising, its alienating effects and its universal failure to convey information about policies to the voters."[33] The advertising industry's loss of revenue, the Committee suggested, "might be democracy's gain."[34] The point was put even more clearly by Senator Kernot, then leader of the Australian Democrats:

> The great majority of political electronic advertising is emotive, manipulative and . . . does not seek to inform but simply aims at the lowest common denominator. It does little to address the issues, and in fact debases the political process.[35]

In the period between the enactment of the Act and its invalidation by the High Court, a State election was held in Tasmania, a Territory election was held in the Australian Capital Territory, and there was one State bi-election in New South Wales.

C. THE FINDINGS

The Act was challenged by a number of commercial television stations which claimed, among other things, that it contravened an implied constitutional guarantee of freedom of communication with regard to political and electoral processes.[36] Six members of the Court agreed, finding either some or all of the Act invalid. Chief Justice Mason, and Justices Deane, Toohey, and Gaudron held the Act wholly invalid because it contravened an implied constitutional guarantee of freedom of communication on matters relevant to political discussion found in Australia's system of "representative democracy." Justice McHugh held the Act invalid because it interfered with the right of an elector to be informed on the merits or otherwise of polices and issues at a federal election

---

[33] Senate Report at 34.

[34] Id at 34.

[35] Dissenting Report—Senator Cheryl Kernot, in Senate Report at 87.

[36] Other grounds for the challenge were that the Act prevented trade between the states in contravention of § 92 of the Constitution, and that the Act was a compulsory acquisition of property without just term within the meaning of § 51(xxxi). The Act was also challenged by the State of New South Wales on the basis that it impeded the State's capacity to function by interfering with its legislative and executive powers. New South Wales argued that §§ 95D (3) and (4) were invalid as they impeded the capacity of the State to function as a State.

and because its "immediate object was to control the States and their people in the exercise of their constitutional functions."[37] Justice Brennan held the Act valid for federal elections but not for State elections because it breached an "implication which protects the functioning of the States from the burden of control by Commonwealth law."[38] Only Justice Dawson was of the opinion that the Act was wholly valid.

III. REPRESENTATIVE DEMOCRACY AND THE IMPLIED
CONSTITUTIONAL GUARANTEE OF FREEDOM
OF POLITICAL COMMUNICATION

In coming to the conclusion that the Act was wholly or partly invalid, the justices of the Australian High Court had no First Amendment with which to work. But they did have the example of U.S. First Amendment jurisprudence. Taking note of the U.S. approach to free speech,[39] the majority of the Justices found within the Australian Constitution an implication of a guaranteed right to freedom of communication on matters relevant to representative democracy. We summarize their arguments to provide the necessary foundation for the analysis that follows, and also because the Justices provide a more general discussion of the relationship between democracy and free speech.

Chief Justice Mason, along with Justices Brennan,[40] Gaudron,[41] and McHugh,[42] based the implication of a guarantee of freedom of political expression on Sections 7 and 24 of the Australian Constitution which explicitly provide that members of both the House of Representatives (Section 24) and the Senate (Section 7) shall be "directly chosen by the people. . . ." Mason argued that these two

---

[37] McHugh J at 241. However, he found the law valid in application to the Australian Territories (McHugh J at 246).

[38] Brennan J at 164.

[39] The Justices also took note of judicial approaches to freedom of communication in other countries, particularly Canada and Great Britain, although considerably less frequently. It is important to note, too, that "paid political advertising is not permitted during election times in the United Kingdom. . . . " Brennan J at 154.

[40] Brennan J in *Nationwide News Pty. Ltd. v Wills* (1992) 177 C.L.R. 1 at 46–47, quoting Stephen J in *Attorney-General (Cth)(Ex rel McKinlay) v Commonwealth* (1975) 135 C.L.R. at 55–56.

[41] Gaudron J at 210.

[42] McHugh J at 227.

provisions form the basis for the principles of representative democracy.[43] Justices Deane and Toohey took a slightly different tack, but likewise concluded that representative democracy was the foundation for the implication of a constitutional right to political discourse.[44] Thus, all of the Justices of the High Court acknowledged that there existed, implicit in the Constitution and based on the text, a right of the people to choose their representatives.[45]

Having established a constitutional basis for the right of the people to choose their representatives, the Justices turned to flesh out its implications. It was here that references to U.S. First Amendment jurisprudence appeared.

Chief Justice Mason led the way. Citing the work of Archibald Cox,[46] Mason argued that "in a representative democracy, public participation in political discussion is a central element of the political process."[47] Quoting his U.S. counterpart, Chief Justice Rehnquist, for the proposition that "freedom of the [sic] speech is indispensable to a free society and its government,"[48] and citing *New York Times v Sullivan*,[49] Mason argued that freedom of communication in relation "to public affairs and political discussion" was "indispensable" to representative government.[50] Mason stressed that the type of communication required for representative democracy was not just "one-way traffic," nor just communication between the elected and their electors, but also communication between all citizens:

---

[43] Mason CJ at 137, citing *Attorney-General (Cth)(Ex rel McKinlay) v Commonwealth* (1975) 135 C.L.R. at 55–56 per Stephen J. Mason, argued that "chosen by the people" signifies "government by the people through their representatives." Mason CJ at 137.

[44] Toohey and Deane in *Nationwide* at 70.

[45] Justice Dawson, too, held that the Constitution provides for the election of members of Parliament "directly chosen by the people" (Dawson J at 186–87), but declined to draw an implication of freedom of political communication from it.

[46] Mason CJ at 139 n 7, citing *The Court and the Constitution* (1987), p 212.

[47] Mason CJ at 139.

[48] *Smith v Daily Mail Publishing Co.*, 443 US 97, 106 (1979), cited in 177 C.L.R. 140, n 11.

[49] 376 US 254 (1964), cited in 177 C.L.R. 140, n 11.

[50] Mason CJ at 138; see also 140. Mason also cited *Monitor Patriot Co. v Roy*, 401 US 265, 272 (1971), and *Buckley v Valeo*, 424 US 1, 15 (1976), for the proposition that the constitutional guarantee to political communication is at its strongest in application to political campaigns. Mason CJ at 144, n 27.

> Absent such a freedom of communication, representative gov-
> ernment would fail to achieve its purpose, namely, government
> by the people through their elected representatives; govern-
> ment would cease to be responsive to the needs and wishes of
> the people and, in that sense, would cease to be truly
> representative.[51]

Likewise, the other Justices found that freedom of political communication "presupposes"[52] and was an "essential,"[53] "necessary,"[54] and "inherent"[55] element of representative government.
For example, Brennan concluded that:

> [t]o sustain a representative democracy embodying the princi-
> ples prescribed by the Constitution, freedom of public discus-
> sion of political and economic matters is essential: it would be
> a parody of democracy to confer on the people a power to
> choose their Parliament but deny the freedom of public discus-
> sion from which the people derive their political judgements.[56]

Deane and Toohey concluded that:

> The people of the Commonwealth would be unable responsi-
> bly to discharge and exercise the powers of governmental con-
> trol which the Constitution reserves to them if each person
> was an island, unable to communicate with any other person.[57]

Similarly, McHugh suggested that the representative government
envisaged by the Constitution requires more than the "right to
mark a ballot paper with a number, a cross or a tick. . . . "[58] For
McHugh, if the business of government is to accord with "representative government" it must be "examinable and the subject of
scrutiny, debate and ultimately accountability at the ballot box."[59]
Before an effective vote can be cast, McHugh held that the
electors:

---

[51] Mason CJ at 139.

[52] Deane and Toohey JJ in *Nationwide* at 72.

[53] Gaudron J at 210–11.

[54] McHugh J at 231.

[55] Brennan J in *Nationwide* at 48.

[56] Brennan J in *Nationwide News Pty. Ltd. v Wills* (1992) 177 C.L.R. 1 at 47, footnotes
omitted.

[57] Deane and Toohey JJ in *Nationwide* at 72.

[58] McHugh J at 226.

[59] McHugh J at 231.

must have access to the information, ideas and arguments which are necessary to make an informed judgment as to how they have been governed and as to what policies are in the interest of themselves, their communities and the nation.[60]

And McHugh concluded that the process included much of the interaction between the governed and the governing and extended to "all forms and methods of communication which are lawfully available for general use in the community."[61]

Justice Dawson recognized that the Constitution does provide for the election of members of Parliament "directly chosen by the people,"[62] but declined to draw an implication of "any guarantee of free communication which operates to confer rights upon individuals or to limit the legislative power of the Commonwealth."[63] He concluded that legislation that denied access to the information necessary to exercise a "true choice" would be contrary to the Constitution. Thus for Dawson the question was "not whether the legislation ought be regarded as desirable or undesirable in the interests of free speech or even of representative democracy." Rather the question was whether the legislation prohibited the electors from making an informed choice.[64] Interestingly, Dawson does not cite U.S. cases.

Apart from Dawson, the other members of the Court believed that this implication, based on representative government, extended to the protection of some form of political discourse. In other words, to give effect to representative government, the electors had a guaranteed freedom to communicate not only with their representatives but also among themselves.

In reaching this position, the Justices, like their Chief, cited U.S. First Amendment cases. For example, *First National Bank of Boston v Bellotti* was cited twice by Justice Gaudron,[65] *Buckley v Valeo* three times by Justice McHugh,[66] *New York Times v Sullivan* by Jus-

---

[60] McHugh J at 321.

[61] McHugh J at 232.

[62] Dawson J at 186–87.

[63] Dawson J at 184.

[64] Dawson J at 189.

[65] 177 C.L.R. 211, 212.

[66] 177 C.L.R. 231, 235, 239.

tice Brennan,[67] and *Mills v Alabama* by Justice McHugh.[68] And this is only a partial list. Other U.S. cases, First Amendment and otherwise, though less directly on point, were cited by the Justices.[69] Overall, the Justices of the High Court made 20 citations to 12 U.S. Supreme Court cases, more citations than to any non-Australian court.[70]

Part of the reason for the numerous citations to U.S. First Amendment jurisprudence may be that the plaintiffs repeatedly invoked them, citing U.S. cases 16 times in their pleadings.[71] These include more recent cases such as *First National Bank of Boston v Bellotti*[72] and *Buckley v Valeo*,[73] somewhat older cases including *Mills v Alabama*,[74] and historic, early twentieth-century cases, such as *Stromberg v California*,[75] *Whitney v California*,[76] and *Abrams v United States*.[77] In addition, some older U.S. cases were cited.[78] But part of the reason may be that the Justices were influenced by First Amendment jurisprudence. On the surface, one might have expected that if the High Court were to look overseas, the United Kingdom, which, like Australia, lacks constitutional guarantees to free speech, would be a more likely source. While we cannot be certain why First Amendment cases were so heavily cited,[79] the

---

[67] 177 C.L.R. 159.

[68] 177 C.L.R. 241.

[69] These include *Red Lion Broadcasting Co. v F.C.C.*, 395 US 367 (1969), cited by Toohey and Deane at 169, numerous citations of *Crandall v Nevada*, 73 US 35 (1867), and cases cited in the next section of the text.

[70] While U.S. cases have traditionally been cited by the High Court, especially in its formative period (see, e.g., the citation of *Marbury v Madison* (note 9 above)), the apparent adoption of First Amendment jurisprudence in *ACTV* is both new and striking given the absence of an explicit guarantee of free speech in the Australian Constitution.

[71] 177 C.L.R. 108–23.

[72] 435 US 765 (1978), cited at 177 C.L.R. 111, 114, 123.

[73] 424 US 1 (1976), cited at 177 C.L.R. 111.

[74] 384 US 214 (1966), cited at C.L.R. 111.

[75] 283 US 359 (1930), cited at C.L.R. 114.

[76] 274 US 357 (1927), cited at C.L.R. 114.

[77] 250 US 616 (1919), cited at C.L.R. 114.

[78] For example, *Crandall v Nevada*, 73 US 35 (1867), cited at C.L.R. 111, 112.

[79] It is possible, for example, that the Justices adopted their analysis and reasoning independently of First Amendment jurisprudence. On this reasoning, the heavy citation of U.S. cases was offered for support of a method of analysis and an outcome that were reached independently of U.S. case law.

number and pattern of citations, and the analysis the High Court Justices offered, are, at the very least, suggestive of influence.

IV. A U.S. Approach to Australian Constitutional Law

After finding an implicit right to freedom of communication in the Australian Constitution, the Justices turned to the issue of applying it to the Act. In so doing, they used the same approach as that taken to free speech by the U.S. Supreme Court. That is, several of the Justices drew the standard U.S. distinction between regulation of content and of format,[80] and applied a balancing test, weighing the interests of the government against the requirements of the constitutional guarantee of freedom of communication. Under this standard, only a compelling justification would suffice to uphold the regulation. But more importantly, in adopting this approach, they implicitly (explicitly in the case of McHugh) adopted a "free-market" notion of speech, assuming that any government regulation of speech was an interference with an unregulated market. And they used this abstract notion to invalidate the Act without making a careful evaluation of the empirical support for the "free market" and the Act's effect on political communication.

Chief Justice Mason drew a distinction between restrictions "on communication which target ideas or information and those which restrict an activity or mode of communication by which the ideas or information are transmitted."[81] Citing U.S. sources,[82] Mason argued that to restrict the content of communication requires "compelling justification"[83] and noted that it would be "extremely difficult to justify restrictions imposed on free communication which operate by reference to the character of the ideas or information."[84] This was particularly the case with regard to elections.

---

[80] See Geoffrey R. Stone, *Content Regulation and the First Amendment*, 25 Wm & Mary L Rev 189 (1983); *Content-Neutral Restrictions*, 54 U Chi L Rev 46 (1987).

[81] Mason CJ at 143.

[82] *Cox Broadcasting Corp. v Cohen*, 420 US 469, 491 et seq (1975), cited at 177 C.L.R. 143 n 24; *Konigsberg v State Bar of California*, 366 US 36, 50–51 (1961), cited at 177 C.L.R. 143 n 25; L. Tribe, *American Constitutional Law* (2d ed 1988) at 790–91, cited at 177 C.L.R. 143 n 25.

[83] Mason CJ at 143.

[84] Mason CJ at 143.

Again citing U.S. cases,[85] including *Buckley v Valeo*, Mason held that "the Court must scrutinize with scrupulous care restrictions affecting free communication in the conduct of elections for political office for it is in that area that the guarantee fulfills its primary purpose."[86] Because "[a]ll too often attempts to restrict the freedom in the name of some imagined necessity have tended to stifle public discussion and criticism of government,"[87] Mason held that in balancing the competing public interests in banning certain political speech, "paramount weight" must be given to protection of that speech.[88]

In examining the Act, Mason accepted the justification given by the Ministers that the ban was aimed at safeguarding the integrity of the political process by restricting the reliance by individuals and parties upon substantial amounts of money to finance expensive campaigns. Further, he accepted the claim that the effect of the Act would be to terminate the relative advantages that wealthy persons or groups enjoyed in access to expensive airwaves, and that modern advertising methods were "trivializing" political debate.[89] However, these were not sufficiently compelling justifications to overcome the fact that the Act "severely impairs the freedoms previously enjoyed by citizens to discuss public and political affairs and to criticize federal institutions."[90] In particular, Mason held that the Act "discriminate[s] against potential participants" in the electoral process.[91] This was because the restrictions not only affect actual candidates but also interest groups or individuals who wish to put their views to the wider community: "Employers' organizations, trade unions, manufacturers' and farmers' organizations, social welfare groups and societies generally are excluded from participation. . . . "[92] These infringements on communication could not, according to Mason, be saved by the "free-time" provisions of

---

[85] *Monitor Patriot Co. v Roy*, 401 US 265, 272; *Buckley v Valeo*, 424 US 1, 15 (1976), cited at 177 C.L.R. 144 n 27.

[86] Mason CJ at 144.

[87] Mason CJ at 145.

[88] Mason CJ at 143. The Chief Justice was more open to format restrictions. Mason CJ at 143–44.

[89] Mason CJ at 144.

[90] Mason CJ at 129.

[91] Mason CJ at 145.

[92] Mason CJ at 132.

the Act because they were heavily weighted in favor of incumbent individuals or parties.[93] The Act, Mason argued, "manifestly favour[s] the status quo."[94]

In addition, Mason was concerned that the allocation of the 10% of the free time not given to incumbent parties would be corrupted. "[A]ccess on the part of those excluded is not preserved," Mason wrote, "except possibly at the invitation of the powerful interests which control and conduct the electronic media."[95] Thus, Mason concluded, the "replacement regime . . . discriminates against new and independent candidates . . . and denies them meaningful access on a non-discriminatory basis. . . ."[96]

Even with regard to the other communication outlets that remained unrestricted to political participants, Mason was unconvinced that they balanced the relative advantage offered to incumbents. Other modes of communication untouched by the Act, Mason noted, "do not have the same striking impact in the short span of an election campaign" as does television.[97] For Mason, the stark contrast between the power of electronic outlets and other forms of communication "underscore[s] the magnitude of the deprivation inflicted on those who are excluded from access to the electronic media."[98]

Four of the other Justices echoed Mason's approach and concerns. Justices Deane and Toohey, as well as Gaudron, who like Mason held the Act to be entirely invalid, focused on the favoritism toward incumbents and the discriminatory effects on everyone else.[99] Justice McHugh made an even broader argument, citing a good deal of U.S. First Amendment case law. Citing *Buckley v Valeo* three times, McHugh argued that the First Amendment provided a "more valid analogy" to the Australian situation than did the case law and experience of other democracies.[100] This was prin-

---

[93] Under the Act, 90% of the free time automatically went to political parties with members sitting in the Parliament. See provisions at page 444.

[94] Mason CJ at 132.

[95] Mason CJ at 146.

[96] Mason CJ at 146.

[97] Mason CJ at 146.

[98] Mason CJ at 146.

[99] Deane and Toohey JJ at 171–72; Gaudron J at 220–21.

[100] McHugh J at 240–41. McHugh never explains why this should be the case.

cipally because McHugh understood the "marketplace of ideas" to be totally unregulated. Further, he understood politics and political campaigns to be entirely private affairs.[101]

Justices Brennan and Dawson voted to uphold the Act, partially and *in toto*, respectively.[102] Interestingly, both explicitly rejected the U.S. analogy, and the First Amendment jurisprudence that followed from it. Dawson, for example, argued that "the Australian Constitution, with few exceptions and in contrast with its American model, does not seek to establish personal liberty by constitutional restrictions upon the exercise of governmental power."[103] Thus, there was "no warrant for the implication of any guarantee of freedom of communication which operates upon individuals or to limit the legislative power of the Commonwealth."[104] While the Constitution did require that electors have access to the "information necessary for the exercise of a true choice,"[105] Dawson was unable to conclude that the Act was "incompatible" with that constitutional requirement.[106]

Justice Brennan also rejected U.S. jurisprudence. Although finding a constitutional implication of "freedom of discussion of political and economic matters which is essential to sustain the system of representative government prescribed by the Constitution,"[107] Brennan distinguished it from the First Amendment: "[U]nlike freedoms conferred by a Bill of Rights in the American model, the freedom cannot be understood as a personal right the scope of which must be ascertained in order to discover what is left for legislative regulation. . . . "[108] Citing the experience of other democracies[109] and a decision of the European Commission of Hu-

---

[101] McHugh J at 236.

[102] Brennan J at 164 found the law invalid as applied to State elections.

[103] Dawson J at 182.

[104] Dawson J at 184. Dawson's position was that the protection of free speech belonged to the people: "The right to freedom of speech exists here because there is nothing to prevent its exercise and because governments recognize that if they attempt to limit it, save in accepted areas such as defamation or sedition, they must do so at their peril." Dawson J at 182–83.

[105] Dawson J at 187.

[106] Dawson J at 189.

[107] Brennan J at 149, citing his opinion in *Nationwide News Ltd. v Wills*.

[108] Brennan J at 150.

[109] Brennan J at 154 notes that "paid political advertising is not permitted during election times in the United Kingdom, Ireland, France, Norway, Sweden, Denmark, Austria, the Netherlands, Israel or Japan."

man Rights,[110] Brennan pointed out that the restrictions imposed by the Act were "not a novel experiment unique to Australia."[111] Rejecting U.S. approaches, Brennan argued that it would be "both simplistic and erroneous to regard any limitation on political advertising as offensive to the Constitution."[112] Freedom of political communication was essential to the maintenance of representative democracy, but it was not "so transcendent a value as to override all interests which the law would otherwise protect."[113]

A. DELIBERATIVE DEMOCRACY

All seven members of the High Court acknowledged that the Australian Constitution was based on representative democracy, and all but one[114] held that representative democracy implied constitutional protection for freedom of political communication. In developing this implication, the majority of the Justices emphasized that it included many aspects of what may be described as "deliberative democracy."[115]

Deliberative democracy presupposes that democracy entails more than just the aggregation of private preferences. Democracy is about more than just casting ballots. It entails the exchange of ideas and political discussion and debate among citizens. In the Westminster system of responsible government, under which the Prime Minister and Cabinet are directly responsible to the Parliament, deliberative democracy requires that voters are informed of, and have wide opportunity to debate, the candidates' and parties' policy proposals. As Chief Justice Mason emphasized, representative government or representative democracy is not limited to "one-way" communications between the elected representatives and their electors, but requires a broad dialogue.[116] It includes the right of citizens to communicate among themselves and with their representatives. The guarantee to such communication is based on

---

[110] Brennan J at 154.

[111] Brennan J at 154.

[112] Brennan J at 159.

[113] Brennan J at 159.

[114] Dawson J.

[115] The phrase is used by Cass Sunstein in *Beyond the Republican Revival*, 97 Yale L J (1988) 1539 at 1548, and *Democracy and the Problem of Free Speech* (1993), chap 3.

[116] Mason CJ at 139.

the right of citizens to criticize or support government decisions, mobilize public opinion against or for governmental decisions, and call for action on the part of government.[117] Legislation that limits such rights, or hinders the ability of citizens to hear, discuss, and debate a wide spectrum of ideas, violates the High Court's understanding of representative government, what we call deliberative democracy. Indeed, much of the concern held by the Justices about the Act was that it would stifle the input into the deliberative process of those interest groups or candidates that were not represented in the Parliament.[118] As Mason puts it, "in a representative government, public participation in political discussion is a central element of the political process."[119]

In the abstract, the case for deliberative democracy is powerful.[120] The questions we address, however, are whether the High Court persuasively applied this understanding to the Act, and whether its analysis of the relationship between political communication and democracy is one that should be followed by other constitutional courts. For two distinct reasons, we argue no. First, on a theoretical level, we argue that the High Court mistook the current situation for a "free market" in speech and mistakenly saw the Act as a regulation that interfered with this unregulated market. Second, on an empirical level, we argue that the High Court failed to analyze the actual effect of the Act. If it had done so, it would have seen that the effect of the Act would have been to

---

[117] Mason CJ at 138–39.

[118] For discussion of this point, see text at pages 453–54. Likewise, Sunstein notes that one of the key requirements of a deliberative democracy is that it bring "alternative perspectives and additional information" to public debate. *Beyond the Republican Revival*, 97 Yale L J 1539, 1549 (1988).

[119] Mason CJ at 139. This view of democracy has a U.S. pedigree as well. Meiklejohn, for example, offers a "town meeting" theory of free speech and democracy which stresses the importance of an informed citizenry. Democracy requires, Meiklejohn suggests, that "all facts and interests relevant to the problem shall be fully and fairly presented [so] that all the alternative lines of action can be wisely measured in relation to one another." The importance to democracy of a full range of ideas being expressed is also highlighted by Meiklejohn: "What is essential is not that everyone shall speak, but that everything worth saying shall be said. To this end . . . it may be arranged that each of the known conflicting points of view shall have, and shall be limited to, an assigned share of the time available." A. Meiklejohn, *Free Speech and Its Relation to Self Government* (Harper & Brothers, 1948) at 22, 25–26; reprinted in A. Meiklejohn, *Political Freedom* (Harper & Brothers, 1960) at 24–28.

[120] We do not address the question of whether the High Court was justified in finding an implied right of political communication in the Constitution. For discussion of this point, see the sources listed in note 7.

further the breadth and depth of political communication that the High Court believed is essential to deliberative democracy. Overall, we suggest that the High Court may have made these mistakes because it was too uncritically enamored of U.S. First Amendment jurisprudence.

B. FREE SPEECH AND "FREE MARKETS"

Informing the Court's view of the Act is the U.S.-derived First Amendment notion of the "marketplace of ideas."[121] The central idea underlying this view is that at present political communication is unregulated. That is, individuals and groups wishing to communicate their ideas have unregulated access to the "marketplace of ideas." Ideas that are persuasive win support and those that fail to persuade languish. It follows that government action to regulate access to political communication "interferes" with this open market. Government regulation decides, arbitrarily or in a discriminatory fashion, which ideas will be heard and which ideas will be barred, favoring some interests and groups and harming others.

The Justices of the High Court viewed the Act in this light. As we have shown, repeatedly they stressed that the Act imposed a regulatory scheme that prevented some views from being put to the public.[122] In particular, the majority of the Justices noted that some "third parties" and all interest groups would be excluded from the political process because they could not put their views to the community by electronic means. Thus, the Justices conceived of the Act as the imposition of regulation into an arena that is essentially free from regulation.

There is, however, an alternative conception of the way in which access to political communication is organized. It is based on the view that political communication is already highly regulated in ways that limit the exchange of ideas. Media outlets, be they television or radio stations, or newspapers, are the creations of government regulation. Their very existence, their corporate structures, and the numerous legal benefits they enjoy, are all the result of government action. There is nothing "free" or unregulated about

---

[121] The phrase the "marketplace of ideas" is not used in the decision, though the argument was put to the High Court by counsel acting for the State of New South Wales (at 114) when they cited *Abrams v United States*, 250 US 616 (1919).

[122] See discussion in text at pages 453–54.

them, and the exchange of views they present is narrow. For instance, the first plaintiffs in this case were holders of exclusive broadcasting licenses under the Broadcasting Act. Their "private" right to broadcast (both commercial and political speech), to decide what views to present and what views to ignore, and to charge others for the right to use "their" airwaves are the outcome of governmental legislation, a quintessentially "public" decision.[123] And, of course, much political communication is regulated by law, ranging from libel and defamation to treason. On this understanding, the question of the constitutionality of the Act is not a conflict between an unregulated market that presents a broad range of ideas and government interference with that market. Rather, it is a question of which regulations, the current ones or those contained in the Act, best further the constitutional goal of deliberative democracy.

The intellectual understandings of the New Deal period usefully illustrate these points about the regulation of political speech. In the era of substantive due process, prior to the New Deal, existing distributions of economic resources were seen as "pre-political" or "natural." There was a "free market" and the Supreme Court held that the Constitution prohibited governmental "interference" with it. The New Dealers rejected this understanding. They saw competing regulatory regimes in which there was nothing neutral, natural, or pre-political about existing distributions. They argued not about government interference with markets, but rather about which set of regulations, the pre–New Deal ones or their New Deal proposals, best furthered constitutional goals.[124]

In the area of political communication, a similar argument can be made. The simplistic binary choices between "free speech" and "regulation" misrepresent reality. "Free speech" is itself a regulatory alternative that supports or endorses a restricted range of ideas. Our point is that it is but one regulatory scheme among many.

---

[123] A particularly poignant example of the content-restrictive effect of this form of regulation occurred in the United States the week before Thanksgiving, 1997. An attempt was made by a group to purchase time for television advertisements on the three major U.S. networks urging Americans not to shop on the Friday following Thanksgiving, traditionally the busiest shopping day of the year. The advertisements did not appear because all three of the networks refused to sell the time.

[124] For further elaboration of this argument, see C. Sunstein, *Democracy and the Problem of Free Speech* (1993).

Another way of stating this position is to recall that for six of the seven Justices deliberative democracy requires that citizens have the opportunity to hear, discuss, and debate a wide spectrum of ideas. Clearly, government action can threaten deliberative democracy by regulating speech in an effort to affect the outcome of public deliberation, but so can the legally sanctioned operation of the "free market" by effectively restricting the range of ideas that is broadcast. Government legislation is by no means the only threat to the practice of deliberative democracy. By too closely following First Amendment jurisprudence, the High Court lost sight of the restrictive effect of current regulations on deliberative democracy.

Returning to *ACTV*, the "regulation" of political speech does not necessarily mean the imposition of a new regime which is fundamentally at odds with political free speech.[125] Yet, those Justices who struck down the regulatory scheme adopted a near absolutist position. That is, they viewed the introduction of new regulation in this area as nearly always being an abridgment of the guarantee of political free speech. This is because they misconstrued existing practice as an unregulated "market." For example, the underlying difficulty with the Act for Mason was that he saw it as an attempt to regulate what is essentially an unregulated market of freedom of communication. Mason argued that the current system was essentially "fair" and preferable to the discriminatory effects of government regulation: "[The replacement regime] plainly fails to *preserve or enhance fair access* . . . [and] does not introduce a 'level playing field.' It is discriminatory. . . ."[126] Only by viewing the current system as "fair" can Mason claim that the Act "fails to *preserve or enhance fair access.* . . ." McHugh went further:

> It is for the electors and the candidates to choose which forms of otherwise lawful communication they prefer to use to disseminate political information, ideas and argument. Their

---

[125] Interestingly, six of the Justices of the High Court acknowledged in the abstract that the right to political free speech in Australia is not absolute (Mason CJ at 142, Brennan J at 150, Deane and Toohey JJ at 169, Gaudron J at 217, McHugh J at 234). And, indeed, in subsequent cases like *McGinty* and *Langer* (cited and summarized in note 6), the High Court did limit the right. But there is nothing in the decision that suggests the Court would uphold legislation regulating access to the media, and the thrust of the free-market conception that permeates the opinions argues against such a reading.

[126] Mason CJ at 146; emphasis added.

> choices are a matter of private, not public, interest. Their
> choices are outside the zone of governmental control.[127]

Similarly, only by viewing televised campaign advertisements as
part of an unregulated market can they be seen as "private," and
not "public," and "outside the zone of governmental control."
McHugh, having adopted the view of political communication as
an unregulated or "laissez-faire" market, saw government regulation as an interference with that market. Although the other members of the High Court were not as explicit as McHugh, their reasoning was similar.

Our second point is that a free-market conception of political
communication leads away, not toward, furthering deliberative democracy. This is because it overlooks the reality of unequal resources and the limitations this places on who can afford to "rent
the microphone" and have their views heard. While we will develop this point in detail in the empirical sections that follow, we
note here that the departure from the constitutional goal is striking. For example, Justices Deane and Toohey argued:

> Nor, in our view, is it to the point to say that the cost of time,
> at least on television, is so high that private individuals would
> not seek to communicate by political advertisement on that
> medium in any event. . . . [I]ndividuals may legitimately come
> together, in employee, industry or other special interest
> groups, to procure political communication by way of adver-
> tisement on television and radio. In any event, the fact that
> the number of groups or individuals who wish to express their
> political views in a particular way is limited does not justify a
> law suppressing the freedom of communication in that particu-
> lar way.[128]

Lost in this analysis is the question of what is the most effective
way of ensuring the constitutional goal, a robust deliberative democracy. Contra Deane and Toohey, "the fact that the number
of groups or individuals who wish to express their political views
in a particular way is limited" raises the precise question of the
constitutional guarantee in a serious way. For if the only voices
that are heard are those who can afford to "rent" the microphone,
how is deliberative democracy protected? If the High Court Jus-

---

[127] McHugh J at 236.

[128] Deane and Toohey JJ at 175.

A----B-------------------C----D-------------------Y----Z

FIG. 1. The distribution of political opinion

tices were concerned with limited access to the electronic media, then the limitations created by the current regulatory system should be of great concern. The "free-market" blinders that the High Court seems to have borrowed from U.S. First Amendment jurisprudence obscured these fundamental points.

It may be helpful to consider our argument schematically. Assume a certain range of opinion on any given subject, designated A–Z in Figure 1. If media presentation of all opinion is prohibited, as would be the case in a total communication ban, clearly there can be no deliberative democracy. That is, voters will not have the opportunity to hear competing views discussed, learn about policy positions, and debate their merits. Lacking such discussion, there can be no informed deliberation and no deliberative democracy.

Instead of a complete prohibition, let's say only views C–D are allowed. Given the paucity of the range of opinion covered, the electorate would be little better off. The same would be true if the only allowed media presentation was of opinion in the range A–B or Y–Z. Indeed, one might worry that allowing only a little information might be worse than prohibiting it all. With all presentation prohibited, it would at least be clear to the voters that informed deliberations were impossible, while with a small amount of information presented voters might be misled into thinking that serious deliberation was in fact occurring.

If the government legislated to allow media presentation of opinion only in the C–D range (or A–B or Y–Z), deliberative democracy would not be possible. Clearly, the High Court would be on strong ground in striking down such legislation as an infringement of the implied right of free speech that derives from the constitutional guarantee of representative government.

In the abstract, these points are uncontroversial. What the High Court failed to analyze in *ACTV*, however, is how similar the real-world situation is to the limited discussion depicted above. That is, in operation, the current system of media presentation of opinion presents only a small part of the range of opinion.[129] This occurs

---

[129] It is possible that the Justices were skeptical that the legislation would enlarge the range of opinion presented on the electronic media. As a logical matter, there is no guarantee that those who received access to the media under the Act wouldn't simply present ideas similar

for one basic reason: access to the media is determined by wealth, and those entities with enough wealth to purchase media access are not evenly spread across the opinion spectrum. In the commercial area, there is little trouble with this. If a company wishes to spend millions of dollars promoting its brand of toothpaste or laundry detergent, representative government is not threatened. Citizens may have cleaner or dirtier teeth and clothes, but the quality of deliberative democratic discussion is not directly affected.

In the political realm, however, if only the wealthy can afford access to the media in a continuous way, two things happen: first, their opinions receive a prominence in the eyes of voters that is difficult, if not impossible, to match; and second, the range of opinions is greatly curtailed. The result is the narrowing of democratic deliberation to only the ideas that the wealthy wish to discuss. While we develop these points in detail in the empirical sections below, we emphasize here the way in which adoption of the free-market conception led the High Court to lose sight of the constitutional goal.

There is another set of problems with a free-market conception of political speech that involves market failure. On an abstract level, one could imagine a market in political communication that might promote deliberative democracy. Each voter might be given a voucher that allowed her some minuscule amount of free air time. Voters could then pool their vouchers to gain enough air time to present their views. On a theoretical level, while clearly extending the range of opinion, such a system might still fail to present a wide range of opinion. This is because not starting from the Rawlsian original position, voters' opinions would not be fully informed. That is, they would likely reproduce the skewed distribution that is seen today. Second, contra Justice McHugh, if a full range of political information is a public good, it is likely that it would be undersupplied. With each voucher worth an infinitesimal amount of time, voters might see little to be gained by acting,

---

to those ideas currently being presented. Although we consider this highly unlikely, our empirical investigation (see text at pages 475–91) will show that even if this were the case, deliberative democracy would be no worse off than under the current regulations. Further, we will show that there is good reason to believe that the range of opinion presented would be extended under the Act. Rather than stressing a logical possibility, however remote, we concentrate on the demonstrated *potential* of the Act and its *likely* consequences.

waiting for others to act.[130] The point that this example illustrates, however, is how far the current system is from presenting a wide range of opinion to the voters.

It is important to reiterate at this point that the Australian Constitution contains no explicit free speech guarantee and that judicial deference to Parliament has been the tradition in Australia. This does not mean that speech has not been protected in Australia. On the contrary, Australia has done an arguably better job in protecting the speech rights of political dissidents than has the United States. Thus, the deep suspicion of government action that pervades First Amendment jurisprudence in the United States has no counterpart in Australian jurisprudence and tradition. Its adoption in *ACTV* suggests that an American-inspired view of the relationship between democracy, free speech, and governmental action has exerted influence over the Justices of the Australian High Court, and changed the way in which they view that relationship.

In sum, the U.S.-inspired free-market view of political deliberation obscures the relationship between current practice and the constitutional concern with deliberative democracy. Rather than focusing on which regulations best further the constitutional guarantee of representative democracy, the Justices of the Australian High Court were diverted by the abstract notion of a free market of political speech. That abstract notion also led the Justices away from a careful examination of the political process the Act affected. We turn now to that.

V. The Debilitating Effects of Televised Campaign Advertising on Deliberative Democracy—Empirical Investigation

The discussion so far has been mostly theoretical. Now, we turn to the empirical reality of television campaign advertising. In the first part of this section we examine what scholars in both the United States and Australia have learned. We argue that the literature provides strong evidence that campaign advertising as practiced makes little positive contribution to deliberative democracy

---

[130] Also, under such a system, one might expect a market to develop for the sale of the vouchers, raising the same wealth problems as before. However, a tax credit rather than a voucher might alleviate the problem.

and may, in fact, be harmful.[131] In the second part, we present data on campaign advertising in Australia that shows that the High Court's concerns about stifling third parties, while compelling in principle, are in practice misplaced. Current practice stifles third parties, and the legislation would have been a step toward correcting the problem.

A. THE NONDELIBERATIVE NATURE OF CAMPAIGN ADVERTISING

1. *The United States.* Since the advent of televised campaign advertising in the 1952 U.S. presidential election, scholars have worked to understand its effects. Because much of the work focuses on the United States, we start our examination there.[132] However, there is a growing consensus in both the United States and Australia of the pervasive nature, if not the persuasive power, of television campaign advertising. In both countries, critics argue that television campaign advertising distorts the issues, lacks substance, and harms the democratic political process.

Concerns about the corrosive effect of television campaign advertising surfaced with its first use. In the 1952 U.S. presidential election, Republican candidate Dwight Eisenhower employed Rosser Reeves to produce television ads. Those ads, Reeves was told by journalist Harlan Cleveland, later Dean of the Maxwell School of Citizenship and Public Affairs at Syracuse University, were objectionable because "their real role 'was selling the President like toothpaste.' "[133] Since then, both television campaign advertising and its critiques have grown in sophistication and voice.

---

[131] We do not mean to imply that pre-television campaign advertising was always ideally supportive of deliberative democracy. Slogans like "Tippicanoe and Tyler too," and "I like Ike," contain little of the kind of information necessary for deliberative democracy. And the Republican campaign slogan in the 1884 presidential campaign against Grover Cleveland, alleging that he fathered an illegitimate child, was hardly a model of positive campaigning: "Ma, ma, where's your pa? Gone to the White House, ha, ha, ha!" The point of the discussion that follows is that campaign advertising on television as practiced today is much more pervasive and harmful to deliberative democracy than other forms of campaigning.

[132] There is a growing literature on televised campaign advertising. In addition to the sources cited in the text, see K. Jamieson, *Packaging the Presidency: A History and Criticism of Presidential Campaign Advertising* (2d ed 1992); K. Jamieson, *Dirty Politics: Deception, Distraction, and Democracy* (1992); M. Kern, *30-Second Politics: Political Advertising in the Eighties* (1989); *New Perspectives on Political Advertising* (L. Kaid, D. Nimmo, and K. Sanders, eds, 1986); D. West, *Air Wars: Television Advertising in Election Campaigns, 1952–1992* (1993).

[133] Quoted in Martin Mayer, *Madison Avenue U.S.A.: The Inside Story of American Advertising* (Bodley Head, 1958) at 287.

There are a number of criticisms that have been raised about television campaign advertising. Some, like the cost of television campaign advertising and the rise to power of the apolitical media consultant, are well documented. There is also evidence that television campaign advertising has led to corruption, a weakening of political parties, the reduction of political participation by citizens, and the debasement of citizen deliberation.[134] The discussion that follows focuses on the effects of television campaign advertising on deliberative democracy.

It is possible to generalize about television campaign advertising. Generally, television campaign advertisements are 30 seconds or less in length. They are crafted around images rather than words. Professional actors and readers do most of the talking, with the candidate's voice and image appearing infrequently, if at all. Issues are discussed in only the vaguest of terms, and specific policy proposals are seldom presented. And the majority of Americans report that they receive the bulk of their information about issues in political campaigns from television campaign advertising.[135]

This format has particular uses and effects. Given the "preference for highly stylized images over the use of verbal messages and facts" in television campaign advertising,[136] Moran underscores the power of images as a mode of communication. Reviewing the U.S. literature in 1992, he found that campaign advertisers "can easily exploit the visual aspect of televised advertising"[137] to

> . . . intensify the effectiveness of what would be barely plausible assertions if made verbally . . . create false and misleading impressions . . . that would probably be too apparent if made verbally . . . [and enable] campaigners to make subtle appeals to the unconscious prejudices or predispositions of a voter.[138]

Impressionistic images also allow for so-called "referential techniques in which either the candidate is associated with something

---

[134] See sources cited in note 132.

[135] Stephen Ansolabehere, Roy Behr, and Shanto Iyengar, *The Media Game: American Politics in the Television Age* (Macmillan, 1993) at 43. Media executives are well aware of this. See, for example, R. Murdoch, News Corporation: Agent of Choice & Change, Address to the National Press Club, Washington, DC (Feb 26, 1996) at 5.

[136] Timothy J. Moran, *Format Restrictions on Televised Political Advertising: Elevating Political Debate Without Suppressing Free Speech*, 67 Ind L J 663, 668 (1992).

[137] Id at 669.

[138] Id at 669, 670.

universally acknowledged to be good or the opponent is linked to something generally acknowledged to be evil."[139]

The 30-second length of the typical television campaign advertisement also has important effects. It is not possible to explain complex issues or make a persuasive case for policy proposals in 30 seconds. At best, slogans can be presented. This reenforces the image content of television campaign advertisements.

The result is that television campaign advertising does not add to deliberative democracy. It appeals to emotion rather than reason and manipulates rather than educates. As Moran puts it, the "commercial techniques that dominate political advertising also make advertising singularly ineffective at promoting meaningful discussion of prospective policy choices."[140] Further, television campaign advertising allows those with money to bring attention to issues with which they are concerned. By bringing attention to issues, they can influence what the media and the voters discuss. Summarizing the findings of the literature on this point, Moran concludes that television campaign advertising "substantially affects the content and the focus of election campaigns."[141]

These general conclusions are well illustrated by any number of studies. For example, Boiney and Paletz examined 196 television campaign ads from the 1984 general elections for three races (Reagan vs. Mondale, U.S. presidency; Helms vs. Hunt, U.S. Senate, North Carolina; Morrison vs. DeNardis, U.S. Congress, Connecticut). They found that "the 'image' content" of the ads was "wide and deep." Overall, 71% of the ads were image-based, with the total reaching 89% in the presidential race. The chance of a viewer hearing a candidate take a specific issue stance was "practically zero."[142]

Similar results were reported by Joslyn, who examined 156 spot ads over several election cycles for presidential, gubernatorial, senatorial, and congressional campaigns. He found that "[w]hat the ads definitely do *not* contain are partisan and specific issue ap-

---

[139] Id at 667.

[140] Id.

[141] Id 664.

[142] John Boiney and David L. Paletz, *In Search of the Model Model: Political Science versus Political Advertising Perspectives on Voter Decision Making*, in Frank Biocca, ed, *Television and Political Advertising* 1 (Lawrence Erlbaum, 1991) at 17, 18. Boiney and Paletz found that only 8% of issue stances were "specific."

peals."[143] For the voter trying to discover a candidate's position on issues, television campaign advertising provides little help. Joslyn found that "only one ad in five contains information specific enough about the policy preferences of candidates that a viewer could use it to predict the candidate's future policy behavior."[144] Distressingly, Joslyn also found that change was for the worse, noting that ads have become "less filled with specific issue information" over time.[145]

The 1996 U.S. Republican presidential primary election campaign illustrates these findings. Steve Forbes, the multi-millionaire publisher of *Forbes* business magazine, despite never having held elected office, used his personal fortune to enter the race. Traveling around the country in an airplane he named "Capitalist Tool," Forbes saturated the airwaves with campaign ads. In the Iowa Caucuses, the first major event of the campaign season, Forbes reportedly spent $4 million on campaign ads, propelling him from an unknown business person to a potential presidential nominee. As one Iowa elected official put it, "Forbes gets you up; he drives you to work, [h]e's on the radio all day at work; he drives you home and he puts you to bed."[146] In the key New Hampshire primary, the typical voter saw Forbes's ads 34 times a week, more than twice as often as ads for Robert Dole and approximately three and a half times as often as ads for leading beer and soft-drink products.[147]

Forbes did not win the nomination (although he did win primaries in Delaware and Arizona). However, he was able to garner a great deal of attention for himself and his issues, attention that was diverted from the other candidates and the eventual nominee, Senator Dole. Writing in the heat of the campaign, a *New York Times* reporter put it this way: "Mr. Forbes continues to set both the tone and the agenda of the campaign with his advertising."[148] And a study by the Center for Media and Public Affairs of 573

---

[143] Richard Joslyn, *Mass Media and Elections* (Addison-Wesley, 1984) at 43; emphasis in original.

[144] Id at 43.

[145] Id at 45.

[146] Quoted in Nancy Gibbs, *Is Forbes for Real?* Time (Feb 12, 1996), p 28.

[147] Id.

[148] Elizabeth Kolbert, *In Campaign Ads, Forbes Is Taking on All Comers*, New York Times (Feb 3, 1996), p 1.

election stories broadcast on the ABC, CBS, and NBC evening news for the first few months of 1996 found that from January 1 through March 4 (Junior Tuesday), when Dole virtually clinched the nomination, reporters' comments were 79% positive on Forbes's chances to win the nomination compared to only 62% positive for Dole.[149]

The non-issue, image-oriented television campaign advertising discussed above is the work of campaign media consultants. Their approach is well captured by Robert Goodman, a leading practitioner. Trumpeting the power of the media, Goodman celebrates its negative effects on political parties and on accountability. Thanks to media, Goodman believes,

> [a]nybody can run for office if they can get enough [financial] backing to get on the tube. They don't have to pay party dues any more; they don't have to come up through the ranks; they don't have to kiss the butts of party bosses or newspaper publishers. They can do their own thing.[150]

For Goodman, "doing their own thing" seems to mean fighting campaigns on often irrelevant and misleading images. "It's more newsworthy," Goodman believes, "when one candidate calls the other a son of a bitch than when he puts out his whitepaper on education."[151] The result of this attitude is campaigns based on "character" rather than on policy choices that give democracy more than superficial meaning. Rather than campaigns being times for reflection and debate about policy, in the hands of media consultants they are opportunities for creative image-making. In colorful language, Goodman puts the point this way: "The fun is be-

---

[149] The study was carried out on behalf of the Markle Presidential Election Watch, a project of the nonpartisan John and Mary Markle Foundation. It can be found on the World Wide Web at http://www.markle.org/markwatc1.html. A critical response to our argument about the Forbes candidacy might argue that he contributed to deliberative democracy by running an issue-oriented campaign, albeit on a single issue, the flat tax. The problem, however, is that Forbes was able to distort the agenda not on the strength of his ideas about the flat tax but on the size of his pocketbook. How can a debate be had when access to the media is dependent on private financial resources that are not equally distributed? Steve Forbes did not enter the deliberative democratic debate; rather, he shouted over the top of it!

[150] Quoted in Edwin Diamond and Stephen Bates, *The Spot: The Rise of Political Advertising on Television* (MIT Press, 1984) at 373.

[151] Quoted in id at 343.

ing out in the field like a bunch of Green Berets, six months before the election, in some wild state that you've never seen before."[152]

The picture painted by the literature discussed above may be too broad. In a set of controlled experiments, Ansolabehere and Iyengar tested the effects of televised negative campaign advertisements on respondents' level of information about candidates' policies, on their vote choice, and on their likelihood of participating in the democratic process.[153] In contrast to the existing literature, Ansolabehere and Iyengar find that "[w]hen advertisements reveal candidates' positions on the issues, voters will become significantly more informed about these positions."[154] However, they also find that "exposure to negative advertising, in and of itself, produces a substantial decrease in voter turnout. . . . [and] that exposure to negative advertising increases voters' cynicism about the electoral process and their ability to exert meaningful political influence."[155] They suggest that "the current marketplace of ideas in which candidates slug it out to woo the support of an increasingly small electorate is gradually eroding the participatory ethos of the American public. . . . "[156]

The Ansolabehere and Iyengar study provides mixed support for the contribution to democracy of paid political advertising on television. Assuming their experiments accurately reflect actual experience,[157] the contribution to voter information that negative political advertisements can convey is accompanied by a growth in cynicism about the democratic process and erosion of participation. In Australia, where voting is legally required, this last point is not relevant. However, since few democracies require voting, the finding is more generally applicable. Further, the growth of

---

[152] Id at 297.

[153] Stephen Ansolabehere and Shanto Iyengar, *Going Negative: How Attack Ads Shrink and Polarize the Electorate* (Free Press, 1995).

[154] Id at 39. The effects on voters of the information, however, are not straightforward. Interestingly, Ansolabehere and Iyengar find that information provided by political advertisements serves to "influence voters in concert with long-standing partisan predispositions." That is, "[a]dvertisements induce few Republicans to vote Democratic and few Democrats to vote Republican." Further, when television stations adopted a policy of evaluating ads and criticizing them when they were misleading, "[t]he candidates whose advertisements were criticized gained support. . . ." Id at 13, 64, 139.

[155] Id at 15.

[156] Id at 16.

[157] By their very nature, controlled experiments cannot duplicate uncontrolled life.

cynicism about politics and the lessening sense of political efficacy caused by paid television campaign advertisements are broadly applicable as well. This at least raises the question of whether the contribution to informing voters is worth the cost of driving them away from the democratic process. It also suggests that democracies might be able to have the best of both worlds. That is, a scheme like that set out in the Act, with two-minute "talking head" advertisements, has the potential to convey information without the debilitating effects of current political advertising. Further, Ansolabehere and Iyengar don't examine the financial resources required to advertise and the insurmountable barrier this presents to all but the major parties. That is, even if current political advertising provides voters with some policy information, it is skewed to those who can afford to advertise.

In sum, the U.S. literature paints a picture of television campaign advertising that adds little to deliberative democracy. More strongly, through its effect on both the agenda and the tone of campaigns, through its use of images and avoidance of policy stands, television campaign advertising may actually harm democracy by making informed deliberation less likely to occur.

2. *Australia.* The literature on television campaign advertising in Australia, although not as extensive, reaches similar conclusions. In general, scholars have criticized the electronic media, both campaign news and ads, for not serving the needs of a robust deliberative democracy. For example, in what is generally considered the standard work on Australian media and politics, Windschuttle argues that what television brings to campaigns is "drama, pathos, tragedy and combat. Television personalizes politics, too, as befits a drama being acted out on a small stage . . . what politicians now try to deliver are images and impressions."[158] More specifically, a study of the five-week 1980 federal election on Sydney TV found that the "electronic media . . . effectively circumscribe rather than facilitate public discussion and debate by diverse, conflicting interests."[159] Television presented "brief, incoherent and fragmentary

---

[158] Keith Windschuttle, *The Media: An Analysis of the Press, Television, Radio and Advertising in Australia* (Penguin, 3d ed 1988) at 312.

[159] Philip Bell, Kathe Boehringer, and Stephen Crofts, *Programmed Politics: A Study of Australian Television* (Sale Publishing, 1982) at 2. The focus of the study was television news, not advertising.

images of the party personalities and policies" with an "emphasis on the 'race' per se rather than the details of party philosophy or policy. . . . "[160] These findings were corroborated in a collection of studies on media and politics in the 1993 Australian federal election.[161] "Political commentators," it was reported, "expressed concern that the media was reducing the election to a decision based on 'style and image, not substance and issue'. . . ."[162] The result, as in the U.S. case, was the disengagement of citizens from political participation and the weakening of deliberative democracy. A constant theme throughout the articles was the voter's "transition from participant to spectator" and "from citizen to consumer."[163] As Ward and Cook put it, "TV advertising diminishes rather than enhances rational political debate. Its use forecloses rather than improves the prospect elections will be decided by informed voters making reasoned judgements at the polls."[164]

The debilitating effect of television campaign advertising on political participation is reflected in interview data on Australian politicians' views of political communication. Open-ended interviews of 22 politicians in 1988 found that communicating political ideas was "seen as an *advertising* process . . . [in which] political ideas and policies need to be advertised and sold to citizens' [sic] in the image of consumers."[165] Missing from these politicians' understandings was the notion of citizens actively engaged in discussion and deliberation about the content of the communication. Rather, the data found that politicians viewed "voting citizens . . . as a passive audience who will 'get' the message if the signal is good."[166] The study concluded that participation, give and take, and deliber-

[160] Id at 13.

[161] Special Section, *Politics and the Media: Election '93*, 20 Australian J Comm (vol 2) 1 (1993).

[162] Julie M. Duck, Michael A. Hogg, and Deborah J. Terry, *Perceptions of Media Influence in the 1993 Australian Federal Election: "Others" as Vulnerable Voters*, in Special Section, *Politics and the Media: Election '93*, 20 Australian J Comm (vol 2) 1 (1993) at 45.

[163] David Sless, *Politics and the Bored Spectator—A Provocation*, in Special Section, *Politics and the Media: Election '93*, 20 Australian J Comm (vol 2) 1 (1993) at 62.

[164] Ian Ward and Ian Cook, *Televised Political Advertising, Media Freedom, and Democracy*, Social Alternatives (vol 11) 1 (April 1992) at 22.

[165] David Rogers and Robyn Penman, *Communication in the Political Arena: Whither Citizenship?* Occasional Paper No 12 (Canberra: Communication Research Institute of Australia, December 1989) at 12; emphasis in original.

[166] Id at 13.

ation are "rare in the political communication process in Australia."[167] Ward and Cook echo this finding, concluding that political advertising "is a form of media-reliant campaigning which is ill-suited to educating, informing, or involving citizens."[168]

The negative impact of television campaign advertising on deliberative democracy in Australia was brought home by the 1991 testimony of two senior political campaign advertisers before the Senate Select Committee examining the legislative proposal that became the Act. Phillip Adams was a partner in Australia's largest advertising agency for 30 years and an active producer of television campaign advertising. Adams, like his U.S. counterparts, emphasized what he called the "image equation" in political advertising,[169] "images which transcend or subvert the normal processes of intellectual or logical communication."[170] Television, Adams told the Committee, "is not good at abstract ideas and information delivery."[171] Illustrating his point, Adams noted that it would be "pointless to do a word count on the most devastating television commercials because they are virtually mimed. Words are not how they communicate."[172] Furthering his indictment of television campaign advertising, Adams, like his U.S. counterpart Goodman, emphasized the irrelevancy of issues. Television campaign advertisements, Adams said, were "written by advertising agencies and by people who often have the dimmest comprehension of the issues involved."[173] The result for deliberative democracy is devastating: "It really is getting to the point where you can have elections won by agencies in which the political process and the politicians themselves are marginalised."[174]

These views were echoed by Rodney Cameron, an advertising executive involved in 54 state and federal elections over a roughly 20-year period for the Australian Labor Party (ALP). Cameron

---

[167] Id at 16.

[168] Ward and Cook (cited in note 164) at 23.

[169] Testimony of Mr. Phillip Adams, Senate Select Committee on Political Broadcasts and Political Disclosures (Oct 23, 1991) at 333.

[170] Adams' Testimony at 334.

[171] Adams' Testimony at 336.

[172] Adams' Testimony at 338.

[173] Adams' Testimony at 338.

[174] Adams' Testimony at 342.

summarized five categories of "ads which work."[175] His list included (1) "the occasionally effective negative ad"; (2) "the late
big scare or big lie"; (3) "the 60-second dramatic Thespian appeal"; (4) "the catchy jingle or slogan"; (5) "some sort of visual
emotional appeal to the heartstrings."[176] "Nowhere in this list of
ads that work," he emphasized to the Senators, "is there any reference to information or to content."[177] He characterized the ads
he produced that he believed were successful like this: "blatant
exaggerations of the truth" that "do not get across anything in
terms of information or rationality"; "pure theatrics which prey
on emotional appeal"; "glib, fairy floss theatrics which had nothing
to do with content or information"; "catchy jingles and slogans
that convey nought in terms of content"; "visual images and emo-
tive positive appeals"; "pure emotional simpatico."[178] The ads
that work, he concluded, are "emotional fairy floss, glib, trite,
nonsense."[179]

In sum, in both the United States and Australia, there is a good
deal of evidence that television campaign advertising harms rather
than helps the democratic process. Scholars of the media and politics in both countries, as well as practitioners, have highlighted its
debilitating effects. Testifying before the Senate Select Committee, two Australian academics put it this way:

> televised political communication actually forecloses rational
> public debate. Its purpose is precisely the opposite of classical
> rhetoric: "not to persuade, but to control; not to stimulate
> thought, but to prevent it; not to convey information, but to
> conceal or distort it."[180]

A striking aspect of *ACTV* is the lack of analysis of this literature. The Report of the Senate Select Committee on Political

---

[175] Testimony of Mr. Rodney Cameron, Senate Select Committee on Political Broadcasts
and Political Disclosures (Nov 10, 1991) at 281.

[176] Cameron Testimony at 281, 282.

[177] Cameron Testimony at 282.

[178] Cameron Testimony at 283.

[179] Cameron Testimony at 284.

[180] Ian Ward and Ian Cook, *Why Banning Televised Political Advertising Will Strengthen
Australian Democracy: A Submission to the Senate Select Committee on Political Broadcasts and
Political Disclosures*, Senate Select Committee on Political Broadcasts and Political Disclo-
sures, Submission No 10 (Sept 20, 1991) at 10, quoting P. Corcoran, *Political Language and
Rhetoric* (Univ of Queensland Press, 1979), xv.

Broadcasts and Political Disclosures was part of the record, and, as noted, there was a law review literature on the effects of campaign advertising on democracy. Yet only Justice Brennan, who voted to uphold the Act in relation to federal elections, mentions it.[181] The other members of the High Court, as we have shown, focused on the abstract notion of a "free" market. This point is further supported by examination of the empirical evidence on campaign advertising.

B. THE MEDIA MONOPOLY OF THE MAJOR POLITICAL PARTIES

The High Court was particularly concerned that the prohibition of electronic advertising would impinge upon the practice of representative democracy. As we have shown, the majority of the Justices held that the Act gave the major parties undue benefit. Further, they expressed grave concern that it disproportionately hindered individuals and third parties to the benefit of the major political parties. The result, the majority believed, would be a crippling of democracy.

In principle, this is a compelling concern. If individuals and groups other than the major political parties are unable to convey their views to the public, then deliberative democracy is stifled. However, as several Justices pointed out, constitutional guarantees must operate in practice, not merely in principle. Justice Gaudron, for example, noted that the "Constitution cannot be construed in a vacuum."[182] And Justice Brennan underscored the same point:

> The Constitution does not operate in a vacuum. It operates in and upon contemporary conditions . . . the implied freedom must be considered in the context of the contemporary and relevant political conditions in which the impugned law operates.[183]

Unfortunately, and despite these claims, the Justices of the High Court did not look to current practice.[184] The Court's analysis was abstract and unconnected to the practice of politics that constitu-

---

[181] Brennan J at 160–61.

[182] Gaudron J at 208.

[183] Brennan J at 158.

[184] Justice Brennan did look at some data, although not in any thorough way. Not surprisingly, he upheld the constitutionality of the Act, as applied to the federal government.

tional provisions protect. While this is no different than the approach taken by the U.S. Supreme Court, the abstract analysis that the High Court offered is particularly problematic. For if the High Court had looked to the actual practice of Australian democracy, the Justices would have discovered that the Act created more opportunities for political speech and deliberation than currently exist. Rather than stifling speech or democracy, the Act would have increased both.

To start, there is no prima facie reason why the U.S. experience should outweigh the experience of other democracies. As the Senate Report pointed out, fully democratic political systems such as Austria, Denmark, France, Israel, Japan, the Netherlands, Norway, Sweden, and the United Kingdom don't allow paid political advertising during election campaigns.[185] This was also noted by Justice Brennan, who listed 10 "liberal democracies" which ban paid political advertising during election periods.[186] Six of these "liberal democracies," Brennan emphasized, "have constitutions guaranteeing the right to freedom of expression."[187] Further, he cited a 1971 European Commission of Human Rights decision holding that there is no "general and unfettered right for any private citizen or organization to have access to broadcasting time on radio and television in order to forward its opinion."[188] What this suggested to Brennan was that the Act was "not a novel experiment unique to Australia."[189] What it suggests to us is that the Court's fears that banning paid political advertising during election periods would cripple democracy are not shared in many other democracies.

In criticizing the Court for not examining the practice of democracy, we are neither asking the Justices to do their own social science research nor demanding that they undertake tasks for

---

[185] Political Advertisements: An International Comparison, Senate Report, App 5, pp 111–23.

[186] Brennan J at 154. In addition to the nine democracies listed in the Senate Report, Brennan added Ireland, which allows paid political advertising during election campaigns but restricts the amount of advertising and allocates it in proportion to representation in Parliament.

[187] Brennan J at 154. The countries Brennan lists are Denmark, Ireland, Japan, The Netherlands, Norway, and Sweden.

[188] Brennan J at 154–55, citing *X and the Association of Z v United Kingdom*, European Commission of Human Rights (July 12, 1971), p 88.

[189] Brennan J at 154.

which they are unequipped. As noted, there was a good deal of research available to the Justices on the effects of televised campaign advertisements on the democratic process, evidence they chose to ignore (Justice Brennan excepted). In terms of statistical work, while there are good arguments that Justices are not trained to understand complex statistical studies, and thus should be wary of them,[190] such studies were not at issue in *ACTV*. Rather, as the next section illustrates, all the Justices needed to do was to look at simple percentages detailing which parties were spending how much money on televised campaign advertisements. Those data were readily available and appropriate for "judicial notice." But more importantly, if justices of constitutional courts wish to decide cases that have major policy ramifications, they must have a solid grasp of existing behavior. Applying constitutional principles to concrete practices requires a firm understanding of those practices. If justices wish to make such applications, it is incumbent upon them to be informed about practice. If they are not, then they should either defer to the legislature or, if appropriate, remand the case to lower courts for further development of the empirical record.[191] This is particularly the case in democratic countries like Australia where there is no bill of rights and courts traditionally defer to parliamentary actions.

In the Australian context, the Justices of the High Court neglected three distinct aspects of Australian political practice relevant to evaluating the constitutionality of the Act. First, under the law at the time of the decision, adopted prior to the enactment of the Act, and under current law, political advertising on the electronic media is already banned during part of the election campaign![192] Under Part 2 of the second Schedule to the Broadcasting

---

[190] Donald L. Horowitz, *The Courts and Social Policy* (Brookings, 1977) (arguing that judges lack the expertise and training to understand such studies, and that the norms of the adversarial process do not permit judges to undertake social science research independent of the material brought to the case by the parties).

[191] It may be the case that the sort of empirical analysis called for above is not part of the Australian legal culture, or the legal culture of many democracies. This is not, however, a persuasive argument for eschewing it. Without such evidence, courts risk undermining rather than furthering the constitutional principles they enunciate. If courts wish to play an active policy role, they must take empirical evidence into account.

[192] At the time the case was decided, § 116 (4) of the Broadcasting Act (Cth) 1942 prohibited broadcasters from broadcasting "political matter" during "the period that commences at the expiration of the Wednesday next preceding the polling day for the election and ends at the close of the poll on that polling day." This section has been replicated in the new Broadcasting Services Act (Cth) 1992.

Services Act (Cth) 1992 there is a prohibition on the broadcasting of election advertisements from midnight on the Wednesday preceding the poll to the close of polls on polling day, always Saturday. According to a parliamentary Report, the rationale for this prohibition on political advertising on the electronic media is that "if the blackout provision did not exist then a party would be able to run negative advertisements up to election day, and the attacked party would have no time to prepare advertisements to reply."[193]

The existence of Part 2, and Section 116, is a crucial point. It means that Australian law already regulates "free speech" to further a vision of democratic deliberation. Under these provisions, paid campaign advertising is banned for a part of the election campaign because of concern for its effects on the exchange of ideas. All the arguments made by the Justices in favor of free speech and for invalidating the Act should apply to these provisions. They stifle political communication, prevent third parties from advertising at a time when voters are most likely to focus on campaign issues, and "severely impair[] the freedoms previously enjoyed by citizens to discuss public and political affairs and to criticize federal institutions."[194] But, in the name of a fuller vision of democracy, political advertising is prohibited for a certain number of days during an election campaign. In other words, if Part 2 and Section 116 do not violate the implied right of political communication, then neither does the Act. The only way to resolve the contradiction caused by upholding Part 2 and Section 116, and invalidating the Act, is to draw a distinction between them based not on any underlying constitutional principle about free speech but rather on the length of time of the prohibition. The distinction comes down to the number of days involved, not the underlying principle. Curiously, only Justice Brennan noted the existence of the prohibition and the inconsistency it creates for invalidating the Act.[195]

---

[193] Who Pays the Piper Calls the Tune—Minimising the Risks of Funding Political Campaigns, Inquiry into the Conduct of the 1987 Federal Election and 1988 Referendums, Rep No 4, Joint Standing Committee on Electoral Matters, Parliament of the Commonwealth of Australia (Canberra: Australian Government Publishing Service, 1989) 109. This is a particularly weak argument. The only effect of the blackout is to change the timing. That is, what is there to stop a party from running negative advertisements in the days before the Wednesday after which political advertisements are banned? That would still leave insufficient time for opponents to respond.

[194] Mason CJ at 129.

[195] Brennan J at 159.

Second, a State election in Tasmania, a Territory election in the Australian Capital Territory, and a State bi-election were held under the Act prior to its invalidation in *ACTV*. In none of these elections was the argument put that the democratic process suffered. In fact, there is some evidence of greater involvement of citizens in these elections. In the Australian Capital Territory, for example, the Australian Labor Party ran ads in movie theaters and on closed-circuit television systems in pubs and clubs.[196] Compared to television advertising viewed in the solitary setting of a home, these ads in public places allowed for the potential of political discussion by citizens in public places. The clearest evidence, however, of the contribution of the Act to a more robust deliberative democracy comes from the Tasmanian State election.

Change was expected in Tasmania. An article in the Hobart *Mercury* suggested that because of the Act, "Candidates actually will have to get out and talk to the people, face to face, without the protection of studios and the advantage of make-up artists and slick TV producers."[197] It appears that this is exactly what happened; the political parties reacted to the Act by investing more time and resources than they had in the recent past in "old-fashioned" politicking, enlisting volunteers to go door-to-door to convince citizens to vote for their party. Candidates had to "get out and about more," and there was a much bigger emphasis on "good old-fashioned rallies in community halls and parks"[198] and other public gatherings than in the past.[199] "[T]he ban on electronic advertising is bringing more politicians back to grassroots campaigning," a newspaper writer noted.[200] For example, debates between citizens and candidates occurred:

> The recent ban on electronic political advertising saw election candidates swapping the television screens for a 15-minute spot on the podium at Speakers' Corner in Salamanca Place. . . .

---

[196] *Follett Sidesteps Political Ad Ban*, Canberra Times (Feb 11, 1992) at 4.

[197] Wayne Crawford, *Now for the Totally Novel Election*, Hobart Mercury (Jan 3, 1992) at 1.

[198] Id.

[199] Authors' conversation with Tasmanian political activist.

[200] Michael Smith, *Ban on the One-Eyed Monster Pushes Pollies on to the Podium*, Hobart Mercury (Jan 19, 1992) at 4.

> We never see anything like this at election time in Queensland
> [said a tourist]. It's terrific.[201]

Rather than stifling the democratic communication that the High
Court found crucial to Australian representative democracy, the
actual effects of the Act seem to have increased it.

A skeptic might interject here that the shift from paid television
advertisements to other forms of campaigning such as the public
rallies and increased candidate appearances in Tasmania does little
to improve deliberative democracy. Rather than creating more
meaningful deliberation, this argument goes, what it does is to create a democratic process that "feels" better to participants and observers. We have two reasons for rejecting this criticism. First, although political rallies, or even door-to-door canvassing, may not
increase deliberation, they have the potential to do so. This is the
case because they are based on active citizen participation in a
shared experience, not on the passive and solitary experience of
watching television in one's home. Second, this is a judgment to
be made by the legislature. It should be respected unless the evidence shows that it makes deliberative democracy worse. If the
experiences in the Australian Capital Territory and in Tasmania
show nothing else, they do show that banning paid televised campaign advertisements did not hurt the democratic process. And
there is additional evidence that the Act improved the democratic
process: its effects on media access.

The enhancement of deliberative democracy the Act brought
about can clearly be seen in the distribution of free television time
under the Act. The Australian Broadcasting Tribunal had 220 minutes of free air time to divide among parties and candidates over
the 24-day Tasmanian campaign. Based on the distribution of first
preference votes in the previous election as required by the Act,
the Liberal Party was awarded 90 minutes of free time (41%),
the Australian Labor Party 70 minutes (32%), and the Green-
Independent Party 30 minutes (14%). In addition, a new party,
the More Jobs Party, received 20 minutes of free time (9%) "to
make a start." The remaining 10 minutes were awarded to an independent candidate, Mr. Ian Jamieson, an unemployed miner.[202]

---

[201] Id.

[202] Rod McGuirk, *Jamieson's Campaign Aloft with Free Air Time*, Hobart Mercury (Jan
18, 1992) at 1. Ten independent candidates applied for the ten minutes of free air time
made available to candidates not affiliated with registered political parties. The Tribunal

Clearly, Mr. Jamieson would have been unable to purchase 10 minutes of television advertising to communicate his ideas to Tasmanian voters. It is also unlikely that the More Jobs Party would have been able to afford 20 minutes of television time. This suggests that the provision of free time under the Act brought a wider spectrum of ideas to the campaign, enhancing rather than limiting political communication.

While few elections were held under the Act, democracy does not appear to have suffered. As a headline in the Hobart *Mercury* noted, under the Act the big loser in the Tasmanian State election was not the citizens or democracy, but rather television stations![203] That is, although television stations lost revenue, democracy was enriched. There was more citizen contact with candidates and presentation of a broader range of ideas than in the past. The effect of the Act was to broaden the spectrum of political communication during the election. Australian deliberative democracy was enhanced by the Act, not stifled. If this is too strong, at the very least, the Tasmanian election held under the provisions of the Act provides no support for the claim that the prohibition in any way harms the political deliberation essential for representative democracy. Unfortunately, the Justices did not look to these examples, focusing their attention on abstract principle, not on the political practice to which constitutional guarantees apply.

1. *Broadcasting.* The most important failing in the High Court's analysis is that it did not carefully examine publicly available data on paid political advertising. Under Commonwealth legislation, the Australian Electoral Commission (AEC) is required to collect certain kinds of relevant data pertaining to election spending. In particular, the AEC collects data on spending by political parties and "third parties."[204] In general, the data show that the four major political parties have a virtual monopoly on electronic advertising. As the left-hand columns of Table 1 show, in the four most recent

---

decided that giving each candidate one minute of free time didn't make sense and instead held a lottery among the ten for the free time.

[203] *State TV Big Loser in Ads Ban Case*, Hobart Mercury (Jan 16, 1992) at 3.

[204] In its most recent Report, for the 1993 federal election, the AEC used the term "third party" to "denote persons, groups or organisations, other than registered political parties, candidates or Senate groups, taking part in an election campaign" (1993 Report, p 17). Its 1990 Report used a similar formulation (p 20) as did the reports on the 1987 (1987 Report, p 24) and 1984 (1984 Report, p 4) federal elections.

TABLE 1

SPENDING ON BROADCASTING AND PUBLISHING BY MAJOR AND THIRD PARTIES, AS A
PERCENTAGE OF TOTAL SPENDING ON BROADCASTING AND PUBLISHING, 1993, 1990, 1987,
AND 1984 FEDERAL ELECTIONS, BROADCASTERS' AND PUBLISHERS' REPORTS

	BROADCASTING		PUBLISHING	
YEAR	% of Total Spent by Four Major Parties	% of Total Spent by Third Parties	% of Total Spent by Four Major Parties	% of Total Spent by Third Parties
1993	92.9	7.1	64.2	35.8
1990	92.1	7.9	77.8	22.2
1987	93.8	6.2	76.9	23.1
1984	96.5	3.5	86.9	13.1

SOURCE.—Compiled from Australian Electoral Commission, *Election Funding and Disclosure Report* for the 1993, 1990, 1987, and 1984 federal elections.

federal elections for which data are available,[205] the four major political parties made over 92% of expenditures for electronic advertising (broadcasting)![206] Under the current system, individuals, interest groups, etc. do not advertise on the electronic media. The
Court's concern that the Act would prevent all but the major political parties from advertising on the electronic media ignores the
fact that this already is the case.

It is further the case that the roughly 3.5%–8% of expenditures
on electronic advertising made by those other than the four major
political parties are concentrated among a tiny handful of groups
closely associated with the major parties. In the 1993 federal election, 243 groups and independent candidates in addition to the
four main political parties reported making election-related expenditures. However, as Table 2 shows, only 38 (15.6%) of these 243
listed any expenditures on electronic advertising, accounting for
24.1% of monies expended by third parties during the campaign.
So, on a general level, the prohibition of expenditures on electronic media by third parties during an election campaign will only
affect roughly one out of every six and a half groups, and only
about one-quarter of all third-party spending.

---

[205] Data are not presently available for the 1996 federal election.

[206] It is important to note, however, that broadcasters appear to underreport the amount
of money spent. In 1990, the AEC compared broadcasters' reports with those of the political
parties, finding that "broadcasters' and publishers' returns disclosed about 70% of the
amount disclosed by political parties, candidates and 'third parties' on broadcasting and
publishing" (1990 Report, p 29). The important, point, however, is that both sets of data
reveal the domination over broadcasting of the four major political parties.

TABLE 2

Third Party Spending on Broadcasting and Publishing, 1993 Federal Election,
Third Party and Publisher's Reports

BROADCASTING		PUBLISHING	
No. of Third Parties Spending on Broadcasting	% of Third Parties Spending on Broadcasting	No. of Third Parties Spending on Publishing	% of Third Parties Spending on Publishing
38	15.6	223	91.8
No. of Third Parties Spending $50,000+ on Broadcasting	% of Total Third-Party Spending by Third Parties Spending $50,000+ on Broadcasting	No. of Third Parties Spending $50,000+ on Publishing	% of Total Third-Party Spending by Third Parties Spending $50,000+ on Publishing
8	85.1	13	57.1

Total No. of Third Parties Reporting Campaign Expenditures: 243

Source.—Compiled from Australian Electoral Commission, *Election Funding and Disclosure Report* for the 1993 federal election.

These modest effects might still raise concerns. For example, if the legislation had been in effect during the 1993 federal election, it would have banned broadcasting of paid political advertisements by 38 groups. Further investigation reveals, however, that broadcasting expenditures were not evenly distributed among these groups, and that very few groups spent sufficient funds to have any hope of getting their message remembered by more than a tiny fraction of Australians.[207] Only four groups spent over $100,000 on electronic advertising, and only another four spent between $50,000 and $100,000. Together, these eight groups spent 85% of the total spent on electronic advertising by third parties (see Table 2). In other words, the prohibition on third-party electronic advertising essentially affects eight groups. Further, three of the four groups which spent over $100,000 were trade unions,[208] while all four of the groups which spent between $50,000 and $100,000

---

[207] Surveys and experiments on media effects make it clear that it takes repeated exposure for viewers to be aware of, and remember, broadcast messages. See Shanto Iyengar and Donald R. Kinder, *News That Matters* (Univ of Chicago Press, 1987).

[208] The ACTU ($171,961.63), the ACTU Future Strategies ($164,095.00), the Fair Go Aust Alliance/Labor Council ($120,873.00), and the Hospital Benefit Fund of Western Australia Inc ($211,895.00). Together these four groups spent $668,824.63, or 57% of total spent by third parties on electronic media.

were trade unions.[209] Given the close connection between unions and the ALP, the prohibition would not greatly hinder these seven groups in getting their message to the public. In other words, the prohibition on electronic broadcasting by third parties in the 1993 federal election would have had only a limited effect on the ability of third parties to advertise their beliefs.[210]

It is quite clear why few individuals, interest groups, or third parties advertise on the electronic media; they can't afford it. Purchasing enough time on the electronic media to convey one's message is beyond the reach of virtually all citizens and most all interest groups. As the Hon. Kim Beazley, then Minister for Transport and Communications, said on the floor of the House in support of the Act: "The exorbitant cost of broadcast advertising precludes the majority of the community and all but the major political parties and large corporate interests from paid access to the airwaves."[211] In the words of the Minister, "[t]he reality is that only the rich can get their message across by . . . means [of electronic advertising]."[212]

Two examples of the inability of third parties and interest groups to make use of broadcasting to disseminate their views illustrate this argument. During the 1996 federal election, for example, one of the most colorful participants was the "No Aircraft Noise Party," which attempted to influence voters in the five seats affected by the noise of Sydney's airport.[213] The Party staged numerous marches, rallies, and protests. However, although the Party was well enough organized and active to gain a great deal of news coverage, the cost of Sydney commercial television advertising was so high as to effectively preclude it from advertising. The Party's

---

[209] The NSW Teachers Federation ($83,250.00), the Public Sector Union ($58,308.00), the Trades and Labor Council of Queensland ($99,109.00), and the United Trades & Labor Council, South Australia ($89,696.00). Together these four groups spent $330,363.00, or 28.1% of the total spent by third parties on electronic media.

[210] Unfortunately, similar data for the 1990, 1987, and 1984 federal elections do not exist.

[211] H Rep (May 9, 1991), p 3479. The passage was also cited in the Report of the Senate Select Committee, p 5.

[212] H Rep (May 9, 1991), p 3480.

[213] Noise at Sydney airport was a major political issue in the several years before the 1996 federal election, with the incumbent Keating (ALP) government building a new runway and closing an old runway, allegedly for safety concerns. The Opposition charged, however, that the old runway was closed because its flight path was over seats held by Ministers in the Labor government. The flight path for the new runway was, of course, over seats held by Members of the Opposition.

entire 1996 federal election advertisement presence in the electronic media consisted of two brief "spot" television commercials, at 1 and 2 A.M. in the morning![214]

Second is the example of the Australian Conservation Foundation (ACF), an environmental group, and the logging industry. As noted in the Senate Report on the Act, in the 1990 federal election the Forest Industries Campaign Association Ltd., an interest group representing the logging industry, spent more than a million dollars on advertising ($1,182,000).[215] In contrast, the ACF spent only $135,536, approximately 11% of the total spent by the logging industry.[216] However, it appears that none of this comparatively meager amount was spent on television. According to the Senate Report, "[m]ost of this expenditure was on newspaper advertising, how-to-vote cards, posters and pamphlet material with approximately $28,000 spent on advertising on FM radio."[217] This huge discrepancy in spending was noted in Parliament in the Second Reading Speech of Minister Beazley,[218] but only by Justice Brennan in the decision.[219]

Given the widespread understanding of the cost of electronic advertising, and the AEC data on the virtual monopoly on such advertising held by the four major parties, it is remarkable that the Justices of the High Court made virtually no mention of it. When they did, they made unsupported and unsupportable claims. For instance, Justices Deane and Toohey argued that the high cost of purchasing broadcast time was not an impediment to doing so:

---

[214] Phone Interview with Campaign Organizer of the No Aircraft Noise Party (Feb 29, 1996). The party relied on print advertisement, handbills, public rallies, and the news coverage they generated to disseminate its policy positions.

[215] Senate Report, p 24. AEC Report for 1990 elections, p 60. Other forestry industry groups reporting campaign advertising include the New South Wales Forest Products Association ($109,820) and the Tasmanian Logging Association ($15,685). AEC Report for 1990 elections, pp 61, 62.

[216] AEC Report for 1990 election, p 59. Other conservation groups reporting campaign advertising include Mountain Residents for Animal Rights ($385), the Wilderness Society ($4,741), and the World League for Protection of Animals ($2,451.20). AEC Report for 1990 election, pp 61, 63.

[217] Senate Report at 24. The Report does note that the ACF was running one television ad "as a community service announcement . . . shown free at the discretion of television stations [with] an estimated 300 other community organisations competing for this discretionary free time." Senate Report at 24.

[218] H Rep (May 9, 1991) at 3480.

[219] Brennan J at 149.

> Nor, in our view, is it to the point to say that the cost of time, at least on television, is so high that private individuals would not seek to communicate by political advertisement on that medium in any event. For one thing, the cost of radio time, especially country radio, is not nearly so high.[220]

As a statement of fact, this is clearly wrong. For example, consider the cost of radio time. The Justices note that radio, and especially country radio, is a cheap alternative to expensive television. The cost of country radio no doubt is cheaper than its metropolitan cousin. However, it is hard to be influenced by cheap political broadcasts when you do not hear them! According to 1990 census data, slightly more than 14% of the Australian population lived in rural areas,[221] the areas presumably covered by "country radio," compared to the 85.4% of the total population who lived in urban areas.[222] Moreover, in 1986 over 10 million people, or 64% of Australia's population, lived in the six State and two Territory capital cities.[223] But more importantly, the data show that the cost of the electronic media, particularly television, precludes virtually everyone from advertising. Clearly, the Justices are correct as a matter of *principle* when they say that groups may come together and buy television time. The question, however, is whether groups are able to come together as a matter of *practice* and buy television time. And the data show that they are not, except for wealthy industry groups and unions. Democracy is to be practiced, not merely praised, but the High Court's following of the U.S.-derived free-market approach diverted the Justices from actual practice.

2. *Publishing.* The data presented above show that third parties make few expenditures on broadcasting. Only a handful of groups make sufficient expenditures to reach the public, and these groups are closely connected to the major parties. In contrast, third parties expend substantially more of their funds on publishing (45.1% in 1993), not affected by the Act. The AEC also compiles data on money spent on publishing activities. These expenditures are mostly for advertisements in the print media, although they may

---

[220] Deane and Toohey JJ at 175. The rest of this paragraph is critically discussed in text at pages 461–62.

[221] Social Indicators, *Australian Bureau of Statistics* (1992) Catalogue No 4101.0 at 17.

[222] Id.

[223] Id.

TABLE 3

THIRD PARTY SPENDING ON PUBLISHING AND BROADCASTING AS A PERCENTAGE OF
TOTAL SPENDING ON PUBLISHING AND BROADCASTING, 1993, 1990, 1987,
AND 1984 FEDERAL ELECTIONS, BROADCASTERS' AND PUBLISHERS' REPORTS

Year	% of Total Spent on Publishing	% of Total Spent on Broadcasting
1993	35.8	7.1
1990	22.2	7.9
1987	23.1	6.2
1984	13.1	3.5

SOURCE.—Compiled from Australian Electoral Commission, *Election Funding and Disclosure Report* for the 1993, 1990, 1987, and 1984 federal elections.

include the printing of palm cards, posters, and the like. The two right-hand columns of Table 1 show expenditures on publishing for the four most recent federal elections.[224]

These numbers show substantially less domination by the major parties, with third parties making nearly one-quarter of total publishing expenditures in 1990 and over one-third in 1993. In the 1993 election, for example, 223 out of 243 groups (91.8%) made publishing expenditures (see Table 2). In contrast to the broadcasting arena, these expenditures were not dominated by just a few groups representing only a limited part of the political spectrum. Five groups spent over $100,000 on publishing,[225] and eight groups spent between $50,000 and $100,000.[226] Together, these 13 groups accounted for 57.1% of the total spent by third parties on publishing, leaving substantially over 40% of total spending to other third parties. What this means is that spending on publishing was not dominated by just a few groups as with broadcasting. Table 3 compares broadcasting and publishing expenditures by third parties.

---

[224] It again appears that publishers underreport the amount of money spent. However, the main point is that even though the numbers differ, both sets of figures show that third parties spend a much larger percentage of campaign expenditures on publishing than on broadcasting.

[225] The Australian Medical Association ($102,995.45), Australia Media Pty. Ltd. ($135,866.20), the Department of Health, Housing & Community Services ($103,836.00), the Medical Benefits Fund of Australia ($231,669.17), and the National Farmers Federation ($120,895.00).

[226] The Australasian Rail Link ($84,827.47), the Australian Asia/Pacific Wholesalers P/L ($76,603.00), the Australian Chamber of Commerce and Industry ($56,987.00), the Australian Economic Analysis Pty. Limited ($51,097.00), the Australian Federal Police ($51,719.00), the Australian Institute of Marine & Power Engineers ($96,588.00), Idameneo (123) Pty. Ltd. ($80,226.00), and Sterling Winthrop Pty. Ltd. ($62,716.00).

Overall, the data show that prohibiting electronic broadcasting has a minimal effect on third parties. Few third parties broadcast. In contrast, most third parties do make advertising expenditures in the print media. Although publishing still sees the disproportionate effect of money, it is to a lesser extent than with broadcasting.

3. *Free-time provisions.* The foregoing discussion was based on the part of the Act prohibiting paid political advertising during election campaigns. There was, however, another part of the Act that created a free-time provision under which 90% of the total time provided for campaign advertisements was allocated to political parties with members in the previous Parliament and which were contesting the current election.[227] In assessing the effect of the Act on the actual practice of Australian democracy, the free-time provision must be evaluated as well.

The majority of the Justices argued that the effect of the free-time provision was to entrench the power of political incumbents at the expense of others by allocating them 90% and 10% of the time, respectively. Chief Justice Mason repeatedly stressed this point, concluding that the Act "manifestly favour[s] the status quo."[228] On its face, Mason argued, the Act "directly exclude[s] potential participants in the electoral process,"[229] "discriminates against new and independent candidates," and "denies them meaningful access on a non-discriminatory basis."[230] Mason's concerns were echoed by Justices Deane and Toohey,[231] Gaudron,[232] and McHugh.[233]

In principle, these are compelling concerns. If the effect of the free-time provision was to bar access to the media on the part of interests other than the four major parties, then the High Court would be on strong ground in invalidating it. Unfortunately, the Justices did not evaluate this claim, basing their conclusion on abstract principle, not actual practice. If they had examined the data,

---

[227] The free-time provisions are set out in text at page 444.

[228] Mason J at 132.

[229] Mason J at 145.

[230] Mason J at 146.

[231] Deane and Toohey JJ at 172.

[232] Gaudron J at 221.

[233] McHugh J at 237, 239.

they would have discovered that the guarantee of 90% of the free time to political parties with members in the previous Parliament who were contesting the current elections was a *decrease* in the amount of broadcast time for these parties. Rather than entrenching incumbents, the effect of the Act would have been to cut back, albeit by only a few percentage points, on the percentage of broadcast time taken by the major parties. Further, by limiting the main parties to 90% of the time, the Act would actually free up time for other individuals and groups. As the data show, in the 1984, 1987, 1990, and 1993 federal elections, such groups were only able to purchase 3.5%, 6.2%, 7.9%, and 7.1% of broadcast time, respectively. Under the Act, they would be eligible for 10% of air time, an increase of more than one-third over the 1993 figure. As the example of Mr. Ian Jamieson, the unemployed miner given 10 minutes of free time in the 1992 Tasmanian State elections, shows, the only realistic hope for most independent candidates to obtain air time is through the free-time provisions of the Act. In *principle* the free-time provision limits access to the media; in *practice*, it enhances it.

It may also be the case that the makeup of incumbents changes over time, with new parties entering Parliament. If so, then the grip of the four major parties over electronic broadcasting will again lessen as they receive a smaller portion of the free time reserved for incumbents. In other words, the free-time provision under the Act is dynamic.

These arguments are strongest in parliamentary systems where independent candidates seldom run for office. In non-parliamentary systems such as the United States, concern might be raised that such a system would make impossible some independent candidacies, including, for example, the 1996 third-party presidential candidacies of Steve Forbes and Ross Perot, and the campaigns of protest candidates like Eugene McCarthy in 1968 and Pat Buchanan in 1992. It is not at all clear, however, that these candidates would be denied air time. For example, there exists in the U.S. a system of government funding of presidential candidates under which all candidates running for president who can meet certain minimum fundraising requirements are eligible to receive federal funds for their campaigns. An equivalent standard could be set for access to free time. Since Buchanan, Forbes, and Perot easily met this funding standard,[234] they would also meet a similar free-time standard. And protest candidates like McCarthy and Buchanan, typically short of financial resources, depend on the enthusiasm of volunteers to spread their message. A free-time scheme is likely to benefit such candidates by providing them access to the media that they lack under the current system. Details aside, the fundamental point is that under current practice in both Australia and the United States there is a close relationship between financial resources and media access and a lack of relationship between private wealth and the promotion of democracy.

In an important sense, the debate boils down to the *possibility* for any individual or group to advertise during a campaign versus the *reality* of who actually does advertise. Critics of the Act, including a majority of the Australian High Court, believed that it was important to protect the possibility of advertising. Our argument, however, is that to focus on the theoretical possibility is to lose sight of the reality of unequal resources. Without intervention of the sort proposed by the Act, the data show that only the wealthy can advertise. A democratic legislature, particularly one in a parliamentary system with a tradition of judicial deference and without an explicit constitutional guarantee of free speech, ought to be able to sever the connection between wealth and access to the media during election campaigns and focus on actual practice, not theoretical possibility.

The Justices expressed concern, too, that the Tribunal empowered to allocate free time might do so in an arbitrary and discriminatory fashion. Indeed, the task of devising objective standards for deciding which individuals or groups are to be given air time does appear daunting, and the dangers real.[235] But given the data presented in this section, this seems somewhat beside the point. That is, if 85% of the broadcast time not taken by the four major parties is taken by eight large groups intimately aligned with the major parties, as in the 1993 federal election, it is hard to see how the Tribunal could make matters worse for deliberative democracy. Indeed, one might suspect that a whole range of groups with sup-

---

[234] There was no such funding available in 1968 when Senator McCarthy ran.

[235] The same could be said about government financing of political campaigns. However, objective standards have been developed in many democracies, including even the United States.

port in segments of the community, from conservationists, pro-choice activists, and supporters of gun control to anti-immigration, pro-life, and pro-gun groups, would have access to the electronic media, *for the first time.* The free time given to the More Jobs Party in the 1992 Tasmanian State election supports this claim. Our point is simple: by failing to evaluate the actual practice of the Australian political system, the Justices prevented the government from improving the nature of democratic deliberation. Paraphrasing Anatole France,[236] the thrust of the High Court's opinion is that the constitutional guarantee of free speech, in its majestic equality, permits the millionaire as well as the homeless person to sleep under bridges, to beg in the streets, and to purchase television air time.

4. *Pointy-headed intellectuals and Utopians.* In response to our argument about the debilitating nature of television campaign advertising on deliberative democracy, it might be argued that prohibiting such advertisements denudes politics of emotion and color. Politics is about images. It stirs passions, not merely intellect. Rational discussion about debate is only one part of politics. To ban television campaign advertising removes from campaigns much of what makes them exciting.[237]

This argument is only partly right. It is certainly the case that politics is about passions. It would be a dull campaign indeed that involved only calm and rational debates about policy. But banning television campaign advertising would have little or no effect on the emotional side of politics. Political passion is not aroused or expressed in the solitary setting of a living room where television campaign advertising is watched. Rather, it is aroused and expressed in public and participatory events such as great speeches, mass rallies, gatherings of the faithful, political concerts, guerilla theater, and the like. A ban on campaign television advertising not only would not diminish these kinds of events, but might also increase their frequency as politicians and political parties sought other avenues for reaching voters.[238] The politics in countries like France, Israel, and Austria are certainly passionate, even though

---

[236] *Le Lys Rouge.*

[237] We thank Desmond Manderson for forcefully presenting this point. The point is also mentioned in passing in *ACTV* by Mason CJ at 145 and Deane & Toohey JJ at 174.

[238] As occurred in the 1992 Tasmanian State Election.

each prohibits paid political advertising during election campaigns. Our point is simple: prohibiting television campaign advertising leaves many other ways of stirring political passions.

A second critique of our argument might be that politicians, if prohibited from spending money on television campaign advertising, will find other ways of influencing voters that will be equally debilitating of deliberative democracy. In particular, one might expect a growth in narrowly targeted direct mail and telephone canvassing. Further, since these forms of campaigning are quintessentially private, lacking even the mass audience of television campaign advertising, the effects on deliberation and participation may be even more severe.[239]

Again, this argument is only partly right. It is plausible, even likely, that a ban on television campaign advertising will lead to an upswing in direct mail and phone canvassing. However, neither is likely to have as powerful a debilitating effect on deliberative democracy as television campaign advertising. This is in large part because neither are visual mediums. Their effectiveness relies less on images and more on words themselves. Specifically, mail requires reading and a level of concentration that is greater than passively watching a television screen. It is also likely that direct mail will be treated by many citizens as junk mail, and discarded without being read. Phone canvassing, unlike television campaign advertising or direct mail, allows for discussion (assuming the caller is a person, not a machine). And the recipient of the phone call can always hang up. Thus, deliberative democracy is unlikely to be weakened if television campaign advertising is replaced by an increase in direct mail and phone canvassing.

A third critique is that our argument romanticizes the past. If televised campaign advertising has been harmful to deliberative democracy, doesn't this imply that democratic practice was more deliberative prior to the television age? And given the closed-door, smoke-filled, back-room politics that characterized at least the United States prior to the television age, and the strict party-line voting followed by a large percentage of the voters, what was so

---

[239] We thank Fiona Wheeler for eloquently presenting this point. In the wake of the only State election held under the Act, in Tasmania, a cartoon in a Tasmanian newspaper showed a television screen talking to a mailbox. When the smiling screen commented, "I had a quiet election, what about you?" the mailbox, buried in a mountain of letters, replied, "I'm stuffed!!" Hobart Mercury (Feb 1, 1992).

deliberative about the old system? To put the point another way, why is it any more debilitating of deliberative democracy for an individual to vote on the basis of the information conveyed in a 30-second television ad than to vote on the basis of the information conveyed in a mere party label about candidates chosen by party bosses?

As before, there is something to this point. Not all pre-television campaign practices contributed to deliberative democracy. But more citizens were more actively involved in the years before television campaign advertising than in the years since. As Ansolabehere and Iyengar find, televised campaign advertising makes voters more cynical about politics, lessens their sense of political efficacy, and, in the United States, produces a "substantial decrease in voter turnout."[240] Thus, even granting that campaign practices in the pre-television age were far from ideal contributors to deliberative democracy, there is evidence that televised campaign advertising has made matters worse.

Further, the law struck down by the Court in *ACTV* attempted to make use of television to further deliberative democracy. It required that all televised campaign ads run for two minutes with candidates themselves talking with a static background and without dramatic enactment or impersonation. This "talking head" format had the potential to further informed discussion of issues and policies. In such a format there are only so many times a candidate can say, "Vote Democratic (or Labor)," or "Vote Republican (or for the Coalition)," without becoming nauseatingly repetitive. Similarly, it's one things for a 30-second spot ad to picture a lovely wilderness setting at dawn, with birds twittering in the background and soft music playing, and with a professional actor intoning the words "It's morning in America (or Australia)," or "I love America (or Australia)." It's quite another for the candidate herself, without the support of pictures or music, to spend two minutes repeating the slogans. The latter would be ineffective, indeed, most likely counterproductive. Thus, without romanticizing the past, our argument is that the Act did contribute to deliberative democracy.

A fourth and final critique is that the notion of deliberative democracy on which our argument is premised demands too much

---

[240] Ansolabehere and Iyengar (cited in note 153) at 15. Their findings are based on a study of the effect of negative advertising. See text at pages 470–71.

of the average voter. In all democracies, this argument goes, the average voter lacks the capacity, interest, and cognitive ability to engage in deliberative democracy. This is an old argument against democracy.[241] And it is a self-fulfilling prophecy. As the level of political discourse drops to negative attack ads, citizens tune out.[242] It is certainly plausible that the average voter has the capacity to acquire and process more information than occurs now. Further, the system is dynamic. As political ads change, so too may political discourse, even among average voters. But this is not for us to decide, for this is the kind of decision that a democratic legislature is entitled to make, and a constitutional court ought to respect.

VI. Conclusion

In this article we examined the relationship between democracy, paid political advertisements on television, and constitutional rights to free speech. Focusing on the Australian High Court's 1992 decision in *ACTV*, we argued that the Court misunderstood the relationship among the three. It did so, not because of any lack of legal acumen, but rather because it too uncritically adopted U.S. understandings of free speech and the relation between free speech and democracy. This led to a particular weakness in its analysis. In following First Amendment jurisprudence, the Australian High Court necessarily adopted, implicitly or explicitly, the concept of free speech as an unregulated "marketplace of ideas." This focused the attention of the Justices on the supposed "interference" with speech the Act created, making it virtually impossible for them to evaluate the Act in the light of the constitutional goal of promoting deliberative democracy. It is ironic that in seeking to promote deliberative democracy in Australia, the High Court adopted the very interpretive means that undermine it.

---

[241] For a colorful rendition of it, see Joseph A. Schumpeter, *Capitalism, Socialism and Democracy* (Harper, [1942] 1975), especially chap 21, where he argues that "the typical citizen drops down to a lower level of mental performance as soon as he enters the political field. He argues and analyzes in a way which he would readily recognize as infantile within the sphere of his real interests. He becomes a primitive again [and tends] to yield to extra-rational or irrational prejudice and impulse." Id at 262.

[242] Ansolabehere and Iyengar (cited in note 153) at 15, discussed in text at pages 470–71.

The adoption of the U.S. concept also focused the High Court on the abstract principle of the free market rather than on the concrete reality of access to the media. The unsurprising result was the unwillingness of all but one member of the High Court to engage in even cursory empirical analysis. Constitutional principles, especially ones as important as political communication and deliberative democracy, must be applied with an understanding of the world in which they operate. As our empirical research has demonstrated, the Act did in fact improve the state of Australian democracy and further the constitutional goal of deliberative democracy. But the High Court, enthralled by the marketplace of ideas, overlooked the reality to which constitutional principles, if they are to have meaning, must apply.

Our argument suggests that because the Australian High Court too closely followed current U.S. Supreme Court understandings of the relationship between democracy and free speech, its decision in *ACTV* was mistaken and should not be followed by other constitutional courts. Even after *ACTV*, the Australian High Court should be cautious in its adoption of First Amendment jurisprudence. Having discovered within the Australian Constitution a rich seam of deliberative democracy, the High Court's challenge is to give it meaning consistent with the Australian experience. It must not be forgotten that during the Cold War the Australian High Court, without the benefit of First Amendment guarantees, gave greater protection to political dissidents than did its U.S. counterpart.[243] It would be sad indeed if the Australian High Court, in a rush to adopt all things American, overlooked its own rich history.

---

[243] Compare *Australian Communist Party v Commonwealth* (1950) 83 C.L.R. 1, in which the Australian High Court invalidated the Communist Party Dissolution Act (1950) (Cth), with *Dennis v U.S.*, 341 US 494 (1951), in which the U.S. Supreme Court upheld the imprisonment of the national leadership of the U.S. Communist Party for its speeches and writings. For an account of the Australian Act and its U.S. counterparts, see Mr. Justice Kirby, *The Anti-Communist Referendum and Liberty in Australia* (1990) 7 Australian Bar Rev 93.